EARLY MIDDLE
ENGLISH TEXTS

LAƷAMON'S BRUT, ll. 1–19

(B. M. Cotton Caligula A ix, ƒ. 1 r)

EARLY MIDDLE ENGLISH TEXTS

EDITED BY

BRUCE DICKINS

& R. M. WILSON

Do way, by Crist and Leonard!
No wil Y lufe na clerc fayllard.

BOWES & BOWES

LONDON

DISCIPVLIS LEODIENSIBVS
ANNORVM XVI
HAVD IMMEMORES

First published 1951 in Great Britain by
BOWES AND BOWES PUBLISHERS LIMITED
42 Great Russell Street, London, W.C.1
Second (revised) impression 1952
Third impression (again revised) 1956
Fourth impression 1959
Fifth impression 1961

PREFACE

THIS book is planned to bridge the gap between the various Old English readers and Kenneth Sisam's admirable *Fourteenth Century Verse and Prose*. At present the only available reader is that of Joseph Hall, which, for all its virtues, is emphatically not a book for any but the specialist who has already received some introduction to early Middle English. Various readers covering the whole period labour under one handicap or another. They are either out of date (as Morris & Skeat), out of print, or prohibitive in price (as are the various American readers) or else, like F. Mossé's excellent work, in a foreign language.

The editors can hardly hope that their choice of extracts will please everyone, though none of the colleagues who have seen the list has had serious criticisms to make. Space had to be considered if the price of the reader were to be kept within reasonable limits. The editors would have liked to include many other pieces, *A Lutel Soth Sermun*, one of the *Lambeth Homilies*, more of the religious lyrics, or longer extracts from some of the works already represented. Each of these was balanced against the extracts included, and, for one reason or another, had to give way. Moreover, it should be emphasized that this book is in no sense intended as an anthology of early Middle English literature. It is hoped that the student, and indeed the general reader, will derive from it a good idea of the varied merits of the literature of an unduly neglected period, but it is expected that it will also be used by those whose interests are linguistic rather than literary, and for them it has been necessary to include a few texts of no great literary value.

The order of arrangement set a difficult problem, and one which we can hardly claim to have settled to our entire satisfaction. On the whole, chronological order would have been the best solution, and one which would have allowed the student to see for himself the gradual change in style and language during the period. But any such arrangement very early proved impracticable. The composition of very few of the texts can be dated at all precisely; any such order could only be hypothetical, one in which the editors would have had little confidence, and one which would have been at the mercy of any competent critic. Nor did arrangement by dialects appear

v

more satisfactory. For many of the shorter pieces there are not sufficient data available by which they can be located with any confidence. Such an arrangement would separate pieces which by subject essentially belonged together, and within the dialect the problem of order would still remain. On the whole the best arrangement appeared to be by subject, with a rough chronological arrangement within each part. The historical pieces, which include the earliest examples of Middle English, naturally come at the beginning, with Laʒamon's *Brut* acting as a bridge between history and romance. Romance is followed by examples of the beast tale, didactic and religious pieces, lyrics, and the sole considerable surviving example of dramatic composition in early Middle English.

In previous readers it has been usual to provide one or two extracts in a normalized spelling, but the value of this practice has not been evident. It is thought that most users of this book will approach by way of Old English, and such students will be familiar with the comparative lack of consistency in orthography and phonology of most medieval texts in the vernacular. Even for those to whom this book may act as an introduction to medieval literature it has seemed of doubtful value to start with a type of language which never in fact existed and must be abandoned almost at once. Similar reasons account for the absence of all length-marks in the texts. It would have been a simple matter to insert length-marks on vowels derived from Old English long vowels and long diphthongs, and on those which, according to the rules, should have been lengthened in Middle English, but again the result would have been a made-up language more or less closely related to the real thing. Variations from the norm, due to stress or the workings of analogy, are sufficiently frequent to cast doubt on the validity of hard-and-fast rules of quantity in Middle English.

The texts themselves h ve been collated with the manuscripts. and some improved readings have been obtained, as at IX. 22 and XII. 264. Emendation has been a rare luxury, but capitalization and punctuation have necessarily been modernized since diplomatic texts would have been out of place in a book of this kind. As far as possible the critical apparatus has been kept subordinate, though the editors have borne in mind that not all students may be using the work for the same purpose. The main attention has been directed towards obtaining accuracy of rendering. This is necessary because of the peculiar difficulties besetting the translation of Middl

English texts, the greatest of which has been aptly called 'the ety-
mological fallacy'. On the whole it is easier to get the drift of a
passage in Middle English than of one in Old English, but the
latter is in general more idiomatically rendered by the student.
The translator of Middle English is too often tempted to use the
corresponding Modern English word, ignoring the considerable
difference which may have developed in meaning, and produces
thereby a bastard language, neither Middle nor Modern. For this
reason particular attention has been paid in the notes to those words
which have survived into Modern English with a widely different
meaning, and the gradual change in sense has usually been traced.
There will be found, too, some notes on syntax. In the present state
of our knowledge an adequate treatment of this subject would have
demanded an inordinate amount of space, while the validity of some
of the statements, appearing as they necessarily must have done in
a dogmatic and summary form, would have been most doubtful.

A general introduction to the spelling and linguistic forms of
early Middle English follows the texts, and linguistic introductions
to the individual extracts are provided at the beginning of each series
of notes. For lack of space no such introduction to the literature
is supplied; the reader may be referred to R. M. Wilson's *Early
Middle English Literature* (London 1939), which covers the ground.

Grammatical abbreviations will be found listed at the beginning
of the Glossary (pp. 244–5), abbreviated titles of books and
periodicals in the bibliography (pp. x–xiii). The convention adopted
in references to the volume and page of periodicals will be unfamiliar to literary students, but it has the merit of eliminating many
needless commas and full stops. I/ or II/ can easily be prefixed to
the volume number if the periodical has more than one series.

We are indebted to the authorities of the British Museum and of
the Bodleian Library for permission to reproduce the facsimiles, and
to the Syndics of the Cambridge University Press for lending the
Laʒamon block.

Some of the further additions and corrections we have been
able to make in this impression we owe to the kindness of friends
and critics.

BRUCE DICKINS   R. M. WILSON
Cambridge   *Sheffield*

November 1954

CONTENTS

FACSIMILES

SELECT BIBLIOGRAPHY

BIBLIOGRAPHICAL AIDS.

F. W. Bateson, *The Cambridge Bibliography of English Literature*, Vol. I. Cambridge 1940.

Carleton Brown & R. H. Robbins, *The Index of Middle English Verse*. New York 1943.

W. L. Renwick & H. Orton, *The Beginnings of English Literature to Skelton 1509*. London 1939. Rev. 1952.

J. E. Wells, *A Manual of the Writings in Middle English 1050–1400*, and *Supplements I–IX*. New Haven 1916–51.

DICTIONARIES

A. L. Mayhew & W. W. Skeat, *A Concise Dictionary of Middle English*. Oxford 1888.

A New English Dictionary on Historical Principles, ed. Sir J. A. H. Murray, H. Bradley, W. A. Craigie, C. T. Onions. Oxford 1888–1933 (NED).

F. H. Stratmann, *A Middle English Dictionary*, revised by H. Bradley. Oxford 1891.

H. Kurath and S. M. Kuhn, *Middle English Dictionary*. Ann Arbor 1952– .

SELECTIONS FROM MIDDLE ENGLISH

A. Brandl & O. Zippel, *Mittelenglische Sprach- und Literaturproben*. 2nd ed. Berlin 1927.

A. S. Cook, *A Literary Middle English Reader*. New York 1915.

O. F. Emerson, *A Middle English Reader*. London 1905, rev. 1915.

W. H. French & C. B. Hale, *Middle English Metrical Romances*. New York 1930.

O. Funke, *A Middle English Reader* (*texts from the 12th to the 14th c.*). Bern 1944.

J. Hall, *Selections from Early Middle English 1130–1250*. Oxford 1920.

R. Morris, *Specimens of Early English*, Part I *1150–1300*. Oxford 1882.

F. Mossé, *Manuel de l'anglais du Moyen Âge: II. Moyen-anglais*. Paris 1949. Transl. J. A. Walker. Baltimore 1952.

K. Sisam, *Fourteenth Century Verse and Prose*. Oxford 1921, frequently reprinted.

OTHER TEXTS OF THE PERIOD

K. Brunner, *Der mittelenglische Versroman über Richard Löwenherz* (*Richard Coer de Lion*). Wien & Leipzig 1913.

A. O. Belfour, *Twelfth-Century Homilies in MS.* Bodley 323. EETS 1909.

A. S. Napier, *History of the Holy Rood-Tree.* EETS 1894.

R. D.-N. Warner, *Early English Homilies from the twelfth century MS. Vesp. D xiv.* EETS 1917.

R. Morris, *Old English Homilies*: I (*Lambeth* and *Vespasian A xxii*). EETS 1867–8.

R. Morris, *Old English Homilies*: II (*Trinity*). EETS 1873.

R. Morris, *An Old English Miscellany.* EETS 1872.

A. F. Colborn, *Hali Meiðhad.* Copenhagen & London 1940.

S. T. R. O. d'Ardenne, *The Liflade ant te Passiun of Seinte Iuliene.* Liège 1936.

E. Einenkel, *The Life of Saint Katherine.* EETS 1884.

R. M. Wilson, *Sawles Warde.* Leeds 1939.

R. Morris, *The Story of Genesis and Exodus.* EETS 1865.

C. Horstmann, *The Early South English Legendary.* EETS 1887.

K. Böddeker, *Altenglische Dichtungen des MS. Harl.* 2253. Berlin 1878.

Carleton Brown, *English Lyrics of the XIIIth Century.* Oxford 1932. [Three more snatches in 4 *Leeds Studies in English* 44–46, and J. Saltmarsh, *Two Medieval Lyrics.* Cambridge 1933.]

H. A. Person, *Cambridge Middle English Lyrics.* Seattle 1953.

G. L. Brook, *The Harley Lyrics.* Manchester 1948.

G. H. McKnight, *Dame Siriz* (in *Middle English Humorous Tales in Verse.* Boston & London 1913).

LITERARY HISTORY

A. C. Baugh, Kemp Malone, etc., *A Literary History of England.* New York 1948.

Cambridge History of English Literature (Cambridge 1907), Vols. I & II.

R. W. Chambers, *On the Continuity of English Prose from Alfred to More and his School.* EETS 1932.

L. A. Hibbard, *Mediaeval Romance in England: a study of the sources and analogues of the non-cyclic metrical romances.* New York 1924.

W. P. Ker, *English Literature, Medieval.* London 1912. Reset 1945.

W. H. Schofield, *English Literature from the Norman Conquest to Chaucer*. London 1906.

A. B. Taylor, *An Introduction to Medieval Romance*. London 1930.

R. M. Wilson, *Early Middle English Literature*. London 1939.

——, *The Lost Literature of Medieval England*. London 1952.

G. Kane, *Middle English Literature*. London 1951.

HISTORY OF THE LANGUAGE

A. C. Baugh, *A History of the English Language*. New York 1935.

O. Jespersen, *Growth and Structure of the English Language*, 9th ed. Leipzig 1938, Oxford 1940.

K. Luick, *Historische Grammatik der englischen Sprache*. Leipzig 1913 ff.

H. C. Wyld, *A Short History of English*, 3rd ed. London 1927.

See also:

J. & E. M. Wright, *An Elementary Middle English Grammar*. 2nd ed. Oxford 1928.

R. Jordan, *Handbuch der mittelenglischen Grammatik*, 2nd ed. Heidelberg 1934.

K. Brunner, *Abriss der mittelenglischen Grammatik*. Halle 1938.

——, *Die englische Sprache*. Halle 1950–51.

S. Moore, S. B. Meech & H. Whitehall, *Middle English Dialect Characteristics and Dialect Boundaries*. Ann Arbor 1935.

J. P. Oakden, *Alliterative Poetry in Middle English*. 2 vols. Manchester 1930–35.

M. S. Serjeantson, *A History of Foreign Words in English*. London 1935.

E. Björkman, *Scandinavian Loan-Words in Middle English*. Halle 1900–2.

MONOGRAPHS ON INDIVIDUAL TEXTS

F. P. Gillespy, *Laʒamon's Brut: a comparative study of narrative art*. (Univ. of California Publications in Modern Philology, Vol. III, No. 4). Berkeley 1916.

G. J. Visser, *Laʒamon: An Attempt at Vindication*. Assen 1935.

W. H. French, *Essays on King Horn*. Ithaca 1940.

K. Huganir, *The Owl and the Nightingale: Sources, Date, Author*.
  Philadelphia 1931.
B. Sundby, *The Date and Provenance of . . . 'The Owl and the Nightingale'*.
  Lund 1950.
O. S. Anderson, *The Proverbs of Alfred*. Lund 1942.
A. K. Moore, *The Secular Lyric in Middle English*. Lexington (Univ.
  of Kentucky Press) 1951.

HISTORICAL BACKGROUND

D. M. Stenton, *English Society in the Early Middle Ages (1066–1307)*.
  London (Pelican) 1951. Rev. and annotated 1952.
  To the excellent short bibliography therein might be added
J. H. Ramsay, *The Foundations of England*, Vol. II; *The Angevin
  Empire; The Dawn of the Constitution*. London 1898, 1903, 1908.
J. R. H. Moorman, *Church Life in England in the 13th Century*.
  Cambridge 1945.
H. S. Bennett, *Life on the English Manor (1150–1400)*. Cambridge
  1937.
D. C. Douglas and G. W. Greenaway, *English Historical Documents
  1042–1189*. London 1953.
G. C. Homans, *English Villagers of the Thirteenth Century*.
  Cambridge (Mass.) 1942.
F. M. Powicke. *The Thirteenth Century*. Oxford 1953.

PERIODICALS AND SERIES

Anglia, and *Anglia-Beiblatt*.
Archiv für das Studien der neueren Sprachen und Literaturen (Archiv).
Early English Text Society (EETS).
A Journal of English Literary History (ELH).
English Place-Name Society volumes (EPNS).
*Essays and Studies by Members of The English Association (Essays
  and Studies)*.
Journal of English and Germanic Philology (JEGP).
Medium Ævum (Med. Æv.).
Modern Language Notes (MLN).
Modern Language Review (MLR).
Publications of the Modern Language Association of America (PMLA).
Review of English Studies (RES).
Rolls Series (RS).

SOME REVIEWS

22 *Med. Æv.* 119–123; 68 *MLN* 575–6; 47 *MLR* 422; NS/4 *RES* 404; *The Times Literary Supplement* for 7 Aug. 1951; *The Year's Work in English Studies* for 1951, pp. 83–84.

ADDITIONS TO SELECT BIBLIOGRAPHY

THE TRUE CORRECTION AND EDITION OF
AUTHORS

Rash diligence hath don gret preiudice. For these *Critiques* haue
often presumed that that which they vnderstand not, is false set
down; As the Priest, that where he found it written of *S. Paul
Demissus est per sportam* [referring to *Acts* ix. 25, and 2 *Corinthians*
xi. 33] mended his book, and made it *Demissus est per portam* because
Sporta was a hard word, and out of his reading; and surely their
errors, though they be not so palpable and ridiculous, yet are of the
same kind. And therefore, as it hath beene wisely noted, the most
corrected copies are commonly the least correct.

[THE Two Bookes of FRANCIS BACON. Of the proficience and
aduancement of Learning, diuine and humane (London 1605), II,
68–69.]

EARLY MIDDLE ENGLISH TEXTS

I. A WORCESTER FRAGMENT

THE *Worcester Fragments* are the remains of a MS., some leaves of which had been cut up and pasted together to form a cover for another book in the Chapter Library at Worcester. These leaves have been collected and now form MS. 174 in that collection. When complete, the MS. evidently contained a copy of Ælfric's *Grammar and Glossary*, the short poem printed below, and a longer one on the *Debate of the Soul and the Body*. The surviving leaves are written in a single hand, dated *c.* 1180, with the metrical sections written continuously though the verse-end is usually indicated by a period. It is clear that the various pieces were composed at a much earlier date. The work of Ælfric was of course in Old English, and it is probable that the poems were also originally composed in the standard WS. literary dialect, though presumably after the Conquest, and roughly modernized by a later scribe writing probably at Worcester. The piece below is written in what is evidently a development of the OE alliterative line, though perhaps derived from the freer and looser type, as developed in oral tradition, rather than from the conventional literary line of most of the extant OE verse. Nothing is known of the author, though the absence of some famous Worcester names, together with the comparatively large number of bishops mentioned who were connected with Winchester, has led to the suggestion that it may originally have been composed in the latter town, presumably towards the end of the eleventh century. In theme a close parallel is to be found in the lament, by William of Malmesbury, on the position of the English at the beginning of the twelfth century:

England is become the dwelling-place of foreigners and the property of strangers. At the present time (i.e. *c.* 1130) there is no Englishman who is either earl, bishop or abbot. Strangers prey upon the riches and vitals of England, nor is there any hope of an end to this misery. (*Gesta Regum*, RS. 90, i, 278.)

All the fragments were printed by Sir Thomas Phillipps, *Fragment*

of Aelfric's Grammar, &c. (London 1838), but the best edition of
this poem is in Hall i, 1; ii, 223 ff.

The Disuse of English

[S]anctus Beda was iboren her on Breotene mid us,
And he wisliche [bec] awende
Þet þeo Englise leoden þurh weren ilerde.
And he þeo c[not]ten unwreih, þe questiuns hoteþ,
5   Þa derne diȝelnesse þe de[or]wurþe is.
Ælfric abbod, þe we Alquin hoteþ,
He was bocare, and þe [fif] bec wende,
Genesis, Exodus, Vtronomius, Numerus, Leuiticus,
Þu[rh] þeos weren ilærde ure leoden on Englisc.
10   Þet weren þeos biscop[es þe] bodeden Cristendom,
    Wilfrid of Ripum, Iohan of Beoferlai, Cuþb[ert] of Dunholme,
Oswald of Wireceastre, Egwin of Heoueshame, Æld[elm] of
Malmesburi, Swiþþun, Æþelwold, Aidan, Biern of Wincæstre,
[Pau]lin of Rofecæstre, S. Dunston, and S. Ælfeih of Cantoreburi.
15   Þeos læ[rden] ure leodan on Englisc,
Næs deorc heore liht, ac hit fæire glod.
[Nu is] þeo leore forleten, and þet folc is forloren.
Nu beoþ oþre leoden þeo læ[reþ] ure folc,
And feole of þen lorþeines losiæþ and þet folc forþ mid.
20   Nu sæiþ [ure] Drihten þus, *Sicut aquila prouocat pullos suos ad
uolandum, et super eo[s uolitat.]*
This beoþ Godes word to worlde asende,
Þet we sceolen fæier feþ [festen to Him.]

---

*Critical footnotes are reduced to a minimum, erasures and corrections in the MSS. being
reported only when they appear significant. Such footnotes are infrequent except in VI and X.
Letters and words within square brackets are editorial additions which do not in general need a
note.*

2 [bec]: *three or four letters are cropped or cut away at the end of each MS. line.*
11 Ripum: *MS.* Sipum.
21 *The beginning of the last surviving MS. line is defective.*

II. THE PETERBOROUGH CHRONICLE

IN 1116 the greater part of the monastery at Peterborough was destroyed by a fire in which perished many or most of its records. But apparently the tradition of historical writing was still vigorous there; a copy of the *Old English Chronicle* was borrowed from some Kentish monastery, probably St. Augustine's, Canterbury, copied up to date, and presumably returned to its original home. The Peterborough MS. itself was continued by various hands until the end of the annal for 1131. It was then laid aside—the unsettled conditions of Stephen's reign were hardly conducive to historical writing—and with the appearance of more settled conditions in 1154 was brought up to date by the insertion of half a dozen annals scattered between the dates 1132 and 1154. Most of the events are dated only approximately, and only two of the annals are of any length, that for 1137 describing the misery of the country during the anarchy, and that for 1140 which gives the main events of the war between Stephen and the Empress Matilda. In all probability the whole of the annals for 1132–1154 were written at one time, soon after 1154. The last few lines of the last annal, which tells of the accession of Henry II and the installation of a new abbot of Peterborough, are only in part legible. Finally there is no good reason to conjecture, as Plummer did, that the MS. has lost one final leaf.

Up to and including the annal for 1131 the *Peterborough Chronicle* is written in what is, in the main, the West Saxon literary language, not perhaps so pure as in the fragment (H) containing the annals for 1113–14. But during the interval this particular literary language appears to have fallen into disuse, and the old spelling traditions to have been almost forgotten. Consequently a new literary language has had to be developed, based in the main on the spoken language of the district, but retaining some vague memory of earlier scribal conventions. The result of this is that, while the earlier annals provide some of the latest examples of the use of the West Saxon literary language, those from 1132 to 1154 are the earliest examples of Middle English, and in that lies the linguistic importance of this particular text. Not that it is negligible as literature. Working under the necessity of developing a new literary language, with a

3

prose tradition only half remembered and a confused syntax, the later annals are not unworthy of the series of capable and sometimes great writers to whom we owe the *Old English Chronicle*. This particular annal is deservedly famous; it has frequently been quoted, often mistranslated, by historians, and well deserves its fame. A faint undertone of querulousness cannot mar the vividness of the description of the state of the country during the anarchy. Historically too, although most of the events are dated only approximately, the work of this continuator is one of the most important sources for the history of the period.

The Peterborough MS. of the *Old English Chronicle* is now preserved as MS. Laud Misc. 636 in the Bodleian Library. Six MSS., including this, were edited by B. Thorpe for the Rolls Series in 1861, but the best edition of the complete text of the Peterborough MS. is in C. Plummer and J. Earle, *Two Saxon Chronicles Parallel* (Oxford 1892). This particular annal is, however, included in most ME readers, and treated in greatest detail in Hall.[1]

The Anarchy

1137. Ðis gære for þe king Stephne ofer sæ to Normandi and ther wes underfangen, forþi ðat hi uuenden ðat he sculde ben alsuic alse the eom wes, and for he hadde get his tresor; ac he to-deld it and scatered sotlice. Micel hadde Henri king gadered
5 gold and syluer, and na god ne dide me for his saule thar-of.

Þa þe king Stephne to Englalande com, þa macod he his gadering æt Oxeneford, and þar he nam þe biscop Roger of Sereberi, and Alexander biscop of Lincol and te canceler Roger, hise neues, and dide ælle in prisun til hi iafen up here castles.
10 Þa the suikes undergæton ðat he milde man was and softe and god, and na iustise ne dide, þa diden hi alle wunder. Hi hadden him manred maked and athes suoren; ac hi nan treuthe ne heolden. Alle he wæron forsworen and here treothes forloren, for æuric riceman his castles makede and agænes him heolden,
15 and fylden þe land ful of castles. Hi suencten suyðe þe uureccemen of þe land mid castel-weorces. Þa þe castles uuaren maked, þa fylden hi mid deoules and yuele men. Þa namen hi þa men þe hi wenden ðat ani god hefden, bathe be nihtes and be dæies, carlmen and wimmen, and diden heom in prisun efter
20 gold and syluer, and pined heom untellendlice pining, for ne

---

[1] The best translation is by G. N. Garmonsway, *The Anglo-Saxon Chronicle* (Everyman 1953), where at p. xli is noted that Ordericus Vitalis's account (viii, 4) of the disorders in Normandy after William I's death is earlier than, and uncommonly close in general outline to part of this annal.

hæued. ðuuȝ ȝchen te ð it gæde to beiærnef. I hi diden heo inquaȝ
terne þar nadȝes ȝ snakef ȝ padef pæȝon inne· ȝ drapen heo ſpa.
Sume hi diden in crucethuȝ ð is in an cęfte þar paf feort ȝ nareu·
ȝun dep. ȝ ðide ſcaȝpe ſtanef þer inne· ȝ þrengde þe man þeȝ
inne· ð hi bȝæcon alle þe limef· Jn mani of þe caſtlef pæron lof
ȝ gȝi· ð pæȝon ȝacheintegef ð tpa oþeȝ thȝe men hadden o noh to
bæron onne· þat paf ſua maced· ð if feftned to an beom· ȝ diden an
ſcaȝp iren abuton þa mannef thȝote· ȝ hif half· ð he inȝ litce nopi
·ðeȝ pardef· ne ſitten ne lien ne ſlepen· oc bæȝon al ð iȝen· Oſ ani
þufen hi drapen mid hungȝ: Jne can ne ine mai tellen alle þe
punder ne alle þe pinef ð hi diden ȝrecce men on þif land· ȝ ð laſte
ðe þa· xix· pintȝe pile Stephne paf king ȝ auȝe it paf uuerſe ȝ
uuerſe· Hi læiden gæildef o the tunef æuertuȝil e ȝ clepeden it
tenſerie· þa þe uuȝecce men ne hadden nã moȝe to gȝuen· þa ȝx
ueden hi ȝ brendon alle the tunef· ð þel þu mihtef faȝen al adaȝf
fare ſculdeſt thu neure finden man intune ſittende· ne land ti
led· þa paf corn dæȝe· ȝ flec ȝ cæſe ȝ butere· for nan ne paf o þe land.
ȝrecce men ſturuen of hungȝ· ſume ȝeden on ælmef þe paȝen ſu
pile ȝicemen· ſume flugen ut of lande· Y ef næuȝ egæt mare pȝ tẽc
lȝed on land· ne næure hethen men þeȝ ſe ne diden þan hi diden·
for ouȝ ſithon ne for laȝen ȝ noruthȝ cȝrce ne cȝȝ ceȝaȝð· oc nam
al þe god ð þaȝ inne paf· ȝ brenden ſychen þe cȝrce ȝ al tẽ gædere·
Ȝe hi ne forbaȝen b land ne abb ne proſtȝf· ac ȝæ ueden munekef
ȝ clerekef· ȝ æuȝic man otheȝ þe ouȝ mihte· Gif tpa men oþeȝ iii
coman ȝidend to an tun· al þe tuniſerpe flugæn for heo· ȝ enden ð
hi pæron ȝæueȝef· þe biſcopef ȝ leȝd men heo cuȝ ſæde æuȝe· oc paf
heo naht þar of· for hi uueronal for curſæd ȝ for ſuoȝen ȝ for lo
ren· paȝ ſæ me tilede· þe erthe ne bar nan corn· for þe land paf al
for don· mid ſuilce dedef· ȝ hi ſæden openlice ð xȝiſt ſlep· ȝ hif ha
lechen· Suile ȝ maȝe þanne þe cumnen ſæm· þe þolenden· xix· pintȝe
                                        ȝ for uȝe ſinnef·

THE PETERBOROUGH CHRONICLE, 1137
(Bodleian Laud Misc. 636, f. 84 v)
Facing page 5

uuæren næure nan martyrs swa pined alse hi wæron. Me henged
up bi the fet and smoked heom mid ful smoke. Me henged bi
the þumbes other bi the hefed, and hengen bryniges on her fet.
Me dide cnotted strenges abuton here hæued and uurythen it
25 ðat it gæde to þe hærnes. Hi diden heom in quarterne þar nadres
and snakes and pades wæron inne, and drapen heom swa. Sume
hi diden in crucethus, ðat is in an cæste þat was scort, and nareu,
and undep, and dide scærpe stanes þerinne, and þrengde þe
man þær-inne, ðat him bræcon alle þe limes. In mani of þe
30 castles wæron lof and grin, ðat wæron rachenteges ðat twa oþer
thre men hadden onoh to bæron onne; þat was sua maced, ðat is
fæstned to an beom, and diden an scærp iren abuton þa mannes
throte and his hals, ðat he ne myhte nowiderwardes, ne sitten ne
lien ne slepen, oc bæron al ðat iren. Mani þusen hi drapen mid
35 hungær. I ne can ne I ne mai tellen alle þe wunder ne alle þe
pines ðat hi diden wreccemen on þis land, and ðat lastede þa xix
wintre wile Stephne was king, and æure it was uuerse and
uuerse. Hi læiden gæildes on the tunes æure umwile, and
clepeden it tenserie. Þa þe uureccemen ne hadden nan more to
40 gyuen, þa ræueden hi and brendon alle the tunes, ðat wel þu
myhtes faren al a dæis fare sculdest thu neure finden man in tune
sittende, ne land tiled. Þa was corn dære and fle[s]c and cæse and
butere, for nan ne wæs o þe land. Wreccemen sturuen of
hungær; sume ieden on ælmes þe waren sumwile ricemen, sume
45 flugen ut of lande. Wes næure gæt mare wreccehed on land, ne
næure hethen men werse ne diden þan hi diden, for ouer sithon
ne forbaren hi nouther circe ne cyrceiærd, oc namen al þe god
ðat þarinne was, and brenden sythen þe cyrce and altegædere.
Ne hi ne forbaren biscopes land ne abbotes ne preostes, ac
50 ræueden munekes and clerekes, and æuric man other þe ouer-
myhte. Gif twa men oþer iii coman ridend to an tun, al þe
tunscipe flugæn for heom—wenden ðat hi wæron ræueres. Þe
biscopes and leredmen heom cursede æure, oc was heom naht
þarof, for hi uueron al forcursæd and forsuoren and forloren.
55 War-sæ me tilede, þe erthe ne bar nan corn, for þe land was al
fordon mid suilce dædes, and hi sæden openlice ðat Christ slep,
and his halechen. Suilc and mare þanne we cunnen sæin, we
þoleden xix wintre for ure sinnes. On al þis yuele time heold
Martin abbot his abbotrice xx wintre and half gær and viii
60 dæis, mid micel suinc, and fand þe munekes and te gestes al þat
heom behoued, and heold mycel carited in the hus, and þoþ-
wethere wrohte on þe circe and sette þarto landes and rentes, and

58 þoleden: *MS.* þolenden

goded it suythe, and læt it refen, and brohte heom into þe neuuæ
mynstre on Sanct PETRES mæssedæi mid micel wurtscipe. Ðat

65 was *anno ab incarnatione domini mcxl, a combustionę loci xxiii.* And
he for to Rome, and þær wæs wæl underfangen fram þe Pape
Eugenie, and begæt thare priuilegies, an of alle þe landes of
þabbotrice, and an-oþer of þe landes þe lien to þe circewican;
and gif he leng moste liuen, alse he mint to don of þe horder-

70 wycan.   And he begæt in landes þat ricemen hefden mid
strengthe. Of Willelm Malduit þe heold Rogingham þæ castel
he wan Cotingham and Estun; of Hugo of Walteruile he uuan
Hyrtlingberi and Stanewig and lx *solidos* of Aldewingle ælc
gær. And he makede manie munekes and plantede winiærd, and

75 makede mani weorkes, and wende þe tun betere þan it ær wæs,
and wæs god munec and god man, and forþi him luueden God
and gode men.

Nu we willen sægen sumdel wat belamp on Stephnes kinges
time. On his time þe Iudeus of Noruuic bohton an Christen cild

80 beforen Estren, and pineden him alle þe ilce pining ðat ure
Drihten was pined; and on Lang-Fridæi him on rode hengen for
ure Drihtines luue, and sythen byrieden him — wenden ðat it
sculde ben forholen, oc ure Dryhtin atywede ðat he was hali
martyr, and to munekes him namen and bebyried him heglice in

85 þe minstre, and he maket þur ure Drihtin wunderlice and
manifældlice miracles, and hatte he Sanct Willelm.

III. THE PROCLAMATION OF HENRY III

This proclamation, issued in 1258, marks the momentary emergence of English as an official language. In the early post-Conquest years English had remained the language of the royal chancery, and many of the official documents of the Conqueror were in English. But during the following reign such documents in the vernacular become scarce and fail entirely with the beginning of the twelfth century. After that Latin, and later Anglo-French, remain the only official languages until the very end of the thirteenth century, the only exceptions being a charter in English, issued in 1155, in which Henry II confirms to the Archbishop of Canterbury and the monks of Christ Church their lands and privileges of jurisdiction, and this proclamation. The *Proclamation*[1] itself was issued in confirmation of the *Provisions of Oxford*, a charter of rights extorted from the king by the barons in 1258. It was issued in French and English, and perhaps also in Latin, and the presence of the English version is no doubt to be connected with the nationalist reaction during the reign of Henry III led by Simon de Montfort, when one of the items on the rebels' programme is said to have been the extirpation of all who could not speak English. As indicated at the end of the *Proclamation* a copy of it was to be sent to every shire in England and to Ireland, and two of these English copies have survived. One, preserved in the Bodleian, was the copy sent to Oxfordshire, while the other, preserved in the Public Record Office, has Huntingdon as its destination, though the note at the end suggests that it may rather have been the version from which the different copies were to be made. It is this copy which is printed below, since it appears to represent the London dialect of the period more nearly than does the Bodleian MS., and the importance of this work linguistically lies in the fact that it gives us the earliest example of the London dialect in Middle English. Originally the London dialect seems to have been mainly southern or south-eastern in character, but by the fourteenth century it had become in the main East Midland, though with some southern forms still remaining. This particular

[1] It is in form Letters Patent (*writ open*) and is entered in the Patent Rolls (43 Henry III, M.15); see H. Hall, *A Formula Book of English Official Historical Documents*, Part I, pp. 60 and 73-4 (Cambridge 1908).

7

text appears to show a mixture of Southern and Midland forms, no doubt characteristic of the London English of the time, and illustrating the gradual transition from a Southern to a Midland basis.

A facsimile of the version in the Public Record Office is given by W. W. Skeat, *English Dialects* (Cambridge 1912), and it has been frequently printed, as for example by Emerson, Brandl and Zippel, etc. The Bodleian version was printed by Skeat in the *Transactions of the Philological Society*, 1880–1. The French version will be found in Brandl and Zippel, and in H. Hall, p. 73.

A Proclamation

Henri, þurȝ Godes fultume King on Engleneloande, Lhoauerd on Yrloande, Duk on Normandi, on Aquitaine, and Eorl on Aniow, send igretinge to alle hise holde, ilærde and ileawede, on Huntendoneschire. Þæt witen ȝe wel alle þæt we willen and
5 vnnen þæt, þæt vre rædesmen alle, oþer þe moare dæl of heom, þæt beoþ ichosen þurȝ us and þurȝ þæt loandes folk on vre kuneriche, habbeþ idon and shullen don in þe worþnesse of Gode and on vre treowþe, for þe freme of þe loande þurȝ þe besiȝte of þan toforeniseide redesmen, beo stedefæst and ile-
10 stinde in alle þinge a buten ænde. And we hoaten alle vre treowe in þe treowþe þæt heo vs oȝen, þæt heo stedefæstliche healden and swerien to healden and to werien þo isetnesses þæt beon imakede and beon to makien, þurȝ þan toforeniseide rædesmen, oþer þurȝ þe moare dæl of heom, alswo alse hit is
15 biforen iseid; and þæt æhc oþer helpe þæt for to done bi þan ilche oþe aȝenes alle men riȝt for to done and to foangen. And noan ne nime of loande ne of eȝte wherþurȝ þis besiȝte muȝe beon ilet oþer iwersed on onie wise. And ȝif oni oþer onie cumen her onȝenes, we willen and hoaten þæt alle vre treowe heom
20 healden deadliche ifoan. And for þæt we willen þæt þis beo stedefæst and lestinde, we senden ȝew þis writ open, iseined wiþ vre seel, to halden amanges ȝew ine hord. Witnesse vsseluen æt Lundene þane eȝtetenþe day on þe monþe of Octobre, in þe two and fowertiȝþe ȝeare of vre cruninge. And þis wes idon
25 ætforen vre isworene redesmen, Boneface Archebischop on Kanterburi, Walter of Cantelow, Bischop on Wirechestre, Simon of Muntfort, Eorl on Leirchestre, Richard of Clare, Eorl on Glowchestre and on Hurtford, Roger Bigod, Eorl on North-

1–32 *All the personal names, with the exception of* Perres, Geffree *and* Iames *are abbreviated in the* MS.   26 Kanterburi: *MS.* Kanterbur'.

folke and Marescal on Engleneloande, Perres of Sauueye,
30 Willelm of Fort, Eorl on Aubemarle, Iohan of Plesseiz, Eorl on
Warewik, Iohan Geffrees sune, Perres of Muntfort, Richard of
Grey, Roger of Mortemer, Iames of Aldithele, and ætforen oþre
inoȝe.

And al on þo ilche worden is isend into æurihce oþre shcire
35 ouer al þære kuneriche on Engleneloande, and ek in-tel Irelonde.

IV. THE SONG OF LEWES

A CONSIDERABLE amount of political poetry has survived from the ME period, and examples are extant in all three of the languages which were then in use. But the surviving ME poems on the subject date mostly from the fourteenth and fifteenth centuries, and vary in length from the pregnant couplet on the fourteenth year of Richard II:

> The ax was sharpe, the stokke was harde,
> In the xiiii yere of Kyng Richarde,

to important works such as *Piers Plowman, Richard the Redeless* (now better known as *Mum and the Sothsegger*), etc. The only political poem dating from the thirteenth century which has survived in its entirety is one celebrating the defeat of Henry III, and more particularly the discomfiture of Richard of Cornwall,[1] at the battle of Lewes. But although this is the earliest extant political poem in English, there are many references to similar poetry of an earlier date, and odd fragments of it still survive.

The *Song of Lewes* is preserved in the British Museum Harley 2253, a famous anthology to which we owe much of our knowledge of the medieval lyric. It was apparently written at Leominster during the first quarter of the fourteenth century, and so in a West Midland dialect, though the rhymes indicate that some of the lyrics were probably composed in other areas. The poem has frequently been printed; most recently by Carleton Brown, but also in various editions of the Harley lyrics, by T. Wright, *Political Songs of England* (Camden Society 1839), and in some ME readers.

The Song of Lewes

> Sitteþ alle stille ant herkneþ to me!
> Þe kyn[g] of Alemaigne, bi mi leaute,
> Þritti þousent pound askede he
> Forte make þe pees in þe countre,
> 5   Ant so he dude more.
> Richard, þah þou be euer trichard,
> Tricchen shalt þou neuermore!

---

[1] For whom see N. Denholm-Young's monograph (Oxford 1947). C. Bémont, *Simon de Montfort* (Oxford 1930) and Sir F. Maurice Powicke, *King Henry III and the Lord Edward* (Oxford 1947) are also valuable for the period.

Richard of Alemaigne, whil þat he wes kyng,
He spende al is tresour opon swyuyng,
10 Haueþ he nout of Walingford o ferlyng;
Let him habbe ase he brew, bale to dryng,
    Maugre Wyndesore.
  Richard, &c.

Þe kyng of Alemaigne wende do ful wel,
He saisede þe mulne for a castel,
15 Wiþ hare sharpe swerdes he grounde þe stel,
He wende þat þe sayles were mangonel,
    To helpe Wyndesore.
  Richard, &c.

Þe kyng of Alemaigne gederede ys host,
Makede him a castel of a mulne-post,
20 Wende wiþ is prude ant is muchele bost,
Brohte from Alemayne mony sori gost,
    To store Wyndesore.
  Richard, &c.

By God þat is abouen ous, he dude muche **synne**
Þat lette passen ouer see þe erl of Warynne;
25 He haþ robbed Engelond, þe mores ant þ[e] fenne.
Þe gold ant þe seluer ant yboren henne,
    For loue of Wyndesore.
  Richard, &c.

Sire Simond de Mountfort haþ suore bi ys chyn,
Heuede he nou here þe erl of Waryn,
30 Shulde he neuer-more come to is yn,
Ne wiþ sheld ne wiþ spere ne wiþ oþer gyn,
    To help of Wyndesore.
  Richard, &c.

Sire Simond de Montfort haþ suore bi ys top,
Heuede he nou here Sire Hue de Bigot,
35 Al he shulde quite here tuelfmoneþ scot,
Shulde he neuermore wiþ his fot pot,
    To helpe Wyndesore.
  Richard, &c.

Be þe luef, be þe loht, Sire Edward,
Þou shalt ride sporeles o þy lyard
40 Al þe ryhte way to Douere ward;
Shalt þou neuermore breke foreward,
    Ant þat reweþ sore.
  Edward, þou dudest ase a shreward,
    Forsoke þyn emes lore.
45   Richard, þah þou be euer trichard,
    Tricchen shalt þou neuermore;

V. THE CHRONICLE OF ROBERT OF GLOUCESTER

THE chronicle which goes under the name of Robert of Gloucester exists in two different versions, the fullest of which contains some 12,000 verses, and it seems probable that Robert himself can have been responsible for part only of it. In all probability the work of at least three different authors is represented in the two extant versions. The first of these was apparently a monk of Gloucester, whose name is unknown, who, towards the end of the thirteenth century, wrote a verse history in some 9,000 lines beginning with the destruction of Troy and ending with the death of Henry I. Soon afterwards a monk named Robert, probably also from Gloucester, revised the work of his predecessor and, by the addition of a further 3,000 lines, carried on the story to the death of Henry III. Then, early in the fourteenth century, still another monk of Gloucester again revised the work of the first writer and added to it a brief independent continuation of some 600 lines. Consequently, although the whole chronicle usually goes under the name of Robert of Gloucester, of whom in any case nothing but the name is known, it must be remembered that he was in fact responsible only for the last 3,000 lines of the longer version, and had nothing whatever to do with the shorter one.

The earlier part of the work appears to be based mainly on Geoffrey of Monmouth, and, when he ends, on various monastic chronicles, though in addition oral tradition has been used fairly freely. Only in the part due to Robert of Gloucester himself, when he begins to deal with more or less contemporary events, is the chronicle of any value as a historical source. Robert had apparently lived through the civil wars of Henry III's reign, and he gives interesting details of the course of events, and especially of the battle of Evesham. From a literary point of view the work is of perhaps more interest than might have been expected. None of the authors was a poet, and in fact they make no attempt at poetry. They write in verse simply because the only other vernacular histories known to them, the Anglo-French ones, were in verse. Nevertheless, they manage their lines capably, and Robert himself has a talent for vivid descriptive detail. But it is perhaps more particularly the reflection of the author's own personality, genuine, sincere, and direct, which adds flavour to his writings.

The longer version, with which alone we are concerned, is preserved in British Museum Cotton Caligula A xi (early fourteenth century), Harley 201 (*c.* 1400), and several later MSS. The Cottonian MS. was edited by W. Aldis Wright in 1887 for the Rolls Series, and the Harleian MS. by T. Hearne (Oxford 1724). The extracts below are taken from the Cottonian MS. and correspond with lines 7537–7547 and 11668–771, in Wright's edition.

The Languages of England
(7537)

Þus com, lo, Engelond in-to Normandies hond:
And þe Normans ne couþe speke þo bote hor owe speche,
And speke French as hii dude atom, and hor children dude also
So þat heiemen of þis lond, þat of hor blod come,   [teche,
5 Holdeþ alle þulke speche þat hii of hom nome;
Vor bote a man conne Frenss me telþ of him lute.
Ac lowe men holdeþ to Engliss, and to hor owe speche ȝute.
Ich wene þer ne beþ in al þe world contreyes none
Þat ne holdeþ to hor owe speche, bote Engelond one.
10 Ac wel me wot uor to conne boþe wel it is,
Vor þe more þat a mon can, þe more wurþe he is.

The Battle of Evesham
(11668)

Þo was Sir Simond is fader at Hereforde iwis,
Mid mani god man of Engelond, and also of Walis.
He wende him out of Hereford mid vair ost inou,
15 And toward Keningwurþe aȝen is sone he drou,
And was hor beire porpos to bi-closi hor fon,
As wo seiþ in eiþer half, and to ssende hom echon.
So þat Sir Simon þe olde com þe Monendai iwis
To a toun biside Wircetre þat Kemeseie ihote is.
20 Þe Tiwesday to Euesham he wende þe morweninge,
And þere he let him and is folc prestes massen singe,
And poȝte to wende norþward is sone vor to mete.
Ac þe king nolde a vot bote he dinede oþer ete,
And Sir Simon þe ȝonge and is ost at Alcestre were,
25 And nolde þanne wende a vot ar hii dinede þere.
Þulke to diners deluol were alas,
Vor mani was þe gode bodi þat þer-þoru islawe was.
Sir Edward and is poer sone come þo ride

To þe norþhalf of þe toun, bataile uor to abide.
30 Þo Sir Simon it iwuste, and hii þat wiþ him were,
Sone hii lete hom armi and hor baners arere.
Þe bissop Water of Wurcetre asoiled hom alle þere,
And prechede hom þat hii adde of deþ þe lasse fere.
Þen wei euene to hor fon a Godes half hii nome,
35 And wende þat Sir Simon þe ȝonge aȝen hom c[ome].
Þo hii come into þe feld, and Sir Simond isei
Sir Edwardes ost and oþere al-so nei,
He avisede þe ost suiþe wel, and þoru Godes grace
He hopede winne a day þe maistrie of þe place.
40 Þo sei he þer biside, as he bihuld aboute,
Þe erles baner of Gloucetre and him mid al is route
As him vor to close in þe oþer half ywis.
'Ouȝ', he sede, 'redi folk and wel iwar is þis,
And more conne of bataile þan hii couþe biuore.
45 Vr soules', he sede, 'abbe God, vor vr bodies beþ hore.
Sir Henri', he sede to his sone, 'þis haþ imad þi prute;
Were þi broþer icome, hope we miȝte ȝute'.
Hii bitoke lif and soule to Godes grace echon,
And in-to bataile smite, vaste among hore fon,
50 And as gode kniȝtes to grounde slowe anon,
Þat hor fon flowe sone þicke manion.
Sir Warin of Bassingbourne, þo he þis isei,
Biuore he gan prikie, and to grede an hei,
'Aȝen traitors, aȝen, and habbeþ in ower þoȝt
55 Hou villiche at Lewes ȝe were to grounde ibroȝt.
Turneþ aȝen and þencheþ þat þut power al oure is,
And we ssole as vor noȝt ouercome vr fon iwis'.
Þo was þe bataile strong in eiþer side alas;
Ac atten ende was bineþe þulke þat feblore was,
60 And Sir Simond was aslawe, and is folk al to grounde;
More murþre are nas in so lute stounde,
Vor þere was werst Simond de Mountfort aslawe, alas,
And Sir Henri is sone, þat so gentil kniȝt was,
And Sir Hue þe Despencer, þe noble iustise,
65 And Sir Peris de Mountfort, þat stronge were and wise,
Sir Willam de Verous, and Sir Rauf Basset also,
Sir [Ion] de Sein Ion, Sir Ion Diue þerto,
Sir [Willam] Trossel, Sir Gileberd of Eisnesfelde,
And mani god bodi were aslawe þere in þulke felde.
70 And among alle oþere mest reuþe it was ido,
Þat Sir Simon þe olde man de-membred was so,

61 are: *MS.* ȝare *with* ȝ *erased.*

Vor Sir Willam Mautrauers, þonk nabbe he non,
Carf him of fet and honde, and is limes manion.
And þat mest pite was, hii ne bileuede nouȝt þis,
75 Þat is priue membres hii ne corue of iwis.
And is heued hii smiten of, and to Wigemor it sende
To Dam Maud þe Mortimer, þat wel foule it ssende;
And of al þat me him bilimede hii ne bledde noȝt, me sede,
And þe harde here was is lich þe nexte wede.
80 Suich was þe morþre of Euesham, uor bataile non it nas,
And þerwiþ Iesu Crist wel vuele ipaied was,
As He ssewede bi tokninge grisliche and gode,
As it vel of Him-sulue, þo He deide on þe rode,
Þat þoru al þe middelerd derkhede þer was inou.
85 Also þe wule þe godemen at Euesham me slou,
As in þe norþwest a derk weder þer aros,
So demliche suart inou þat mani man agros,
And ouercaste it poȝte al þut lond, þat me miȝte vnneþe ise,
Grisloker weder þan it was ne miȝte an erþe be,
90 An vewe dropes of reine þer velle grete inou.
Þis tokninge vel in þis lond, þo me þis men slou,
Vor þretti mile þanne, þis isei Roberd,
Þat verst þis boc made, and was wel sore aferd.
Louerdinges þer were inome at Euesham manion,
95 As Sir Vnfrai de Boun, Sir Ion le FizIon,
And Simondes sone, de Mountfort Sir Gwy,
Sir Baudewine de Wake, Sir Ion de Vescy,
Sir Henri de Hastinges, and Sir Nicole iwis
De Segraue was þere inome, and also Sir Piers
100 And Sir Roberd þat Sir Peris de Mountfort sones were.
Þuse and wel mo were inome in þulke morþre þere.
Ac þe Welsse fot-men þat þer were manion
At þe bigininge of þe bataile bigonne to fle echon,
And come þoru Teuskesburi, and þere men of þe toune
105 Slowe hom al to grounde, þat þere hii leie þer doune,
So þicke bi strete þat reuþe it was to se,
And grace nadde non of hom, to fiȝte ne to fle.
Þo þe bataile was ido, and þe godemen aslawe were,
Sir Simond þe ȝonge com to mete is fader þere.
110 He miȝte þo at is diner abbe bileued al-so wel,
As me seiþ, 'Wan ich am ded make me a caudel'.
And þo me tolde him bi þe wei, wuch þe ende was þer,
He turnde aȝen to Keningwurþe, wel longe him þouȝte e[r].
He miȝte segge wan he com, 'Lute ich abbe iwonne;
115 Ich mai honge vp min ax, febliche ich abbe agonne'.

VI. LAȜAMON'S BRUT

NOTHING is known of Laȝamon's career apart from the information given in the opening lines of his work. He lived towards the end of the twelfth century and was a parish priest of what is now Areley Kings in Worcestershire; his name suggests that he had some Scandinavian blood. Being interested in history he decided to deal with the history of the Britons, for which he quotes authorities in his preface (ll. 16–27). Yet his only written source appears to have been the metrical translation by Wace of Geoffrey of Monmouth's *Historia Regum Britanniae*, and it seems certain that the text of Wace used by Laȝamon differed a good deal from that printed by Le Roux de Lincy. In any case, Laȝamon treats his source freely enough, with frequent omissions and expansions, and in addition seems to have drawn independently on the floating oral traditions (Welsh as well as English) of the neighbourhood, and so to have introduced much new material into his work (see G. J. Visser, *Laȝamon: an Attempt at Vindication*, Assen 1935). The result is a poem of some 16,000 alliterative lines telling the history of Britain from the landing of Brutus—hence the title which has been given to it—to the death of Cadwallader; undoubtedly one of the most significant and important of ME. poems. Its more specifically English characteristics have been emphasized (see H. C. Wyld, 6 *RES* 1 ff.) and perhaps exaggerated. His use of the alliterative line, vivid descriptions of the sea, delight in arms, armour and battle, the insistence on the part played by Fate, and an emphasis on loyalty and the bonds of kinship, no doubt owe much to native models. But in addition Laȝamon has certainly been influenced by contemporary French romance. Many of his characters show the influence of the French romances of chivalry; his predilection for the marvellous connects him with the romance rather than with the epic; and the fact that he writes his history in verse, not prose, is probably due to the influence of his source.

One particular importance of the work lies in the fact that it is the first use in English of the subjects which were later to be developed as the Matter of Britain. Laȝamon follows his authorities in devoting a disproportionate amount of space to Arthur. Many new details are added to the story, and the characterisation of the king has been completely changed. In Wace, naturally enough, he is pictured as a contemporary feudal king: in Laȝamon he has been made into a more individual figure and approaches rather to the Germanic hero than to the knight of chivalry.

The alliterative verse used by Laȝamon appears to derive rather from the popular poetry of OE and early ME than from the strict classical line as seen for example in *Beowulf*. Although very little of it has survived, there appears to have existed in OE, by the side of the purely literary poetry, a much looser popular type which retained its hold on the common people long after the literary tradition had been shattered by the Conquest. Certainly there are considerable differences between the alliterative line as used in Laȝamon and the usual type in OE. Stylistically the parallelism which is so characteristic a feature of OE poetry has been almost completely lost, enjambement is rare, much of the specifically poetic vocabulary has vanished, and along with it the kenning has fallen into almost complete disuse, though on the other hand similes are rather more common. Metrically the rhythm has become purely accentual, the structure of the line has become freer with a greater number of unaccented syllables; most of the specific OE types of half-line have disappeared, and rhyme and assonance are more common.

The *Brut* is extant in two MSS., the British Museum Cotton Caligula A ix (*c.* 1225), and Cotton Otho C xiii (*c.* 1250), which suffered a good deal in the Cottonian fire; the earlier of these appears to have been written in approximately the same dialect as that which must have been used by the author. The scribe of the later MS., however, was not content with the mechanical copying usual with medieval scribes, but abbreviated and altered his original considerably. More particularly he often substituted a less archaic word or phrase, changed a specifically poetic word for one nearer to the language of everyday life, or replaced the English word of his original by a French loan-word. The result is that a comparison of the two texts throws considerable light on the changes of vocabulary which have taken place during the years separating them. Nevertheless, despite such alterations the two versions are obviously closely connected, and are probably independent copies of the same original.

The only complete edition of the two texts is that by Sir Frederic Madden (London 1847), but selections were edited by J. Hall (Oxford 1924), and extracts appear in most ME readers. A new edition of the two MSS. is in preparation by Professor G. L. Brook for the Early English Text Society.[1]

The extracts below are taken from Caligula A ix, but it has seemed desirable to illustrate the variation between the two texts by printing on the opposite page the version of the first extract from Humfrey Wanley's printed copy of the burnt leaf of Otho C xiii, and by indicating in the other extracts omissions and changes made by the later scribe, omitted lines and passages being shown by the use of single quotes at the beginning and at the end.

Wanley's transcript from Otho C xiii, f. 1, is printed at p. 237 of G. Hickes, *Antiquæ Literaturæ Septentrionalis Liber Alter* (Oxford 1705). It should be noted that Wanley, while using the continental capital in *God* (10, 25) and *Godes* (30), prints *ȝode* (3), *enȝelond* (7), *enȝlene* (9), *ȝan* (14), *enȝlisse* (17), *finȝres* (26), *toȝedere* (27), *ȝodne* (29), *seȝȝe toȝadere* (32), after the fashion of his time. As in none of these forms does ȝ represent a semi-vowel or a front or back voiced spirant and as elsewhere in Otho these words are written with the continental *g* (see, for example, the facsimile facing p. xxxviii in the first volume of Madden's edition), it is believed that the spellings given at p. 21 represent more faithfully what was in the burnt original.

[1] J. S. P. Tatlock, *The Legendary History of Britain* (University of California Press 1950), has a long and important chapter of Laȝamon.

The Author and his Sources (C)

Incipit hystoria brutonum.

An preost wes on leoden, Laȝamon wes ihoten.
He wes Leouenaðes sone; liðe him beo Drihten.
He wonede at Ernleȝe, at æðelen are chirechen,
Vppen Seuarne-staþe, sel þar him þuhte,
5   On-fest Radestone, þer he bock radde.
Hit com him on mode, and on his mern þonke,
Þet he wolde of Engle þa æðelæn tellen;
Wat heo ihoten weoren and wonene heo comen,
Þa Englene londe ærest ahten,
10   Æfter þan flode þe from Drihtene com,
Þe al her a-quelde quic þat he funde,
Buten Noe and Sem, Japhet and Cham,
And heore four wiues þe mid heom weren on archen.
Laȝamon gon liðen wide ȝond þas leode,
15   And bi-won þa æðela boc, þa he to bisne nom.
He nom þa Englisca boc, þa makede seint Beda.
An oþer he nom on Latin, þe makede seinte Albin,
And þe feire Austin, þe fulluht broute hider in.
Boc he nom þe þridde, leide þer amidden,
20   Þa makede a Frenchis clerc,
Wace wes ihoten, þe wel couþe writen,
And he hoe ȝef þare æðelen Ælienor[e]
Þe wes Henries quene, þes heȝes kinges.
Laȝamon leide þeos boc, and þa leaf wende;
25   He heom leofliche bi-heold, liþe him beo Drihten.
Feþeren he nom mid fingren, and fiede on boc-felle,
And þa soþere word sette to-gadere,
And þa þre boc þrumde to are.
Nu biddeð Laȝamon alcne æðele mon,
30   For þene almiten Godd,
Þet þeos boc rede, and leornia þeos runan,
Þet he þeos soðfeste word segge to sumne,
For his fader saule, þa hine forð brouhte,
And for his moder saule, þa hine to monne iber,
35   And for his awene saule, þat hire þe selre beo.
                              AmeN.

29 biddeð: *MS.* bidded.

The *Author and his Sources* (O)

*Incipit **Prologus** libri Brutonum*

A prest was in londe, Laweman was hote.
He was Leucais sone; lef him beo Driste.
He wonede at Ernleie wid þan gode cniþte
Uppen Seuarne—merie þer him þohte—
5 Faste bi Radistone, þer heo bokes radde.
Hit com him on mode and on his þonke,
Þat he wolde of Engelond þe ristnesse telle;
Wat þe men hi-hote weren and wanene hi comen.
Þe Englene lond ærest afden
10 After þen flode þat fram God com,
Þat al ere acwelde cwic þat hit funde,
Bote Noe and Sem, Iaphet and Cam,
And hire four wifes þat mid ham þere weren.
Loweman gan wende, so wide so was þat londe.
15

And nom þe Englisse boc þat makede seint Bede.
Anoþer he nom of Latin, þat makede seint Albin.
Boc he nom þan þridde, an leide þar amidde,
Þat makede Austin, þat follost broste hider in.
20

Laweman þes bokes bieolde, an þe leues tornde.
25 He ham loueliche bi-helde; fulste God þe miþtie.
Feþere he nom mid fingres and wrot mid his hande,
And þe soþe word sette togedere,
And þane hilke boc tock us to bisne.
Nu biddeþ Laweman echne godne mon
30 For þe mistie Godes loue
Þat þes boc redeþ
Þat he þis soþfast word segge togadere,
And bidde for þe saule
                      þat hine to manne strende,
35 And for his owene soule, þat hire þe bet bifalle.
                                        Amen.

8 wanene: *Wanley* wanene.

Arthur's Court

(19930)

Þa þe Arður wes king, hær[c]ne nu seollic þing,
He wes mete-custi ælche quike monne,
Cniht mid þan bezste, wunder ane kene.
He wes þan ʒungen for fader, þan alden for frouer,
40   And wið þan vnwise wunder ane sturnne;
Woh him wes wunder lað, and þat rihte a leof.
'Ælc of his birlen, and of his bur-þæinen,
And his ber-cnihtes, gold beren an honden,
To ruggen and to bedde, iscrud mid gode-webbe,'
45   Nefde he neure nænne coc, þet he nes keppe swiðe god;
'Neuær nanes cnihtes swein, þat he næs bald þein.'
Þe king heold al his hired mid hæʒere blise,
And mid swulche þinges he ouer-com alle kinges,
Mid ræhʒere strengðe, and mid riche dome.
50   'Swulche weoren his custes þat al uolc hit wuste.'
Nu wes Arður god king; his hired hine lufede,
Æc hit wes cuð wide of his kinedome.

The Battle with Colgrim

(20070)

Þer com Arður him aʒein, ʒaru mid his fehte.
In ane brade forde þa ferden heom imetten;
55   Fastliche on sloʒen 'snelle heore kenpen,'
Feollen þa uæie, 'uolden to grunde.'
Þer wes muchel blod-gute, balu þer wes riue,
'Brustlede scæftes, beornes þer ueollen.'
Þat isæh Arður, on mode him wes unneðe.
60   Arður hine biðohte whæt he don mahte,
And thehte hine a bacward in enne uald brade.
Þa wenden his feond þat he flæn walde;
Þa wes glad Colgrim, and al his ferde mid him.
'Heo wenden þat Arður mid arhreðe weore afallæd þere',
65   And tuʒen ouer þat water alse heo wode weoren.
Þa Arður þat isah, þat Colgrim him wes swa neh,
And heo weoren beien bihalues þan wateren,
Þus seide Arður, aðelest kingen:

---

40 C. winder ane: O. wonderliche.   41 O. Woh him was swiþe loþ, and riht him was
swiþe leof.   45 swiðe: C. swide.   47 hired: O. folk. O. to-gadere mid blisse.
51 his hired: O. al folk.   53b O. redi to fihte.   57 blod-gute, balu: O. blod
iʒote, and wowe.   59b O. þat ʒam lute lofuede.   61 thehte, uald: O. teh, felde.
62 feond: O. fon.   63 al his ferde: O. his iveres.   65a O. and after him wende.
67 bihalues: O. in on half.   68b O. and spac to his cnihtes.

"Iseo ȝe mine Bruttes, here us bihalfues,
70 Ure iuan uulle—Crist heom aualle—
Colgrim þene stronge ut of Sæx-londe.
His cun i þisse londe ure ælderne aqualden;
Ah nu is þe dæi icumen þe Drihten haueð idemed,
Þat he scal þat lif leosen, and leosien his freonden,
75 Oðer we sculle dæde beon, ne muȝe we hine quic iseon.
Scullen Sæxisce men sorȝen ibiden,
'And we wreken wurhliche ure wine-maies'."
Vp bræid Arður his sceld foren to his breosten,
And he gon to rusien swa þe runie wulf,
80 Þenne he cumeð of holte, bihonged mid snawe,
And þencheð to biten swulc deor swa him likeð.
Arður þa cleopede to leofe his cnihten:
"Forð we biliue, þeines ohte,
'Alle somed heom to; alle we sculleð wel don,
85 And heo uorð hælden swa þe hæȝe wude
Þenne wind wode weieð hine mid mæine'."
Fluȝen ouer þe woldes þritti þusend sceldes,
And smiten a Colgrimes cnihtes, þat þa eorðe aȝæn quehte;
'Breken braden speren, brustleden sceldes',
90 Feollen Sæxisce men, folden to grunden.
Þat isah Colgrim, þer-uore wa wes him,
'Þe alre hendeste mon þe ut of Sexlonde com'.
Colgrim gon to flænne, feondliche swiðe,
And his hors hine bar mid hæhȝere strengðe
95 Ouer þat water deope, and scelde hine wið dæðe.
Saxes gunnen sinken, sorȝe heom wes ȝiueðe.
Arður wende his speres ord, and for-stod heom þene uord;
Þer adruncke Sexes, fulle seoue þusend.
Summe heo gunnen wondrien swa doð þe wilde cron
100 I þan moruenne þenne his floc is awemmed,
And him haldeð after hauekes swifte,
Hundes in þan reode mid reouðe hine imeteð.
Þenne nis him neouðer god, no þat lond no þat flod;
Hauekes hine smiteð, hundes hine biteð,

69 Iseo: O. ne se. bih-: C. bil-. 70 uulle, aualle: O. folle, acwelle. 72 aqualden: O. afulde. 74 O. þat hii hit solle abugge, if ich mote libbe. 75 we, we: O. ich, ich. 79 rusien, runie: O. rese, wode. 80 þenne: O. wane. 81 swulc deor swa: O. woch seap þat. 83 C. Ford . . .: O. Wende we blifue, and do ȝam vt of lifue. 84 somed: C. someð. 87 woldes: O. feldes. 88 a Colgrimes: O. Colgrim his. 93 Colgrim feondliche: O. and he, wonderliche. 94 hæȝere: O. mochelere. 95 scelde hine wið: O. readde hine fram. 96 O. Arður to þan watere hiȝede swiþe. 97 Arður wende his: O. and tornde þe. 100 þenne, floc: O. wane, fliht. 101 haldeð: C. halded.

105   Þenne bið þe kinewurðe foȝel fæie on his siðe.
      Colgrim ouer feldes flæh him biliues,
      Þat he com to Eouerwic riden swiðe sellic.
      He wenden into burȝe and faste heo biclusde.
      Hafuede he binnen ten þusend monnen,
110   'Burh-men mid þa bezste þe him bihalues weoren'.
      Arður halde after mid þritti þusend cnihten,
      'And ferde riht to Eouerwic mid folke swiðe sellic',
      And bilæi Colgrim þe weorrede aȝæin him.

                    The Humbling of Childric
      (20825)
      Þa loh Arður ludere stefene:
115   "Iþonked wurðe Drihtene þe alle domes waldeð,
      Þat Childric þe stronge is sad of mine londe.
      Mi lond he hafeð to-dæled al his duȝeðe-cnihtes;
      Me-seoluen he þohte driuen ut of mire leoden,
      'Halden me for hæne and habben mine riche,
120   And mi cun al for-uaren, mi uolc al fordemed'.
      Ah of him bið iwurðen swa bið of þan voxe,
      Þenne he bið baldest ufen an þan walde,
      And hafeð his fulle ploȝe and fuȝeles inoȝe;
      For wildscipe climbið and cluden iseheð;
125   I þan wilderne holȝes him wurcheð;
      Faren wha-swa-auere fare, naueð he næuere nænne kare.
      He weneð to beon of duȝeðe baldest alre deoren.
      Þenne siȝeð him to segges vnder beorȝen,
      Mid hornen, mid hunden, mid haȝere stefenen.
130   Hunten þar talieð, hundes þer galieð,
      Þene vox driueð ȝeond dales and ȝeond dunes.
      He ulih to þan holme and his hol iseheð,
      I þan uirste ænde, i þan holle wendeð.
      Þenne is þe balde uox blissen al bideled,
135   And mon him to-delueð on ælchere heluen.
      Þenne beoð þer forcuðest deoren alre pruttest."

---

105 bið, fæie on his siðe: *O.* his, adrad in eche side.   106 biliues: *O.* wel swiþe.
108 biclusde: *O.* bi-tunde.   109 binnen: *O.* þar inne.   111 halde: *O.* him heol.
113 bilæi:*O.* bi-lay at Euerwich.   115 Iþonked wurðe: *O.* Ich þonki mine.   117 *O.*
idealed amang his freo cnihtes.   118 mire leoden: *O.* mine cuþþe.   122 þenne:
O. wane.   123 fulle ploȝe:*O.* folle pleay.   124 *C.* iseched:*O.* he secheþ.   125 *O.*
in þan wilde cleues holes he secheþ.   127 to beon of duȝeðe: *O.* þat he be þanne.
128 þenne, segges vnder beorȝen: *O.* ac wane, hontes onder borewe.   132 holme,
hol iseheð his: *O.* cleoue, his hol secheþ.   133 *O.* into þan forrest ende of þan hole.
135 ælchere: *O.* euereche.

The Arming of Arthur

(21129)

Þa dude he on his burne ibroide of stele,
Þe makede on aluisc smið mid aðelen his crafte;
He wes ihaten Wygar, þe Witeȝe wurhte.
140 His sconken he helede mid hosen of stele.
Calibeorne his sweord he sweinde bi his side,
Hit was iworht in Aualun mið wiȝele-fulle craften.
Halm he set on hafde, hæh of stele.
Þer-on wes moni ȝimston al mid golde bi-gon;
145 'He wes Vðeres, þas aðelen kinges',
He wes ihaten Goswhit, ælchen oðere vnilic.
He heng an his sweore ænne sceld deore,
His nome wes on Bruttisc Pridwen ihaten,
Þer wes innen igrauen mid rede golde stauen
150 An on-licnes deore of Drihtenes moder.
His spere he nom an honde, þa Ron wes ihaten.
Þa he hafden al his i-weden, þa leop he on his steden.
Þa he mihte bihalden, þa bihalues stoden,
Þene uæireste cniht þe verde scolde leden.
155 'Ne isæh næuere na man selere cniht nenne,
Þene him wes Arður, aðelest cunnes'.

The Haunted Mere

(21739)

Þat is a seolcuð mere, iset a middelærde,
Mid fenne and mid ræode, mid watere 'swiðe' bræde,
'Mid fiscen and mid feoȝelen, mid uniuele þingen'.
160 Þat water is unimete brade, nikeres þer baðieð inne,
'Þer is æluene ploȝe in atteliche pole'.
Sixti æit-londes beoð i þan watere longe,
In ælc of þan æit-londe is a clude hæh and strong
Þer næstieð arnes and oðere græte uoȝeles.
165 Þe ærnes habbeoð ane laȝe bi æuerælches kinges dahȝen,
Whænne swa æi ferde fundeð to þan ærde,
Þeonne fleoð þa fuȝeles feor i þan lufte,

---

137 O. And he warp on him one brunie of stele.   138 aðelen his: O. his wise.
140 sconken: O. legges.   142 wiȝele-fulle craften: O. witfolle crafte.   145 Vðeres:
C. Vderes.   146 ælchen: O. alle.   149 O. igraued on anlichnisse of golde.   150 O.
þat was mid isoþe Drihtene moder.   153 þa bihalues stoden: O. þat þar bi-halues
were.   154 scolde: O. sal.   157 seolcuð, middelærde: O. wonder, middilerþe.
160 C. badieð inne: O. wonieþ.   162 C. æit-londes beod, watere: O. eyllondes
beoþ, mere.   163 æit-londe, hæh and: O. yllond, swiþe.   164 næstieð: O. nestleþ.
166 ærde: O. erþe.   167 i: O. in to.

'Moni hundred þusen, and muchel feoht makieð.
Þenne is þat folc buten wene, þat reouðe heom is to cumene,
170   Of summes cunnes leoden þe þat lond wulleð i-sechen.'
Tweien dæȝes oðer þreo þus scal þis taken beo,
'Ær unkuðe men to þan londe liðen'.
Ȝet þer is sellic to suggen of þan watere,
Þer walleð in þan mæren, 'a moni are siden,
175   Of dalen and of dunen and of bæcchen deopen',
Sixti wateres 'alle þer isomned,
Swa neuere ut of þan mære na man no uindeð'
Þat þer ut wenden, buten an an ænde
'An imetliche broc þe of þan mere ualleð,
180   And swiðe isemeliche into sæ wendeð.'
Þa Scottes weoren 'to-deled mid muclen vniselen',
Ȝeond þa monie munten 'þa i þan watere weoren'.

Arthur's Last Battle

(28526)
Arður for to Cornwale mid uni[me]te ferde.
Modred þat iherde, and him toȝeines heolde
185   Mid vnimete folke,—þer weore monie uæie.
Uppen þere Tanbre heo tuhten to-gadere;
Þe stude hatte Camelford, euer mare ilast þat ilke weorde.
And at Camelforde wes isomned sixti þusend,
And ma þusend þer-to—Modred wes heore ælder.
190   Þa þiderward gon ride Arður þe riche,
Mid unimete folke, uæie þah hit weore.
Uppe þere Tambre heo tuhte to-somne;
'Heuen here-marken, halden to-gadere',
Luken sweord longe, leiden o þe helmen;
195   Fur ut sprengen, speren brastlien,
'Sceldes gonnen scanen, scaftes to-breken.
Þer faht al to-somne folc vnimete.'
Tambre wes on flode mid vnimete blode.
Mon i þan fihte non þer ne mihte ikennen nenne kempe,
200   No wha dude wurse no wha bet, swa þat wiðe wes imenged.
For ælc sloh adun-riht, weore he swein weore he cniht.

174 walleð of: O. falleþ in.   176 sixti: O. many cunnes.   178 O. and vt noþing
ne goþ in neuere one side.   181b O. þar ine weren Scottes.   182 O. oueral þan
muntes.   183 for: O. wende.   186 heo tuhten: O. icome.   188 O. were
mid Arthur sixti þousend manne.   189 O. þousendes ȝite in Modred his syde.
191 uæie þah hit weore: O. of cnihtes wel bolde.   192 tuhte to-somne: O. smite
to-gadere.   194 luken, leiden: O. drowen, smiten.   195 O. þat þe fur vt sprong,
þe swippes were bitere.   199 ikennen: O. icnowe.   200 wiðe: O. weder.

Þer wes Modred of-slaȝe, and idon of lif-daȝe,
[And alle his cnihtes islaȝe] in þan fihte.
Þer weoren of-slaȝe alle þa snelle,
205 Arðures hered-men heȝe [and laȝe],
And þa Bruttes alle of Arðures borde,
And alle his fosterlinges of feole kineriches.
And Arður forwunded mid wal-spere brade,
Fiftene he hafde feondliche wunden,
210 Mon mihte i þare laste twa glouen iþraste.
Þa nas þer na mare i þan fehte to laue,
Of twa hundred þusend monnen, þa þer leien to-hauwen,
Buten Arður þe king ane, and of his cnihtes tweien.
Arður wes for-wunded wunder ane swiðe,
215 Þer to him com a cnaue þe wes of his cunne,
He wes Cadores sune, þe eorles of Cor[n]waile,
Constantin hehte þe cnaue, he wes þan kinge deore.
Arður him lokede on, 'þer he lai on folden',
And þas word seide 'mid sorhfulle heorte':
220 "Costæntin, þu art wilcume, þu weore Cadores sone;
Ich þe bitache here mine kineriche,
And wite mine Bruttes a to þines lifes,
'And hald heom alle þa laȝen þa habbeoð istonden a mine daȝen,
And alle þa laȝen gode þa bi Vðeres daȝen stode'.
225 And ich wulle uaren to Aualun 'to uairest alre maidene',
To Argante þere quene, 'aluen swiðe sceone',
And heo scal mine wunden makien alle isunde,
Al hal me makien mid haleweiȝe drenchen.
And seoðe ich cumen wulle to mine kineriche,
230 'And wunien mid Brutten mid muchelere wunne'."
Æfne þan worden, þer com of se wenden,
Þat wes an sceort bat liðen sceouen mid vðen,
And twa wimmen þer-inne wunderliche idihte,
And heo nomen Arður anan, and ane ouste hine uereden,
235 And softe hine adun leiden, and forð gunnen hine liðen.
Þa wes hit iwurðen þat Merlin seide whilen,
Þat weore unimete care of Arðures forðfare.

203 *Bracketed words supplied from O.*   205 and laȝe *supplied from O. and* loȝe.
206 C. Ardures: O. Arthur his.   208 wal-spere: O. one spere.   211 i þan fehte to
laue: O. ileued in þan fihte.   212 leien tohauwen: O. lay to-hewe.   214 wunder
ane: O. wonderliche.   215 þer to him com a: O. þer com a ȝong.   216 Cadores:
O. Cador his.   217 O. Constantin he hehte, þe king hine louede.   218 Arður him
lokede on: O. þe king to him bi-heold.   222 a to þines lifes: O. wel bi þine liue.
225 uaren: O. wende.   227 scal: C. slal.   232 O. a lu.. sort bot wandri mid Þ. .
beres.   233 idihte: O. igynned.   234 ane ouste hine uereden: O. . . . þan bote
bere.   235 gunnen . . . liðen: O. . . . gan wende.   236 þa wes hit iwurðen: O. þo
was . . . onde.   237 weore unimete: O. solde beon mochel.

Bruttes ileueð ʒete þat he bon on liue,
And wunnien in Aualun mid fairest alre aluen,
240 'And lokieð euere Bruttes ʒete whan Arður cumen liðe'.
Nis nauer þe mon iboren, of nauer nane burde icoren,
Þe cunne of þan soðe of Arðure sugen mare;
Bute while wes an witeʒe, Mærlin ihate,
He bodede mid worde, his quiðes weoren soðe,
245 Þat an Arður sculde ʒete cum Anglen to fulste.

---

239 aluen: O. cwene.   241 of nauer nane burde icoren: O. ne of womman icore.
244 bodede, quiðes: O. saide, saʒes.   245 Anglen to fulste: O. Bruttes . . . for to
healpe.

VII. KING HORN

King Horn, the earliest of the extant romances in ME, tells how the king of Suddene is slain by pirates, and his son Horn captured. Because of his beauty Horn is spared, but fearing his strength the pirates set him adrift with two companions. They come ashore in Westernesse and are welcomed and cared for by the king whose daughter Rimenhild falls in love with Horn. After some difficulty she succeeds in making known her love, but Horn refuses to plight troth until he shall have proved his prowess. Thereupon Rimenhild persuades her father to knight Horn and his companions, and he sets out to seek adventures. He meets a band of paynim whom he slays; but the next day the love of Horn and Rimenhild is betrayed to the king, and Horn is banished. He takes refuge in Ireland, slays a giant, and rescues the country from the Saracens, but, when offered the daughter of the king in marriage, is faithful to Rimenhild and postpones acceptance for seven years. In the meantime Rimenhild is wooed by another prince and contrives to send word to Horn, who arrives in Westernesse, disguised as a pilgrim, in time for the wedding feast. He enters the hall, and the extract below describes how he makes himself known to Rimenhild. The rival wooer is slain, and Horn sets out to recover his heritage. This is soon done, and he is reunited with his mother who has escaped the pirates and is living in a cave by the sea. But Rimenhild is again pursued by an unwelcome suitor, and Horn, warned of this in a dream, enters the castle of his rival disguised as a harper, slays him, and is at last wedded to his beloved.

The romance appears also in a thirteenth-century French version, *Horn et Rimel*, and was re-written in English in the fourteenth century as *Horn Childe*. No direct connection can be traced between the different versions, but all are probably based ultimately on a story that survived for some time only by oral tradition, the variations in names and localities being due to the different minstrels through whose hands the story has passed. As a romance it belongs to the so-called Matter of England—romances dealing with the earlier history of the country—and the story is usually supposed to be based on events which took place during the Anglo-Saxon conquest or the Viking raids. This is possible enough, but any basis of fact that there might originally have been can hardly now be distinguished from the mass of folk-tale with which it has been overlaid, nor is it possible to localize the events.

As a story its chief merit is its rapidity of movement, and in general it has some of the merits of the later ballads. It was evidently written for a popular audience and is primitive, simple, and unsophisticated, with none of the courtly elements of French romance. The love element is treated briefly and cursorily and the emphasis is on the adventure and fighting, as is usual in romances composed particularly for the less cultivated classes.

The short couplets in which it is written are often said to be a development of the native alliterative line, strongly influenced by French prosody. The two parts of the original four-stress line have been separated and end-rhyme added to turn them into couplets. This is a possible, though not very probable, line of development, and W. H. French, *Essays on King Horn* (New York 1940), has shown that the affinities of the metre are with contemporary French and Anglo-French rather than with OE verse.

This particular version of the romance is contained in three MSS., University Library, Cambridge, Gg. 4. 27, Part II (end of thirteenth century), Bodleian Laud Misc. 108 (*c.* 1300–20), and British Museum Harley 2253 (*c.* 1310), of which the relationship is uncertain. They appear to be independent copies, at various removes, of the original, though Laud and Harley may be more closely related to each other than to the Cambridge MS. The best edition of all three MSS. is that by J. Hall (Oxford 1901), while the Cambridge text is printed also in W. H. French and C. B. Hale, *Middle English Metrical Romances* (New York 1930), pp. 25–70. The extract below, corresponding with ll. 1107–1214 on pp. 64–8 of Hall's edition, is taken from the Harley MS. which, though not the oldest, appears in some ways to represent the original better than the other two.

The Banquet

(1107) Rymenild ros of benche,
    Þe béér al forte shenche:
    After mete in sale
    Boþe wyn ant ale
  5 An horn hue ber an honde,
    For þat wes lawe of londe.
    Hue dronc of þe béére

To knyht ant skyere.
Horn set at grounde,
10   Him þohte he wes ybounde.
     He seide, 'Quene so hende,
To me hydeward þou wende;
Þou shenh vs wiþ þe vurste:
Þe beggares bueþ afurste.'
15   Hyre horn hue leyde adoune,
Ant fulde him of þe broune
A bolle of a galoun,
Hue wende he were a glotoun.
Hue seide, 'Tac þe coppe,
20   Ant drync þis ber al vppe;
Ne seh y neuer, y wene,
Beggare so kene.'
Horn toc hit hise yfere,
Ant seide, 'Quene so dere,
25   No béér nullich ibite
Bote of coppe white.
Þou wenest ich be a beggere,
Ywis icham a fysshere,
Wel fer come by weste
30   To seche mine beste.
Min net lyht her wel hende,
Wiþ-inne a wel feyr pende.
Ich haue leye þere
Nou is þis þe seueþe ȝere.
35   Icham icome to loke
ȝef eny fyssh hit toke.
ȝef eny fyssh is þer-inne
Þer-of þou shalt wynne;
For icham come to fyssh:
40   Drynke nully of dyssh,
Drynke to Horn of horne,
Wel fer ich haue y-orne'.
     Rymenild him gan bihelde;
Hire herte fel to kelde.
45   Ne kneu hue noht is fysshyng,
Ne him-selue noþyng;
Ah wonder hyre gan þynke,
Why for Horn he bed drynke.
Hue fulde þe horn of wyne,

41 drynke: *MS.* drynkes.   44 fel: *L.* bigan.

50 Ant dronke to þat pelryne.
    Hue seide, 'Drync þi felle,
    Ant seþþen þou me telle
    ʒef þou Horn euer seʒe
    Vnder wode leʒe'.
55   Horn dronc of horn a stounde,
    Ant þreu is ryng to grounde,
    Ant seide, 'Quene, þou þench
    What y þreu in þe drench'.
    Þe quene eode to boure,
60 Mid hire maidnes foure.
    Hue fond þat hue wolde,
    Þe ryng ygraued of golde,
    Þat Horn of hyre hedde.
    Fol sore hyre adredde
65 Þat Horn ded were,
    For his ryng was þere.
    Þo sende hue a damoisele
    After þilke palmere.
    'Palmere', quoþ hue, 'So trewe,
70 Þe ryng þat þou yn þrewe,
    Þou sey wer þou hit nome,
    Ant hyder hou þou come'.
    He seyde, 'By Seint Gyle!
    Ich eode mony a myle,
75 Wel fer ʒent by weste,
    To seche myne beste,
    Mi mete forte bydde,
    For so me þo bitidde.
    Ich fond Horn knyht stonde
80 To shipeward at stronde.
    He seide he wolde gesse
    To aryue at Westnesse.
    Þe ship nom in to flode
    Wiþ me ant Horn þe gode;
85 Horn by-gan be sek ant deʒe,
    Ant for his loue me preʒe
    To gon wiþ þe rynge
    To Rymenild þe ʒynge.
    Wel ofte he hyne keste,
90 Crist ʒeue is soule reste.'
    Rymenild seide at þe firste,

50 dronke: *MS.* dronkes.

'Herte, nou to-berste!
Horn worþ þe no more,
Þat haueþ þe pyned sore'.
95 Hue fel adoun a bedde,
Ant after knyues gredde
To slein mide hire kyng loþe,
Ant hire-selue boþe,
Wiþinne þilke nyhte,
100 Come ȝef Horn ne myhte.
To herte knyf hue sette.
Horn in is armes hire kepte;
His shurte lappe he gan take,
Ant wypede awey þe foule blake
105 Þat wes opon his suere,
Ant seide, 'Luef so dere,
Ne const þou me yknowe?
Ne am ich Horn þyn owe?'

VIII. THE LAY OF HAVELOK THE DANE

THE historical element in *Havelok*, slight though it may be, is more pronounced than in any other of the romances of the so-called Matter of England. It appears to contain vague memories of the union of England and Denmark under Swegen and Canute, while the name Birkabeyn, given to the father of Havelok, is presumably taken from the ON. *Birkibeinar*, the followers of King Sverre of Norway (1184–1202), whose own career was romantic enough.[1] Moreover, the name Havelok is an Anglicized form of the Irish Abloc, a name often substituted for the ON. Óláfr, and it seems probable that the hero is intended to represent Óláfr Cuaran, a famous Viking of the tenth century.[2] Yet the story as a whole is simply a folk-tale of a common type, and none of the happenings in it can be connected with anything known to us of the life of Óláfr Cuaran. Presumably historical names and some vague historical material have simply been included to increase the interest of the story. In any case *Havelok* is the best of the romances of its class, simple, straightforward, with the emphasis on fighting and adventure and with all the sentimental possibilities completely ignored. The background is that of the common man in thirteenth-century England, and the romance throws a good deal of light on social life. It was obviously written for the uncultivated, as is shown by the author's familiar address to his audience, and by his use of popular proverbs and conventional rhyming tags.

In all the extant versions the story is localized in Lincolnshire. It provides an eponymous founder for Grimsby, and much of the action takes place there and at Lincoln.[3] Certainly by the reign of Edward I the connection had become so firmly established that the seal of the town (reproduced in Skeat-Sisam), which dates from that period, shows representations of Havelok, Grim, and Goldeboru. The extant English version has passed through the hands of various scribes, but so far as we can tell the dialect appears to be that of North Lincolnshire. As for its date, the MS. is of the early

[1] At one stage 'his condition most resembled that of royal children in the old stories, under the curses of stepmothers' (*Sverrissaga*, c. 7).
[2] He bears the nickname Cuaran(t) 'rawhide sandal' in Gaimar and *Le Lai d' Havelot*, Coraunt in the *Lambeth Interpolation*, mentioned below.
[3] For the background see J. W. F. Hill, *Medieval Lincoln* (Camb. 1948).

fourteenth century, but echoes of the Havelok story in Robert
Mannyng's *Chronicle*, finished in 1338, show that it must have
been in existence before that date. References in the work itself
have been used in an attempt to date its composition more precisely,
but their evidence has been shown to be inconclusive, and no more
accurate date than 'towards the end of the thirteenth century' is as
yet possible.

The earliest known version of the story is that inserted into his
Estoire des Engleis by the twelfth-century Anglo-French writer
Geffrei Gaimar, who, like Robert Mannyng, came from Lincolnshire; and an unknown author of the same century re-wrote it in the
form of a Breton lai (for both see A. Bell, *Le Lai d'Haveloc*, Manchester 1925). Both appear to be derived from a common original,
now lost, and from the same lost original is derived an English
version interpolated into a copy of Robert Mannyng's *Chronicle*
preserved in Lambeth MS. 131, ff. 204 ff., and so known as the
Lambeth Interpolation (Skeat-Sisam, pp. xvii–xviii). All these are
apparently quite unconnected with the version from which selections
are printed below. The bulk of this is preserved only in the Bodleian
MS. Laud Misc. 108, though sixty lines of it are also to be found in
some MS. scraps in the University Library, Cambridge. Various
editions of this English version have appeared, the handiest being
that by W. W. Skeat, revised by K. Sisam (Oxford 1923), while the
most recent and most conservative is in W. H. French and C. B.
Hale, *Middle English Metrical Romances*, pp. 73–176. In addition,
annotated selections have appeared in most ME readers. The
extracts below correspond with ll. 1–105, 999–1058, 1793–1859,
2320–2345, 2984–3001, of the Skeat-Sisam edition.

Introduction

    Herknet to me, godemen,
    Wiues, maydnes, and alle men,
    Of a tale þat ich you wile telle,
    Wo-so it wile here and þer-to duelle.
5   þe tale is of Hauelok imaked;
    Wil he was litel, he yede ful naked.
    Hauelok was a ful god gome:
    He was ful god in eueri trome;
    He was þe wicteste man at nede
10 þat þurte riden on ani stede.
    Þat ye mowen nou yhere,

And þe tale ye mowen ylere.
At þe biginning of vre tale,
Fil me a cuppe of ful god ale;
15 And wile [Y] drinken, her Y spelle,
Þat Crist vs shilde alle fro helle!
Krist late vs heuere so for to do
Þat we moten comen Him to;
And, wit þat it mote ben so,
20 *Benedicamus Domino!*
Here Y schal biginnen a rym;
Krist us yeue wel god fyn!
The rym is maked of Hauelok,
A stalworþi man in a flok;
25 He was þe stalworþeste man at nede
Þat may riden on any stede.
     It was a king bi are-dawes,
Þat in his time were gode lawes,
He dede maken an ful wel holden;
30 Hym louede yung, him louede holde,
Erl and barun, dreng and tayn,
Knict, bondeman and swain,
Wydues, maydnes, prestes and clerkes,
And al for hise gode werkes.
35 He louede God with al his micth,
And holi kirke and soth ant ricth;
Ricth-wise men he louede alle,
And oueral made hem forto calle;
Wreieres and wrobberes made he falle,
40 And hated hem so man doth galle;
Vtlawes and theues made he bynde,
Alle that he micthe fynde,
And heye hengen on galwe-tre;
For hem ne yede gold ne fe.
45 In þat time a man þat bore
[Wel fifty pund, y wot, or more,]
Of red gold upon hijs bac,
In a male with or blac,
Ne funde he non þat him misseyde,
50 N[e] with iuele on hond leyde.
Þanne micthe chapmen fare
Þuruth Englond wit here ware,
And baldelike beye and sellen,

31 tayn: *MS.* kayn.   37 ricth-: *MS.* rirth-.   46 *Supplied by Skeat.*

Oueral þer he wilen dwellen,
55   In gode burwes, and þer-fram
Ne funden he non þat dede hem sham,
Þat he ne weren to sorwe brouth,
An pouere maked, and browt to nouth.
Þanne was Engelond at hayse;
60   Michel was svich a king to preyse,
Þat held so Englond in grith!
Krist of heuene was him with.
He was Engelondes blome;
Was non so bold louerd to Rome
65   Þat durste upon his [londe] bringhe
Hunger ne here, wicke þinghe.
Hwan he felede hise foos,
He made hem lurken, and crepen in wros:
Þe[i] hidden hem alle, and helden hem stille,
70   And diden al his herte wille.
Ricth he louede of alle þinge,
To wronge micht him no man bringe,
Ne for siluer, ne for gold,
So was he his soule hold.
75   To þe faderles was he rath,
Wo-so dede hem wrong or lath,
Were it clerc, or were it knicth,
He dede hem sone to hauen ricth;
And wo diden widuen wrong,
80   Were he neure knicth so strong
Þat he ne made him sone kesten
And in feteres ful faste festen;
And wo-so dide maydne shame
Of hire bodi, or brouth in blame,
85   Bute it were bi hire wille,
He made him sone of limes spille.
He was te beste knith at nede
Þat heuere micthe riden on stede,
Or wepne wagge, or folc vt lede;
90   Of knith ne hauede he neuere drede,
Þat he ne sprong forth so sparke of glede,
And lete him [knawe] of hise hand-dede,
Hw he couþe with wepne spede;
And oþer he refte him hors or wede,
95   Or made him sone handes sprede,

57 weren: *MS*. weren sone.   64 louerd: *MS*. lond.   86 He: *MS*. **Ke.**
87 He was te: *MS*. Ke waste.

And 'Louerd, merci!' loude grede.
He was large, and no wicth gnede;
Hauede he non so god brede,
Ne on his bord non so god shrede,
100   Þat he ne wolde þorwit fede
Poure þat on fote yede,
Forto hauen of Him þe mede
Þat for vs wolde on rode blede,
Crist, that al kan wisse and rede
105   Þat euere woneth in ani þede.

[On his death Athelwold entrusts his daughter Goldeboru to the care of Godrich, Earl of Cornwall, commanding him to marry her to the fairest and strongest man he can find, and then to hand the government of the country over to her. The earl, desiring to seize England for his son, imprisons Goldeboru in Dover castle; and the romance goes on to tell of Havelok. King Birkabeyn of Denmark has appointed Earl Godard as guardian of his son Havelok and his two daughters. Godard seizes the kingdom, kills the two daughters, and hands Havelok over to a fisherman, Grim, with orders that he is to be drowned. The sight of a mysterious flame issuing from the mouth of the sleeping child convinces Grim of his royal birth. Thereupon he and his wife adopt the child, set sail for England, and found the town of Grimsby. Havelok works as a fisherman until a famine causes him to secure the place of a scullion in Earl Godrich's kitchen at Lincoln, where he wins all hearts by his beauty, strength, and charm.]

Medieval Sports

(999) In þat time al Hengelond
Þerl Godrich hauede in his hond,
And he gart komen into þe tun
Mani erl and mani barun;
110   And alle þat liues were
In Englond þanne wer þere
Þat þey haueden after sent
To ben þer at þe parlement.
With hem com mani champioun,
115   Mani with ladde, blac and brown;
An fel it so þat yunge men,
Wel abouten nine or ten,
Bigunnen þe[re] for to layke:
Þider komen boþe stronge and wayke:
120   Þider komen lesse and more
Þat in þe borw þanne weren þore;
Chaunpiouns and starke laddes,
Bondemen with here gaddes,
Als he comen fro þe plow;
125   Þere was sembling inow!
For it ne was non horse-knaue,

99 non: *MS.* n̄.   114 champioun: *MS.* chābioun.

Þo þei sholden in honde haue,
Þat he ne kam þider þe leyk to se.
Biforn here fet þanne lay a tre,
130 And pulten with a mikel ston
Þe starke laddes, ful god won.
Þe ston was mikel and ek greth,
And al-so heui so a neth;
Grund-stalwrþe man he sholde be
135 Þat mouthe liften it to his kne;
Was þer neyþer clerc ne prest,
Þat mithe liften it to his brest.
Þerwit putten the chaunpiouns
Þat þider comen with þe barouns;
140 Hwo-so mithe putten þore
Biforn anoþer an inch or more,
Wore he yung, wore he hold,
He was for a kempe told.
Al-so þe[i] stoden an ofte stadden,
145 Þe chaunpiouns and ek the ladden,
And he maden mikel strout
Abouten þe alþerbeste but,
Hauelok stod and lokede þer-til;
And of puttingge he was ful wil,
150 For neuere yete ne saw he or
Putten the ston, or þanne þor.
Hise mayster bad him gon þer-to,
Als he couþe þer-with do.
Þo hise mayster it him bad,
155 He was of him sore adrad;
Þerto he stirte sone anon
And kipte up þat heui ston
Þat he sholde puten wiþe;
He putte, at þe firste siþe,
160 Ouer alle þat þer wore
Twel fote and sumdel more.
Þe chaunpiouns þat put sowen;
Shuldreden he ilc oþer and lowen:
Wolden he no more to putting gange,
165 But seyde, 'We dwellen her to longe!'

[Havelok is now reputed the strongest and fairest man in England, whereupon
Godrich determines to fulfil his oath by marrying Goldeboru to the supposed scullion.
Havelok at first refuses, but finally takes Goldeboru to wife and the pair depart for
Grimsby. At night Goldeboru sees the light from Havelok's mouth and a birthmark

144 stadden *Sisam*: MS. stareden.

in the shape of a golden cross on his shoulder, while an angel tells her of good fortune
to come, and Havelok in a dream sees his future greatness. They leave for Denmark,
accompanied by the sons of Grim, and are there befriended by Earl Ubbe. However,
during the night they are attacked in their lodgings by a band of thieves, one of whom
shivers the door with a great boulder.]

The Defence of the Lodgings

(1793) Auelok it saw and þider drof,
   And þe barre sone vt-drow,
   Þat was unride and gret ynow,
   And caste þe dore open wide
170 And seide, 'Her shal Y now abide:
   Comes swiþe vn-to me;
   Daþeyt hwo you henne flel'
   'No,' quodh on, 'þat shaltou coupe,'
   And bigan til him to loupe,
175 In his hond his swerd ut-drawe;
   Hauelok he wende þore haue slawe.
   And with [him] comen oþer two,
   Þat him wolde of liue haue do.
   Hauelok lifte up þe dore-tre,
180 And at a dint he slow hem þre;
   Was non of hem þat his hernes
   Ne lay þer-ute ageyn þe sternes.
   Þe ferþe þat he siþen mette,
   Wit þe barre so he him grette
185 Bifor þe heued þat þe rith eye
   Vt of þe hole made he fleye,
   And siþe clapte him on þe crune
   So þat he standed fel þor dune.
   Þe fifte þat he ouer-tok
190 Gaf he a ful sor dint ok
   Bitwen þe sholdres, þer he stod,
   Þat he speu his herte blod.
   Þe sixte wende for to fle,
   And he clapte him with þe tre
195 Rith in þe fule necke so
   Þat he smot hise necke on to.
   Þanne þe sixe weren doun feld,
   Þe seuenþe brayd ut his swerd,
   And wolde Hauelok riht in þe eye;
200 And Haue[lok] le[t þe] barre fleye,
   And smot him sone ageyn þe brest,
   Þat hauede he neuere sch[r]ifte of prest;

171 me: MS. me datheit.

For he was ded on lesse hwile
Þan men mouthe renne a mile.
205   Alle þe oþere weren ful kene:
A red þei taken hem bitwene
Þat he sholde[n] him bihalue,
And brisen so þat wit no salue
Ne sholde him helen leche non.
210   Þey drowen ut swerdes, ful god won,
And shoten on him so don on bere
Dogges þat wolden him to-tere
Þanne men doth þe bere beyte.
Þe laddes were kaske and teyte,
215   And vmbiyeden him ilkon.
Sum smot with tre, and sum wit ston;
Summe putten with gleyue in bac and side
And yeuen wundes longe and wide
In twenti stedes and wel mo,
220   Fro þe croune til þe to.
Hwan he saw þat, he was wod,
And was it ferlik hw he stod,
For þe blod ran of his sides
So water þat fro welle glides;
225   But þanne bigan he for to mowe
With þe barre, and let hem shewe
Hw he cowþe sore smite;
For was þer non, long ne lite,
Þat he mouthe ouer-take,
230   Þat he ne garte his croune krake,
So þat on a litel stund
Felde he twenti to þe grund.

[Because of this attack Havelok and his company are taken into the house of Earl
Ubbe, and again the miraculous light from his mouth while asleep proclaims him to
be the rightful heir. Ubbe sees the light, is convinced, does homage, and raises the
country against Godard who is defeated and hanged. Havelok is crowned king, and
the next extract describes the rejoicings at his coronation.]

The Coronation

(2320) Hwan he was king, þer mouthe men se
Þe moste ioie þat mouhte be:
235   Buttinge with sharpe speres,
Skirming with taleuaces þat men beres,
Wrastling with laddes, putting of ston,
Harping and piping, ful god won,

215 vmbiyeden: *MS.* vn bi yeden.

Leyk of mine, of hasard ok,
240   Romanz-reding on þe bok;
        Þer mouthe men here þe gestes singe,
        Þe glevmen on þe tabour dinge;
        Þer mouthe men se þe boles beyte,
        And þe bores, with hundes teyte;
245   Þo mouthe men se eueril gleu.
        Þer mouthe men se hw grim greu;
        Was neuere yete ioie more
        In al þis werd þan þo was þore.
        Þer was so mike yeft of cloþes,
250   Þat, þou I swore you grete othes,
        I ne wore nouth þer-offe troud.
        Þat may I ful wel swere, bi God!
        Þere was swiþe gode metes;
        And of wyn þat men fer fetes,
255   Rith al-so mik and gret plente
        So it were water of þe se.
        Þe feste fourti dawes sat;
        So riche was neuere non so þat.

[Havelok then sails with a large army to England. Godrich is defeated, captured, and burned, and the story ends with the marriages of the minor characters.]

The Conclusion

(2984) Nu haue ye herd þe gest al þoru
260   Of Hauelok and of Goldeborw:
        Hw he weren born and hw fedde,
        And hwou he woren with wronge ledde
        In here youþe, with trecherie,
        With tresoun and with felounye;
265   And hwou þe swikes haueden tith
        Reuen hem þat was here rith,
        And hwou he weren wreken wel,
        Haue ich sey[d] you euerildel;
        And forþi ich wolde biseken you
270   Þat hauen herd þe rim[e] nu,
        Þat ilke of you, with gode wille,
        Seye a *Pater Noster* stille
        For him þat haueth þe rym[e] maked,
        And þer-fore fele nihtes waked,
275   Þat Iesu Crist his soule bringe
        Biforn His Fader at his endinge.
                A-M-E-N.

251 troud *Sisam*: *MS.* croud.   265 tith: *MS.* thit.

IX. FLORIZ AND BLAUNCHEFLUR

THE English version of *Floriz and Blauncheflur* is an excellent example of those romances based on oriental material which may be classified as the Matter of the East. It is hardly to be expected that an exact source should be found in eastern literature (the transmission is too complicated), but the strong resemblances to the typical Arabic love-tales makes the ultimately eastern origin obvious enough. Nor is it possible to say by exactly which route the story reached Western Europe, whether carried there orally by crusaders or pilgrims, or in a written form through Constantinople or Sicily or Spain. What is certain is the popularity of the story in Western Europe where two distinct versions existed, one preserving the more original form and intended for an aristocratic audience, the other adapted to suit the taste of a less cultured audience. The two versions are represented by extant French romances, and it is on the aristocratic version that the English romance is based. The English adaptor, however, has severely pruned his original, to such a degree that occasionally details vital to the plot have been omitted. Moreover, he was obviously writing for a lower class than that for which his original was made, and concentrates therefore on incident and adventure, drastically curtailing the descriptive passages. Nevertheless, some of his omissions have the effect of tightening and unifying the plot; the simplicity of the theme benefits from the simple unaffected style of the English poet; and most of the crucial passages retain their full dramatic effect. But on the whole the mediocrity of the English adaptor is made obvious by frequent unintelligent cutting, and the slightness of his poetic gift by an excessive use of rhyming tags and an attempt whenever possible to retain the rhymes of his original.

The story tells of the attack by a Saracen king on a band of pilgrims, which includes a young widow whose father is killed in the attack. The remainder of the pilgrims are carried off into Spain, and soon afterwards the widow gives birth to a daughter Blaunche-flur, while on the same day the Saracen queen gives birth to a son Floriz. The two children are brought up together and fall in love. Attempts to cure Floriz of his infatuation having failed, Blauncheflur is sold as a slave during his temporary absence. On his return Floriz is told that she is dead, and being shown an empty tomb

inscribed with her name, attempts to kill himself. His parents
thereupon tell him the truth, and promise help to regain Blauncheflur. He follows her purchaser in disguise, and at last discovers
her in the harem of the emir of Babylon. He bribes the porter
and is carried in a basket into the harem where he is reunited with
Blauncheflur, but the lovers are discovered by the emir, and the
story ends with the passage given below.

The original English version was apparently made about the
middle of the thirteenth century, and probably in a dialect of the
South-East Midlands. Four MSS. are extant containing the romance:
the British Museum Cotton Vitellius D III (second half of thirteenth
century); University Library, Cambridge, Gg. 4, 27, Part 2 (early
fourteenth century); Auchinleck MS. in the National Library in
Edinburgh (c. 1325–50); British Museum Egerton 2862 (first half
of fifteenth century). Of these the Cottonian MS. was almost completely destroyed in the fire of 1731, and the first 366 lines of the
romance are found only in Egerton. All MSS. go back to a single
lost original, but the wide discrepancies between them suggest that
the intervening links were more probably oral than written. The
Cambridge, Egerton, and Cottonian MSS. were re-edited for the
Early English Text Society in 1901 by G. H. McKnight, and the
Auchinleck MS., with missing lines supplied from other MSS., by
A. B. Taylor (Oxford 1927). The extract below is taken from the
Cambridge MS., and corresponds with ll. 639–824 of McKnight's
edition.

The Judgment

(639) After his barnage he haþ isend,
　　　 To awreke him wiþ iugement.
　　　 And let hem þe while binde faste,
　　　 And in-to prison ben icaste.
　　5 His palais þat was so faire ibuld,
　　　 Of erles and barons hit was ifuld.
　　　 Vp he stod among hem alle,
　　　 Bi semblaunt wel wroþ wiþ-alle.
　　　 'Lordinges,' he sede, 'wiþ muchel honur,
　 10 Ʒe habbeþ iherd of Blauncheflur,
　　　 Hu ihc hire boʒte apliʒt,
　　　 For seuesiþe of gold hire wiʒt.
　　　 To hire was mi meste wene,
　　　 For to habbe to mi quene.
　 15 Nis noʒt ʒore þat I ne com

And fond hire wiþ hordom,
Me to schame and deshonur,
In hire bedde on mi tur.
Ihc habbe ȝou told hu hit is went;
20 Awrekeþ me wiþ jugement.'
Þanne spak a freo burgeis,
Þat was hende and curt[eis],
'Sire, are hi beo to diþe awreke,
We mote ihere þe children speke.
25 Hit nere noȝt elles rist iugement,
Biþuten ansuare to acupement.'
Þe king of Nubie sede þo,
'For soþ, ne schal hit noȝt go so.
Hit is riȝt pureȝ alle þing
30 Felons inome hond-habbing,
For to suffre jugemenᴛ
Biþute ansuere oþer acupement.'
      After þe children ńu me sendeþ;
Hem to berne fir me tendeþ.
35 Seide Floriz to Blauncheflur,
'Of vre lif nis no sucur;
Ac min is þe guld and þe vnmeþ
Þat þu for me schalt þolie deþ.
Ac if cunde hit þolie miȝte,
40 Ihc oȝte deie tuye wiþ riȝte,
O deþ for þe, on oþer for me;
For þis þu þolest nu for me.
For if I nere in-to þis tur icume,
Wiþ mireȝþe þu miȝtest her-inne wune.'
45 He droȝ forþ a riche ring
His moder him ȝaf at his parting.
'Haue þis ring, lemman min,
Þu ne miȝt noȝt deie þe while he is þin.'
Þe ring he haueþ forþ araȝt
50 And to Blauncheflur bitaȝt.
'Þe ring ne schal neure aredde me,
For deþ ne mai ihc se on þe.'
Þe ring heo wolde aȝe reche,
And to Floriz him biteche.
55 Ac for al þat heo miȝte do,
He him nolde aȝen ifo;
And þe ring bi one stunde

22 [eis]: *MS.* ais *erased but visible under ultra-violet.*

Fel adun to þe grunde.
A duc stupede and him vp nom,
60 And was þer-of wel bliþe mon.
    Nu þes childre forþ me bringeþ
To here dom, al wepinge.
Ac þer nas non so sturne mon,
Þat hem lokede vpon,
65 Þat nolde þo suþe faȝe
Þat iugement were wiþdraȝe.
For Floriz was so faire ȝongling,
And Blauncheflur so suete þing.
Of men and wimmen þat buþ nuþe,
70 Þat goþ and seoþ and spekeþ wiþ muþe,
Ne buþ so faire in here gladnesse,
So hi were in here sorinesse.
Ac þe Admiral was so wroþ and wod,
He quakede for grame þer he stod,
75 And het hem binde wel faste
And in-to þe fire caste.
Þe duc þat þe ring funde
Com to þe Admiral and runde,
And al togadere he gan him schewe
80 Of þat þe children were biknewe.
Þe Admiral let hem aȝen clepe,
For he wolde wiþ Floriz speke.
    'Sire,' quaþ Floriz, 'for soþ ihc telle,
Þu noȝtest noȝt þat maide quelle.
85 Of al þis gilt ihc am to wite;
Ihc oȝte deie and he go quite.'
Quaþ Blauncheflur, 'Aquel þu me,
And let Floriz aliue be.
Ȝef hit nere for mi luue,
90 He nere noȝt fram his londe icome.'
Quaþ þe Admiral, 'So ihc mote go,
Ȝe schulle deie togadere bo.
Miself ihc wulle me awreke;
Ne schulle ȝe neure go ne speke.'
95 Floriz forþ his nekke bed,
And Blauncheflur wiþdraȝe him ȝet.
Blauncheflur bid forþ hire suere,
And Floriz aȝen hire gan tire.
Neiþer ne miȝte þere þole
100 Þat oþer deide bifore.
Þo þe Admiral, þeȝ he wroþ were,

Þer he chaungede his chere.
For eyþer wolde for oþer deie,
And for he seȝ mani wepinde eie,
105 And for he luuede so muche þat mai,
Al wepinge he turnde away.
His swerd fel of his hond to grunde;
Ne miȝte he hit holde þulke stunde.
Þe duc þat here ring hadde
110 For hem to speke wille he hadde.
    'Sire Admiral,' he sede, 'iwis
Hit is þe wel litel pris
Þis feire children for to quelle;
Ac betere hit is þat hi þe telle
115 Hu he com in-to þi tur
To ligge þer bi Blauncheflur.
His engin whan þu hit wite,
Þe betere wiþ oþere þu miȝt þe wite.'
Alle þat herde wordes his
120 Bisecheþ þat he granti þis.
He het him telle his engin,
Hu he to Blauncheflur com in,
And ho him radde and help þarto.
'Þat,' quaþ he, 'nelle ihc neure do,
125 For þing þat me mai me do,
Bute hit hem beo forȝiue also.'
Alle þoþere bisecheþ þis,
And of þe Admiral igranted is.
Nu ord and ende he haþ hem itold,
130 Hu Bla[un]cheflur was fram him isold,
And hu he was of Spaygne a kinges sone,
For hire luue þuder icume,
To fonden wiþ sume ginne,
Hu he miȝte hure awinne,
135 And hu, þureȝ þe cupe and þureȝ þe gersume,
Þe porter was his man bicume,
And hu he was in a cupe ibore;
Alle þes oþere lowe þeruore.
    Þe Admiral þo, wel him bitide,
140 Þat Child he sette bi his side,
And haþ forȝiue his wraþþe bo,
Floriz and Blauncheflur also.
And sede wiþ him hi scholde be.

103 For: *MS.* For he seȝ þat.   133 ginne: *MS.* ginne.

Þe beste of al his maine.

145 And Floriz he makeþ stonde vpriȝt,
And þer he dubbede him to kniȝt.
Nu boþe togadere þes childre for blisse
Falleþ to his fet hem to kisse.
He let hem to one chirche bringe,

150 And spusen hem wiþ one gold-ringe.
Þureȝ þe red of Blauncheflur
Me fette Clariz adun of þe tur.
Þe Admiral hire nam to quene.
Þilke feste was wel breme,

155 For þer was alle kunnes gleo,
Þat miȝte at eni briddale beo.
Hit nas þerafter noþing longe
Þat þer come to Floriz writ and sonde,
Þat þe king his fader was ded,

160 And þat he scholde nimen his red.
Þanne seide þe Admiral,
'If þu dost bi mi consail,
Bilef wiþ me; ne wend naȝt hom,
Ihc wulle ȝeue þe a kinedom

165 Also long and also brod
Also eure ȝet þi fader ibod.'
Ac Floriz nolde for no winne;
Leuere him were wiþ his kinne.
Þe Admiral he bid god day,

170 And þonkede Clariz þat faire may,
And to hire he haþ iȝolde
Twenti pond of ride golde.
And to Daris þat him so taȝte
Twenti pund he araȝte.

175 And alle þat for him duden eidel,
He ȝeld here while suþe wel.
He bitaȝte hem alle Godalmiȝte,
And com hom whane he miȝte.
He was king with muchel honur,

180 And heo his quene Blauncheflur.
Nu ȝe habbeþ iherd þane ende
Of Floriz and his lemman hende,
Hu after bale comeþ bote.
God leue þat vs so mote,

185 Þat we Him mote louie so
Þat we mote to heuene go. Amen.
E-X-P-L-I-C-I-T.

X. THE OWL AND THE NIGHTINGALE

THE debate form in which the *Owl and the Nightingale* is written was widely popular during the twelfth and thirteenth centuries. Under different names it was essentially a contest in verse in which the rival views of two or more speakers were expounded, with or without final judgment. Such debates are not infrequent in Latin and French, but the *Owl and the Nightingale* is the first to appear in English. While retaining the conventional framework, the English poem enlivens the dialogue by the introduction of a good deal of narrative detail, and particularly noteworthy is the fact that its procedure closely follows that of a twelfth-century lawsuit, with a consistent use of legal terminology. The poem is obviously allegorical in intention, though what exactly may be symbolized is doubtful—perhaps the old conflict between pleasure and asceticism, between an active and a contemplative life, between a secular and a monastic life, between art and philosophy, or more probably between the newer lyric and the older didactic and religious poetry, with the owl defending the latter, the nightingale the former.

Questions of date, provenance, and author are still in dispute. Various references to contemporary events which can be found or suspected in the poem are not very definite, and at present all that can be said is that it was probably composed some time between the death of Henry II and the accession of Henry III. Attempts to prove an earlier or more precise date are so far unconvincing. As far as the provenance is concerned there is no doubt that the dialect of the extant versions is south-western, but the evidence of rhymes suggests that this was not the dialect of the original, which must have come from some district a good deal further to the east, one in which south-eastern forms were to be found, i.e. the eastern parts of Surrey or Sussex. Such a provenance is supported by what can be deduced about the author. In neither of the extant MSS. is any clue given to this. A certain Master Nicholas of Guildford, mentioned in the poem, is, however, referred to in a way that makes it quite certain that one of the author's objects in writing the poem was to bring Nicholas to the notice of his ecclesiastical superiors and so obtain promotion for him. A knowledge of the ways of medieval authors would lead one to suspect that it was Nicholas himself who had adopted this method of drawing attention to his merits. The only other name that has been mentioned in this connection is that of a certain John of Guildford. In the later of the two MSS. a seventeenth-century owner has noted that 'on parte of a broaken leafe of this MS. I found these verses written, whereby the Author may bee guesst at. (viz.)

> Mayster Johan eu greteþ of Guldeuorde þo,
> And sendeþ eu to seggen þat synge nul he mo.
> Nu on þisse wise he wille endy his song;
> God Louerd of Heuene beo vs alle among. Amen.'

Such an attribution would provide a fellow-townsman of Nicholas anxious to obtain promotion for him, but there is no evidence that the verses had anything to do with the *Owl and the Nightingale*, and much against it. On the whole, Nicholas of Guildford is as probable an author as anyone, but there is little definite evidence in his favour, nor has it been possible to identify him. (See also p. 57.)

Scholars have united in praise of the narrative skill of the author, his characterization and sense of form. The allegory is firmly kept in its place, and vivid circumstantial details throw into relief the scene of the dispute, the figures of the characters, and the life of the times, whilst incidental allusions help to provide a realistic historical background. But probably the most notable achievement of the author is the skill with which he has blended English and French elements in his work. He has borrowed his metre and form from the French and is one of the earliest English poets to use the octo-syllabic couplet, though in his use of it there is no suggestion of the novice. In the poem we find reminiscences of various other French literary types, and its outlook and atmosphere agree rather with contemporary French than English verse. The author has made his own the light ironic and humorous style, learned from the French, with which no other English poet succeeded before Chaucer. Nevertheless, it is essentially an English poem; the background is English, the progress of the debate is modelled on the procedure of a twelfth-century English lawsuit, and it shows some little influence from the native alliterative verse. Not before the fourteenth century do we again find so successful a mingling of the literatures.

The poem is preserved in two MSS., Cotton Caligula A IX in the British Museum (*c.* 1220), and MS. 29 from the library of Jesus College, Oxford (*c.* 1275), the differences between the two texts throwing much valuable light on the development of the vocabulary during the fifty years which separate them. Both texts go back to a common original which was not the author's autograph copy, though how many copies intervened in either case it is not possible to say. The text has several times been edited, the most comprehensive edition being that by J. W. H. Atkins (Cambridge 1922), the handiest that by J. E. Wells (Boston and London 1907), while a diplomatic version of the texts appears in the edition by J. H. G. Grattan and G. F. H. Sykes for the Early English Text Society (1935). C. T. Onions made 'An Experiment in Textual Reconstruction' of lines 1–446, 707–42, 1707–94, in 22 *Essays and Studies* 86–102. The extracts below are based on the Cotton MS., and correspond with lines 1–90, 995–1042, 1717–94, of the complete poem. It should be noted, however, that in the C. text there are two systems of spelling, the earlier covering lines 902–60 and 1184–end, the later lines 1–901 and 961–1183.

The Setting of the Scene

    Ich was in one sumere dale,
    In one suþe diȝele hale,
    Iherde ich holde grete tale
    An hule and one niȝtingale.
5   Þat plait was stif an starc an strong,
    Sum-wile softe an lud among;
    An aiþer aȝen oþer sval,
    An let þat vuele mod ut al.
    An eiþer seide of oþeres custe
10   Þat alre-worste þat hi wuste:
    An hure an hure of oþere songe
    Hi holde plaiding suþe stronge.
      Þe niȝtingale bigon þe speche,
    In one hurne of one breche,
15   An sat up one vaire boȝe,
    —Þar were abute blosme inoȝe—
    In ore vaste þicke hegge
    Imeind mid spire an grene segge.
    Ho was þe gladur uor þe rise,
20   An song a uele cunne wise:
    Bet þuȝte þe dreim þat he were

4 niȝtingale: *J.* nyhtegale (*regularly*).   7 *J.* eyþer: *C.* asþer.   8 *J.* uvele: *C.* wole.
10 alre: *MS.* alere *with first* e *cancelled*.   11 *J.* oþres.   14 *J.* beche.   17 *J.* vaste:
C. waste.   21 *J.* Bet: *C.* Het.

Of harpe an pipe þan he nere:
Bet þuȝte þat he were ishote
Of harpe and pipe þan of þrote.
25   [Þ]o stod on old stoc þarbiside,
Þar þo vle song hire tide,
An was mid iui al bigrowe;
Hit was þare hule eardingstowe.
    [Þ]e niȝtingale hi iseȝ,
30   An hi bihold an ouerseȝ,
An þuȝte wel wl of þare hule,
For me hi halt lodlich an fule.
'Vn-wiȝt,' ho sede, 'a-wei þu flo!
Me is þe wrs þat ich þe so.
35   Iwis for þine wle lete
Wel oft ich mine song forlete;
Min horte atfliþ an falt mi tonge,
Wonne þu art to me iþrunge.
Me luste bet speten þane singe
40   Of þine fule ȝoȝelinge.'
    Þos hule abod fort hit was eve,
Ho ne miȝte no leng bileue,
Vor hire horte was so gret
Þat welneȝ hire fnast at-schet,
45   An warp a word þar-after longe,
'Hu þincþe nu bi mine songe?
We[n]st þu þat ich ne cunne singe,
Þeȝ ich ne cunne of writelinge?
Ilome þu dest me grame,
50   An seist me boþe tone an schame.
Ȝif ich þe holde on mine uote,
(So hit bitide þat ich mote!)
An þu were vt of þine rise,
Þu sholdest singe an oþer w[i]se.'
55   Þe niȝtingale ȝaf answare:
'Ȝif ich me loki wit þe bare,
An me schilde wit þe blete,
Ne reche ich noȝt of þine þrete;
Ȝif ich me holde in mine hegge,
60   Ne recche ich neuer what þu segge.
Ich wot þat þu art un-milde
Wiþ hom þat ne muȝe from þe schilde;
An þu tukest wroþe an vuele,

31 wl: _J._ ful.   40 ȝoȝelinge: _J._ howelynge.   47 _C._ west þu: _J._ wenestu.
48 þeȝ: _J._ þe.   51 _J._ vote: _C._ note.   54 _J._ wise: _C._ wse.   62 _J._ þe: _C._ se.

THE OWL AND THE NIGHTINGALE, ll. 1–67

(B. M. Cotton Caligula A. IX, f. 233 r)

Whar þu miȝt, over-smale fuȝele.
65 Vorþi þu art loþ al fuel-kunne,
    An alle ho þe driueþ honne,
    An þe bi-schricheþ an bigredet,
    An wel narewe þe biledet;
    An ek forþe þe sulue mose,
70 Hire þonkes, wolde þe totose.
    Þu art lodlich to biholde,
    An þu art loþ in monie volde;
    Þi bodi is short, þi swore is smal,
    Grettere is þin heued þan þu al;
75 Þin eȝene boþ colblake an brode,
    Riȝt swo ho weren ipeint mid wode;
    Þu starest so þu wille abiten
    Al þat þu mist mid cliure smiten:
    Þi bile is stif an scharp an hoked,
80 Riȝt so an owel þat is croked;
    Þar-mid þu clackes oft an longe,
    An þat is on of þine songe.
    Ac þu þretest to mine fleshe,
    Mid þine cliures woldest me meshe.
85 Þe were icundur to one frogge
    [Þat sit at mulne vnder cogge,]
    Snailes, mus an fule wiȝte,
    Boþ þine cunde an þine riȝte.
    Þu sittest adai an fliȝt aniȝt,
90 Þu cuþest þat þu art on vnwiȝt.

[The nightingale goes on to discuss the personal habits of the owl, and tells of the hawk who reared an owl in her nest but had to cast it out because of its filthy habits. She then bursts into song and is challenged to trial by battle. This is declined, and after some discussion it is agreed that the case shall be judged by Nicholas of Guildford, but before proceeding to judgement the nightingale again attacks the song of the owl and her preference for the dark. In defence the owl claims that by her song she gives warning of impending dangers to men, does not cheapen it by over-use, and can see all that is necessary. The nightingale then complains of the mournfulness of the owl's song, heard only during the winter and never in summer. The obvious reply is that the winter is the very time when people most need cheer, and summer leads only to wantonness—the theme of the nightingale's song. In winter the latter flies away, but the owl stays and helps people in their misery. She emphasizes the uselessness of her adversary and again refutes the charge of uncleanliness, flinging back the accusation at the other. The nightingale in reply claims that her single accomplishment, which makes her loved by all, is better than the many which the owl claims to possess. A fox has any number of tricks, a cat but one, yet the fox loses his skin while the cat saves his. In reply the owl claims that her song leads men to repentance and a better life; as for the nightingale she sings only of worldly things, and if her song is so wonderful there are plenty of people in the far north whom she neglects. The owl on the other hand is known everywhere and sings to all men. The nightingale replies]

74 þan: *J.* ne.   78 mist: *J.* myht.   80 owel: *J.* ewel.   81 clackes: *J.* clechest.
86 *Supplied from J.*   89 fliȝt: *J.* flyhst.

The Barbarous North

(995)   'Ʒut þu aisheist wi ich ne fare
       In-to oþer londe an singe þare?
       No! wat sholde ich among hom do,
       Þar neuer blisse ne com to?
95   Þar lond nis god, ne hit nis este,
       Ac wildernisse hit is an weste:
       Knarres an cludes houen[e]tinge,
       Snou an haʒel hom is genge.
       Þat lond is grislich an unuele,
100   Þe men boþ wilde and unisele,
       Hi nabbeþ noþer griþ ne sibbe:
       Hi ne reccheþ hu hi libbe.
       Hi eteþ fihs an flehs unsode,
       Suich wulues hit hadde to-brode:
105   Hi drinkeþ milc an wei þarto,
       Hi nute elles wat hi do:
       Hi nabbeþ noþ[er] win ne bor,
       Ac libbeþ al-so wilde dor:
       Hi goþ bitiʒt mid ruʒe uelle,
110   Riʒt suich hi comen ut of helle.
       Þeʒ eni god man to hom come,
       So wile dude sum from Rome,
       For hom to lere gode þewes,
       An for to leten hore unþewes,
115   He miʒte bet sitte stille,
       Vor al his wile he sholde spille:
       He miʒte bet teche ane bore
       To weʒe boþe sheld an spere,
       Þan me þat wilde folc ibringe
120   Þat hi me wolde ihere singe.
       Wat sol ich þar mid mine songe?
       Ne sunge ich hom neuer so longe,
       Mi song were ispild echdel:
       For hom ne mai halter ne bridel
125   Bringe vrom hore wude-wise,
       Ne mon mid stele ne mid ise.
       Ac þar lond is boþe este an god,
       An þar men habbeþ milde mod,

97 J. houene-: C. houen-.   100 unisele: J. vnsele.   106 nute: J. nuteþ.   107
C. noþ: J. noht.   117 bore: J. beore.   118 weʒe boþe: J. bere.   119 þan
me: J. þane.   120 J. me wolde: C. me segge wolde.   122 sunge: J. singe.
126 ise: C.J. ire.   127 J. lond: C. long.

Ich noti mid hom mine þrote,
130 Vor ich mai do þar gode note,
An bringe hom loue-tiþinge,
Vor ich of chirche-songe singe.
Hit was iseid in olde laʒe,
An ʒet ilast þilke soþsaʒe,
135 Þat man shal erien an sowe,
Þar he wenþ after sum god mowe;
For he is wod þat soweþ his sed
Þar neuer gras ne sprinþ ne bled.'

[The owl then follows up the charge of wantonness, and tells how a lady was led astray by the song of a nightingale. In revenge the bird was seized by the husband and torn asunder by wild horses. But a different version is given by the nightingale; the knight was so punished for his cruelty that no one now dares to harm her, the owl, on the other hand, is universally hated because in her song she foretells only misfortunes to come. The owl admits this, but claims that by her power of foreseeing future events she is able to help mankind, whereupon the nightingale accuses her of witchcraft, and goes on to defend herself against the charge of wantonness by claiming that she protects maidens from folly. In return the owl claims to help married women, and even though disliked by men, yet in death helps them by acting as a scarecrow. At this the nightingale claims victory on the ground that the owl has boasted of her own disgrace. She sings so loudly that all the song-birds, including the wren, flock to her. The owl threatens to summon the birds of prey, whereupon the wren intervenes.]

The Conclusion

(1717) Þe wranne, for heo cuþe singe,
140 Þar com in þare moreʒen[i]nge
To helpe þare niʒtegale;
For þah heo hadde steuene smale,
Heo hadde gode þorte an schille,
An fale manne song a wille.
145 Þe wranne was wel wis iholde,
Vor þeg heo nere ibred awolde,
Ho was itoʒen among man[k]enne,
An hire wisdom brohte þenne;
Heo miʒte speke hwar heo walde,
150 To-uore þe king þah heo scholde.
'Lusteþ,' heo cwaþ, 'lateþ me speke.
Hwat! wulle ʒe þis pes to-breke,
An do þan [kinge] swuch schame?
Ʒe, nis he nouþer ded ne lame.
155 Hunke schal i-tide harm an schonde,
Ʒef ʒe doþ griþ-bruche on his londe.

131 loue-tiþinge: J. leue-tydinge.   134 an: J. þat.   140 moreʒeninge: C. more ʒennge, J. moreweninge.   142 For þah: J. Vor.   143 þorte: J. þrote.   146 þeg: J. þeih.   147 mankenne: C. mannenne, J. mankunne.   153 þan kinge: C.J. þanne.   154 C. ʒe nis he: J. yet nys heo.   156 ʒe: J. we.

Lateþ beo, an beoþ isome,
An fareþ riht to ower dome,
An lateþ dom þis plaid to-breke,
160   Al-swo hit was erur bispeke.'
    'Ich an wel,' cwað þe niȝtegale,
'Ah, wranne, naþt for þire tale,
Ah do for mire lahfulnesse.
Ich nolde þat unriht-fulnesse
165   Me at þen ende ouer-kome;
Ich nam of-drad of none dome.
Bi-hote ich habbe, soþ hit is,
Þat Maister Nichole, þat is wis,
Bi-tuxen vs deme schulle,
170   An ȝet ich wene þat he wule.
Ah war mihte we hine finde?'
Þe wranne sat in ore linde:
'Hwat! nuȝte ȝe,' cwaþ heo, 'his hom?
He wuneþ at Portes-hom,
175   At one tune ine Dorsete,
Bi þare see in ore ut-lete:
Þar he demeþ manie riȝte dom,
An diht an writ mani wisdom,
An þurh his muþe and þurh his honde
180   Hit is þe betere in-to Scot-londe.
To seche hine is lihtlich þing;
He naueþ bute one woning.
Þat his bischopen muchel schame,
An alle þan þat of his nome
185   Habbeþ ihert, an of his dede.
Hwi nulleþ hi nimen heom to rede,
Þat he were mid heom ilome
For teche heom of his wisdome,
An ȝiue him rente a uale stude,
190   Þat he miȝte heom ilome be mide?'
    'Certes,' cwaþ þe hule, 'þat is soð;
Þeos riche men wel muche misdoð,
Þat leteþ þane gode mon,
Þat of so feole þinge con,
195   An ȝiueþ rente wel misliche,

---

158 ower: *C.* oþer, *J.* eure.   161 an: *J.* unne.   162 naþt, þire: *J.* nouht, þine.
163 ah: *J.* ac.   169 vs deme **schulle:** *C.* vs deme schulde, *J.* eu deme schulle.
170 ȝet ich wene: *C.* ȝef ich þene, *J.* yet ic wene.   171 war: *C.J.* þar.   173 nuȝte
ȝe: *J.* mihte yet.   183 his: *J.* is.   184 *J.* þan: *C.* wan.   187 *J.* teche: *C.* theche,
first h *deleted.*   192 wel muche: *J.* muchel.

An of him leteþ wel lihtliche.
Wið heore cunne heo beoþ mildre,
An ȝeueþ rente litle childre;
Swo heore wit hi demþ adwole,
200 Þat euer abid Maistre Nichole.
Ah ute we þah to him fare,
For þar is unker dom al ȝare.'
     'Do we,' þe niȝtegale seide;
'Ah wa schal unker speche rede,
205 An telle to-uore unker deme?'
     'Þarof ich schal þe wel icweme,'
Cwaþ þe houle, 'for al, ende of orde,
Telle ich con, word after worde;
An ȝef þe þincþ þat ich mis-rempe,
210 Þu stond aȝein an do me crempe.'
     Mid þisse worde forþ hi ferden,
Al bute here an bute uerde,
To Portes-ham þat heo bi-come.
Ah hu heo spedde of heore dome,
215 Ne chan ich eu namore telle;
Her nis na more of þis spelle.

---

199 *J.* adwole: *C.* adpole.   201 *J.* we: *C.* þe.   202 þar: *J.* þat.
210 *J.* do me: *C.* dome.   216 þis: *J.* þisse.

Addendum to Page 50

There was a *Magister Nicholas*, a canonist working in England *c.* 1200 and cited in *Quaestiones Londinenses* (B.M. Royal 9 E vii, ff. 191-198, on which see W. Ullmann, *Medieval Papalism*, pp. 13 and 200-1). But S. Kuttner (7 Traditio 317-20) thinks he " may well be Nicholas de Aquila, . . . presumably the dean of Chichester *c.* 1197-1217, who was elected bishop of that see in 1209 but apparently never consecrated ". Nicholas de Aquila was not an Englishman and so an unpromising candidate for the authorship of *The Owl and the Nightingale*.

XI. THE BESTIARY

BESTIARIES appear to have been one of the most popular types of medieval literature, and their general characteristics can be seen from the extracts below. They consisted of descriptions of birds, beasts, and reptiles, and more particularly of the legends connected with them, these being then allegorized in a following section. The earliest bestiaries were in Greek, and probably originated in Egypt some time during the second century A.D. A Latin version was made, perhaps as early as the fifth century, and through it bestiary literature made its way into most of the Western European languages. Fragments of a bestiary appear already in OE verse, and although only one ME version exists, preserved in a single MS., material drawn from it is frequent enough in other vernacular works. The ME work is, in the main, derived from the metrical Latin version by Thetbaldus, an Italian monk of the eleventh century, whose work appears to have superseded all other Latin versions. In some 700 lines the ME author deals with the lion, eagle, adder, ant, hart, fox, spider, whale, mermaid, elephant, turtle-dove, and panther of his original, adding a further section, taken from the *De Naturis Rerum* of Alexander Nequam, on the dove. The popularity of this type of literature, with its plentiful supply of marvels, is not surprising, but its main importance lies in the fact that the legends continued in literary use long after their origin had been forgotten.[1]

The extant ME version has passed through the hands of so many copyists that we can say little of its date or provenance. In all probability it was composed during the first half of the thirteenth century, somewhere in the East Midlands. The Latin original uses a variety of metres, and the English adaptor does the same, even improving on his model by mixing the different kinds of verse in the description of the same creature, cf., for example, the mixture of alliteration and rhyme in the description of the fox. The most recent edition is that by Hall, i, 176–96; ii, 579–626, and extracts appear in most ME readers. The passages below are taken from the sole surviving MS., British Museum Arundel 292, and correspond with lines 296–354 and 382–439, in Hall's edition.

[1] A convenient introduction to the Bestiary and its influence is P. A. Robin, *Animal Lore in English Literature* (London 1932).

Natura Wulpis

(296) A wilde der is, ðat is ful of fele wiles,
    Fox is hire to name, for hire qweðsipe
    Husebondes hire haten, for hire harm-dedes.
    Ðe coc and te capun
5   Ge feccheð ofte in ðe tun,
    And te gandre and te gos,
    Bi ðe necke and bi ðe nos,
    Haleð is to hire hole. For-ði man hire hatieð,
    Hatien and huten bothe men and fules.
10   Listneð nu a wunder ðat tis der doð for hunger.
    Goð o felde to a furg, and falleð ðar-inne,
    In eried lond er in erðchine, forto bilirten fugeles.
    Ne stereð ge nogt of ðe stede a god stund deies,
    Oc dareð so ge ded were, ne drageð ge non onde.
15   Ðe rauen is swiðe redi, weneð ðat ge rotieð,
    And oðre fules hire fallen bi, for to winnen fode,
    Derflike wiðuten dred, he wenen ðat ge ded beð.
    He wullen on ðis foxes fell, and ge it wel feleð.
    Ligtlike ge lepeð up, and letteð hem sone.
20   Gelt hem here billing
    Raðe wið illing,
    Tetoggeð and tetireð hem mid hire teð sarpe.
    Fret hire fille,
    And goð ðan ðer ge wille.

Significacio

25   Twifold forbisne in ðis der,
    To frame we mugen finden her,
    Warsipe and wisedom
    Wið deuel and wið iuel man.
    Ðe deuel dereð dernelike,
30   He lat he ne wile us nogt biswike.
    He lat he ne wile us don non loð,
    And bringeð us in a sinne, and ter he us sloð.
    He bit us don ure bukes wille,
    Eten and drinken wið unskil,
35   And in ure skemting
    He doð raðe a foxing.
    He billeð one ðe foxes fel,
    Wo-so telleð idel spel,

9 huten *Hall*: *MS.* hulen.   31 don: *MS.* ðon.

And he tireð on his ket,
40 Wo-so him wið sinne fet.
And deuel geld swilk billing
Wið same and wið sending,
And for his sinfule werk
Ledeð man to helle merk.

Significacio

45 Ðe deuel is tus ðe [fox] ilik,
Mið iuele breides and wið swik.
And man[i] al-so ðe foxes name
Arn wurði hauen to same.
For wo-so seieð oðer god,
50 And ðenkeð iuel on his mod,
Fox he is and fend iwis—
Ðe boc ne legeð nogt of ðis.
So was Herodes fox and flerd
Ðo Crist kam into ðis middel-erd.
55 He seide he wulde him leuen on,
And ðogte he wulde him fordon.

Natura cetegrandie

(382) Cethegrande is a fis,
Ðe moste ðat in water is;
Ðat tu wuldes seien get,
60 Gef ðu it soge wan it flet,
Ðat it were á neilond
Ðat sete one ðe se-sond.
Ðis fis ðat is vnride,
Ðanne him hungreð he gapeð wide;
65 Vt of his ðrote it smit an onde,
Ðe swetteste ðing ðat is o londe.
Ðer-fore oðre fisses to him dragen,
Wan he it felen he aren fagen;
He cumen and hoven in his muð,
70 Of his swike he arn uncuð.
Ðis cete ðanne hise chaueles lukeð,
Ðise fisses alle in sukeð;
Ðe smale he wile ðus biswiken,
Ðe grete maig he nogt bigripen.
75 Ðis fis wuneð wið ðe se-grund,
And liueð ðer eure heil and sund,

Til it cumeð ðe time
Ðat storm stireð al ðe se,
Ðanne sumer and winter winnen.
80 Ne mai it wunen ðer-inne,
So droui is te sees grund;
Ne mai he wunen ðer ðat stund,
Oc stireð up and houeð stille,
Wiles ðar weder is so ille.
85 Ðe sipes ðat arn on se fordriuen—
Loð hem is deð, and lef to liuen—
Biloken hem and sen ðis fis,
A neilond he wenen it is.
Ðer-of he aren swiðe fagen,
90 And mid here migt ðar-to he dragen,
Sipes on festen,
And alle up gangen.
Of ston mid stel in ðe tunder
Wel to brennen one ðis wunder;
95 Warmen hem wel and heten and drinken.
Ðe fir he feleð and doð hem sinken,
For sone he diueð dun to grunde;
He drepeð hem alle wið-uten wunde.

Significacio

Ðis deuel is mikel wið wil and magt,
100 So witches hauen in here craft;
He doð men hungren and hauen ðrist,
And mani oðer sinful list,
Tolleð men to him wið his onde,
Wo-so him folegeð he findeð sonde.
105 Ðo arn ðe little in leue lage,
Ðe mikle ne maig he to him dragen;
Ðe mikle, I mene ðe stedefast
In rigte leue mid fles and gast.
Wo-so listneð deueles lore,
110 On lengðe it sal him rewen sore;
Wo-so festeð hope on him,
He sal him folgen to helle dim.

48 hauen to *Hall*: *MS.* to hauen.   86 deð: *MS.* ded.

XII. THE VOX AND THE WOLF

THE comparative lack of beast tales in ME is particularly surprising when contrasted with their popularity abroad. In English there is only the *Vox and the Wolf*, Chaucer's *Nun's Priest's Tale*, and the as yet unpublished *Fox and Geese*, but occasional references make it clear that these are merely the accidental survivors of a much greater number. The plot of the *Vox and the Wolf* is a not uncommon one in folk-lore, and no doubt derives ultimately from the east. A version of it appears in the *Roman de Renart*, and, judged from other versions in the *Fables* of Odo of Cheriton and Nicholas Bozon, along with a passing reference to the 'tale of the fox and the wolf in the well-buckets' in the *Summa Predicantium* of John Bromyard, the story was evidently popular in England. In all probability the English story depends ultimately on some French version which cannot now be identified but probably had the same ultimate original as the episode in the *Roman de Renart*. Certainly, whether translating from another language or using a native folk-tale, the English adaptor does not give so satisfactory a version as that to be found in the French, and some of the variations suggest unintelligent cutting of a written original. For example, from later references in the poem we gather that the fox has succeeded in disposing of some of the hens, probably three, but no mention is made of this in the episode itself. Moreover, the French version gives a much more reasonable explanation for some of the events than is to be found in the English. The fox is trapped in a more plausible way. It is a clear starlight night, and as he peers over the rim of the well he takes his reflection in the water to be his wife Hermeline, while the echo of his voice he takes to be her reply. Consequently he gets into the bucket and goes down to see what is wrong. Similarly the wolf is persuaded to get into the bucket by the fox's explanation that the two buckets are God's balance of good and evil in which souls must be weighed before they can enter Paradise. Nevertheless, despite the faults of the English adaptor, inartistic cutting, lack of proportion, etc., there is much to enjoy in his version, whether it be due to himself or to his original. The dialogue is natural and unforced, the octosyllabic metre in perfect keeping with the subject-matter, and the whole poem has a lightness of touch which makes it a worthy representative in English of the beast tale. Above all, the characterization is excellent, whether of the cock, the fox, or the wolf; the somewhat pompous disapproval of the cock at the slaughter of the hens, the hopeful attempt of the fox to add him to his bag, as well as the cringing manner in which the wolf makes his confession in hope of being admitted to the unlimited food of Paradise.

Nothing is known of the author of the English version, which is extant only in a single Bodleian MS., Digby 86 (*c.* 1250–75), from which it is here printed. As it stands it appears to be in a western dialect, but rhymes indicate that it was originally composed in some district in which south-eastern and Midland forms could be used, at any rate for the sake of the rhyme. It was edited by G. H. McKnight, *Middle English Humorous Tales in Verse* (Boston and London 1913), and is to be found also, complete or in part, in most ME readers.

Of þe vox and of þe wolf

A vox gon out of þe wode go,
Afingret so þat him wes wo;
He nes neuere in none wise
Afingret erour half so swiþe.
5 He ne hoeld nouþer wey ne strete,
For him wes loþ men to mete;
Him were leuere meten one hen,
Þen half an oundred wimmen.
He strok swiþe ouer-al,
10 So þat he ofsei ane wal;
Wiþinne þe walle wes on hous,
The wox wes þider swiþe wous;
For he þohute his hounger aquenche,
Oþer mid mete, oþer mid drunche.
15 Abouten he biheld wel ȝerne;
Þo eroust bigon þe vox to erne.
Al fort he come to one walle,
And som þer-of wes afalle,
And wes þe wal ouer-al to-broke,
20 And on ȝat þer wes i-loke;
At þe furmeste bruche þat he fond,
He lep in, and ouer he wond.
Þo he wes inne, smere he lou,
And þer-of he hadde gome i-nou;

25 For he com in wiþouten leue
     Boþen of haiward and of reue.
       On hous þer wes, þe dore was ope,
     Hennen weren þerinne i-crope,
     Fiue, þat makeþ anne flok,
30 And mid hem sat on kok.
     Þe kok him wes flowen on hey,
     And two hennen him seten ney.
     'Wox,' quod þe kok, 'wat dest þou þare?
     Go hom, Crist þe ȝeue kare!
35 Houre hennen þou dest ofte shome.'
     'Be stille, ich hote, a Godes nome!'
     Quaþ þe wox, 'Sire Chauntecler,
     Þou fle adoun, and com me ner.
     I nabbe don her nout bote goed,
40 I have leten þine hennen blod;
     Hy weren seke ounder þe ribe,
     Þat hy ne miȝtte non lengour libe,
     Bote here heddre were i-take;
     Þat I do for almes sake.
45 Ich haue hem letten eddre-blod,
     And þe, Chauntecler, hit wolde don goed.
     Þou hauest þat ilke ounder þe splen,
     Þou nestes neuere daies ten;
     For þine lif-dayes beþ al ago,
50 Bote þou bi mine rede do;
     I do þe lete blod ounder þe brest,
     Oþer sone axe after þe prest.'
     'Go wei,' quod þe kok, 'wo þe bi-go!
     Þou hauest don oure kunne wo.
55 Go mid þan þat þou hauest nouþe;
     Acoursed be þou of Godes mouþe!
     For were I adoun, bi Godes nome,
     Ich miȝte ben siker of oþre shome.
     Ac weste hit houre cellerer,
60 Þat þou were i-comen her,
     He wolde sone after þe ȝonge,
     Mid pikes and stones and staues stronge;
     Alle þine bones he wolde to-breke;
     Þene we weren wel awreke.'
65   He wes stille, ne spak namore,
     Ac he werþ aþurst wel sore.
     Þe þurst him dede more wo

Þen heuede raþer his hounger do.
Ouer-al he ede and sohvte;
70   On auenture his wiit him brohute
To one putte wes water inne,
Þat wes i-maked mid grete ginne.
Tuo boketes þer he founde,
Þat oþer wende to þe grounde,
75   Þat wen me shulde þat on opwinde,
Þat oþer wolde adoun winde.
He ne hounderstod nout of þe ginne,
He nom þat boket, and lep þerinne,
For he hopede i-nou to drinke.
80   Þis boket biginneþ to sinke,
To late þe vox wes biþout,
Þo he was in þe ginne i-brout.
I-nou he gon him bi-þenche,
Ac hit ne halp mid none wrenche;
85   Adoun he moste, he wes þerinne.
I-kaut he wes mid swikele ginne.
Hit miȝte han i-ben wel his wille
To lete þat boket hongi stille.
Wat mid serewe and mid drede,
90   Al his þurst him ouer-hede.
Al þus he come to þe grounde,
And water i-nou þer he founde.
Þo he fond water, ȝerne he dronk!
Him þoute þat water þere stonk,
95   For hit wes to-ȝeines his wille.
'Wo worþe,' quaþ þe vox, 'lust and wille,
Þat ne con meþ to his mete!
Ȝef ich neuede to muchel i-ete,
Þis ilke shome neddi nouþe,
100   Nedde lust i-ben of mine mouþe.
Him is wo in euche londe,
Þat is þef mid his honde.
Ich am i-kaut mid swikele ginne,
Oþer soum deuel me broute her-inne.
105   I was woned to ben wiis,
Ac nou of me i-don hit hiis.'
    Þe vox wep, and reuliche bigan;
Þer com a wolf gon after þan,
Out of þe depe wode bliue,
110   For he wes afingret swiþe.

Noþing he ne founde in al þe niȝte,
Wer-mide his honger aquenche miȝtte.
He com to þe putte, þene vox i-herde,
He him kneu wel bi his rerde,
115 For hit wes his neiȝebore,
And his gossip, of children bore.
Adoun bi þe putte he sat.
Quod þe wolf, 'Wat may ben þat
Þat ich in þe putte i-here?
120 Hertou cristine, oþer mi fere?
Say me soþ, ne gabbe þou me nout,
Wo haueþ þe in þe putte i-brout?'
Þe vox hine i-kneu wel for his kun,
And þo eroust kom wiit to him;
125 For he þoute mid soumme ginne,
Him-self houpbringe, þene wolf þer-inne.
Quod þe vox, 'Wo is nou þere?
Ich wene hit is Sigrim þat ich here.'
'Þat is soþ,' þe wolf sede,
130 'Ac wat art þou, so God þe rede?'
      'Al' quod þe vox, 'ich wille þe telle,
On alpi word ich lie nelle,
Ich am Reneuard, þi frend,
And ȝif ich þine come heuede i-wend,
135 Ich hedde so i-bede for þe,
Þat þou sholdest comen to me.'
'Mid þe?' quod þe wolf, 'War-to?
Wat shulde ich ine þe putte do?'
Quod þe vox, 'Þou art ounwiis,
140 Her is þe blisse of paradiis;
Her ich mai euere wel fare,
Wiþ-outen pine, wiþouten kare;
Her is mete, her is drinke,
Her is blisse wiþ-outen swinke;
145 Her nis hounger neuermo,
Ne non oþer kunnes wo;
Of alle gode her is i-nou.'
Mid þilke wordes þe volf lou,
      'Art þou ded, so God þe rede,
150 Oþer of þe worlde?' þe wolf sede.
Quod þe wolf, 'Wenne storue þou,
And wat dest þou þere nou?
Ne beþ nout ȝet þre daies ago,

Þat þou and þi wif also,
155 And þine children, smale and grete,
Alle togedere mid me hete.'
'Þat is soþ,' quod þe vox,
'Gode þonk, nou hit is þus,
Þat ihc am to Criste vend;
160 Not hit non of mine frend.
I nolde, for al þe worldes lond,
Ben ine þe worlde, þer ich hem fond.
Wat shuldich ine þe worlde go,
Þer nis bote kare and wo,
165 And liuie in fulþe and in sunne?
Ac her beþ ioies fele cunne,
Her beþ boþe shep and get.'
Þe wolf haueþ hounger swiþe gret,
For he nedde ȝare i-ete,
170 And þo he herde speken of mete,
He wolde bleþeliche ben þare.
'A!' quod þe wolf, 'gode i-fere,
Moni goed mel þou hauest me binome,
Let me adoun to þe kome,
175 And al ich wole þe for-ȝeue.'
'Ȝe,' quod þe vox, 'were þou i-sriue,
And sunnen heuedest al forsake,
And to klene lif i-take,
Ich wolde so bidde for þe,
180 Þat þou sholdest comen to me.'
        'To wom shuldich,' þe wolf seide,
'Ben i-knowe of mine misdede?
Her nis noþing aliue,
Þat me kouþe her nou sriue.
185 Þou hauest ben ofte min i-fere,
Woltou nou mi srift i-here,
And al mi liif I shal þe telle?'
'Nay,' quod þe vox, 'I nelle.'
'Neltou,' quod þe wolf, 'þin ore,
190 Ich am afingret swiþe sore;
Ich wot to-niȝt ich worþe ded,
Bote þou do me somne reed.
For Cristes loue be mi prest.'
Þe wolf bey adoun his brest,
195 And gon to siken harde and stronge.

161 lond: *MS. goed.*

'Woltou,' quod þe vox, 'srift ounderfonge,
Tel þine sunnen on and on,
Þat þer bileue neuer on.'
    'Sone,' quod þe wolf, 'wel i-faie,
200 Ich habbe ben qued al mi lifdaie;
Ich habbe widewene kors,
Þerfore ich fare þe wors.
A þousent shep ich habbe abiten,
And mo, ӡef hy weren i-writen,
205 Ac hit me of-þinkeþ sore.
Maister, shal I tellen more?'
    'Ӡe,' quod þe vox, 'al þou most sugge,
Oþer elles-wer þou most abugge.'
    'Gossip,' quod þe wolf, 'forӡef hit me,
210 Ich habbe ofte sehid qued bi þe.
Men seide þat þou on þine liue
Misferdest mid mine wiue;
Ich þe aperseiuede one stounde,
And in bedde to-gedere ou founde.
215 Ich wes ofte ou ful ney,
And in bedde to-gedere ou sey.
Ich wende, al-so oþre doþ,
Þat ihc i-seie were soþ,
And þerfore þou were me loþ.
220 Gode gossip, ne be þou nohut wroþ.'
      'Vuolf,' quod þe vox him þo,
'Al þat þou hauest her-bifore i-do,
In þohut, in speche, and in dede,
In euche oþeres kunnes quede,
225 Ich þe for-ӡeue at þisse nede.'
    'Crist þe forӡelde!', þe wolf seide,
'Nou ich am in clene liue,
Ne recche ich of childe ne of wiue.
Ac sei me wat I shal do,
230 And ou ich may comen þe to.'
    'Do?' quod þe vox, 'Ich wille þe lere.
I-siist þou a boket hongi þere?
Þer is a bruche of heuene blisse,
Lep þerinne mid i-wisse,
235 And þou shalt comen to me sone.'
    Quod þe wolf, 'Þat is liӡt to done.'
He lep in, and way sumdel—

199 i-faie: *MS.* I fare.

Þat weste þe vox ful wel.
Þe wolf gon sinke, þe vox arise;
240 Þo gon þe wolf sore agrise.
Þo he com amidde þe putte,
Þe wolf þene vox opward mette.
'Gossip,' quod þe wolf, 'Wat nou?
Wat hauest þou i-munt? Weder wolt þou?'
245 'Weder ich wille?' þe vox sede,
'Ich wille oup, so God me rede!
And nou go doun wiþ þi meel,
Þi biȝete worþ wel smal.
Ac ich am þerof glad and bliþe,
250 Þat þou art nomen in clene liue.
Þi soule-cnul ich wille do ringe,
And masse for þine soule singe.'
Þe wrecche bineþe noþing ne vind
Bote cold water, and hounger him bind.
255 To colde gistninge he wes i-bede,
Wroggen haueþ his dou i-knede.
    Þe wolf in þe putte stod,
Afingret so þat he ves wod.
I-nou he cursede þat þider him broute;
260 Þe vox þer-of luitel route.
Þe put him wes þe house ney,
Þer freren woneden swiþe sley.
Þo þat hit com to þe time,
Þat hoe shulden arisen, prime,
265 For to suggen here houssong,
O frere þer wes among,
Of here slep hem shulde awecche,
Wen hoe shulden þidere recche.
He seide, 'Ariseþ on and on,
270 And komeþ to houssong heuereuchon.'
Þis ilke frere heyte Ailmer,
He wes hoere maister curtiler.
He wes hofþurst swiþe stronge,
Riȝt amidward here houssonge.
275 Alhone to þe putte he hede,
For he wende bete his nede.
He com to þe putte and drou,
And þe wolf wes heui i-nou.
Þe frere mid al his maine tey,

264 prime: *MS.* ·Ime.

280   So longe þat he þene wolf i-sey.
       For he sei þene wolf þer sitte,
       He gradde, 'Þe deuel is in þe putte!'
          To þe putte hy gounnen gon,
       Alle mid pikes and staues and ston,
285   Euch mon mid þat he hedde,
       Wo wes him þat wepne nedde.
       Hy comen to þe putte, þene wolf op-drowe,
       Þo hede þe wreche fomen i-nowe,
       Þat weren egre him to slete
290   Mid grete houndes, and to bete.
       Wel and wroþe he wes i-swonge,
       Mid staues and speres he was i-stounge.
       Þe wox bicharde him mid i-wisse,
       For he ne fond nones kunnes blisse,
295   Ne hof duntes forȝeuenesse. explicit.

THE *Thrush and the Nightingale* is an example of the debate which is much closer to the conventional French and Latin models than is the *Owl and the Nightingale*. In comparison with the latter it contains practically no connecting narrative, and few of the personal touches to be found in the earlier poem. The matter is completely conventional, and is found frequently enough elsewhere during the medieval period, whilst the fact that nearly all the speeches are complete within the stanza recalls the formalism of the Latin models. Nevertheless, it is an excellent example of the formal debate poem, though perhaps slightly more dramatic and realistic than the majority of such poems. It is said to have been influenced by the *Owl and the Nightingale*, though the only likeness discernible lies in the fact that the disputants in both cases are birds, and in reality its affinities are rather with such lyrical poems as the *Debate between the Clerk and the Maiden* and *The Nut-Brown Maid*.

The poem appears to have been composed somewhere in the south during the last quarter of the thirteenth century, though definite evidence on either point is lacking. It is found complete only in the Bodleian MS. Digby 86 (1272–83), from which it is here printed, but 74 lines appear also in the Auchinleck MS. in the National Library in Edinburgh. The best edition of the earlier version is in Carleton Brown, pp. 101–07, and of the later by H. Varnhagen, 4 *Anglia* 208 ff.

> *Ci comence le cuntent parentre le Mauuis & la russinole*
> Somer is comen wiþ loue to toune,
> Wiþ blostme, and wiþ brides roune
>   Þe note of hasel springeþ,
> Þe dewes darkneþ in þe dale.
> 5 For longing of þe niʒttegale,
>   Þis foweles murie singeþ.
>
> Hic herde a strif bitweies two—
> Þat on of wele, þat oþer of wo—
>   Bitwene two i-fere.
> 10 Þat on hereþ wimmen þat hoe beþ hende,
> Þat oþer hem wole wiþ miʒte shende;
>   Þat strif ʒe mowen i-here.

Þe niȝtingale is on bi nome
Þat wol shilden hem from shome,
15   Of skaþe hoe wole hem skere;
Þe þrestelcok hem kepeþ ay,
He seiþ bi niȝte and eke bi day,
    Þat hy beþ fendes i-fere.

For hy biswikeþ euchan mon
20   Þat mest bi-leueþ hem ouppon,
    Þey hy ben milde of chere.
Hoe beþ fikele and fals to fonde,
Hoe wercheþ wo in euchan londe;
    Hit were betere þat hy nere.

25   'Hit is shome to blame leuedy,   *[Nightingale]*
For hy beþ hende of corteisy;
    Ich rede þat þou lete.
Ne wes neuere bruche so strong,
I-broke wiþ riȝte ne wiþ wrong,
30   Þat wimmon ne miȝte bete.

Hy gladieþ hem þat beþ wrowe,
Boþe þe heye and þe lowe,
    Mid gome hy cunne hem grete.
Þis world nere nout ȝif wimen nere;
35   I-maked hoe wes to mones fere,
    Nis no þing al-so swete.'

'I ne may wimen herien nohut,   *[Thrush]*
For hy beþ swikele and false of þohut,
    Als ich am ounderstonde.
40   Hy beþ feire and briȝt on hewe,
Here þout is fals and ountrewe;
    Ful ȝare ich haue hem fonde.

Alisaundre þe king meneþ of hem—
In þe world nes non so crafti mon,
45   Ne non so riche of londe.
I take witnesse of monie and fele
Þat riche weren of worldes wele,
    Muche wes hem þe shonde.'

30 wimmon: *A.* wimmen, *B.* mon.   31 wrowe: *MS.* wroþe.

Þe niȝtingale hoe wes wroþ:
50 'Fowel, me þinkeþ þou art me loþ   [*Nightingale*]
    Sweche tales for to showe.
Among a þousent leuedies i-tolde
Þer nis non wickede I holde
    Þer hy sitteþ on rowe.

55 Hy beþ of herte meke and milde,
Hem-self hy cunne from shome shilde
    Wiþinne boures wowe.
And swettoust þing in armes to wre
Þe mon þat holdeþ hem in gle.
60   Fowel, wi ne art þou hit i-cnowe?'

'Gentil fowel, seist þou hit me?   [*Thrush*]
Ich habbe wiþ hem in boure i-be,
    I-haued al mine wille.
Hy willeþ for a luitel mede
65 Don a sunfoul derne dede,
    Here soule forto spille.

Fowel, me þinkeþ þou art les;
Þey þou be milde and softe of pes,
    Þou seyst þine wille.
70 I take witnesse of Adam,
Þat wes oure furste man,
    Þat fonde hem wycke and ille.'

'Þrestelcok, þou art wod,   [*Nightingale*]
Oþer þou const to luitel goed,
75   Þis wimmen for to shende.
Hit is þe swetteste driwerie,
And mest hoe counnen of curteisie.
    Nis noþing also hende.

Þe mest murþe þat mon haueþ here,
80 Wenne hoe is maked to his fere
    In armes for to wende.
Hit is shome to blame leuedi,
For hem þou shalt gon sori—
    Of londe ich wille þe sende.'

72 wycke: *MS.* wycle.

85 'Niȝttingale, þou hauest wrong!   [*Thrush*]
      Wolt þou me senden of þis lond
         For ich holde wiþ þe riȝtte?
      I take witnesse of Sire Wawain,
      Þat Iesu Crist ȝaf miȝt and main
90   And strengþe for to fiȝtte.

      So wide so he heuede i-gon,
      Trewe ne founde he neuere non
         Bi daye ne bi niȝtte.'
      'Fowel, for þi false mouþ   [*Nightingale*]
95   Þi sawe shal ben wide couþ;
         I rede þe fle wiþ miȝtte.

      Ich habbe leue to ben here,
      In orchard and in erbere
         Mine songes for to singe.
100   Herdi neuere bi no leuedi
      Bote hendinese and curteysi,
         And ioye hy gunnen me bringe.

      Of muchele murþe hy telleþ me;
      Fere, al-so I telle þe,
105   Hy liuieþ in longinge.
      Fowel, þou sitest on hasel-bou,
      Þou lastest hem, þou hauest wou,
         Þi word shal wide springe.'

      'Hit springeþ wide, wel ich wot,   [*Thrush*]
110   Þou tel hit him þat hit not!
         Þis sawes ne beþ nout newe.
      Fowel, herkne to mi sawe,
      Ich wile þe telle of here lawe,
         Þou ne kepest nout hem i-knowe.

115   Þenk on Costantines quene—
      Foul wel hire semede fow and grene—
         Hou sore hit gon hire rewe.
      Hoe fedde a crupel in hire bour,
      And helede him wiþ couertour.
120   Loke war wimmen ben trewe!'

         105 longinge: *MS.* longinginge.

'Þrestelkok, þou hauest wrong,   [*Nightingale*]
Al-so I sugge one mi song,
   And þat men witeþ wide.
Hy beþ briȝttore ounder shawe
125 Þen þe day wenne hit dawe,
   In longe someres tide.

Come þou heuere in here londe,
Hy shulen don þe in prisoun stronge,
   And þer þou shalt abide.
130 Þe lesinges þat þou hauest maked,
Þer þou shalt hem forsake,
   And shome þe shal bitide.'

'Niȝttingale, þou seist þine wille,   [*Thrush*]
Þou seist þat wimmen shulen me spille.
135   Daþeit wo hit wolde!
In holi bok hit is i-founde,
Hy bringeþ moni mon to grounde,
   Þat proude weren and bolde.

Þenk oupon Saunsum þe stronge,
140 Hou muchel is wif him dude to wronge,
   Ich wot þat hoe him solde.
Hit is þat worste hord of pris
Þat Iesu makede in parais
   In tresour for to holde.'

145 Þo seide þe niȝttingale:
'Fowel, wel redi is þi tale;   [*Nightingale*]
   Herkne to mi lore!
Hit is flour þat lasteþ longe,
And mest i-herd in eueri londe,
150   And louelich ounder gore.

In þe worlde nis non so goed leche,
So milde of þoute, so feir of speche,
   To hele monnes sore.
Fowel, þou rewest al þi þohut,
155 Þou dost euele, ne geineþ þe nohut,
   Ne do þou so nammore!'

154 þi: *MS.* mi.

'Niȝtingale, þou art ounwis   [*Thrush*]
On hem to leggen so muchel pris,
    Þi mede shal ben lene.
160 Among on houndret ne beþ fiue,
Nouþer of maidnes ne of wiue,
    Þat holdeþ hem al clene,

Þat hy ne wercheþ wo in londe,
Oþer bringeþ men to shonde,
165   And þat is wel i-seene;
And þey we sitten þerfore to striuen,
Boþe of maidnes and of wiue,
    Soþ ne seist þou ene.'

'O fowel, þi mouþ þe haueþ i-shend!   [*Nightingale*]
170 Þoru wam wes al þis world iwend?
    Of a maide meke and milde.
Of hire sprong þat holi bern
Þat boren wes in Bedlehem,
    And temeþ al þat is wilde.

175 Hoe ne weste of sunne ne of shame,
Marie wes ire riȝte name;
    Crist hire i-shilde!
Fowel, for þi false sawe
Forbeddi þe þis wode-shawe;
180   Þou fare into þe filde.'

'Niȝttingale, I wes woed,   [*Thrush*]
Oþer I coupe to luitel goed,
    Wiþ þe for to striue.
I suge þat icham ouercome
185 Þoru hire þat bar þat holi sone,
    Þat soffrede wundes fiue.

Hi swerie bi His holi name
Ne shal I neuere suggen shame
    Bi maidnes ne bi wiue.
190 Hout of þis londe willi te,
Ne rechi neuere weder I fle;
    Awai ich wille driue.'

170 wes: *MS.* wel.

XIV. THE PROVERBS OF ALURED

It is unlikely that Alfred the Great had anything to do with the so-called *Proverbs of Alured*, the ascription in all probability resting simply on the tradition of his wisdom. That the tradition was widespread is suggested by the frequent ascription to him of isolated proverbs in other works, as for example in the *Owl and the Nightingale*. Alfred is represented, at the beginning of the work, as sitting in council with his thanes, and most of the following sections of uneven length into which it is divided open with the words 'Thus said Alfred', followed by passages of homely advice and conventional moralizing. The chief emphasis is on the uncertainty of life, the fleetingness of worldly things, and the fickleness of woman, the matter rarely departing much from the conventional medieval treatment of such subjects. The *Proverbs* are written in a mixture of the alliterative long line, with or without rhyme, and rhyming couplets, though the fact that the extant MSS. have passed through the hands of numerous scribes, most of whom have evidently not recognized the metrical intentions of the author, has made the original scheme difficult to recover. Because of this it has seemed better to print the selections below in short lines rather than to attempt, with Hall, to reconstruct the original plan.

The MSS. vary a good deal between themselves; obviously this kind of compilation lends itself very readily to interpolation and omission. So far as we can tell the original was probably of the twelfth century, and composed in some southern dialect. Four MSS. are known: Trinity College, Cambridge, B. 14, 39 (beginning of thirteenth century); MS. A 13 in the Maidstone Museum (thirteenth century); Jesus College, Oxford, MS. 29 (*c.* 1275); while fragments of another version have been preserved from a text in the British Museum MS. Cotton Galba A xix, now destroyed. Various editions have appeared, the most recent one of all MSS. being that in Brandl and Zippel. Among other editions may be noted that of the Trinity and Jesus MSS. by R. Morris for the Early English Text Society in *An Old English Miscellany* (1872), and the same, along with the surviving fragments from Galba A xix, were edited by E. Borgström (Lund 1908). The Maidstone version was printed by Carleton Brown (21 *MLR* 249 ff.), and with full introductory and

77

critical apparatus by H. P. South (New York 1931). The extracts
below, corresponding with Sections i, vii, xiv, xv, xviii, of the full
text, are taken from the Jesus MS. Although probably the latest of
the extant MSS., it preserves a fuller version of the work than is
to be found in the Maidstone MS., while the version in the Trinity
MS., written by a scribe with many orthographical peculiarities, is
needlessly difficult.

Incipiunt Documenta Regis Aluredi

At Seuorde sete
Þeynes monye,
Fele Biscopes,
And feole bok-ilered,
5 Eorles prute,
Knyhtes egleche.
Þar wes þe eorl Alurich,
Of þare lawe swiþe wis,
And ek Ealured,
10 Englene hurde,
Englene durlyng,
On Englenelonde he wes kyng.
Heom he bi-gon lere,
So ye mawe ihure,
15 Hw hi heore lif
Lede scholden.
Alured he wes in Englenelond
An king wel swiþe strong.
He wes king, and he wes clerek.
20 Wel he luuede Godes werk.
He wes wis on his word
And war on his werke.
He wes þe wysuste mon
Þat wes Englelonde on.

VII

25 Þus queþ Alured:
'Wyþ-vte wysdome
Is weole wel vnwurþ;
For þey o mon ahte
Huntseuenti acres,
30 And he hi hadde isowen

18 An: *MS.* And.

Alle myd reade golde,
And þat gold greowe
So gres doþ on eorþe,
Nere he for his weole
35 Neuer þe furþer
Bute he him of frumþe
Freond iwrche.
For hwat is gold bute ston
Bute if hit haueþ wismon.'

XIV

40 Þus queþ Alured:
'If þu hauest seorewe
Ne seye þu hit nouht þan arewe.
Seye hit þine sadelbowe,
And ryd þe singinde forþ.
45 Þenne wile wene,
Þet þine wise ne con,
Þat þe þine wise
Wel lyke.
Serewe if þu hauest,
50 And þe erewe hit wot,
By-fore he þe meneþ,
By-hynde he þe teleþ.
Þu hit myht segge swyhc mon
Þat þe ful wel on,
55 Wyþ-vte echere ore
He on þe muchele more.
By-hud hit on þire heorte,
Þat þe eft ne smeorte.
Ne let þu hyne wite
60 Al þat þin heorte by-wite.'

XV

Þus queþ Alured:
'Ne schal tu neuere þi wif
By hire wlyte cheose,
For neuer none þinge
65 Þat heo to þe bryngeþ.
Ac leorne hire custe,
Heo cuþeþ hi wel sone.
For mony mon for ayhte
Vuele i-auhteþ,

70　And ofte mon oþ fayre
　　Frakele icheoseþ.
　　Wo is him þat vuel wif
　　Bryngeþ to his cotlyf.
　　So him is alyue
75　Þat vuele ywyueþ;
　　For he schal vppen eorþe
　　Dreori i-wurþe.
　　Monymon singeþ
　　Þat wif hom bryngeþ;
80　Wiste he hwat he brouhte
　　Wepen he myhte.'

XVIII

　　Þus queþ Alured:
　　'Eure þu bi þine lyue
　　Þe word of þine wyue
85　To swiþe þu ne arede,
　　If heo beo i-wreþþed
　　Myd worde oþer myd dede.
　　Wymmon wepeþ for mod
　　Oftere þan for eny god,
90　And ofte lude and stille
　　For to vordrye hire wille.
　　Heo wepeþ oþer-hwile
　　For to do þe gyle.
　　Salomon hit haueþ i-sed,
95　Þat wymmon can wel vuelne red.
　　Þe hire red foleweþ
　　Heo bryngeþ hine to seorewe.
　　For hit seyþ in þe loþ,
　　As scinnes forteoþ.
100　Hit is ifurn iseyd
　　Þat cold red is quene red.
　　Hu he is vnlede
　　Þat foleweþ hire rede.
　　Ich hit ne segge nouht for þan,
105　Þat god þing nys god wymmon,
　　Þe mon þe hi may icheose,
　　And icouere over oþre.

88 mod: *first minim erased in MS.*　　99 scinnes: *MS.* scumes.
105 nys: n *erased in MS.*

XV. THE ORRMULUM

'Þiss boc iss nemmnedd Orrmulum, forrþi þatt Orrm itt wrohhte', but apart from the information given in his dedication, and the fact that his name suggests that he was of Scandinavian descent, nothing is known of the author. He calls himself indifferently Orrm and Orrmin, and says that he has written the book at the request of his brother Walter, who is, like himself, an Augustinian canon. Definite information as to date or provenance is lacking, but on palæographical grounds the MS. has been dated *c*. 1210, and it seems possible that Orrm may have been a canon of Elsham Priory in North Lincolnshire. On the other hand, it has been pointed out that Walter, prior of the Augustinian canons at Carlisle between 1150 and 1170, had a brother Orm who may also have been an Augustinian canon and possibly the author of this work. As far as the language is concerned it is the dialect that we should expect to have been spoken in North Lincolnshire *c*. 1200; but so little is known of the Northern dialect in Middle English before the fourteenth century that we cannot say with confidence that Orrm's is definitely a Midland and not a Northern work. But the majority of scholars would place it somewhere in the northern part of the East Midland dialect area.

The work itself is a collection of homilies intended as a course of sermons to be read aloud in church. In the dedication, Orrm explains that he intends to give an English version of the Gospels for the whole year, each followed by an interpretation and an application. His table of contents lists 242 homilies, but of these only 1–32 are represented in the Junius MS., 32 being a fragment mostly illegible. The 20,512 short lines counted by White-Holt are only about an eighth of the whole work envisaged—and possibly completed—by the author, who was a determined character.

Almost alone among Middle English poets Orrm uses neither rhyme nor alliteration; he is a merciless syllable-counter. His model is the Latin septenarius; his line has fifteen syllables, neither more nor less, and he does little to vary the rhythm. Such a vehicle calls for subject-matter of high interest if the work is to be at all endurable, and that it is far from having. It contains, to be sure, a good deal of the best (if, already in Orrm's time, old-fashioned) medieval religious teaching drawn from various authors, mainly Gregory the Great and Bede, but every other virtue has been sacrificed to clarity. The author is so determined that nothing shall remain obscure that he constantly repeats himself, and the result is an intolerably diffuse and tedious work.

From a linguistic point of view, however, the work is highly important; the author's autograph copy has probably survived, and he uses a highly individual orthography, the most noticeable characteristic of which is the frequent doubling of consonants. Various theories have been suggested to account for this; that Orrm intended to mark the length of the vowels, that he wished to mark the length of the consonants, or a compromise of the two. But on the whole the most plausible suggestion is that these various orthographical devices are simply intended to help preachers in reading aloud to the congregation (see 9 *RES* 4 ff.). Complaints of the way in which preachers stumbled and mumbled when reading sermons are frequent enough in the Middle Ages, and the careful Orrm has decided to give them every help in reading his work. The first necessity is a consistent spelling system with the divisions between the words clearly marked. In reading aloud, the length of the vowel is obviously important, and consequently it is made clear by doubling the consonant after a short vowel in closed syllables. But in open syllables this might lead to ambiguity, and instead a breve was sometimes added above the vowel. Latin vowels before a final -*t* are usually short, and, since English words with a long vowel in such a position might give difficulty to a Latin-trained cleric, Orrm helps by placing double[1] or treble acute accents over such long vowels. His phonetic care is further illustrated by his use of three separate symbols for sounds that could be represented by the insular ʒ in OE.:

'ʒ' for the semi-vowel [j] as in 'ʒet', 'ʒiff', 'modiʒnesse'.

'ʒʒ' for the second element of an -*i* diphthong, 'maʒʒ', 'þeʒʒ' 'twiʒʒess'.[2]

'ʒh' for the voiced spirant that became *w*, as in 'reʒhellboc', 'follʒhen'.

---

[1] Represented in the extract by a circumflex. The trebly accented vowel does not occur in it.

[2] Similarly 'ww' for the second element of a -*u* diphthong as in 'Awwstin', 'trowwenn'. The whole problem is well treated by A. S. Napier, *Transactions of the Philological Society*, 1891-4 (Appendix II).

'ḡ' (a compromise between the insular 'ȝ' and the continental 'g')
for the stop, as in 'ḡod', 'Ennḡlisshe', 'amanḡ'.
'ḡḡ' as in 'triḡḡ' (from ON *tryggr*).
'g' (continental) is found only in 'gyn' (7087) which Napier
rightly takes to be a French loanword, from (*en*)*gin*.
'gg' for the sound in Mod. E. *edge*, as in 'egge'. (Neither 'g' nor
'gg' happens to occur in the extract given below, but the three
symbols are well illustrated on the Bodleian postcard from
Junius I, f. 65*a*, which in ll. 7866–82 shows 'Ḡodd', 'bodiȝ',
'biggenn', 'laȝheboc', 'Aȝȝ'.[1])

The single medieval MS. containing the work is preserved in the
Bodleian as MS. Junius I, and the only complete edition of that MS.
is by R. M. White and R. Holt (Oxford 1878). A collation by E.
Kölbing appeared in 1 *Englische Studien*, 1 ff.; note also S. Holm,
Corrections and Additions in the Ormulum Manuscript (Uppsala 1922).
N. R. Ker, 'Unpublished Parts of the *Ormulum* printed from MS.
Lambeth 783' (9 *Medium Ævum* 1–22), gives 539 short lines from
extracts made by the Dutch scholar, Jan van Vliet, a seventeenth-
century owner, before certain folios of Junius I had been lost.

Dedication

Nu broþerr Wallterr, broþerr min, affterr þe flæshess kinde,
Annd broþerr min i Crisstenndom þurrh fulluhht annd þurrh trowwþe,
Annd broþerr min i Ḡodess hus, ȝêt o þe þride wise,
Þurrh þatt witt hafenn tăkenn ba an reȝhellboc to follȝhenn,
5 Vnnderr kanunnkess had annd lif, swa summ Sannt Awwstin sette;
Icc hafe don swa summ þu badd, annd forþedd te þin wille,
Icc hafe wennd inntill Ennḡlissh Ḡoddspelless hallȝhe láre,
Affterr þatt little witt tatt te min Drihhtin hafeþþ lenedd.
Þu þohhtesst tatt itt mihhte wel till mikell frame turrnenn
10 Ȝiff Ennḡlissh follc, forr lufe off Crist, itt wollde ȝerne lernenn,
Annd follȝhenn itt, annd fillenn itt, wiþþ þohht, wiþþ word, wiþþ
[dede.
Annd forrþi ȝerrndesst tu þatt icc þiss werrc þe shollde wirrkenn;
Annd icc itt hafe forþedd te, acc all þurrh Cristess hellpe;
Annd unnc birrþ baþe þannkenn Crist þatt itt iss brohht till ende.
15 Icc hafe sammnedd o þiss boc þa Ḡoddspelless neh alle,
Þatt sinndenn o þe messeboc inn all þe ȝer att messe.
Annd aȝȝ affterr þe Ḡoddspell stannt þatt tatt te Ḡoddspell meneþþ,
Þatt mann birrþ spellenn to þe follc off þeȝȝre sawle nede;

---

[1] God, body, buy, law-book, ever.

Annd ʒêt tær tekenn mare inoh þu shallt tæronne findenn,
20 Off þatt tatt Cristess hallʒhe þed birrþ trowwenn wel annd follʒhenn.
Icc hafe sett her o þiss boc amang Goddspelless wordess,
All þurrh mesellfenn, maniʒ word þe ríme swa to fillenn;
Acc þu shallt findenn þatt min word, eʒʒwhær þær itt iss ekedd,
Maʒʒ hellpenn þa þatt redenn itt to sen annd tunnderrstanndenn
25 All þess te bettre, hu þeʒʒm birrþ þe Goddspell unnderrstanndenn;
Annd forrþi trowwe icc þatt te birrþ wel þolenn mine wordess,
Eʒʒwhær þær þu shallt findenn hemm amang Goddspelless wordess.
Forr whase môt to læwedd follc larspell off Goddspell tellenn,
He môt wel ekenn maniʒ word amang Goddspelless wordess.
30 Annd icc ne mihhte nohht min ferrs aʒʒ wiþþ Goddspelless wordess
Well fillenn all, annd all forrþi shollde icc well offte nede
Amang Goddspelless wordess don min word, min ferrs to fillenn.
Annd te bitæche icc off þiss boc, heh wikenn alls itt semeþþ,
All to þurrhsekenn illc an ferrs, annd to þurrhlokenn offte,
35 Þatt upponn all þiss boc ne be nan word ʒæn Cristess lare,
Nan word tatt swiþe wel ne be to trowwenn annd to follʒhenn.
Witt shulenn tredenn unnderrfôt annd all þwerrt ût forrwerrpenn
Þe dom off all þatt laþe flocc, þatt iss þurrh niþ forrblendedd,
Þatt tæleþþ þatt to lofenn iss, þurrh niþfull modiʒnesse.
40 Þeʒʒ shulenn lætenn hæþeliʒ off unnkerr swinnc, lef broþerr;
Annd all þeʒʒ shulenn takenn itt onn unnitt annd onn idell;
Acc nohht þurrh skill, acc all þurrh niþ, annd all þurrh þeʒʒre sinne.
Annd unnc birrþ biddenn Godd tatt he forrgife hemm hĕre sinne;
Annd unnc birrþ baþe lofenn Godd off þatt itt wass biʒunnenn,
45 Annd þannkenn Godd tatt itt iss brohht till ende, þurrh Hiss hellpe;
Forr itt maʒʒ hellpenn alle þa þatt bliþelike itt herenn,
Annd lufenn itt, annd follʒhenn itt wiþþ þohht, wiþþ word, wiþþ dede.
Annd whase wilenn shall þiss boc efft oþerr siþe writenn,
Himm bidde icc þatt hêt wríte rihht, swa summ þiss boc himm tæcheþþ
50 All þwerrt ût affterr þatt itt iss vppo þiss firrste bisne,
Wiþþ all swillc ríme alls her iss sett, wiþþ all-se fele wordess;
Annd tatt he loke wel þatt he an bocstaff wríte twiʒʒess,
Eʒʒwhær þær itt uppo þiss boc iss wrĭtenn o þatt wise.
Loke he wel þatt hêt write swa, forr he ne maʒʒ nohht elless
55 Onn Ennglissh wrítenn rihht te word, þatt wite he wel to soþe.
Annd ʒiff mann wile wĭtenn whi icc hafe don þiss dede,
Whi icc till Ennglissh hafe wennd Goddspelless hallʒhe lare;
Icc hafe itt don forrþi þatt all Crisstene follkess berrhless
Iss lang uppo þatt an, þatt teʒʒ Goddspelless hallʒhe lare
60 Wiþþ fulle mahhte follʒhe rihht þurrh þohht, þurrh word, þurrh dede.
Forr all þatt æfre onn erþe iss ned Crisstene follc to follʒhenn
I trowwþe, i dede, all tæcheþþ hemm Goddspelless hallʒhe lare.
Annd forrþi whase lerneþþ itt annd follʒheþþ itt wiþþ dede,
He shall onn ende wurrþi ben þurrh Godd to wurrþenn borrʒhenn.
65 Annd tærfore hafe icc turrnedd itt inntill Ennglisshe spæche,
Forr þatt I wollde bliþeliʒ þatt all Ennglisshe lede

Wiþþ ære shollde lisstenn itt, wiþþ herrte shollde itt trowwenn,
Wiþþ tunge shollde spellenn itt, wiþþ dede shollde itt follȝhenn,
To winnenn unnderr Crisstenndom att Godd soþ sawle berrhless.
70 Annd ȝiff þeȝȝ wilenn herenn itt, annd follȝhenn itt wiþþ dede,
Icc hafe hemm hollpenn unnderr Crist to winnenn þeȝȝre berrhless.
Annd I shall hafenn forr min swinnc god læn att Godd onn ende,
Ȝiff þatt I, forr þe lufe off Godd annd forr þe mede off heffne,
Hemm hafe itt inntill Ennglissh wennd forr þeȝȝre sawle nede.
75 Annd ȝiff þeȝȝ all forrwerrpenn itt, itt turrneþþ hemm till sinne,
Annd I shall hafenn addledd me þe Laferrd Cristess are,
Þurrh þatt icc hafe hemm wrohht tiss boc to þeȝȝre sawle nede,
Þohh þatt teȝȝ all forrwerrpenn itt þurrh þeȝȝre modiȝnesse.

For corrections we are indebted to Mr. R. W. Burchfield.

XVI. VICES AND VIRTUES

THE *Vices and Virtues* is extant in a single MS. of the early thirteenth century, BM. MS. Stowe 34, of which the beginning is missing. The work is in dialogue form, and opens in the middle of the confession by a Soul to Reason of a formidable array of sins. The Soul then asks Reason how it can be reconciled with Christ, and is urged to cherish the three Christian virtues which are described in turn. The Soul promises this, and Reason then goes on to describe the other Christian virtues as chief components of the Temple of God whose foundation is the Soul. The Body protests that Body and Soul are of different natures, but Reason shows how both should work in accord, and goes on to discourse of Peace, Prudence, Righteousness, and various other virtues. In conclusion it recommends the Soul to practice its counsels and to thank and praise God.

There is little continuity in the work, which is really a series of expositions on the various subjects, loosely bound together by the dialogue device which makes the best of a not particularly interesting subject. However, the author is master of a clear straightforward prose style, and can use skilfully the allegory of which he is so fond. The extract printed below, the allegory of the four virtues disputing about man's redemption before God, is the first use in ME of a theme which became popular and was frequently treated later, e.g. in the *Cursor Mundi, Piers Plowman*, etc. However, there is no reason to suppose that it is original with the unknown author of this work which, in fact, probably contains very little that is new. The author derives much of his material from Latin religious writers, and much, too, from the OE homiletic tradition. In fact his work is a continuation of that tradition, and occasional archaic forms near the beginning suggest that it might even be the modernization of a work composed originally during the OE period. Whether this be so or not the work as it stands is particularly interesting from a linguistic point of view, since it provides a lengthy specimen of the Essex dialect, in which area it was probably composed.

The complete text was edited, with a translation, by F. Holthausen for the Early English Text Society in 1888, the extract below beginning on f. 37 of the MS. and comprising p. 113/30 to p. 117/24 of that edition.

An Allegory of Mercy

(113/30) Misericordia nam mid hire Pietatem and Pacem, and comen
before Gode, and swiðe eadmodliche him besohten, and se
eadiȝe Mildce hire astrehte sone teforen Gode, and ðus sæde:
'Hali, hali Lauerd, haue are and milce of Adame, ðine forgilte
5 manne, ðe swo maniȝe hundred wintre hafð iðoled þo ðesternesse of helle, ðe was iscapen to ðare muchele eadinesse of ðine
riche! Ac noht he one, ac all his ofspreng hafð dieuel swo on his
walte, ðat non ne mai cumen into ðare riche ðe hie to waren
iscapen; ac alle he bringþ into helle, baðe gode and euele.
10 Hlauerd, haue ore and rewhþe and mildce of ðin handiwerc!
Æure hie habbeð hope ðat tu scule habben ore and milce of
hem.'

Anon hire bemande Rewðe, and sade: 'Ælle, ðu, Lauerd,
angin and welle of alle godnesse, haue rewðhe and milce of ðe
15 wrecche Adames soule, ðe was iscapen after ðine andlicnesse,
and of ðine patriarches and of ðine profietes, and mani þusend
hali saules, ðe alle þolieð pine for Adames gelte, mid gode rihte,
for his unhersumnesse! Alle hie wepeð and wonið, and hopieð
to ðire muchele milce and to ðe lokið allhwat ðu send hem
20 sume aliesendnesse. Hi me reweð swa swiðe ðat ic reste ne mai
habben.'

'Lauerd, ȝif hit is ðin wille', sæde Sibsumnesse, 'þis ne mai
noht bien on ðine riche. Ðin sibsumnesse is swo swiðe michel
ðat on-lepi þoht ne mai ðer bien bute mid alle sofnesse and mid
25 alle eadinese. Make seihte betwen Milce and Rihwisnesse, and
Dom and Rewðe make wel togedere! Naðelæs, ic hit wot wel ðat
tu wilt hauen ore of mankenne. Þin godnesse hit ne mai noht
læten.'

Ðat sede Rihtwisnesse: 'Mid michel riht ðoleð Adam ðat he
30 ðoleð, for ðan he was his sceppend unhersum. Godd he unwurðede ða þa he ðolede ðat his wiðerwine him ouercam,
wiðuten strencþe. His louerd he dede arst michel harm, he
slou arst himseluen, and seððen all mankenn, and for his unhersumnesse he bereauede Godes riche of himseluen and of all
35 his ofsprenge, þat naure mo he ne mai aȝean cumen be rihte
dome.'

Ða sade Soð: 'Ðat is riht ðat Godes milce bie aure heier and
more ðanne his rihte dom. Hlauerd, hit is soð ðat tu behete
Abraham, ðine lieue frend, þat þurh an of his kenne scolde bien
40 iblesced all mankenn. Eft ðu behete Dauiðe, the rihtwise kyng:
De fructu uentris tui ponam super sedem tuam, 'Of ðo wastme of

ðine wombe ic wille setten uppe ðine setle.' Eft he seið an
oðer stede: *Dominus dixit ad me*: '*Filius meus.*'

Ða spac almihti Godd, and sade: 'Ðies dai haueð aure ibien
45 mid me and æure ma wurð. Hit is soð ðat tu seiest: 'On ðese
daiʒe ic ðe habbe istriend on heuene, wið-uten moder'. Swa ðu
scalt on ierðe, wið-uten fader istriend of moder. On ðelliche
wise ðu scalt becumen soð mannes sune swo swo ðu art soð
Godes sune. Ne bidde ich non oðer loc for Adames gelte bute
50 ðe. *Postula a me*, and besiech at me swo muchel folc swo ðu
wilt after ʒiernen, and ic ðe wile ʒiuen to ðin eruename, and
ðu scalt wealden all middeneard and all ðat ðar-inne is.'

Tunc dixi: *ecce, uenio*. Ðo sade Soð: 'Hlauerd, fader, ðu ne
woldest non oðer loac ne oðer ofrende bute ðat ic underfenge
55 mannes lichame and his saule, and ðat ic ðe her offrede for here
gelte. *Ecce venio*, loke, ic am i-radi ðine wille to werchen, and
mankenn to aliesen.'

Ðat sade Godes Rihwisnesse: 'Nv ðu wilt mann becumen, ðu
scalt deað þolien after ðine auʒene dome, ʒif ðat wunder mai
60 bien soð þat eche lif mai ðoliʒen deað; and ðu scalt on alle
wise bieten ðe he haueð tebroken. Hoal ði godnesse!'

Ðat sade Soð: 'Hierto ic am all iradi, te bien hersum Godd
anon to ðe deaðe for mankenn to aliesen.' *Iusticia et Pax osculate
sunt*; ðe profiete seið ðat Rihtwisnesse and Sibsumnesse kesten
65 hem to-gedere.

XVII. ANCRENE RIWLE AND ANCRENE WISSE

THE *Ancrene Riwle* is undoubtedly the most influential and important of the prose works of the early ME period. Written originally at the request of three noble maidens who had abandoned the world to live as anchoresses, it was early revised (as the *Ancrene Wisse*) for the use of a larger community, adapted for the use of a male community, and translated into French and Latin. During the fourteenth and fifteenth centuries its influence on devotional literature is evident, and this influence persists into the sixteenth century. The reasons for its popularity are obvious. Written by a humane and cultured cleric during the twelfth century, it provides a tolerant and enlightened rule, with a decided emphasis on the necessity for moderation in all things. Much of it consists of the ordinary medieval religious teaching, the exposition of scriptural texts and the use of allegory, but brought to life by the descriptive powers of the author, his homely illustrations and lively touches. The first and the last of the eight parts into which the work is divided are concerned with what the author calls the 'outer rule,' as distinct from the 'inner rule' of the other six. The first part deals with the formal religious duties of the anchoresses, whilst the last is concerned with practical advice on their everyday life, their clothes, their health, their maids, etc., providing many sidelights on the social life of the time. But, however interesting this part may be to the modern reader, it is clear that it was of little importance to the author as compared with the 'inner rule'. He devotes very little space to the 'outer rule', and constantly emphasizes the supreme importance of the 'inner rule'.

The only problem connected with the work which has been definitely settled is the fact that it was originally composed in English, and that the French and Latin versions are translations from that language (see D. M. E. Dymes, 9 *Essays and Studies* 31 ff.) As far as the questions of date and authorship are concerned it is unlikely that definite answers will ever be possible. Identifications of the three noble ladies for whom the rule was composed have been suggested, and the most plausible would equate them with the ladies Emma, Gunhild and Christina, who were responsible for the foundation of Kilburn Priory (*c.* 1130). There are striking similarities between the anchoresses of the *Ancrene Riwle* and those of Kilburn, but the evidence is not conclusive and there are grave objections. On the whole the internal evidence, references to the writings of St. Ailred, quotations from the works of St. Bernard and from Geoffrey of Auxerre, indicates that the work can hardly have been written before 1160, and was probably somewhat later. As for the author, although various names have been suggested, there is not the slightest evidence in favour of any one of them.

As far as the provenance of the *Rule* is concerned J. R. R. Tolkien (14 *Essays and Studies* 104 ff.) has argued that the earliest of the extant MSS. is that containing the revised version for a larger community, Corpus Christi College, Cambridge, MS. 402 (*c.* 1230) This MS. is written in an extraordinarily consistent dialect and orthography such as is found elsewhere only in texts which are the holographs of the authors. The Corpus MS. is certainly not that, but equally certainly the consistency and lack of scribal corruption suggest a particularly simple textual history. Even more significant is the use of the same dialect and orthography in the Bodley MS. of the *Katherine Group*, also dated *c.* 1230. Obviously the two MSS. must be closely connected both in time and place, and there appear to be only three possible explanations for the remarkable consistency of spelling. First, that these MSS. are the autograph copies of the authors—which they are certainly not. Second, that the present similarity is due to accurate translation of the original texts into this dialect—but such accurate and consistent translation is most improbable, nor would it be easy to suggest a reason for it. Third, that the vanished originals of the two MSS. were written in the same dialect as the extant texts, and near enough in date for there to be no trace of archaism or modernization in the extant texts, i.e. not later than the last quarter of the twelfth century. The present dialect of these two MSS. is certainly West Midland, but it is hardly possible to localize it more exactly on linguistic evidence alone. Both MSS. are connected with Herefordshire, in that the Bodley MS. was there in the sixteenth century, while the Corpus MS. was at Wigmore Abbey by about 1300. It may well be that both originals and copies were written in the Herefordshire dialect, though definite evidence on the point is as yet lacking.

It seems likely enough that the *Ancrene Riwle* and the texts of the

Katherine Group were originally composed in the West Midland dialect area, but Tolkien has perhaps dismissed too easily the possibility of translation from one dialect into another (see J. R. Hulbert, 45 *JEGP* 411 ff.). There is some evidence for such translation in ME., and for a standard western dialect into which texts from other dialects might well have been translated, while the assumption that the Corpus MS.[1] retains the dialect and inflexions of the original leads to difficulties in that more archaic forms seem to appear in other MSS. of this text.

The French and Latin versions were edited by J. A. Herbert and C. D'Evelyn respectively for the Early English Text Society in 1934. The only English version so far available is that of the Nero MS. which was edited by J. Morton in 1852, by M. Day in 1952, but all the extant English MSS. are to be published by the EETS. The first of the following extracts is taken from the BM. MS. Cotton Nero A xiv (early thirteenth century) and corresponds with Morton, p. 86/1 to p. 90/4. The second extract is taken from the Corpus Christi College, Cambridge, MS. 402, and corresponds with Morton, p. 288/20 to p. 294/1.

Flatterers and Backbiters [2]

(86/1) Uikelares beoð þreo kunnes. Þe uorme beoð vuele inouh, þe
oðre þauh beoð wurse, þe þridde ȝet beoð alrewurste. Þe
uorme, ȝif a mon is god, preiseð hine biuoren himsulf, and
makeð hine, inouh reðe, ȝet betere þen he beo, and ȝif he seið
5 wel oðer deð wel he hit heueð to heie up mid ouerpreisunge
and herunge. Þe oðer is, ȝif a mon is vuel, and seið and deð so
muche mis þet hit beo so open sunne þet he hit ne mei nonesweis allelunge wiðsiggen: he þauh, biuoren þe monne sulf,
makeð his vuel lesse. 'Nis hit nout nu,' he seið, 'so ouer vuel
10 ase me hit makeð. Nert tu nout i þisse þinge þe uorme ne þe
laste. Þu hauest monie ueren. Let iwurðe, gode mon. Ne
gest tu nout þe one. Moni deð muche wurse.' Þe þridde cumeð
efter, and is wurst fikelare, ase ich er seide, vor he preiseð þene
vuele and his vuele deden, ase ðe seið to þe knihte þet
15 robbeð his poure men, 'A sire! hwat tu dest wel! Uor euere me
schal þene cheorl pilken and peolien, uor he is ase þe wiði þet
sprutteð ut þe betere þet me hine ofte croppeð'. Þus ðe ualse

---

[1] On the dialect of Corpus, see M. S. Serjeantson, 1 *London Medieval Studies* 225–48.
[2] D. S. Brewer (22 *Med. Æv.* 123) suggests a probable source for part of the 'Backbiters' passage, in St. Bernard's *Sermones in Cantica* (Migne's *Patrologia Lat.* CLXXXIII, col. 896 B and C)

uikelare ablendeð þeo ðe ham hercneð, ase ich er seide, and
wrieð hore fulðe þet heo hit ne muwen stinken; and tet is
20 muchel unselhðe. Vor ȝif heo hit stunken, ham wolde wlatien
þer aȝean: and so eornen to schrifte, and speouwen hit ut þer,
and schunien hit þer-efter.

Bacbitares, þe biteð oþre men bihinden, beoð of two
maneres; auh þe latere beoð wurse. Þe uorme cumeð al open-
25 liche, and seið vuel bi an-oðer, and speouweð ut his atter, so
muchel so him euer to muðe cumeð, and gulcheð al ut somed
þet þe attri heorte sent up to þe tunge. Ac þe latere cumeð forð
al an oþer wise, and is wurse ueond þen ðe oþer, auh under
ureondes huckel, weorpeð adun þet heaued, and foð on uor te
30 siken er he owiht sigge, and makeð drupie chere; bisaumpleð
longe abuten uor te beon ðe betere ileued. Auh hwon hit
alles cumeð forð þeonne is hit ȝeoluh atter. 'Weilawei, and
wolawo,' heo seið, 'wo is me þet he, oðer heo, habbeð swuch
word ikeiht. I-nouh ich was abuten, auh ne help me nout to
35 don her-one bote. Ȝare hit is þet ich wuste her-of; auh þauh
þuruh me ne schulde hit neuer more beon i-upped; auh nu hit is
þuruh oþre so wide ibrouht forð, ich hit ne mei nout wiðsaken.
Vuel me seið þet hit is; and ȝet hit is wurse. Seoruhful ich am
and sori þet ich hit schal siggen, auh for soðe so hit is, and tet
40 is muche seoruwe. Uor ueole oþre þing he, oðer heo, is swuðe
to herien, auh nout for þisse þinge, and wo is me ðereuore.
Ne mei ham no mon werien.' Þis beoð þes deofles neddren þet
Salomon spekeð of. Vre Louerd, þuruh His grace, holde ou our
earen urom hore attrie tungen, and ne leue ou neuer stinken
45 þene fule put þet heo unwreoð, ase þe uikelares wreoð and
helieð, ase ich er seide; vnwreon to hamsuluen þeo þet hit to
iimpeð and helien hit oðre. Þet is a muche þeau, and nout to
þeo þet hit schulden smellen, and hatien þet fulðe. Nu, mine
leoue sustren, urom al vuel speche, þet is þus þreouold, idel,
50 and ful, and attri, holdeð feor our earen. Me seið upon ancren
þet euerich mest haueð on olde cwene to ueden hire earen,
ane maðelild þet maðeleð hire alle ðe talen of ðe londe, ane
rikelot þet cakeleð hire al þet heo isihð oþer ihereð. So þet me
seið ine bisauwe, 'Vrom mulne and from cheping, from
55 smiððe and from ancre-huse, me tiðinge bringeð.' Þet wot
Crist, þis is a sori tale: þet ancre-hus, þet schulde beon onlukust
stude of alle, schal beon i-ueied to þeo ilke þreo studen þet
mest is inne of cheafle. Auh ase quite ase ȝe beoð of swuche,
leoue sustren, weren alle ðe oðre, ure Louerd hit ðe.

18 ablendeð: MS. ablenðeð   36, 37, 43 þuruh: MS. þ with horizontal stroke through the
descender   45 uikelares: MS. uikerares   46 vnwreon: interlinear hit follows in later hand.

The Dog of Hell

(288/20) Cunsence, þet is skiles ʒettunge, hwen þe deliti þe lust is igan
se ouerforð þet ter nere nan wiðseggunge ʒef þer were eise to
fulle þe dede. Þis is hwen þe heorte draheð to hire unlust, as
þing þe were amainet, ant feð on as to winkin to leote þe feond
iwurðen, and leið hire seolf duneward, buheð him as he bit,
65 ant ʒeieð 'crauant, crauant', ase softe swohninde. Þenne is he
kene þe wes ear curre. Þenne leapeð he to, þe stod ear
feorren to, ant bit deaðes bite o Godes deore spuse, iwiss
deaðes bite, for his teð beoð attrie as of a wed dogge. Dauið i
þe sawter cleopeð hine dogge. *Erue a framea deus animam meam*
70 *et de manu canis unicam meam.*

For þi, mi leoue suster, sone se þu eauer underʒetest þet
tes dogge of helle cume snakerinde wið his blodi flehen of
stinkinde þohtes, ne li þu nawt stille, ne ne site nowðer to
lokin hwet he wule don, ne hu feor he wule gan. Ne sei þu
75 nawt slepinde, 'Ame dogge, ga her-ut; hwet wult tu nu her-
inne?' Þis tolleð him inward. Ah nim anan þe rode-steaf mid
nempnunge i þi muð, mid te mearke i þin hond, mid þoht i þin
heorte, ant hat him ut heterliche, þe fule cur-dogge, ant liðere
to him luðerliche mid te hali rode-steaf stronge bac-duntes.
80 Þet is, Rung up, sture þe; hald up ehnen on heh ant honden
toward heouene. Gred efter sucurs. *Deus in adiutorium meum*
intende. Domine ad adiuuandum. Veni Creator Spiritus. Exurgat
Deus et dissipentur inimici eius. Deus in nomine tuo saluum me fac.
Domine, quid multiplicati sunt. Ad te, Domine, leuaui animam
85 *meam. Ad te leuaui oculos meos. Leuaui oculos meos in montes.*
ʒef þe ne kimeð sone help, gred luddre wið hat heorte.
Vsquequo Domine obliuisceris me in finem? usquequo auertis faciem
tuam a me? ant swa al þe salm ouer, *Pater noster, Credo, Aue*
Maria, wið halsinde bonen o þin ahne ledene. Smit smeortliche
90 adun þe cneon to þer eorðe, ant breid up þe rode-steaf, ant
sweng him o fowr half aʒein helle-dogge. Þet nis nawt elles
bute blesce þe al abuten wið þe eadi rode-taken. Spite him
amid te beard to hoker ant to scarne, þe flikereð swa wið þe
ant fikeð dogge-fahenunge, hwen he for se liht wurð, for þe
95 licunge of a lust ane hwile-stucche, chapeð þi sawle, Godes
deore bune þet he bohte mid his blod ant mid his deorewurðe deað o þe deore rode. Aa bihald hire wurð þet he paide
for hire, ant dem þrefter hire pris, ant beo on hire þe deorre.
Ne sule þu neauer se eðeliche his fa, ant þin eiðer, his deore-
100 wurðe spuse þet costnede him se deore. Makie deofles hore of

hire is reowðe ouer reowðe. To unwreast mid alle ha is þe mei,
wið to heouen up hire þreo fingres, ouercumen hire fa, ant ne
luste for slawðe. Hef for þi wið treowe ant hardi bileaue up
þine þreo fingres, ant wið þe hali rode-steaf, þet him is laðest
105 cuggel, lei o þe dogge-deouel. Nempne ofte Iesu, cleope his
passiunes help, halse bi his pine, bi his deorewurðe blod, bi his
deað o rode. Flih to his wunden. Muchel he luuede us þe lette
makien swucche þurles in him forte huden us in. Creop in
ham wið þi þoht. Ne beoð ha al opene? Ant wið his deore-
110 wurðe blod biblodde þin heorte. *Ingredere in petram, abscondere*
[*in*] *fossa humo.* 'Ga in to þe stan,' seið þe prophete, 'ant hud te
i þe deoluen eorðe,' þet is i þe wunden of ure Lauerdes flesch,
þe wes as idoluen wið þe dulle neiles, as he i þe sawter longe
uore seide. *Foderunt manus meas et pedes meos,* þet is, ha duluen
115 me baðe þe vet ant te honden. Ne seide he nawt þurleden, for
efter þis leattre, as ure meistres seggeð, swa weren þe neiles
dulle þet ha duluen his flesch ant tobreken þe ban mare þen
þurleden, to pinin him sarre. He him-seolf cleopeð þe toward
teose wunden: *Columba mea, in foraminibus petre, in cauernis*
120 *macerie.* 'Mi culure', he seið, 'cum hud te i mine limen þurles, i
þe hole of mi side.' Muche luue he cudde to his leoue culure,
þet he swuch hudles makede. Loke nu þet tu, þe he cleopeð
culure, habbe culure cunde, þet is wið-ute galle, ant cum to him
baldeliche, ant make scheld of his passiun, ant sei wið Ieremie,
125 *Dabis scutum cordis laborem tuum.* Þet is, 'þu schalt ʒeoue me,
Lauerd, heorte-scheld aʒein þe feond, þi swincfule pine.'
Þet hit swincful wes, he schawde hit witerliche inoh, þa he
sweatte, ase blodes swat, dropen þe runnen to þer eorðe. Me
schal halden scheld i feht up abuuen heaued, oðer aʒein þe
130 breoste, nawt ne drahen hit bihinden. Al riht swa, ʒef þu
wult þet te rode-scheld ant Godes stronge passiun falsi þe
deofles wepnen, ne dragse þu hit nawt efter þe, ah hef hit on
heh buue þin heorte-heaued i þine breoste-ehnen. Hald it
up toʒein þe feond, schaw hit him witerliche. Þe sihðe prof
135 ane bringeð him o fluhte.

Seinte Marherete is one of a number of texts found in MS. Bodley 34,
all apparently composed at approximately the same time and in the
same dialect, to which the title of the *Katherine Group* has been
given. This group includes lives of the three virgin saints, Katherine,
Juliana, Margaret, and the prose homilies *Hali Meiðhad* and *Sawles
Warde.* The only one for which no Latin source has yet been found
is *Hali Meiðhad,* but in the other texts the various originals are
dealt with so freely that they are adaptations rather than translations.
S. Marherete is based on that particular version of the Latin life
first printed by Mombritius in his *Sanctuarium* (1490) and preserved
in many MSS., but the English adaptor has not hesitated to rearrange
his material and to select and elaborate at will. More particularly
in his power of vivid description he is far superior to his original,
and most of the vivifying details are due to him. This independence
and sureness of touch is due to the fact that he is using a prose
tradition which goes back to pre-Conquest times, and so is freed
from the close dependence on his original so common in other
vernacular literature. He makes effective use of alliteration and
rhythm, to such an extent that some scholars have assumed him to
be writing verse rather than prose. But it is clear that there is no
underlying principle of rhythm and alliteration such as would make
possible its arrangement as verse, while the MS. punctuation is
clearly not metrical but a prose one of natural stops in reading.
In fact the texts of this group appear to continue that tradition of
poetic homiletic prose which had been established by Ælfric in his
homilies. Nothing is known of the author of any of the works in
the group, nor can we be certain whether they are all by one man or
not. Stylistic differences within the group have led to their attribution to different authors, and various names have been mentioned
in this connection. But argument from apparent differences of style
is notoriously unsafe, and there is not the slightest evidence in
support of any of the names which have at various times been put
forward.

Most of the texts of this group are preserved in three MSS.,
some only in two, and the earliest of them, MS. Bodley 34 written

during the first quarter of the thirteenth century, displays an extraordinarily consistent dialect, one which agrees very closely with that used in the Corpus MS. of the *Ancrene Riwle*. For the conclusions as to date and provenance which have been drawn from this see the introduction to the extracts from the *Ancrene Riwle*. The present dialect of the Bodley MS. is certainly West Midland, but attempts which have been made to localize it more accurately must, in the present state of our knowledge, be accepted with considerable reserve. Sixteenth-century scribblings on the margins of the MS. connect it with Herefordshire, and it may well represent the thirteenth-century dialect of that county, though there is no real evidence on the point.

The text of *S. Marherete* is found in two MSS., both written *c.* 1230, MS. Bodley 34 and MS. Royal 17 A xxvii, which appear to be independent copies of the original, with an unknown number of intermediate texts. The best edition of both MSS. is that by Dr. F. M. Mack for the Early English Text Society in 1934, and this contains also a Latin version in an appendix. The extract below, describing one of the experiences of the saint while in prison, is taken from the Bodleian MS. and corresponds with p. 20/16 to p. 24/19 of Dr. Mack's edition.

The Dragon

(20/16) [H]ire uostermoder wes an þet frourede hire, ant com to þe cwalmhus ant brohte hire to fode bred ant burnes drunch, þet ha bi leuide. Heo, þa, ant monie ma biheolden þurh an eilþurl as ha bed hire beoden. Ant com ut of an hurne hihendliche

5 towart hire an unwiht of helle on ane drakes liche, se grislich þet ham gras wið þet sehen þet unselhðe glistinde as þah he al ouerguld were; his lockes ant his longe berd blikeden al of golde, ant his grisliche teð semden of swart irn. His twa ehnen steareden steappre þen þe steoren ant ten ʒimstanes, brade ase

10 bascins, in his ihurnde heaued on eiðer half on his heh hokede nease. Of his speatewile muð sperclede fur ut, ant of his nease- þurles þreste smorðrinde smoke, smecche forcuðest. Ant lahte ut his tunge se long þet he swong hire abuten his swire, ant semde as þah a scharp sweord of his muð scheate, þe

15 glistnede ase gleam deð ant leitede al o leie. Ant al warð þet stude ful of strong ant of stearc stench, ant of þes schucke

---

1 [H]ire: *space left for initial in MS.*   5 ane: *MS.* ana.

schadewe schimmede ant schan al. He strahte him ant sturede
toward tis meoke meiden, ant geapede wið his genow upon hire
ungeinliche, ant bigon to crahien ant crenge wið swire, as þe þe
20 hire walde forswolhe mid alle. ʒef ha agrisen wes of þet
grisliche gra nes na muche wunder. Hire bleo bigon to blakien,
for þe grure þet grap hire; ant, for þe fearlac offruht, forʒet hire
bone þet ha ibeden hefde þet ha iseon moste þen unsehene
unwiht, ne nawt ne þohte þron, þet hire nu were ituðet hire
25 bone, ah smat smeortliche adun hire cneon to þer eorðe ant hef
hire honden up hehe toward heouene, wið þeos bone to Crist
þus cleopede.

'[U]nseheliche Godd, euch godes ful, hwas wreaððe is se
gromful þet helle-ware ant heouenes ant alle cwike þinges
30 cwakieð þeraʒeines, aʒein þis eisfule wiht, þet hit ne eili me nawt,
help me, mi Lauerd. Þu wrahtest ant wealdest alle worldliche
þing; þeo þet te heieð ant herieð in heouene, ant alle þe þinges
þe eardið on eorðe, þe fisches þe i þe flodes fleoteð wið finnes,
þe flihinde fuheles þe fleoð bi þe lufte, ant al þet iwraht is,
35 wurcheð þet ti wil is ant halt þine heastes bute mon ane. Þe
sunne reccheð hire rune wið-uten euch reste. Þe mone ant te
steorren, þe walkeð bi þe lufte, ne stutteð ne ne studegið, ah
sturieð aa mare, ne nohwiðer of þe wei þet tu hauest iwraht ham,
ne wrencheð ha neaure. Þu steorest þe sea-strem þet hit flede
40 ne mot fir þen þu merkest. Þe windes, þe wederes, þe wudes,
ant te weattres buheð þe ant beið. Feondes habbeð fearlac ant
engles of þin eie. Þe wurmes ant te wilde deor þet o þis wald
wunieð libbet efter þe lahe þet tu ham hauest iloket, luuewende
Lauerd; ant tu loke to me ant help me, þin hondiwerc, for al
45 min hope is o þe. Þu herhedest helle ant ouercome ase kempe þe
acursede gast þe fundeð to fordo me. Ah her me nu ant help me,
for nabbe ich i min nowcin nanes cunnes elne bute þin ane.
Wið þis uuel wite me, for ich truste al o þe, ant ti wil iwurðe hit,
deorwurðe Lauerd, þet ich þurh þi strengðe mahe stonden wið
50 him, and his muchele ouergart þet ich hit mote afeallen. Low,
he fundeð swiðe me to forsweolhen, ant weneð to beore me into
his balefulle hole þer he wuneð inne. Ah o þin blisfule nome ich
blesci me nuðe.' Ant droh þa endelong hire, ant þwertouer
þrefter, þe deorewurðe taken of þe deore rode þet he on reste.
55 Ant te drake reasde to hire mið tet ilke, ant sette his sariliche
muð ant unmeaðlich muchel on heh on hire heaued, ant rahte

---

28 [U]n-: *space for initial.*   wreaððe: *MS.* wreaðe.   30 wiht: *MS.* whit.

ut his tunge to þe ile of hire helen, ant swengde hire in, ant
forswelh into his wide wombe. Ah Criste to wurðmund ant
him to wraðerheale, for þe rode-taken redliche arudde hire, þet
60 ha wes wið iwepnet, ant warð his bone sone, swa þet his bodi
tobearst omidhepes o twa, ant þet eadi meiden allunge unmerret, wiðuten eauereuch wem, wende ut of his wombe,
heriende on heh hire Healent in heouene.

XIX. A KENTISH HOMILY

MS. Bodley Laud Misc. 471 contains, with other homiletic material, five sermons which are all translations from French versions of sermons composed in Latin by Maurice de Sully, bishop of Paris (1160–96). These sermons dealt with the Gospels for the Sundays and other festivals of the Christian year, and were apparently intended for the use of the priests in his diocese. Judged by the number of manuscript copies which have survived, they became very popular, and free translations of them into French were made by various preachers. The five which have been turned into English are all on the same general plan, a gospel story followed by a brief allegorical exposition and concluded by an exhortation.

Nothing is known of the English translator, except that he was evidently working sometime before 1250, and was a native of the Kentish dialect area. In fact the particular importance of these texts is linguistic rather than literary, since they provide excellent specimens of early Kentish, though they also have their value in the history of the development of medieval sermon literature. The sermons deal with (i) the appearance of the star to the Three Kings; (ii) the story of the marriage at Cana; (iii) the healing of the leper after the sermon on the mount; (iv) the stilling of the tempest; and (v) the parable of the vineyard. All five sermons were edited by R. Morris, *An Old English Miscellany* (EETS 1872), pp. 26–36, and again by Hall, i, 214–22; ii, 57–75. The particular sermon given below was also printed by Emerson.

The Parable of the Vineyard

Dominica in sexagesima. Sermo

Simile est regnum celorum homini patrifamilias, qui exijt primo mane conducere operarios in uineam suam.

Hure Lord Godalmichti to us spekeþ ine þo holi godespelle of teday, and us se⸍weth one forbisne; þet yef we uilleth don his seruise, þet we sollen habbe þo mede wel griat ine heuene-For so seyth ure Lord ine þo godspelle of todai, þet on good-
5 man was þat ferst uut yede bi þe moreghen for to here werk.

men into his winyarde for ane peny of forewerde, and also he
hedde imad þise forewerde so ha sente hi into his wynyarde.
So ha dede at undren and at midday also. Þo þat hit was ayen
þan euen, so ha kam into þe marcatte, so he fond werkmen þet
10 were idel. Þo seyde he to hem, 'Wee bie ye idel?' And hie
answerden and seyde, 'Lord, for we ne fonden tedai þat us
herde.' 'Goþ nu,' ha seide se godeman, 'into mine wynyarde,
and hic þat richt is yu sal yeue.' Þos yede into þise wynyarde
mid þo oþre, þo þet hit wes euen. Þo seide þe lord to his ser-
15 gant, 'Clepe þo werkmen and yeld hem here trauail, and agyn
to hem þat comen last and go al to þo ferste, yef eueriche of
hem ane peny.' Se sergant dede þes lordes commandement,
so paide þo werkmen and yaf euerich ane peny. And so hi
seghen þo þet bi þe morghen waren icomen, þet hi þet waren
20 last icume hedden here euerich ane peny, þo wenden hi more
habbe. Þo gruchchede hi amenges hem, and seyden, 'Þos
laste on ure habbeþ itravailed, and þu his makest velaghes to
us þet habbeth al deai ibye ine þine wynyarde, and habbeþ
ipoled þe berdene of þo pine and of þo hete of al þo daie.'
25 Þo ansuerede se godeman to on of hem, 'Frend', ha seide, 'I ne
do þe noon unricht. Wat forþingketh þat hic do min iwil?'
And also ure Lord hedde itold þise forbisne, so he seide efter-
ward, so sulle þo uerste bie last and þo laste ferst. Fele bieþ
iclepede, ac feaue bieþ icorene.
30   Nu ihereþ þe signefiance. Þes godeman betockneþ Godalmichti ure Lord. Se winyard betockneþ þe seruise of ure
Lorde. Þe werkmen betockneþ alle þo þet doþ Cristes seruise.
Þo tides of þo daie betokneþ þe time of þis world. Bie þe
morghen iherde ure Lord werkmen into his winyarde, þo
35 ha sente þe patriarches ate begininge of þis wordl ine is
seruise, þet þurch gode beleaue him seruede, and seden his
techinge to alle þo þet hi hedden hit to siggen. Also at undren
and at midday iherede he werkmen into is winyarde þo ha
sente be þo time þet Moyses was and Aaron, and i þe time of
40 his prophetes dede he mani god man into his seruise, þet þurch
griate luue to him helden and deden his seruise. Toyenes þan
euen Godalmichti ihierde werkmen into his winyarde, þo þat
He a last of þis wordle naam fles and blod ine þe maidene
Seinte Marie, and seauede ine þis world. Þo fond he men þet
45 al day hedden ibe idel. Werefore he fond þet heþen folk þet
be þo time þet was igo hedden ibe ut of Godes biliaue and of
his luue and of his seruise. Hi ne hedden nocht ibe idel for to

14 hit wes: MS. hi wel.   23 habbeþ: MS. habbetþ.   29 icorene: MS. icornee.
26 beleaue: MS. beleauee.

done þo deueles werkes. Ac þerefore seith þet godspel þet
hedden ibe idel þo þet hi nedden bileued ane Godalmichti, ne
50 Him louie ne Him serui. For al þat is ine þis wordle þet man
is, bote yef ha luuie Godalmichti and him serui, al hit him may
þenche forlore and idelnesse. Þo aresunede ure Lord þe paens
bi ise apostles vrefore hi hedden ibe so longe idel, þo þet hi ne
hedden ibe in his seruise. Þo ansuerden þe paens, þet non ne
55 hedden iherd hij, þet is to sigge þet hi ne hedden neuer te
iheerd prophete ne apostle ne prechur þet hem seaude ne hem
tachte hu i solden ine Gode beleue ne him serui. 'Goþ', a seide
ure Lord, 'inte mine winyarde, þet is inte mine beleaue, and
hic yw sal yeue yure peni, þet is heueriche blisce.' Þo heþen
60 men yeden be þa daghen into Cristes seruise, and we þet of
hem bieþ icume, and habbeþ cristendom underfonge, bieþ
i-entred into Cristes seruise, þerfore we sollen habbe ure peni,
þet is þe blisce of heuene, also wel ase þo þet comen bi þe
morghen. For also we hopieð for te habbe heueriche blisce
65 ase þo patriarches and þo prophetes and þo apostles and þo
gode men þet hwilem ine þis world Godalmichti serueden.
     So as we habeþ iseid of diuers wordles, þet God almichti
dede werkmen into his winyarde, so we mowe sigge of þo
elde of eueriche men. For Godalmichti deþ werkmen into
70 his winyarde bi þe morghen, wanne ha clepeþ of swiche þer
bieþ into his seruise ine here childhede, wanne hi of þis world
wendeþ, be swo þet hi ne be ine no diadlich senne. At undren
ha sent men into his winyarde, þet a turneþ into his seruise
of age of man. At middai, wanne þo dai is alþer hotest
75 betokneð þo men of xxxᵗⁱ wyntre, oþer of furti, for þe nature
of man is of greater strengþe and of greater hete ine þo age.
So euen bitockneþ elde of man, þet is se ende of þe liue.
Vre Lord deþ werkmen into his winyarde agenes þo euen,
wanne fele ine here elde wendeþ ut of here senne into Cristes
80 seruise. Also solle hi habbe þo blisce of heuene ase þo þet
ferst comen into þe winyarde. Nocht for þan, for þise griate
bunte þet ure Lord yefþ, ne solde no man targi for to wende
to Godalmichti ne him to serui, for also seid þet holi writ
þet non ne wot þane dai of his diaþe, for man mai longe liues
85 wene and ofte him legheþ se wrench.
     Nu, gode men, ye habbeþ iherd þet godspel and þe for-
bisne. Nu lokeþ yef ye bieþ withinne þo winyarde, þet is
þet yef ye bieþ ine Godes seruise, yef ye bieþ withute diadliche

---

55 iherd: *MS.* iheed.   74 hotest: *MS.* hotestd.   75 betokneð: *MS.* betokned.
80 Also: *MS.* As so.

senne, yef ye hatieþ þat he hateþ, yef ye luuieþ þet he luueþ,
90   and doþ þet he hot, and, bute ye do, ye bieþ hut of his winyarde,
þe[t] is ut of his seruise. And ye doþ þet ure Lord hoot, so ye
ofserueþ þane peni, þet is heueriche blisce. Ye ofserueþ þet
good þet noon herte ne may iþenche ne noon yare ihere ne
tunge telle, þo blisce þet God halt alle þo þet hine luuieþ.
95   Þider Lord granti us to cumene. *Quod ipse prestare dignetur, per.*

XX. A LUUE-RON

THE vanity of earthly things has seldom been better expressed than in this poem by Thomas de Hales, written at a time when the theme had long been popular in England, but before it had become hackneyed. In fact, the *ubi sunt qui ante nos* theme is a universal one, and during the Middle Ages was utilized from Boethius to Villon. In OE it occurs already in the *Wanderer* and is frequent in ME down to the very end of the period. This particular treatment is of especial interest in that it occurs in one or the very few English poems of the thirteenth century which was still remembered at the end of the fourteenth. J. E. Wells (9 *MLR* 236 ff.) has drawn attention to the fact that *Clene Maydenhod* in the Vernon MS. shows the same sequence of ideas, close verbal parallels, and even the use of the same rhyme words.

Little is known of the author beyond the information given in the note at the beginning of the poem. He was a friar of the Franciscan order, and presumably derived his name from Hailes in Gloucestershire. An Anglo-Norman sermon in St. John's College, Oxford, MS. 190, ff. 179 ff., is ascribed to one of the same name (30 *MLR* 212 ff.), and some Latin sermons in the same MS. may also be his. Adam Marsh (*d.* 1257–8) mentions a certain Thomas de Hales as one of his personal friends, and a Thomas de Hales joined with the guardian and prior of his house in London in a letter to Fulk Bassett who was bishop of London from 1244 to 1258. It is impossible to prove that these various references are to the same man, but it is likely enough.

The references to King Henry (ll. 82, 101) must presumably be to Henry III (1216–72), and so show the poem to have been composed some time between those dates, but more exact dating is hardly possible. It is extant in a single MS., Jesus College, Oxford, MS. 29, ff. 260 ff., from which it is here printed. The most recent edition of the complete poem is in Carleton Brown, pp. 68–74, but extracts are to be found in most ME readers.

Incipit quidam cantus quem composuit frater Thomas de Hales de ordine
fratrum Minorum, ad instanciam cuiusdam puelle deo dicate

A mayde Cristes me bit yorne
    Þat ich hire wurche a luue-ron,
For hwan heo myhte best ileorne
    To taken on-oþer soþ lefmon,
5   Þat treowest were of alle berne
    And best wyte cuþe a freo wymmon.
Ich hire nule nowiht werne,
    Ich hire wule teche as ic con.

Mayde, her þu myht biholde
10   Þis worldes luue nys bute o res
And is by-set so fele-volde,
    Vikel and frakel and wok and les.
Þeos þeines þat her weren bolde
    Beoþ aglyden so wyndes bles,
15   Vnder molde hi liggeþ colde
    And faleweþ so doþ medewe-gres.

Nis no mon iboren o lyue
    Þat her may beon studeuest,
For her he haueþ seorewen ryue,
20   Ne tyt him neuer [ro ne rest].
Toward his ende he hyeþ blyue
    And lutle hwile he her ilest;
Pyne and deþ him wile of-dryue
    Hwenne he weneþ to libben best.

25   Nis non so riche, ne non so freo,
    Þat he ne schal heonne sone away,
Ne may hit neuer his waraunt beo,
    Gold ne seoluer, vouh ne gray.
Ne beo he no þe swift, ne may he fleo,
30   Ne weren his lif enne day.
Þus is þes world, as þu mayht seo,
    Al-so þe schadewe þat glyt away.

Þis world fareþ hwilynde—
    Hwenne on cumeþ an-oþer goþ;
35   Þat wes bi-fore nv is bihynde,
    Þat er was leof nv hit is loþ.

        20 ro ne rest *in a later hand.*

Forþi he doþ as þe blynde
   Þat in þis world his luue doþ;
Ye mowen iseo þe world aswynde—
40   Þat wouh goþ forþ, abak þat soþ.

Þeo luue þat ne may her abyde,
   Þu treowest hire myd muchel **wouh;**
Al-so hwenne hit schal to-glide,
   Hit is fals and mereuh and frouh,
45 And fromward in vychon tide.
   Hwile hit lesteþ is seorewe inouh;
An ende, ne werie mon so syde,
   He schal to-dreosen so lef on bouh.

Monnes luue nys buten o stunde:
50   Nv he luueþ, nv he is sad,
Nu he cumeþ, nv wile he funde,
   Nv he is wroþ, nv he is gled.
His luue is her and ek a lunde,
   Nv he luueþ sum þat he er bed;
55 Nis he neuer treowe ifunde—
   Þat him tristeþ he is amed.

Yf mon is riche of worldes weole,
   Hit makeþ his heorte smerte and **ake;**
If he dret þat me him stele,
60   Þenne doþ him pyne nyhtes wake;
Him waxeþ þouhtes monye and fele,
   Hw he hit may witen wiþvten sake.
An ende hwat helpeþ hit to hele?
   Al deþ hit wile from him take.

65 Hwer is Paris and Heleyne
   Þat weren so bryht and feyre on bleo,
Amadas and Ideyne,
   Tristram, Yseude and alle þeo,
Ector, wiþ his scharpe meyne,
70   And Cesar, riche of wordes feo?
Heo beoþ iglyden vt of þe reyne
   So þe schef is of þe cleo.

67 Ideyne: *MS.* Dideyne.

Hit is of heom also hit nere;
  Of heom me h7aueþ wunder itold,
75 Nere hit reuþe for to heren,
  Hw hi were wiþ pyne aquold,
And hwat hi þoleden alyue here.
  Al is heore hot iturnd to cold.
Þus is þes world of false fere—
80   Fol he is þe on hire is bold.

Þeyh he were so riche mon
  As [is] Henry vre kyng,
And also veyr as Absalon,
  Þat neuede on eorþe non euenyng,
85 Al were sone his prute agon;
  Hit nere on ende wrþ on heryng.
Mayde, if þu wilnest after leofmon,
  Ich teche þe enne treowe king.

A swete, if þu iknowe
90   Þe gode þewes of þisse Childe!
He is feyr and bryht on heowe,
  Of glede chere, of mode mylde,
Of lufsum lost, of truste treowe,
  Freo of heorte, of wisdom wilde,
95 Ne þurhte þe neuer rewe,
  Myhtestu do þe in His ylde.

He is ricchest mon of londe,
  So wide so mon spekeþ wiþ muþ,
Alle heo beoþ to His honde,
100   Est and west, norþ and suþ.
Henri, king of Engelonde,
  Of Hym he halt and to Hym buhþ.
Mayde, to þe He send His sonde
  And wilneþ for to beo þe cuþ.

105 Ne byt He wiþ þe lond ne leode,
  Vouh, ne gray, ne rencyan;
Naueþ He þer-to none neode,
  He is riche and wel[i man].

103 sonde: *MS.* schonde.   **108** *Bracketed letters in later hand.*

If þu Him woldest luue beode
110   And by-cumen His leouemon,
He brouhte þe to suche wede
Þat naueþ king ne kayser non.

Hwat spekestu of eny bolde
Þat wrouhte þe wise Salomon
115   Of iaspe, of saphir, of merede golde,
And of mony on-oþer ston?
Hit is feyrure of feole-volde
More þan ich eu telle con;
Þis bold, mayde, þe is bihote
120   If þat þu bist His leouemon.

Hit stont vppon a treowe mote
Þar hit neuer truke ne schal;
Ne may no mynur hire vnderwrote,
Ne neuer false þene grundwal.
125   Þar-inne is vich balewes bote,
Blisse and ioye and gleo and gal.
Þis bold, mayde, is þe bihote
And vych o blisse þar wyþ-al.

Þer ne may no freond fleon oþer,
130   Ne non fur-leosen his iryhte;
Þer nys hate ne wreþþe nouþer,
Of prude ne of onde, of none wihte.
Alle heo schule wyþ engles pleye,
Some and sauhte in heouene lyhte.
135   Ne beoþ heo, mayde, in gode weye
Þat wel luueþ vre Dryhte?

Ne may no mon Hine iseo,
Al-so He is in His mihte,
Þat may wiþ-vten blisse beo
140   Hwanne he isihþ vre Drihte.
His sihte is al ioye and gleo,
He is day wyþ-vte nyhte.
Nere he, mayde, ful sley
Þat myhte wunye myd such a knyhte?

143 sley: *MS.* seoly.

145   He haueþ bi-tauht þe o tresur
       Þat is betere þan gold oþer pel,
    And bit þe luke þine bur,
       And wilneþ þat þu hit wyte wel,
    Wyþ þeoues, wiþ reueres, wiþ lechurs,
150   Þu most beo waker and snel;
    Þu art swetture þane eny flur
       Hwile þu witest þene kastel.

    Hit is ymston of feor iboren,
       Nys non betere vnder heouene grunde,
155   He is to-fore alle oþre i-coren,
       He heleþ alle luue wunde.
    Wel were alyue iboren
       Þat myhte wyten þis ilke stunde;
    For habbe þu hine enes for-loren,
160   Ne byþ he neuer eft ifunde.

    Þis ilke ston þat ich þe nemne
       Mayden-hod i-cleoped is;
    Hit is o derewurþe gemme,
       Of alle oþre he berþ þat pris,
165   And bryngeþ þe wiþ-vte wemme
       In-to þe blysse of paradis.
    Þe hwile þu hyne witest vnder þine hemme,
       Þu ert swetture þan eny spis.

    Hwat spekstu of eny stone
170   Þat beoþ in vertu oþer in grace—
    Of amatiste, of calcydone,
       Of lectorie and tupace,
    Of iaspe, of saphir, of sardone,
       Smaragde, beril and crisopace?
175   Among alle oþre ymstone,
       Þes beoþ deorre in vyche place.

    Mayde, also ich þe tolde,
       Þe ymston of þi bur,
    He is betere an hundred-folde
180   Þan alle þeos in heore culur;

168 þan: MS. þat.   170 grace: MS. pris *in later hand.*   172 tupace: MS. *adds* y-wys *in later hand.*

He is i-don in heouene golde
   And is ful of fyn amur.
Alle þat myhte hine wite scholde,
   He schyneþ so bryht in heouene bur.

185 Hwen þu me dost in þine rede
   For to cheose a leofmon,
Ich wile don as þu me bede,
   Þe beste þat ich fynde con.
Ne doþ he, mayde, on vuele dede,
190   Þat may cheose of two þat on,
And he wile wiþ-vte neode
   Take þet wurse, þe betere let gon?

Þis rym, mayde, ich þe sende
   Open and wiþ-vte sel;
195 Bidde ic þat þu hit vntrende
   And leorny bute bok vych del;
Her-of þat þu beo swiþe hende
   And tech hit oþer maydenes wel.
Hwo-so cuþe hit to þan ende,
200   Hit wolde him stonde muchel stel.

Hwenne þu sittest in longynge,
   Drauh þe forþ þis ilke wryt;
Mid swete stephne þu hit singe,
   And do al-so hit þe byt.
205 To þe He haueþ send one gretynge;
   God almyhti þe beo myd,
And leue cumen to His brudþinge
   Heye in heouene þer He sit.

And yeue him god endynge,
210   Þat haueth iwryten þis ilke wryt. Amen.

XXI. IACOB AND IOSEP

Iacob and Iosep is probably the most interesting of the early ME paraphrases of biblical material, certainly a good deal more entertaining than the better known and roughly contemporary *Genesis and Exodus*. Much of its attraction is no doubt due to the fact that it continues the OE tradition of dealing with biblical stories Just as, in Anglo-Saxon times, bible stories were approximated as closely as possible to the manners of the heroic age, so here the background has been completely medievalized Knights, minstrels and medieval castles appear; Jacob is a lord who 'sits in hall', and Pharaoh goes hunting 'with bowe ybent'. By describing scenes which were familiar to him the author has given life and movement to the Old Testament story, whilst the fact that he deals only with certain chosen incidents of the story has preserved him from the tedious comprehensiveness all too common in medieval literature. As told here the story differs in some details from the biblical version, but the additions are probably not original since they occur also in contemporary French versions as well as in the episode as told in the *Cursor Mundi*. Nothing is known of the author except that he apparently wrote in some southern or south-west Midland dialect during the first half of the thirteenth century.

The poem is extant in a single MS., Bodley 652 (from which a leaf is missing), written during the second half of the thirteenth century. The best edition is that by A. S. Napier (Oxford 1916), and the extracts below include the first twenty lines of introduction and the account of the visit of the sons of Jacob to Egypt to buy corn, corresponding with lines 1–20 and 352–428 of Napier's edition.

Introduction

> Wolle ȝe nou ihere wordes swiþe gode
> Of one patriarke after Noees flode?
> Nellic ȝou nouȝt tellen of þis flodes grame,
> Bote of one patriarke, Iacob was his name.
> 5 While men loueden meti song, gamen and feire tale;
> Nou hem is wel leuere gon to þe nale,
> Vcchen out þe gurdel and rume þe wombe,

Comen erliche þider and sitte þer ful longe.
Þat is þe soule ful loþ, and lef þe licame,
10 Bote we hit bileuen, hit biþ a luþer game.
To fullen oure wombe hit is lutel pris,
And seþþe ligge slepe, such hit were a gris.
Þus ferden ure aldren bi Noees dawe,
Of mete and of drinke hi fulden here mawe.
15 And for ȝiuernesse þei weren riȝt wod;
For þi sende oure Louerd Noees flod.
Þo hi miȝten drinke þat hi weren fulle,
Hi floten swiþe riued bi dich and bi pulle.
Þer nas in þis world hul non so heiȝ,
20 Þat tis vnirude flod muchel ne ouersteiȝ.

The Brothers' Visit to Egypt

(352) Feire fareþ þis ȝungemen bi dai and bi niȝt,
Into Egipte lond þat hi comen riȝt.
Muche was þe blisse and muche was þe gome
In water and in londe of wilde and of tome.
25 Muche was þe blisse þat hi þar iseye,
Bernes ful riche and mowen ful heye.
Muche was þe blisse after here swinke
Þat hi þare funden of mete and of drinke.
Hem oftok a menestral, his harpe he bar a-rugge.
30 'Whennes be ȝe, ȝunge men? Ich bidde þat ȝe me sigge.
Me þuncheþ bi ȝoure assen þat corn ȝe wolde begge,
And ich ȝou wole bringe to þe tu-brugge.
Þar þe hendeste man þat euere is aliue
Ȝou wole gistni to-niȝt and make ȝou ful bliþe.
35 Ȝe þuncheþ ferrene men and alle freboren,
To-niȝt ssal mani kniȝt-child knele ȝou biforen.'
He brouȝtem to þe castel ase he hem bihet,
And spac wiþ þe porter in þat he hem let.
Hi seyen in þe castel mani riche þing,
40 And Iosep sitten in halle, such hit were a king.
Ac if hi wenden Iosep þer for to sen,
Leuere hem were alle at hom on hunger ded to ben.
Alle þese ten breþren comen into þe halle,
To-fore Ioseppes fet a kne hi valleþ alle.
45 'Ariseþ vp,' seide Iosep, 'sitte ȝe nouȝt a-kne,
Ac telleþ me wel feire wat ȝoure wille be.'
'From Ierusalem,' quod Ruben, 'we beþ hider icome;

33 Þar þe: *MS.* Þarle.

Let sullen vs corn, louerd, for Godes loue.
Old man is oure fader and corn naþ he non;
50 For muchel one nede we beþ hider igon.'
Þenne seide Iosep, such hit were his gome,
'Wat is,' he seide, 'ȝoure faderes nome?'
'Vre fader heiȝte Iacob, vre moder Rachel,'
Mid þat ilke worde he knew hem ful wel.
55 Þo Iosep iherde þat his fader was aliue,
Nas neuere for his fader child al-so bliþe.
He goþ in-to þe boure and wepeþ for blisse,
Sore he is alonged his breþren to kisse.
Iosep cam into halle, þe water he lette bringe.
60 And halde to here honden mid his wite vingres.
Feire beþ þis ȝungemen iserued þilke niȝt;
Of mete ne of drinke trukede hem nowiȝt.
Iosep ful riche win lette to him bringe,
And so he bad þis children on Ebrewisse singe.
65 And so hi sungen alle ase Iosep hem bad,
Seþþe he cam into Egipte nas Iosep so glad.
Al of rede wete here assen he lette seme,
For to meten here corn nam he none ȝeme.
Nou dude Iosep a swiþe wonder þing,
70 He nam a guldene nap, was Pharaones þe king,
And putte in þones sakke wiþ-inne þe prenne,
And þerof come þis ȝungemen swiþe muche tene.
Feire hi nomen leue to wenden here way
Toward here contre a lutel ere day.
75 Ase hi ferden here wai in þe morewentide,
Þenne seyen hi twolf ȝungemen after hem ride
Mid helm and mid brunie, mid swerdes outdrawe,
Þo wenden þese ten breþren alle to ben islawe.
'Abideþ,' hi seiden, 'þeues, abideþ, ȝe beþ inome.
80 To-fore þe stiward aȝein ȝe ssulen alle come
For a guldene nap þat ȝe habbeþ inome.
Ȝif ȝe in þis londe mid þefþe beþ ifonge,
Ȝoure dom is idemed, alle ȝe worþeþ anhonge;
For ȝoure assen isemed al of rede golde
85 Of Faraones lond þe king faren ȝe ne ssolde.'
Alle þese ten breþren turneþ ham aȝein
Mid reuþfule wepe and mid dreri drem,
To-fore þe stiward aȝein hi beþ alle ibrouȝt,
Þe nap in here sakke sone hit is isouȝt.
90 Þe nap is ifunde sone and anon,

Nou wringeþ hi here honden þis breþren eueruchon.
Iosep sauȝ his breþren wepe, sore hit him gan rewe,
He nolde in none wise ȝit þat hi him knewe.
Iosep feng þene nap, mid pal he was biweued,
95 He lokede on his breþren, and ssok on hem his heued.
Awaried worþe swikedom and þat hit erest funde,
So mani gultelese man hit bringeþ to þe grunde!

XXII. CURSOR MUNDI

THE most comprehensive versification of biblical material and early Christian legend during the ME period is to be found in the *Cursor Mundi*. The prologue, printed below, gives the author's reasons for writing, and it is evident that he is deliberately competing with the popular secular romances of the time, whose influence he thinks is not always for good. The complete work, running to some 30,000 lines, consists of a prologue and seven parts, divided according to the seven ages of the world, along with four appendices and seven further additions, some of which are not included in all the MSS. This encyclopædic poem deals at length with all the principal incidents of the Old and New Testaments, and includes also treatments of numerous topical religious subjects. In general it bears an obvious resemblance to some of the later cycles of miracle plays and may have influenced them. The author draws his material from various sources, more particularly from the *Vulgate* and the *Historia Scholastica* of Petrus Comestor, but also from the apocryphal gospels and from other sources, English as well as French and Latin. Perhaps the most surprising thing about the work is that it is so far from being as dull as might have been feared. No doubt this is partly due to the diversity of topics and tales to be found in it, but something is due also to the skill of the author. From an extensive reading he has selected those elements which would make the widest appeal to his audience, and woven together this diverse material with remarkable skill. He shows a sense of form unusual for the period, though it may be suspected that in this particular he owes as much to his originals as to his own literary sense. Though not a great poet he is a capable enough versifier, writing in a plain, straightforward style. The skilful adaptation of his material, and its lively treatment, no doubt explain the popularity of the work, this being evidenced by the survival of at least ten MSS.

Few of the problems connected with the work can as yet be considered settled. Much remains to be done on the relationship of the various MSS., on the date of composition, and on the provenance. The name of the author is unknown; he was certainly a cleric and wrote somewhere in the north, perhaps in Co. Durham, during the last quarter of the thirteenth century. The most complete version of the poem is that preserved in the British Museum MS. Cotton Vespasian A III (1300–1350), which probably best represents the dialect of the original and is the source of the extract below. Four of the MSS. (British Museum Cotton Vespasian A III; Bodl. MS. Fairfax 14; Göttingen MS. theol. 107; Trinity College, Cambridge, MS. R 3. 8) were edited for the Early English Text Society by R. Morris in 1874–93.

The Cursur o the World

Man yhernes rimes for to here,
And romans red on maneres sere,
Of Alisaundur þe conquerour;
Of Iuly Cesar þe emparour;
5 O Grece and Troy the strang strijf,
Þere many thosand lesis þer lijf;
O Brut þat bern bald of hand,
Þe first conquerour of Ingland;
O Kyng Arthour þat was so rike,
10 Quam non in hys tim was like,
O ferlys þat hys knythes fel,
Þat aunters sere I here of tell,
Als Wawan, Cai and oþer stabell,
For to were þe ronde tabell;
15 How Charles kyng and Rauland faght,
Wit Sarazins wald þai na saght;
O Tristrem and hys leif Ysote,
How he for here be-com a sote,
O Ioneck and of Ysambrase,
20 O Ydoine and of Amadase.
Storis als o serekin thinges
O princes, prelates and o kynges;
Sanges sere of selcuth rime,
Inglis, Frankys, and Latine,
25 To rede and here ilkon is prest,
Þe thynges þat þam likes best.
Þe wisman wil o wisdom here,
Þe foul hym draghus to foly nere,
Þe wrang to here o right is lath,
30 And pride wyt buxsumnes is wrath;
O chastite has lichur leth
On charite ai werrais wreth;

21 serekin: *MS*. ferekin, *F*. mony, *G*. diuers, *T*. dyuers.

Bot be the fruit may scilwis se,
O quat vertu is ilka tre.
35 Of alkyn fruit þat man schal fynd
He fettes fro þe rote his kynd.
O gode pertre coms god peres,
Wers tre, vers fruit it beres.

XXIII–XXXVII. LYRICAL POETRY

THE earliest surviving examples of ME. secular lyric date from the thirteenth century, though there are references enough to show that it was not uncommon in the twelfth, and a few short fragments from that period have been preserved. The religious lyric had naturally enough a better chance of survival, and, on a strictly arithmetical calculation, the proportion of secular lyric printed below is unduly high. But the secular lyric of the thirteenth century has a quality of its own which it is desirable to have represented as fully as possible. With the exception of the first, all of those given below were printed by Carleton Brown, and many have also been printed elsewhere. Most are extant only in a single MS. The first, taken from the records of a medieval lawsuit as reported by Robert of Graystanes, a fourteenth-century historian of Durham, is a single stanza from a lament said to have been composed *c.* 1272 on the death of the then Lord Neville. It was printed by J. Raine (9 *Surtees Society* 112), and is included here because of the paucity of secular lyrics before the fourteenth century and because of its affinities with the later ballads, also mainly northern. 24, 25, 26 are among the few early lyrics which are provided with musical notation in the MSS. 27 occurs also in the British Museum Addit. MS. 11579 in a Latin exemplum which was printed by T. Wright, *Latin Stories* (8 *Percy Society*). 33 is one of the best and earliest of the macaronic poems. It appears to have remained popular for some two centuries and was still being copied and adapted during the fifteenth century. 34 is said by Carleton Brown to be the anglicization of some Latin verses which are given above it in the MS., but which in fact read more like a translation from the English. 35 is an excellent example of the *Ubi sunt* theme (illustrated also in the *Luue-Ron*), and stanzas from it are not infrequently incorporated in poems on the 'Sayings of St. Bernard'. 36 is perhaps the best of the Crucifixion dialogues, whilst 37 is an example of the penitential lyric. 28, 29, 30, 31, 32 are all taken from the British Museum Harley 2253, for which see p. 10. The MS. was probably written during the first quarter of the fourteenth century, and consequently Dr. K. Sisam includes two of the best known of the secular lyrics, but almost certainly the poems

in it were composed during the preceding century. Along with the
two printed by Sisam these comprise practically all the secular
lyrics in the MS. Of these, 31 is one of the few examples of the
purely comic poems which have survived from the period, while
32 is one of the earliest examples of political satire in English.

XXIII. A LAMENT

(York Cathedral Chapter Library, MS. XVI, I. 12)

Wel, qwa sal thir hornes blau
   Haly Rod thi day?
Nou is he dede and lies law
   Was wont to blaw thaim ay.

XXIV. THE CUCKOO SONG

(BM. MS. Harley 978)

Svmer is icumen in,
   Lhude sing cuccu!
Groweþ sed and bloweþ med
   And springþ þe wde nu.
5 Sing cuccu!

Awe bleteþ after lomb,
   Lhouþ after calue cu,
Bulluc sterteþ, bucke uerteþ.
   Murie sing cuccu!
10 Cuccu, cuccu,
   Wel singes þu cuccu.
Ne swik þu nauer nu!

XXV. WINTER COMES

(Bodl. MS. Rawlinson G. 22)

[M]irie it is while sumer ilast
   Wið fugheles song,
Oc nu necheð windes blast
   And w[e]der strong.
5 Ej! ej! what þis nicht [is] long!
And ich wið wel michel wrong
   Soregh and murne and [fast].

XXVI. SORROW
(Bodl. MS. Douce 139)

Foweles in þe frith,
Þe fisses in þe flod,
And I mon waxe wod.
Mulch sorw I walke with
5   For beste of bon and blod.

4 Mulch: *MS*. Multh.

XXVII. SILENCE IS GOLDEN
(Trinity College, Cambridge, MS. 323)

Say me, viit in þe brom,
Teche me wou I sule don
Þat min hosebonde
Me louien wolde.
5   Hold þine tunke stille
And hawe al þine wille.

XXVIII. BLOW, NORTHERN WIND
(BM. MS. Harley 2253)

Blow, northerne wynd,
Sent þou me my suetyng!
Blow, norþerne wynd,
Blou! blou! blou!

5 Ichot a burde in boure bryht
Þat fully semly is on syht,
Menskful maiden of myht,
    Feir ant fre to fonde;
In al þis wurhliche won,
10 A burde of blod ant of bon
Neuer ȝete Y nuste non
    Lussomore in londe.
      Blou, &c.

Wiþ lokkes lefliche and longe,
Wiþ frount ant face feir to fonde,
15 Wiþ murþes monie mote heo monge—
    Þat brid so breme in boure,

Wiþ lossom eye grete ant gode,
Wiþ browen blysfol vnder hode.
He þat reste Him on þe rode
20   Þat leflich lyf honoure!
     Blou, &c.

Hire lure lumes liht
Ase a launterne a-nyht,
Hire bleo blykyeþ so bryht,
   So feyr heo is ant fyn.
25 A suetly suyre heo haþ to holde,
Wiþ armes, shuldre ase mon wolde
Ant fyngres feyre forte folde.
   God wolde hue were myn!

Middel heo haþ menskful smal,
30 Hire loueliche chere as cristal;
Þeȝes, legges, fet ant al,
   Ywraht wes of þe beste.
A lussum ledy lasteles
Þat sweting is ant euer wes;
35 A betere burde neuer nes,
   Yheryed wiþ þe heste.

Heo is dereworþe in day,
Graciouse, stout ant gay,
Gentil, iolyf so þe jay,
40   Worhliche when heo wakeþ.
Maiden murgest of mouþ;
Bi est, bi west, by norþ ant souþ,
Þer nis fiele ne crouþ
   Þat such murþes makeþ.

45 Heo is coral of godnesse,
Heo is rubie of ryhtfulnesse,
Heo is cristal of clannesse
   Ant baner of bealte;
Heo is lilie of largesse,
50 Heo is paruenke of prouesse,
Heo is solsecle of suetnesse
   Ant ledy of lealte.

To Loue, þat leflich is in londe,
Y tolde him, as ych vnderstonde,
55   Hou þis hende haþ hent in honde
On huerte þat myn wes;
Ant hire knyhtes me han so soht,
Sykyng, Sorewyng ant Þoht,
Þo þre me han in bale broht
60   Aȝeyn þe poer of Péés.

To Loue Y putte pleyntes mo,
Hou Sykyng me haþ siwed so,
Ant eke Þoht me þrat to slo
Wiþ maistry, ȝef he myhte,
65   Ant Serewe sore in balful bende
Þat he wolde, for þis hende,
Me lede to my lyues ende
Vnlahfulliche in lyhte.

Loue me lustnede vch word,
70   Ant beh him to me ouer bord,
Ant bed me hente þat hord
Of myne huerte hele,
Ant bisecheþ þat swete ant swote,
Er þen þou falle ase fen of fote,
75   Þat heo wiþ þe wolle of bote
Dereworþliche dele.

For hire loue Y carke ant care,
For hire loue Y droupne ant dare,
For hire loue my blisse is bare,
80   Ant al ich waxe won;
For hire loue in slep Y slake,
For hire loue al nyht ich wake,
For hire loue mournyng Y make
More þen eny mon.

69 Loue: *MS.* hire loue.

XXIX. DE CLERICO ET PUELLA
(BM. MS. Harley 2253)

'My deþ Y loue, my lyf ich hate, for a leuedy shene;
Heo is brith so daies liht, þat is on me wel sene;
Al Y falewe so doþ þe lef in somer when hit is grene.
Ȝef mi þoht helpeþ me noht, to wham shal Y me mene?

5 Sorewe ant syke ant drery mod byndeþ me so faste
Þat Y wene to walke wod ʒef hit me lengore laste;
My serewe, my care, al wiþ a word he myhte awey caste.
Whet helpeþ þe, my suete lemmon, my lyf þus forte gaste?'

'Do wey, þou clerc, þou art a fol, wiþ þe bydde Y noht chyde;
10 Shalt þou neuer lyue þat day mi loue þat þou shalt byde.
Ʒef þou in my boure art take, shame þe may bityde.
Þe is bettere on fote gon, þen wycked hors to ryde.'

'Weylawei! whi seist þou so? Þou rewe on me, þy man!
Þou art euer in my þoht in londe wher ich am.
15 Ʒef Y deʒe for þi loue, hit is þe mykel sham;
Þou lete me lyue ant be þi luef, ant þou my suete lemman.'

'Be stille, þou fol, Y calle þe riþt; cost þou neuer blynne?
Þou art wayted day ant nyht wiþ fader ant al my kynne.
Be þou in mi bour ytake, lete þey for no synne
20 Me to holde, ant þe to slon; þe deþ so þou maht wynne.'

'Suete ledy, þou wend þi mod, sorewe þou wolt me kyþe;
Ich am also sory mon so ich was whylen blyþe.
In a wyndou þer we stod we custe vs fyfty syþe—
Feir biheste makeþ mony mon al is serewes mythe.'

25 'Weylawey! whi seist þou so? Mi serewe þou makest newe.
Y louede a clerk al par amours, of loue he wes ful trewe,
He nes nout blyþe neuer a day bote he me sone seʒe;
Ich louede him betere þen my lyf—whet bote is hit to leʒe?'

'Whil Y wes a clerc in scole, wel muchel Y couþe of lore;
30 Ych haue þoled for þy loue woundes fele sore.
Fer from [hom] ant eke from men, vnder þe wode-gore,
Suete ledy, þou rewe of me—nou may Y no more.'

'Þou semest wel to ben a clerc, for þou spekest so scille;
Shalt þou neuer for mi loue woundes þole grylle.
35 Fader, moder, ant al my kun ne shal me holde so stille
Þat Y nam þyn, ant þou art myn, to don al þi wille.'

33 scille: *MS*. stille.

XXX. LOVE IN SPRING
(BM. MS. Harley 2253)

When þe nyhtegale singes þe wodes waxen grene,
Lef ant gras ant blosme springes in Aueryl, Y wene,
Ant loue is to myn herte gon wiþ one spere so kene;
Nyht ant day my blod hit drynkes, myn herte deþ me tene.

5 Ich haue loued al þis ȝer, þat Y may loue na more,
Ich haue siked moni syk, lemmon, for þin ore;
Me nis loue neuer þe ner, ant þat me reweþ sore.
Suete lemmon, þench on me, ich haue loued þe ȝore.

Suete lemmon, Y preye þe of loue one speche;
10 Whil Y lyue in world so wyde oþer nulle Y seche.
Wiþ þy loue, my suete leof, mi blis þou mihtes eche;
A suete cos of þy mouþ mihte be my leche.

Suete lemmon, Y preȝe þe of a loue-bene;
ȝef þou me louest ase men says, lemmon as Y wene,
15 Ant ȝef hit þi wille be, þou loke þat hit be sene.
So muchel Y þenke vpon þe, þat al Y waxe grene.

Bituene Lyncolne ant Lyndeseye, Norhamptoun ant Lounde,
Ne wot Y non so fayr a may as Y go fore ybounde.
Suete lemmon, Y preȝe þe þou louie me a stounde.
20   Y wole mone my song
       On wham þat hit ys on ylong.

13 preȝe: *MS.* preeȝe.

XXXI. THE MAN IN THE MOON
(BM. MS. Harley 2253)

Mon in þe mone stond ant strit,
  On is bot-forke is burþen he bereþ;
Hit is muche wonder þat he nadoun slyt,
  For doute leste he valle, he shoddreþ ant shereþ.
5 When þe forst freseþ, muche chele he byd;
  þe þornes beþ kene, is hattren to-tereþ.
Nis no wyþt in þe world þat wot wen he syt,
  Ne, bote hit bue þe hegge, whet wedes he wereþ.

Whider trowe þis mon ha þe wey take?
10 He haþ set is o fot is oþer to-foren;
For non hiþte þat he haþ ne syþt me hym ner shake,
  He is þe sloweste mon þat euer wes yboren.

Wher he were o þe feld pycchynde stake,
For hope of ys þornes to dutten is doren,
15   He mot myd is twybyl oþer trous make,
Oþer al is dayes werk þer were yloren.

Þis ilke mon vpon heh when er he were,
Wher he were y þe mone boren ant yfed,
He leneþ on is forke ase a grey frere.
20   Þis crokede caynard sore he is adred.
Hit is mony day go þat he was here.
Ichot of is ernde he naþ nout ysped,
He haþ hewe sumwher a burþen of brere;
Þarefore sum hayward haþ taken ys wed.

25   Ʒef þy wed ys ytake, bring hom þe trous,
Sete forþ þyn oþer fot, stryd ouer sty.
We shule preye þe haywart hom to vr hous
Ant maken hym at heyse for þe maystry,
Drynke to hym deorly of fol god bous,
30   Ant oure Dame Douse shal sitten hym by.
When þat he is dronke ase a dreynt mous,
Þenne we schule borewe þe wed ate bayly.

Þis mon hereþ me nout þah ich to hym crye;
Ichot þe cherl is def, þe Del hym to-drawe!
35   Þah ich ȝeȝe vpon heþ nulle nout hye,
Þe lostlase ladde con nout o lawe.
Hupe forþ Hubert, hosede pye!
Ichot þart amarscled in-to þe mawe.
Þah me teone wiþ hym þat myn teh mye,
40   Þe cherld nul nout adoun er þe day dawe.

XXXII. THE FOLLIES OF FASHION
(BM. MS. Harley 2253)

Lord þat lenest vs lyf ant lokest vch-an lede,
Forte cocke wiþ knyf nast þou none nede,
Boþe wepmon ant wyf sore mowe drede
Lest þou be sturne wiþ strif for bone þat þou bede
5   In wunne,
Þat monkune
Shulde shilde hem from sunne.

Nou haþ prude þe pris in euervche plawe,
By mony wymmon vnwis Y sugge mi sawe,
10   For ȝef a ledy lyne is leid after lawe,
Vch a strumpet þat þer is such drahtes wl drawe;
     In prude
        Vch a screwe wol hire shrude
Þah he nabbe nout a smok hire foule ers to hude.

15   Furmest in boure were boses ybroht,
Leuedis to honoure, ichot he were wroht;
Vch gigelot wol loure bote he hem habbe soht,
Such shrewe fol soure ant duere hit haþ aboht.
        In helle
20   Wiþ deueles he shulle duelle,
For þe clogges þat cleueþ by here chelle.

Nou ne lackeþ hem no lyn boses in to beren;
He sitteþ ase a slat swyn þat hongeþ is eren.
Such a ioustynde gyn vch wrecche wol weren,
25   Al hit comeþ in declyn þis gigelotes geren.
        Vp o lofte
        Þe Deuel may sitte softe
Ant holden his halymotes ofte.

Ȝef þer lyþ a loket by er ouþer eȝe,
30   Þat mot wiþ worse be wet for lac of oþer leȝe,
Þe bout ant þe barbet wyþ frountel shule feȝe.
Habbe he a fauce filet he halt hire hed heȝe
        To shewe
        Þat heo be kud ant knewe
35   For strompet in rybaudes rewe.

                30 lac: *MS*. lat.

XXXIII. STELLA MARIS

(BM. MS. Egerton 613)

Of on þat is so fayr and briȝt
   velud maris stella,
Briȝter þan þe dayis liȝt,
   parens et puella,

5   Ic crie to þe, þu se to me,
     Leuedy, preye þi sone for me,
        tam pia,
     Þat ic mote come to þe,
        Maria.

10   Of kare conseil þou ert best,
        felix fecundata;
     Of alle wery þou ert rest,
        mater honorata.
     Bisek Him wit milde mod
15   Þat for ous alle sad Is blod
        in cruce,
     Þat we moten komen til Him
        in luce.

     Al þis world was forlore
20   *Eua peccatrice*
     Tyl our Lord was ybore
        de te genitrice;
     With *Aue* it went away,
     Þuster nyth, and comȝ þe **day**
25   *salutis,*
     Þe welle springet hut of þe
        uirtutis.

     Leuedi, flour of alle þing,
        rosa sine spina,
30   Þu bere Iesu, heuene-king,
        gratia diuina.
     Of alle þu berst þe pris,
     Leuedi, quene of parays
        electa,
35   Mayde milde moder *es*
        effecta.

     Wel He wot He is þi sone
        uentre quem portasti;
     He wyl nout werne þe þi bone
40   *paruum quem lactasti.*
     So hende and so god He his,
     He hauet brout ous to blis
        superni;
     Þat hauet hi-dut þe foule put
45   *inferni.*

XXXIV. THE GRAVE

(Trinity College, Cambridge, MS. 323)

Wen þe turuf is þi tuur,
And þi put is þi bour,
Þi wel and þi wite þrote
Ssulen wormes to note.
5   Wat helpit þe þenne
Al þe worilde wnne?

XXXV. UBI SUNT QUI ANTE NOS FUERUNT?

(Bodl. MS. Digby 86)

Uuere beþ þey biforen vs weren,
Houndes ladden and hauekes beren
And hadden feld and wode?
Þe riche leuedies in hoere bour,
5   Þat wereden gold in hoere tressour
Wiþ hoere briȝtte rode;

Eten and drounken and maden hem glad;
Hoere lif was al wiþ gamen ilad,
Men keneleden hem biforen,
10   Þey beren hem wel swiþe heye—
And in a twincling of on eye
Hoere soules weren forloren.

Were is þat lawing and þat song,
Þat trayling and þat proude ȝong,
15   Þo hauekes and þo houndes?
Al þat ioye is went away,
Þat wele is comen te weylaway,
To manie harde stoundes.

Hoere paradis hy nomen here,
20   And nou þey lien in helle ifere,
Þe fuir hit brennes heuere.
Long is 'ay' and long is 'ho',
Long is 'wy' and long is 'wo'—
Þennes ne comeþ þey neuere.

25 Dreȝy here, man, þenne if þou wilt,
    A luitel pine þat me þe bit,
      Wiþdrau þine eyses ofte,
    Þey þi pine be ounrede;
    And þou þenke on þi mede
30   Hit sal þe þinken softe.

    If þat fend, þat foule þing,
    Þorou wikke roun, þorou fals egging,
      Neþere þe haueþ icast,
    Oup and be god chaunpioun!
35 Stond, ne fal namore adoun
      For a luytel blast.

    Þou tak þe rode to þi staf,
    And þenk on Him þat þereonne ȝaf
      His lif þat wes so lef.
40 He hit ȝaf for þe, þou ȝelde hit Him,
    Aȝein His fo þat staf þou nim,
      And wrek Him of þat þef.

    Of riȝtte bileue, þou nim þat sheld,
    Þe wiles þat þou best in þat feld
45   Þin hond to strenkþen fonde,
    And kep þy fo wiþ staues ord,
    And do þat traytre seien þat word.
      Biget þat mvrie londe.

    Þereinne is day wiþhouten niȝt,
50 Wiþouten ende strenkþe and miȝt,
      And wreche of euerich fo,
    Mid God himselwen eche lif,
    And pes and rest wiþoute strif,
      Wele wiþouten wo.

55 Mayden moder, heuene quene,
    Þou miȝt and const and owest to bene
      Oure sheld aȝein þe fende;
    Help ous sunne for to flen,
    Þat we moten þi sone iseen
60   In ioye wiþouten hende.

        33 Neþere: *MS.* Þere neþere.

XXXVI. THE CRUCIFIXION
(BM. MS. Harley 2253)

'Stond wel, moder, vnder rode,
Byholt þy sone wiþ glade mode,
   Blyþe moder myht þou be!'
'Sone, hou shulde Y bliþe stonde?
5 Y se þin fet, Y se þin honde
   Nayled to þe harde tre.'

'Moder, do wey þy wepinge.
Y þole deþ for monkynde,
   For my gult þole Y non.'
10 'Sone, Y fele þe dedestounde,
Þe suert is at myn herte grounde
   Þat me byhet Symeon.'

'Moder, merci! Let me deye,
For Adam out of helle beye
15 Ant his kun þat is forlore.'
'Sone, what shal me to rede?
My peyne pyneþ me to dede.
   Lat me deʒe þe byfore.'

'Moder, þou rewe al of þi bern,
20 Þou wosshe awai þe blody tern;
   Hit doþ me worse þen my ded.'
'Sone, hou may Y teres werne?
Y se þe blody stremes erne
   From þin herte to my fet.'

25 'Moder, nou Y may þe seye,
Betere is þat ich one deye
   Þen al monkunde to helle go.'
'Sone, Y se þi bodi byswngen,
Fet ant honden þourhout stongen;
30 No wonder þah me be wo!'

'Moder, now Y shal þe telle,
ʒef Y ne deʒe, þou gost to helle;
   Y þole ded for þine sake.'
'Sone, þou art so meke ant mynde,
35 Ne wyt me naht, hit is my kynde,
   Þat Y for þe þis sorewe make.'

'Moder, nou þou miht wel leren
Whet sorewe haueþ þat children beren,
   Whet sorewe hit is wiþ childe gon.'
40 'Sorewe ywis Y con þe telle;
Bote hit be þe pyne of helle,
   More serewe wot Y non.'

'Moder, rew of moder kare,
For nou þou wost of moder fare,
45   Þou þou be clene mayden-mon.'
'Sone, help at alle nede
Alle þo þat to me grede,
   Maiden, wif, and fol wymmon.'

'Moder, may Y no lengore duelle,
50 Þe time is come Y shal to helle;
   Þe þridde day Y ryse vpon.'
'Sone, Y wil wiþ Þe founden,
Y deye ywis for Þine wounden,
   So soreweful ded nes neuer non.'

55 When He ros, þo fel hire sorewe,
Hire blisse sprong þe þridde morewe.
   Blyþe moder were þou þo!
Leuedy, for þat ilke blisse,
Bysech þi sone of sunnes lisse;
60   Þou be oure sheld aȝeyn oure fo!

Blessed be þou, ful of blysse.
Let vs neuer heuene misse,
   Þourh þi suete sones myht!
Louerd, for þat ilke blod
65 Þat Þou sheddest on þe rod,
   Þou bryng vs in-to heuene lyht!
                   Amen.

XXXVII. PENITENCE
(Bodl. MS. Digby 2)

No more ne willi wiked be,
Forsake ich wille þis worldis fe.
Þis wildis wedis, þis folen gle;
   Ich wul be mild of chere,
5 Of cnottis scal mi girdil be,
   Becomen ich wil frere.

Frer menur I wil me make,
And lecherie I wille asake;
To Iesu Crist ich wil me take
10   And serue in holi churche,
Al in mi ouris for to wake,
    Goddis wille to wurche.

Wurche I wille þis workes gode,
For Him þat boþht us in þe rode;
15 Fram His side ran þe blode,
    So dere He gan vs bie—
For sothe I tel him mor þan wode
    Þat hantit licherie.

XXXVIII. AN INTERLUDE

THE importance of this fragment is that it is one of the very few examples of secular drama that have survived from the ME period; till recently it was believed to be the only surviving example of drama of any kind in the vernacular before the fourteenth century.[1] Although only a fragment remains, the general outline of the plot is clear enough, since there is evidently a close connection between this work and the thirteenth-century fabliau *Dame Siriʒ*. There are verbal resemblances and even identity of lines between the two, and although it is quite clear that neither is to be derived directly from the other, the probability is that both are derived independently from a common original—probably an interlude, since *Dame Siriʒ* is fairly obviously the re-working of an earlier interlude into a fabliau. Whether this original was derived from French or English is impossible to say. The theme is found in contemporary French fabliaux, but must certainly have been known also in this country. Nor do the personal names in the two extant versions give any help; some are English, some French, but all were in use in England during the ME period.

Nothing is known of the author; the date of the MS. is *c.* 1300, and it is impossible to say how much earlier this particular version of the story was in existence. As far as the provenance is concerned the only available evidence is that of the dialect in which the text is written, and this suggests North Lincs., or South Yorks.; at any rate some district in which Northern forms were usual, but in which some Midland forms were also to be found. The interlude is preserved in a single MS., British Museum Add. 23986, and has frequently been printed, e.g. by G. H. McKnight, *Middle English Humorous Tales in Verse* (Boston, U.S.A., 1913), and in many ME readers. The stage directions given below are not in the MS.

SCENE I

Maiden's home: enter Cleric and Maiden

CLER. Damishel, reste wel!
MAID. Sir, welcum, by Saynt Michel!

---

[1] But see R. H. Robbins, 'An English Mystery Play Fragment ante 1300' (65 *MLN* 30-35).

CLER. Wer es ty sire? Wer es ty dame?
MAID. By Gode, es noþer her at hame.
5 CLER. Wel wor suilc a man to life,
    Þat suilc a may mithe haue to wyfe!
MAID. Do way, by Crist and Leonard!
    No wil Y lufe na clerc fayllard;
    Na kep I herbherg clerc in huse no y flore,
10   Bot his hers ly wit-uten dore.
    Go forth þi way, god sire,
    For her hastu losyt al þi hire.
CLER. Nu, nu, by Crist and by Sant Jhon,
    In al þis land ne wist I none,
15   Mayden, þat hi luf mor þan þe;
    Hif me micht euer þe bether be!
    For þe hy sory nicht and day;
    Y may say, 'Hay, wayleuay!'
    Y luf þe mar þan mi lif,
20   Þu hates me mar þan gayt dos chnief.
    Þat es noutt for mysgilt.
    Certhes, for þi luf ham hi spilt.
    A, suythe mayden, reu of me,
    Þat es ty luf, hand ay sal be!
25   For þe luf of þe moder of efne,
    Þu mend þi mode, and her my steuene.
MAID. By Crist of heuene, and Sant Jone!
    Clerc of scole ne kep I non,
    For many god wymman haf þai don scam—
30   By Crist, þu michtis haf be at hame!
CLER. Syn it n[o] oþir gat may be,
    Jesu Crist bytech Y þe,
    And send neulic bot tharinne,
    Þat Y be lesit of al my pine.
35 MAID. Go nu, truan, go nu, go,
    For mikel canstu of sory and wo!

SCENE II

Mome Helwis' house: enter Cleric and Helwis

CLER. God te blis, mome Helwis.
MOME HELWIS. Son, welcum, by San Dinis!

12 losyt, hire: *MS*. losye, wile. 20 gayt: *MS*. yayt *apparently though* y *is badly rubbed.*
25 þe moder: *MS*. þ mod. 31 syn: *MS*. synt. 33 neulic: *MS*. neulit. 34 Y:
MS. yi.

CLER.   Hic am comin to þe, mome;
40   Þu hel me noth, þu say me sone.
          Hic am a clerc þat hauntes scole;
          Y lydy my lif wyt mikel dole;
          Me wor lever to be dedh
          Þan led the lif þat hyc ledh,
45   For ay mayden with and schen—
          Fayrer ho lond haw Y non syen.
          Yo hat mayden Malkyn, Y wene—
          Nu þu wost quam Y mene;
          Yo wonys at the tounes ende,
50   Þat suyt lif, so fayr and hende;
          Bot if yo wil hir mod amende,
          Neuly Crist my ded me send!
          Men send me hyder vytuten fayle,
          To haf þi help an ty cunsayle.
55   Þarfor am Y cummen here,
          Þat þu salt be my herandbere,
          To mac me and þat mayden sayct,
          And hi sal gef þe of myn ayct,
          So þat hever, al þi lyf,
60   Saltu be þe better wyf;
          So help me Crist—and hy may spede
          Riche saltu haf þi mede!
MOME HELWIS. A, son, vat saystu? *Benedicite*!
          Lift hup þi hand, and blis þe!
65   For it es boþt syn and scam
          Þat þu on me hafs layt thys blam;
          For Yc am an ald quyne and a lam;
          Y led my lyf wit Godis gram;
          Wit my roc Y me fede;
70   Can I do non othir dede
          Bot my *Pater Noster* and my *Crede*,
          (To say Crist for missedede),
          And myn *Avy Mary*
          (For my scynnes hic am sory).
75   And my *De Profundis*
          (For al that yn sin lys);
          For can I me non oþir þink,
          Þat wot Crist, of hevene kync,
          Jesu Crist, of hevene hey,

80

Gef that þay may heng hey,
And gef þat hy may se
Þat þay be heng on a tre
Þat þis ley as leyit onne me,
For aly wyman am I on.

CHARACTERISTICS OF EARLY MIDDLE ENGLISH

THE Norman Conquest marks an important stage in the history of the English language, though its full effects are not apparent till later than might have been expected. It has been usual to speak of the OE period as extending to 1100, but 1150 is probably a better limit. During the first half of the century vernacular literature is still being written in the WS standard literary language, and no literature that survives in ME is earlier than the middle of the century. Moreover, the chief effects of the Conquest are to be seen in other than the obvious places. It is, of course, responsible for the presence of numerous French loan words, though these begin to appear in the language before the Conquest and do not become unduly numerous till the fourteenth century. More important is the fact that with the Conquest Wessex loses both its political and its literary supremacy. No one dialect has a claim to be considered superior to the rest, and each author is free to use his own. By the end of the ME period the increasing importance of London means that henceforward the dialect of the capital will be supreme. This had originally been a Southern—mainly South-Eastern—dialect, but by the fourteenth century it had become mainly East Midland in character. Consequently modern Standard English is to be derived, not from WS, but, in the main, from an East Mercian dialect. On the orthography, too, the Conquest had a considerable influence which was expressed in two ways. Before the end of the OE period the spelling had become more or less fixed, and was in consequence some 150 to 200 years behind the actual pronunciation. The gradual disappearance of English-trained scribes and their replacement by professional French-trained scribes brought about the breakdown of the old convention, and a new orthography had to be developed based on the spoken language. The result is that sound-changes which had taken place during the OE period, but were not yet represented in the written language, are first regularly recorded in the more phonetic spelling of post-Conquest scribes. Moreover, this spelling is strongly influenced by the French. For example OE *c* under certain conditions had been fronted to the *tch* sound, but was still represented by *c*. Consequently that symbol in OE stood for two entirely different sounds, [k] and [tʃ]. Post-Conquest scribes coming across the latter sound represented it in the way in which it was represented in France, namely by *ch*. Hence the later scribes were responsible for two different types of change, the discrimination between sounds originally identical but long since fallen apart, and the introduction of new characters and scribal devices. Palaeographically, too, the Conquest is responsible for a change in script. Anglo-Saxon England had obtained much of its learning from Ireland, and used a script Latin in origin but considerably modified by Celtic influence. From the tenth century use is occasionally made of the new Carolingian script which had been developed on the continent. After the Conquest this continental script was naturally used by French-trained scribes, and it remained in use, with some changes, until the fifteenth and sixteenth centuries. On English syntax, too, it is probable that French influence was appreciable, though until the publication of the projected Middle English dictionary it will be impossible to assess this influence properly. On the other hand there is not the slightest evidence to show that the Conquest had any effect on the accidence or the phonology. ME is marked by a general tendency to level all inflexional vowels under -*e*, but it is clear that the tendency to analogize grammatical forms has always been inherent in the language. It is to be seen at work already in lOE, and was no doubt greatly accelerated by the close intermixture of Danes and Anglo-Saxons in the Danelaw. Similarly with the phonology. Although ME is characterized by widespread changes in phonology, the beginnings of those changes are to be found in the OE period. What the Conquest did was to break down a spelling convention.

Early ME orthography is based partly on the traditional OE, and partly on Anglo-French. Many of the OE vowels and diphthongs continue to be written, especially in the earlier texts, long after they must have changed in sound, but it is important to remember that in ME many of the changes in the form of the word are merely orthographical and do not indicate any corresponding change in the pronunciation.

OE *y* had the sound represented in Fr. by *u*, and consequently when AF scribes came across the sound in ME they represented it in the way in which it was represented in their own language. The result is that where the high-front-rounded sound remains in ME it is always written *u*, never *y*, and similarly *ȳ* is written *u, ui, uy* These spellings had become usual by the end of the twelfth century and the scribes then had a spare letter, *y*, available. This they used as a spelling for *i* in positions where the use of *i* might have been ambiguous, i.e. before and after nasals, *u* and *w*, which, consisting as they did of a series of strokes similar to that used for *i*, could be easily misread in the neighbourhood of the latter letter. The writing of *y* for *i* in these positions became common, and by the fourteenth century it had come to be used in positions where there was no risk of ambiguity. In ME *y* never stands for the high-front-rounded sound but is invariably a spelling for *ĭ*. For similar reasons *u* in the same positions is written *o*,[1] a spelling which becomes common during the thirteenth century. In the fourteenth *o* is often written for *u* where there is no danger of ambiguity, and note, too, that initial *u* is frequently written *v*. In the thirteenth century *ū* comes to be written *ou/ow*.

In the consonants many ambiguities of the OE consonant system were cleared up. OE *c* had been used for both the front and the back sounds; in ME the front *c* is regularly represented by *ch* (medially by *cch*, later *tch*), while the back sound continues to be represented by *c*, though at a comparatively early date *k* is used interchangeably with *c*. Before long the use of the two is standardized, *c* being used before back vowels and liquids, *k* before front vowels and *n*, but Fr. *c* is also used for *-ts-*, e.g. *blecen*, etc., and for *s*, e.g. *ice*, etc. Similarly OE *cw-* is represented by *qu-*. OE *g* was used for three different sounds, a voiced back stop [g], a front spirant [j], and a voiced back spirant [ʒ], and these are usually represented differently in ME. The back stop continues to be spelled *g*, but for the front spirant a new symbol, known as *yogh/ʒok* and represented by ʒ, is developed from the OE insular *g*. By the fourteenth century this tends to be replaced by *i/y*, and ʒ gradually disappears from English during the fifteenth century. It remains in use in Scots until the introduction of printing, and the early printers represented it by ʓ, this being the letter already present in their founts of type which was nearest to it in appearance. Some words and names, with ʓ standing for an earlier ʒ, are still so spelled (as Dalziel, capercailzie, gaberlunzie, Menzies, McKenzie, Kirkgunzeon, etc.), and, though

[1] As an example of the confusion which this spelling was designed to avoid cf. Sir Henry Newbolt's historical novel, *The New June*, which centres round the London house of one of the great magnates of the late fourteenth and early fifteenth century. The name appears to be due to the misreading of capital *I* as *J* and of *nn* as *un*. The building was really called *The New Inne*, a much more probable name for a medieval house.

the historically correct pronunciation would be [j], a new spelling
pronunciation has not infrequently developed. The voiced back
spirant, OE *g* between back vowels, is normally vocalized to *u* in
eME, and joins with the preceding vowel to form a diphthong, but
in early texts it is sometimes represented by ȝ, e.g. *daȝes*, *laȝe*, etc.
OE *-cg* is regularly written *gg* in ME, and the same sound in Fr.
loans is represented initially by *i/j*, medially by *gg*, e.g. ME *seggen*,
ioye, *jugge*, etc. In ME *h* comes to be used as a spelling for the
aspirate only, though it should be noted that initial *h-* is often prefixed in ME to words which had none in OE; this was due to the
influence of French, in which initial *h-* was already silent. The OE
voiceless spirant, whether back or front, was represented by ȝ (less
frequently *h*) in the early period, by *gh* later, e.g. *fiȝt/fight*, *poȝte/*
poughte, etc. The OE voiceless consonants *hl-*, *hn-*, *hr-*, are voiced in
most dialects and fall in with the ordinary voiced *l-*, *n-*, *r-*. *Hw-* is
also voiced in some ME dialects and represented by *w*, but it
remains as a voiceless sound in most, spelled *wh-*. In Northumbrian, however, the sound represented was a spirant plus *w* [χw]
and this remains in the N dialect of ME represented by *qu-*, *quh-*, *qw-*,
etc. Hence OE *hwæt*, ME. *wat*, *what*, *quhat*, etc. OE *sc* is usually
written *sch* in eME, later *ssh*, *sh*, but in the SE and neighbouring
dialects *s*, *ss*, are not uncommon. *s* is normally written for both the
voiced and the voiceless sounds, but *ȝ* is occasionally found for
the former. In OE *f* similarly was used for both the voiced and
voiceless sounds, but in ME was restricted to the voiceless sound,
the voiced sound being written *v/u* initially and *u* medially. The
runic *þ* (*þorn*) continues to be used side by side with *ð* until well into
the thirteenth century, when *ð* falls into disuse. In the fourteenth
century *th* is used more and more frequently by the side of *þ*. The
latter, however, continues in use throughout the period, especially
initially, and is still used by the early printers in abbreviations—
which eased the 'justification' of their lines. The letter in their
founts most resembling it is *y*, and hence such forms as *yᵉ*, *yᵗ* (for
the, *that*), appear in printed works for some time, the former surviving into current English as the pseudo-archaic *Ye*. The runic
letter *p* (*wynn*) continues in use until the end of the thirteenth
century, often confused with *þ* and *y*. But after the Conquest *u*,
uu, and *w*, are also used, and in the fourteenth century *w* becomes
the normal spelling. It should be emphasized that these are the usual
orthographical developments, but that in some (more particularly

the earlier) ME texts there are often distinctive peculiarities in the spelling, especially in the representation of the spirants: e.g. *Driste* 6/2, *mist* 10/78, *mistie* 6/30, *rist* 9/25, *ristnesse* 6/7, *follost broste* 6/19, for *Driʒte*, etc., and conversely *nuʒte* 10/173, for *nuste*; *cnipte* 6/3, *hipte* 31/11, *miptie* 6/25, *ript* 29/17, *sypt* 31/11, *wypt* 31/7, *heþ* 31/35 (beside *heh* 31/17), *napt* 10/162, *bopht* 37/14, *popwethere* 2/61, for *cniʒte*, etc., and conversely *comʒ* 33/24, for *comþ*; *þurhte* 20/95, for *þurfte*; *wurhliche* 28/9, *worhliche* 28/40, for *wurð*.[1] These peculiarities, which were partly at any rate due to the unfamiliarity of French-trained scribes with the English back and front spirants, have sometimes fared ill at the hands of modern editors, though they should be regarded as genuine spelling variants and as such preserved.

The conventional grouping of the ME dialects corresponds roughly with that of the OE ones:

1. *Northumbrian* splits into *Scots* and *Northern English*, but it seems probable that the distinction does not arise till after the end of this period. In any case no Northern texts earlier than the end of the thirteenth century have been preserved, and Scots literature does not begin until the latter part of the fourteenth.

2. *Mercian* is divided into *East Midland* and *West Midland*. By the end of the Danish wars Mercia had been partitioned, East Mercia having been overrun by the Danes and forming part of the Danelaw, while West Mercia had been incorporated into the West Saxon kingdom. The East Midland dialect approximates more closely to Northern English, whereas the West Midland dialect has much in common with Southern speech.

3. *West Saxon* is the basis of the *South Western* and *Central Southern* dialects.

4. *Kentish* is the basis of the *South Eastern* dialects.

The sound changes which, conventionally, distinguish OE from ME—it must be emphasized again that many of them had taken place already during the lOE period—can conveniently be divided into quantitative and qualitative. Of the former the most important was the lengthening of short vowels which took place:

1. Before certain consonant groups. Already by the end of the OE period, lengthening appears to have taken place before any liquid or nasal plus single voiced consonant, e.g. *ld*, *rd*, *rl*, *mb*,

---

[1] The Laʒamon forms all come from the later text (O).

etc. However, most of such vowels were shortened again during the eME period, and lengthening usually remained only before:

-*ld*, where it is preserved in all dialects throughout the period, e.g. Ang. *áld*>ME *ọ́ld*>NE *old*; OE *féld*>NE *field*; OE *wílde*>NE *wild*.

-*mb*, preserved in all dialects throughout the period, e.g. OE *cámb*> ME *cọmb*; OE *clímban*>ME *clímben*, etc.

-*nd*. During the thirteenth century all vowels except *i* and *u* were shortened again in the N and NM dialects, and during the four-teenth century these shortened forms made their way southwards into the London dialect. Hence NE *bind, bound*, as compared with *send, hand, bond*.

-*ng*. Lengthening remains in most dialects during most of the period, but by the end of the fourteenth century all such length-ened vowels have been shortened again.

Lengthening does not take place if a third consonant follows, e.g. OE *cíld*>NE *child*, but OE *cíldru*>NE *children*. The short vowel remains also in trisyllabic words, e.g. NE *alderman*, cf. NE *old*, and in unaccented words, e.g. *and, wolde, sholde*, etc.

2. In open syllables of disyllabic words. This lengthening took place in most dialects in the first half of the thirteenth century. The comparative lateness of this lengthening is shown by the fact that, whereas vowels lengthened before consonant groups fell in with OE long vowels and shared their development, those lengthened in open syllables were kept apart. Note, too, that in the case of *ē* and *ō* ME had long tense vowels—conventionally represented by *ẹ̄, ọ̄*—and long slack vowels—conventionally represented by *ẹ̣, ọ̣*. In the case of the *ē* sounds the difference between the two corresponds fairly closely with the difference in sound between OE *ē* and *ǣ*. The distinction between the tense and slack sounds is important in that they have different developments during the modern period. Consequently it is important to remember that *e, o* lengthened before consonant groups are lengthened to the tense vowels, but in open syllables to the slack vowels. Lengthening of *i* and *u* occurs mainly in the N, and is accompanied by a change in quality to tense *ē* and tense *ō* respectively, e.g. OE *biden*>ME *bẹ̄den*; OE *duru*>ME *dọ̄re*, etc. Occasional words showing the change made their way south-wards and thence into StE, e.g. *beetle, evil, wood*, etc. As far as the general lengthening is concerned many analogous forms are to be found in the ME dialects. Disyllabic words would become trisyllabic

when inflected, and consequently would have a lengthened vowel in the n. but a short one in the oblique cases. Similarly words might be monosyllabic in the n. but disyllabic in the oblique cases, e.g. *staf/stāves* and again analogical forms might develop in both directions. Such analogical forms are reflected in NE, where such words may be from a long or a short vowel in ME, cf. e.g. NE *staff/ stave, saddle/cradle, seven/beaver*, where each pair of words has the same accented vowel or diphthong in OE.

The tendency towards the shortening of long vowels is much less important and consistent. The earliest change seems to have been a shortening before three consonants. This was followed by shortening before double consonant plus *r*, before two consonants in polysyllabic words, before double consonants, before two consonants in monosyllabic and disyllabic words, and finally before single consonants in polysyllabic words. Hence such NE forms as *bramble, adder, brought, taught, thought, holiday, empty*, etc., all had in OE long vowels which were shortened.

The changes in quality are much more extensive and important than the changes in quantity. The following are the more important, and it should be noted that the forms in modern StE are normally derived from EM forms:

OE *a* appears as *o* before a nasal in the WM, e.g. *mon, con*, etc. In the SW *a/o* forms appear side by side; *a* is usual in all other dialects. Some *o* forms appear in StE, e.g. *strong, long, song*, etc., and cf. also the personal names *Long, Strong*, but *Lang* (Sc. *Laing*), *Strang*. In these cases the *o* forms in StE are probably due rather to lengthening of *a* before *ng*, the subsequent rounding of *ā* to *ō*, and later shortening.

OE *æ* gave *e* in the SE and SWM. In the latter this *e* was replaced by *a* from about 1300, and in the former from about 1400. In early SW texts *a/e* forms appear side by side, but the *e* forms gradually disappear. In the N/EM/NWM, *a* forms are regular.

OE *y* gave *i* in N/EM, *e* in SE, and remained spelled *u* in SW/WM. The *i* forms will be normal in StE, but some *e* forms remain (*merry, knell, left*, etc.) and some *u* forms (*cudgel, rush, shut*, etc.), whilst in *bury, busy*, the SW/WM spelling has survived, but in the former the SE pronunciation, in the latter the normal EM.

OE *ā* was rounded to slack *ō* south of the Humber, i.e. in EM/WM/ SE/SW, probably during the twelfth century, but remained in the N. The distinction remains in modern dialects, the N having a

front diphthong developed from ME $\bar{a}$, the M and S a back diphthong from ME $\bar{o}$. Cf. also Sc. *laird, raid*, but S/M *lord, road*.

OE $\bar{æ}$ comes from two different sources, the fronting of $\bar{a}$ and the *i*-
mutation of $\bar{a}$. These had different developments in the different
OE dialects, and consequently different results appear in ME.
The $\bar{æ}$ from fronting—conventionally referred to as $\bar{æ}^1$—remained
only in WS; in all other dialects it was raised to $\bar{e}$ in PrOE. The
$\bar{æ}$ from *i*-mutation—conventionally $\bar{æ}^2$—was raised to $\bar{e}$ in K,
but remained elsewhere. Where OE had $\bar{æ}$ the corresponding
ME dialect will have slack $\bar{e}$; where OE had $\bar{e}$ the result will be
tense $\bar{e}$ in ME. Consequently $\bar{æ}^1$ and $\bar{æ}^2$ fall together in tense $\bar{e}$ in
the SE, and in slack $\bar{e}$ in the SW, but in the N and M the two are
differentiated, $\bar{æ}^1$ appearing as tense $\bar{e}$, $\bar{æ}^2$ as slack $\bar{e}$. The difference
in quality between the two vowels is important in that they have
different developments in the later language, but in ME texts
it is not as a rule easy to tell whether the vowel be tense or slack,
since the spelling is usually the same in any case. Only in rhyme
is it perhaps possible to distinguish them, and even here there are
difficulties. It is frequently said that a good medieval poet would
not rhyme the tense and slack vowels together—a statement more
easily made than proved. It may be true that poets such as
Chaucer and Gower would not rhyme the two if they could help
it, but it is quite clear that many medieval poets in fact did, and
not all the examples of such rhymes can be emended away or
explained by the postulation of further sound changes. It must
remain doubtful whether tenseness or slackness in a vowel can
in fact be deduced from the rhyme, and arguments based thereon
cannot safely be used to determine the dialect of a ME text.

OE $\bar{o}$ remains as tense $\bar{o}$ in all dialects except the N, where it is raised
and fronted to [$\bar{y}$], spelled *u, ui, uy*, e.g. *flode/flude, boke/buik*, etc.

OE $\bar{y}$ has the same development as the short vowel; it is unrounded
to $\bar{\imath}$ in the N/EM, lowered to $\bar{e}$ in the SE, and remains spelled *ui,
uy*, in the SW/WM.

The OE diphthongs were all monophthongized in ME and, except
to some extent in the SE, never gave diphthongs in ME[1]: *ie*
occurred mainly in WS and had already been monophthongized

---

[1] But place-name evidence suggests that in some dialects OE *ea* may have given a
diphthong in ME, though no evidence for this appears in the literary texts; see H. Hall-
qvist, *Studies in Old English Fractured* ea (Lund 1948), and *The Place-Names of Devon*
(8 EPNS), p. xxxiii.

to *i/y* by the time of Alfred. In the main ME simply developes differences originating in OE.

OE *ea* had been monophthongized to *æ* before the end of the OE period. This fell in with OE *æ*, and like it developed to *a* in the N/EM/WM, and to *e* in the SE/SWM/SW, though *a* forms make their way into these dialects at an early date, and variation between *e* and *a* is not uncommon, e.g. *yard/yerd*, *harm/herm*, etc. Before *l* + cons. there were differences in OE; fronting, and fracture of *a* did not take place in Anglian before *l* + cons. (occasionally also before some *r* groups), hence WS/K *eald*, *ceald*, Ang. *ald*, *cald*. Moreover, in these cases lengthening of the vowel or diphthong would take place before the lengthening group and the result would fall in with the OE long vowel or diphthong and have the same development. Hence

WS/K *eald*>lWS/K *ēald*>SW *ēld*, SE *eald*; cf. NE *Weald*.

Ang. *ald* >lAng. *ǻld* > EM/WM *ǭld*, N *ǻld*; cf. NE *Wolds*.

The mutation is to *ie* in WS, hence WS *dierne*>lWS *dyrne*>SW *durne*, but to *e* in nWS, hence nWS *derne*>N/EM/WM/SE *derne*. Before *l* + cons. WS/K will have mutation of *ea* (to *ie* in the former, to *e* in the latter), whereas in Ang. the mutation will be of *a* to *æ*. Hence

WS *wielle*>lWS *wylle*>SW *wulle*.

K *welle*   >   SE *welle*.

Ang. *wælle*   >   (N/EM) WM *walle*.

e forms appear to have been frequent also in the S. Midlands and to have made their way at a very early date into the EM and N, with the result that *a* forms in ME are distinctively WM.

OE *eo* became *e* in N/EM/SE during the twelfth century, but in the SW/WM it was monophthongized to a rounded sound *ö*, spelled *eo*, *o*, *ue*, *u*, which remained until the fourteenth century, when it was gradually replaced by *e* forms from the other dialects.

Mutation was to *ie* in WS, but elsewhere to *io* which appears to have remained in the N but otherwise became *eo* again. Hence

WS *hierde*, *ierre*>lWS *hyrde*, *yrre*>SW *hurde*, *urre*.

Nh *hiorde*, *iorre*   >   N *hirde*, *irre*.

M/K *heorde*, *eorre* > EM/SE *herde*, *erre*; WM *heorde*, *eorre*.

OE *ēa* was monophthongized to *ǣ* in lOE. This fell together with *ǣ*[2] and, like it, gave slack *ē* in all dialects in ME except the SE. In the SE OE *ēa* appears to have become a rising diphthong during the twelfth century, perhaps (*ie*), spelled *ea*, *ia*, *ya*, *yea*.

This remains initially and after a dental but otherwise became tense *ē*. Hence

OE *dēad, hēafod*>N/EM/WM/SW *dẹ̄de, hẹ̄ued*: SE *dyead, heaued*. The mutation was to *ie* in WS, but elsewhere to *ē*. Hence

WS *hīeran*>lWS *hȳran*>SW *huiren*.

Ang./K *hēran* > N/EM/WM/SE *hēren*.

OE *ēo* had the same development as short *eo*, except that the diphthong did not exist in K, which had *īo*. Hence

WS/M/Nh *dēop*>N/EM *dēpe*; SW/WM *deope*.

K *īo* became the *ie* diphthong in eME. This became *ī* finally, but remained initially and after a dental, otherwise becoming *ē*. Hence

K *dīop*>SE *dyepe*. K *flīon*>SE *vlȳ*.

The WS mutation was to *ie*, but in other dialects, apart from K, the result was *ēo*. Hence

WS *dīere*>lWS *dȳre*>SW *duyre*.

Nh/M *dēore*>N/EM *dēre*; WM *deore*.

K *dīore* > SE *dyere*.

ME developments from the distinctively WS forms are comparatively rare, even in early SW texts. At an early period forms derived from non-WS mutated forms appear to have made their way into the SW and are found side by side with the forms that might have been expected to be regular, ousting them completely at a comparatively early date. The same is true of forms developed from OE fractured forms before *l* + cons. Here again unfractured forms appear early and become usual. It is doubtful whether such forms are really to be regarded as intrusions from nWS districts. In all probability the comparative regularity of the late WS written language was not shared by the spoken language. In the early period fractured and unfractured forms appear to have existed side by side, and the mutations were by no means regular. In the later literary language the irregularities have been smoothed out, but probably still continued to exist in the spoken language, and it is from the spoken, not the written, language that the SW dialect of ME is developed.

It should be clear, too, that the conventional division into five dialects during the ME period is much more convenient than real. Each of the main dialectal areas would be made up of a number of dialects, agreeing in some characteristics but varying to a greater or lesser extent between themselves. It is clear, for example, that there

F

were considerable differences between the northern and the southern forms of the WM dialect, and the same was probably true of the EM dialect. Nor would it be possible to indicate on a map the exact boundaries of these dialects, though for the sake of convenience approximate ones are often enough given. In reality, of course, a dialect rarely has precise boundaries, the characteristics of the different dialects shading gradually into each other. There was hardly such a thing as a pure consistent dialect in ME, any more than in NE, nor is there any reason why there should have been. An occasional text has been preserved in a comparatively consistent orthography, but in such cases it was written near the middle of the dialect area, e.g. Dan Michel's *Aȝenbite*, or else its very consistency suggests the use of some 'standard' dialect, as in the case of the Corpus MS. of the *Ancrene Wisse*. Away from the centre of the area any dialect will tend to be influenced by its neighbours, so that the actual spoken language will be of a mixed type dialectally. More-over, in the extant MSS. confusion is increased by the scribes. Throughout the period a book could be made known to its readers only by the slow and costly multiplication of manuscripts. The copyist might work long after the date of the original composition of the work, and he would then be likely to modernize the language, though unlikely to do this consistently. Again, if the dialect of the original were unfamiliar to the copyist, words and forms from his own dialect would tend to creep into the text, whether intentionally or not. The general result is that the dialect of any ME text is to a greater or less extent the product of its own textual history. Certainly, almost all the extant ME texts show a mixed dialect, and, though in the past it has been usual to attribute this to scribal corruption, it seems probable that in most cases the language of the author was also mixed, and not all the aberrant forms are to be attributed to later scribes—some of whom, in fact, may rather have tended to regularize the language of the text which they were copying. The result of all this is that in the present state of our knowledge it is impossible to localize exactly, on linguistic evidence alone, any ME text. In the absence of external evidence all that we can do is to assign it in general terms to one of the major dialectal divisions, and a more precise localization is always to be suspect.

Along with the monophthongization of the OE diphthongs went the development of a large number of new diphthongs of an entirely different type from the OE, with a second element in *-i* or *-u* (sometimes written -*y*, -*w*). It is probable that all ME diphthongs were short; some are occasionally marked long in the text-books, but this only indicates that the first element was long before the diphthong was formed, and there is no reason to believe that it remained long. The formation of new diphthongs in ME is due mainly to the following causes:

1. Intervocalic and final postvocalic -*w* combined with the preceding vowel to form a diphthong of the -*u* type during the first half of the twelfth century, e.g. OE *sāwol*>ME *soule*; OE *dēaw*> ME *deu*; OE *hēow*>ME *heu*; OE *blōwan*>ME *blowen*, etc.

2. OE front *g*, and the voiced back spirant represented by *g*, were vocalized to *i* and *u* respectively. In the former case the *i* combined with the preceding vowel to form an *i* diphthong, in the latter case a *u* diphthong was the result. Hence OE *dæg*>ME *dai*; OE *weg*>ME *wei*; OE *ægþer*>ME *eiþer*; OE *lagu*>ME *lawe*; OE *dagas*>ME *dawes*; OE *boga* >ME *bowe*, etc.

3. A glide developed between a vowel and a following front or back *h*. In the former case the result was an *i* diphthong, in the latter a *u* diphthong, but in some of the N and EM dialects diphthongization in these positions did not invariably take place. Hence lOE *seh*>ME *seigh*; OE *dohtor*>ME *doughter*; OE *þōhte*> *pouȝte*, etc.

In accidence ME occupies an intermediate position between the well-developed inflexional system of OE and the almost complete loss of inflexions to be observed in NE. The following points may be noted. In some dialects grammatical gender appears to have been lost early in the period, but in the southern ones remnants of it may survive till the end of the thirteenth century. As far as the inflexions are concerned, a g. in -*es* is usual, but the only other is an occasional gpl. in -*ene* (OE -*ena*); though the n/apl. without ending of the OE long stem neuters is found occasionally in such words as *þing*, *word*, etc., as late as the fourteenth century. Similarly the old gf. still survives occasionally, even into NE, e.g. *Ladyday* (cf. *Lord's Day*). But most ME masc. nouns fall within a pattern, sg. in consonant or -*e* and pl. in -*es*, and most fem. and neuter nouns have come over into this declension. More of the mutation plurals survive than are to be found in NE, e.g. *bec*, *geet*, *ky*, as well as *feet*, *men*, etc., and a relic of the OE weak declension pl. in -*an* is still to be found in NE *oxen*; while *brethren*, *children*, *kine*, which were strong in OE took a weak ending in ME. In the N dialects of ME most weak nouns very early go over to the strong declension and take a pl. in *-es*, the only common nouns to retain the weak ending throughout the period being *oxen* and *een*, while *shoon*, although a strong noun in OE, is also not infrequent. In the S weak plurals are much more frequent and remain longer, while it is not uncommon for nouns originally strong to go over to the weak declension and to take a pl. in *-en*, e.g. *deoflen*, *englen*, etc. It should be noted, too, that some of the old inflexions remain in fossil form, even in NE; e.g. *seldom*, *whilom*, retain the old dpl. which in OE was often used adverbially. Similarly the g. remains in *needs* (*must*), (*early*) *days*, *once* (OE *ānes*), *twice*, *thrice*, etc. NE *alive* is OE *on life* d., cf. NE *life*, where the variation between *f* and *v* shows that *alive* represents the inflected dative, and must have become established as an independent word before the loss of inflexions; in *abed*, *asleep*, *aboard*, no trace of the inflexion remains.

In general the adjectival inflexions are lost at an early date in ME. The strong adjective ending in a consonant has no inflexion in the sg.; otherwise *-e* is usual both strong and weak, sg. and pl. Occasional survivals of the OE declension are to be found, more particularly in some of the early texts, and it is sometimes possible to distinguish survivals of the weak declension, but in general the adj., even in eME, is well on its way to the uninflected forms of NE.

In the pronouns the most important variations are to be found in the feminine pronoun, and in the pl. of the 3rd personal pronoun. In ME the feminine pronoun of the third person can have one of two basic forms:

1. It can be the regular descendant of OE *hēo* which appears in a variety of forms. The commonest are SE *hi*, *he*; SW *heo*, *ha*, *he*; WM *hue*, *ho*, *he*, *heo*; EM *he*, *ʒho*, *ge*.

2. By far the commonest forms in EM are the ancestors of NE *she*, and only *sch-* forms are found in N. The etymology of the word is doubtful: semantic difficulties are in the way of deriving it from OE *sēo* or ON *sjá*. It may be a direct descendant of OE *hēo*,[1] or conceivably due to some blend of *sēo* and *hēo*. It appears first in the EM about the middle of the twelfth century under the form *scæ*, and spreads rapidly into other dialects in such forms as *sche*, *scho*, *sge*, *she*, etc. By the end of the thirteenth century *sch*-forms are regular

---

[1] See A. H. Smith, 1 *RES* 437–440, and *The Place-Names of the East Riding and York* (14 EPNS 95 and 228).

in the N (*scho*, less frequently *sche*), and EM (*sche*, less frequently *scho*), while *h*- forms, derived from OE *hēo*, remain regular in the S and WM.

The pl. of the 3rd personal pronoun similarly can have one of two basic forms:

1. The descendants of OE *hīe*, *hēo*, appearing in ME as *he*, *hi*, *heo*, *hue*, *ho*, etc.

2. The ON loanwords *þei(r)*, *þeir(r)a*, *þeim*, of which *þei* appears first in the EM about the beginning of the thirteenth century, and the oblique forms in that dialect later in the century, though Orrm already has occasional *þ*-forms side by side with *h*- forms, e.g. *þeȝȝre/heore*, *þeȝȝm/hemm*. By the end of the thirteenth century the normal state of affairs is that the N has *þ*-forms throughout *þei/þai*, *þeire/þaire*, *þeim/þaim*. The M normally have *þ*-forms in the nom. and *h*- forms in the oblique cases, *þei*, *here/heore*, *hem/heom*, though *þ*- forms have begun to spread into the oblique cases. In the S *h*- forms are usual throughout.

Already in OE the dual of the 1st and 2nd personal pronouns are becoming obsolete, but in eME they continue to be employed, though rather infrequently, and it should be noted that the oblique cases of the 1st dual, *unc*, *uncer*, are sometimes used for the 2nd person dual.

In the verbs the following are the more important dialectal variations:

	N	EM/WM	SE/SW
Inf.	*bind*	*binde(n)*	*binden; louien, lokin*
prp.	*-and*	*-ende*	*-inde*
3pr.	*-is*	*-eþ, -es*	*-eþ*
prpl.	*-e, -is*	*-en*	*-eþ*
ptp.	*bounden*	*bounden*	*ybounde*

In the N -*n* of the inf. had already been lost in OE, and the -*a* is weakened to -*e* and lost in eME, hence the ME type which is the bare stem of the verb. In the M -*n* is lost during the ME period, and forms appear both with and without it. In the N and M the 2nd Weak Class (OE *lufian*) has taken the same endings as the other verbs. Hence the inf. of OE *lufian* appears regularly as N *luf*, M *luue(n)*. In the S and SWM -*n* of the inf. remains longer, and the 2nd Weak Class is kept separate until late in the period with an inf. in -*in*, -*ien*.

In the prp. the N -*and* is a borrowing from ON; M -*ende* is from OE, as also is S -*inde*, where however raising of *e* to *i* before the nasal has taken place. The modern -*ing* appears first in the EM during the thirteenth century, and spreads rapidly throughout the South. It is probably taken from the ending of the OE verbal noun -*ing*/-*ung*.

The 3pr. in the N is -*is*, from which are derived the -*s* endings of the modern forms. The M and S forms are descended from the OE (*e*)*þ*. The -*is* forms spread rapidly and are early found in the NMid. dialects. Syncopated forms, from WS, are found in the South throughout the period, but are always in a minority.

The ending of the prpl. in the M is derived from the OE subjunctive pl., while the S forms are from the corresponding OE indicative forms. The initial *ge*- of the ptp., originally perfective in meaning, remains in the South as *y*-, but was early lost in the N and M, where however the final -*n* remained.

NOTES TO THE TEXTS

I. A WORCESTER FRAGMENT

Dialect: West Midland of Worcester.

Inflexions:

Verbs: 3pr. *sæiþ* 20.
prpl. *hoteþ* 4, 6, *losiæþ* 19.
ptp. *iboren* 1.
Pronouns: 3 pl. poss. *heore* 16.
The definite article retains its dpl. inflexion in *þen* 19.
Nouns: *cnotten* 4, retains the pl. ending of weak nouns, and *leoden*, *leodan* 3, 9, etc., has gone over to the weak declension. *word* 22, retains the lack of ending in the pl. of OE long-stem neuters, and the mutated vowel remains in *bec* 7. Grammatical gender survives in *þet folc* 19.

Sounds:

æ usually remains, *næs* 16, *fæire* 16, etc., but *was* 1, 7, and *þet* 10, 17, 23.
y is *u* in *Cantoreburi* 14.
ā is regularly *o*, *hoteþ* 4, 6, *glod* 16, but *leore* 17.
$\bar{æ}^1$ is *e* in *weren* 3, 9, etc.
$\bar{æ}^2$ is *æ* in *ilærde* 9, *lærden* 15, *læreþ* 18, but *e* in *ilerde* 3.
WS *ea*/Ang. *a* before *l*+cons. is *a* in *Oswald* 12, *o* in *Æþelwold* 13. The mutation before *r*+cons. is *e* in *derne* 5. *ea* due to front diphthongization appears in *Wireceastre* 12, but *æ* in *Wincæstre* 13, *Rofecæstre* 14.
eo remains in *deorc* 16, *feole* 19.
ēa is *e* in *unwreih* 4.
ēo is regularly *eo*, *leoden* 3, etc., *beoþ* 18, 22.

Orthography: OE *sc* remains in *Englisc* 9, *biscopes* 10, *sceolen* 23, but *s* appears in *Englise* 3. The front spirant is still represented by *h* in *liht* 16, *unwreih* 4. *th* appears for *þ* in *this* 22.

Notes

1. *Sanctus Beda*. Like many of the early saints Bede, despite his European reputation, was never officially canonized. He was evidently regarded as a saint in popular tradition, but is usually referred to as "the Venerable", a title given to those who have completed the first stage towards canonization.
2. *bec*. The outer margin of the folio having been cropped, letters are

missing from the words at the end of the lines, and here a complete word is gone. Hall supplies *writen* which fits in well with the alliteration, but is certainly too long. Elsewhere the cropping has destroyed three or four letters, and it is difficult to believe that there could have been six here. Hence *bec*, suggested by other editors, is more probable. According to Hall the author is here thinking of the translation of St. John's Gospel and of extracts from Isidore of Seville with which Bede is said to have been occupied on his death-bed. But reference to this is found only in a letter, by Bede's disciple Cuthbert to Cuthwine, which is unlikely to have been known to this twelfth-century writer. More probably he is thinking of Bede's translation of the Lord's Prayer and the Creed referred to in the *Ecclesiastical History*.

3. *þet ... þurh*. Note the separation of the preposition from its relative, a common construction in ME.

4. *questiuns*. During the seventh and eighth centuries it seems to have been fashionable for scholars to circulate lists of questions on theological or Biblical subjects, either to elicit information or to show their own ingenuity. As Hall suggests, the reference here may be to Bede's *In Libros Regum Quaestiones Triginta*, answering questions put by Nothelm, or perhaps to the *Bedae Quaestiones in utrumque Testamentum*.

6. *Ælfric*, c. 955–1020, the greatest prose-writer of the OE period. *Alquin*, a Latinization of OA Alhwine (735–804), was educated at York. He is now better known as an important assistant to Charlemagne in the latter's educational reforms than for his own numerous writings in Latin. The confusion with Ælfric is probably due to the fact that Alcuin's *Sigewulfi Interrogationes* was translated into English by Ælfric, and copies of this translation were still being made as late as the twelfth century. A new life of Alcuin by Professor E. S. Duckett has appeared (New York 1951).

7. *fif*. A word at the end of the line has been cropped, and *fif* is usually supplied by editors on the basis of the five books mentioned in the following line. In point of fact at least the first seven books of the OT. were translated under Ælfric's direction, though perhaps not actually by himself. However, any form of 'seven' would certainly be too long for the space available.

8. *Vtronomius*, for *Deutronomius*. Probably a scribal error.

10. *þet weren*. This use of *þet* as the anticipatory subject is not unusual in OE or ME, and the pronoun remains in the singular though the verb, as in this case, may be in the pl. agreeing with the real subject. Cf. Wulfstan's Voyage in the OE version of Orosius, "þæt wæron eall Finnas", and note also Fr. *c'étaient*.

11 ... For these bishops see Index of Names. No particular order is to be discerned in the list.

18. *opre leoden*, '(people of) other languages'.

20ff. ... *Deuteronomy* xxxii, 11.

23. ... 'that we should place our full trust in Him'.

II. THE PETERBOROUGH CHRONICLE

Dialect: East Midland of Peterborough.

Inflexions:

Verbs: inf. *finden* 41, *sitten* 33, *slepen* 34, etc.
prpl. *lien* 68.
prp. *sittende* 42, *ridend* 51.

Pronouns: 3pl. nom. *hi* 15, etc.; poss. *her* 23, *here* 24; obj. *heom* 19, etc.

Nouns: *wunder* 11, retains the lack of ending of the OE long-stem neuter nouns, and cf. also *wintre* 37, 58, 59 (OE *wintru*). The dpl. inflexion survives in *sithon* 46, and the gpl. in *Engla-* 6. Survivals of the weak declension appear in *halechen* 57, *circewican* 68, *horderwycan* 70.

Sounds:

a/o is invariably *a*, *nam* 7, *man* 10, *-lande* 6, etc.

æ is indifferently *a*, *e*, *æ*, *was* 31, *bar* 55; *wes* 2, *hefden* 18; *æt* 7, *wæs* 43, etc.

y is *i*, *yuele* 17, *sinnes* 58, etc.

ā is indifferently *a* or *o*, *stanes* 28, *mare* 45; *more* 39, etc.

ǣ¹ is *æ* or *e*, *wæron* 21, *bræcon* 29, *flesc* 42, *uueron* 54, etc. *þar* 25, *waren* 44, *þarof* 54, etc., are due to early shortening.

ǣ² is usually *æ*, *næure* 21, *ær* 75, etc., but *neure* 41, *leredmen* 53, *hethen* 46. *ani* 18, is due to early shortening or to the influence of *ān*.

gyuen 40, *gif* 69, and perhaps *gæildes* 38, are from front-diphthongized forms in OE.

WS *ea*/Ang. *a* before *l*+cons. is usually *a*, *alse* 21, *hals* 33, *half* 59, etc., but *ælle* 9, *manifældlice* 86. Before *r*+cons. *a* appears in *quarterne* 25, *nareu* 27, *-wardes* 33, but *æ* in *scærpe* 28, *scærp* 32, *-iærd* 47, 74. Before *h* the mutation appears as *i* in *nihtes* 18, *myhte* 33, *myhtes* 41.

eo is *eo* in *-weorces* 16, *weorkes* 75, but *e* in *erthe* 55. *clepeden* 39, is from a form with non-WS back-mutation. The mutation appears as *e* in *uuerse* 37, 38, *werse* 46.

ēa is *e* or *æ*, *hæued* 24, *ræueden* 40; *hefed* 23, *estren* 80, etc., but *eo* appears in *eom* 3, *beom* 32. The mutation is *y* in *atywede* 83.

ēo is *eo* in *heolden* 13, 14, *deoules* 17, *preostes* 49, *heold* 58, 61, but *e* in *ben* 2, 83, *undep* 28, *thre* 31, and *æ* in *gæde* 25. The mutation appears as *æ* in *dære* 42, and *e* in *neuuæ* 63.

Diphthongization of *o* does not appear in *wrohte* 62, *brohte* 63, *bohton* 79.

Consonants: OE *hw* appears as *w* in *nowiderwardes* 33, *wile* 37, *-wile* 44, *warsæ* 55, *þopwethere* 61, *wat* 78. Final -*n* has been lost in *o* 43, final -*d* in *þusen* 34, and final -*h* in *þur* 85. *þ* has been assimilated to *t* initially in *te* 60, and medially in *wurtscipe* 64. Medial -*pp*- has been simplified in *sythen* 48, 82, and already in OE *g* had been lost before *d* in *sæden* 56.

Orthography: *æ* is used as a spelling for *e* in *bæron* 31, *læiden* 38, *wæl* 66, *sæin* 57, *sægen* 78, and for *ē* in *læt* 63, *gæt* 45. OE front *c* continues to be represented by *c*, e.g. *riceman* 14, *circe* 47, etc., and *sc* by *sc* as in *scort* 27, *biscopes* 49, etc. *w* is frequently represented by *uu*, *uuaren* 16, *uury-then* 24, *uuerse* 37, etc., and is regularly *u* after *s*, *suencten* 15, *suyðe* 15, *sua* 31, etc. *th* is used for *þ* in *bathe* 18, *thre* 31, *hethen* 46, etc., and *þ* is used as a spelling for the back voiceless spirant in *poþwethere* 61. OE front *g* is represented by *i* or *g*, *ieden* 44, *iafen* 9, *-iærd* 47, 74, *gæde* 25, *gyuen* 40, *gif* 51, *gestes* 60. *ch* is used for OE back *c* in *rachenteges* 30, and for the voiced back spirant in *halechen* 57. OE medial *f* is represented by *f* in *hefed* 23, *iafen* 9.

Notes

For comparison with the language of the *Peterborough Chronicle* we include here the twelfth-century additions to the C and D MSS. The C MS. (BM. MS. Cotton Tiberius B. i), copied about the middle of the eleventh century, probably at Abingdon, ends abruptly in the middle of the annal for 1066 describing the battle of Stamford Bridge. A twelfth-century scribe has completed the annal by adding the well-known description of the Norwegian who held the bridge against the English. The D MS. (BM. Cotton Tiberius B iv), copied during the middle of the eleventh century somewhere in the diocese of Worcester, probably at Worcester itself, ends mutilated in the annal for 1079, though probably with little lost. A twelfth-century scribe has then added a note on the rebellion of Angus, Earl of Moray, in 1130 (miswritten 1080).

(a) . . . *and þa Normen/flugon þa Englisa. Ða wes þer an of Nor-wegan þe widstod þet Englisce folc, þet hi ne micte þa brigge ofer-stigan, ne sige gerechen. Ða seite an Englisce mid anre flane, ac hit nactes ne wid-stod. And þa com anoþer under þere brigge end hine þurðstang enunder þere brunie. Ða com Harold Engla chinge ofer þere brigge end hys furde forð mid hine, end þere michel wel geslogon, ge Norweis, ge Flæming, end þes cyninges sunu þe[1] het Mundus let Harold faran ham to Norweie mid alle þa scipe.*

(b) MILLESIMO. LXXX. *Her werþ Anagus of-sleien fram Scotta éére, and þer werþ micel weell ofsleigen mid him. Þer wes Codes riþt gesochen in him for þet he wes all forswóórn.*

3. *get.* Ambiguous, 'because he still had his treasure', or 'because he had obtained his treasure'. In the last section of the *Chronicle* WS *ea* after front *g* is normally *a* or *æ*, so that the former is the more probable, but the orthography is too confused for certainty to be possible. According to William of Malmesbury the treasure taken over by Stephen from his uncle Henry I amounted to £100,000, which must be multiplied by at least thirty to obtain the modern equivalent. For what happened to some of the *tresor* see E. Panofsky, *Abbot Suger* (Princeton 1946), pp. 58–59.

4. *Henri king.* The OE word order, with the title following and in apposition to the name, is still retained, see also line 78. But l. 6, etc., show the modern word order already in use.

[1] sunu þe: *the second minim of* n *and the second* u *of* sunu, *and* þe *have been erased but are clearly visible under the ultra-violet lamp.* (See 5 *Proc. Leeds Philosophical Society, Lit.-Hist.* 148–9.)

7. *Oxeneford.* The Council of Oxford, June 1139. Alexander, Bishop of Lincoln (d. 1148), had been adopted and brought up by his uncle, the justiciar Roger of Salisbury, but the chancellor Roger was the nephew (*nepos, vel plusquam nepos*) of the justiciar only by courtesy. The castles surrendered included Sleaford, Newark, Banbury, Sherborne, Malmesbury and Devizes. The last was surrendered only after a vigorous defence by Nigel, bishop of Ely, another of the justiciar's nephews, and Maud of Ramsbury, mother of the chancellor and mistress of the justiciar.

8. *Sereberi.* The regular development of OE *Searobyrig*. The medial *s* of the modern form appears already in *Domesday*, and *l* for *r* is due to dissimilation in Anglo-French. *Sarum* (for *Sarisburia*) is due to a misunderstanding of the medieval abbreviation for *-isburia* which was very similar to the more frequently used one for *-um*.

9. *hise neues.* *his* has evidently developed into a possessive pronoun, and is here given a pl. inflexion. The same thing had earlier happened to *min* and *þin*.

11. *na iustise ne dide.* Hall has shown this to be a partial translation of Fr. *faire justise* 'to inflict punishment'. For similar partial translations of Fr. phrases cf. ME *fowe and gris* (Fr. *vair et gris*), *in good point* (Fr. *en bon point*), etc. For a sidelight on Stephen's character which affords a good illustration of the chronicler's remark see 2 *RES* 341.

11. *wunder*, 'atrocities', a development from the earlier sense 'omen, portent'. This particular sense is not infrequent in ME; cf. *Sir Gawain and the Green Knight*, 14ff., "Bretayn . . ./Where werre & wrake & wonder/Bi syþeʒ hatʒ wont þerinne".

16. *castel-weorces*, 'forced labour on the building of castles', a common grievance of the time which was specifically condemned by Pope Eugenius III in a letter to four of the English prelates in 1147; see J. H. Round, *Geoffrey de Mandeville* (London 1892), p. 416.

18. *be nihtes and be dæies.* Note the reinforcement of the old adverbial genitive by a preposition.

19–20. For this reading see N. R. Ker, 3 *Med. Æv.* 137.

24. See Ker, *loc. cit.*

27. *crucethus.* Apparently a form of L. *cruciatus* with the ending due to popular etymology.

30. *lof and grin.* Obviously unusual terms since the chronicler felt that they needed fuller explanation. The former is no doubt to be connected with the gloss *redimicula: wrædas oððe cynewiððan, lofas* occurring in MSS. of Aldhelm's *De Laudibus Virginitatis*. In classical Latin *redimiculum* usually has the sense 'fillet, string (of bonnet)', but later it seems to have developed the sense 'bond, fetter', no doubt the meaning of *lof* here. The latter word appears as *grī* in the MS., and is by some editors expanded to *grim*. But if *lof* is a noun, presumably this word is too, and it is therefore better expanded as *grin*, a common ME word for 'halter, snare', still surviving in the AV. (1611), where modern reprints substitute *gins* for *grins* at *Job* xviii, 9; *Psalms* cxl, 5; cxli, 9. The two words would presumably be a

technical term for some species of fetter encircling the neck of the prisoner (2 *RES* 341-2).

30-1. *ðat . . . onne*, 'which two or three men could support only with difficulty'. *rachenteges*, OE *racente* 'chain, rope' + OE *tēag* 'fetter', but the gloss *collario: racentege* in MS. Bodl. Digby 146 may be significant of the exact sense of the word in this particular context.

34. *bæron*, OE *beran*, inf.; some such word as *sculde* is to be understood before it.

35. *I ne can ne I ne mai*, 'I do not know how to, nor am I able', preserving the OE distinction between *cunnan* and *magan*.

36-7. *ðat lastede . . . king*. This shows clearly that the account cannot have been composed before the death of Stephen (1154). Cf. also line 58, and the reference to the length of Martin's abbacy (59-60). No doubt, as Round suggested, this account of the misery of the country, despite the fact that it is dated 1137, owes much to the chronicler's memory of the ravaging of the Fen District in 1144 by Geoffrey de Mandeville.

38. *æure umwile*, 'at regularly recurring intervals'.

39. *tenserie*, 'protection money', a derivative of L *tensare* 'to protect, exact tribute for protection'. The meaning and etymology of the word were first worked out by Round, *op. cit.*, pp. 414-6. For a similar development in meaning from 'protection' to 'robbery' cf. *blackmail*.

44. *ieden on ælmes*, 'lived on alms, charity'.

46. *hethen men*. A reference to the Viking invasions with which so much of the earlier part of the *Chronicle* is concerned.
ouer sithon. Emerson emends to *ower* which he takes to be OE *āhwǣr* and translates 'everywhere thereafter, afterwards', but Hall's suggestion is better. He takes the phrase to be from OE *ofer sīþan* 'contrary to experience', here perhaps rather 'contrary to custom'.

47 . . . As consecrated ground the church and churchyard should have been safe from plunderers. Consequently in times of civil disturbance they were not infrequently regarded as places of safety in which people could deposit their treasures. But mercenaries of the period were evidently prepared to commit sacrilege for the sake of plunder; cf. the account of the sack of Cambridge by Geoffrey de Mandeville in the *Gesta Stephani*, and see also the account of the sack of Worcester by Milo of Gloucester.

50-1. *ouer-myhte*. Necessity for emendation to *ower myhte* is avoided if we take this as OE *ofer-mihte* 'had the power' (2 *RES* 342).

52. *tunscipe*, 'the inhabitants of the village', hence the plural verb following; the use of a pl. verb with a collective noun is frequent both in OE and in ME.

53-4. *oc . . . þarof*, 'but they cared nothing for it'.

56-7. *hi . . . halechen*. A popular saying. Some of the Latin chroniclers give it as said by the wicked, others by the good.

59. *Martin abbod*. Martin of Bec, so-called because previously prior of St. Neot's, a cell of Bec. He was a native of the Isle of Wight and

succeeded Henry of Poitou in the abbacy after the latter had been deposed by Henry I in 1132. An account of Martin's abbacy, very similar to this, appears in the chronicle of Hugh Candidus (ed. W. T. Mellows, Oxford 1949) who used this text as one of his sources.

60. *fand*, 'provided for', a not uncommon sense of the verb in ME; cf. the *Nun's Priest's Tale* (CT. VII, 2828–9): "By housbondrie of swich as God hire sente/She foond hirself and eek hir doghtren two". The sense survives in MnE., mainly in the phrase 'all found' in advertisements.

61. *carited*. Probably 'alms-giving', but L *caritas* had the further sense 'monastic allowance or measure of food or drink', and also the technical one of 'commemoration feasts at the anniversaries of benefactors'.

62. *sette . . . rentes*, 'set apart for the expenses of the building the income from various estates, and also other moneys'. *rentes* has the usual ME sense 'revenue, income'; cf. Chaucer, *CT*. VII, 2210, "Kyng, God to thy fader sente/Glorie and honour, regne, tresour, rente".

64. *mynstre*, L *monasterium*, and 'monastery' is the usual sense of the word in OE. But already it is found occasionally with the meaning 'church of a monastery' which it has here.

Sanct Petres mæssedæi, June 29. The fire took place on Aug. 4, 1116, so that according to this the monks began to use the new church on June 29, 1140, but other Peterborough chroniclers give the date as 1143. Only the choir of the church was built under Martin, the transepts being added by his successor.

66. *for to Rome*. Not before 1145, when Eugenius III became Pope.

67. *priuilegies*, 'a grant of special rights or immunities', a legal term borrowed directly from L *privilegium*. The two documents, dated 1146, are given in full by Hugh Candidus, pp. 109 ff. The former protects the lands, property and rights of the monastery in general, these being given in detail, whilst the latter recounts and confirms that part of the properties which was specifically allocated for the expenses of the sacrist. In addition to providing an income for the necessary expenses of the office another motive for appropriating certain revenue to a particular office within the monastery was to prevent it falling into the king's hands during a vacancy in the abbacy. A suit on this point between the monks of Abingdon and the crown, during the reign of Henry II, was decided in favour of the monastery.

68. *circewican*, literally 'the office of sacrist', but the context suggests that it is the sacrist himself, the custodian of the sacred vessels, vestments, etc., of the church, who is meant here, rather than his office.

69. *horderwycan*. 'Office of treasurer', but *hordere* is used in various senses. Elsewhere it is found glossing *cellerarius*, and judging from Hugh Candidus it is here used for *camerarius*, the officer in charge of the stores of clothing and bedding for the monastery. Martin

assigned two manors for the provision of clothes, but did not live long enough to obtain a privilege for his appropriation.

71. *Willelm Malduit.* Constable of the King's castle of Rockingham and Warden of the Forest. In *Domesday* the abbey has holdings in Cottingham, Easton Maudit, Irthlingborough, Stanwick, and Aldwinkle.

72. *Hugo of Walteruile.* Hugh of Waterville, the twelfth-century lord of the manor of Addington Parva and Thorp Waterville, and perhaps a relation of William of Waterville, the successor of Martin at Peterborough.

74. *winiærd.* Medieval references suggest that many of the southern monasteries had vineyards and prepared wine from them, and certainly vineyards are found in this country as late as the eighteenth century; see E. Hyams, *The Grape Vine in England* (London 1949).

75. *weorkes.* In the not uncommon ME sense 'domestic buildings'. According to Hugh Candidus Martin's buildings included a room for the abbot and a hall for the monks.

wende þe tun. Martin is said to have changed the site of the town from the east to the west of the monastery.

78ff. . . . Accusations of ritual murder are not infrequently brought against the Jews in medieval chronicles. According to Thomas of Monmouth, *St. William of Norwich*, ed. A. Jessopp and M. R. James (Cambridge 1896), this particular event took place in 1144; but other chroniclers date it 1146.

78. *on Stephnes kinges time.* Note the retention of the OE idiom with the genitive inflexion on both nouns. The normal ME usage was to place it on the first noun only, *for my lordes loue Sir Orfeo*, where the modern idiom would place it only on the last, *for my lord Sir Orfeo's love.*

81. *Lang-Fridæi.* Good Friday, so-called from the length of the fasts and services; cf. Danish *Langfredag*, ON *Fǫstudagr inn langi, Langafrjddagr.* But the English use is probably the earlier.

83ff. . . . According to Thomas a miraculous light in the sky led to the discovery of the body. It was first buried in the wood where it was found, then in the cemetery of the monks, and six years later translated to the chapter-house.

84. *to.* Perhaps a mistake for *te* 'the', or it may be from OE *þā*, plural of *se*, with rounding of *ā* and assimilation of *þ* to *t* after the preceding *d*.

III. THE PROCLAMATION OF HENRY III

Dialect: London.

Inflexions:

Verbs: inf. *healden* 12, *foangen* 16, *werien* 12, *makien* 13, and note also the survival of the dative inf. in *to done* 15, 16.

3pr. *send* 3. prpl. *hoaten* 10, 19, *senden* 21, but *habbeð* 7.

prp. *ilestinde* 9, *lestinde* 21.

ptp. *ichosen* 6, *isworene* 25.

Pronouns: 3 pl. nom. *heo* 11; obj. *heom* 5, 14, 19.
    Some pronominal inflexions still survive in the def. art., am. *þane* 23; dm. *þan* 9, 13; df. *þære* 35.
Nouns: *þinge* 10, shows the lack of ending of the OE long-stem neuter plurals. A gpl. inflexion appears in *Englene-* 1, 29, 35, and a dpl. inflexion in *worden* 34. *ifoan* 20, retains the weak pl.

Sounds:

    a/o before lengthening groups is usually *oa/o*, *-loande* 1, *foangen* 16, *Irelonde* 35, but *amanges* 22, *and* 2, etc.
    æ is usually *a*, *þæt* 4, *-fæst* 9, etc., but *e* appears in *wes* 24.
    y is *u* in *kuneriche* 7, 35, *-buri* 26, but *i* in *king* 1.
    ā is indifferently *oa* or *o*, *lhoauerd* 1, *oþe* 16, etc.
    $\bar{æ}^1$ and $\bar{æ}^2$ are *æ* in *rædes-* 5, 14, *dæl* 5, 14, *ilærde* 3, *æurihce* 35, but *e* in *redes-* 9, 25, *ilestinde* 9, *lestinde* 21, *wher-* 17, *eȝte* 17, and *ea* in *ileawede* 3.
    WS *ea/*Ang. *a* before *l+*cons. is *ea* in *healden* 12, 20, but otherwise *a* in *halden* 22, *alle* 3, etc., Before *h e* appears in *eȝtetenþe* 23.
    ēa is *ea* in *deadliche* 20, *ȝeare* 24, but *e* in *ek* 35.
    ēo is *eo* in *beoþ* 6, *beo* 9, *beon* 13, 18, *o* in *fower-* 24, and *e* in *ȝew* 21, 22 The mutation is *eo* in *treowþe* 8, 11, *treowe* 11, 19.
Consonants: A prosthetic consonant has been developed in *ȝew* 21, 22. OE *hl* is represented by *lh* in *lhoauerd* 1. The *s* in *ichosen* 6, is due to analogy, while inf. *foangen* 16, is also analogical.

Orthography: OE *e* is represented by *æ* in *ænde* 10, unless this represents the *æ* stage of the mutation of *a/o*. *ō* is frequently represented by *oa*, *moare* 5, *lhoauerd* 1, etc., and *ē* appears as *ee* in *seel* 22. OE *hl* is represented by *lh* in *lhoauerd* 1, front *c* by *hc* in *æhc* 15, *æurihce* 34, and *sc* by *shc* in *shcire* 34.

Notes

1. *on*, 'of'. Not unusual in this sense in ME.
5. *þæt*, 'that which'.
    rædesmen. A reference to the Council of Twenty-four, twelve elected by the barons and twelve appointed by the king, who had drawn up the Provisions of Oxford.
6. *þæt loandes folk on vre kuneriche*. Fr. *le commun de nostre reaume*.
9. *besiȝte*. Fr. *sicum il ordenera*.
10. *vre treowe*. Fr. *nos feaus et leaus*.
11. *in þe treowþe*, 'by the loyalty'.
12. *isetnesses*. Fr. *establissemenz*.
15–6. . . . 'and that each should help the other, by the same oath, to act so towards all men, to do right and to receive it'. Fr. *cuntre tutte genz dreit fesant et parnant*.
17–8. *þis besiȝte muȝe beon ilet*. Fr. *ceste purveance puisse estre desturbee*.
18. *oni oþer onie*. Note the distinction between sg. and pl., 'If any man, or if any men, . . .'

21. *open*, i.e. letters *patent* as compared with letters *close*. Writs from the royal chancery were sealed, *patent* if they were to be kept and exhibited as was the case with this, but *close* if they contained simple orders to do this or that. The reason for the difference was not altogether one of secrecy but one of economy also. Letters *close* needed much less wax to seal, and were more easily carried by messenger.

24. 42 Henry III ran from Oct. 28, 1257, to Oct. 27, 1258.

25ff. . . . The same thirteen, in the same order, sign as witnesses to the Oxford copy, so that presumably all the copies of the English version were alike in this respect. The French version, however, is signed by sixteen, and includes, in addition to the thirteen here, Humphrey de Bohun, earl of Hereford, Roger de Quency, earl of Winchester, and Hugh le Despenser.

35. *kuneriche*. OE *cynerice* is known only as a neuter noun. Either it has changed gender in lOE, or *þære* (df.) is a scribal error.

IV. THE SONG OF LEWES

Dialect: Southern.

Inflexions:

   Verbs: inf. *make* 4, *habbe* 11, *helpe* 17, etc.
     3pr. *haueþ* 10, *haþ* 25, 28, etc.
     ptp. *yboren* 26, *suore* 28.
   Pronouns: 3 pl. poss. *hare* 15.

Sounds:

   a/o is *o* in *mony* 21.
   æ is *e* in *wes* 8, *gederede* 18, *heuede* 29, 34.
   y is *u* in *mulne* 14, 19, *muche* 23, etc., but *i* in *kyng* 2, 8, etc., *synne* 23 (r.w. *Warynne*). *dude* 5, 23, etc., *dudest* 43, are from lOE forms in *y*.
   ā is regularly *o*, *more* 5, *sori* 21, etc.
   $\bar{æ}^1$ and $\bar{æ}^2$ are *e*, *were* 16; *euer* 6, *neuer* 7, etc.
   WS. *ea*/Ang. *a* before *l*+cons. is *a* in *alle* 1, etc., but *e* in *stel* 15. Before *r*+cons. *a* appears in *sharpe* 15, *ward* 40.
   eo is regularly *e*, *ferlyng* 10, *swerdes* 15, *erl* 29, etc.
   ēa is *e* in *shreward* 43, *emes* 44. *þah* 6, etc., shows early shortening.
   ēo is *e* in *brew* 11, but *ue* in *luef* 38.
   Diphthongization before the back spirant has not taken place in *brohte* 21, *þah* 6, etc.
   Consonants: Final unaccented *-d* is unvoiced in *ant* 5, etc., and an inorganic final *-d* has been added in *Simond* 28, 33. In *dryng* 11, *ng* is an inverted spelling for *-nk*. Initial *h-* has been lost in *is* 9, *ys* 18, etc.

Orthography: *w* is written *u* after *s* in *suore* 28, 33, and short *u* is written *o* in *opon* 9.

Notes

2. *kyng of Alemaigne.* Richard of Cornwall, brother to Henry III, was crowned King of the Romans, but never received the imperial diadem.

3. *pritti.* Richard is said to have asked £30,000 as the price of his mediation between Henry III and the barons, but the only other authority to mention this is Thomas Wykes.

5. . . . 'and he asked for more as well'.

6. *trichard.* Richard was accused by the barons of treachery in that he had broken his oath to abide by the provisions of the Statutes of Canterbury.

9. . . . Thomas Wykes makes similar complaints of Richard's character, but other authorities complain of his uxoriousness—he married three wives.

10. *Walingford.* The honour and castle of Wallingford had come into Richard's hands as early as 1231, and formed an important part of his vast estates. After Lewes he was imprisoned in his own castle there by the victorious barons.

11. *dryng* 'drink'. An inverted spelling showing the unvoicing of final -*ng* to -*nk*. The rhyme must presumably be *ferlynk*: *drynk*.

13ff. . . . After the defeat at Lewes Richard took refuge in a windmill, and there, after some show of defence, was captured by the barons.

15. *grounde þe stel*, 'he made his position secure'.

16. *mangonel.* A siege-engine working by torsion and consisting of two posts joined by a set of ropes. A beam placed between them is drawn back so as to twist the ropes in opposite directions. When the beam is let go a missile placed in a hollow or attached to a sling on it will be thrown forward with considerable force. Presumably the top sail of a windmill is thought to be like the beam of a mangonel after it has been operated.

24. *erl of Warynne.* John of Warenne, earl of Surrey. After the defeat at Lewes he succeeded in making his way to Pevensey, and thence escaped to France.

34. *Hue de Bigot.* Hugh de Bigot, former justiciar, who succeeded in escaping from Lewes with Warenne.

35. . . . 'He would readily pay their board and lodging for a year', i.e. would imprison them.

40. . . . Prince Edward had first been imprisoned at Wallingford, but was moved to Dover after the beginning of 1265. This poem must, then, have been composed after that date.

44. *emes*, 'uncle's'. Simon de Montfort had married Eleanor, sister of Henry III.

V. ROBERT OF GLOUCESTER

Dialect: South-West Midland of Gloucester.

Inflexions:

Verbs: inf. *speke* 2, *singe* 21, etc.
   3pr. *telþ* 6, *seiþ* 17, 111, *haþ* 46.
   prpl. *holdeþ* 5, 7, 9.
   ptp. *iwonne* 114, *inome* 94, etc., *islawe* 27, *ihote* 19.
   The distinctive vowel of the ptpl. is still preserved in *smite* 49,
   smiten 76. *corue* 75, *bigonne* 103.

Pronouns: 3 pl. n. *hii* 3, etc.; poss. *hor* 2, etc., *hore* 49; obj. *hom* 5, etc.
   The npl. of the demonstrative appears as *þis* 91, *þuse* 101. The am. of
   the definite article appears in *þen* 34, and the d. in *atten* 59.

Nouns: *fon* 16 (r.w. *echon*), and *massen* 21, retain the pl. ending of the
   weak masculine nouns.

Sounds:

a/o is *o* before lengthening groups, *hond* 1, *strong* 58, etc., and usually
   a elsewhere, *man* 6, 13, *can* 11, etc., but *mon* 11.
æ is regularly *a*, *þat* 4, *was* 16, 59 (r.w. *alas*), etc.
y is *e* in *werst* 62, *verst* 93; *u* in *vuele* 81; *i* in *king* 23. *iwuste* 30, *sulue*
   83, *wuch* 112, are from forms with *y* in lOE.
ā is regularly *o*, *wot* 10, *fon* 16, etc.
ǣ[1] and *ǣ*[2] are regularly *e*, *here* 79, *strete* 106, *speche* 2 (r.w. *teche*); *arere*
   31 (r.w. *were*), *mest* 70, etc. *ar* 25 is due to early shortening.
ȳ is *u* in *lute* 6 (r.w. *ʒute*), 61. *wule* 85 is from a lOE form with *ȳ*.
WS *ea*/Ang. *a* before *l*+cons. is *o* before lengthening groups, *holdeþ*
   5, 9, *olde* 18, 71, etc., but otherwise *a*, *alle* 5, *half* 17, etc.: the mutation
   is to *e* in *Welsse* 102. Before *r*+cons. *a* appears in *carf* 73, *harde* 79,
   suart 87, but *e* in *middelerd* 84. Before *h ei* appears in *isei* 36, etc.,
   sei 40.
eo is *e* in *derk* 86, *erles* 41, *erþe* 89, but *i* appears in *kniʒtes* 50, etc., *fiʒte* 107.
ēa is regularly *e*, *deþ* 33, *heued* 76, etc. The mutation is *e* in *nexte* 79,
   vnneþe 88.
ēo is regularly *e*, *prestes* 21, *beþ* 45, etc., but *u* appears in *bihuld* 40,
   þuse 101.
Diphthongization of *o* before the back spirant is lacking in *poʒte* 22,
   noʒt 57.
ʒute 7 (r.w. *lute*), 47 (r.w. *prute*), is presumably from an OE form with
   front diphthongization.
Consonants: Initial *f* frequently appears as *u/v*, *uor* 10, *vair* 14, etc.,
   and once as *w*, *werst* 62. Initial *h* is frequently omitted, as in *atom* 3,
   is 21, *adde* 33, etc., and the back voiceless spirant has been vocalized
   to *u* in *þoru* 27, 38, etc. OE *hw* appears as *w* in *wo* 17, *wan* 111, 114,
   wuch 112. Final inorganic *-d* has been added in *Simond* 62, etc.
   Medial *s* has been lost in *Wurcetre* 32, *Wircetre* 19, *Gloucetre* 41; medial
   w in *to* 26; while already in OE *g* had been lost before *d* in *sede*
   45, 46, 78 (r.w. *wede*).

Orthography. OE *sc* is regularly represented by *ss*, *ssende* 17, 77, *bissop* 32, etc. *ī* appears as *ii* in *hii* 3, etc. *ū* is *v* in *vr* 45, *o* in *bote* 2, 6, etc., but *ou* in *coupe* 2, *toun* 19, etc. Short *u* is *o* in *poru* 27, etc. *w* after *s* is *u* in *suart* 87, *suipe* 38; and initial *v* (from *f*) is written *w* in *werst* 62.

Notes

1ff. . . . Robert is not to be trusted in his account of the linguistic position during the second half of the eleventh century. There is a good deal of contemporary evidence to suggest that on the contrary the Norman settlers early learned English and abandoned French. See R. M. Wilson, "English and French in England 1066–1300" (28 *History* 37 ff.)

3. *hor . . . teche*, 'had their children also taught (French)'.

11. . . . Reminiscent of Alfred's remark in the Introduction to the *Pastoral Care*, "ond woldon ðæt her ðy mara wisdom on londe wære ðy we ma geðeoda cuðon".

12. *is* 'his', i.e. Simon de Montfort the younger. In the preceding lines Robert has been telling of his defeat at Kenilworth, and now goes on to speak of the elder Simon de Montfort. At the beginning of the campaign the position seems to have been that Simon de Montfort, earl of Leicester, was on the Welsh side of the Severn, and the river crossings were held against him by Prince Edward and the Earl of Gloucester. The younger Simon was besieging Pevensey, and messages were sent ordering him to join his father, whose army was much too small to make headway against the royalists. After some delay the younger Simon reached Kenilworth, and encamped there for the night. Prince Edward, leaving the Severn crossings unguarded, thereupon marched with his whole army against the baronial army at Kenilworth, and completely surprised and almost annihilated it, the younger Simon, almost alone of the leaders, managing to escape into the castle. In the meantime Simon the elder, taking advantage of Prince Edward's absence, had managed to transport his army across the Severn, and was on his way to join his son at Kenilworth when he encountered the royalist army at Evesham. Robert of Gloucester apparently thought that, despite the defeat at Kenilworth, Simon the younger still had a considerable army under his command, but this was not the case.

13. *Walis.* Simon de Montfort had allied himself with Llywelyn, Prince of Wales, since the Royalist Lords of the Marches were enemies to both of them. The greater part of Simon's infantry was made up of Welsh subjects of Llywelyn.

17. *as wo seip*, 'as if anyone says', 'as is commonly said', a fairly common idiom in ME.

21. . . . 'He caused the priests to sing mass for himself and his army'.

23. *king.* After Lewes Henry III and Prince Edward had been in the hands of the baronial party. In March, 1265, Simon set out to hunt down insurgents in the Welsh marches and took with him Henry III

and the Prince Edward who, though nominally free, were never
allowed to stir far from his side. At Hereford Prince Edward
managed to escape, but Henry III remained a prisoner with the
baronial army until freed by Evesham, in which battle he was
wounded and almost slain by the Royalists before being recognized.

26-7. . . . 'The same two dinners were calamitous, alas, for many a good
man was slain because of them'. Apparently Robert considered that
the delay involved was responsible for the two armies being unable
to unite before being attacked by the Royalists. *to* is obviously for
two, with *w* lost before a following rounded vowel. Such forms
appear early, and are found occasionally until the sixteenth century.
After that *w* is regular in the spelling, but the pronunciation is still
usually without the *w*; cf. modern English *two*, *sword*, etc.

28. *come po ride*, 'came riding'. Note the use, as in OE, of the inf. following and defining the sense of a verb of motion, where modern
English always, and ME often, has a present participle. This construction, however, is not infrequent in ME; cf. *Judas*, "In him
com ur Lord gon".

31. *lete . . . armi*, 'caused themselves to be armed'. In ME *let* plus the
inf. regularly has the sense 'to cause something to be done'.

32. *Water of Wurcetre*. Walter of Cantelupe, bishop of Worcester. This
form of the personal name, without the *-l-*, is evidently due to
Northern French *Wautier* (Central Fr. *Gautier*). Modern surnames
such as *Waters*, *Waterson*, along with *Watson*, *Watkins*, *Watts*, etc.,
derived from the diminutive *Wat*, suggest that this may have been
the usual form of the name during the ME period. That the
pronunciation survived until at any rate the end of the sixteenth
century is shown by the pun on *Walter* and *water* in Shakespeare,
2 *Henry VI*, IV, i, 31-35.

35. . . . Simon was ignorant of his son's defeat, and at first took the
Royalist army to be that of his son, a mistake encouraged by the
fact that Prince Edward had ordered the banners captured at Kenilworth to be carried in the van. Consequently when the royal banner
over the main army was seen it was too late to retreat.

39 . . But other authorities make it clear that Simon had no hope of
victory, and indeed the discrepancy in numbers, 7 or 8 to 1, made
this impossible; cf. line 45.

41. *erles baner of Gloucetre*. For this idiom see note to II. 78. Gilbert de
Clare, earl of Gloucester, had been one of Montfort's firmest
supporters and had fought on his side at Lewes. He had become
discontented, and on Prince Edward's escape met him at Ludlow,
did homage, and concluded a formal alliance with him against
Montfort.

42. . . . The Royalist army was in three divisions, under Edward,
Gloucester, and Mortimer, and had marched on Evesham from
different directions. The Prince approached from the north,
Gloucester from the north-west, and Mortimer from the west.

44. . . . A reference to the ease with which the King's army had been

surprised at Lewes as compared with Prince Edward's masterly generalship during this campaign. Other authorities suggest that Simon believed the Prince to have benefited from his teaching, but in fact, as a general, Prince Edward was far in advance of Earl Simon.

46. *þis . . . prute*, 'your pride has brought this about', but no reason is known why Simon should have blamed his son, if indeed he is doing so.

52. . . . . Simon and his followers, despite the disparity in numbers, charged into the middle of the Prince's division so fiercely that the Royalists wavered and had to be rallied by Warin of Bassingbourn who taunted them with their defeat at Lewes, and so stung them into steadiness.

61. *are.* MS. *ȝare* with ȝ erased. The MS. form suggests that OE *gēara* 'formerly' may to some extent have survived in eME. But if the form here were intended for that word it appears no longer to have been understood, and the erasure of initial ȝ has made the word into *are*, a by-form, with early shortening, of OE *ǣr* 'formerly'.

74. *hii . . . þis*, 'they did not hesitate to do this'.

77. *Dam Maud.* Wife of Sir Roger Mortimer of Wigmore. In ME *dame* 'lady' was regularly used as a title of rank; cf. the modern D.B.E. The form of the word used here has now been particularized to mean 'the female parent of an animal'. *Maud* is the colloquial form of the name which usually appears in medieval documents in the Latinized form *Mathilda*.

78. . . . . 'And despite the fact that he was dismembered it is said that he bled not at all'.

84. *middelerd.* OE *middangeard* literally 'middle enclosure', i.e. between the upper air and the nether pit; cf. ON *miðgarðr*. But in ME the exact sense of the word is forgotten and the second element is taken as a form of OE *eard* 'country'.

85. . . . . 'Similarly at the time when these noble men were slain at Evesham . . .'. *wule* is evidently OE *hwīl* 'space of time'. Presumably in eME initial *hw* has been voiced to *w*, and *ī* then rounded to *ȳ* between *w* and *l*. For a similar rounding of *ī* cf. lOE *swȳþe*.

88. *poȝte.* The form of OE *þencan* 'to think', but the sense and construction of *þyncan* 'to seem'. The two verbs are often confused in ME.

96. *Sir Gwy.* For his later career in Italy see F. M. Powicke, *Ways of Medieval Life and Thought*, pp. 69–88.

111. . . . . A proverbial saying. A caudle was a warm drink consisting of thin gruel mixed with wine or ale, sweetened and spiced, and given chiefly to sick people. Obviously the phrase expressed the idea that something necessary had been done, but much too late to do any good.

113. *wel . . . er*, 'it seemed to him too long before he arrived there'.

115. *honge vp min ax.* A popular saying, 'make no further effort, confess myself beaten'; cf. *Owl and Nightingale* 658, "Hong up þin axl nu þu miȝt fare".

VI. LAȜAMON'S BRUT

Dialect: South West Midlands (Worcestershire).

Inflexions:

Verbs: Inf. Usually with *-n, tellen* 7, *liðen* 14, etc., but *ride* 190.
 Second Weak Class still kept distinct with ending *-ien, wondrien* 99, *leosien* 74, *rusien* 79, etc.
 3pr. Normally *-eð, biddeð* 29, *pencheð* 81, *haueð* 73, etc., but *ulih* 132, *climbið* 124.
 prpl. *-eð* usual, *biteð* 104, *ileueð* 238, *habbeð* 223, but *fleoð* 167. Sec. Weak Class regularly, *-ieð, talieð* 130, *baðieð* 160, *lokieð*, 240, etc.
 ptp. Initial *i–* invariable, final *-n* usual, *icoren* 241, *iwurðen* 121, *ihoten* 1, etc., but *ihate* 243.

Pronouns: Fem. *hoe* 22.
 3 pl. n. *heo* 8, etc.; poss. *heore* 13, etc.; obj. *heom* 13, etc.
 Many of the pronominal inflexions survive, e.g., am. *hine* 34, 51, etc., df. *hire* 35.
 Def. art.: am. *pene* 30, 71, etc.; gm. *pas* 145, *pes* 23; dm/n. *pan* 121, 122, 125, etc.; n/an. *pat* 74, 95, etc.; af. *pa* 15; df. *pare* 22; npl. *pa* 27, 224; dpl. *pan* 39, 67, etc.
 Demonst. art.: nf. *peos* 24, 31; n/apl. *pas* 219.

Nouns: Grammatical gender still to some extent survives, e.g. *peos boc* 24, 31, *pat water* 65, etc. The dpl. is usually *-en* (OE *-um*), *ruggen* 44, *cnihten* 82, *wateren* 67, *breosten* 78, etc., and other inflexions are occasionally to be distinguished, e.g. gpl. *Englene* 9, *kingen* 68, *deoren* 127, 136, *æluene* 161.
 Some long-stem neuters retain their npl. without ending, e.g. *word* 219, but cf. *pinges* 48.
 The pl. ending of the weak declension survives in *-en* (OE *-an*), e.g. *hunten* 130, *birlen* 42, *speren* 89, etc., and some original strong nouns have gone over to the weak declension, e.g. *feperen* 26, *runan* 31, *laȝen* 224, *freonden* 74, etc.

Adjectives: The weak forms of the adjective are often to be distinguished, e.g. *pa ædela boc* 15, and many of the strong inflexions survive, e.g. am. *alcne* 29, *nænne* 45, *enne* 61, etc., gm. *heȝes* 23; g/df. *ludere* 114, *ælchere* 135, *hæȝere* 47, *haȝere* 129, *muchelere* 230, etc.; gpl. *alre* 92, 136, etc.; dpl. *deopen* 175, *muclen* 181, etc.

Sounds:

a/o is regularly *o, gon* 14, *mon* 29, *ponke* 6, *londe* 9, etc.
æ is indifferently *æ, e, a, æðelen* 3, *næs* 46, *wes* 1, *pet* 7, *onfest* 5, *at* 3, *pat* 11, *stape* 4, etc.
y is usually *u, ruggen* 44, *cun* 72, etc., but *i* appears in *uirste* 133. *king* 36, 51, etc., *kine–* 105, 207, etc., are from forms with *i* in lOE. *wuste* 50, *suggen* 173, *sugen* 242, are from forms with *y* in lOE.
ā is indifferently *a* and *o, lað* 41, *brade* 54, *ihoten* 1, etc. *bræde* 158, is probably due to the analogy of the verb.

ā[1] is usually *e*, *þer* 5, *weren* 13, *beren* 43, etc. *weoren* 8, etc., is probably due to the rounding influence of *w*. In *þar* 4, etc., *radde* 5, etc., early shortening has taken place.

ā[2] is usually *æ*, *ærest* 9, *sæ* 180, etc., but *e* forms are not infrequent, *neure* 45, *bideled* 134, *se* 231, etc. *lasten* 210, *bitache* 221, *nauer* 241, are due to early shortening.

ȳ is *u* in *fur* 195.

WS *ea*/Ang. *a* before *l*+cons. is normally *a*, *alden* 39, *bald* 46, *bihalues* 67, etc., but *e* appears in *aquelde* 11, *heluen* 135, *æ* in *ælderne* 72, *ælder* 189, and *o* in *woldes* 87; the mutation is *ai* n *aluisc* 138, *walleð* 174, but *æ* in *hælden* 85, *æluene* 161. Before *r*+cons. *æ* appears in -*ærde* 157, *ærde* 166, *ærnes* 165, *a* in *ȝaru* 53, *arnes* 164, -*marken* 193, *art* 220, etc., and *e* in *Ernleȝe* 3; the mutation is *a* in *afallæd* 64, *arhredðe* 64, *aualle* 70, but *e* in *ferde* 63, etc. Before *h* *æ* appears in *Sæxlonde* 71, *isæh* 59, 155, *a* in *isah* 66, 91, *Saxes* 96, *faht* 197, and *e* in *thehte* 61, *quehte* 88, *Sexlonde* 92, *Sexes* 98; the mutation appears as *a* in *mahte* 60, as *æ* in *Sæxisce* 76, etc.

eo is usually *eo*, *leornia* 31, *beornes* 58, etc. Before *ht* *i* appears in *cniht* 38, etc., *fihte* 203, but *e* in *fehte* 53, 211, and *eo* in *feoht* 168.

cleopode 82, etc., *seoþe* 229, are from OE forms with non-WS back-mutation.

weorrede 113, *seollic* 36, *seolcuð* 157, show rounding of *e* through the influence of the adjacent consonants.

seoluen 118, shows non-WS fracture of *e* before *lf*.

weorde 187, *feoȝelen* 159, are probably scribal errors.

ēa appears as *ea* in *leaf* 24, as *æ* in *æc* 52, *dæde* 75, *hæȝe* 85, etc., and as *e* in *neh* 66, *rede* 149, etc. *hafde* 143, *þah* 191, are due to early shortening. The mutation is *e* in *iherde* 184.

ēo is usually *eo*, *preost* 1, *leoden* 1, *beo* 2, etc., but *æo* appears in *ræode* 158, *æ* in *flæn* 62, *flænne* 93, *e* in *þre* 28, and *o* in *four* 13, *ȝond* 14, *bon* 238. Diphthongization of *o*, *e*, before *h* has not taken place in *biðohte* 60, *þohte* 118, *thehte* 61, *quehte* 88.

Consonants: OE *hw* appears as *w* in *wat* 8, *wonene* 8, etc. Initial *f* is frequently voiced, *uolc* 50, *uæie* 56, etc. Medial *þ* appears as *h* in *wurhliche* 77. Medial *m* is assimilated in *keppe* 45, and medial *f* in *wimmen* 233. Medial *n* is lost in *Costæntin* 220 (but cf. Welsh *Cystennin*), and medial spirant in *broute* 18, *almiten* 30. Final -*sc* appears as *s* in *Frenchis* 20; final *n* has been lost in *a* 88, 174, 223, *seoue* 98; final *þ* in *ulih* 132; and final *d* in *þusen* 168. Medial *n* has been doubled in *wunnien* 239.

Orthography: *æ* is used as a spelling for *e* in -*þæinen* 42, *afallæd* 64, *ænde* 133, 178, *næstieð* 164, *æfne* 231. *o* for OE *u* would not have been expected in *foȝel* 105, *uoȝeles* 164. The voiceless back stop [k] is represented by *ck* in *bock* 5, *adruncke* 98, and by *ch* in *archen* 13, OE medial *f* is represented by *fu* in *bihalfues* 69, *hafuede* 109, and by *f* in *hafeð* 117, 123; OE *g* between back vowels by *hȝ* in *dahȝen* 165; *ts* by *ȝs* in *beȝste* 38, 110; and medial *w* by *uw* in *tohauwen* 212.

Notes

2. *Leouenaðes.* OE *Lēofnōþ*, a not uncommon name in OE. *Leucais* (O) is presumably g. of *Lēofeca*, a pet-form of *Lēofnōþ*. *Lēoueca* is recorded in Florence of Worcester, s.a. 1006, and Lewknor, Oxon., is (*æt*) *Leofecan oran*, c. 994.

3. *Ernleʒe.* The modern Areley Kings, near Bewdley in Worcestershire.
at . . . chirechen. The order adj., pronoun, noun, is not uncommon in Laʒamon. It is characteristic of OE verse, but survives into modern English only in the archaic "Good my Lord".

5. *Radestone.* A high cliff of red sandstone near the Severn, where the parishes of Astley and Areley Kings join, at Redstone Ferry.
þer he bock radde, 'said his mass', so Hall, who gives *bock* 'missal', though such a sense seems without parallels in OE or ME. On the other hand it is not infrequently used in the sense 'Bible', and it may be better to take it in that sense here—'where he read his Bible'.

14. *gon liðen*, 'journeyed'. A common construction in ME, where *gon* (pt. of OE *ginnan*) plus the inf. regularly has the simple preterite sense.

15. . . . 'And he obtained those noble books which he took as his models', i.e. which he used as his sources.

16. . . . No doubt the reference here is to the English version of Bede's *Historia Ecclesiastica* made, probably under the guidance of King Alfred, towards the end of the ninth century.

17. *Albin.* Abbot of St. Augustine's, Canterbury, 708–32. He was never canonized, nor is he known to have been an author. He was, however, one of Bede's most important sources for events in the south, and in the *H.E.* Bede duly acknowledges his debt. This mention has, perhaps, led Laʒamon to attribute the Latin text of that work to Albinus rather than to Bede.

18. *Austin.* The regular ME form of *Augustinus*, and the origin of the modern surname. The only reason for St. Augustine's connexion with the book here would appear to be the fact that Bede necessarily has much to say about him.

19ff. . . . A reference to the *Brut* by Wace, a twelfth-century writer known also as the author of other historical and hagiological works in Norman-French. The *Brut* is a versified Norman-French version, with some additions, of Geoffrey of Monmouth's *Historia Regum Britanniae*, and in fact was practically the sole written source of Laʒamon, who uses his other authorities hardly at all. This is the only evidence for Wace's presentation of his book to Eleanor, wife of Henry II.

23. *þes heʒes kinges.* In apposition to *Henries* and so, as in OE, put into the same case. But such agreement in ME is found only in the earliest texts.

28. *þrumde to are*, 'compressed into one', *are* for *anre*.

33. *for his fader saule*, 'for his father's soul'. As in OE there is no ending

in the g. of *fader*; cf. similarly *his moder saule* in the following line. But analogical forms with -*es* appear early.

38. *wunder ane.* A common intensifying phrase in Laʒamon. *wunder* is the adv. 'wonderfully', whilst *ane* is an adverbial derivative of *ān* 'one' in the extended sense 'uniquely, exceptionally'.

42. *bur-þæinen.* OE *būr-þegn* 'chamberlain', but the context suggests that the word has degenerated in meaning and has here more the sense 'attendants' in general.

44. *to ruggen and to bedde,* 'on their back and on their bed', i.e. as garments and bed-clothes. OE *hrycg* 'back' has been obsolete in that sense since the seventeenth century.

49. *riche* 'noble' gives adequate sense, but emendation to *rihte* 'just' would improve it considerably.

53. *fehte* 'army', a sense of the word not otherwise recorded. Perhaps due to the fact that Fr. *bataile* had early developed the sense 'army in battle array', a meaning found in English by the fourteenth century.

61. . . . 'he retreated into a more open place'.

63. *Colgrim.* ON Kolgrímr, not a Saxon name at all.
ferde. In OE usually used of the defending army, *here* being used of the invading army, but as a rule in ME this particular sense appears to have been forgotten, and the word is used quite generally of any kind of an army, though the distinction between the two may, perhaps, still be kept in the *Owl and the Nightingale.*

67. . . . Either 'they were both on the same side of the stream', or 'Colgrim's men were on both sides of the stream', i.e. some of them had crossed, others were waiting to do so, and Arthur charged them whilst they were only partly across. The second translation would certainly make better sense of the account of the battle.

70. *uulle.* OE *full*, of a foe 'avowed, open'; cf. R. Morris, *An Old English Miscellany*, p. 42, "þer him cumeþ Iudas, þat is my vulle i-fo".

77. *wine-maies,* 'members of the retinue'. A distinctively poetic word in OE with this same sense, due no doubt to the fact that in early times the retinue of the chieftain would consist mainly of relatives. Only in Laʒamon does any considerable proportion of the OE poetic vocabulary survive in ME.

79. . . . This type of simile appears to be unknown in OE, and is first noted in Laʒamon, who may have derived it from Latin epic.

85–6. . . . 'They shall fall (lean over) like the lofty forest, when the furious wind presses upon it with its strength'.

89. *brustleden,* i.e. bristled with the arrows and darts sticking in them. though *NED* does not give *bristle* in this sense until the seventeenth century.

100. C *floc*, but O *fliht* 'power of flight' gives better sense with *awemmed*, since OE *awemman* means 'to disfigure, to corrupt'.

105. *on his siðe* 'in his journey', but perhaps for *on þis siðe* 'at this time'.

107. *Eouerwic.* York, OE *Eoforwic*, the Anglicized form of L *Eburacum*, ultimately a Celtic place-name.

114ff. . . . This passage is not in Wace, and appears to be original.

116. *Childric.* A sixth-century Childeric the Saxon is several times mentioned in Gregory of Tours.
is sad of, 'is satiated with, has had enough of'.

117. . . . 'He has divided my kingdom amongst all his best warriors'.

127. . . . 'He considers himself to be in valour the bravest of all beasts'.
deoren 'animals'. This general sense of the word is regular in OE,
and usual in ME up to the sixteenth century, when, except in the
phrase *small deer,* it becomes obsolete; cf. Shakespeare, *K. Lear* III,
iv, 144, " . . . Mice, and Rats, and such small deare". But this
general sense was perhaps a conscious archaism in Shakespeare
since already in the thirteenth century *deer* is found in the modern
sense, and after the fifteenth that becomes the regular one.

133. *i þan uirste ænde,* 'in the nearest place', i.e. he makes for the earth
which chances to be nearest to him. O has a simpler reading.

139. *Wygar. Wigheard* 'tough in battle' would be a more appropriate
name for a mail-coat than *Wïggār* 'battle-spear' (for the loss of final
-d, cf. *þusen* 168).
Witeʒe. Perhaps to be identified with the Germanic hero *Widia/Wudga*
(*Widsith* 124–30, *Waldere B,* 4–10) who was presumably identical
with the *Vidigoia* of Jordanes. Nothing is known to show that he
was regarded as a skilled smith, but in English tradition he appears
to have been thought of as the son of Weland and Beaduhild, and it
may be that Weland's fame has been passed on to the son. In the ME
tail-rime romance *Torrent of Portugal* 421–439 the good sword *Adolake,*
given to the hero, is described as *thorrow Velond wroght.*

141. *Calibeorne.* The name of Arthur's sword which, along with his
spear Ron and his shield Pridwen, appears already in Geoffrey of
Monmouth. All, as their names suggest, come ultimately from
Welsh tradition, though there Pridwen seems to have been the name
of Arthur's ship, not of his shield as in Geoffrey. On the other hand
Wygar and Goswhit, i.e. OE *Gōs-hwīt* 'goose-white', are known
only in Laʒamon, and, if not his own invention, must, judged from
the names, come from English tradition.

153. . . . 'Then those who stood by his side could see . . .', but if so *le
mihte* must be pl. and so should, perhaps, be emended to *heo mihten.*

160. *nikeres.* OE *nicor* 'a water monster', but by the Germanic peoples
the name appears to have been applied to any strange water creature
from a mermaid to a hippopotamus (see R. W. Chambers on *Beowulf*
422).

169. . . . 'Then the people know without doubt that sorrow is to come to
them'.

174. *a moni are siden,* 'on many a side'.

186. *Tanbre.* The River Tamar between Devon and Cornwall.

187. *Camelford.* Modern Camelford in the north of Cornwall, which, of
course, has no connexion with the River Tamar. According to
Geoffrey of Monmouth the battle took place near the river *Cambula,*

and in the different MSS. of Wace this appears in such forms as *Camblan, Tambre, Tamble,* etc., where the latter forms are probably due to the common confusion between *c* and *t* in medieval MSS. Presumably Laʒamon used a MS. of Wace with the form *Tambre.* This he identified as the Tamar, and hence the discrepancies in his description of the place of battle.

191. *uæie . . . weore,* 'although they were doomed'. *hit* refers to *folke,* a neuter sg. in OE.

199. . . . 'No one could distinguish any outstanding warrior in the battle'.

200. *swa . . . imenged,* 'whoever was joined in battle with one another'. The O scribe has apparently not understood this use of *wiðe* and taken it to be a mistake for *weder* 'weather', though in that case *imenged* gives no good sense in the context.

210. *i þare laste,* 'in the least, smallest of them'.

215. *cnaue* 'youth, young warrior', the usual sense of the word in OE, but even then it has already developed the sense 'servant', a sense which survives until the end of the seventeenth century; cf. Dryden, *Virg. Past.* iii, 21, "What Nonsense would the fool thy Master Prate,/ When thou, his Knave, canst talk at such a rate". Side by side with these two senses the modern meaning had developed in the ME period and is now the sole survivor.

222. . . . 'Ever protect my Britons, even with your own life'.

227ff. . . . The British hope that Arthur will come again, here put into Arthur's own mouth, does not appear in Geoffrey of Monmouth, though Wace has it. Whatever its source, it evidently formed part of the British Arthurian tradition, for in 1113 a monk from Laon got into trouble at Bodmin for denying that Arthur still lived. The mention of *Argante,* on the other hand, appears to be an addition by Laʒamon.

228. *haleweiʒe.* Prob., as suggested by F. P. Magoun (171 *Archiv* 29), for *hale-wæge* in the OE charm *Wiþ wæterælf-adle,* a compound of OE *wæge,* so 'healthgiving cup'; but cf. ON *heilvágr,* MHG *heil(a)wāc,* where the second element is presumably cognate with OE *wæg* 'wave'. In either case the sense is the same.

VII. KING HORN

Dialect: Southern with SE and Midland forms.

Inflexions:

    Verbs: inf. *ibite* 25 (r.w. *white*), *loke* 35 (r.w. *toke*), *wynne* 38, etc.
        3pr. *worþ* 93, *lyht* 31, *haueþ* 94. prpl. *bueþ* 14.
        ptp. *ybounde* 10, *icome* 35, *y-orne* 42, but *leye* 33.
    Pronouns: Fem. *hue* 5, 7, etc.
        The am. of *he* appears as *hyne* 89.

Sounds:

a/o is usually *o*, *mony* 74, *honde* 5, *dronc* 7, etc., but *a* appears in *gan* 43, 47, 103, *bygan* 85.

æ is usually *a*, *after* 3, *at* 9, *was* 66, etc., but *e* appears in *wes* 6, 10, 105, *ber* 5, *hedde* 63, *set* 9, *bed* 48, and *o* in *quoþ* 69.

v is *u* in *vurste* 13, *afurste* 14, *fulde* 16, 49, *shurte* 103, but *i* in *firste* 91 (r.w. *toberste*), *kyng* 97, and *e* in *felle* 51 (r.w. *telle*), *keste* 89 (r.w. *reste*).

ā is regularly *o*, *ros* 1, *boþe* 4, etc.

ǣ[1] and *ǣ*[2] are regularly *e*, *were* 18, *seȝe* 53, *adredde* 64; *neuer* 21, *eny* 36, etc.

WS *ea*/Ang. *a* before *l*+cons. is *a* in *al* 20, but *e* in *bihelde* 43, *kelde* 44. Before *r*+cons. *a* is regular, *hydeward* 12, *shipeward* 80, *armes* 102. Before *h* *e* appears in *seh* 21; the mutation appears as *i* in *nyhte* 99, *myhte* 100.

eo is regularly *e*, *fer* 29, 42, 75, *herte* 44, 92, 101, but *i* appears before *ht* in *knyht* 8, 79, and *weor-* appears as *wor-* in *worþ* 93.

ēa is *e* in *ded* 65, *leȝe* 54, *ȝere* 34, but *ei* in *slein* 97.

ēo is usually *e*, *be* 27, *fel* 44, *sek* 85, etc. *eo* appears in *eode* 59, 74, *ue* in *hue* 5, etc., *bueþ* 14, *luef* 106, and *o* in *foure* 60. The mutation appears as *e* in *dere* 24, 106.

No diphthongization has taken place in *þohte* 10, *noht* 45.

Consonants: OE *hw* appears as *w* in *wer* 71. Initial *h* is lost in *is* 45, etc. Final unaccented *-d* is unvoiced to *-t* in *ant* 16, etc., *ȝent* 75. Initial *f* is voiced in *vurste* 13; final *þ* is assimilated to *t* in *lyht* 31, and medial *r* lost in *hydeward* 12.

Orthography:

Long *e* is written *ee* in *beer* 2, 25, *beere* 7. Short *u* is represented by *o* in *fol* 64, *opon* 105, and *ū* by *o* in *bote* 26. OE *sc* is indifferently *sh*, *ssh*, as in *shenh* 13, *fyssh* 36, etc. OE front *c* appears as *h* in *shenh* 13.

Notes

1ff. . . . The episode of the banquet appears to have been particularly popular, and formed the basis of the later *Hind Horn* ballads. The theme is not uncommon in folk-tales, and a particularly close parallel is to be found in the visit of Gram in Saxo Grammaticus, ed. A. Holder, pp. 12ff. In the early Middle Ages it was the custom to admit a few beggars to the wedding feast, and these were served by the bride.

6. *lawe* 'custom'. For this not unusual sense in ME cf. Laȝamon, *Brut* 14,353ff., "& þurh þa ilke leoden, þa laȝen comen to þissen londe,/ Wæs-hail & drinc-hæil".

10. . . . 'It seemed to him that he was overpowered', i.e. he felt overcome by his feelings.

13. *wiþ þe vurste*. Ambiguous. Either 'along with those whom you serve first', or 'along with those who are first, i.e. highest, in rank'.

15. . . . Rimenhild has been pledging the people of rank in a drinking·

horn full of wine, but now lays this down and fills a bowl of ale for
the beggars as being more suitable to their condition. Horn refuses
to accept this (40ff.), and insists on a drinking-horn full of wine,
thereby hinting to Rimenhild that he is of higher rank than he
seems.

23. *toc . . . yfere*, 'handed it to his companion'.

25. *ibite* 'taste', a rare sense of the word in ME, but cf. *Havelok* 1730,
"Was þer-inne no page so lite/þat euere wolde ale bite". Perhaps
used in this sense only for the sake of the rhyme.

26. *coppe white*. Drinking horns, made of the horns of animals, would
naturally be whitish, whereas medieval pottery was usually brown.

29. *by weste*, 'westward', a not unusual meaning of the phrase in ME.

31. . . . Earlier in the romance Rimenhild's love has been likened to a
net, and here the word is probably best taken as referring in turn to
Horn's love for her. 'My love has been here like a net for seven
years; now I have come to see whether it has caught anything; if it
has caught you you will be the gainer'.

31-2. . . . Most editors adopt the reading of the other MSS., and assume
that the original read *honde : ponde*. But it is difficult to believe that
a scribe would replace the comparatively familiar *by honde* by the rarer
wel hende. The word here is possibly *pende* 'arch, covered passage or
entrance'. *NED* knows it only as a Scots word, recorded from the
sixteenth century onwards, but it may well have existed in ME,
perhaps with a wider meaning, or maybe influenced by *pen*
'enclosure'.

44. *fel*. C *bigan* is obviously the word needed. It is difficult to find a
satisfactory meaning for *fel* in the context, and French is probably
correct in taking it as a mistake for *gan*, though it is not easy to see
how such a mistake may have come about.

45-6. . . . 'She recognized neither the allusion to fishing nor Horn
himself'.

50. *pelryne*, Fr. *pèlerin*. But ME usually has a form borrowed from the
earlier Fr. *pelegrin*.

54. *vnder wode leȝe*. The usual ME phrase is *under wode boȝe*, but cf.
Ancren Riwle, ed. J. Morton, p. 96, "euer is þe eie to þe wude leie".

56. *to grounde*, 'to the bottom (of the drinking horn)'.

59-60. *boure : foure*. It is difficult to see how this could ever have been a
good rhyme.

67-8. *damoisele : palmere*. Since these words appear in all MSS., the lack
of rhyme presumably appeared in their common original, which
therefore could hardly have been the author's autograph copy.
French suggests reading *chambrere* 'woman attendant' for *damoisele*,
and this would give good enough rhyme and sense.

72. *hou*. But B *wi*, C *whi* 'why', perhaps gives better sense in the context.

73. *Seint Gyle*. The abbey of St. Gilles, near Nîmes in Provence, was
one of the most popular resorts of pilgrims during the Middle Ages.

75. *ȝent*, 'at a distance', a by-form of *yond*. 'I travelled many a mile, a
long distance westwards'.

79–80. *stonde to shipeward*, 'standing near the ship', i.e. about to embark.

83. *nom in to flode*, 'set out to sea'. This use of *niman* in the sense 'betake oneself, go' is not unusual in ME, and may, perhaps, be due to ellipsis of an original *niman weg* 'to take one's way', though no such idiom has yet been found in OE or eME.

88. *ȝynge*. OE *ging*, a by-form of *geong*, said to be Northumbrian in *NED*. The examples of the form in Bosworth-Toller give no support to this, though in ME the form certainly appears to be northern or northerly.

91–2. *firste* : *toberste*. Original rhyme *ferste* : *toberste* with the south-eastern *ferste* for the sake of the rhyme. A later scribe has replaced the distinctively SE form by the form from his own dialect, and by so doing has spoiled the rhyme.

94. . . . 'Who (i.e. Horn) has been longing for you'.

100–01. . . . 'If Horn should not come back she would stab (herself) to the heart'.

102. . . . B *And Horn hire gan lette*, 'Horn stopped her' gives better rhyme and sense, and no doubt preserves the reading of the original.

VIII. HAVELOK THE DANE

Dialect: East Midland of North Lincs.

Inflexions:

Verbs: Inf. Indifferently with or without final -*n*, e.g. *telle* 3, *here* 4, *riden* 10, *drinken* 15, etc.

3pr. *woneth* 105, but *glides* 224 (r.w. *sides*).

prpl. *dwellen* 165, *hauen* 270, *taken*, 206, but *beres* 236 (r.w. *speres*), *fetes* 254 (r.w. *metes*).

ptp. *slawe* 176, *born* 261, *wreken* 267.

Pronouns: 3 pl. nom. *he* 54, etc., but also *þey* 112, 210, *þei* 127, 206, *þe(i)* 69, 144; poss. *here* 52, etc.; obj. *hem*. 38, etc.

Nouns: *þinghe* 66, 71, retains the pl. without ending of the OE long-stem neuters. *ladden* 145 (r.w. *stadden*), has the pl. ending of the weak nouns, and *liues* 110 is an adverbial genitive.

Sounds:

a/*o* is *a* or *o* before lengthening groups, *handes* 95, *gange* 164, *hond* 50, *wronge* 72, etc., otherwise *a* is invariable, *man* 9, *sham* 56, etc.

æ is normally *a*, *was* 8, *after* 112, etc., but *e* in *festen* 82.

y is normally *i*, *fil* 14, *iuele* 50, etc., but *beye* 53.

ā is usually *o*, *holi* 36, *ston* 130, etc., but *a* in *stan-* 188, *lath* 76.

ǣ[1] and *ǣ*[2] both appear as *e*, *were* 28, *wepne* 89; *ylere* 12 (r.w. *yhere*), *se* 256 (r.w. *plente*), etc. *late* 17, *ani* 10, 105, *adrad* 155 (r.w. *bad*), are due to early shortening, *þor-* 100, *þore* 121, 140, are from OE forms with *ā*.

ȳ is regularly *i*, *litel* 6, *unride* 168, etc.

WS *ea*/Ang. *a* before *l*+cons. is regularly *o* before lengthening groups, *holden* 29, *bold* 64, etc., but *baldelike* 53; elsewhere *a* is regular, *alle* 2, *falle* 39, etc.; the mutation appears as *e* in *welle* 224, *feld* 197, 232. Before *r*+cons. *a* is usual, *sparke* 91, *starke* 122, etc.   Before *h* *a* appears in *saw* 150, 166, 221; the mutation appears as *i* in *nihtes* 274.

eo is normally *e*, *werkes* 34, *heuene* 62, etc.; *i* appears before *ht* in *knict* 32. *siluer* 73, may be from an OE form with *y*, and *bores* 244 is probably a scribal error.

ēa is usually *e*, *red* 47, *gret* 168, etc., but *a* in *chapmen* 51, and note also *shewe* 226 (r.w. *mowe*). The mutation appears as *e* in *here* 4, 241, *yhere* 11, etc.

ēo is regularly *e*, *prestes* 33, *theues* 41, etc., but *o* in *fourti* 257.

Consonants: OE *hw* frequently appears as *w*, *woso* 4, *wil* 6, etc. Medial or final *þ* is not infrequently assimilated or dissimilated to *t*, *witþat* 19, *wit* 52, *þerwit* 138, etc., and note also *tayn* 31, etc. The back spirant has been lost medially in *browt* 58, and finally in *þou* 250, *plow* 124, and been vocalized to *u* in *þoru* 259, *borw* 121. Medial *w* has been lost in *to* 196, medial *l* in *werd* 248, and final -*l* in *mike* 249, *mik* 255. Medial double *þ* has been simplified in *siþen* 183, *siþe* 187, and medial double *t* in *puten* 158. Final -*d* has been lost in *an* 29, etc., and final -*f* in *twel* 161. Medial *þ* has developed in *alþerbeste* 147, and the back stop in *biseken* 269 is due to the influence of the 2/3pr.

Orthography:

Numerous scribal peculiarities appear. *g* is occasionally written *gh*, *bringhe* 65, *þinghe* 66. Initial *h* is often omitted, *Auelok* 166, or wrongly added, *heuere* 17, *holde* 30, etc. *th* is not infrequently used by the side of *þ*, *soth* 36, *theues* 41, *grith* 61, etc. OE -*ht* is indifferently *th, cth, ct*, *brouth* 84, *micth* 35, *knict* 32, etc. Final -*t* appears as *th* in *greth* 132, *neth* 133, *þuruth* 52, and final -*d* as *dh* in *quodh* 173. *w* is represented by *v* in *svich* 60, and by *u* in *duelle* 4, and *wu* by *w* in *stalwrþe* 134. *i* is represented by *ij* in *hijs* 47. *ū* is normally *ow*/*ou*, *nou* 11, *brown* 115, etc., but spellings with *u*/*v* are not infrequent, *fule* 195, *dune* 188, *vt* 186, etc., and *w* appears in *hw* 93, and *wou* in *hwou* 262, 265, 267. In *sholdres* 191, *o* is used for *u* where it would not be expected, and the same may be true of *dore* 169, *dore-tre* 179, *boles* 243, *þoru* 259, *borw* 121.

Notes

1ff. . . . Such a prologue by the minstrel in a romance designed for the lower classes is not unusual, though this is rather fuller than most. As French and Hale point out, this follows the usual convention of such prologues by including (i) a request for attention, (ii) an announcement of the subject, (iii) an interesting fact or two about the story to whet the interest of the audience, (iv) a prayer for the company.

7. *gome*. OE *guma* 'man', one of the few specifically poetic words of OE

which survived into the ME period. This particular word was in poetic use from OE times to the sixteenth century. Similarly as the second element of OE *brȳdguma* it survived in the ME *bridegome* until the sixteenth century when, through popular etymology, it was replaced by the unrelated *-groom*, *gome* having become obsolete.

9–10. . . . A favourite couplet of the author, repeated with variations fairly frequently, cf. 25–6, 87–8, and found elsewhere in medieval romance. Apparently a translation of the common OF phrase "Ce fu li mieudres qui sor destrier sist".

24. *flok.* Until the seventeenth century regularly used in the sense 'body, company of people', but after that the term was restricted to animals.

25. *stalworpeste.* On the analogy of lines 9–10 Skeat-Sisam emends to *wihtest*, unnecessarily so in view of the variation found in lines 87–8, 1970–1, etc.

27ff. . . . As French and Hale point out, this portrait of a good king has more in common with the kings of OE heroic poetry than with the good kings of French romance.

It was, 'there was', the anticipated subject is regularly expressed by *it* in ME.

28. *þat in his time,* 'in whose time'. The ME relative *þat,* being uninflected, had to be supplemented by the personal pronoun if it were desired to show its case. Hence *þat he* 'who', *þat his* 'whose', *þat him* 'whom', etc. Cf. the similar use with the indeclinable relative *þe* in OE.

29. . . . 'which he caused to be made and to be well kept'.

31. *tayn.* MS. *kayn.* The original apparently had *tayn,* with partial assimilation of initial *þ* to the preceding final *-d.* In ME *c* and *t* are easily confused in writing, and a scribe has mistaken the *t* for *c*, which he, or another, has written *k*.

38. . . . 'and summoned them from everywhere'. So French and Hale. Sisam translates 'and everywhere had them summoned to preferment', but there seems to be no support in ME for such a sense of *calle.*

39. *wrobberes* 'informers'. There is no need to emend to *robberes* as do some editors, since *wreȝen and wrobben/wrabben* was evidently an alliterative phrase in eME; see 9 *Med. Æv.* 15, and 10 *Med. Æv.* 159–160.

44. . . . 'Neither gold nor treasure went for them', i.e., there was no possibility of ransom.

45ff. . . . Similar stories were told of any strong king during the medieval period; cf. Bede on King Edwin and the *Peterborough Chronicle* (*s.a.* 1135) on Henry I.

47. *red gold.* The conventional description of gold in ME, but perhaps originally more than a mere conventional epithet. Medieval gold is said to have been frequently alloyed with copper, and this gave it a reddish tinge. Moreover, the sources of gold are now different; most medieval gold came from Asia, whereas modern gold is rather from S. Africa and Australia.

55–6. *fram* : *sham*. Sisam suggests influence from ON *skamm-* on ME *shame*, since the latter should have a long *a*, due to lengthening in open syllables, and elsewhere in the romance it does rhyme with *ā*. But this could equally well be a Northern form with early loss of *-e* and so no lengthening.

63–4. *blome* : *Rome*. Since *blome* (ON *blómi*) must have had a tense vowel in ME Sir William Craigie (quoted in Skeat-Sisam) argues that the rhyme-word in 64 is not the verb 'to roam' but *Rome* which regularly has tense *ō* in ME; further, that *lond* is due to a scribe's misreading of *lou'd* (*louerd*). The translation is then 'There was no lord so bold as far as Rome'; with *to Rome*; cf. *desi k'a Rome* elsewhere in Le Lai d'Haveloc 371.

65 is metrically incomplete as it stands in the MS. and Skeat-Sisam supplies [*menie*] after *his*. If, however, it be assumed that the original read "Þat durste upon his londe bringhe" we restore the prosody and account for the corruption (by anticipation) in 64.

66. . . . Most editors emend to *Hunger ne othere wicke þinghe*, but *wicke þinghe* is to be taken in apposition to *hunger ne here*, a not uncommon alliterative phrase in OE and eME.
On 63–6 see 4 *Leeds Studies in English* 75–6.

74. . . . 'He was so careful of the good of his soul'.

80–1. . . . As Sisam points out, this is a confused construction: *were* requires *he made him*, while *þat he ne made him* would normally follow *was*.

86. . . . On loss of testicles as a legal punishment for rape, cf. *Chronicle* 1086 E, "Gif hwilc carlman hæmde wið wimman hire unðances, sona he forleas þa limu þe he mid pleagode".

87–8. . . . Cf. lines 9–10. The following nineteen lines, rhyming on the same vowel, may be a deliberate imitation of the French assonant tirades.

94. . . . A reference to the fact that in tournaments the arms, armour and horse of the vanquished knight became the prize of the victor.

113. . . . . This mention of a parliament at Lincoln has been used in attempts to date the composition of the poem. But it has been shown that several parliaments were in fact held at Lincoln, the earliest in 1213, so that even if the reference be to an actual historical event—and this is far from certain—it would not help in the dating.

115. *blac and brown*. A characteristic tag of the poet of which the exact meaning is doubtful. Sisam takes it to mean 'everyone', and points out that the poet liked to indicate inclusiveness by coupling terms of opposite meaning. This is possible enough; 'black' is generally agreed to refer to peasants only, and 'brown' was a proper enough complexion for knights in medieval romance; cf. for example the Nut-Brown Maid, who was a baron's daughter. But in most ballads and romances, as French and Hale point out, brown and black complexions are for the peasantry, red and white for the nobles. Consequently the phrase may rather mean 'all the lesser folk'.

126ff. . . . 'For there was no horse-boy, whatever work there might be on hand, who didn't come there to see the sports'.

127. *þo*, 'though'. Some editors unnecessarily emend to *þouh*, but *þo* in this sense is found elsewhere (e.g. in *Cursor Mundi*) and presumably represents a northern form of ON *þóh* with early loss of the final spirant which caused diphthongization.

130. *pulten*. Usually emended to *putten*, probably unnecessarily since the two words appear to coincide in many of their meanings.

138. *chaunpioun*, 'a competent athlete', but apparently the *kempe* (143) was an outstanding one. For an illustration of putting the stone in medieval times see the British Museum MS. Royal 10 E. iv, f. 96 (reproduced on a postcard).

144–5. *stadden : ladden*. MS. *stareden*, but, as Sisam points out, if this be replaced by *stadden* (ptpl. of ON *steðja*) 'looked on', it improves the rhyme, retains the alliteration, and gives good sense. In addition it is easy to see why a southern scribe might replace the ON word by one more familiar.

149. . . . 'And he was quite ignorant of (the art of) putting'.

153. . . . 'To do as well as he could with it'.

161. *twel*. This could be a genuine form of the word with loss of *-f* due to the following *fot*. Consequently there is no need to emend to *twelue*, even though this would improve the metre.

162–3. *sowen : lowen*. An example of slack and tense *ō* rhyming together. Because of this most editors suggest that some emendation is needed, but no satisfactory one has yet been suggested. In any case there is no real reason to believe that the author would have hesitated to rhyme the two vowels together.

172. *you* is object, '(flee from) you'; cf. *NED*, *flee* II, 7.

192. *speu*. Most editors read *spen* and emend to *spende*. Sisam suggested *speu* as involving less change, and this in fact appears to be the MS. reading.

197–8. *feld : swerd*. E. J. Dobson (1 *English and Germanic Studies* 58–9) suggests that 198 should be read *þe seuenþe brayde up his scheld* or *þe seuenþe uppe brayd his scheld*, either of which would give the rhyme required.

199. . . . As in modern English, verbs of action in OE and ME were often omitted when their auxiliaries are expressed, and the omission of the verb here may be due to the influence of that idiom. But Dobson (*loc. cit.*) suggests emendation of *riht* to *pliht* 'endanger, harm, injure', or *diht* 'harm, injure'.

211ff. . . . A reference to bear-baiting, a common medieval sport, in which the bear was chained by the neck or hind legs and dogs turned loose to worry him.

224. *glides*. This northerly form of the ending of the 3pr. is proved by the rhyme to be due to the author.

225–6. *mowe : shewe*. By the side of regular *scēawian* lOE also had *scāwian* with shift of stress to the second element of the diphthong and later absorption of the front element of the diphthong by the preceding palatal. The two forms regularly gave ME *shēwen/shōwen* which remained in use side by side throughout the period. In modern English *show* became the regular pronunciation, though *shew* remained in the spelling until the middle of the nineteenth century, and perhaps even later. Here the original rhyme must have been *mowe* : *showe*.

33ff. . . . Such descriptions of festivities are not infrequent in medieval romances.

35–6. . . . Tilting and sword-and-buckler play were recognized amusements for younger men. Their obvious danger led to their prohibition by Edward I, but like many such prohibitions this appears to have been ineffective.

37. . . . For another example of the coupling of these two sports see the eME homily on two lines of a popular song:

> "Atte wrastlinge mi lemman I ches,
> And atte ston-kastinge I him forles." (42 *Anglia* 152.)

39. *mine, hasard.* Gambling games played with dice and a board.

40ff. . . . Note that some of the romances are sung, others read. The drummers of 242 were presumably a different kind of entertainment altogether.

43. . . . The bull was fastened to a stake and attacked by dogs. These tried to seize the bull's nose and jaw, pinning them together, and holding on until the bull gave up. Baiting was supposed to make the flesh more wholesome, and the sale of bull-beef was forbidden unless baiting had taken place.

44. *bores.* Obviously for *beres.* The form could be from OE *beora* with non-WS back-mutation, and the *eo* remaining as a rounded vowel. But such a form would be completely isolated in this text, and is more probably due to confusion of *e* and *o* by some scribe.

46. *hw grim greu.* 'how fury, rage, increased', referring to the bear-baiting.

51. *troud.* MS. *croud*, which Sisam suggests is a scribal error for *troud*, *c* and *t* being easily confused; this in turn has been substituted for *trod* 'believed', a shortened form of the pt. of OEN *tróa.* This would give good sense and a reasonable rhyme.

IX. FLORIZ AND BLAUNCHEFLUR

Dialect: South-East Midland.

Inflexions:

Verbs: inf. Usually in -*e*, *awreke* 2, *binde* 3, etc., but *fonden* 133.
2 Weak Class in -*ie*, *polie* 38, 39, *louie* 185.
3pr. Usually -*eþ*, *bringeþ* 61, *sendeþ* 33, etc., but syncopated forms appear in *bid* 97, *haþ* 1.
prpl. Regularly -*eþ*, *spekeþ* 70, *falleþ* 148, etc., but *seoþ* 70.
prp. *wepinge* 62 (r.w. *bringeþ*), 106, *wepinde* 104.
ptp. *inome* 30, *icume* 43, etc.

Pronouns: Fem. *heo* 53, 55, *he* 86.

3pl. nom. *hi* 23, etc.: poss. *here* 62, etc.; obj. *hem* 3, etc.

Note the retention of the am. of the definite article in *þane ende* 181.

Nouns: *þing* 29, retains the pl. without ending of the OE long-stem neuters. Similarly *childre* 61, 147, retains the historically correct form of the pl. (OE *cildru*); cf. *children* 24, 80, 113.

Sounds:

a/o is regularly *o* before lengthening groups, *fond* 16, *longe* 157, etc.; otherwise *a* and *o* forms appear side by side, *nom* 59, *mon* 60, *grame* 74, *mani* 104, etc.

æ is invariably *a*, *after* 1, *was* 5, etc.

y is usually *u*, *ibuld* 5, *ifuld* 6, *muchel* 9, etc., but *i* forms also occur *mireȝþe* 44, *gilt* 85, etc.

ā is regularly *o*, *wroþ* 8, *hom* 163, etc. *naȝt* 163, shows early shortening, and *biknewe* 80 is probably analogical.

$\bar{æ}^1$ and $\bar{æ}^2$ both appear as *e*, *vnmeþ* 37, *were* 66, *red* 160 (r.w. *ded*); *meste* 13, *neure* 51, etc. *radde* 123, *are* 23, *bitaȝt* 50, etc., are probably due to early shortening.

ȳ is regularly *i*, *fir(e)* 34, 76, *litel* 112, etc., but *suþe* 65, 176, from a lOE form with *ȳ*.

WS *ea*/Ang. *a* before *l*+cons. is *o* before lengthening groups, *told* 19, *isold* 130, *itold* 129, otherwise *a* is usual, *alle* 7, *falleþ* 148, etc., but *e* appears in *ȝeld* 176, *help* 123. Before *h* *e* appears in *seȝ* 104; the mutation is *i* in *miȝte* 39, *miȝtest* 44, etc.

eo is regularly *e*, *erles* 6, *swerd* 107, etc., but *i* appears before *ht* in *kniȝt* 146. *clepe* 81 (r.w. *speke*), is from a form with non-WS back-mutation in OE.

ēa is usually *e*, *deþ* 38, *ded* 159 (r.w. *red*), etc., but *i* appears in *diþe* 23, *ride* 172. The mutation is *e* in *ihere* 24, *iherd* 10.

ēo is *e* in *ben* 4, *se* 52, etc.; *eo* in *freo* 21, *seoþ* 70, etc., and *u* in *buþ* 69, 71. *forȝiue* 126, 141 (cf. *ȝeue* 164), is from an OE form with front diphthongization.

Diphthongization of *o* before the back spirant has not taken place in *boȝte* 11, *noȝt* 15, etc.

Consonants: Final *-t* has been voiced in *guld* 37. *w* has been lost before the following rounded vowel in *suþe* 65, 176, and already in OE *g* had been lost before a following *d* in *sede* 9, 27, etc. In *lemman* 47, 182, *hadde* 109, 110, assimilation of *fm* and *fd* has taken place. OE *hw* appears in *h* in *ho* 123, whilst *iȝolde* 171 has *ȝ* by analogy with the pr. and pt.

Orthography:

OE front *c* regularly appears as *hc* in *ihc* 11, 19. etc. *-ht* is written *-st* in *rist* 25. *w* is regularly written *u* after *s*, *ansuare* 26, *suete* 68, etc., and once after *t* in *tuye* 40.

Notes

1. *isend. isent* is obviously required for the rhyme.

13–14. . . . 'It was my best hope to have her as my queen'.

21. *freo burgeis.* Only in this MS., the others making the speaker a king. On the whole this gives the better sense; the citizen, with a strong sense of justice, demands that the lovers be heard in their own defence, while the King of Nubie, because of the dishonour to a fellow ruler, would have them condemned out of hand.

26. *biputen,* 'without'. The form occurs occasionally in ME, but the etymology is puzzling. *NED* merely says that it is an altered form of *without* with *by-* substituted for *wi-*, which explains nothing at all.

30. *hond-habbing,* a survival of OE *hand-hæbbende,* a technical legal term used of the thief taken with stolen property in his hands. Hence 'in the act, red-handed'.

39–40. . . . 'But if human nature could endure it I ought rightly to die twice'.

45ff. . . . This was a magic ring given to Floriz by his mother when he set out in search of Blauncheflur. It had the property of preserving the wearer from almost any kind of death.

51–2. . . . 'This ring shall never save me, for I could not bear to see you die'. The other MSS. make it clear that these lines are spoken by Blauncheflur.

61–2. . . . E *pus pe children wepyng com/To pe fire and hur[e] doom* probably represents the original, and certainly gives a better rhyme.

73. *Admiral,* 'emir', a borrowing from the Arabic *amir* "commander", with the initial *am-* treated as if it were the usual Fr. *am-* from L *adm-*, and *-al* due to the fact that the Arabic title was often followed by *al* '(of) the', and this was taken as part of the title. Under Edward III the title was used specifically of the commander at sea, following French and Genoese usage imitating the Arabic, hence "Amyrel of the Sea". Later, about 1500, after the original sense became obsolete, *admiral* was used as a naval title without any qualification.

95–6. *bed : ȝet.* A *bet : ȝet* probably retains the original rhyme, though in this MS. Blauncheflur offers herself first.

97–8. *suere : tire.* Read *suire : tire,* as in the other MSS.

99–100. . . . E *And seide, 'I am man: I shal byfore,/With wrong hast pou py lyf loore'* certainly gives a much better rhyme.

103. *he seȝ pat* is not in the other MSS. and is better omitted.

125. . . . 'Despite anything that may be done to me'.

129. *ord and ende,* 'from beginning to end', a common alliterative phrase, found already in OE and surviving into the fifteenth century.

135. *cupe.* A marvellous cup given to Floriz by his father when he set out in search of Blauncheflur. With it he had bribed the porter of the emir to have him carried into the harem in a basket of flowers. But the *cupe* of 137 is OE *cūpe* 'basket', a different word.

152. *Clariȝ.* An inmate of the harem who had helped Floriz in his search for Blauncheflur.

160. *nimen his red*, 'adopt as a plan, decide'. Obviously something like 't
return home' must be understood here. Other MSS. read *þe barnag*
ʒaf him red/Þat he scholde wenden hom/And vnderfongen his kyndom.
The omission of the second two lines is probably due to unintelligen
cutting by the copyist of C.

173. *Daris*. A bridge-porter at Babylon (a medieval name for Cairo) wh
had befriended and helped Floriz, more particularly by introducin
him to the porter of the harem and advising him how to proceed.

181ff. . . . The conventional romance-ending. With it should be com
pared the ending of *Havelok*.

X. THE OWL AND THE NIGHTINGALE

Dialect: Southern.

Inflexions:

Verbs: inf. Indifferently with and without final *-n*, *singe* 39, *biholde* 7*
speten 39, *smiten* 78, etc. 2 Weak Class *-ien* in *erien* 135.

3pr. *-eþ* in *soweþ* 137, *demeþ* 177, etc., but syncopated forms a*
frequent, *falt* 37, *sprinþ* 138, *writ* 178, etc.

prpl. *-eþ* regular, *driueþ* 66, *eteþ* 103, etc.

ptp. *ishote* 23, *itoʒen* 147.

Pronouns: Fem. *ho* 19, etc., *heo* 142, etc.

3pl. nom. *hi* 10, etc., *ho* 66, 76, *heo* 197; poss. *hore* 114, *heore* 197, 19*
obj. *hom* 62, etc., *heom* 186, 187.

Some of the OE pronominal inflexions survive, e.g. definite artic*
am. *þen* 165, *þane* 193; df. *þare* 31, 140, etc.; dpl. *þan* 184. Indefinit
article, df. *ore* 17, 172, 176. Possessive pronouns, df. *þire* 162, *mi*
163. Note also am. *hine* 171, 181.

Nouns: Grammatical gender is still to some extent observed, an
occasional examples of the distinctive OE inflexions are to be foun
e.g. *wiʒte* npl. *i*-stems 87, *eʒene* npl. wk. nouns 75, *bischopen* dpl. 18*
þinge 194, has not yet taken the *-es* ending of the pl., and cf. als
childre 197 (OE *cildru* pl.).

Sounds:

a/o is regularly *o* before lengthening groups, *strong* 5, *þonkes* 70, etc
Otherwise *a* and *o* forms appear side by side, *man* 135, *grame* 4*
bigon 13, *monie* 72, etc.

æ is invariably *a*, *was* 1, *sat* 15, etc.

y is normally *u*, *hurne* 14, *cunne* 20, etc., but *i* in *kinge* 153. *wuste* 1*
sulue 69, *nute* 106, *wulle* 152, *stude* 189, are from lOE forms in *y*.

ā is regularly *o*, *one* 1, *lop* 72, etc.

ā[1] and *ā*[2] appear as *e*, *were* 16, *lete* 35, *lere* 113, *teche* 117, etc. Earl
shortening has taken place in *þar* 16, etc., *lateþ* 151, etc., *ofdrad* 16*
ilast 134, etc.

ȳ is *u* in *suþe* 2, 12, *ʒut* 91, from forms with *ȳ* in lOE.

WS *ea*/Ang. *a* before *l*+cons. is *o* before lengthening groups, *holde* 3, *volde* 72, etc., otherwise *a*, *al* 8, *halt* 32, etc. Before *r*+cons. *a* is usual, *starc* 5, *harpe* 22, etc., but *earding-* 28; the mutation is *e* in *uerde* 212. Before *h e* appears in *iseʒ* 29, *ouerseʒ* 30; the mutation is *i* in *miʒte* 42, *aniʒt* 89, etc.

eo is usually *o*, *horte* 37, *hore* 114, etc., but *eo* in *feole* 194. *milc* 105 is from an OE form with *io*. The mutation is *o* in *-worste* 10, and *u* in *wrs* 34.

ēa is regularly *e*, *grete* 3, *atschet* 44, etc. *dreim* 21 is presumably a scribal error, and early shortening has taken place in *þah* 142, 150. The mutation is *e* in *ihere* 120, etc.

ēo is *o* in *holde* 12, *bihold* 30, etc., but *eo* in *beo* 157, *beoþ* 157, and *e* in *eu* 215. The mutation is *i* in *atfliþ* 37, *fliʒt* 89.

ʒiue 189, *ʒif* 51, etc., *schilde* 57, etc., are from forms with WS front diphthongization, but cf. *ʒeueþ* 198, etc., *ʒef* 156, etc., *sheld* 118.

Consonants: Initial *f* is frequently voiced as in *vaire* 15, *uor* 19, etc. OE *hw* is indifferently *w* and *wh*, *wi* 91, *wat* 93, *what* 60, *whar* 64, etc. Loss of *g* before *d* had taken place already in OE in *sede* 33, etc., *tobrode* 104, and later loss of *g* appears in *sprinþ* 138, *imeind* 18, *fuel-* 65. Loss of *w* before a rounded vowel has taken place in *suþe* 2, 12. Initial *h* is frequently misplaced, *hule* 4, *h·nke* 155, etc. *fihs* 103, *flehs* 103, may represent genuine dialectal forms with metathesis. Medial *d* has been lost in *answare* 55, and medial *h* already in Ang. in *atfliþ* 37. Final *d* is lost in *an* 7, etc., and an intrusive *n* appears in *niʒtingale* 4, etc., but *niʒtegale* 141, etc. Final *þ* has become *t* in *fort* 41, *wit* 56, and final *d* unvoiced to *t* in *ihert* 185.

Orthography:

w is used as a spelling for *wu-*, *wi-*, *vu-*, e.g. *wrs* 34, *wse* 54, *wle* 35. After *s w* is written *u/v* in *suich* 104, 110, *sval* 7. OE *sc* appears as *s* in *sol* 121. *ū* is usually represented by *u*, but *ou* appears in *houle* 207, and *ē* is written *ee* in *see* 176.

Notes

1. *sumere dale*, 'summer valley', perhaps a valley open to the south, cf. *summer-wall*, *-side* 'wall, side facing south', but more probably 'valley used for summer grazing'; cf. such place-names as *Somerton* '*tūn* used only in summer', *Somercotes* 'huts used in summer', etc. But Atkins prefers to take it as lWS *sumere*, df. of *sum* 'a certain'.

2. *hale*, OE *h(e)alh*, as a place-name element in the south usually with the sense 'nook, recess, remote valley', but in the north it developed the meaning 'flat alluvial land by the side of a river'. A common place-name element, as in *Hale*, *Hailes*, *Halton*, etc.

3. *tale*, 'conversation, talk', a sense obsolete since the seventeenth century; but cf. Shakespeare, *Rom. & Jul.*, II, iv, 99, "Thou desirs't me to stop in my tale against the haire".

8. J *vuele*. C *wole* is usually explained as due to the C scribe having taken the *uv* of *uvele* as *vu*, and then written *w* for the *vu-*, a spelling found occasionally in this text, while the *o* is simply a careless writing for *e*.

13. *speche*, 'law-suit, plea', a regular legal term with this meaning already in OE.

14. *breche*. Probably OE *bræc* 'fallow-ground', connected with the modern SW dialect *breach* 'land ploughed but not yet sown', with OHG *brāhha*, and found in such place-names as *Bircham*, *Braxted*, etc., in that sense. J *beche* seems to be an attempt at emendation by a scribe to whom the C word was unfamiliar.

15. *up* 'upon', an unaccented form of OE *uppan*.

17. J *vaste* (OE *fæst*, 'close, thick') gives better sense than C *waste* 'deserted, solitary', the latter form probably being due to a misspelling of *w* for *v*.

18. *mid*. Throughout the poem, with few exceptions, *mid* and *wiþ* are kept distinct, retaining their OE meanings, *mid* 'with', *wiþ* 'against'.

20. . . . 'And sang many different tunes'.

26. *tide*, 'the services recited at the canonical hours', a meaning of the word which had already been developed in OE; cf. Ælfric, *Lives of Saints*, ii, 344, "Nu wille ic þæt þu . . . singe þær þine tida". Elsewhere in the poem the owl is represented as uttering her cries at the canonical hours observed by the regular clergy for devotion and prayer.

30. . . . 'Scanned her and looked scornfully at her'.

31. *þuȝte*. An impersonal construction, 'it seemed (to her) very foul concerning the owl', i.e. she thought poorly of the owl. Impersonal constructions are common in the poem, though in this particular instance the absence of 'to her' suggests that it may be an example of the equally common confusion between *pencan* and *pyncan*.

32. *me*. The usual indefinite pronoun in ME. Usually explained as a weakening of *men*, itself an unaccented form of OE *man*.

43. . . . 'For her heart was so swollen with anger'.

45. *warp a word*. A common alliterative phrase in English, and probably already in PrGmc. since it appears in ON *varpa orð*, though there the alliteration has been lost.

54. *an*. J *on* 'in'. WS normally has only *on*, which is used for both 'on' and 'in', the use of *in* as a preposition in OE being characteristically Anglian. Hence the use of *an, on,* for 'in' in this poem is a continuation of the WS practice, but *in* is also found side by side with *on*. Atkins interprets in this way, but better sense would be obtained if *an oþer* were taken together 'you would sing another tune'.

64. *over-smale*. As it stands the MS. gives good sense, the only objection being that *tukien* is not normally construed with *over* in ME. Hence it is perhaps better to take *over-smale* as a compound 'very small'; cf. OE *ofereald, oferceald*, etc.

65–6. *kunne : honne*. The imperfect rhyme is presumably due to scribal corruption. OE *cynn* would give N/EM *kinne*, SE *kenne*, SW/WM *kunne*, whereas OE *heonan* would give N/EM/SE *henne*, SW/WM *honne/heonne*. The author must presumably have used the SE forms *kenne : henne*, and a later scribe, replacing them by the SW/WM forms, has spoiled the rhyme.

70. *hire ponkes*, 'willingly', a common idiom in OE and in ME.

72. *in monie volde*, 'in many respects'.

73. . . . It has been suggested that in this line *bodi* and *swore* should be transposed, since the neck of an owl in full plumage looks 'short' not 'thin', and the body is 'thinner' not 'shorter' than the face.

74. J *ne* in the sense 'than', as in many modern dialects, may perhaps better represent the original.

80. *owel*, 'flesh-hook', as invariably in ME; cf. Chaucer, *Summoner's Tale* (C.T. III, 1730 ff.): "Ful hard it is with flesshhook or with oules/To been yclawed, or to brenne or bake".

82. . . . 'And that is all there is in your song'.

85. . . . 'A frog would be more natural to you'.

88. . . . 'Are natural to you and your proper food'.

91ff. . . . This account of Norway and the far North is reminiscent of the OE account of the voyage of Ohthere, and that these ideas survived into the ME period is suggested also by the account of the mission of Cardinal William to Hákon the Old in 1247, "It was told him by the Englishmen for envy's sake against the men of Norway that he would get no honour there and hardly any meat, and no drink but sour whey; and the English dissuaded him . . . against going to Norway and frightened him both with the sea and the grimness of the folk". Moreover at Hákon's coronation feast "it was told me that I should see few men . . . (and) they would be more like to beasts in their behaviour than men" (88 RS 241, 248). Compare also the papal legate who, in 1154, was sent "that he might rescue the Norwegians from their barbarism" (1 *Surtees Society* 108).

103. . . . Cf. William of Malmesbury, according to whom enthusiasm for the First Crusade was so great that "the Welshman left his hunting; the Scot his fellowship with vermin; the Dane his drinking party; the Norwegian his raw fish" (90 RS ii, 399).

111ff. . . . Some definite papal mission seems to be referred to here, and the passage has been used in attempts to date more exactly the composition of the poem. It is unlikely that the reference is to the mission of Cardinal Guala in 1218, but it might refer to that of Cardinal Vivian in 1176-7, or to that of Nicholas Breakspeare in 1152-4.

117-8. *bore* : *spere*. Read *bere* : *spere*. *bore* (for *beore*) would be from *beora*, a form with non-WS back mutation.

According to Atkins the illustration may have been suggested by the author's reading of Alexander Nequam, *De Naturis Rerum* (Bk. ii, cap. 129), where an account is given of a jongleur who trained two apes to fight in a mimic tournament with shield, sword and spear. In the following chapter the bear is described as a type of cruelty, and this idea may have suggested itself as adding point to the illustration.

122. . . . 'However long I might sing to them'.

125. *wude-wise*. J *wode wyse*. C is usually taken as a scribal error, and J *wode* 'mad', as the correct reading. But perhaps C represents OE *wuduwāsa* 'savage, wild man of the woods', for which ME examples

give forms with a second element in -*wise*, though the word does not elsewhere appear to be used as an adj. However, such a development would not be unusual, and would help to explain the change by the J scribe who had not recognized the rare word.

126. *ise*. C J *ire*, but the rhyme shows that the original must have had *ise* 'iron'. In OE *iren* appears to have been distinctively Anglian, *isern* WS, but in ME *ysen, yse, ise*, appear to have been distinctively SE, whereas *ire* is SW. Presumably this is another instance where a SW scribe has altered a SE form, and spoiled the rhyme.

142. *smale* 'thin, of little strength'. For this sense cf. Chaucer (*C.T.* I, 688), "A voys he hadde as smal as hath a goot".

146-7. . . . 'For though she was not bred in the woods she had been brought up among mankind, and derived her wisdom thence'. Presumably the general sense is that though by her place of birth the wren was not skilled in woodcraft she had learned wisdom from the men with whom she had been brought up. There is some reference to a story connected with the wren not now known.

wolde 'woodland', the original sense of the word. Later apparently 'wooded upland', and as this was cleared it retained its name, whence the word came to denote an elevated tract of open country, whether wooded or not, as in the Yorkshire/Lincolnshire Wolds. But the original sense, along with the distinctively southern form, still survives in the Weald (of Kent and Sussex).

152-3. . . . It is likely enough that some definite peace is indicated by these two lines, and consequently they have been used in attempts to date the poem more exactly. But which particular peace is intended? Perhaps that established by Henry II, in consequence of his legal reforms, from 1170 onwards; perhaps that established by the justiciar Hubert Walter during the reign of Richard I, 1194-8. The question is made more difficult by the fact that *kinge* is a modern emendation, a word having been omitted in the common original of our two MSS.

155. *hunke*. Historically the dat. of the 1st dual 'to us two', and explained by Atkins as used loosely of speaker and those addressed. But in ME, whether due to confusion with OE *inc* or not, this form appears also to have been used as the 2nd dual; cf. *Havelok* 1882, "Gripeth eyþer unker a god tre", where Huwe is addressing Robert and William. Certainly the 2nd dual gives the sense required here.

168. *Maister*. The use of the title at this date presumably indicates that Nicholas had received a degree qualifying him to teach in a University.

173. *nuȝte*. Onions suggests that *nuȝte ȝe* is a mistake for *nuste ȝit* 'did you two not know?', while Grattan reads *miȝte* and takes it to be a case of ellipsis, with a different ellipsis from that in modern English because of a difference in the word order, '(where) could you (find) his home'. On the whole it seems best to take it, with Atkins, as a form for *nuste* with ȝ as an inverted spelling for *s* due to the fact that in early texts *s* is not infrequently used as a spelling for the spirant.

174ff. . . . This description of the position of Portisham has given trouble
to editors, mainly because Portisham, a small town in Dorset, is not
on the coast, and the nearest inlet of the sea is some distance away.
The usual explanation is that, although Portisham is not on the
coast, it is on the sea side of a coastal ridge running from Lulworth
to Swyre with an average height of 500 feet, and so could be
described as 'by the sea' as compared with places on the further side
of the coastal ridge. Similarly *utlete* is probably used with reference
to the coastal ridge which has openings at Upway, Swyre and
Portisham, so that the description here would indicate that the
place was situated on an outlet from Frome Vale to the sea. This is
ingenious, but the description is close enough, and it is difficult to
see why minute topographical detail should be expected.

179–80. . . .'And because of his words and because of his deeds things
are the better as far as Scotland'.

186. . . . 'Why will they not adopt as a plan for themselves . . .' For
this use of *nimen to rede* cf. IX 160.

191ff. . . . It is significant that the owl and the nightingale, who agree
on nothing else, should agree on the merits of Master Nicholas.

197ff. . . . Complaints of nepotism and the presentation of benefices to
minors are common in contemporary writings.

199. . . . 'Thus their intelligence adjudges them in error (i.e. directs them
falsely) in that Master Nicholas ever awaits preferment'.

212. *uerde.* The supporters of the nightingale, who had joined her when
she claimed to have triumphed over the owl. *here* refers to the birds
of prey whom the owl had threatened to summon to her aid. It
may be that the OE distinction between the two words is here still
retained, but if so it need imply nothing as to the sympathies of the
poet, since *here* would in any case be more appropriate for the owl's
army.

213. *þat*, 'until', a rare sense of the word, found occasionally in OE (cf.
Blickling Homilies 237, "Nu þry dagas to lafe syndon þæt hie þe willaþ
acwellan") and ME.

XI. THE BESTIARY

Dialect: East Midland.

Inflexions:

   Verbs: inf. *winnen* 16, *finden* 26, etc.
   3pr. -*eð* usual, *falleð* 11, *bringeð* 32, *cumeð* 77, etc., but some syncopated
forms appear, *smit* 65, *flet* 60, *gelt* 20, etc. In 2 Weak Class *hatieð* 8,
rotieð 15, retain -*ieð*, but others have taken the -*eð* ending, *wuneð* 75,
hungreð 64, etc.
   prpl. *winnen* 79, *haten* 3, *wenen* 88, *sen* 87, but *hatien* 9.
   Pronouns: Fem. *ge* 5, etc.
   3pl. nom. *he* 17, 18, etc.; poss. *here* 20, 90; obj. *hem* 19, 20.
   Note also *is* 'them', 8.

Sounds:

a/o is *o* before lengthening groups, *lond* 12, *sond* 62, etc., otherwise *a*, *name* 2, *man* 8, etc.

æ is usually *a*, *ðat* 1, *was* 53, etc., but *festen* 91, *festeð* 111.

y is usually *i*, *iuel* 28, *sinne* 32, etc., but *stereð* 13.

ā is usually *o*, *loð* 86, *ston* 93, etc., but *gast* 108 (r.w. *stedefast*).

ǣ[1] and *ǣ*[2] are regularly *e*, *-dedes* 3, *were* 14; *ledeð* 44, *sees* 81, etc. *ðar-* 11, 90, is due to early shortening. *moste* 58 is probably analogical.

ȳ is *i*, *vnride* 63 (r.w. *wide*), *fir* 96, etc.

WS *ea*/Ang. *a* before l+cons. is *a* in *falleð* 11, *fallen* 16, *alle* 72, 92. Before *r*+cons. *a* appears in *harm-* 3, *sarpe* 22, but *e* in *merk* 44, *flerd* 53, *-erd* 54; the mutation is *e* in *dernelike* 29, but *a* in *warmen* 95. Before *h* *a* appears in *magt* 99.

eo is regularly *e*, *erð-* 12, *werk* 43. The mutation is *u* in *wurði* 48.

ēa is *e* in *ded* 14, *lepeð* 19, etc., but *a* in *chaueles* 71. The mutation is *e* in *leuen* 55.

ēo is regularly *e*, *der* 1, *beð* 17, etc.

Diphthongization of *o* has not taken place before the back spirant in *nogt* 13, etc., *ðogte* 56.

Consonants: OE *hw* appears as *w* in *woso* 38, etc., *wan* 60, *wiles* 84. Medial *g* has been lost or vocalized to *u* in *fules* 9, 16, cf. *fugeles* 12. Initial *þ* has been assimilated or dissimilated to *t* in *tis* 10, *ter* 32, *tus* 45, *te* 4, 6. Final *-dþ* had already become *-t* in OE in *gelt* 20, *bit* 33, *fet* 40. Initial *n* in *neilond* 61, is due to misdivision of syllable. The back stop in *mikel* 99, *mikle* 106, 107, *dernelike* 29, *ligtlike* 19, is probably due to Scandinavian influence.

Orthography

OE *sc* regularly appears as *s*, *sarpe* 22, *fles* 108, etc. *th* appears in *bothe* 9. In addition to its use for the back stop *g* is used as a spelling for OE front *g* in *fagen* 89, for OE front *h*, *migt* 90, *ligtlike* 19, and for OE back *h*, *nogt* 13, etc., *furg* 11, etc. In *ge* 5, etc., it probably represents a *hj*-sound.

Notes

2. *hire.* Presumably due to the fem. gender of L *vulpes*; in OE *fox* was regularly masculine.

3. *husebondes.* The earliest sense, 'master of a house, head of a household', passes easily into the modern sense which is found already by the thirteenth century. But side by side with this the word also has, from the thirteenth to the seventeenth centuries, the sense 'farmer, cultivator of the soil' as here.

5. *tun.* A word whose wide variety of possible meanings often gives trouble in OE and in ME. The original sense was 'enclosure', and this passes into the sense 'farmyard', as here, and also 'farmstead',

'hamlet', 'village', and so to the modern sense of the word, which probably appears already in ME side by side with the other senses.

9. *huten.* MS. *hulen* is known only in the sense 'to remove the hull, skin', and is unlikely to be the word intended in the context. Suggested emendations are *hunten, hurlen,* 'drive', *huten* 'revile', of which the last gives the most satisfactory meaning.

12. *eried,* 'ploughed, cultivated', a word which survives in this sense until the seventeenth century or later; cf. Shakespeare, *Ant. & Cl.* I, iv, 49, "Make the Sea serue them; which they eare and wound/With keeles".

13. *a god stund deies,* 'a good part of the day'.

16. *fallen bi,* 'alight near', but this is a strained sense of the phrase which is used only because of the demands of the alliteration.

18. *wullen.* Perhaps a verb of motion, such as 'alight on', is to be understood after *wullen,* and the omission of verbs of motion after *will* and *shall* is frequent both in OE and ME. But such a form as *wulle* for 'will' is unlikely in this text, so that the word is more probably a mistake for *pullen* 'tug, pull'.

26. . . . 'We can find here to our benefit'.

32. *bringeð . . . sloð,* 'causes us to sin, and slays us in our sin', i.e. before we have time for absolution.

35–6. . . . 'And while we are amusing ourselves, he plays us a trick like that of the fox'.

39. *ket,* 'carrion', still common in northern dialects, as also *ketmonger* 'dealer in carrion'; cf. *Ketmongergate,* the name of a former street in York (14 EPNS 291).

40. . . . '. . . whoever feeds himself with sin'.

53. . . . '. . . such was the trickery and treachery of Herod'.

57. *cethegrande.* Apparently the *cetegrandie* of the heading has been taken by the writer to be a single word.

57–8. *fis : is.* The rhyme may indicate the Northern change of final *-sc* to *s*; see note to XXII/24. But in a text such as this it is perhaps unwise to place much reliance on the rhymes.

60. *soge.* Presumably due to confusion between WS *sāwe* and non-WS *sēge.*

65. . . . '. . . a breath comes forth from his throat'.

68. *felen,* 'perceive by smell or taste', a common sense of the word from the thirteenth to the nineteenth century, but now obsolete.

70. . . . 'They are ignorant of his treachery'.

79. . . . 'When winter and summer strive together,' i.e. at the equinoctial gales.

93–4. . . . 'With flint and steel in the tinder (they cause a fire) to burn well on this wonderful creature'; but Hall suggests *welm* 'blazing fire', N. Davis (19 *Med. Æv.* 58–9) *bel* 'bonfire', for *wel.*

100. *hauen.* As Hall points out, this gives a fair sense with *wil and magt* as object, but he suggests that it is probably a mistake for *taunen* 'show' rendering the *monstrant* of the original.

105. . . . 'Those weak in faith are, as it were, the small fishes'.

XII. THE VOX AND THE WOLF

Dialect: South-West Midland.

Inflexions:

> Verbs: inf. Usually in -*e*, *mete* 6 (r.w. *strete*), *drinke* 79, etc., but some -*en* forms, *meten* 7, *comen* 136, etc. 2 Weak Class distinguished in *hongi* 88, *liuie* 165. The dat. inf. appears in *to done* 236.
> 3pr. *worþ* 248, *ofþinkeþ* 205, *haueþ* 122, 168. prpl. *makeþ* 29.
> ptp. Usual type *iloke* 20, etc., but *icomen* 60, *iwriten* 204, *flowen* 31, *leten* 40, *letten* 45, *bore* 116, *nomen* 250.
> Pronouns: 3 pl. nom. *hy* 41, etc., *hoe* 264, 268; poss. *here* 43, 267, *hoere* 272; obj. *hem* 30, 162, 267.
> Other pronominal inflexions which can be distinguished are am. *hine* 123, *þene* 113, etc.
> Nouns: The pl. ending of weak nouns (OE -*an*) appears as -*en* in *hennen* 28, 32, 35, 40, *sunnen* 177, 197, *freren* 262; cf. also gpl. *widewene* 201. *get* 167 retains its mutated pl.
> Adjectives: Remnants of the strong declension survive in am. *anne* 29, *somne* 192.

Sounds:

> *a/o* is regularly *o* before lengthening groups, *fond* 21, *wond* 22, etc.; otherwise *a* and *o* appear side by side, *gon* 1, *shome* 35, *can* 97, *bigan* 107, etc. *founde* 73, 92 (r.w. *grounde*), etc., has apparently the vowel of the pl.
> *æ* is usually *a*, *þat* 44, *spak* 65, etc., but *e* forms are not infrequent, *wes* 2, *heuede* 68, etc. *quod* 33, 53, has *o* due to the rounding influence of the preceding *w*.
> *y* is normally *u*, *drunche* 14 (r.w. *aquenche*), *kun* 123 (r.w. *him*), *putte* 282 (r.w. *sitte*), etc., but *i* appears in *afingret* 2, etc. *sugge* 207, *suggen* 265, are from lOE forms with *y*.
> *ā* is regularly *o*, *wo* 2, *hom* 34, etc.; *ane* 10, *anne* 29, etc., are from unaccented forms with early shortening.
> *ǣ¹* and *ǣ²* are regularly *e*, *strete* 5 (r.w. *mete*), *weren* 28; *neuere* 3, *erour* 4, etc. *þare* 33 (r.w. *kare*), 171 (r.w. *ifere*), *gradde* 282, are from forms with early shortening.
> *ȳ* is *ui* in *luitel* 260.
> WS *ea*/Ang. *a* before *l*+cons. is regularly *o* before lengthening groups, *cold* 254, *colde* 255, but otherwise *a*, *half* 4, *afalle* 18, *halp* 84, etc. Before *r*+cons. *a* appears in -*ward* 26, 242, *art* 130, 149, *harde* 195, but *e* in *werþ* 66, *hertou* 120; the mutation is *a* in *bicharde* 293. Before *h* *e* is regular, *ofsei* 10, *sey* 216 etc.; the mutation is *i* in *miȝte* 87, *niȝte* 111, etc.
> *eo* is usually *e*, *ȝerne* 15 (r.w. *erne*), *rerde* 114, etc. *weor-* is *wor-* in *worþe* 96, 191, *worlde* 150, 162. The mutation is *o* in *wors* 202, *worþ* 248, but *ii* in *isiist* 232.

ēa is regularly *e*, *leue* 25, *grete* 155 (r.w. *hete*), etc. The mutation is *e* in *iherde* 113, *ihere* 119 (r.w. *fere*), etc.

ēo is usually *e*, *leuere* 7, *biheld* 15, etc., but *oe* appears in *hoeld* 5, and *o* in *ou* 214, 215.

weste 59, 238, *dede* 67, show a lowering of OE *i* to *e*. *nelle* 132 (r.w. *telle*), 188, *neltou* 189, are from OE forms with *e*.

gistninge 255, is from a form with front diphthongization in OE, and cf. also *forȝeue* 175 (r.w. *isriue*).

Consonants: Initial *f* is not infrequently voiced, *vox* 1, *vind* 253, etc. OE *hw* frequently appears as *w*, *wat* 33, *wen* 75, *wo* 122, etc. *h* is omitted initially in *oundred* 8, *ou* 230, and before *t* in *route* 260, and wrongly added in *houre* 35, *heddre* 43, etc. It has been lost medially in *afingret* 2, etc., and added medially in *ouerhede* 90, *alhone* 275. Already in OE *g* had been lost before *d* in *sede* 129, 150 (r.w. *rede*); *n* has been lost medially in OE in *alpi* 132, and finally in *a* 36, *ifaie* 199, *ope* 27. Medial *bb* has been simplified in *libe* 42, and lost in *han* 87, whilst single *t* has been doubled in *miȝtte* 42, 112, *letten* 45. Assimilation has taken place in *gossip* 209, etc., *houssong* 265, etc., *wimmen* 8, *hadde* 24, etc. Final *-d* has been unvoiced in *pousent* 203, *afingret* 2, etc.; final *-þ* appears as *-t* in *fort* 17. *quod* 33, etc. has *d* by analogy with the pl., while *ounderfonge* 196, has *-ng* on analogy with the ptp.

Orthography:

ī is represented by *ii* in *wiis* 105, *liif* 187, *ounwiis* 139, *paradiis* 140, *isiist* 232, and short *i* by *ii* in *wiit* 70, 124, *hiis* 106. *ē* is represented by *ee* in *reed* 192, *meel* 247. *oe* is used as a spelling for *ō* in *goed* 39, etc., and *o* for *u* where it would not be expected in *bote* 39, *opwinde* 75, *opward* 242, etc. Short *u* is occasionally represented by *ou*; in such words as *oundred* 8, *hounger* 13, etc., this may indicate a lengthening of the vowel before a lengthening group, but that can hardly be the explanation of such forms as *soum* 104, *houpbringe* 126, etc. *w* is represented by *u* in *tuo* 73, and used as a spelling for *v* in *wox* 12, etc., *wous* 12, *wroggen* 256, and alternatively *v* is used as a spelling for *w* in *volf* 148, *vend* 159, *ves* 258. OE *sc* appears as *s* in *isriue* 176, *sriue* 184, *srift* 186, and OE front *c* is spelled *hc* in *ihc* 159. *þohute* 13, *sohvte* 69, etc., are probably merely orthographical variants.

Notes

5. . . . . 'He avoided both path and road'. *strete* is here used in its earlier sense 'paved road, highway'. It has been obsolete in that sense since the sixteenth century, except where preserved in the proper names of Roman roads, e.g. Watling Street, Ermine Street, etc.

13–14. *aquenche* : *drunche*. Read *aquenche* : *drenche*. By the side of the usual *drync* OE has also a by-form *drenc*, and this latter was obviously the form used by the author.

22. *wond*, 'went, proceeded'. This sense of OE *windan* survives until the seventeenth century; cf. Shakespeare, *A.Y.L.*, III, iii, 104, "But winde away, bee gone I say".

26. *haiward.* Strictly speaking the officer of the manor whose duty it was to look to the hedges and fences, more particularly to see that the cattle did not break into the common fields, though some references suggest that his police duties may have been rather more extensive than the name might suggest. His badge of office was a horn.

31ff. . . . A gap in the sense. The fox has eaten three of the hens and the remaining two, along with the cock, have flown on to the beams out of his reach. It is impossible to say whether the omission is due to unintelligent cutting by the author, or by a later scribe.

37. *Chauntecler*, 'the clear, tuneful singer', the usual name of the cock in medieval beast-epic.

40. . . . Blood-letting was not only the invariable medieval remedy for almost any kind of ill, but also the means by which health was preserved. Monastic rules prescribe the frequency and occasion of blood-letting.

43. *heddre*, 'vein'. Some editors insert *blod* after *heddre*, though this is perhaps hardly necessary. From 'vein' the word might very easily come to have the sense 'blood from the vein', though other examples of its use in this sense do not apparently occur.

47. . . . According to Galen the spleen helped to purify the blood manufactured by the liver by secreting the thick and melancholic juices. See generally on this A. P. Robin, *The Old Physiology in English Literature*, pp. 66–72 (London 1911).

48. *nestes*, 'build a nest', so McKnight and *NED*, but the word is probably used here as the avian equivalent of 'go to bed (with a woman)'.

51. . . . 'I advise you to have blood let from the breast'.

59. *cellerer.* The officer of the monastery who looked after the cellar and the provisions. The reference here would suggest that he looked after the poultry as well.

66. *he*, i.e., the fox; but in the preceding line it refers to the cock.

68. *raper*, 'earlier', the literal sense of the word which is the comparative of OE *hraðe*. The latter remains in use throughout the ME period, and is not infrequent in poetry after that time; cf. Milton, *Lycidas* 142, "the rathe primrose that forsaken dies", Swinburne, *On the Cliffs* 114, "The labours, whence men reap/Rathe fruit of hopes and fears", etc.; but apart from its use in poetry the word is now only dialectal. The comparative similarly remains in this sense until the sixteenth century; cf. Spenser, *S.C.*, Feb. 83, "The rather Lambes bene starved with cold".

84. . . . 'There was no trick that would help him'.

89–90. . . . 'What with sorrow and with fear his thirst disappeared completely'.

93. *ʒerne* must be ironical if the MS. reading be kept.

96. . . . 'May pleasure and delight change to misery for the man who knows no moderation in his eating'.

    lust, 'pleasure, delight', a frequent sense of the word down to the seventeenth century; cf. Shakespeare, *Lucrece* 1384, "Gazing upon the Greeks with little lust". Side by side with this meaning the

modern sense also appears throughout the OE and ME periods,
and after the seventeenth century is regular.

105-6. *wiis* : *hiis*. The imperfect rhyme is probably due to the comparative
lack of words with *ī*.

106. .... 'But now it is finished concerning me', i.e. now I am finished.

107. *bigan*. Some such word as *lament* is to be understood.

108. *com . . . gon*. For this idiom see note on V/28.

112. *aquenche*, 'to satisfy, assuage, hunger', a rare use of the word, but
found occasionally in ME.

116. *gossip*, OE *godsibb*, literally 'one who has contracted spiritual affinity
with another by acting as a sponsor at baptism', but already during
the ME period this passes into the sense 'familiar acquaintance,
friend". Thence in the sixteenth century into 'one who delights in
idle talk', and in the nineteenth to 'idle talk'. It is impossible to be
certain whether it is the original sense which is intended here, or
the derived sense of 'friend'.

of children bore, 'from the time we were children'.

123-4. *kun* : *him*. N/EM. *kin* would give the nearest approximation to a
rhyme. *him* may, perhaps, be for earlier *hin* (OE *hine*), though one
would not have expected the am. here.

128. *Sigrim*. In the *Roman de Renart* the wolf's name is *Isengrim*, and the
fact that this name for him is found only here may indicate that the
author took the story from oral English tradition rather than from a
French version. Similarly the fox is *Reneward* in this version as
compared with *Reynart* in the French.

132. *alpi*. An early reduced form of OE *ānlīepig* 'single'. It appears in the
form *ælpig* already in the *Chronicle*, 1086E.

133. *frend*. Probably here in the sense 'kinsman', a sense due to the
influence of ON *frœndi* of which this is the only meaning. Cf.
Shakespeare, *Two Gent.* III, i, 106, "She . . . is promis'd by her
friends/Vnto a youthfull Gentleman of worth".

140. .... A conventional description of the Happy Land such as is not
infrequently met with in OE (e.g. *Phoenix* 1-84) and in ME.

151. *storue*, 'died', used in the general sense throughout the ME period,
but from the sixteenth century *starve* comes to be used in the special-
ized sense 'to die from, or kill by, hunger', now the only meanings
in Received Standard.

160. .... 'None of my kindred knows of it', i.e. that I am dead.

161. *lond* (MS. *goed*). The lack of rhyme shows that some emendation
is needed.

167. *get*, 'goats', the historically correct form from the OE mutated pl.
gæt, which survives in use until the sixteenth century, but as early as
the thirteenth an analogical *gotes* is also found.

171-2. *pare* : *ifere*. Read *pere* : *ifere*.

175-6. *forȝeue* : *isriue*. *forȝiue* would give the required rhyme.

181-2. *seide* : *misdede*. Evidently *sede* from an OE form with loss of *g*
before a following *d* and lengthening of the preceding vowel.

192. .... 'unless you give me some advice'.

208. . . . 'Or else you will have to atone (pay) for it elsewhere', i.e. you will have to suffer for it in hell.

218. *þat þat ihc iseie*, 'that which I saw', would improve the metre.

233. . . . 'There is an opening into the joy of heaven'. This is the obvious meaning, but such a sense for *bruche* does not seem to be recorded elsewhere before the sixteenth century.

241. . . . 'When he got half-way down the well'.

244. . . . 'What are you intending to do? Where are you going?'

246. . . . See note to XI/18.

247. *wiþ þi meel*, 'towards your meal', though *NED* records *with* in the sense 'towards' only in OE.

254. *bind*. Presumably in the figurative sense 'makes helpless'.

264. *prime* (MS. *·Ime*), 'the first hour of the day', perhaps used loosely for 'very early'. Other editors, not recognizing the abbreviation, have emended to *ine*, to the detriment of the rhyme.

265. *houssong*, OE *ūhtsong* 'matins', with inorganic *h*, loss of spirant, and assimilation of *-ts-* to *-ss-*.

271. *Ailmer*. OE *Æþelmær*/*Ægelmær*. It is unusual to find a distinctively English name at this date, and it is possible that the author derived his story from English rather than from French sources.

272. *curtiler*. OF *courtillier* 'gardener', the monk in charge of the garden of the monastery. The *curtal friar*, however, was one with a short (curtailed) habit, and had nothing to do with this word.

273. . . . 'He was terribly thirsty'.

XIII. THE THRUSH AND THE NIGHTINGALE

Dialect: West Midland.

Inflexions:

Verbs: inf. Usually *-e*, *shende* 11 (r.w. *hende*), *ihere* 12, etc., but *-en* is not infrequent, *shilden* 14, *striuen* 166 (r.w. *wiue*), etc. *herien* 37 retains the ending of the 2 Weak Class.

3pr. *-eþ* regular, *springeþ* 3, *holdeþ* 59, etc., but *seiþ* 17.

prpl. *bringeþ* 137, 164, *sitteþ* 54, *darkneþ* 4; but *gladieþ* 31, *liuieþ* 105.

ptp. *ibroke* 29, *icnowe* 60, *iknowe* 114, *ifounde* 136, but *comen* 1, *boren* 173, *ounderstonde* 39.

Pronouns: Fem. *hoe* 10, etc.

3 pl. nom. *hy* 18, etc., *hoe* 77; poss. *here* 41, etc.; obj. *hem* 11, etc.

Nouns: *þing* 58, *word* 108, retain the lack of ending in the pl. of the OE long-stem neuters.

Sounds:

a/o is regularly *o* before lengthening groups, *strong* 28, *fonde* 22, etc., otherwise *o* is usual, *nome* 13, *mon* 19, etc., but with occasional *a* forms, *name* 176, *shame* 175, *man* 71. *founde* 92 is due to analogy.

æ is *a* in *þat* 8, *crafti* 44, *bar* 185, but *e* in *wes* 28, etc., *heuede* 91, *nes* 44.
y is usually *u*, *murie* 6, *furste* 71, etc., but *e* appears in *euele* 155, *wercheþ* 23, 163, and *i* in *king* 43; *dude* 140, and *sweche* 51, are from OE forms in *y* and *e* respectively.
ā is regularly *o*, *wo* 8, *holi* 136, etc.
ǣ[1] and *ǣ*[2] both appear as *e*, *were* 24, *rede* 27; *mest* 20, *neuere* 28, etc. *lasteþ* 148 is due to early shortening.
ȳ is *ui* in *luitel* 64, 74, etc.
WS *ea*/Ang. *a* before *l*+cons. is *o* before lengthening groups, *itolde* 52, *holdeþ* 59, etc., otherwise *a*, *also* 36, 78, etc. Before *r*+cons. *a* is usual, *darkneþ* 4, *armes* 58, etc., but *e* appears in *bern* 172; the mutation is *e* in *derne* 65. Before *h* the mutation is *i* in *miȝte* 11, *niȝte* 17, etc.
eo appears as *e* in *herte* 55; *i* appears before *ht* in *fiȝtte* 90, and *weor-* appears as *wor-* in *world* 34, *worldes* 47, etc. The mutation is *o* in *worste* 142.
ēa is regularly *e*, *dewes* 4, *eke* 17, etc. *showe* 51 (r.w. *rowe*), is from an OE form with *ā*. The mutation appears as *e* in *ihere* 12 (r.w. *ifere*).
ēo is regularly *e*, *beþ* 10, *fle* 96, etc., but *oe* in *hoe* 10, etc. The mutation appears as *e* in *trewe* 92, *newe* 111, etc.
shilden 14, *shilde* 56, *ishilde* 177, are from forms with front-diphthongiza-tion in OE, whilst *weste* 175, shows a lowering of OE *i*.
Consonants: OE *hw* is frequently *w*, *wi* 60, *wenne* 80, etc. Initial *h* is lost in *ire* 176, *is* 140, and frequently added wrongly as in *hic* 7, *heuere* 127, etc. Medial *t* has been doubled in *niȝttingale* 85, *riȝtte* 87, etc. An intrusive *n* appears in *niȝtingale* 13, etc. Medial *fm* has been assimilated in *wimmen* 10, etc., medial *nm* in *nammore* 156, and *mm* simplified in *wimen* 34, 37. Similarly medial *nn* has been simplified in *mones* 35. Medial *þ* has been lost in *war* 120, and medial *n* in *Costantines* 115. Final -*d* is unvoiced in *þousent* 52, *houndret* 160, and the back spirant has been vocalized to *u* in *þoru* 170, 185, and lost before *t* in *þout* 41.

Orthography:

OE *ō* is written *oi* n *goed* 72, etc., *woed* 181. *u* is written *o* where it would not be expected in *bote* 101, *þoru* 170, 185, and is not infrequently represented by *ou*. In *founde* 92, *ounder* 124, etc., this may indicate lengthening before -*nd*, but that can hardly be the explanation of such forms as *sunfoul* 65, *foul* 116, *oupon* 139, *ounwis* 157, etc., while it is also used to represent OE unaccented *o* in *swettoust* 58. Tense *ē* appears as *ee* in *iseene* 165. Forms such as *nohut* 37, *þohut* 38, etc., are probably mere orthographical variants.

Notes

1. . . . . A *Le(nten is come)n wiþ love (to toun)* is even more reminiscent of the well-known lyric in MS. Harley 2253.
2. *roune.* OE *rūn* 'dark, mysterious saying' had apparently developed the

sense 'speech', at first with a secret connotation, and then that of 'song', as here, though this sense appears rarely and only in ME.

3. It could equally well mean 'The melody (note) comes from the hazel-tree', or 'The hazel-nut begins to form'.

5. *niʒttegale*. OE *nihtegale*, with the second element related to OE *galan* 'to sing', hence 'the singer by night'. For the intrusive -*n*- in the modern form cf. *popinjay*, *messenger*, etc.

6. *foweles*, 'birds (in general)', the usual sense of OE *fugol*, and one which survives until the eighteenth century. But from the seventeenth century the word tends to become restricted more especially to poultry, and, except in such compounds as *waterfowl*, that is now its invariable sense.

   murie has a wide variety of meanings in ME and can rarely be translated by the modern 'merry'. The usual sense is 'pleasing, pleasant', as originally in the phrase *Merry England*. The word here is the adverb 'pleasantly, tunefully'.

7. *strif*. One of the regular technical terms for this type of debate poem.

10–11. *Þat on . . . Þat oþer* are represented in Scots by *the tane* and *the tither*, and the second survives in colloquial English in *the tother from which* 'the one from the other'.

13. *is on bi nome*, 'is the name of the one'.

16. *kepeþ*, 'lies in wait, ambush for', a comparatively rare meaning of the word; but cf. Robert of Gloucester 1964, "A gret erl him kepte þer in a wode bi syde".

22. *fals to fonde*, 'false when put to the test'.

30. A *wimmen* gives better sense.

31. *gladieþ*, 'rejoice, make happy', is possible, but A *ysauʒten* 'reconcile' fits the context better.

   wrowe : lowe. Carleton Brown suggested replacing MS. *wroþe* by *wrowe*, which has much the same sense. This gives a satisfactory rhyme.

39. *ounderstonde*. In ME regularly used in the passive in the sense 'to be 'informed, advised'; cf. *OE Miscellany* 52/518, "We beoþ vnderstonde þes ilke swike seyde . . .".

43. *Alisaundre*. Presumably a reference to the outwitting of Alexander by Candace, as in the ME *King Alisaunder*.

   hem : mon. The rhyme would be improved if *wimmon* were read for *hem*.

44. *crafti*, 'mighty, powerful', a rare but certain sense of the word in OE and in ME. The usual sense is 'skilful, dexterous', though already by the fourteenth century the word has acquired the depreciative sense which is the only one to survive in current speech.

48. . . . 'Great was the disgrace to them', i.e. they were greatly disgraced by them.

53. *wickede*. If this be taken as a form of *wickedhede* 'wickedness' it will improve the metre considerably, and the meaning remain much the same.

59. *holdeþ . . . gle*, 'regards them with pleasure'.

60. . . . 'Why don't you confess it?'

69. . . . 'You say what you wish'.

85–6. *wrong* : *lond*. Read *shond* : *lond*, 'You will have disgrace if you send me from the land'.

87. . . . 'I maintain what is right'.

88. *Wawain*. The ONF form of the name corresponding to Central Fr. *Gauvain*, cf. *wage/gage*, *warden/guardian*, etc. The particular reference here is obscure; Gawain was certainly deceived by a lady at the castle of the Green Knight, and perhaps also in *The Weddinge of Sir Gawane*, but neither of these seems obvious enough to be the incident referred to here.

114. . . . 'You don't bother to understand them'.

115. . . . As Carleton Brown points out, this reference belongs to the large class of stories which tell of queens who loved a cripple or deformed person. See also Kemp Malone (43 *PMLA* 397ff.). The story is found connected with Constantine's queen in a number of OF poems, notably in *Auberi le Bourguignon*.

116. *fow and grene*. The usual phrase is *fowe and grai*, a translation of the common OF phrase *vair et gris* 'variegated fur and grey fur', the first being fur made from the grey back and white belly of a sort of squirrel, the second from the grey back alone. Side by side with this phrase there appears to have been another, *grene and grai*, used in the sense 'sumptuous clothing'. This is apparently a mixture of the two phrases used, perhaps, for the sake of rhyme.

124. . . . Apparently an imitation of the common phrase *schene under schete* altered to fit the bird characters, and perhaps also for the sake of the rhyme.

142ff. . . . 'She is the worst sort of treasure that Jesus ever created to be accounted precious in paradise'. Perhaps some sort of pun on *hoard* and *whore* is intended by the author.

149. *iherd*, i.e. *ihered* 'praised'.

150. *ounder gore*, 'under clothes', a common ME tag; cf. *Alysoun* 35, "geynest vnder gore".

154. *rewest*. Carleton Brown takes this as a form of *riuen* 'pull apart, tear to pieces', but though examples of *w* as a spelling for *v* appear elsewhere in the MS., the *e* is difficult. A better sense is obtained by emending the MS. *mi* to *þi* and taking the verb as ME *rewen* 'repent, be sorry for'. Although *rewen* is usually impersonal, personal uses of it are not infrequent in ME. The sense would be 'Bird, you will be sorry for all your thoughts (against women)'.

166–7. *striuen* : *wiue*. Read *striue* : *wiue*.

173. *Bedlehem*, 'Bethlehem', not infrequently with -*d*- in ME, and it is from this -*d*- form that the modern *bedlam* is derived, the development of meaning being due to the fact that the hospital of St. Mary of Bethlehem in London was used as an asylum for the insane.

180. *filde*. OE *gefilde* 'plain', cf. *The Fylde* (Lancs.); but it is difficult to be certain that this OE word survived in the ordinary vocabulary of ME, since its forms would tend to become confused with those of OE *feld*.

XIV. THE PROVERBS OF ALURED

Dialect: South-Western.

Inflexions:

Verbs: inf. Usually -*e*, *lere* 13, *lede* 16, etc., but *wepen* 81.
3pr. *icheoseþ* 71, *bryngeþ* 65, *meneþ* 51, etc., but *seyþ* 98.
prpl. *forteoþ* 99.
prp. *singinde* 44.
ptp. *isowen* 30.

Pronouns: Fem. *heo* 65, etc.
3pl. nom. *hi* 15, etc.; poss. *heore* 15; obj. *heom* 13.
Other pronominal inflexions occasionally survive, e.g. am. *hyne* 59,
etc., *hine* 97. Definite article am. *þan* 42, g/df. *þare* 8. Possessive
pronoun df. *þire* 57.

Nouns: *þinge* 64, has not yet taken the -*es* ending of the pl.
The gpl. ending survives in *Englene* 10, etc., *Engle-* 24.

Adjectives: Occasional examples of the strong declension survive,
am. *vuelne* 95, df. *echere* 55.

Sounds:

a/*o* is regularly *o* before lengthening groups, -*londe* 12, *strong* 18, etc.
Otherwise *o* is usual, *monye* 2, *bigon* 13, *mon* 23 (r.w. *on*), etc., but *can*
95, *þan* 89, 104.

æ is indifferently *e* or *a*, *wes* 7, *queþ* 25, *war* 22, *at* 1, etc. *ea* appears in
Ealured 9.

y is usually *u*, *custe* 66, *ifurn* 100, etc., but *i* in *kyng* 12, *king* 18, 19.
vordrye 91 has been influenced by OE *forðian*.

ā is regularly *o*, *ston* 38, *wot* 50, etc. *ahte* 28 is due to early shortening.

ǣ[1] and *ǣ*[2] both appear as *e*, *sete* 1, *dede* 87; *lere* 13, *lede* 16, etc. *þar* 7,
þare 8, etc., show early shortening.

ȳ is regularly *u*, *byhud* 57, *cupeþ* 67.

WS *ea*/Ang. *a* before *l*+cons. is *a* in *alle* 31. Before *r*+cons. *a* appears
in *arewe* 42, but *e* in *erewe* 50. Before *h a* is found in *iauhteþ* 69; the
mutation is *i* in *myht* 53, *myhte* 81.

eo is *e* in *fele* 3, -*seuenti* 29, but *eo* in *feole* 4, *eorles* 5, etc. *weor-* is *wer-* in
werk 20, *werke* 22, but *wur-* in *iwurþe* 77. Before *h i* appears in *knyhtes* 6.
The mutation is *u* in *hurde* 10.

ēa is *ea* in *reade* 31, but *e* in *ek* 9. The mutation is *u* in *ihure* 14.

ēo is usually *eo*, *greowe* 32, *freond* 37, *cheose* 63, but *loþ* 98. The mutation
is *u* in *durlyng* 11.

Consonants: Already in OE *g* had been lost before *d* in *ised* 94. Initial
f has been voiced in *vordrye* 91, and medial -*fd-*, -*fm-*, have been
assimilated in *hadde* 30, *wymmon* 88, etc. Initial *þ* appears as *t* in *tu* 62.

Orthography:

OE *ū* is written *w* in *hw* 15, whilst *wu-* is represented by *w* in *iwrche* 37.
OE *sc* remains in *biscopes* 3. Front *g* is represented by *y* in *ye* 14, and
front *c* by *hc* in *swyhc* 53. *clerek* 19 may be due to an attempt to
indicate a strongly trilled *r*.

Notes

1. *Seuorde*, other MSS. *Sif(f)orde*. The place has been variously identified with Seaford (Sx.), Shefford (Beds., Berks.), and Shifford (Ox.). But the spelling and the alliteration show that the original form must have had *s*, not *sc*, and hence Seaford (Sx.) is no doubt correct, the *i* forms being due to scribes who were more familiar with Shefford/Shifford. W. H. Stevenson (*Asser's Life of Alfred*, p. lxxii, n. 5) has pointed out that there is historical evidence for a connexion between Alfred and Seaford, since Asser is said to have first met the king at a royal manor called *Dene*, in Sussex, and this has been identified with Eastdean near Seaford (6 EPNS 47, and 7 EPNS 363 and 417).

2. *þeynes*, 'thanes'. The original sense of the word was "servant", but at an early date it was applied especially to the servants of the king, and hence became a title of honour; cf. *marshal, minister*, etc.

5. *eorles*. OE *eorl*, originally 'man of noble rank, warrior'; but already in lOE, through the influence of ON *jarl*, it has come to be used as a title of rank synonymous with OE *ealdorman*, and no doubt is used in that sense here.

7. *Alurich*. It is, perhaps, possible to identify him with one of Alfred's followers, but it is doubtful whether the author had any definite person in mind.

14. *ihure; ihere* from the non-WS form would give a better rhyme.

18. *an* 'a, one', MS. *and*. The other MSS. have *a*, which is obviously correct in the context, and no doubt the J scribe has mistaken the *an* of his original for a shortened form of *and*.

23–4. *mon : on*. Such a rhyme would suggest that the original must have been composed in some district in which rounding of *a* to *o* before a single nasal had taken place. But in a text such as this it is unwise to depend on the evidence of rhymes.

29. *huntseuenti*. The element *hund-* (so far unexplained, but to be compared with *ant-* in the Old Saxon numerals 70 and 80) was regularly prefixed in OE to the numerals from 70 (*hund-seofontig*) to 120 (*hund-twelftig*). Few such forms survive in ME, none later than the thirteenth century.

35. *furþer*, 'further, more forward', gives adequate sense, but the other MSS. have *wurþere*, 'more worthy', which has the advantage of providing alliteration, and no doubt represents the original.

36–7. . . . 'Unless from the beginning he makes friends for himself'. *frumþe*, OE *frymþ* 'beginning'. Other MSS. have forms with *e*, *fremðe*, etc., which at first sight appear preferable, 'unless he makes friends of strangers with it'. But the point is not that we should make friends out of strangers, since the line is merely a variation on the biblical theme that we should make friends of the mammon of unrighteousness.

43. *sadelbowe*, 'the arched front of the saddle'.

45–6. . . . 'Then he will think, who does not know your way of life . . .'.

For *wile wene* T has *sait þe mon,* 'the man will say', which gives as good
sense and provides a rhyme.

53–6. . . . . 'You can tell it to such a man whom (you think) wishes you
full well; without any mercy he wishes you much more (sorrow)'.

54. *on*, 'wishes', from OE *unnan* 'to grant', rare in ME, but found occasionally as late as the fourteenth century.

57. T *for-hele hit wið þin areʒe* probably represents the original more
nearly than J since it provides the necessary antecedent for the *hyne*
of the following line. The change in J was probably to provide a
rhyme for *smeorte*.

61ff. . . . These two sections contain much typically medieval satire on
women. For a description and bibliography of this type of literature
see F. L. Utley, *The Crooked Rib* (Columbus, Ohio, 1944).

64–5. . . . i.e. for her dowry. C has *Ne for non athte/to þine bury bringen*,
and *ahte* and *bury*, being less usual words, no doubt more nearly
represented the original. J gives, however, adequate sense.

69. *vuele iauhteþ*, 'estimates falsely', i.e. makes a bad bargain.

70–1. . . . 'And often a man when he choses beauty choses wickedness'.

74. *So.* Holthausen (78 *Archiv* 370) suggests emendation to *wo*. This
gives better sense and a common ME phrase, but, since all MSS.
have *so*, the mistake, if mistake it be, must have been present in their
common original.

78ff. . . . Almost identical lines appear in the *Proverbs of Hending*, st. 18:
Monimon syngeþ/When he hom bringeþ/Is ʒonge wyf;/Wyste wat
he broʒte,/Wepen he mohte/Er his lyf syþ.
Presumably borrowing has taken place, but in which direction it is
impossible to say.

80–1. *brouhte : myhte.* Read *brouhte : mouhte.*

83ff. . . . T has only two lines, *Vretu noth to swiþe/þe word of þine wiue*,
'Don't listen (OE *hïer þū*) too quickly to the words of your wife',
and is perhaps nearer to the original.

88. *mod*, 'anger', a sense which becomes obsolete during the seventeenth century, though still found in Shakespeare, *Two Gent.* IV, i,
51, "Who, in my moode, I stabb'd vnto the heart". This sense was
later revived by Scott and is found in Tennyson.

94. *Salomon*, 'Solomon', the usual ME form, Latin and Greek having
a/o forms side by side. One of the sources of such modern surnames
as *Salmon, Salmond, Sammond*, etc. As a Christian name it appears to
have died out in England by the beginning of the fourteenth century,
but was revived by the Puritans in the seventeenth.

99. MS. *scumes.* Various suggestions have been made towards a solution
of this crux, of which the most probable are those of Brandl-Zippel
and Anderson. The former suggest that *as scumes* is a mistake for
as cuenes (OE *cwene* 'woman'), and *loþ* would then be a reference to
Proverbs, more particularly to c. vii, in which Solomon deals with
the deceitfulness of evil women. But in that case *as* must have the
sense 'how, that' which is difficult to parallel. Consequently

Anderson suggests that the word should be read *scinnes* (OE *scinn(a)* 'spectre, evil spirit, phantom'), the retention of *sc* in the spelling being due to the scribe's ignorance of the word.

100–01. *iseyd* : *red.* Read *ised* : *red.*

101. ... A common medieval proverb; cf. Chaucer, *Nun's Priest's Tale* (*C.T.* VII, 3256), "Wommennes conseils been ful ofte colde", etc. The proverb occurs also in ON, and may have been borrowed thence into English. If so, the ON meaning of *kaldr*, 'baneful, hostile, cruel', would add point to the proverb.

104ff. ... 'Despite all this I do not say that a good woman is not (*nys*) a good thing for the man who can chose her and win her from others'. But for line 106 T has ... *cnowen ant chesen hire from opere*, which gives a better meaning since the whole point of the advice in this section is that, since women often deceive men, it is essential to know her before choosing her in preference to others.

XV. THE ORRMULUM

Dialect: East Midland of North Lincolnshire.

Inflexions:

Verbs: inf. *turrnenn* 9, *findenn* 19, *þolenn* 26, etc.
    3pr. *meneþþ* 17, *semeþþ* 33, etc., but some syncopated forms occur, *stannt* 17, *birrþ* 14, etc. prpl. *herenn* 46.
    ptp. *writenn* 53, *hollþenn* 71, etc.
Pronouns: 3 pl. nom. *þeȝȝ* 40, etc., *teȝȝ* 59, 78; poss. *þeȝȝre* 18, etc., *here* 43; obj. *hemm* 27, etc., *þeȝȝm* 25.
    Note the retention of the duals *witt* 4, 37; *unnc* 14, 43, 44; *unnkerr* 40.
Nouns: A weak pl. occurs in *wikenn* 33.

Sounds:

a/o is invariably *a*, *mann* 18, *maniȝ* 22, *þannkenn* 14, etc.
æ is invariably *a*, *affterr* 1, *þatt* 4, etc.
y is invariably *i*, *kinde* 1, *fillenn* 11, etc.
ā is invariably *a*, *had* 5, *lare* 7, etc.
ǣ[1] and *ǣ*[2] are usually *æ*, *flæshess* 1, *lætenn* 40; *bitæche* 33, *tæleþþ* 39, etc., but *e* in *dede* 11, etc., *redenn* 24; *meneþþ* 17, *lenedd* 8. *badd* 6, is probably due to analogy.
ȳ is *i* in *little* 8.
WS *ea*/Ang. *a* before *l*+cons. is *a* in *all* 13, etc., *alle* 15, etc., *alls* 33, etc. Before *h a* appears in *mahhte* 60; the mutation is *i* in *mihhte* 9, 30.
eo is regularly *e*, *ȝerne* 10, *lernenn* 10. *weor-* is *-wer* in *forwerrpenn* 75 *werrc* 12, but *wur-* in *wurrþenn* 64. The mutation appears as *u* in *wurrþ* 64.
ēa is usually *e*, *tekenn* 19, *neh* 15, etc., but *æ* in *ære* 67, *ȝæn* 35, *læn* 72 The mutation is *e* in *ekenn* 29, *herenn* 46, etc.

ēo is *e* in *sen* 24, *lef* 40, *þed* 20, but *o* in *trowwþe* 2, 62, *trowwenn* 20, etc., *trowwe* 26.

Diphthongization of *o* before *h* does not occur in *þohht* 11, *brohht* 14, etc.

Elision is not infrequent, hence such forms as *tunnderrstanndenn* 24, *tekenn* 19, *het* 49, etc.

Consonants: Initial *þ* is regularly *t* after a word ending with *d* or *t*, *te* 6, *tatt* 9, *tu* 12, *tær* 19, *teʒʒ* 59, *tiss* 77, etc. The *k* in *bliþelike* 46, *wirrkenn* 12, *þurrhsekenn* 34, may be due to Scandinavian influence, or is perhaps analogical.

Orthography:

Most of the distinctive characteristics of Orrm's orthography have been dealt with at pp. 82-3.

Notes

1ff. . . . Usually taken to mean that Wallterr was Orrm's brother, his brother Christian, and his brother in religion in that both were canons of an Augustinian house. But Emerson suggests that blood-relationship is not necessarily indicated, and he compares *Philemon* 16, where Philemon is requested to receive Onesimus as brother "both in the flesh, and in the Lord".

4. *witt* 'we two'. The dual pronouns, already growing obsolete in OE, do not survive in ME after the thirteenth century. The use of *ba* 'both' in the same line may indicate that *witt* was already archaic, and Orrm was not certain that it would be understood.

reʒhellboc, 'rule of an order'. No detailed rule had in fact been written by St. Augustine: on the rule followed by Augustinian canons see J. C. Dickinson, *The Origin of the Austin Canons and their Introduction into England* (London 1950).

5. *swa summ*, 'just as', a common phrase in the *Orrmulum*, *summ* being OEN *sum* (OWN *sem*).

Awwstin, 'Augustine'. On this form of the name see VI/18.

7. *hallʒhe*. Evidently the weak form of the adj., OE *hālga*, with shortening before the consonant group. The strong form *hālig* would give *haliʒ* in this text.

8. *Drihhtin*. OE *dryhten*, but Orrm's spelling indicates *ī* in the ending of his form, and this is usually explained as due to the influence of ME *allmihtīn* in which *ī* is from OE am. *ælmihtigne* becoming *ælmihtīne*. In lOE *-ig* normally becomes *ī*, but the explanation remains unconvincing.

14. *unnc birrþ*, 'it behoves us two', OE *byrian*, an impersonal verb, and a favourite with Orrm.

15ff. . . . Orrm is here describing his method, first to give an English version of the gospel for the day, and then to comment on its signification.

28. *læwedd*, 'unlearned'. Originally 'lay, not in holy orders', and from that, at a time when literacy was almost the monopoly of the clergy,

it developed the sense, 'unlearned, untaught'. Both these senses
became obsolete during the sixteenth century, but from the latter
was developed the meaning 'common, low, vulgar', hence 'ill-bred,
ill-mannered', so to 'bad, evil, wicked', and ultimately 'lascivious,
unchaste', the only surviving meaning of the word.

30. *ferrs. fers* is the regular development in OE and ME of the loan-
word from L *versus*, later replaced by F *vers*, the source of modern
verse.

3 . *wel*. Found in the *Orrmulum* side by side with *well*. Holthausen
(13 *Anglia-Beiblatt* 16) has shown that the former is usual in both
stressed and unstressed positions, and is used in independent positions, whilst the latter is used when modifying an adj. or adv.

annd all forrþi. 'And because of this I was often compelled of necessity
to include my own words among the words of the Gospel in order to
fill out the metre'.

33. . . . 'And I entrust to you concerning this book what seems to me
to be an important duty'.

40ff. . . . The editors take these lines as an indication that some of his
contemporaries were jealous of Orrm, and suggest that the loss of
part of the work may be due to them. But on the whole it is unlikely
that the work, as envisaged by Orrm in his list of contents, was ever
completed, though on the other hand it is certain that not all he
wrote has survived; see N. R. Ker, 9 *Med. Æv.* 1–22.

lætenn, 'think, judge', uncommon meanings for OE *lǣtan*, but common
enough for ON *láta*.

42. *skill*, 'reason, power of discrimination', the usual sense in ME, but
obsolete by the sixteenth century. The modern sense 'cleverness,
expertness' seems to be found already in ME, but does not become
frequent before the sixteenth century.

48ff. . . . Despite Orrm's plea that the copyist should copy his work
exactly there is no evidence that any medieval scribe had the courage
to attempt it.

52. *bocstaff*. OE *bōcstæf* 'letter', a common Gmc. word which still survives in some languages, cf. G *Buchstabe*, but which was rare already
in OE and in ME appears only here and in Laȝamon.

58ff. . . . 'I have done it (i.e. translated the gospel) because the salvation
of all Christian people is dependent upon this alone, that they
should follow properly the true teaching of the gospel . . .'

berrhless, 'salvation', found only in the *Orrmulum*, the first element
being presumably connected with OE *beorgan* 'to protect'.

61. . . . 'For everything which there is on the earth which is necessary
for Christian men to follow . . .'

69. *att Godd*, 'from God', a not unusual use of the preposition until almost
the present day; cf. Coverdale, *Judith* x, 7, "They axed no question
at her, but let her go". Now replaced by *of, from*, except in the phrase
at the hand(s) of.

76. *addledd*, 'earned, acquired'. A word found only in N writers in ME
and now exclusively dialectal.

XVI. VICES AND VIRTUES

Dialect: Essex.

Inflexions:

Verbs: inf. *cumen* 8, *setten* 42, *habben* 11, etc., but 2 Weak Class *þolien* 59, *ðoliȝen* 60.

3pr. *reweð* 20, *ðoleð* 29, 30, *haueð* 44, 61, but *bringþ* 9, *hafð* 5, 7, *seið* 42, 64

prpl. *habbeð* 11, *wepeð* 18, *þolied* 17, *hopieð* 18, *woniþ* 18, *lokið* 19. ptp. *iscapen* 6, 9, 15.

Pronouns: 3 pl. nom. *hie* 8, etc., *hi* 20; poss. *here* 55; obj. *hem* 12, 19. Some pronominal inflexions remain: def. art., nm. *se* 2, df. *ðare* 6, 8. Reflexive, -*seluen* dpl. 33, 34. Possessive, df. *ðire* 19.

Nouns: The neuter pl. -*u* survives as *e* in *wintre* 5.

Sounds:

a/o is usually *a*, *hand-* 10, *manne* 5, *mani* 16, but *wombe* 42.

æ is regularly *a*, *was* 6, *after* 15, etc.

y is usually *e*, *euele* 9, *kenne* 39, etc., but *u* appears in *muchele* 6, 19, *muchel* 50, and *i* in *forgilte* 4, *michel* 23, *kyng* 40.

ā is indifferently *a* or *o*, *hali* 4, *are* 4, *swo* 5, *ore* 10, etc. *oa* appears in *loac* 54, *hoal* 61.

$\bar{æ}^1$ and $\bar{æ}^2$ are usually *a*, *waren* 8, *sade* 13; *arst* 32, *naure* 35, etc., but *æ* appears in *sæde* 3, 22, *læten* 28, *æure* 11, 45, and *e* in *sede* 29, *ðer* 24, *togedere* 26.

WS *ea*/Ang. *a* before *l*+cons. is *ea* in *wealden* 52, but otherwise *a*, *walte* 8, *alle* 9, etc.; the mutation is *e* in *welle* 14. Before *r*+cons. *ea* appears in -*eard* 52, but *a* in *harm* 32, *art* 48; the mutation is *e* in *eruename* 51. Before *h* *e* appears in *astrehte* 3; the mutation is *i* in *almihti* 44.

eo is *e* in *heuene* 46, but *ie* in *ierðe* 47. *weor-* is *wur-* in *unwurðede* 31, but *wer-* in -*werc* 10. The mutation is *u* in *wurð* 45, but *ie* in *ȝiernen* 51.

ēa is regularly *ea*, *eadiȝe* 3, *deað* 59, etc. The mutation appears as *e* in *unhersumnesse* 18, 34, *unhersum* 30, *onlepi* 24, but as *ie* in *aliesendnesse* 20, *aliesen* 57, 63.

ēo is *ie* in *dieuel* 7, *bien* 23, etc., but *e* in *rewhþe* 10, etc. The mutation is *ie* in *istriend* 47, but *e* in *ðesternesse* 5.

ȝif 22, 59, *ȝiuen* 51, are from forms with front diphthongization.

Diphthongization of *o* before *h* does not appear in *besohten* 2, *noht* 7, 23, *þoht* 24.

Consonants: Already in OE *g* had been lost before *d* in *sæde* 3, *sade* 13, *sede* 29, etc. OE *hl* remains in *hlauerd* 10, 38, 53. Medial *d* has been lost in *milce* 4, etc. (cf. *mildce* 3, 10), and medial *h* added in *rewhþe* 10. Medial -*ng*- has been unvoiced in *strencþe* 32, and initial *þ* has become *t* in *tu* 11, etc.

Orthography:

sc is used to represent OE *sc* regularly, *scule* 11, *iscapen* 6, etc., and as a spelling for *ss* in *iblesced* 40. The final *-d* of *Godd* 30, etc., has been doubled in order to distinguish it from the adj. *gōd*. OE *ē* is frequently represented by *ie*, *bisiech* 50, *bieten* 61, etc.

Notes

4ff. . . . According to the apocryphal gospels Adam was imprisoned in hell for five thousand years, and only released at Christ's Harrowing of Hell after the Crucifixion (see J. A. MacCulloch, *The Harrowing of Hell*, Edinburgh 1930).

5. *wintre*. The OE use of *winter* as a synonym for 'year' remains in use until the sixteenth century. When found later it is chiefly poetical and rhetorical with reference to advanced age or to a lengthy period of hardship or misfortune.

6. *ðe*, 'who', referring back to Adam. The ordinary indeclinable relative of OE.

9. *he*, i.e. the devil.

10. *handiwerc* (OE *hand-geweorc*). The only example of the survival in current English of the OE unaccented prefix *ge-* is in *handiwork* whence *handi-craft*, *handy*.

16ff. . . . According to medieval belief no salvation was possible for man after the fall of Adam until Christ had been crucified, since salvation is possible only through Christ. Hence the patriarchs and prophets must necessarily suffer in hell, and could only be released on the Harrowing of Hell by Christ.

18. *hopieð to*. The usual construction in OE, but in ME *to* and *after* gradually cease to be used with *hopien*, and *for* becomes the usual construction.

19. *allhwat*, 'until', cf. *Ayenbite*, p. 52, "He uesteþ . . . alhuet niȝt".

27–8. *Þin . . . læten*, 'Thy goodness cannot cease'.

29. *ðat*, 'that which', a common sense down to the sixteenth century, cf. A.V. *Job* xlii, 3, "Therefore haue I vttered that I vnderstood not". Now archaic or poetic and usually replaced by *what*.

39–40. *þat þurh . . . mankenn*. *Genesis* xxii, 18.

41. . . . Vulgate *Psalm* cxxxi, 11 (A.V. cxxxii, 11).

42. *setle*. OE *setl* remains throughout the ME period in the general sense 'seat', and in the earlier part of the period is not uncommon in the sense 'high seat, throne'. But in this sense it is gradually replaced by OF *throne* from the thirteenth century, and the modern sense 'bench' is first recorded for it in the sixteenth century.

43. . . . *Psalm* ii. 7.

44–5. . . . 'This day has ever been with Me, and ever more will be'.

45ff. . . . Cf. Ælfric, *Homilies* ii, 6, " . . . his Sunu, wæs æfre of him acenned, buton ælcere meder. Þeos acennednys, þe we nu todæg wurðiað, wæs of eorðlicere meder, buton ælcum eorðlicum fæder".

But the author is not necessarily borrowing directly from Ælfric, since similar sentiments are found in other writers, e.g. in Alcuin.

50ff. . . . *Psalm* ii, 8.

53ff. . . . Vulgate *Psalm* xxxix, 6–8 (A.V. xl, 6-8), cf. *Hebrews* x, 5–10.

60ff. . . . *Philippians* ii, 8.

63. . . . Vulgate *Psalm* lxxxiv, 11 (A.V. lxxxv, 10).

XVII. ANCRENE RIWLE

Dialect: South West Midland.

Inflexions:

Verbs: inf. *stinken* 19, *siggen* 39, etc., but 2 Weak Class *peolien* 16, *wlatien* 20, *herien* 41, etc.

    3pr. *bringeð* 55, *cumeð* 12, *makeð* 9, etc. Some syncopated forms, *isihð* 53, *sent* 27, etc.

    prpl. *biteð* 23, *makeð* 4, *hercneð* 18, *preiseð* 3, but *helieð* 46, and *wreoð* 45, *unwreoð* 45.

    Pronouns: Fem. *heo* 33, etc.

    3 pl. nom. *heo* 19, 20; poss. *hore* 19, 44; obj. *ham* 18, 20.

    Some pronominal inflexions survive, am. *hine* 3, 17. Def. art., am. *pene* 13, 16, 45. Reflexive, dpl. *-suluen* 46.

    Nouns: Grammatical gender occasionally survives, *pet heaued* 29, *pet fulðe* 48, etc. *þing* 40, retains the pl. without ending of the OE long-stem neuters. Some of the OE weak nouns retain a pl. in *-en*, *ueren* 11, *tungen* 44, *earen* 44, 50, 51, and some original strong nouns have gone over to the weak declension, *deden* 14, *sustren* 49, 59, *talen* 52, *studen* 57, *ancren* 50.

    Adjectives: A gpl. inflexion remains in *alre-* 2.

Sounds:

    a/o is invariably *o*, *londe* 52, *longe* 31, *mon* 3, etc.

    æ is *e* in *þet* 7, *efter* 13, etc., but *a* in *hwat* 15, *was* 34, *latere* 24, 27.

    y is regularly *u*, *kunnes* 1, *vuele* 1, *sunne* 7, etc. *wuste* 35, *-sulf* 3, etc., *-suluen* 46, are from forms with *y* in lOE.

    ā is regularly *o*, *wo* 33, *louerd* 43, etc. *ane* 52, is probably due to early shortening.

    ǣ¹ and *ǣ²* both appear as *e*, *deden* 14, *weren* 59; *lesse* 9, *gest* 12, etc. *laste* 11 is due to early shortening.

    swuðe 40 is from a lOE form with *ȳ*.

    WS *ea*/Ang. *a* before *l*+cons. is *o* before lengthening groups, *holde* 43, *olde* 51, etc., but otherwise *a*, *alle* 52, etc., except for *help* 34. Before *r*+cons. *e* appears in *nert* 10. After front *c ea* appears in *cheafle* 58.

eo is *eo* in *cheorl* 16, *heorte* 27, *feor* 50. *weor-* is *wur-* in *iwurðe* 11. *i* appears before *h* in *knihte* 14. The mutation is *u* in *wurse* 2, etc., *wurst* 13, *alrewurste* 2, but *eo* in *weorpeð* 29, and *i* in *isihð* 53. *peolien* 16, *peonne* 32, are from forms with non-WS back-mutation.

ēa is *ea* in *heaued* 29, *earen* 44, *peau* 47. Early shortening has taken place in *pauh* 2, etc. The mutation appears as *e* in *ileued* 31, *ihereð* 53, *cheping* 54.

ēo is normally *eo*, *beop* 1, *deofles* 42, etc., but *o* in *our* 43, 50, *ou* 43. The mutation is *i* in *wrieð* 19.

Consonants: Initial *f* is often voiced, *uikelares* 1, *uorme* 1, etc., and initial *þ* appears as *t* in *tu* 10, 12, 15, *tet* 19, 39. Medial *l* has been lost in *swuche* 58, and final *l* in *muche* 12, 40. An inorganic final *h* appears in *ʒeoluh* 32, and a glide vowel has been developed before a back *h* in *þuruh* 36, 37, 43.

Notes

3–4. *preiseð . . . beo,* 'praise him to his face, and quickly enough make him out to be better than he is'.

11. *Let iwurðe,* 'let be'. A not uncommon idiomatic use of *iwurðen* in ME.

11–12. *Ne . . . one,* 'You are not alone in this'.

15. *hwat.* OE *hwæt* 'lo, behold', used to introduce or call attention to a statement. Rare in ME; but cf. Chaucer (*C.T.* I, 853–4), "He seyde 'Syn I shal bigynne the game,/What! welcome be the cut a goddes name' ".

19. *stinken,* 'to smell'; this transitive sense is not recorded in *NED.*

34ff. *Inouh . . . bote,* 'I tried hard enough, but that did not help me to effect any improvement here'.

43. Solomon in *Ecclesiastes* x, 11.

47. *þeau,* 'virtue', OE *þēaw* 'custom, usage' regularly developed the sense 'habit, quality', and by the seventeenth century had come to be used of general physique, 'habit of body, bodily proportions, etc.' The word then fell out of use but was revived later by Scott, who regularly linked it with *sinews,* so that the meaning was then taken to be 'muscles, tendons'.

56. *onlukust.* Apparently OE *ānlīc* 'solitary', which has been influenced by *ān,* and given the ordinary comparative and superlative of words in *-līc, -luker, -lukest.*

57. *iueied,* 'joined, united', but this appears to be the latest text in which this sense of the word survives. It is perhaps a mistake for *i-euened* 'likened'.

58. *cheafle,* 'idle, malicious talk'. OE *ceafl* 'jaw', modern *jowl,* though the exact development from the OE to the modern English form is obscure.

XVII. ANCRENE WISSE

Dialect: West Midland (of Hereford?).

Inflexions:

   Verbs: inf. *iwurðen* 64, *halden* 129, *huden* 108, but 2 Weak Class *makie* 100, *makien* 108, *winkin* 63, *lokin* 74, *pinin* 118.
     3 pr. *bringeð* 135, *draheð* 62, etc., but some syncopated forms, *bit* 64, 67, *leið* 64, *seið* 111, 120.
     prpl. *seggeð* 116.
     prp. *stinkinde* 73, *slepinde* 75, etc.
     ptp. *idoluen* 113, *deoluen* 112.
   Pronouns: Fem. *ha* 101.
     3 pl. nom. *ha* 109, 114, 117; obj. *ham* 109.
     Some pronominal inflexions survive, am. *hine* 69. Def. art., df. *þer* 90, 128.
   Nouns: *ehnen* 80, 133, retains the weak pl in -*en*, and some original strong nouns have gone over to the weak declension, *honden* 80, 115, *bonen* 89, *cneon* 90, *wunden* 107, 112, 119, *limen* 120, *dropen* 128, *wepnen* 132.

Sounds:

   a/o is regularly *o*, but examples occur only before lengthening groups *hond* 77, *stronge* 79, etc.
   æ is usually *e*, *wes* 66, *hwet* 74, etc., but *a* in *bac* 79, and *ea* in -*steaf* 76, 79, 104.
   y is usually *u*, *stucche* 95, *cunde* 123, etc., but *i* in *kimeð* 86. *wule* 74, *wult* 75, are from forms with *y* in lOE.
   ā is regularly *a*, *hali* 79, *stan* 111, etc.
   ǣ[1] is regularly *e*, *were* 61, *dede* 62, etc. *leote* 63, is usually explained as due to analogy with such verbs as *beoren*, etc.
   ǣ[2] is regularly *ea*, *ear* 66, *eauer* 71, etc.
   ȳ is regularly *u*, *huden* 108, *luðerliche* 79, etc.
   WS *ea*/Ang. *a* before *l*+cons. is invariably *a*, *hald* 80, *baldeliche* 124, *galle* 123, etc. Before *r*+cons. *ea* appears in *mearke* 77, *beard* 93, but *a* in -*ward* 64, etc.
   eo is usually *eo*, *heorte* 62, *heouene* 81, etc., *weor*- is *wur*- in *iwurðen* 64. -*seolf* 64, etc. is from a form with non-WS fracture before *lf*, *ʒeoue* 125, *heouen* 102, *cleopeð* 69, 118, 122, *cleope* 105, are from forms with nWS back-mutation. *deoluen* 112 is presumably a scribal error for *doluen*.
   ēa is usually *ea*, *deaðes* 67, *eadi* 92, etc., but *e* before *h* in *flehen* 72, *ehnen* 80, 133, *heh* 80, 133, and *a* after OE *sc* and front *c* in *schawde* 127, *schaw* 134, *chapeð* 95. The mutation is *e* in *eðeliche* 99.
   ēo is usually *eo*, *feond* 63, *beoð* 68, etc., but *i* appears before *h* in *flih* 107, and *o* before *w* in *fowr* 91. The mutation is *eo* in *deore* 67, *treowe* 103, etc.
   Diphthongization of *o* before *h* does not appear in *bohte* 96, *þoht* 109, *inoh* 127.

Consonants: The OE back spirant *g* appears regularly as *h*, *draheð* 62, *flehen* 72, *drahen* 130, etc. Final *n* is lost in *a* 95, *o* 67, etc., *i* 68, etc., final *l* in *muche* 121, and medial *l* in *swucche* 108, *swuch* 122. Final *d* is unvoiced in *ant* 63, and a glide consonant has developed in *nempnunge* 77, *nempne* 105.

Orthography:

OE *ā* is written *aa* 97, and Fr. *e* appears as *ea* in *leattre* 116. Medial *ss* appears as *sc* in *blesce* 92, and OE front *c* is *cch* in *swucche* 108 (cf. *swuch* 122).

Notes

62. *unlust*, 'evil desire', so *NED* because of the reading of the French translation, *a son mal desir*, and certainly the translator must have thus understood the word. But such a sense would occur only here, and the usual meaning of the word 'disinclination to do something, slothfulness' fits much better into the context.

63. *amainet*, 'maimed, crippled', seems to give rather better sense than N *amaset* 'bewildered'.
    ant feð . . . iwurðen, 'and begins as it were to close his eye and to let the devil do as he pleases'.

65. *crauant*. Presumably to be connected with *crave*, OE *crafian*. The *-ant* would be a Normanization of the prp., so that the original sense would be 'craving (mercy)'.

66–7. *þe stod ear feorren to*, 'who stood previously afar off (leaps) to (him)'.

69. . . . Vulgate, *Psalm* xxi, 21 (A.V. xxii, 20).

72. *snakerinde*, 'approaching stealthily', a word found apparently only in the *Ancrene Riwle*.

75. *slepinde*, i.e. sleepily, in a sleepy fashion.
    ame. Formally this could be the masc. of a ptp. of which the fem. *amee* is recorded by Godefroy as appearing in OF. But it is much more likely to be the conventional representation of a yawn.

77. *nempnunge . . . muð*, 'invoking the holy name'.
    mearke, 'sign', i.e. the crucifix.

81ff. . . . With the exception of *Veni Creator*, which is the opening of a hymn, these are phrases taken from various *Psalms*, the following being the Vulgate references in order: lxix, 2; lxvii, 2; liii, 3; iii, 2; xxiv, 1; cxxii, 1; cxx, 1.

82. . . . The *Veni Creator Spiritus*, which is tenth-century at latest, has taken deeper hold of the Western Church than any other medieval hymn.

87. . . . Vulgate, *Psalm* xii, 1 (A.V. xiii, 1).

89. *ledene*, 'language'. The word is OE *lǣden* 'Latin', but it was very early used in the more general sense, one which survived until the sixteenth century; cf. Spenser, *F.Q.*, IV, xi, 19, "he . . . could the ledden of the Gods vnfold".

96. *bune*. N *spuse* is the usual word in the context, but C *bune* 'purchase',

a rare word, found, apart from the *Ancrene Riwle*, only in the *Lambeth Homilies*, gives good sense and probably represents the original, since other MSS. have *bugging* and the Latin version *mercem*.

98. *ant beo on . . . deorre*, 'and value the soul at a dearer price'.

110. . . . *Isaiah* ii, 10.

114. . . . Vulgate *Psalm* xxi, 17 (A.V. xxii, 16).

118. *þurleden* 'pierced', OE *þyrlian*, a formation from *þyrel* 'hole, aperture', the latter remaining in modern English only as the second element of *nostril*. The verb survives, in a metathesized form, as the modern *thrill*, which retained its original literal sense until the sixteenth century; cf. Spenser, *F.Q.* IV, vii, 36, "in her wrath she thought them both haue thrild,/With that selfe arrow, which the Carle had kild". The word is now used only in the metaphorical sense, 'to affect with a sudden wave of emotion'.

119. . . . *Canticles* ii, 14.

123. . . . In medieval bestiaries the dove has no gall, and so is always gentle and mild.

125. . . . *Lamentations* iii, 65.

132. *dragse.* If this be a scribal error, it is one for which it is difficult to account. Perhaps the *s* may be due to the following *þu*, the scribe first assuming it to have been an ordinary 2 pr., then realizing that it was an imperative but forgetting to erase the *s* which he had already written. If *dragse* be a genuine form, one might postulate a *-sian* suffix; cf. *hrēowsian* beside *hrēowan* (Wright, *OE Grammar*, sect. 659).

XVIII. SEINTE MARHERETE

Dialect: West Midland (of Hereford?).

Inflexions:

Verbs: inf. *beore* 51, *forswolhe* 20, *stonden* 49, *forsweolhen* 51, but 2 Weak Class *crahien* 19, *blakien* 21.

3 pr. *fundeð* 51, *weneð* 51, etc., but *halt* 35.

prpl. *fleoteð* 33, *wurcheð* 35, *habbeð* 41, etc., but *herieð* 32, *wunieð* 43; *eardið* 33, *studegið* 37, etc.

prp. *flihinde* 34, *glistinde* 6, but *heriende* 63.

ptp. *ibeden* 23.

Pronouns: Fem. *ha* 3, etc., *heo* 3.

3 pl. obj. *ham* 6, 43.

Some pronominal inflexions survive. Def. art., df. *þer* 25.

Nouns: *ware* 29, retains the OE pl. form, whilst *smecche* 12 keeps the distinctive ending of the gpl. (OE *-a*). *deor* 42, *þing* 32 (cf. *þinges* 32), retain the pl. without ending of the long-stem neuters. *ehnen* 8, *steoren* 9, *steorren* 37, retain the pl. ending of the weak nouns, and some original strong nouns have gone over to the weak declension, *beoden* 4, *cneon* 25, *honden* 26, *helen* 57.

ounds:

a/o is regularly *o*, *stonden* 49, *longe* 7, *monie* 3, etc.

æ is usually *e*, *wes* 1, *bed* 4, etc., but *ea* in *weattres* 41, *tobearst* 61.

y is regularly *u*, *-þurl* 3, *hurne* 4, etc. *stude* 16 is from a form with *y* in lOE.

ā is regularly *a*, *twa* 8, *brade* 9, etc.

ǣ¹ is usually *e*, *were* 7, *iwepnet* 60, etc., but *ea* in *fearlac* 22, 41, *reasde* 55, *unmeaðlich* 56.

ǣ² is regularly *ea*, *heastes* 35, *neaure* 39, etc.

ȳ is *u* in *fur* 11, *ituðet* 24.

WS *ea*/Ang. *a* before *l*+cons. is normally *a*, *wald* 42, *halt* 35, *alle* 20, etc., but *e* appears in *forswelh* 58; the mutation appears as *ea* in *wealdest* 31, *afeallen* 50. Before *r*+cons. *a* appears in *towart* 5, *swart* 8, *scharp* 14, *warð* 15, 60, but *ea* in *stearc* 16, *eardið* 33, and *e* in *berd* 7, *sperclede* 11; the mutation is *e* in *merkest* 40, *unmerret* 62. Before *h a* appears in *iwraht* 34, etc. *steareden* 9, *nease* 11, *geapede* 18, are from forms with Mercian back-mutation of *æ*.

eo is usually *eo*, *steoren* 9, *eorðe* 25, etc. *weor-* is *wur-* in *iwurðe* 48, but *weor-* in *sweord* 14, and *wer-* in *-werc* 44. *cleopede* 27, *beoden* 4, *beore* 51, are from forms with nWS back-mutation. The mutation appears as *i* in *fir* 40.

ēa is usually *ea*, *heaued* 10, *scheate* 14, etc., but *e* appears in *bred* 2, *-strem* 39, and regularly before *h*, *hehe* 26, *heh* 56, etc. *þah* 6, 14, is due to early shortening. The mutation is *e* in *her* 46.

ēo is usually *eo*, *beheolden* 3, *bleo* 21, etc., but *i* before *h* in *flihinde* 34. The mutation is *eo* in *deor-* 49, etc., *steorest* 39.

Diphthongization of *o* before *h* does not appear in *þohte* 24.

Consonants: Initial *f* is occasionally voiced, *uoster-* 1, and final unaccented *d* is frequently unvoiced, *towart* 5, *healent* 63, etc. OE back spirant *g* regularly appears as *h*, *ehnen* 8, *fuheles* 34, *lahe* 43, etc., whilst OE front *g* appears as *h* in *herhedest* 45. Initial *þ* is *t* in *tis* 18, *te* 32, *tu* 38, *ti* 35, *tet* 55, etc., and final *þ* has become *t* in *libbet* 43. Final *n* is lost in *o* 15, *i* 33, etc., and final *l* in *muche* 21, while medial *rr* has been simplified in *steoren* 9.

rthography:

ā is written *aa* in *aa* 38. *sc* is used as a spelling for *s* in *bascins* 10, and for *ss* in *blesci* 53. The final *d* of *Godd* 28 has been doubled to distinguish it from the adj. *gōd*.

Notes

-3. *þet* . . . *leuide*, 'by means of which she lived'. Most editors emend *leuide* to *liuede*, but the former is possible as a development from OE *leofode*, pt. of *leofian/lifian*.

. *eilþurl*. As Dr. Mack has pointed out, this is a hybrid form with OF *ueil* 'eye' and OE *þyrel* 'hole'. OE *ēagþyrl* has had its first element replaced by the corresponding OF word.

4. *beoden.* Ang. *gebeodu,* 'prayers'. The modern sense of the word *bead* is due to the transference of meaning from the prayer itself to the objects, beads on a rosary, with which the various prayers were enumerated; cf. *to tell one's beads,* 'to number one's prayers'.
6. *ham gras . . . unselhðe,* 'they were horrified because of it, those who saw that evil creature'.
9. *steareden,* translating L *splendebant.* As Mack points out the use of the word in the sense 'shine' appears to have been peculiar to the WM dialects between the thirteenth and the fifteenth centuries.
   steappre, 'more brilliant', a sense of the word that survives until the end of the sixteenth century; cf. Skelton, *Philip Sparowe,* 1014, "He eyen gray and stepe".
10. *on,* 'of', not infrequent in this sense in ME, due to a difference of idiom. But a similar use after the sixteenth century is probably due to confusion because of the reduction of both *of* and *on* to *o* in colloquial speech.
12. *Ant lahte ut.* Omission of a pronominal subject before a verb is not unusual in this group of texts.
13. *hire,* referring to *tunge* which was fem. in OE.
15. *leitede . . . leie,* 'glittered with fire'.
16. *schucke,* 'devil, fiend', obsolete in StE since the thirteenth century but surviving in some dialects, and a not uncommon element in place-names, e.g. *Shuckburgh* (Wa.), *Shucknall* (He.), etc.
20. *mid alle,* 'altogether, entirely', a common phrase from the tenth to the fourteenth century.
21. *blakien,* OE *blācian* 'to grow pale', a derivative of *blāc* 'white' and related to *blǣcan* 'to bleach'.
22. *ant . . . offruht,* 'rendered helpless with fear'.
25. *smat . . . eorðe,* 'fell to her knees'.
29. *cwike,* 'living', the original sense of the word, now obsolete except in such phrases as *quickset hedge, the quick and the dead,* etc.
35–6. *þe sunne . . . reste,* 'the sun continues on its course without any rest'.
37. *walkeð,* in the now obsolete general sense 'journey'; cf. *Meid Margret* xlix, "Muchel ich habbe iwalken bi water ant bi londe".
   lufte. R *weolcne* fits in better with the alliteration and no doubt represents the original. B *lufte* may be due to the occurrence of that word in line 30.
39–40. *Þu steorest . . . merkest.* Perhaps a reminiscence of *Genesis* i, 9–10.
42. *Þe wurmes ant te wilde deor.* Cf. *Beowulf* 1430, "wyrmas ond wildeor". Note that both words are used in their now obsolete general sense. OE *wyrm* 'reptile, anything from a worm to a dragon', survived in that sense until the modern period; cf. Milton, *P.L.* vii, 475, "A once came forth whatever creeps the ground,/Insect or worme" Yet already in OE the word was used also in the restricted sense 'earthworm'. OE *dēor* 'wild animal' had been particularized to its modern sense already in ME., and, by the close of the period, that had become its usual meaning.

o þis wald. Emendation to *world* is tempting; but the Royal MS. reads *on þeos wilde waldes.*

3. *luuewende*, 'loving, beloved', a rare word found only in the Katherine Group. It is significant that the R scribe has substituted *luuiende.*

5. *kempe*, 'champion', probably used here in the distinctively legal sense 'one who does battle for another in a judicial duel'.

3. *blesci*, 'make the sign of the Cross as a protection'.

8. *wombe*, 'belly'. The modern sense of 'womb', found already in OE, did not oust the older and wider sense (which persists in the Scots *wame*) till the eighteenth century.

8–9. *Ah . . . wraðerheale*, 'but (it was) to the glory of Christ and to his own confusion'.

1. *o midhepes*, 'in the midst', translating L *per medium*. As Mack points out, OE *on middan hēapes* has evidently been weakened in meaning and can now be used as merely synonymous with OE *on middan, a middan.* The Saint's emblem is a dragon, out of which she is often represented as emerging.

XIX. A KENTISH HOMILY

Dialect: Kentish.

Inflexions:

Verbs: inf. *yeue* 13, *wene* 85, etc., but *siggen* 37, and 2 Weak Class *louie* 50, *serui* 50, 57, *targi* 82. Note the retention of the dative inf. in *to done* 48, *to cumene* 95.

3 pr. *legheþ* 85, *spekeþ* 1, etc., but occasional syncopated forms, *yefþ* 82, *halt* 94, *sent* 73, *seyth* 4, etc.

prpl. *ofserueþ* 92, *habbeth* 22, etc., but *hopieð* 64, *hatieþ* 89, *luuieþ* 89, 94. ptp. *icomen* 19, *icume* 20, 61, *icorene* 29.

Pronouns: 3 pl. nom. *hi* 18, etc., *i* 57, *hie* 10; poss. *here* 15, etc.; obj. *hem* 10, etc.

Some pronominal inflexions survive, am. *hine* 94, apl. *his* 22. Def. art., am. *þan* 9, 41, *þane* 84, 92.

Nouns: *wyntre* 75 retains the distinctive ending of the neuter pl., and forms of the dpl. appear in *hwilem* 66, *daghen* 60.

Sounds:

a/o is *o* before lengthening groups, *fond* 9, *longe* 53, etc., but otherwise *a*, *kam* 9, *man* 82, etc. *e* appears in *amenges* 21.

æ is *e* in *þet* 2, *hedde* 7, *hedden* 20, *efter-* 27, etc., but *a* in *was* 5, *þat* 5, *ate* 35, etc., and *ea* in *deai* 23.

y is *e*, *berdenne* 24, *senne* 72, etc.

ā is *o*, *Lord* 1, *holi* 1, etc.

ǣ¹ and *ǣ²* both appear as *e*, *were* 10, *fles* 43; *heþen* 45, *neuer* 55, etc. *waren* 19, *last* 16, 20, 28, *laste* 22, 28, *last* 43, *tachte* 57, are due to early shortening.

ȳ is usually *e*, *here* 5, *herde* 12, etc., but *ie* in *ihierde* 42, and *ee* in *wee* 10.

WS *ea*/Ang. *a* before *l*+cons. is *o* before lengthening groups in *itol*
27, otherwise *a*, *alle* 32, *halt* 94, etc.; the mutation is *e* in *elde* 69, etc
Before *r*+cons. *a* appears in -*yarde* 6, etc., -*ward* 28, but *e* in -*werde* 7
Before *h* the mutation is *i* in *almichti* 1, etc.

eo is regularly *e*, *heuene* 3, *herte* 93, etc. *weor-* is *wor-* in *world* 33, etc., bu
wer- in *werkmen* 5, etc. *clepe* 15, *clepeþ* 70, *iclepede* 29, etc., are from
forms with nWS back-mutation.

ēa appears as *ea* in *seaweth* 2, *beleaue* 36, etc., but *ia* in *griat* 3, *diadlich* 72
etc., *ya* in *yare* 93, and *e* in *beleue* 57. The mutation is *e* in *ihereþ* 30
bileued 49, etc.

ēo appears as *ie* in *bie* 10, *bieþ* 28, etc., as *e* in *frend* 25, *ibe* 45, etc., as
in *furti* 75, *yu* 13, *yure* 59, and as *w* in *yw* 59.

Consonants: Initial *f* is voiced in *uerste* 28, *velaghes* 22. Metathesis o
ld to *dl* appears in *wordl* 35, *wordle* 43, 50. OE *hw* appears as *w* i
wanne 70, 71, 74, *wat* 26, *werefore* 45. Medial *fd* has been assimilate
in *hedde* 7, *hedden* 20, etc.; medial *bb* has been simplified in *habeþ* 6·
a glide consonant developed in *alþer* 74, and already in OE *g* ha
been lost before *d* in *seden* 36. Final *n* has been lost in *i* 39, medial
in *heueriche* 64, 92, and medial *l* in *swiche* 70.

Orthography:

Initial *h* is occasionally omitted, *is* 35, *ise* 53, etc., and frequentl
wrongly added, *hure* 1, *hic* 13, etc. *w* is represented by *u* initially i
uilleth 2, and after *s* in *ansuerede* 25, *ansuerden* 54. OE front *g* is
in *yef* 2, *yeue* 13, etc., and back spirant *g* is represented by *gh*, *daghen* 6·
moreghen 5, etc. OE *sc* is regularly *s*, *seaweth* 2, *sal* 13, *fles* 43, etc
and the voiceless spirant, back or front, is represented by *ch*
þurch 36, *tachte* 57, *richt* 13, etc. Front *c* is spelled *c* in *hic* 13, etc
and double front *c* by *chch* in *gruchchede* 21, while back *c* is repre
sented by *ck* in *betockneþ* 30, etc., and *nc* by *ngk* in *forþingketh* 2·
th appears in *uilleth* 2, *seyth* 4, etc., and OE *ss* appears as *sc* in *blisce* 5·
etc. *ē*, *ō* are written *ee*, *oo* in *iheerd* 56, *wee* 10, *good-* 4, *noon* 2·
hoot 91, etc., and *ī* is *ij* in *hij* 55, *ū* is *uu* in *uut* 5, and short *a* is *aa* i
naam 43.

Notes

1. *godespelle of teday.* *Matthew* xx, 1, as indicated by the Latin rubri·
2-3. *þet . . . þet.* Similar repetition of *þet* is characteristic of the Englis
translator, and may be due to the influence of Fr. *ke . . . ke.*
4. *goodman*, 'head of the household', the earliest recorded example of th
word in this particular sense.
6. *winyarde*, OE *wīngeard*, the usual word in ME until the beginning o
the fifteenth century. During the fourteenth century *vineyard* begi·
to take its place, and becomes invariable during the followir
century.

   for . . . forewerde. Fr. *au couenant dun denier*, 'at the agreement of a pen·
each'.

8. *ayen* 'towards, drawing near', a sense of this word which is rare in ME, but is not infrequent for *against*.

14. *hit wes*, Fr. *quant uint au seir*. As Hall points out the MS. *hi wel* is obviously to be emended to *hit wes*. A scribe has omitted the final *-t* of *hit* and misread a long *s* as *l*.

   sergant, 'servant', the original sense of the word, ultimately from L. *servientem*. By the thirteenth century the word had come to mean 'ordinary soldier', and also 'tenant by military service under the rank of knight', especially one of this class attending on a knight in the field. The modern military sense of the word does not appear until the sixteenth century, and may originally have indicated a higher rank than now.

15–16. *agyn . . . ferste*, 'begin with those who came last, and go thence in order to the first'.

19. *þo . . . icomen*, 'those who had come during the morning'.

22. *velaghes*, 'equals, co-workers', the original sense of the word, but already by the fourteenth century it had come to be used in a depreciatory sense.

26. *Wat . . . iwil*, 'What displeases you in that I do my pleasure?'

33. *tides*, 'hours', a not uncommon sense of the word in ME, but obsolete since the fifteenth century. Fr. *les diuerses ores del ior*.

33–4. *Bie þe morghen*, 'during the morning', Fr. *par matin*.

37. *þet . . . siggen*, 'to whom they had the duty of announcing it'. Fr. *a toȝ cels a qui il auoient a dire*.

38–9. *þo . . . was*, 'whom he sent in the days of Moses'.

41. *to him helden*, 'inclined to him'. Fr. *a lui se tindrent*.

43. *a last of þis wordle*, 'towards the end of the world'. Fr. *uer la fin del siecle*.

44. *seauede*, Fr. *se demustra*. As Hall suggests, *him* has probably been omitted before *ine*.

45–6. *þet . . . igo*, 'during all the time that was past'. Fr. *qui par le tens qui est ore trepasse*.

48. *Ac þerefore*, 'but because of this'. Fr. *Mes por ceo*.

49. *þo þet*, 'because'. Fr. *car*.

50–1. *þet man is*. Fr. *ce que hom faet*. Hall suggests that the translator misread *faet* 'does' as *seit* 'is'.

52. *þenche*, 'seem'. Confusion of *þencan* and *þyncan* is not unusual in ME.
   aresunede, 'questioned, called to account', a bye-form of *arraign*.

57. *a seide ure Lord*. Fr. *dist seil nostre sire*.

60. *be þa daghen*, 'during the course of the day'.

67. *diuers wordles*, 'of the different ages of the world'. Fr. *del diuers tens del siecle*.

68. *dede*, 'put, placed' (Fr. *mist*), a sense of the word obsolete except in dialect since the seventeenth century.

70–1. *per bieþ*. Hall suggests that the translator has misread the *ia* 'already' of his original as *i a* 'there is'.

71–2. *wanne . . . senne*. Not in the French.

72. *be swo þet*, 'since, because', hardly 'provided that' as Hall.

80. *Also . . . ase*, 'as much . . . as'.
81. *Nocht . . . yefþ.* As it stands the English hardly makes sense, but the Fr. shows the meaning intended, *Neporquant ceste grant bunte damledeu quil il done as ons come as autres.*
84–5. *for . . . wrench.* A popular proverbial saying of the period.
91. *and*, 'if', a not uncommon sense of the word from the thirteenth to the eighteenth century; cf. Shakespeare, *Com. Errors* I, ii, 94, "And you will not, sir, Ile take my heeles".
92–4. Cf. 1 Corinthians ii, 9.
94. *halt*, 'keeps in reserve', so Hall, Fr. *promet et estore.*

XX. A LUUE-RON

Dialect: South-West or South West Midlands.

Inflexions:

Verb: inf. Indifferently *-e* or *-en*, *ileorne* 3, *abyde* 41, *weren* 30, *heren* 75, etc. *wunye* 144 retains ending of 2 Weak Class.

3 pr. Usually *-eþ*, *heleþ* 156, *weneþ* 24, etc., but many syncopated forms, *glyt* 32, *bit* 1, *isihþ* 140, etc.

prpl. *liggeþ* 15, *falewiþ* 16.

prp. *hwilynde* 33 (r.w. *bihynde*).

ptp. *iglyden* 71, *iwryten* 210, *icoren* 155, etc., but *ifunde* 55 (r.w. *a lunde*), 160.

Pronouns: Fem. *heo* 3, 135.

3 pl. nom. *heo* 71, 133, *hi* 15, 76, 77; poss. *heore* 78, 180; obj. *heom* 73, 74.

Some pronominal inflexions survive, e.g. am. *hine* 137, 183, *hyne* 167. Def. art., am. *þene* 124, 152, *þan* 199. Indef. art. am. *enne* 30, 88; gm. *enes* 159.

Nouns: *seorewen* 19 has the weak pl. in *-en*.

Sounds:

a/o is usually *o*, *con* 8, *mon* 47, etc., but *hwan* 3, *þane* 151, *þan* 199.

æ is indifferently *a* or *e*, *was* 36, *sad* 50 (r.w. *gled*), *hwat* 63, etc., but *wes* 35, *glede* 92, etc.

y is *u* in *wurche* 2, *muchel* 42, 200, *suche* 111, *vuele* 189, but *i* in *ylde* 96 (r.w. *wilde*), *Drihte* 140, *king* 88, etc. *nule* 7, *wule* 8, are from lOE forms in *y*.

ā is usually *o*, *gap* 34, *ston* 116, etc.

ǣ¹ and *ǣ²* appear as *e*, *were* 5, *dret* 59; *teche* 8, *ilest* 22, etc., but *bitauht* 145, shows early shortening.

ȳ is *u* in *lutle* 22, *brudþinge* 207.

WS *ea/*Ang. *a* before *l*+cons. is *o* before lengthening groups, *biholde* 9, *bolde* 13, etc., but otherwise *a*, *alle* 5, *halt* 102, etc. Before *r*+cons. *e* appears in *berne* 5, *mereuh* 44, *ert* 168, but *a* in *scharpe* 69, *-ward* 21, 45; the mutation is *e* in *werne* 7. Before *h* *a* appears in *waxeþ* 61; the mutation is *i* in *myhte* 3, *myht* 9, etc. *mayht* 31, is probably a scribal error.

eo usually remains, *ileorne* 3, *eorþe* 84, etc., but is *o* in *yorne* 1, *e* in *smerte* 58, and *i* before *h* in *knyhte* 144. *icleoped* 162, is from a form with nWS back mutation in OE. The mutation is *u* in *wurse* 192.

ēa is regularly *e*, *les* 12, *deþ* 23, etc. The mutation appears as *e* in *heren* 75.

ēo is usually *eo*, *freo* 6, *beoþ* 14, *neode* 107, etc., but *e* in *lefmon* 4, *reuþe* 75, *eu* 118. The mutation is *eo* in *treowe* 55, etc., but *e* in *dere-* 163.

Consonants: Initial *f* is often voiced, *vouh* 28, *vikel* 12, etc. Medial *l* is lost in *wordes* 70, medial *l* and *w* in *suche* 111, and initial *h* in *ylde* 96. Final *-n* is lost in *Dryhte* 136, etc., and medial *fm* assimilated in *wymmon* 6. Note the distinctively WS retention of *h* in *isihþ* 140.

Orthography:

OE *ū* is represented by *o* in *-ron* 2, and by *w* in *hw* 62, 76. In *wrþ* 86, *w* is used as a spelling for *wu*, and in *lost* 93 short *u* is represented by *o*. *th* appears in *haueth* 210, and *ph* is used as a spelling for *f* in *stephne* 203.

Notes

2. *luue-ron*, 'song of love'. The compound is found elsewhere only in the pl. in *The Life of St. Katherine* (see p. xi above), translating L. *amatoria carmina*, but the sense 'song, cry' is not unusual for *rune* in the fourteenth century.

The rhyme of *-ron* : *-mon* is curious, and if anything more than an assonance were intended we must presume that in the one case the second element of a compound has been shortened from *ū* and obscured and in the other *o* has been obscured.

6. *freo*, 'noble', the usual sense in ME, rather than the modern 'free'. The virgin addressed is obviously a nun, who in the ME period would almost certainly be of gentle birth.

13. *peines*. OE *þegn* survives in ME in its various senses, but by the end of the thirteenth century has become obsolete in England and remains so until revived by sixteenth-century antiquaries. In Scotland, however, in the sense 'person holding lands of the king and ranking with an earl's son, chief of a clan', it remains in use until the nineteenth century. Cf. Shakespeare, *Macbeth* I, ii, 46, "The worthy thane of Ross".

21. *blyue*, for *bi liue*, literally 'with life, liveliness', hence 'quickly, with speed'. For the meaning cf. modern *look alive* 'be quick'. The word survives in English until the seventeenth century, but after that is apparently found only in Scots.

24. . . . 'When he has the greatest expectation of life'.

28. *vouh ne gray*. For this phrase see note to XIII/116.

29. *Ne . . . swift*, 'however swift he may be'; *þe* is here the OE instrumental of the definite article used adverbially.

33. . . . 'This world is full of ups and downs'.

49. . . . 'Man's love lasts only a short time'.

50. *sad*, 'sated, tired'; the modern sense does not appear before the end of the fourteenth century.

50–2. *sad : gled*. Read *sad : glad* or *sed : gled*.

53. *a lunde*. Carleton Brown takes this as for *on londe*, but in that case the sense is difficult and the rhyme bad. It is more probably for *on lunde* (ON *lundr*) 'in the grove', i.e. in the forest, away. The ON word is a common place-name element, e.g. *Lound* (Nt.), *Lund* (ERY), *Swanland* (ERY), etc. This gives the required rhyme, but the sense is still difficult. Moreover, the word does not seem to be otherwise known in ME except as a place-name element, and it could, perhaps, be taken as one here; cf. XXX/17, "Bituene Lyncolne and Lynde-seye, Norhamptoun and Lounde". Stratmann-Bradley cites *Lunde* as a ME form of *London*, and this would give excellent sense and rhyme. Unfortunately, one of their two examples is certainly, and the other probably, for a *Lound/Lund*.

57. *weole*, 'wealth, riches, possessions'; the original concrete sense of the word has been obsolete since the seventeenth century.

67. *Ideyne*. MS *Dideyne* due to a misdivision of *and Ideyne*. Amadas and Idoine are hero and heroine of an extant French romance. They are frequently referred to in ME as outstanding examples of faithful lovers.

69. *meyne*. Formally it might be from OE *mægen* 'strength', or OF *meyne* 'retinue'. Carleton Brown takes it as the former. But the adj. is found in OE and in ME in the sense 'eager, impetuous, violent' used of warriors, and this would fit 'retinue' better than 'strength'.

72. *cleo*. Carleton Brown and *NED* derive from OE *clif, cleofu*, and translate 'as the sheaf is from the hillside'. For the unusual form *NED* compares *Clee Hills* and *Cleobury Mortimer* in Shropshire. But Ekwall derives these from OE *clǣg* 'clay', and *cleo* would certainly be a surprising development from OE *clif, cleofu*. Kemp Malone (2 *ELH* 60) takes the word to be from OE *clēo* 'hook', with reference to an agricultural implement. This would give good sense, 'as the sheaf is (cut) by the reaping hook', and a satisfactory form. But it is doubtful whether the word can bear this particular sense. It is a variant of OE *clēa, clawe*, and should presumably mean 'a claw-hook' rather than a reaping hook—a different sort of implement. None of the examples of the word seems to give the kind of sense required.

73. *also*, 'as if', a rare meaning of the word found only in ME.

80. . . . 'Foolish is anyone who trusts in it'.

90. *Childe*. 'youth of noble birth'. In OE the word appears to have been used as a kind of title, and in the thirteenth and fourteenth centuries is not infrequently applied to a young noble awaiting knighthood, especially in romances. From these it appears to have been taken over by the ballads and used as a title, this use having been borrowed from them by modern poets in such names as *Childe Harold, Childe Roland*.

94. *wilde*. Carleton Brown takes this as for *filde*, 'filled with wisdom', with voicing of initial *f* (not infrequent in this text), and representa-

tion of the *v* by *w* (a spelling not otherwise recorded in this text). This gives good sense, but the spelling is eccentric. Menner (55 *MLN* 244) takes the word as OE *wield* 'powerful, mighty', occurring rarely elsewhere in ME. Again this would give excellent sense, but a distinctively WS form would be surprising in this text.

99. *to His honde*, 'in His power'.

102. *of Hym he halt*, 'is His vassal', apparently a translation of the Latin legal formula *X tenet de Y*.

105. *ne byt He wiþ þe*, 'He does not ask with you', i.e. 'He demands no dowry with you'. But the convent generally did.

106. *rencyan*. Some kind of particularly fine cloth, but exactly what is not known.

111. *wede*, 'clothing, dress'; after the seventeenth century, apart from the phrase *widow's weeds*, the word is found in this sense only dialectally and in verse.

112. *king ne kayser*. A common alliterative phrase already in OE; cf. *Seafarer* 82, "cyningas ne caseras". Here the second word has been replaced by the cognate ON *keisari*.

113. *bolde*, 'building', here presumably 'temple'. The word has been obsolete since the fourteenth century, but is frequent enough in place-names, e.g. *Bold, Bolton, Newbold, Wychbold*, etc.

121. *mote*, 'hill, eminence', as in *Liddel Moat* (Cu.). It appears to be the same word as modern 'moat', and may have developed the sense 'ditch, moat' already in AN. For similar changes in meaning cf. *dam, dike*.

135. *in gode weye*, 'in a favourable position'.

143. *sley*. MS. *seoly*, is taken by Carleton Brown as OE *sǣlig* 'happy, blessed' which gives good sense but an improbable rhyme, while the representation of OE *ǣ* by *eo* would be eccentric. More probably the word intended is *sley* (ON *slœgr*) 'skilful, dexterous'. This would give a fair rhyme, though not perhaps quite so satisfactory a meaning.

146. *pel*. As Kemp Malone (2 *ELH* 60) points out this is rather OE *pæll/ pell* 'rich, purple cloth', than AF *pell* 'fur'. In modern *pall* the OE word has been particularized in meaning, but the original sense survives until the end of the sixteenth century; cf. Spenser, *Shep. Cal.*, July 173, "They bene yclad in purple and pall".

153. *ymston*, a variant of *ȝimstone*. For similar loss of initial ȝ- cf. modern *if, itch*, and place-names such as *Ideford* (De.), *Ilchester* (So.), *Ing* (Ex.), *Ipswich* (Suf.), etc.

154. *vnder heouene grunde*, 'beneath the lowest part of heaven'.

164. . . . 'It carries away the prize from all other things', i.e. excels.

170. *beoþ*, 'excels', but this sense of the word is not recorded by *NED*. *vertu*. Probably here in the sense, 'occult efficacy or power, as in the prevention or cure of disease, etc.', a quality which the Middle Ages frequently attributed to various kinds of precious stones.

172. *lectorie*, from L *alectoria* (from Gk. *alektōr*) 'cock-stone', said to be found in the gizzard of a cock.

181. . . . 'It is set in heavenly gold'.

185. *dost in þine rede*, 'ask, desire'.

194. *open.* See note to III/21.

196. *bute bok*, 'without book', i.e. by heart.

200. *stonde muchel stel*, 'be very useful', a common idiom from the thirteenth to the fifteenth century; cf. *Owl and Nightingale* 1631, "Ah þu
neuer mon to gode/Lyues ne deþes stal ne stode", and see also
modern *stand in good stead.*

XXI. IACOB AND IOSEP

Dialect: South West Midland.

Inflexions:

Verbs: inf. Indifferently *-e* or *-en*, *comen* 8, *tellen* 3, *sitte* 8, *drinke* 17,
etc.

3 pr. *bringeþ* 97, *wepeþ* 57, *þuncheþ* 31, 35, but *naþ* 49.

prpl. *wringeþ* 91, *valleþ* 44, *turneþ* 86, etc.

ptp. *ifunde* 90, *icome* 47, etc.

Pronouns: 3 pl. nom. *hi* 14, etc., *þei* 15; poss. *here* 27, etc.; obj. *hem* 6,
etc., *-em* 37.

Note also definite article, am. *þene* 94.

Nouns: *þing* 39, retains the OE long-stem neuter pl. without ending,
but cf. *wordes* 1. *mowen* 26, *assen* 31, etc., *honden* 60, 91, *breþren* 43,
etc., *aldren* 13, *children* 64, have the weak pl. ending in *-en* (OE *-an*),
whether historically correct or due to analogy.

Sounds:

a/o is regularly *o* before lengthening groups, *song* 5, *wombe* 7, *lond* 22,
etc. Otherwise *a* and *o* forms appear side by side, *grame* 3, *name* 4,
gome 23, *tome* 24, etc.

æ is regularly *a*, *after* 2, *was* 4, etc. *quod* 47, is due to the rounding
influence of *w*.

y is normally *u*, *gurdel* 7, *hul* 19, etc., but *e* in *meri* 5, *begge* 31, and *i* in
king 40 (r.w. *þing*), etc., *kisse* 58 (r.w. *blisse*). *sullen* 48, *dude* 69, are
from lOE forms with *y*.

ā is regularly *o*, *gon* 6, *hom* 42, etc.

ǣ[1] and *ǣ*[2] both appear as *e*, *þer* 8, *slepe* 12; *bileuen* 10, *euere* 33, etc.
þar 25, 33, *þare* 28, are due to early shortening.

ȳ is regularly *u*, *lutel* 11, *vnirude* 20, etc.

WS *ea*/Ang. *a* before *l*+cons. is *o* before lengthening groups, *old* 49,
otherwise *a*, *halle* 40, *valleþ* 44, etc.; the mutation is *a* in *aldren* 13,
halde 60. Before *r*+cons. *a* is regular, *harpe* 29, etc.; the mutation is *a*
in *awaried* 96. Before *h a* appears in *sauȝ* 92; the mutation is *i* in
miȝten 17, *niȝt* 21, 61.

eo is *e* in *ferrene* 35, but *i* before *ht* in *kniȝt-* 36. *weor-* is *wor-* in *world* 19,
worþeþ 83, *worþe* 96, but *wer-* in *swerdes* 77. *seþþe* 12, 66, is from a
form with nWS back-mutation.

ĕa is *e*, *ded* 42, *heued* 95 (r.w. *biweued*), etc. The mutation is *e* in *ihere* 1, *seme* 67, etc., but *v* in *vcchen* 7.

ēo is *e*, *leuere* 6, *lef* 9, etc. The mutation is *e* in *þefþe* 82.

gistni 34, *ʒif* 82, come from OE forms with front diphthongization, whilst the *o* in *twolf* 76 is probably due to the rounding influence of *w*.

Consonants: Initial *f* is voiced in *valleþ* 44, *vingres* 60. OE *hw* appears as *w* in *wat* 46, 52, *wite* 60, *wete* 67. Initial *þ* is *t* in *tis* 20, and *h* has been lost in *-em* 37. The *-d* of *quod* 47 is analogical. Medial *w* and *l* have been lost in *such* 12, etc., final *l* in *muche* 23, etc., and final *n* in *seþþe* 12, 66.

Orthography:

OE *sc* is regularly written *ss*, *ssal* 36, *ssok* 95, etc. Front *c* is represented by *c* in *nellic* 3, and front *g* by *g* in *gistni* 34.

Notes

1. *wolle*. *o* forms of the present of this verb are not uncommon in ME, presumably having developed in unaccented positions from OE *wylle*, ME *wulle*. They survive until the seventeenth century; cf. Shakespeare, *Hamlet* V, i, 299, "Woo't drink up eisil, eat a crocodile", but in modern English are found only in the negative *won't* (*wol not*).

6. *to þe nale*. OE *to þæm ealoþ*, ME *to þen ale*, with misdivision of syllable as in modern English *nickname*; *apron*, *adder*, *umpire*, etc., show the reverse process.

7–8. *wombe* : *longe*. Presumably the author intended nothing more than an assonance here. In any case he was obviously not a skilled versifier, as is shown by the number of poor rhymes in these comparatively short extracts. See lines 33–4, 47–8, 59–60, 86–7, etc.

10. . . . 'Unless we abandon this way of life it will prove a dangerous sport'.

13. *dawe*. OE *dæg* sg., *dagas* pl., regularly give ME *dai* sg., *dawes* pl., but analogical *daies* came early into use. Here we have apparently a regular development of the dpl. *dagum*.

17. . . . With this cf. OE *Andreas*, 1532ff.

18. *riued*, 'in great numbers', a word found occasionally in ME, and an irregular formation from *rive*, an obsolete form of *rife*.

32. *tu-brugge*, 'drawbridge', found elsewhere apparently only in Robert of Gloucester. The first element is presumably connected with OE *tēon*, *togian* 'to draw'.

35. *freboren*. For this word *NED* gives only 'of free birth, born free', but the sense here seems rather 'of noble birth'; cf. *frēo* (XX/6).

40. *Iosep*. The usual form of the name in ME, and found occasionally also in OE.

45. *sitte a-kne*, 'to be in a kneeling posture', a common idiom from the ninth to the seventeenth centuries, but after that surviving only in dialect.

48. *let . . . corn*, 'cause corn to be sold to us'.

50. *for muchel one nede*, 'for a great need'. For the position of the article Napier compares *many (such) a need*.

51. *such . . . gome*, 'such was his pleasure', or perhaps 'as if it were in sport'.

61. *þilke*, i.e. *þe ilke* 'the same'. OE *ilca* 'same', now obsolete except in the Scots phrase *of that ilk* used chiefly in the names of landed families, e.g. *Guthrie of that ilk* 'Guthrie of Guthrie', etc.

67. *rede wete*. Modern wheat can be roughly divided into white and red, i.e. with the grain covered by white or red chaff. Unless the adjective here is to be taken as purely conventional it would suggest that the ordinary medieval wheat was of the second kind.

70. *Pharaones þe king*. For this idiom see note to II/78.

71. *þones*, i.e. *þe ones*, 'the sack of one of them'.

79–81 rhyme together, but the sense is apparently complete.

85. *of Faraones lond þe king*. In ME two genitives in apposition are usually separated by the governing substantive; cf. Chaucer, *Book of the Duchess* 282, "The kynges metynge Pharao", 'the dream of King Pharaoh'.

XXII. CURSOR MUNDI

Dialect: Northern.

Inflexions:

Verbs: inf. *here* 1, *rede* 25, etc., but *red* 2, *tell* 12.
3 pr. *beres* 38, *werrais* 32, *coms* 37, *draghus* 28, etc.
prpl. *lesis* 6.
Pronouns: 3 pl. nom. *þai* 16; poss. *þer* 6; obj. *þam* 26.

Sounds:

a/o is invariably *a*, *man* 1, *many* 6, *hand* 7, etc.
æ is *a*, *þat* 7, *was* 9, etc.
e is raised to *i* before *ng* in *Ingland* 8, *Inglis* 24.
y is invariably *i*, *kynd* 36 (r.w. *fynd*) *alkyn* 35, etc.
ā is *a* in *lath* 29, *wrath* 30, *na* 16, but *o* in *non* 10, *so* 9.
ǣ[1] and *ǣ*[2] both appear as *e*, *red* 2, *þere* 6; *leth* 31, etc.
WS *ea*/Ang. *a* before *l*+cons. is *a* in *bald* 7, *als* 13. Before *h a* appears in *faght* 15.
eo is *e* in *yhernes* 1, *bern* 7, etc., but *i* before *ht* in *knythes* 11; the mutation appears as *e* in *wers* 38, *vers* 28.
ēa is *e* in *nere* 28. The mutation is *e* in *here* 1, etc.
ēo is *e* in *fel* 11, *lesis* 6, *tre* 34, but *ei* in *leif* 17.
Consonants: OE *hw* is the spirant + *w*, represented by *qu*, in *quam* 10, *quat* 34. Final *f* is lost in *o*, *5*, etc., and final *þ* appears as *t* in *wit* 16, *wyt* 30. Final *-sc* appears as *s* in *Inglis* 24, *Frankys* 24, and initial *w* is represented by *v* in *vers* 38. *rike*, 9 *like* 10, show the northern preference for back *c*.

Orthography:

OE/OF *ī* is represented by *ij* in *lijf* 6, *strijf* 5, *ū* by *o* in *thosand* 6, *ronde* 143
OE *ēo* by *ei* in *leif* 17, and Fr. *o* by *ou* in *foul* 28. OE front *g* is represented by *yh* in *yhernes* 1, and back spirant *g* by *gh* in *draghus* 28.
OE *ht* is represented by *ght* in *right* 29, *faght* 15, *saght* 16, but by *th* in
knythes 11. *th* appears in *lath* 29, *thynges* 26, etc.

Notes

2ff. . . . Lists of heroes of romance, such this, are not infrequent in ME
literature, but this is one of the most comprehensive. On the various
themes and heroes mentioned see A. B. Taylor, *An Introduction to
Medieval Romance* (London 1930), and J. E. Wells, *A Manual of the
Writings in Middle English* 1050–1400 (New Haven, Conn., 1916).

    romans. Originally 'the vernacular language of France as opposed to
Latin'; then the word was applied, as here, to tales in verse describing
the adventures of some hero of chivalry, because they were originally
written in that vernacular. The modern meaning of the word does
not appear before the seventeenth century.

3. *Alisaundur*. The Alexander legend, derived in the main from the
pseudo-Callisthenes, was one of the most popular themes of medieval
romance. Among the ME writings on the subject are *King Alisaunder*
in short couplets, and fragments of three alliterative poems.

5. . . . The siege of Troy was another favourite subject of medieval
romance, the details as a rule being ultimately derived from the
apocryphal accounts of Dares Phrygius and Dictys Cretensis.

7. *Brut*. According to the legend popularized by Geoffrey of Monmouth
Brutus, grandson of Aeneas, was expelled from Rome, and thereupon
sailed westwards with his companions. He landed in this country,
then called Albion, found it inhabited by giants whom he killed,
and settled the land which henceforth was called Britain after him.
Since many of the later chronicles began with this legendary conquest
by Brutus, *Brut* became a common term for a chronicle.

10. . . . 'Incomparable during his lifetime'.

13. *Wawan*. The Northern French form of the name *Gawain*, several
times used in *Sir Gawain and the Green Knight*. In all probability
Gawain was originally the hero of an independent cycle, but was
early attracted into the Arthurian legend and in England became
the most popular of all Arthur's knights.

    Cai. Better known under the spelling *Kay*. One of the most important
of Arthur's knights in early French romance and Welsh tradition,
the degeneration of his character appearing only in comparatively
late works.

15. . . . A reference to the romances of the Charlemagne cycle, and to
Roland, the most famous of his paladins.

17. . . . Tristram and Iseult were early famous in French romance, but
appear in English, before Malory, only in the early fourteenth-century
Sir Tristrem.

19. *Ioneck*. Yonec, the hero of one of the lais of Marie de France, not apparently found among the surviving English romances.

Ysambrase. Isumbras, the hero of a popular medieval romance exemplifying the virtue of patience.

20. . . . On Amadas and Idoine see note to XX/67.

21. *serekin*, 'of various kinds', a rare compound in ME, as is shown by the fact that other MSS. avoid it and use instead *mony/diuers/dyuers*.

24. *Inglis*, 'English'. The change of final or unaccented *sc* to *s* is characteristic of the northern dialects. An example of the change survives in the personal name *Inglis*, which was originally the Scots or northern English form of the surname found as *English* in the south.

30. *buxsumnes*, 'obedience'. Derived from OE *būgan* 'to bend', hence the original meaning of the word is 'pliancy' which passes into the above sense by the twelfth century. Later it develops the sense 'well-favoured' and so by the sixteenth century the modern meaning 'plump, healthy'.

XXIII. LYRICAL POETRY

Dialect: Northern.

Inflexions:

Verbs: inf. *blau* 1, *blaw* 4. 3 pr. *lies* 3.
Pronouns: 3 pl. obj. *thaim* 4.

Sounds:

æ is *a* in *was* 4.
ā remains as *a* in *haly* 2, *law* 3, *blau* 1, *blaw* 4.
ēa is *e* in *dede* 3.
Consonants: OE *hw* is the spirant + *w*, represented by *qw* in *qwa* 1. Unaccented OE *sc* appears as *s* in *sal* 1.

Orthography:

th is used in *thir* 1, *thi* 2.

Notes

For an account of the fourteenth-century law-suit during the course of which this stanza was adduced as evidence, see R. M. Wilson, *Early Middle English Literature* (London 1939), pp. 272ff.

1. *thir*, 'these'. This demonstrative pronoun, of obscure origin, is found only in Scots and northern English dialects from the thirteenth century onwards.

2. *Haly Rod*. Holy Cross Day, September 14.

XXIV. LYRICAL POETRY

Inflexions:

Verbs: 3 pr. *springþ* 4, *lhouþ* 7, *groweþ* 3, *bloweþ* 3, *bleteþ* 6, *sterteþ* 8, *uerteþ* 8.
ptp. *icumen* 1.

Sounds:

a/o is *o* in *lomb* 6.
æ is *a* in *after* 6, 7.
y is *e* in *sterteþ* 8, but *u* in *murie* 9.
ǣ¹ is *e*, *sed* 3, *med* 3.
ǣ² is *a* in *nauer* 12, probably due to early shortening.
WS *ea*/Ang. *a* before *l*+cons. is *a* in *calue* 7.
ēo appears as *a* in *awe* 6.
Consonants: OE *hl* remains, represented by *lh*, in *lhude* 2, *lhouþ* 7.
Initial *f* is voiced in *uerteþ* 8.

Orthography:

w is used as a spelling for *wu* in *wde* 4.

Notes

This, probably the best known of all early ME lyrics, is preserved in a commonplace book formerly belonging to Reading Abbey. Below the English words the same scribe has added an alternative religious text in Latin. The most reasonable suggestion as to the relationship between English words, Latin words, and music, is that we have here a learned adaptation of a popular lyric by some composer, the Latin text, which does not fit the tune too well, being the result of an unskilful attempt to convert the lyric to religious uses, while the careful instructions for the singing of the song which are found in the MS. suggest that it was of an unusual type for the time. Frequently printed, most recently by M. F. Bukofzer (Univ. of California Press 1944), who dates the music at *c.* 1310, though the song is usually dated at *c.* 1225.

3. *bloweþ*. OE *blōwan*, 'burst into flower, blossom'. Since the sixteenth century a distinctively poetic word; cf. Tennyson, *Daisy* 16, "Here and there . . . A milky-bell'd amaryllis blew".

XXV. LYRICAL POETRY

Inflexions:

Verbs: 3 pr. *necheð* 3.

Sounds:

a/o is *o* before lengthening groups, *song* 2, *strong* 4, etc.
æ is *a* in *fast* 7.

y is *i* in *mirie* 1, *michel* 6.
ǣ² is *a* in *ilast* 1, *blast* 3, presumably due to early shortening.
The mutation of *ea* before *h* is *i* in *nicht* 5.
ēa is *e* in *necheð* 3.

Orthography:

The back voiced spirant is represented by *gh* in *fugheles* 2, *soregh* 7, and
the front voiceless spirant by *ch* in *necheð* 3, *nicht* 5.

Notes

Preserved on a single sheet which has been bound up as a fly-leaf of
another MS., the contents of which suggest connexion with Thorney
Abbey. Previously printed in E. K. Chambers and F. Sidgwick, *Early
English Lyrics* (London 1907, etc.).

4. *strong*, 'cold, severe'. For this sense cf. *Owl and Nightingale* 523, "Ac
wane niȝtes cumeþ longe,/An bringeþ forstes starke an stronge".
6. *wið*, 'because of, as a result of'. 'And I because of a great wrong . . .'.

XXVI. LYRICAL POETRY

Sounds:

y is *u* in *mulch* 4.
ā is *o* in *bon* 5.
WS *ea*/Ang. *a* before *l*+cons. is *a* in *walke* 4. Before *h a* appears in
waxe 3.
Consonants: An intrusive *l* appears in *mulch* 4, perhaps due to metathesis of *muchel*.

Orthography:

OE *sc* is represented by *ss* in *fisses* 2, and *th* is found in *frith* 1, *with* 4.

Notes

Previously printed in Chambers and Sidgwick.

3. *mon*, 'must', ON *munu*, appearing elsewhere only in Northern or
Midland texts; dialectal since the seventeenth century.

XXVII. LYRICAL POETRY

Inflexions:

Verbs: inf. 2 Weak Class *louien* 4.

Sounds:

æ is *a* in *þat* 3.
ǣ² is *e* in *teche* 2.

WS *ea*/Ang. *a* before *l*+cons. is *o* before a lengthening group in *hold* 5, but otherwise *a* in *al* 6.

Consonants: -*ng* is unvoiced to -*nk* in *tunke* 5. Initial *h* is lost in *wou* 2, and the front spirant in *viit* 1.

Orthography:

ii is used as a spelling for *i* in *viit* 1, and *wou* for *hū* in *wou* 2, the same long vowel being represented by *o* in *hosebonde* 3. *w* is represented by *v* in *viit* 1, and *v* by *w* in *hawe* 6. OE *sc* appears as *s* in *sule* 2.

Notes

These lines appear also, in a slightly different form, in a Latin exemplum from BM. Addit. MS. 11579, printed by T. Wright, *Latin Stories* (8 *Percy Society*), No. 22, and Carleton Brown. A woman complains to a fortune-teller about her husband, and is told to go to a wood and repeat her complaint there. She does this, and the dialogue follows.

XXVIII. LYRICAL POETRY

Inflexions:

Verbs: inf. *fonde* 8, *holde* 25, etc.
3 pr. *wakeþ* 40, *makeþ* 44, etc., but *blykyeþ* 23, *lumes* 21, and *haþ* 25, etc. prpl. *han* 57, 59.
Pronouns: Fem. *heo* 15, etc., *hue* 28.
Nouns: *shuldre* 26 retains its historically correct pl.

Sounds:

a/*o* is invariably *o*, *fonde* 8, *longe* 13, *mon* 26, etc.
æ is *e* in *wes* 32, 34, 56, *nes* 35, but *a* in *smal* 29.
y is *u*, *murþes* 15, *lustnede* 69, etc. *nuste* 11 is from a lOE form with *y*.
ā is *o*, *bon* 10, *sore* 65, etc.
ǣ[1] and *ǣ*[2] appear as *e*, *were* 28; *neuer* 11, *hele* 72, etc. *clannesse* 47 is due to early shortening.
WS *ea*/Ang. *a* before *l*+cons. is *o* before lengthening groups, *holde* 25, *folde* 27, *tolde* 54, but *a* in *al* 31, *falle* 74. Before *r*+cons. *a* appears in *armes* 26. Before *h* *a* appears in *ywraht* 32, *waxe* 80; the mutation appears as *i* in *myht* 7, *anyht* 22, etc.
eo is *ue* in *huerte* 56, 72, but *i* appears before *ht* in *knyhtes* 57.
ēa is regularly *e*, *grete* 17, *eke* 63, etc. *þrat* 63 is probably due to early shortening.
ēo is usually *e*, *fre* 8, *lefliche* 13, etc., but *eo* in *bleo* 23, and *u* in *lure* 21. The mutation is *e* in *dere*- 37, 76.
Consonants: Final -*d* is unvoiced in *sent* 2, *ant* 8, etc. Medial *þ* appears as *h* in *wurhliche* 9, *worhliche* 40. Medial *v* is lost in *ledy* 33, 52, and -*fs*-assimilated in *lussomore* 12, *lossom* 17, *lussum* 33.
No diphthongization of *o* before *h* has taken place in *soht* 57, *þoht* 58, 63, *broht* 59.

Orthography:

> *w* is represented by *u* after *s* in *suetyng* 2, *suetly* 25, *suyre* 25, etc. *th* appears in *northerne* 1, and *o* appears as a spelling for *u* where it would not be expected in *lossom* 17.

Notes

For an account of MS. Harley 2253 see Introduction to IV. This particular lyric has frequently been printed, most recently by G. L. Brook,

1–4. . . . Usually said to be the refrain of a popular song which has here been used for a more sophisticated lyric, but no evidence for such a statement has ever been produced.

6. *fully.* G. V. Smithers (3 *English and Germanic Studies* 81) reads *sully* 'strangely'; cf. *seollic* VI/36.

9. *wurhliche won*, 'the world'. A not uncommon alliterative phrase, usually in the form *worthly/worldly wone*, used in this sense.

14. *frount*, 'forehead'. In this sense now archaic or poetic; cf. Milton, *Samson Agonistes* 496, "The mark of fool set on his front!"

15. . . . 'With many pleasant things must she mingle', i.e. be likened to.

29. *smal*, 'slender', a not uncommon sense of the word in OE and in ME; cf. the fox's "snowte smal" in Chaucer's *Nun's Priest's Tale*.

43. *fiele.* Perhaps for *fipele*, 'fiddle'; but, as Brook points out, it could perhaps be a spelling for OF *viele*, 'a stringed musical instrument'.
    croup. Welsh *crwth*, apparently an early form of fiddle. At this date it appears to have had six strings, four of which were played with a bow, and two by plucking with the fingers.

45ff. . . . Similar comparisons of the lady with a list of precious stones are found in French lyrics.

48. *baner.* Difficult to translate in the context. It might, perhaps, be a scribal mistake for some such word as *burde* 'lady' which would then balance the *ledy* of 52.

53–76. . . . An allegory in which the poet complains to Love that his lady has taken possession of his heart.

57. *soht*, 'attacked', a common sense of the word in OE and in ME, but obsolete since the seventeenth century; cf. Shakespeare, *Ant. and Cleo.* II, ii, 161, "Of vs must Pompey presently be sought,/Or else he seekes out vs".

65. *sore* has usually been taken as an adverb or adjective, but a verb 'swore', parallel with *hap siwed* (62) and *prat* (63), gives better sense; there are in ME plenty of examples of the loss of *w* between *s* and a rounded vowel, notably *soote* from OE *swōte* 'sweet'.

69. MS. *hire* appears to be unnecessary, and may be due to the eye of the scribe having been caught by the frequent *hire loue* of the following **stanza.**

XXIX. LYRICAL POETRY

Inflexions:

Verbs: inf. *lyue* 10, *byde* 10, *blynne* 17, etc.
  3 pr. *helpeþ* 4, 8, *makeþ* 24.
  prpl. *byndeþ* 5.
  ptp. *take* 11, *ytake* 19.
Pronouns: Fem. *heo* 2.
  3 pl. nom. *þey* 19.
Nouns. The dpl. inflexion, used adverbially, survives in *whylen* 22.

Sounds:

a/o is *o* before a lengthening group in *londe* 14; otherwise *a* and *o* forms
  occur side by side, *shame* 11, *man* 13, *mon* 22, *mony* 24, etc.
æ is *a* in *faste* 5, *fader* 18, *was* 22, but *e* in *whet* 8, 28, *wes* 26, 29, *nes* 27.
y is *i* in *mykel* 15, *kynne* 18, *synne* 19, but *u* in *custe* 23, *muchel* 29, *kun* 35.
ā is regularly *o*, *gon* 12, *sore* 30, etc.
ǣ[1] and *ǣ*[2] both appear as *e*, *grene* 3, *lete* 16; *neuer* 10, *leuedy* 1, etc. *laste* 6,
  is due to early shortening.
ȳ is *i* in *kype* 21.
WS *ea*/Ang. *a* before *l*+cons. is *o* before a lengthening group, in *holde*
  20, 35, otherwise *a*, *falewe* 3, *walke* 6, *al* 18. Before *r*+cons. *a* appears
  in *care* 7, *art* 9, etc. Before *h* *a* appears in *maht* 20; the mutation is
  i in *myhte* 7, *nyht* 18.
eo is *e* in *fer* 31.
ēa is *e*, *deþ* 1, *lef* 3, etc. The mutation is *e* in *shene* 1.
ēo is usually *e*, *drery* 5, *be* 17, etc., but *ue* in *luef* 16. The mutation is *e*
  in *newe* 25, *trewe* 26.
Consonants: Initial *h* is lost in *is* 24, and medial *n* in *cost* 17. Medial
  fm has been assimilated in *lemmon* 8, *lemman* 16. *mykel* 15 probably
  owes the *k* to Scandinavian influence.

Orthography:

OE *sc* is represented by *sc* in *scille* 33, and *w* after *s* is represented by *u*
  in *suete* 8, etc.

Notes

2. *þat* . . *sene*, 'that is very obvious from her effect on me'.
6. *walke wod*, 'live as a madman, become mad'; cf. 'to run mad'.
9. *wiþ* . . . *chyde*, 'I don't chose to argue with you'. For this idiom see
  1 *English and Germanic Studies* 101ff.
12 . . . Evidently proverbial.
15. *sham*. For this form with a short vowel see note to VIII/55–6.
19. *lete* . . . *synne*, 'the fact that it is a sin will not prevent them'.
20. *þe deþ*; *þi deþ* would, perhaps, give better sense in the context, but
  emendation is not strictly necessary.
24. . . . Perhaps another proverbial saying.

26. *par amours.* A common phrase in medieval romance, usually with the technical sense, 'to love a person of the opposite sex by way of sexual love', sometimes even 'to have an affair with'.

28. *whet . . . leȝe,* 'what is the good of lying about it?'

31. *hom.* Some word has been omitted by the scribe. Carleton Brown supplies *bour,* but other editors prefer *hom* 'home' as being more general.

33. *scille,* 'eloquently'. But Brook points out that OE *sc* in this text is otherwise regularly represented by *sh-* and prefers to read the MS. *stille* 'softly', though this, perhaps, hardly gives the sense required.

XXX. LYRICAL POETRY

Inflexions:

   Verbs: 3 pr. *singes* 1, *drynkes* 4, but *reweþ* 7.
       prpl. *springes* 2, *says* 14, but *waxen* 1.
       ptp. *ybounde* 18.

Sounds:

   a/o is usually *o, song* 20, *moni* 6, etc.
   æ is *a* in *gras* 2.
   y is *u* in *muchel* 16. *nulle* 10, is from a lOE form with *y.*
   ā is usually *o, gon* 3, *ore* 6, etc., but *wham* 20.
   ǣ¹ and *ǣ²* both appear as *e, speche* 9 (r.w. *seche*), *grene* 1, 16, *neuer* 7.
   WS *ea*/Ang. *a* before *l*+cons. is *a* in *al* 5. Before *h a* appears in *waxe* 16; the mutation is *i* in *nyht* 4, *myhtes* 11, etc.
   eo is *e* in *herte* 3, 4; *weor-* is *wor-* in *world* 10.
   ēa is regularly *e, lef* 2, *ner* 7, etc. The mutation is *e* in *eche* 11.
   ēo is usually *e, tene* 4, *be* 12, etc., but *eo* in *leof* 11.
   Consonants: Final *-d* is unvoiced in *ant* 3, 15, 17; medial *-fm-* has been assimilated in *lemmon* 6, 8, etc.

Orthography:

   w after *s* is represented by *u* in *suete* 8, etc., and after *t* in *bituene* 17.

Notes

2. *Aueryl,* OF *avril* 'April', but already by the fourteenth century the word has been refashioned after L *aprilis* with initial *apr-.*

4. *myn . . . tene,* 'my heart causes me grief'.

7. *me . . . ner,* 'love is no nearer to me'.

13. *preȝe.* As Brook points out, *preȝe* in ME is regularly followed by *of* and then the thing desired, where in modern English *for* would be regular.

16. *grene,* 'pale, sickly', a not uncommon sense of the word; cf. Shakespeare, *Macbeth* I, vii, 37, " . . . And wakes it now to looke so greene and pale!" For the change in meaning cf. Gk. *chlōros* 'green, pale'.

17. *Lounde*. The modern Lound in Notts., Lincs., or Suffolk, perhaps
    the last. Evidently this lyric was originally composed in the EM
    area.
18. *as . . . ybounde*, 'as the one who has taken me prisoner'.
20. Note the substitution of a short couplet for the last line of the lyric.
    Brook suggests that this may be due to the influence of the *envoi*.
    on . . . ylong, 'to the one who is the cause of it'.

XXXI. LYRICAL POETRY

Inflexions:

Verbs: inf. *shake* 11, *make* 15, but *maken* 28, *sitten* 30.
   3 pr. *bereþ* 2, *freseþ* 5, etc., but *stond* 1, *byd* 5, *syt* 7, etc.
   ptp. *yboren* 12, *yloren* 16, *ytake* 25, *boren* 18, *taken* 24, *take* 9, *hewe* 23,
   dronke 31.
Nouns: *hattren* 6, *doren* 14, have the *-en* ending of the weak pl.

Sounds:

a/o is invariably *o*, *stond* 1, *mon* 1, etc.
æ is usually *a*, *was* 21, *at* 28, etc., but *e* in *whet* 8, *wes* 12.
y is regularly *u*, *burþen* 2, *muche* 3, etc. *nulle* 35, *nul* 40, are from lOE
   forms with *y*.
ā is regularly *o*, *wot* 7, *sore* 20, etc.
ǣ[1] and *ǣ*[2] are both *e*, *were* 13, *adred* 20; *leste* 4, *euer* 12, etc. *þare-* 24 is
   due to early shortening.
WS *ea*/Ang. *a* before *l*+cons. is *a* in *valle* 4, *al* 16. Before *r*+cons. *a*
   appears in *-wart* 27, *þart* 38.
eo is *e* in *cherl* 34, *cherld* 40. *weor-* is *wor-* in *world* 7, but *wer-* in *werk* 16.
ēa is regularly *e*, *hewe* 23, *def* 34, etc. *þah* 33, 35, 39, *-lase* 36, are due to
   early shortening.
ēo is *e* in *freseþ* 5, *beþ* 6, *Del* 34, *eo* in *deorly* 29, *teone* 39, and *ue* in *bue* 8.
Consonants: OE *hw* is *w* in *wen* 7. Initial *h* is lost in *is* 2, etc., *ys* 14.
   Final *-d* is unvoiced in *haywart* 27, *ant* 28, 30, and final *þ* appears as *h*
   in *teh* 39. Initial *f* is voiced in *valle* 4. Medial *v* is lost in *ner* 11, *-er* 17,
   Del 34, and medial *þ* in *wher* 13, 18, and medial front *c* in *dreynt* 31,
   deorly 29. *tþ* appears as *t* in *ate* 32. Final *n* is lost in *y* 18, final *l* in
   muche 3, 5, and an inorganic final *-d* has been added after *-l* in
   cherld 40.

Orthography:

OE *-ht* is represented by *-þt* in *wyþt* 7, *hiþte* 11, etc. *o* is used as a spelling
   for *u* where it would not be expected in *fol* 29, *lostlase* 36.

Notes

According to a widespread folk-tale the man in the moon is supposed
to be a peasant who has been banished there because he has stolen the
thorns or brushwood which he is still carrying on his fork. The poem

has been frequently printed, most recently by G. L. Brook, *op. cit.*;
see also the valuable article on the interpretation of the poem by R. J.
Menner in 48 *JEGP* 1ff.

1. *stond ant strit*, 'stands and strides', is the usual translation, though in
   the context this does not give very good sense. Possibly a mistake
   for *stond astrit* 'stands astride', though *NED* gives no examples of
   astride before the seventeenth century.

8. . . . 'Nor, unless it be the hedge, what clothes he wears'. Menner
   suggests that the point is improved if we take it as implying that the
   peasant has stolen his clothes from the hedge, like Falstaff's soldiers
   who "will find linen enough on every hedge".

9. *ha*, for *haþ* 'has', the loss of final -*þ* probably being due to the initial *þ*
   of the following *þe*.

11. *for . . . haþ*, 'despite his efforts'.

14. . . . Menner translates 'in expectation of his thorns to close his gaps',
    and points out that it was the duty of the tenants of the manor to
    keep the hedges in repair and the gaps closed so that cattle could
    not break through. OE *duru/dor(a)* is not recorded elsewhere in the
    sense 'gap (in a hedge)', but Menner points out that the words were
    used in the sense 'pass, gate', and that OE *geat* is a common word for
    a passage in a fence or hedge. Hence he concludes that "in the con-
    text *to dutten is doren* can only mean 'to stop up his gaps', whether
    these were the weak places in the hedge that needed repair . . . or
    the temporary gates that were blocked up at certain times of the
    year".

15. *trous*. Menner points out that the word is used here of the hedge-
    cuttings of brush or thorns which the man places over the quickset
    hedge which he has planted, to prevent the live plants being eaten off
    by sheep or cattle, when 'his day's work would be lost'.

17. . . . 'This same man, whenever he is aloft, where he was born and
    bred in the moon'.

22–3. . . . The peasant has cut a bundle of briars where he had no right,
    and has been caught in the act by the hayward, to whom he has
    given a pledge. ME *wed*, L *vadium*, was a legal term with the sense
    'security for the payment of a fine '.

25ff. . . . The poet here addresses the Man in the Moon directly, and
    apparently promises to help him get the hayward drunk, and then to
    steal from him a coin with which the pledge can be redeemed.

28. *for the maystry*, 'as if aiming at mastery', i.e. in the highest degree,
    extremely. A common ME idiom.

30. *Douse*. Most editors take this as the adj., OF *dous* 'sweet, pleasant',
    in which case we should expect it to precede the noun. In any case
    Douce is a common enough feminine name in ME.

31. *dronke . . . mous*, 'as drunk as a drowned mouse', evidently a common
    proverbial expression; cf. Chaucer, *Wife of Bath's Prologue* (C.T.
    III, 246), "Thou comest hoom as dronken as a mous".

32. . . . 'Then we shall redeem the pledge from the bailiff'. It was part of
    the bailiff's duties to keep such pledges, these being handed over to

him by the hayward. For the form *bayly*, with loss of final *-f*, cf. the personal name *Bailey*, and also modern English *hasty, tardy, jolly*, etc.

35. *nulle.* Either *he* is to be understood, or *nulle* taken for *nulle he.*

36. . . . 'The lazy fellow can't change his custom'. So Menner, but this seems rather forced, and it is more natural to translate as 'The lazy fellow knows nothing of the law', i.e. he doesn't realize what a serious position he is in and so won't hasten.

37. *Hubert.* Evidently a traditional name, though whether for the magpie or for the man in the moon is uncertain.

hosede, 'provided with hose', usually taken as a reference to the black legs of the magpie below the white belly, which give him the appearance of wearing stockings.

38. *amarscled.* Carleton Brown takes it to mean 'marshalled, summoned', though in that case both form and meaning are difficult. Brook follows *NED* in translating 'stuffed full (of drink)', but neither offers any suggestion as to the etymology. Meroney (62 *MLN* 184ff.), followed by Smithers (2 *English and Germanic Studies* 64ff), takes it to be a metathesized form of ME. *malscred* 'bewildered', and translates 'I know you are crazy to the core'. Menner relates it to West Midland *mascle* (OF *mascle*) 'stain, spot', and translates 'stained into its maw', taking this as a reference to the black of the magpie's breast which contrasts sharply with the white of the belly. Not one of these explanations is really convincing.

XXXII. LYRICAL POETRY

Inflexions:

Verbs: inf. *hude* 14, *sitte* 27, etc., but *beren* 22, *weren* 24, *holden* 28.

3 pr. *lackeþ* 22, *sitteþ* 23, etc., but *haþ* 8, 18, *lyþ* 29, *halt* 32.

prpl. *cleueþ* 21.

ptp. *knewe* 34.

The historically correct vowel of the 2 pt. remains in *bede* 4 (r.w. *drede*).

Pronouns: Fem. *heo* 34.

3 pl. nom. *he* 16; poss. *here* 21; obj. *hem* 7, etc.

Nouns: *eren* 23, *geren* 25, have the *-en* ending of the pl. of weak nouns.

Sounds:

a/o is invariably *o, mony* 9, *hongeþ* 23, etc.

æ is *a* in *nast* 2, *after* 10.

y is regularly *u, sturne* 4, *wunne* 5, etc. *sugge* 9, is from a form with *y* in lOE.

ā is regularly *o, Lord* 1, *sore* 3, etc.

ǣ[1] and *ǣ*[2] both appear as *e, drede* 3, *were* 15; *lenest* 1, *ledy* 10, etc.

ȳ is *u* in *shrude* 13, *hude* 14, *kud* 34.

WS *ea*/Ang. *a* before *l*+cons. is *o* before a lengthening group in *holden* 28, but *a* in *halt* 32, *hal-* 28. Before *h a* appears in *drahtes* 11.

ēa is *e*, *screwe* 13, *eren* 23, etc. *þah* 14, is due to early shortening.
ēo is *e*, *lede* 1, *cleueþ* 21, etc. The mutation is *ue* in *duere* 18.
shilde 7 is from a form with front diphthongization in OE.
Diphthongization of *o* before *h* has not taken place in *wroht* 16, *soht* 17, etc.
Consonants: Initial *h* is lost in *is* 23, and final -*d* unvoiced in *ant* 1. Medial *v* is lost in *hed* 32, and medial *w* and *l* in *such* 11, etc., while *fm* has been assimilated in *wymmon* 9.

Orthography:

w after *d* is represented by *u* in *duelle* 20, whilst *w* is used as a spelling for *wu* in *wl* 11. The representation of short *u* by *o* in *fol* 18 would not have been expected. OE *sc* is represented by *sc* in *screwe* 13.

Notes

1. *lokest . . . lede*, 'watches over, guards, every nation', a sense of *lokest* that has been obsolete since the fifteenth century.
2. . . . i.e. God has no need of physical means of defence,
9. . . . 'I utter my verdict from the example of many a foolish woman'.
10–11. . . . Carleton Brown suggests 'If a lady's clothes are according to fashion, every low-class person will imitate them, at whatever cost'.
13. *screwe*. OE *scrēawa* 'shrew mouse', but superstitions as to the malignant influence of the animal led to the usual ME sense 'evil-doer, rogue', referring to either sex. The modern sense, 'scolding woman', has been regular only since the seventeenth century.
15. *boses*, 'bosses', evidently padding of some kind or other, but its exact purpose and use is unknown.
18. . . . 'Such a slut will pay for it very bitterly and dearly'.
21. *chelle*. *NED* suggests, rather improbably, derivation from OE *ceafl* 'jaw'. Perhaps a scribal variant of *kelle* 'woman's hair-net', since the alliteration seems to demand a word beginning with *k*- rather than with *ch*. If so, the general sense of the line would be 'because of the wooden ornaments which stick to their hair-nets'.
22. . . . 'Now they have no lack of linen padding to wear'.
24. *ioustynde*. Carleton Brown's 'justing' gives no sense in the context unless we translate as 'a device used in jousting', i.e. presumably some kind of padding used to minimize the danger of wounds in that sport.
25. *al . . . declyn*, 'everything goes to the bad'.
28. *halymotes*, 'the court of the lord of the manor held in the hall'.
29. . . . 'If there lies a lovelock (hanging) by ear or eye'. Kemp Malone's translation (2 *ELH* 66) gives good sense and fits the forms better than that of Carleton Brown.
30. *leȝe*. As Menner (55 *MLN* 244) shows, this is OE *lēag* 'lye', and the significance of this line rests in the fact that lye was used as a cosmetic and dressing for the hair during the Middle Ages. Moreover there was a common association of lye with urine, since urine or chamber-lye was a familiar kind of lye used for cleaning and as a cosmetic.

Hence Menner translates '(lock) that must be wet with worse or inferior (lye) for lack of other lye', and the implication is that the 'worse lye' is urine.

31. *barbet*, 'part of a woman's headdress', so Carleton Brown; but the word suggests rather connexion with *barbe* 'piece of white plaited linen passed over or under the chin and reaching midway to the waist'. The *bout* would then be the front of the headdress and the *frountel* the band across the forehead, all of which must match.

XXXIII. LYRICAL POETRY

Inflexions:

Verbs: inf. *come* 8, *werne* 39, but *komen* 17.

3 pr. *springet* 26, *hauet* 42, 44, but *comȝ* 24.

The historically correct vowel of the 2 pt. remains in *bere* 50. ptp. *ybore* 21.

Nouns: *þing* 28 retains the lack of ending in the pl. of the long-stem neuters.

Sounds:

a/o is *a* in *þan* 3.

æ is *a* in *was* 19.

y is *u* in *put* 44, but *i* in *-king* 30.

ā is *o*, on 1, *Lord* 21, *wot* 37.

ǣ[1] and *ǣ*[2] appear as *e*, *bere* 30; *leuedy* 6, *leuedi* 28, 33.

WS *ea*/Ang. *a* before *l*+cons. is *a* in *alle* 12, etc.; the mutation is *e* in *welle* 26. Before *r*+cons. *a* appears in *kare* 10, but *e* in *ert* 10, 12; the mutation is *e* in *werne* 39. Before *h* the mutation is *i* in *nyth* 24.

eo is *e* in *heuene-* 30. *weor-* is *wor-* in *world* 19.

ēo is *e* in *se* 5. The mutation is *u* in *þuster* 24.

Consonants: Initial *h* has been added in *hut* 26, *hidut* 44, and lost in *Is* 15, etc. Final *-þ* appears as *t* in *wit* 14, *comet* 24, *springet* 25, *hauet* 42, 44.

Orthography:

OE *sc* is represented by *s* in *sad* 15, and *-ht* by *th* in *nyth* 24.

Notes

Frequently printed, usually from the Egerton MS. There is a slightly different version in Trinity College, Cambridge, MS. 323.

5. *se to*. An early example of the use of this phrase in the sense 'provide for the wants of', which does not otherwise appear before the fifteenth century. T *I crie þe grace of þe* gives good enough sense but poor metre, and is unlikely to represent the original.

10. . . . 'Thou art the best help (advice) in grief'. T *In car ant consail þou art best* hardly gives the sense required.

23ff. . . . 'The dark night (of sin) passed away, and the day of salvation came with the *Ave Maria*'. *Ave Maria*, the opening words of the

Archangel Gabriel when he announced to Mary the coming birth of Christ.

37. T *Vuel þou wost he is þi sone.* But line 39 suggests that E is more likely to represent the original.

37–9. *sone : bone.* If this be intended as a rhyme rather than as an assonance it would seem that we must assume here the distinctively northern lengthening and lowering of *u* to tense *ō* in open syllables. The rhyme would then be on tense *ō* in both words.

XXXIV. LYRICAL POETRY

Inflexions:

Verbs: 3 pr. *helpit* 5.

Sounds:

æ is *a* in *wat* 5.

y is *u* in *put* 2, *wnne* 6 (r.w. *þenne*), but *o* in *wormes* 4.

WS *ea*/Ang. *a* before *l*+cons. is *a* in *al* 6.

weor- is *wor-* in *worilde* 6.

Consonants: OE *hw* is *w* in *wen* 1, *wite* 3, *wat* 5. Final *-þ* is *-t* in *helpit* 5. The glide vowels in *turuf* 1, *worilde* 6, may indicate a strongly trilled *r*.

Orthography:

OE *ū* is represented by *uu* in *tuur* 1. *w* is used as a spelling for *wu* in *wnne* 6, and OE *sc* is represented by *ss* in *ssulen* 4.

Notes

Previously printed only by Carleton Brown. A Latin version of the lines is written directly above the English in the MS., but this is probably not the original as was suggested by Carleton Brown. It reads much more like a translation from the English: Cum sit gleba tibi turris/tuus puteus conclauis,/pellis et guttur album/erit cibus vermium./Quid habent tunc de proprio/hii monarchie lucro?

6. *wnne.* Presumably for *wunne*, but the rhyme shows that the original must have had the SE *wenne*.

XXXV. LYRICAL POETRY

Inflexions:

Verbs: inf. *flen* 58, *þinken* 30, *seien* 47, *strenkþen* 45.

3 pr. *bit* 26, *haueþ* 33.

prpl. *comeþ* 24, *lien* 20.

ptp. *comen* 17.

Pronouns: 3 pl. nom. *þey* 1, etc., *hy* 19; poss. *hoere* 4, etc.; obj. *hem* 7, etc.

Sounds:

a/*o* is *o* before lengthening groups, *song* 13, *londe* 48, etc., but otherwise *a*, *manie* 18, *man* 25.

æ is usually *a*, *glad* 7, *was* 8, etc., but *e* in *wes* 39.

y is *u* in *mvrie* 48, *sunne* 58, but *i* in *pinken* 30.

ā is *o*, *wo* 23, *fo* 41, etc.

ǣ[1] and *ǣ*[2] appear as *e*, *weren* 1, *beren* 2; *leuedies* 4, *heuere* 21, etc.

ȳ is *ui*/*uy*, *fuir* 21, *luitel* 26, *luytel* 36.

WS *ea*/Ang. *a* before *l*+cons. is *a* in *al* 8, *fal* 35. Before *r*+cons. *a* appears in *harde* 18. Before *h* the mutation is *i* in *niȝt* 49, *miȝt* 50, 56.

eo is *e* in *heuene* 55, but *oe* in *hoere* 4, etc.

ēa is regularly *e*, *bileue* 43, *eye* 11, etc.

ēo is regularly *e*, *beþ* 1, *lef* 39, etc., but *ee* in *iseen* 59.

Consonants: OE *hw* is *w* in *were* 13, *wiles* 44, and *uu* in *uuere* 1. Initial *h* is added wrongly in *heuere* 21, *hende* 60, and medially in *wiþhouten* 49, while final -*h* appears to have been vocalized in *þorou* 32. Medial -*fd*- has been assimilated in *hadden* 3, and medial *k* lost in *maden* 7. In *strenkþen* 45, *strenkþe* 50, -*ng* has been unvoiced to *nk*.

Orthography:

OE *u* is written *ou* in *ounrede* 28, *ouþ* 34, and in *rode* 6, *þorou* 32, the spelling with *o* would not have been expected. *ē* is represented by *ee* in *iseen* 59. OE *sc* appears as *s* in *sal* 30; *w* is represented by *uu* in *uuere* 1, and used as a spelling for -*v*- in *himselwen* 52.

Notes

A shorter version of the poem is found in the Auchinleck MS., while in three others, Laud 108, Harley 2253, Vernon MS., it is annexed to, or incorporated in, the *Sayings of St. Bernard*, a poem in a similar metre. This particular version has frequently been printed elsewhere.

9. *keneleden.* The spelling is probably due to a French-trained scribe's lack of familiarity with initial *kn*-.

18. *stoundes*, 'times of hard trial or pain', still used in this sense by Spenser, *F.Q.* I, viii, 25, "Such percing griefe her stubborne hart did wound,/That she could not endure that dolefull stound".

23. *wy* 'woe'!, L *vae*. On the vowel see Kemp Malone, *A Grammatical Miscellany dedicated to O. Jespersen*, pp. 45–54.

25-6. *wilt : bit.* A *wit : bit* improves the rhyme, but spoils the sense.

28-29. *ounrede : mede*, OE *ungerȳde : mēd*, a SE rhyme.

29-30. . . . 'If you think about the reward the pain will seem little to you'.

40ff. . . . 'He gave it (i.e. His life) for you, repay Him for it, Take that staff against His foe, and avenge Him on that thief'.

46. *kep.* Presumably in the sense 'meet in resistance, opposition', a sense found occasionally in ME; cf. *Sir Gawain and the Green Knight* 307, "When non wolde kepe hym with carp he coȝed ful hyȝe".

47. . . . 'And cause that traitor to utter the word (of surrender)'.

XXXVI. LYRICAL POETRY

Inflexions:

Verbs: inf. *stonde* 4, *beye* 14, *deye* 13, *werne* 22, but *leren* 37, *founden* 52.
3 pr. *pyneþ* 17.
prpl. *haueþ* 38.
prp. *wepinge* (r.w. -*kynde*) 7.
ptp. *stongen* 29.

Nouns: The weak pl. appears in *tern* 20 (cf. *teres* 22), *honden* 29, *children* 38, *wounden* 53.

Sounds:

a/o is regularly *o*, *stond* 1, *sprong* 56, -*mon* 45, etc.
æ is *a* in *glade* 2, *what* 16, but *e* in *whet* 38, 39, *nes* 54.
y is *u* in *gult* 9, *kun* 15, -*kunde* 27, *sunnes* 59, but *i* in -*kynde* 8, 35, and *e* in *beye* 14.
ā is regularly *o*, *wo* 30, *more* 42, etc.
ǣ[1] and *ǣ*[2] appear as *e*, *rede* 16 (r.w. *dede*); *leren* 37, *leuedy* 58, etc.
WS *ea*/Ang. *a* before *l*+cons. is *o* before lengthening groups in *byholt* 2, otherwise *a*, *al* 19, 27, *alle* 46, 47. Before *r*+cons. *a* appears in *harde* 6, *art* 34, but *e* in *bern* 19 (r.w. *tern*); the mutation is *e* in *werne* 22. Before *h* the mutation is *i* in *myht* 3, 63, *miht* 37.
eo is *e* in *suert* 11, *herte* 11, 24, *heuene* 62, 66. The mutation is *o* in *worse* 21.
ēa is *e*, *deþ* 8, *stremes* 23, etc. *þah* 30 is due to early shortening.
ēo is regularly *e*, *se* 5, *rewe* 19, etc.
o in *wosshe* 20, is due to the rounding influence of *w*.

Consonants: Final -*d* is unvoiced in *byholt* 2, *suert* 11, *ant* 15, 29.
Medial -*t*- has been lost in *wost* 44, and -*fm*- assimilated in *wymmon* 48.

Orthography:

w is represented by *u* after *s* in *suert* 11, *suete* 63, and after *d* in *duelle* 49, while in *byswngen* 28, *w* is used as a spelling for *wu*. Short *u* is represented by *ou* in *þourhout* 29, *þourh* 63.

Notes

An English version of the sequence *Stabat iuxta Christi crucem*. There are other texts in Digby 36, Royal 12 E i, and an incomplete version in St. John's College, Cambridge, MS. 111. The Royal and the Cambridge versions also include music. Frequently printed.

8. R *for mannes thinge* improves the rhyme and metre but weakens the sense, while D *for monnes kuinde* is an improvement on the metre of H.
10. *dedestounde*, 'hour of death', but Kemp Malone (2 *ELH* 60) suggests that it may be a mistake for *dedes stounde*, 'the pangs of death'.
12. . . . See *Luke* ii, 25–35.
16ff. . . . D *Sone, wat sal me þe stounde?/þine pinen me bringeþ to þe grounde,/ Let me dey þe bifore.* On the whole H seems preferable.
19ff. . . . D *Moder, do wei þine teres,/þou wiþ awey þe blodi teres.* Although identical rhymes are not uncommon in ME, this is a good deal

weaker than H. On the other hand H *tern*, though perhaps possible as a weak pl. of *tere* 'tear', looks suspiciously as if it had been invented by the scribe for the purposes of the rhyme.

21. *doþ*, 'causes'. Presumably some such word as 'sorrow' is to be understood.

26-7. . . . 'It is better that I alone should die than that all mankind should go to hell'.

39. *wiþ childe gon*, 'to carry a child (in the womb)', but here probably rather in the sense 'to bear a child'.

43-5. . . . D *Moder, of moder þus I fare./Nou þou wost wimmanes kare,/þou art clene mayden on.* If the *þou* of the third line in D be taken as a haplography for *þou þou* 'though thou', D probably gives a better reading here than H or R.

56. *morewe*, 'morning', the original sense of OE *morgen*. Obsolete or archaic in this sense since the seventeenth century.

XXXVII. LYRICAL POETRY

Inflexions:

Verbs: inf. *forsake* 2, *wurche* 12, etc., but *becomen* 6.
   3 pr. *hantit* 18.

Nouns: The ending *-es* of g. and pl. appears as *-is* in *worldis* 2, *wedis* 3, *Goddis* 12. The weak pl. ending appears in *folen* 3.

Sounds:

a/o is regularly *a*, *fram* 15, *ran* 15, *gan* 16.

y is *u* in *wurche* 12, 13, *churche* 10, but *i* in *girdil* 5, *bie* 16. *wul* 4 is from a lOE form in *y*.

ā is regularly *o*, *more* 1, *holi* 10, etc.

ǣ[1] is *e* in *wedis* 3.

weor- is *wor-* in *worldis* 2, *workes* 13.

ēo is *e* in *be* 1, *gle* 3, etc. The mutation is *e* in *dere* 16.

Consonants: Final *þ* appears as *-t* in *hantit* 18. Medial *d* has been doubled in *Goddis* 12.

Orthography:

OE *sc* is represented by *sc* in *scal* 5, and *-th* is used in *sothe* 17. OE *hʒ* is written *pht* (rather than *yht*, as previously read) in *bopht* 14.

Notes

2. *fe*, 'goods, possessions', obsolete in this sense since the sixteenth century, but cf. Drayton, *Legends* iv, 74, "Whose labour'd Anvile only was His fee".

3. *wildis*. Presumably used here as a noun, 'wantons', a sense not recorded in *NED*.

17-8. . . . 'In truth I account him more than mad who has anything to do with lechery'.

XXXVIII. AN INTERLUDE

Dialect: North East Midland.

Inflexions:

> Verbs: inf. *haf* 30, *mac* 57, *gef* 58, etc., but *haue* 6, *lufe* 8.
>   3 pr. *wonys* 49, *lys* 76, *hauntes* 41, *as* 83.
>   prpl. *haf* 29, *send* 53.
>   ptp. *comin* 39, *cummen* 55, *syen* 46, *henge* 83.
> Pronouns: Fem. *yo* 47, 49, 51.
>   3 pl. nom. *þai* 29, *þay* 80, 82.

Sounds:

> *a/o* is usually *a*, *land* 14, *man* 5, etc., but *lond* 46.
> *æ* is *a* in *þat* 15, 21.
> *y* is *i*, *mysgilt* 21 (r.w. *spilt*), *syn* 65, etc.
> *ā* is indifferently *a* or *o*, *hame* 4 (r.w. *dame*), *mar* 19, *non* 28 (r.w. *Jone*),
>   *sory* 74 (r.w. *Mary*), etc.
> *ǣ¹* and *ǣ²* appear as *e*, *dede* 70 (r.w. *fede*), *euer* 16, *hel* 40, etc., but *i* is
>   found in *lydy* 42. *þar-* 33, 55, shows early shortening.
> WS *ea*/Ang. *a* before *l*+cons. is *a*, *ald* 67, *al* 12, etc. Before *h* the
>   mutation is *i* in *nicht* 17, *micht* 16, etc.
> *eo* is *e* in *herbherg* 9, *efne* 25, *heuene* 27.
> *ēa* is *e*, *dedh* 43, *ded* 52, *hey* 79, 80. The mutation is *e* in *her* 26, *lesit* 34, etc.
> *ēo* is regularly *e*, *be* 16, *lever* 43, etc. The mutation is *e* in *neulic* 33,
>   *neuly* 52.
> *ē* appears as *i* in *suyt* 50, *quyne* 67, etc.
> Consonants: OE *hw* appears as *w* in *wer* 3, *with* 45, as *v* in *vat* 63, and
>   as *qu* in *quam* 48. *w* appears for *v* in *haw* 46, and is written *v* in *vytuten*
>   53. *þ* appears as *t* initially in *ty* 3, etc., *te* 37, medially in *vytuten* 53,
>   *wituten* 10, and finally in *wyt* 42, etc. OE *sc* appears as *s* in *sal*
>   24, 58, *salt* 56, *saltu* 60, 62. -*ng* has been unvoiced in *þink* 77,
>   *kync* 78. An inorganic initial *h* appears in *ho* 46, *hi* 15, *hand* 24, etc., and
>   initial *h* has been lost in *as* 83, *aly* 84, *efne* 25, etc. Inorganic final -*t*
>   appears in *synt* 31; final -*n* is lost in *y* 9, *ho* 46, final -*d* in *an* 54, and
>   final front *c* in *neuly* 52. -*fm*- has been assimilated in *wymman* 29,
>   and the *mm* simplified in *wyman* 84. *n* has been doubled in *onne* 83,
>   whilst the back consonant in *mikel* 36, 42, is probably due to Scandi-
>   navian influence.

Orthography:

> *b* and *d* are represented by *bh*, *dh*, in *herbherg* 9, *dedh* 43, *ledh* 44. OE -*ht*
>   is represented by *th* in *mithe* 6, *noth* 40, by -*cht* in *micht* 16, *nicht* 17,
>   etc., and by *ct* in *sayct* 57, *ayct* 58. *w* is represented by *u* after *s* in *suilc*
>   5, 6, *suythe* 23, *suyt* 50. OE *sc* is *sc* in *scam* 29, etc., whilst the *sc* in
>   *scynnes* 74 is a spelling for *s*. *t* is written *th* in *bether* 16, *suythe* 23, *with*
>   45, and *th* appears for *þ* in *forth* 11, *thys* 66, etc. OE front *c* is
>   represented by *c* in *hyc* 44, 74, *neulic* 33, whilst the *y* in *yo* 47, etc., is
>   probably a spelling for *hj-*.

Notes

3. *sire, dame,* 'father', 'mother', distinctively poetic senses of the words since the sixteenth century; cf. Shakespeare, *Lucrece,* 1477, "The sire, the sonne, the dame and daughter die".

5–6. . . . 'It would be well for such a man to live who could have such a maiden as his wife', i.e. such a man would have a happy life.

7. *Leonard.* The patron saint of poor prisoners. According to legend a noble at the court of Clovis who was converted, formed a religious community at Noblac, and died there *c.* 550. St. Leonard's-on-Sea is one of the numerous English medieval dedications.

9. *na kep I,* 'I don't care to'.

9–10. *flore : dore.* OE had *duru* by the side of *dor(a),* and the two appear to have become confused in ME where such forms as *dure* and *dore* are found side by side. The confusion was, perhaps, assisted by the fact that in the north OE *duru,* by lengthening and lowering of *u* to tense *ō* in open syllables, would have the same spelling as OE *dor(a),* though the quality of the latter vowel should have been slack. Modern *door* apparently owes its form to OE *duru,* but its pronunciation to OE *dor(a).* If we could be certain that the author would not have rhymed tense and slack *ō* together the rhyme here would be N, since OE *flōr* could only give the tense vowel in ME.

12. *hire.* MS. *wile* 'time' gives good sense, but the obvious emendation to *hire* 'wages, money' is needed for the rhyme.

16. . . . 'If I am ever to be any better off'.

17. *for þe hy sory,* 'because of you I feel sorrowful'. *sory* can hardly be from OE *sorgian,* but must represent *sorry* v. which *NED* cites only from the sixteenth century.

28. . . . 'I care nothing for university students'.

29–30. *scam : hame.* Read *scame : hame* or *scam : ham.* In *æt ham* the dative inflexion had already been lost in OE. The rhyme shows that the author must have used the northern *ham(e).*

30. . . . 'You would have done better to stay at home'.

31. *gat* 'way, road', ON *gata.* A frequent element in street names of northern and midland towns, e.g. *Gallowgate, Kirkgate, Briggate,* etc., but otherwise remaining in modern English only in the form *gait* with a derived meaning.

37. *Helwis.* A not uncommon personal name in medieval times, usually Latinized as *Helwisia;* equivalent to French *(H)eloise,* and one of the sources of the modern surname *Elwes.*

38. *San Dinis.* The patron saint of France. Originally St. Dionysius, traditionally an Athenian sent to convert the Parisians, and by them martyred during the third century. For the loss of the final -*t* of *saint,* cf. the modern surname *Sinclair.*

39. *mome.* The rhyme indicates that *mone* should be read here. Both forms are known in ME, *mome* apparently being a reduplicated form of the first syllable of OE *mōder,* whilst *mone* is ON *móna.*

40. . . . 'Conceal nothing from me, tell me immediately'.

I

41. .... 'I am a student who frequents the Schools', i.e. the University.

44. The insertion of *nu* before *ledh* would improve the metre.

47. *Malkyn*. The diminutive suffix *-kin*, added to *Mal*, one of the pet-forms of Mary. In the thirteenth-century *A Lutel Soth Sermun* Malkin is used as a generic term for girl.

49. *tounes ende*, 'the outskirts of the town'.

50. *lif*. The sense 'beloved, dearest', for OE *līf* is apparently found in ME before the sixteenth century only in *The Early-English Life of St. Katherine*, 1531, "He is mi lif ant mi luue", and again later in the same work. Hence the word here is perhaps OE *lēof* with an early raising of tense *ē* to *ī* as seen in the preceding word.

60. *wyf*, 'woman', the original general sense of the word, now obsolete except in dialect and in such compounds as *housewife, fishwife, old wife's tale*, etc.

63. *Benedicite*. When the word appears in verse it is clear that in the spoken language it had often been reduced to *bencite*, cf. Chaucer, *Nun's Priest's Tale* (*C.T.* VII, 3392), "So hydous was the noyse, a, *benedicitee*!/Certes, he Jakke Straw and his meynee/Ne made nevere shoutes half so shrille,/Whan that they wolden any Flemyng kille . . ."

66. *blam*, 'shame, culpability, sin', cf. Shakespeare, *All's Well* V, iii, 36, "My high repented blames/Deere soueraigne pardon to me".

67. *quyne*, 'woman', already in eME used as a term of disparagement or abuse. Derived from OE *cwene*, and to be distinguished in ME from modern English *queen* (OE *cwēn*) by the possession of open *ē* as compared with the tense *ē* of the latter. In modern English the words have been differentiated in spelling, *quean* as compared with *queen*. For the difference in meaning cf. *Piers Plowman* C ix, 46, "At churche in the charnel cheorles aren vuel to knowe/ . . . other a queyne fro a queene".

68. *wit Godis gram*, 'in the fear of God'.

73–4. .... The rhyme points to the use by the author of northern *sari*, a form which has been changed by some later scribe.

75. *De Profundis*. The first words of Vulgate *Psalm* cxxix (A.V. cxxx), a penitential psalm.

83–4. .... A reasonable rhyme is obtained by transposing the *onne me* of 83.

GLOSSARY

_HIS glossary is not intended to be an *index verborum*, but it is hoped that
will suffice, even for the beginner, for whose benefit numerous cross-
ferences are included. Whenever possible the etymology is given; and
hen it is noted as obscure, the student should refer to *NED*. The
ative form is cited which best illustrates the ME example, and often
is is not WS; forms cited as OE are either WS or common to all
alects. ON words are cited in the form found in Geir T. Zoëga's *A*
oncise Dictionary of Old Icelandic (Oxford 1910) (except that ǫ and ø
e not lumped together as ö); but here again it should be realized
at ME loanwords from Scandinavian were almost always borrowed
om a form of the language more archaic than that represented in
oëga, and from OEN, not OWN. Long vowels in ON (except æ and œ,
hich always represented long vowels) and original short vowels length-
ed before consonant groups in lOE are distinguished by an acute
cent, while the vowels historically long in OE are marked by a macron;
us ON *lágr, ætla, slœgr,* and OE *féld, ā.* Verbal prefixes are usually left
nmarked since their length at any particular stage of OE must be
nsidered doubtful.

In the glossary *æ* follows *ad-* initially and medially; initial ȝ has a
parate alphabetical place following *g,* and medially it also follows *g;*
itial *þ-* has a separate alphabetical place following *t,* but medially it
llows *-tȝ-.*

The following possible variations, due to changes in orthography
d/or phonology, should be noted:

a may vary with (i) *o* before nasals, *land/lond,* (ii) with *æ* or *e* in such
   words as *was/wæs/wes.*
a (=*ā*) may vary with *o, oo, oa,* according partly to date and partly to
   dialect, *mare/more/moare/,* etc.
ai/ay may vary with *ei/ey, dai/dei.*
au before *m, n* (usually in F words) may vary with *a, daunse/danse.*
be- prefix varies with *bi-.* In the glossary the word will be found under
   bi- unless *be-* forms are the only ones which occur.
c varies with *k, come/kome.*
e (=OE *ǣ*) may vary with *ea* or *a* (in Essex), and in Essex and Kent
   original *ē* may vary with *ie.*
f initially varies with *u* (=*v*), but such forms are regularly given under
   f unless *u* forms are the only ones which occur. Medially *u* is normal,
   though *f* is found occasionally in early texts.
ȝ initially may vary with *i/y.*
. Initial *h* is often lost, but words are glossed under it unless forms
   without *h-* are the only ones to appear.
-ht appears also as *-ȝt, -gt, -ght, -cht, -st, -pt,* etc.

11. *i* is indifferently *i* or *y*, whether independently or as the second element of a diphthong. Words beginning indifferently with *i* and *y* are glossed under *i*; those which are found only with *y*- are glossed under *y*-. Medially *i* and *y* are alike glossed after *-h-*.

12. *qu-* may vary with *cw-*.

13. *sh* varies with *sch*, *s*, *ss*.

14. *þ* is indifferently *þ*, *ð*, *th*.

15. *u* as the second element of a diphthong varies with *w*.

u, *v* (=*v*) are used indifferently. In the glossary they have been conventionalized, *v* appearing initially, *u* medially.

u. v (=*u*) vary with each other and with *o* (especially before *m*, *n*). Initially such words are entered in the glossary under *u*.

ū is indifferently *u* and *ou*.

16. *w* medially may vary with *gh* or *ʒh* according to date.

17. OE *y* appears indifferently as *i*, *e*, *u*, according to dialect.

18. *eo* may vary with *e*, *u*, *o*.

19. *ea* may vary with *æ*, *e*, *a*.

20. Single consonant or vowel may vary with double consonant or vowel, but the regular double consonants of Orrm may be ignored.

Abbreviations

To economize space the part of speech is indicated by a superior figure, thus:

noun[1] adjective[2] verb[3] adverb[4] pronoun[5] relative pronoun[6] preposition[7] conjunction[8] interjection[9]

In the etymologies a roman 1, 2, 3, 4, 5, 6, 7, denotes the class of strong verb, a capital A, B, C, the first, second, third, class of weak verbs.

A	1st Class of weak verbs.	contr.	contracted.	instr.	instrumental.
a.	accusative (singular).	*d.*	dative (singular).	*int.*	intransitive.
		def.	definite.	K	Kentish.
adv.	adverb(ial).	*df.*	dative (singular) feminine.	L	Latin.
am.	accusative (singular) masculine.			lOE	late Old English.
		dial.	dialect(al).	M	Midland(s).
apl.	accusative plural.	dpl.	dative plural.	ME	Middle English.
art.	article.	EM	East Midland(s).	MHG	Middle High German.
AN	Anglo-Norman.	eME	early Middle English.		
B	2nd Class of weak verbs.	F	French.	MLG	Middle Low German.
		G	German.	N	North(ern).
C	3rd Class of weak verbs.	*g.*	genitive (singular).	n	note.
cf.	in etymologies indicates uncertain or indirect relationship.	ger.	gerund (inflected infinitive).	*n.*	nominative; see note.
				Nh	Northumbrian.
		gf.	genitive (singular) feminine.	NE	New (Modern) English.
CM	Central Midland(s).	gpl.	genitive plural.	NEM	North East Midland(s).
comp.	comparative.	imp.	imperative (singular).		
CS	Central South(ern)			NM	North Midland(s).
CWM	Central West Midland(s).	imppl.	imperative plural.	NWM	North West Midland(s).
		ind.	indefinite.		
cons.	consonant.	inf.	infinitive.	nWS	non-West Saxon.

OA	Old Anglian.	*prspl.*	present subjunctive plural.	*sup.*	superlative.
bj.	objective.			Sw	Swedish.
OE	Old English.	*pt.*	past (preterite) indicative (singular).	SW	South West(ern).
OEN	Old East Norse.			SWM	South West Midland(s).
OF	Old French.				
OK	Old Kentish	*ptp.*	past participle.	*tr.*	transitive.
OM	Old Mercian.	*ptpl.*	past (indicative) plural.	*unacc.*	unaccented.
ON	Old Norse.			W	West(ern).
ONF	Old Northern French.	*pts.*	past subjunctive (singular).	WM	West Midland(s).
OWN	Old West Norse.	*ptspl.*	past subjunctive plural.	WS	West Saxon.
bl.	plural.				
boss.	possessive.	*r.w.*	rhyming with.	*	prefixed to forms hypothetically reconstructed.
br.	present indicative (singular).	S	South(ern).		
		Sc.	Scots.		
brp.	present participle.	SE	South East(ern).	+	between the elements shows that a compound or derivative is first recorded in Middle English.
brpl.	present(indicative) plural.	SEM	South East Midland(s).		
brs.	present subjunctive (singular).	*sg.*	singular.		
		StE	Standard English.		

a,⁴ ever, always 3/10, 6/41, 61, 222, aa 17/97, 18/38 [OE *ā*].

a⁵, he 19/57, 73 [unacc. form of ME *ha*].

a⁵, *ind. art.*, a(n) 2/41, 4/14, etc., ay 38/45 [OE *ān*].

a⁷, on, in 5/34, 6/157, etc., from 6/174, during 6/223; *a last of*, towards the end of 19/43; *a lunde*, elsewhere 20/53n; *a wille*, to the pleasure of 10/144 [unacc. form of OE *on*].

a,⁹ ah 12/131, 172, etc. [OF *a*].

aa. *See* a⁴.

abak⁴, backwards 20/40 [OE *on bæc*].

abbe. *See* habbe(n).

abbod, abbot¹, abbot 1/6, 2/59; abbotes g. 2/49 [OE *abbod*].

abbotrice¹, abbacy 2/59, þabbotrice, abbot's domain 2/68 [OE *abbodrīce*].

abide³, to wait, stay 8/170, 13/129, 20/41, to await, experience 5/29; abid 3*pr.* 10/200; -eþ *imppl.*, stop 21/79; abod 3*pt.* 10/41 [OE *abīdan* 1].

abiten³, to bite 10/77; *ptp.*, worried 12/203 [OE *abītan* 1].

ablendeð³ 3*pr.*, blinds 17/18 [OE *abléndan* A].

abod. *See* abide.

abouen, abuuen⁴, above, over 4/23, 17/129 [OE *abūfan*].

aboute(n), abute(n), abuton⁴, about, round, on all sides 5/40, 10/16, 12/15, 17/31, 34, 92. As⁷, about, round, concerning 2/24, 32, 8/117, 147, 18/13 [OE *abūtan*].

abugge³, to atone for 12/208; aboht *ptp.*, bought 32/18 [OE *abycgan* A].

ac⁸, but 1/16, 2/3, etc. [OE *ac*].

acoursed, acursede³ *ptp.*, accursed 12/56, 18/46 [OE *a + cúrsian* B].

acres¹ *pl.*, acres 14/29 [OE *æcer, acer*].

acupement¹, accusation 9/26, 32 [OF *acoupement*].

acwelde. *See* aquel.

adai⁴, during the day 10/89 [OE *on dæge*].

adde. *See* habbe(n).

addledd³ *ptp.*, deserved 15/76 [ON *øðla-st*].

admiral¹, emir 9/73n, 78, etc. [OF *amiral*].

adoun(e), adun⁴, down 7/15, 95, etc., nadoun 31/3; *weorpeð adun* hangs 17/29 [OE *of-dūne, adūne*].

adredde³ 3*pt.*, feared 7/64; adrad,
 adred *ptp.*, afraid 8/155, 31/20
 [OE *ondrǣdan* A].
adruncke³ 3*ptpl.*, drowned 6/98
 [OE *adrincan* 3].
adunriht⁴, fiercely, violently 6/201
 [OE *adūne* + *riht*].
adwole⁴, in error 10/199 [OE *on
 dwolan*].
æc. *See* ek(e).
æfne,⁴ at the same moment 6/231
 [OE *efne*].
æfre; æfter; æhc. *See* euer(e);
 after⁷; euch(e).
æi², any 6/166 [contr. form of OE
 ǣnig].
æitlonde¹, island 6/163; -es *pl.*
 6/162 [OE *iggað* + *lónd*].
ælc, ælche, ælchere, ælchen. *See*
 euch(e).
ælder¹, leader 6/189 [OE * éaldor*].
ælderne¹, ancestors 6/72 [OA
 ældran].
ælle,⁹ alas 16/13 [OE *ēala*].
ælle. *See* al².
ælmes¹, alms, charity 2/44; *for
 almes sake*, for charity's sake
 12/44 [OE *ælmesse*].
æluene, aluen¹ *gpl.*, of uncanny
 creatures 6/161, of fairies 6/226,
 239 [OE *ælf*].
ænde; ænne; ær. *See* ende; an; er(e).
ærde¹, country 6/166 [OE *éard*].
ære; ærest. *See* er; er(e)⁴.
ærnes, arnes¹ *pl.*, eagles 6/164, 165
 [OE *éarn*].   æt. *See* at.
ætforen⁷, in the presence of 3/25,
 32 [OE *ætforan*].
æðela, æðele², noble, excellent
 6/15, 29; aðelen *g.* 6/145;
 æðelen, -æn, aðelen *d.* 6/3, 7,
 22, 138; aðelest *sup.* 6/68, 156
 [OE *æpele*].
æueralches; æure; æuric, æurihce; afallæd. *See* euerich(e);
 euer(e); euerich(e); afeallen.
afalle³ *ptp.*, fallen down 12/18 [OE
 af(e)allan 7].

afden. *See* habbe(n).
afeallen³, to cast down 18/5
 aualle 3*prs.* 6/70; afallæd *ptp*
 stricken 6/64 [OA *afællan* A].
aferd³ *ptp.*, afraid 5/93 [OE *afǣre*
 A].
afingret³ *ptp.*, hungry 12/2, 4, et
 [OE *ofhingrian* B].
after, efter⁴, afterwards 10/13
 17/13 [OE *æfter*].
after, æfter, efter⁷, behind, after (
 place) 17/132, (of time) 6/10, 7/
 10/208, in pursuit of, after 7/6
 9/1, 33, 17/81, 24/6, 7, for 2/1
 7/96, 12/52, according to 15/
 16/59, 17/116, 18/43, 32/1
 after the manner of 16/15; *affte
 patt*, according to, as 15/8, 5
 after ʒiernen, to desire 16/51; *hald
 after*, pursue 6/101; *pat . . . afte
 for whom 8/112 [OE *æfter*].
afurste. *See* apurst.
age¹, age 19/74, 76 [OF *age*].
ageyn; agenes, agænes. *S
 aʒeyn; aʒenes.
agyn³ *imp.*, begin 19/15; agonn
 ptp. 5/115 [OE *onginnan* 3].
aglyden³ *ptp.*, passed away 20/
 [OE *aglīdan* 1].
ago(n)³ *ptp.*, gone, past 12/49, 15
 20/85 [OE *agān*].
agrise,³ to be afraid 12/240; -gr
 3*pt.* 5/87; -grisen *ptp.*, horrifi
 18/20 [OE *agrīsan* 1].
aʒein, aʒen, aʒæn,⁴ back, aga
 5/54, 113, 6/88, etc. [OE
 gegn, ongēn].
aʒeyn, aʒen⁷, against, in oppo
 tion to 6/113, 10/7, 17/91, etc., t
 wards, in the direction of 5/
 35, 6/53, on 8/201, in front
 17/129, ayen, near (of tim
 19/8, ageyn, in the sight
 8/182; *aʒe reche*, to hand ba
 9/53; *stond aʒein*, object 10/2
 aʒean cumen, to return 16/
 per aʒean, with it 17/21 [C
 ongegn, ongēn].

aȝenes, agenes, agænes[7], against, in opposition to 2/14, 3/16, near (of time) 19/78 [OE *ongēn* + adv. *-es*].

aȝȝ[4], 15/17, 30. *See* ai.

ah[8], but 7/47, 10/162, etc. [OE *ah*].

ǝhne; ahte(n). *See* owe; owest.

ai[4], ever, always 13/16, etc. [ON *ei*].

ay[9], alas 35/22.

ay; ayen. *See* a[5]; aȝeyn.

ayhte[1], possessions, treasure 14/68, ayct 38/58 [OE *ǣht*].

aisheist[3] 2*pr.*, ask 10/91 [OE *ǣscian* B].

aiþer. *See* eiþer.

ake[3], to ache 20/58 [OE *acan* 6].

al, all, alle[1], everything 2/60, 10/207, etc.; *al abuten*, on all sides 17/92; *mid alle*, in everything 17/101 [OE (*e*)*all*].

al, all, alle[2], all 2/34, 47, etc., ælle 2/9; alle *pl.* 2/11, 29, etc.; alre *gpl.* 6/92, 127, etc., alþer 19/74; alle *dpl.* 10/184; *al*, a whole 2/41, 19/23; *al to*, along to 19/16; as[1], everyone 3/4, 16/9, 38/76 [OE (*e*)*all*].

al, all, alle[4], entirely, quite 2/13, 55, 4/35, etc.; *al riht swa*, similarly 17/130; *al þus*, in this way 12/91; *mid alle*, whole 18/20 [OE (*e*)*all*].

alas[9], alas 5/26, 58 [OF *a las*].

alcne; ald. *See* euch(e); old(e).

aldren[1] *pl.*, ancestors 21/13 [OA *ældran*].

ale,[2] ale 7/9, 8/19, nale 21/6n [OE *ealu*].

alhone[4], alone 12/275 [OE (*e*)*all*+ *ān*].

aly. *See* hali.

aliesen[3], to redeem, ransom 16/57, 63 [nWS *alēsan* A].

aliesendnesse[1], redemption 16/20 [cf. nWS *alēsednes*].

aliue[2], alive 9/88, 12/183, 20/77, 21/33, 55, whilst living 14/74, into life 20/157 [OE *on līfe*].

alkyn[2], of all kinds 22/35 [OE (*e*)*alra cynna*].

allelunge[4], completely 17/8 [cf. OE (*e*)*allunga*].

alles[4], entirely, fully 17/32 [OE (*e*)*alles*].

allhwat[8], until 16/19 [OE (*e*)*all* + *hwæt*].

allunge[4], completely 18/61 [OE (*e*)*allunga*].

almichti, almihti[2], almighty 16/44, 19/1, etc. [OE *ælmihtig*].

almiȝte[2], almighty 9/177; almiten *am.* 6/30 [OE *ælmiht*].

almes. *See* ælmes.

alonged[3] *ptp.*, filled with longing 21/58 [OE *alángian* B].

alpi[2], single 12/132 [OE *ǣlpig*].

alreworste, -wurste[2], worst of all, 10/10, 17/2 [OE (*e*)*alra* + *wyrst*].

als, alse, also[4], also, as well 5/3, 13, 9/126, etc.; similarly, likewise 2/69, 5/85, thus, so 8/144, 13/36, 78; *also nei*, so near 5/37; *also wel*, equally well 5/110; *also . . . so*, as soon as 19/6 [OE (*e*)*alswā*].

als, alse, also, alswo[8], as, like 2/3, 21, 8/133, etc., as if 6/65, 20/73, just as 8/124, 9/165, 10/160, 20/43, so 21/56, when 19/27; *alswo alse*, even as 3/14; *also . . . so*, as . . . as 29/22 [OE (*e*)*alswā*].

altegædere[1], everything 2/48 [OE (*e*)*all* + *tōgæd*(*e*)*re*].

alþer. *See* al[2].

alþerbeste[2], best of all 8/147 [OE (*e*)*alra* + *betst*].

aluen. *See* æluene.

aluisc[2], fairy 6/138 [OE *ælf* + *-isc*].

alsuic[8], just such 2/3 [OE (*e*)*all* + *swylce*].

am[3] 1*pr.*, am 5/111, 7/108, etc., ham 38/22 [OA *am*].

amainet[3] *ptp.*, crippled 17/63 [OF *a* + *mayner*].

amang. *See* among.

amanges, amenges⁷, amongst
3/22, 14/21 [OE *onmáng* + adv.
-es].

amarscled³ *ptp.*, 31/38n.

amatiste¹, amethyst 20/171 [OF
amatiste].

ame, 17/75n.

amed³ *ptp.*, mad 20/56 [cf. OE
gemǣd].

amende³, to soften 38/51 [OF
amender].

amid⁷, in the middle of 17/93 [OE
onmiddan].

amidde(n)⁴, in the midst 6/19,
half-way down 12/241 [OE *onmiddan*].

amidward⁷, in the middle of 12/
274 (OE *onmiddan* + *w(e)ard*].

among⁴, at intervals 10/6; as⁷,
among 5/49, 9/7, etc., **amang**
15/21, etc., along with 5/70, with
10/Int. 4, among them 12/266,
compared with 20/175 [OE *onmáng*].

amur¹, love 20/182 [OF *amur*].

an³ *1pr.*, grant 10/161; on *3pr.*,
wishes 14/54, 56; **vnnen** *1prpl.*
3/5; **võe** *3pts.* 17/59 [OE *unnan*;
ann; *ūðe*]

an, ane⁵ *ind. art.*, a(n) 2/27, 32,
etc.; **anne, ænne, enne** *am.*
6/61, 147, 12/29, 20/30, 88; **are**
df. 6/3, 28, 174 [OE *ān*].

an⁵, one (thing or person) 2/67,
15/59, etc.; as², single 15/34 [OE
ān].

an⁷, in 6/122, 7/5, etc., on 5/89,
6/147; *an hei*, loudly 5/53; *an
honde*, in his hand 6/151; *ane
ouste*, in haste 6/234 [OE *on*].

an, and, ant⁸, and 1/2, 4/5, etc.,
hand 38/24, if 19/91, 35/29,
38/61 [OE *and*].

anan, anon⁴, at once, straightway
5/50, 6/234, etc., even 16/63
[OE *on ān*].

ancre-hus(e)¹, hermitage 17/55,
56 [OE *ancor* + *hūs*].

ancren¹ *pl.*, anchoresses 17/50
[OE *ancre*, f. of *ancra*].

and. *See* an⁸.

andlicnesse¹, image 16/15 [OE
andlīcnes].

ane², alone, only 6/213, 17/135,
18/35, 47; *wunder ane*, exceptionally 6/38n, 40,214 [OE *āna*].

angin¹, origin 16/14 [OE *anginn*].

anhonge³ *ptp.*, hanged 21/83 [OE
onhōn 7].

ani, eny², any 2/18, 8/10, etc.,
oni(e) 3/18, every 8/105 [OE
ānig, ǣnig].

aniȝt, anyht⁴, during the night
10/89, 28/22 [OE *on niht*].

anoþer², another 2/68, 8/141,
17/25, 20/34 [OE *ān* + *ōþer*].

ansuare, ansuere, answare¹,
answer 9/26, 32, 10/55 [OE
an(d)swaru].

ansuerede³ *3pt.*, answered 19/25;
ansuerden, answerden *3ptpl.*
19/11, 54 [OE *an(d)swerian* B].

aperseiuede³ *1pt.*, spied upon
12/213 [OF *apercevoir*].

apliȝt⁴, in truth 9/11 [OE *on* +
pliht].

apostle¹, apostle 19/56; -es *pl.*,
19/53, 65 [OE *apostol*].

aquel³ *imp.*, kill 9/87; **aquelde,
acwelde** *3pt.*, 6/11, o 11; **aqualden** *3ptpl.* 6/72; **aquold** *ptp.*
20/76 [OE *acwellan* A].

aquenche³, to assuage 12/13, 112
[OE *acwencan* A].

ar(e)⁴, before 5/25, 9/23, formerly
5/61 [OE *ǣr*].

araȝte³ *3pt.*, gave, handed 9/174;
araȝt *ptp.* 9/49 [OE *arǣcan* A].

archebischop¹, archbishop 3/25
[OE *ærcebisceop*].

archen¹ *d.*, ark 6/13 [OF *arche*].

are. *See* an⁵.

are¹, mercy 15/76, 16/4 [OE *ār*].

are-dawes¹ *pl.*, former days 8/27
[ON *ár* + OE *dagas*].

aredde³, to save, rescue 9/51; **arudde** 3*pt.* 18/59 [OE *ahreddan* A].

arede³ *imp.*, receive as advice 14/85 [OE *arǣdan* A].

aren, arn³ 3*prpl.*, are 11/48, 68, etc. [OA *aron*].

arere³, to raise 5/31 [OE *arǣran* A].

aresunede³ 3*pt.*, questioned 19/52 [OF *aresoner*].

arewe, erewe¹, enemy 14/42, 50 [OE (*e*)*arg*].

arhredŏe¹, cowardice 6/64 [cf. OE (*e*)*arg* and WS *iergŏ*(*o*)].

arise(n),³ to rise 12/239, 264; -eþ *imppl.* 12/269, 21/45; **aros** 3*pt.* 5/86 [OE *arīsan* 1].

aryue³, to arrive, get to 7/82 [OF *ariver*].

armes¹ *pl.*, arms 7/102, 13/58, etc. [OE (*e*)*arm*].

armi³, to be armed 5/31 [OF *armer*].

arnes; arst. *See* **ærnes; er(e)⁴**.

art, ert³ 2*pr.*, art 6/220, 10/38, etc., **hertou** 12/120 [OE (*e*)*art*].

arugge⁴, on the back 21/29 [OE *on hrycge*].

as. *See* **habbe(n)**.

as, ase⁸, as, like 4/43, 5/3, etc., as if 5/42, 17/63, 65, as it were 5/86, 17/113, 128, as for instance 5/95, that which 4/11; *as vor noȝt*, as if they were nothing 5/57; *so as . . . so*, just as . . . so 19/67 [OE (*e*)*alswā*].

asake³, to forsake, give up 37/8 [OE *a* + *sacan* 6].

assen¹ *pl.*, asses 21/31, 67, 89 [OE *assa*].

asende³ *ptp.*, sent 1/22 [OE *aséndan* A].

askede³ 3*pt.*, asked 4/3 [OE *āscian* B].

aslawe³ *ptp.*, slain 5/60, 62, 69, 108 [OE *aslēan* 6].

asoiled³ 3*pt.*, absolved 5/32 [OF *asoiler*].

astrehte³ 3*pt.*, prostrated 16/3 [OE *astreccan* A].

aswynde³, to vanish 20/39 [OE *aswindan* 3].

at, æt⁷, at 3/23, 5/12, etc., from 15/69, 72, 16/50, on 7/9; *atten, ate*, at the 5/59, 19/35, from the 31/32; *at þe firste*, first of all 7/91; *at a dint*, with a single blow 8/180; *at alle (þisse) nede*, at need 12/225, 36/46 [OE *æt*].

atflip³ 3*pr.*, flies away, sinks 10/37 [OE *ætflēon* 2].

aŏelen, aŏelest; athes. *See* **æŏela; oþe**.

aþurst, afurste³ *ptp.*, thirsty 7/14, 12/66 [OE *ofþyrst*].

atywede³ 3*pt.*, showed 2/83 [OE *ætīewan* A].

atom. *See* **hom**.

atschet³ 3*pt.*, vanished 10/44 [OE *ætscēotan* 2].

atteliche², terrible 6/161 [OE *atol*(*l*)*īc*].

atter¹, poison 17/25, 32 [OE *ātor*].

attri(e)², poisonous 17/27, 44, 50, 68 [OE *ātor* + -*ig*, or *ǣtrig*].

aualle. *See* **afeallen**.

aue, Avy Mary¹, Ave Maria 33/23n, 38/73.

auenture¹, chance; *on auenture*, by chance 12/70 [OF *aventure*].

aueryl¹, April 30/2 [OF *avril*].

auȝene. *See* **owe**.

auh⁸, but 17/24, 28, etc. [OE *ah*].

avisede³ 3*pt.*, observed 5/38 [OF *aviser*].

aunters¹ *pl.*, adventures 22/12 [OF *aventure*].

aure. *See* **euer(e)**.

away, awey⁴, away 7/104, 9/106, etc. [OE *on weg, aweg*].

awaried³ *ptp.*, cursed 21/96 [OA *awærgan* A].

awe¹, ewe 24/6 [cf. OE *ēowe*].

awecche³, to awaken 12/267 [OE *aweccan* A].

awemmed³ *ptp.*, impaired 6/100n [OE *awemman* A].

awene. *See* owe.

awende³ *3pt.*, translated 1/2 [OE *awéndan* A].

awinne³, to rescue 9/134 [OE *awinnan* 3].

awolde⁴, in the woods 10/146 [OE *on* + OA *wáld*].

awreke³, to avenge 9/2, 93; -eþ *imppl.* 9/20; awreke *ptp.* 12/64, condemned 9/23 [OE *awrecan* 5].

ax¹, axe 5/115 [OE *æcs*].

axe³, to ask 12/52 [OE *āxian* B].

ba. *See* bo.

bac,¹ back 8/47, 217 [OE *bæc*].

bacbitares¹ *pl.*, backbiters 17/23 [OE *bæc* + *bīt-* + *-ere*].

bac-duntes¹ *pl.* blows on the back 17/79 [OE *bæc* + *dynt*].

bacward⁴, backwards 6/61 [OE *bæc* + *w(e)ard*].

bæcchen¹ *dpl.*, vales 6/175 [obscure].

bæron. *See* beren.

bayly¹, bailiff 31/32 [OF *bailif*].

bald(e), bold(e)², brave 6/46, 134, etc.; baldest *sup.* 6/122, 127 [OA *báld*].

baldeliche, -like⁴, boldly, openly 8/53, 17/124 [OA *báldlíce*].

bale, balu¹, danger, misfortune 6/57, 9/183, sorrow 4/11, torment 28/59; balewes *g.* 20/125 [OE *b(e)alu*].

bal(e)ful(le)², noisome 18/52, deadly 28/65 [OE *b(e)aluful*].

ban. *See* bon.

baner¹, banner 5/41, 28/48n; -s *pl.* 5/31 [OF *banere*].

bar. *See* beren.

barbet¹, part of headdress 52/31n [cf. OF *barbe*].

bare², absent 28/79; as¹, open spaces 10/56 [OE *bær*].

barnage¹, baronage 9/1 [OF *barnage*].

barre,¹ bar 8/167, etc. [OF *barre*].

barun¹, baron 8/31, etc.; barons, barouns *pl.* 8/139, 9/6 [OF *barun*].

bascins¹ *pl.*, basins 18/10 [OF *bacin*].

bat¹, boat 6/232 [OE *bāt*].

bataile¹, battle 5/29, 49, 58, art of war 5/44 [OF *bataille*].

baþe. *See* boþe.

baðieð³ *3prpl.*, swim 6/160 [OE *baþian* B].

be, be-. *See* bi, bi-.

be(n), beo(n)³, to be 2/2, 3/18, etc., bene 35/56, bie(n) 16/23, 24, etc.; best, bist *2pr.* 35/44, will be 20/120; beþ, beoþ, bið *3pr.* 6/105, 136, etc., excels 20/170; bieþ *1prpl.* 19/61; beþ, beoð, bieþ *2prpl.* 17/58, 19/87, etc.; beþ, beoþ *3prpl.* 3/6, 5/45, etc., bieþ 19/28, 29, 71, boþ 10/75, 88, 100, bueþ 7/14, buþ 9/69, 71; be *imp.* 12/36, 56, etc.; beoþ *imppl.* 10/157; be *1prs.* 7/27, 38/34; *2prs.* 4/6, 13/68, etc., beo 20/197; be, beo *3prs.* 3/20, 4/38, etc., bie 16/37, bue 31/8, bon 6/238; be, bie *2prspl.* 19/10, 21/30; be(n), beo(n) *3prspl.* 13/21, 120, etc.; be(n) *ptp.* 12/185, 200, 38/30, ibe(n) 12/87, 100, etc., ibye 19/23, ibien 16/44 [OE *bēon*].

bealte¹, beauty 28/48 [OF *bealte*].

beard, berd¹, beard 17/93, 18/7 [OE *béard*].

bebyried³ *3ptpl.*, buried 2/84 [OE *bebyrian* B].

bec; bed. *See* boc; beode.

bedde¹, bed 7/95, 9/18, etc., bed-clothes 6/44 [OE *bedd*].

beer(e)¹, beer 7/2, 7, 25, ber 7/20, bor 10/107 [OE *bēor*].

begæt. *See* biget.

beggare, -ere¹, beggar 7/22, 27, -es *pl.* 7/14 [obscure].

begge, beye, bie³, to buy 8/53, 21/31, 37/16, to ransom 36/14; **boȝte** 1*pt.* 9/11; **bohte, bopht** 3*pt.* 17/96, redeemed 37/14; **bohton** 3*ptpl.* 2/79 [OE *bycgan* A].

beh. *See* buheð.

behete³ 2*pt.*, promised 16/38, 40; **bihet** 3*pt.* 21/37, 36/12; **bihote** *ptp.* 10/167, 20/119, 127 [OE *behātan* 7].

behoued³ 3*pt.*, was necessary 2/61 [OE *behōfian* B].

bey. *See* buheð.

beien², both 6/67; **beire** *gpl.* 5/16 [OE *bēgen*].

beyte³, to bait 8/213, 243 [ON *beita*].

beið³ 3*prpl.*, obey 18/41 [OF *obeir*].

belamp³ 3*pt.*, happened 2/78 [OE *belimpan* 3].

beleue³, to believe 19/57; **bileuep** 3*pr.* 13/20; **bileued** *ptp.* 19/49 [nWS *belēfan* A].

bemande³ 3*pt.*, lamented 16/13 [OE *bemǣnan* A].

benche¹, bench 7/1 [OE *benc*].

bende¹ *pl.*, bonds 28/65 [OE *bend*].

benedicite⁹, bless me 38/63 [L *benedicite*].

beo(n). *See* be(n).

beode³, to offer, give 20/109; **bid** 3*pr.* 9/97; **bed** 3*pt.* 9/95, offered battle 20/54 [OE *bēodan* 2].

beoden¹ *pl.*, prayers 18/4 [nWS *beodu*].

beom¹, beam 2/32 [OE *bēam*].

beore. *See* beren.

beorȝen¹ *pl.*, hills 6/128 [OE *beorg*].

beornes; beoð; ber. *See* bern; be(n); beer(e).

ber-cnihtes¹ *pl.*, footmen 6/43 [OE *bǣr-* + *cniht*].

berdene¹, burden 19/24 [OE *byrðen*].

bere, bore¹, bear 8/211, 213, 10/117; **bores** *pl.* 8/244n [OE *be(o)ra*].

bereauede³ 3*pt.*, deprived 16/34 [OE *berēafian* B].

beren, beore³, to carry, bear 18/51, 32/22, **bæron** 2/31, 34; **berst** 2*pr.*, carry off 33/32; **berþ, -eþ, -es** 3*pr.* 20/164, 22/38, 31/2; **-es** 3*prpl.* 8/236; **-en** 3*prspl.* 36/38; **bere** 2*pt.* 33/30; **bar** 3*pt.* 6/94, 13/185, 21/29, **ber** 7/5, **bore** 8/45, produced 2/55; **beren** 3*ptpl.* 35/2, 10; **ibore(n), bore(n), born** *ptp.* 4/26, 9/137, 20/153, born 1/1, 6/241, etc. [OE *beran* 4].

beril¹, beryl 20/174 [OF *beril*].

bern¹, child 13/172, 36/19 [OE *bēarn*].

bern¹, man, warrior 22/7; **-e,** **beornes** *pl.* 6/58, 20/5 [OE *béorn*].

berne³, to burn 9/34 [OE *bærnan* 3].

bernes¹ *pl.*, barns 21/26 [OE *bere-ærn*].

berrhless¹, salvation 15/58, 69, 71 [cf. OE *be(o)rgan* 3].

besiȝte¹, wisdom, advice 3/9, judgment 3/17 [OE *be* + *sihð*].

best. *See* be(n).

best(e)² *sup.*, best 8/87, 9/144, 33/10; as¹, gain, profit 7/30, 76, best (person) 26/5; *mid þa(n) beȝste,* among the best (people) 6/38, 110; *(of) þe beste,* in the best way 20/188, 28/32; as⁴, best, most readily 20/3, 6, 24, 22/26 [OE *betst*].

bet⁴ *comp.*, better 6/0 35, 200, 10/39, 115, more easily 10/117; *bet puȝte,* seemed rather 10/21, 23 [OE *bet*].

bete, bieten³, to remedy, atone for 12/276, 13/30, 16/61 [OE *bētan* A].

betere, better(e)² *comp.*, better 9/114, 118, etc., **bether** 38/16, to a better position 2/75; *hit is þe betere,* things are the better 10/180; as⁴, 13/24, 29/28, 36/26, **bettre** 15/25 [OE *betera*].

betockneþ³ *3pr.*, signifies 19/30, 31, etc., **betokneð** 19/75 [OE *betācnian* B].

bi, bie, be⁷, by, by means of 2/22, 23, 5/82, 11/7, 19/53, 22/33, etc., (in oaths) 4/2, 23, 7/73, etc., because of 14/63, 21/31, 32/9, about, concerning 10/46, 12/210, 13/189, 17/25, according to 3/15, 9/162, 12/50, 16/35, during 6/224, 8/27, 19/5, 33, etc., at, in (of time) 2/18, 6/165, (of place) 21/18, near 9/116, 10/176, 11/16, 32/29, throughout 18/34, 37, through, from 13/100, 28/42, to 32/21; *bi strete*, along the street 5/106; *bi þe wei*, on the road 5/112; *bi semblaunt*, by his appearance 9/8; *bi one stunde*, at that time 9/57; *þet . . . bi*, by means of which 18/2; *be swo þet*, provided that 19/72 [OE *bi*].

biblodde³ *imp.*, sprinkle with blood 17/110 [OE *bi* + *blōd*-].

bicharde³ *3pt.*, tricked 12/293 [OE *bi* + OA *cærran* A].

biclosi³, to surround 5/16; -**clusde** *3ptpl.*, shut themselves in 6/108 [OE *bi* + OF *clos*-].

bycumen, be-³, to become 16/48, 58, 20/110, **becomen** 37/6; **becom** *3pt.* 22/18; **bicome** *3ptpl.*, arrived at 10/213; **bicume** *ptp.* 9/136 [OE *becuman* 4].

bid. *See* **beode.**

bidde(n)³, to pray, beg, ask 7/77, 12/179, 15/43; **bidde** *1pr.* 15/49, 16/49, etc.; **bit, bid, biddeð** *3pr.* 6/29, 20/1, etc., bids 9/169, 11/33, 17/64, 20/147; **bede** *2pt.* 20/187, ordered 32/4; **bad, bed** *3pt.* 15/6, 18/4, **bade** 7/48, 8/152, etc.; **ibede(n)** *ptp* 12/135, 18/23, invited 12/255 [OE *biddan* 5].

byde³, to experience 29/10; **byd** *3pr.* 31/5 [OE *bīdan* 1].

bideled³ *ptp.*, deprived of 6/134 [OE *bedǣlan* A].

bie; bie(n), bieð; bieten. *See* **begge; be(n); bete.**

bifalle³ *3prs.*, may happen 6/0 35 [OE *bef(e)allan* 7].

bifore(n), bifor(n), biuore(n)⁷, before, in front of 2/80, 8/129, etc.; *bifor þe heued*, in the face 8/185. As⁴, earlier, previously 3/15, 5/44, 9/100, to the front 5/53, to the face 14/51, in front 20/35, earlier than 35/1 [OE *beforan*].

biget³ *imp.*, obtain 35/48; **begæt** *3pt.* 2/67; *begæt in*, recovered 2/70 [OE *beg(i)etan* 5].

biginnen³, to begin 8/21; -**eþ** *3pr.* 12/80; **bigan, -gon** *3pt.* 8/174, 225, etc.; **bigonne, bigunnen** *3ptpl.* 5/103, 8/118, 15/44 [OE *beginnan* 3].

biginning(e)¹, begininge, beginning 5/103, 8/13, 19/35 [OE *beginn-* + *-ing*].

bigo³ *3prs.*, may befall 12/53; **bigon** *ptp.*, set 6/144 [OE *begān*].

bigredet³ *3prpl.*, scold 10/67 [OE *be* + *grǣdan* A].

bigripen³, to grip 11/74 [OE *begrīpan* 1].

bigrowe³ *ptp.*, overgrown 10/27 [OE *be* + *grōwan* 7].

biȝete¹, gain, acquisition 12/248 [cf. OE *beg(i)etan* 5].

bihalden, biholde³, to see, behold 6/153, 10/71, 20/9, **bihelde** 7/43; **bihald, byholt** *imp.* 36/2, consider 17/97; **bihe(o)ld, bihold, bihuld** *3pt.* 5/40, 6/25, 12/15, scanned 10/30; **biheolden** *3ptpl.* 18/3 [OE *behéaldan*, OA *behǎldan* 7].

bihalfues, etc. *See* p. 330.

biheste¹, promise 29/24 [OE *behǣs*].

bihet. *See* **behete.**

bihinde(n)⁴, behind 17/23, 130, 20/35, to one's back 14/52 [OE *behindan*].

bihold. *See* **bihalden.**

bihonged³ *ptp.*, covered 6/80 [OE *be* + *hángian* B].

byhud³ *imp.*, hide 14/57 [OE *behýdan*].

biknewe³ *ptp.*, confessed 9/80 [OE *becnāwan* 7].

bilæi³ *3pt.*, besieged 6/113 [OE *belicgan* 5, with the sense of *belecgan* A].

bile¹, bill 10/79 [OE *bile*].

bileaue,-liaue¹, belief, faith 17/103, 19/46, bileue 35/43, beleaue 19/36, 58 [OE *be* + *lēafa*].

biledet³ *3prpl.*, pursue 10/68 [OE *belǣdan* A].

bileue³, to remain 10/42; *3prs.*, may be passed over 12/198; -en *1prspl.*, abandon 21/10; bilef *imp.* 9/163; bileuede *3ptpl.*, hesitated 5/74; bileued *ptp.* 5/110 [OE *belǣfan* A].

bileued, bileueþ. See beleue.

bilimede³ *3pt.*, dismembered 5/78 [OE *be* + *lim-*].

bilirten³, to ensnare 11/12 [OE *belyrtan* A].

biliue(s)⁴, quickly 6/83, 106 [OE *be* + *līfe* + adv. *-es*].

billeð³ *3pr.*, pecks 11/37 [cf. OE *bile*].

billing¹, pecking 11/20, 41 [OE *bile* + *-ing*].

biloken³ *3prpl.*, look around 11/87 [OE *belōcian* B].

binde³, to bind, imprison 8/41, 9/3, 75; bind *3pr.*, makes helpless 12/254; -eþ *3prpl.* 29/5; ybounde *ptp.* 7/10, 30/18 [OE *bindan* 3].

binepe⁴, underneath 5/59, below 12/253 [OE *beneoþan*.]

binnen⁴, within 6/109 [OE *binnan*].

binome³ *ptp.*, deprived of 12/173 [OE *beniman* 4].

byrieden³, *3ptpl.*, buried 2/82 [OE *byrgan* A].

birlen¹ *pl.*, cup-bearers 6/42 [OE *byrele*].

birrþ³ *3pr.*, befits, behoves 15/14, 18, etc. [OE *byrian* A].

bisaumpleð³ *3pr.*, moralizes 17/30 [OE *be* + OF *saumple*].

bisauwe¹, proverb 17/54 [OE *be* + *sagu*].

bischop, biscop¹, bishop 2/7, 8, 3/26, bissop 5/32; -es *pl.*, 1/10, 2/49, 53, 14/3; -en *dpl.* 10/183 [OE *biscop*].

bischricheþ³ *3prpl.*, shriek at 10/67 [OE *be* + **scrician* B].

biseken³, to beg, beseech 8/269; bisecheþ *3pr.* 28/73; *3prpl.* 9/120, 127; bysech, bisek *imp.* 33/14, 36/59, besiech 16/50; besohten *3ptpl.* 16/2 [OE *besēcan* A].

byset³ *ptp.*, beset 20/11 [OE *besettan* A].

biside⁴, nearby 5/40; as⁷, near 5/19 [OE *be* + *sīdan*].

bisne¹, example 15/50; *to bisne*, as a guide 6/15, o 28 [OE *bisen*].

bispeke³ *ptp.*, agreed 10/160 [OE *besp(r)ecan* 5].

bist. See be(n).

biswike(n)³, to deceive 11/30, 73; -eþ *3prpl.* 13/19 [OE *be* + *swīcan* 1].

byswngen³ *ptp.*, scourged 36/28 [OE *beswingan* 3].

biteche³, to hand over, entrust to 9/54; bytech, bitæche, bitache *1pr.* 6/221, 15/33, 38/32; bitaȝte *3pt.*, committed to the protection of 9/177; bitaȝt, bitauht *ptp.* 9/50, 20/145 [OE *betǣcan* A].

bite¹, bite 17/67, 68 [OE *bite*].

biten³, to bite 6/81; bit *3pr.* 17/67; -eð *3prpl.* 6/104, 17/23 [OE *bītan*].

bitide³, to happen 13/132, 29/11; *3prs.* 9/139, 10/52; bitidde *3pt.* 7/78 [OE *be* + *tīdan* A].

bitiȝt³ *ptp.*, clothed 10/109 [OE **betyhtan* A].

bitoke³ *3ptpl.*, entrusted 5/48 [OE *be* + ON *taka*].

bituene, bitwen(e)[7], between 8/191, 206, 13/9, etc. [OE *betwēonan*].

bituxen[7], between 10/169 [OE *betwux* + -*an*].

bitweies[7], between 13/7 [OE *betweoh* + adv. -*es*].

bið. See be(n).

biþenche[3], to reflect 12/83; **biðohte** 3*pt.* 6/60; **biþout** *ptp.* 12/81 [OE *beþencan* A].

biþute(n)[7], without 9/26n, 32 [obscure].

biweued[3] *ptp.*, covered 21/94 [OE *bewefan* 5].

bywite[3] 3*prs.*, may guard 14/60 [OE *bewitan*].

biwon[3] 3*pt.*, acquired 6/15 [OE *be* + *winnan* 3].

blac[2], black 8/48; *blac and brown* 8/115n; as[1], **blake**, dirt 7/104 [OE *blæc*].

blakien[3], to grow pale 18/21 [OE *blācian* B].

blam(e)[1], sin, shame 38/66; *brouth in blame*, caused to sin 8/84 [OF *blasme*].

blame[3], to blame 13/25, 82 [OF *blasmer*].

blast[1], storm 25/3, wind 35/36 (OE *blǣst*].

blau, blaw[3], to blow 23/1, 4; **blou, blow** *imp.* 28/1, 3, 4 [OE *blāwan* 7].

bled[1], flower 10/138 [OE *blǣd*].

blede[3], to bleed 8/103; **bledde** 3*pt.* 5/78 [OE *blēdan* A].

bleo[1], face 18/21, 20/66, 28/23 [OE *blēo*].

bles[1], gust (of wind) 20/14 [OE *blǣs*].

blesce[3], to bless, make the sign of the cross 17/92; **blesci** 1*pr.* 18/53; **blis** *imp.* 38/37, 64; **blessed, iblesced** *ptp.* 16/40, 36/61 [OE *bletsian* B].

blete[1], hard weather 10/57 [OE *blēat*].

bleteþ[3] 3*pr.*, bleats 24/6 [OE *blǣtan* A].

bleþeliche. See bliþeliȝ.

blykyeþ[3] 3*pr.*, gleams 28/23; **blikeden** 3*ptpl.* 18/7 [OE *blīcian* B].

blynde[2], blind (men) 20/37 [OE *blind*].

blynne[3], to stop 29/17 [OE *blinnan* 3].

blis. See blesce.

blis, blisce, blisse[1], joy 9/147, 10/94, etc., **blise** 6/47; -**en** *pl.* 6/134 [OE *bliss*].

blysfol, blisfule,[2] blessed 18/52, lovely 28/18 [OE *bliss* + *full*].

bliþe[2], happy 9/60, 12/249, etc. [OE *blīþe*].

bliþeliȝ, -like[4], gladly 15/46, 66, **bleþeliche** 12/171 [OE *blīþelīce*].

bliue[4], quickly 12/109, 20/21 [OE *be* + *līfe*].

blod(e)[1], blood 6/198, 8/192, etc., ancestry 5/4; *blodes swat*, bloody sweat 17/128 [OE *blōd*].

blod-gute[1], bloodshed 6/57 [OE *blōdgyte*].

blodi[2], bloody 17/72, 36/20, 23 [OE *blōdig*].

blome[1], flower 8/63 [ON *blóm*].

blos(t)me[1] *pl.*, flowers 10/16, 13/2, 30/2 [OE *blōstm*].

blou, blow. See blau.

bloweþ[3] 3*pr.*, bursts into flower 24/3 [OE *blōwan* 7].

bo[2], both 9/92, **ba** 15/4; as[4], as well 9/141 [OE *bā*].

boc[1], book 5/93, 6/15, etc., **bock** 6/5n; *pl.* 6/28, **bec** 1/2, 7 [OE *bōc*].

bocare[1], writer 1/7 [OE *bōcere*].

bocfelle[1], parchment 6/26 [OE *bōcfell*].

bokilered[1] *pl.*, learned men 14/4 [OE *bōc* + *gelǣred*].

bocstaff[1], letter, character 15/52 [OE *bōcstæf*].

bodede³ 3*pt.*, foretold 6/244; -eden
3*ptpl.*, preached 1/10 [OE *bodian*
B].

bodi¹, body 8/84, etc., man, person
5/27, 69; -es *pl.* 5/45 [OE *bodig*].

boȝe, bouh¹, bough 10/15, 20/48
[OE *bōg*].

bohte, bohton, bopht. *See* begge.

boket¹, bucket 12/78, etc.; -es *pl.*
12/73 [OF *buket*].

bold(e)¹, hall, temple 20/113, 119,
127 [OE *bóld*].

bold(e). *See* bald(e).

boles¹ *pl.*, bulls 8/243 [OE *bula*].

bolle¹, bowl 7/17 [OE *bolla*].

bon. *See* be(n).

bon¹, bone 26/5, 28/10; -es *pl.*
12/63, ban 17/117 [OE *bān*].

bondeman¹, farmer 8/32; -men
pl. 8/123 [ON *bóndi* + OE
mann].

bone¹, prayer 18/23, 25, etc.,
command 32/4; -en *pl.* 17/89 [ON
bón].

bone¹, slayer 18/60 [OE *bana*].

bor. *See* beer(e).

bord(e)¹, table 6/206, 8/99, 28/70
[OE *bórd*].

bore(n); bore(s). *See* beren; bere.

borewe³, to redeem 31/32 [OE
borgian B].

born. *See* beren.

borrȝhenn³ *ptp.*, saved 15/64 [OE
be(o)rgan 3].

borw. *See* burȝe.

boses¹ *pl.*, padding 32/15, 22 [OF
boce].

bost¹, ostentation 4/20 [obscure].

bot(e)¹, remedy 9/183, 17/35, etc.
[OE *bōt*].

bot(e). *See* bute(n).

bot-forke¹, forked stick 31/2 [ME
bat + OE *forca*].

bop. *See* be(n).

bope, bape²,⁵ both 5/10, 7/4, etc.,
bopt 38/65; bopen *dpl.* 12/26
[ON *báði-r*].

bouh. *See* boȝe.

bour(e), bur¹, room, ladies' cham-
ber 7/59, 13/62, etc.; boures *g.*
13/57 [OE *būr*].

bous¹, liquor, strong drink 31/29
[obscure].

bout¹, part of woman's headdress
32/31 [obscure].

brade, brod(e)², broad, wide 6/54,
61, etc., braden *pl.* 6/89 [OE
brād].

bræde³ *ptp.*, extended 6/158, staring
10/75 [OE *brǣdan* A].

bræid, brayd. *See* breid.

brastlien³ 3*prspl.*, may clash 6/195
[OE *brastlian* B].

breche¹, fallow ground 10/14n
[OE *bræc*].

bred¹, bread 18/2 [OE *brēad*].

brede¹, roast meat 8/98 [OE *brǣde*].

breid³ *imp.*, raise 17/90; bræid 3*pt.*
6/78; brayd ut, drew 8/198 [OE
bregdan 3].

breides¹ *pl.*, tricks 11/46 [OE
brægd].

breke³, to break 4/41; -en, bræcon
3*ptpl.* 2/29, 6/89; ibroke *ptp.*,
committed 13/29 [OE *brecan* 5].

breme², splendid 9/154, passionate
28/16 [OE *brēme*].

brennen³, to burn 11/94; -es 3*pr.*
35/21; brendon 3*ptpl.* 2/40 [ON
brenna].

brere¹, briars 31/23 [OE *brēr*].

breoste, brest¹, breast 8/137, 201,
etc.; breosten *d.* 6/78 [OE *brēost*].

brepren. *See* broper.

brew³ 3*pt.*, brewed 4/11 [OE
brēowan 7].

brid¹, bride 28/16 [OE *brȳd*].

briddale¹, wedding 9/156 [OE
brȳdeala].

bridel¹, bridle 10/124 [OE *brīdel*].

brides¹ *pl.*, birds 13/2 [OE *bridd*].

bryht, briȝt, brith², fair, beautiful
13/40, 20/66, etc., briȝtte 35/6,
radiant 29/2, 33/1; briȝter, briȝttore *comp.* 13/124, 33/3 [OE
byrht, beorht].

bryht⁴, brightly 20/184 [OE *byrhte, beorhte*].

bringe³, to bring 8/72, 10/125, etc., bringhe 8/65, guide 21/32; -eþ, bringþ 3*pr.* 9/61, 14/65, etc.; -eþ 3*prpl.* 13/164; -e 3 *prs.* 8/275; bring *imp.* 31/25, 36/66; brohte, brouhte, broute 3*pt.* 4/21, 6/18, etc., brouʒtem=brouʒt hem 21/37, broste 6/0 19, brouth 8/84, brohute 12/70, installed 2/63, derived 10/148; brouhte 3*pts.* 20/111; (i)brout, (y)broht *ptp.* 12/82, 15/14, etc., ibroʒt 5/55, ibrouʒt 21/88; *to sorwe brouth,* punished 8/57; *let . . . bringe,* had them brought 9/149; *bringeð us in a sinne,* causes us to sin 11/32; *ibrouht forð,* made known 17/37; *bringeð . . . o fluhte,* causes to flee 17/135 [OE *bringan* A].

bryniges. *See* brunie.

brisen³, to bruise 8/208 [OE *brȳsan* A].

broc¹, stream 6/179 [OE *brōc*].

brod(e); broht(e), brohute. *See* brade; bringe.

brom¹, broom, brushwood 27/1 [OE *brōm*].

broste. *See* bringe.

broþer¹, brother 5/47, etc.; breþren *pl.* 21/43, etc. [OE *brōþor*].

brouʒtem, brouhte. *See* bringe.

broune, brown², brown (vessel), 7/16, 8/115n [OE *brūn*].

browen¹ *pl.,* eyebrows 28/18 [OE *brū*].

bruche¹, opening 12/21, 233, sin 13/28 [OE *bryce*].

brudþinge¹, bridal 20/207 [OE *brȳdþing*].

brunie, burne¹, corselet 6/137, 21/77; bryniges *pl.* 2/23 [ON *brynja,* OE *byrne*].

brustlede(n)³ 3*ptpl.,* bristled 6/58, 89 [cf. OE *byrst*].

bucke¹, stag 24/8 [OE *bucca*].

bue(þ). *See* be(n).

buheð, buhþ³ 3*pr.,* bends, obeys 17/64, 20/102; 3*prpl.* 18/41; beh, bey 3*pt.* 12/194, 28/70 [OE *būgan* 2].

bukes¹ *g.,* of the belly 11/33 [OE *buc*].

bulluc¹, bullock 24/8 [OE *bulloc*].

bune¹, purchase 17/96n [obscure].

bunte¹, kindness 19/82 [OF *bontet*].

bur. *See* bour(e).

burde¹, maiden 6/241, 28/5, etc. [obscure, ? OE *byrde*].

burgeis¹, citizen 9/21 [OF *burgeis*].

burʒe, borw¹, town, fortress 6/108, 8/121; burwes *pl.* 8/55 [OE *burg, burh*].

burhmen¹ *pl.,* garrison 6/110 [OE *burhmann*].

burne. *See* brunie.

burnes¹ *g.,* of the stream 18/2 [OE *burn*].

bur-pæinen¹ *pl.,* attendants 6/42 [OE *būrþegn*].

burþen¹, burden 31/2, 23 [OE *byrþen*].

but¹, throw, putt 8/147 [OF *bout*].

but, bute(n)⁴, only, but 8/165, 10/182, 20/10, 49, bote 5/2 [OE *būtan*].

bute(n)⁷, without 3/10, 6/169, 10/212, 20/196 [OE *būtan*].

bute(n), bot(e)⁸, except, unless 5/9, 23, 6/12, etc., but 19/90, but, however, yet 6/243, 21/4, 22/33; *bot if, bote yef, bute if,* unless 14/39, 19/51, 38/51 [OE *būtan*].

butere¹, butter 2/43 [OE *bute re*].

buttinge¹, thrusting 8/235 [? OF *bouter*].

buþ. *See* be(n).

buue⁴, above 17/133 [OE *bufan*].

buxsumnes¹, obedience 22/30 [OE **buhsum + -nes*].

cæse¹, cheese 2/42 [nWS *cēse*].

caynard¹, idler 31/20 [OF *cagnard*].

cakeleð³ 3pr., cackles 17/53 [eME cakelen].

calcydone¹, chalcedony 20/171 [OF calcidoine].

calle³, to call 8/38; 1pr., name 29/17 [lOE ceallian B, from ON kalla].

calue¹, calf 24/7 [OA calf].

cam; can. See cumen; conne.

canceler¹, chancellor 2/8 [ONF canceler].

canstu. See conne.

capun¹, capon 11/4 [OE capun].

care, kare¹, grief, sorrow 6/126, 237, 12/34, etc. [OE caru].

care³ 1pr., grieve 28/77 [OE carian B].

carf³ 3pt., cut 5/73; **corue** 3ptpl. 5/75 [OE ceorfan 3].

carited¹, alms-giving 2/61n [OF carited].

carke³ 1pr., grieve 28/77 [OF carkier].

carlmen¹ pl., men 2/19 [ON karl + OE mann].

caste, kesten³, to throw, cast 8/81, 9/76, 29/7; 3pt. 8/169; **icast(e)** ptp. 9/4, 35/33 [ON kasta].

castel¹, castle 2/71, 4/14, etc., **kastel** 20/152; -es pl. 2/9, etc. [ONF castel].

castel-weorces¹ pl., forced labour on the castles 2/16n (ONF castel + OE weorc]

caudel¹, warm drink for invalids 5/111n (ONF caudel).

cellerer¹, cellarer 12/59 [OF celerer].

certes, certhes⁴, certainly 10/191, truly 38/22 [OF certes].

ceste¹, chest 2/27 [nWS cest].

cete¹, whale 11/71 [OF cete].

cethegrande¹, whale 11/57 [OF cete grande].

champioun, chaunpioun¹, champion 8/114, 35/34; -s pl. 8/122, 138, etc. [OF champiun].

chan. See conne.

chapeð³ 3pr., bargains for 17/95 [OE cēapian B].

chapmen¹ pl., merchants 8/51 [OE cēapmann].

charite¹, charity 22/32 [OF charite].

chastite¹, chastity 22/31 [OF chastete].

chaueles. See cheafle.

chaungede¹ 3pt., changed 9/102 [OF changier].

cheafle¹, gossip 17/58; **chaueles** pl., jaws 11/71 [OE ceafl].

chele¹, cold 31/5 [nWS cele].

chelle.¹ See note to 32/21.

cheorl, cherl¹, man, peasant 17/16, 31/34, **cherld** 31/40 [OE ceorl].

cheose³, to choose 14/63, 20/186, 190; **icoren(e)** ptp. 6/241, 19/29, 20/155, **ichosen** 3/6 [OE cēosan 2].

cheping¹, market 17/54 [OE cēapung].

chere¹, face, appearance 13/21, 20/92, 28/30, 37/4, mood 9/102; makeð drupie chere, puts on a dismal look 17/30 [OF chere].

chyde³, to argue 29/9 [OE cīdan A].

child(e),¹ child, youth 9/140, 12/228, etc., **cild** 2/79; **childre(n)** pl. 5/3, 9/61, etc. [OE cild, cildru].

childhede¹, childhood 19/71 [OE cildhād].

chyn¹, chin 4/28 [OE cinn].

chirche-songe¹ pl., hymns 10/132 [OE cirice + sáng].

chirechen. See circe.

chnief¹, knife 38/20 [OE cnīf].

christen; cild. See crisstene; child(e).

circe, chirche¹, church 2/47, 48, 62, 9/149, **churche** 37/10; **chirechen** d. 6/3 [OE cirice].

cyrceiærd¹, churchyard 2/47 [OE cirice + géard].

circewican¹ d., office of sacrist 2/68 [OE cirice + wīce].

clackes³ 2*pr*., gabble 10/81 [cf. F *claquer*].

clannesse¹, purity 28/47 [OE *clǣnnes*].

clapte³ 3*pt*., struck 8/187, 194 [ON *klappa*].

clene², pure, innocent 12/227, 250, etc., chaste 13/162, **klene** 12/178 [OE *clǣne*].

cleo. *See* note to 20/72.

clepe³, to call 9/81; **cleopeð, clepeþ** 3*pr*. 17/69, 118, 19/70, names 17/122; **clepe** *imp.* 19/15, **cleope**, call for 17/105; **cleopede** 3*pt*. 6/82, 18/27; **clepeden** 3*ptpl*. 2/39; **icleoped, iclepede** *ptp*. 19/29, 20/162 [OA *cleopian* B].

clerc¹, cleric, learned man 6/20, 8/77, etc., **clerek** 14/19, scholar 29/9, 29, etc.; **clerekes, clerkes** *pl*. 2/50, 8/33; *clerc of scole*, university student 38/28 [OE *cler(i)c*, L *clericus*].

cleueþ³ 3*prpl*., cleave to 32/21 [OA *cleofian* B].

climbið³ 3*pr*., climbs 6/124 [OE *climban* 3].

cliure(s)¹ *pl*., claws 10/78, 84 [OE *clifras*].

clogges¹ *pl*., blocks of wood 32/21 [obscure].

clos³, to surround 5/42 [cf. OF *clos*].

clopes¹ *pl*., clothes 8/249 [OE *clāþ*].

clude¹, rock 6/163; **-en, -es** *pl*. 6/124, 10/97 [OE *clūd*].

cnaue¹, youth 6/215, 217 [OE *cnafa*].

cneon¹ *pl*., knees 17/90, 18/25 [OE *cnēo(w)*].

cniht, cnipte. *See* **knyht(e)**.

cnotted³ *ptp*., knotted 2/24 [cf. OE *cnotta*].

cnotten, -is¹ *pl*., knots 37/5, difficulties 1/4 [OE *cnotta*].

coc¹, cook 6/45 [OE *cōc*].

coc, kok¹, cock 11/4, 12/30, etc. [OE *cocc*].

cocke³, to fight 32/2 [cf. OE *cocc*].

cogge¹, cog-wheel 10/86 [obscure].

col-blake², black as charcoal 10/75 [OE *col* + *blæc*].

cold(e)², cold 12/254, 255, 20/15, useless 14/101; **as**¹, coldness 20/78 [OA *cáld*].

com, come(s), comen, comeþ. *See* **cumen.**

come¹, coming 12/134 [cf. OE *cuman* 4].

commandement¹, commands 19/17 [OF *comandement*].

conne³, to know, know how to, be able to 5/10; **can, con** 1*pr*. 2/35, 10/208, etc., **chan** 10/215; **const** 2*pr*. 7/107, 13/74, 35/56, **cost** 29/17, **canstu**, can (inflict) 38/36; **can, con** 3*pr*. 5/11, 10/194, etc., **kan** 8/104; **cunnen** 1*prpl*. 2/57; **conne, cunne** 3*prpl*. 5/44, 13/33, 56, **counnen** 13/77; **cunne** 1*prs*. 10/47, 48; 3*prs*. 6/242, **conne** 5/6; **couþe** 1*pt*. 13/182, 29/29; **couþe, cuþe** 3*pt*. 6/21, 8/93, 153, etc., **kouþe** 12/184; **couþe** 3*ptpl*. 5/2, 44; **cuþe** 3*pts*., might understand 20/199; **couþ** *ptp*. 13/95 [OE *cunnan*; *can, con*; *cūþe*].

conquerour¹, conqueror 22/3, 8 [OF *conquereor*].

consail, conseil¹, advice 9/162, 33/10, **cunsayle** 38/54 [OF *conseil*].

countre, contre¹, country 4/4, 21/74; **contreyes** *pl*. 5/8 [OF *co(u)ntree*].

coppe. *See* **cu(p)pe.**

coral¹, coral 28/45 [OF *coral*].

corn¹, corn 2/42, 55, etc. [OE *córn*].

corteisy; corue. *See* **curteisi(e); carf.**

cos¹, kiss 30/12 [OE *coss*]

cost. *See* **conne.**

costnede³ 3*pt.*, cost 17/100 [OE *costnian* B].

cotlyf,¹ cottage 14/73 [OE *cotlīf*].

counnen. *See* conne.

couertour¹, coverlet 13/119 [OF *coverture*].

coupe³, to pay dearly for 8/173 [ON *kaupa*].

coup(e). *See* conne.

craft(e)¹, skill, knowledge 6/138, 11/100; -en *dpl.* 6/142 [OE *cræft*].

crafti², powerful 13/44n [OE *cræftig*].

crahien³, to stretch out 18/19 [obscure].

crauant², craven 17/65n [cf. OE *crafian* B].

crede¹, the Creed 38/71 [OE *crēda*, from L *credo*].

crempe³, to stop 10/210 [OE **crempan* A].

crenge³, to draw in 18/19 [OE **crengean* A].

crepen³, to creep, lurk 8/68; creop *imp.* 17/108; icrope *ptp.* 12/28 [OE *crēopan* 2].

crie³ 1*pr.*, speak, pray 31/33, 33/5 [OF *crier*].

crisopace¹, chrysoprase 20/174 [OF *crisopace*].

cristal¹, crystal 28/30, 47 [OF *cristal*].

cristendom¹, christianity 1/10, 15/2, 69, 19/61 [OE *crīstendōm*].

crisstene², Christian 15/58, 61, christen 2/79, cristine 12/120 [OE *crīsten*].

croked(e)², crooked 10/80, deformed 31/20 [cf. ON *krók-r*].

cron¹, crane, heron 6/99 [OE *cran*].

croppeð³ 3*pr.*, polls 17/17 [ON *kroppa*].

croune, crune¹, crown of the head 8/187, 220, 230 [OF *coroune*].

croup¹, early form of fiddle 28/43 [Welsh *crwth*].

crucethus¹, torture-box 2/27 [cf. L *cruciatus*].

cruninge¹, reign 3/24 [OF *coroune-* + OE *-ing*].

crupel¹, cripple 13/118 [OE *crypel*].

crune. *See* croune.

cu¹, cow 24/7 [OE *cū*].

cuccu⁹, cuckoo 24/2, 5, etc. [imitative].

cudde. *See* kype.

cuggel¹, stick, club 17/105 [OE *cycgel*].

culur¹, brilliance 20/180 [OF *colour*].

culure¹, dove 17/120, 121, 123 [OE *culfre*].

cumen, come(n), kome(n)³, to come 6/229, 7/100, etc., to return 4/30, cum 6/245, to enter 16/8; cumene *ger.* 6/169, 19/95; cumeð, comeþ 3*pr.* 6/80, 9/183, etc., comȝ 33/24, kimeð 17/86; cumen, comeþ, coms 3*prpl.* 11/69, 22/37, escape 35/24; come 2*prs.* 13/127; cume(n) 3*prs.* 6/240, 17/72; come 3*prspl.* 5/4; cum, com *imp.* 12/38, 17/120, 123; komeþ, comes *imppl.* 8/171, 12/270; com 1*pt.* 9/15; come 2*pt.* 7/72; com(e), kom 3*pt.* 2/6, 5/1, etc., cam, kam 8/128, 11/54, etc.; come(n) komen 3*ptpl.* 5/28, 6/8, etc., coman 2/51; come 3*pts.* 5/35, 10/111; icume(n), icome(n), come(n) *ptp.* 5/47, 6/73, etc., cummen 38/55, comin 38/39, descended 19/61, changed 35/17; com . . . to, arrived at 5/18; com . . . aȝein, came towards 6/53; cumeð forð, shows himself 17/27 [OE *cuman* 4].

cun(ne), kenne, kinne¹, kindred 6/72, 120, etc., descendants 16/39; cunnes *g.*, kind(s) of 6/170, 9/155, etc., race 6/156;

kunne *pl.* 12/54; cunne *gpl.*,
kinds of 10/20, 12/166 [OE *cynn*].
cunde, kind(e)¹, nature 9/39,
10/88, etc. [OE *(ge)cýnd*].
cunne(n); cunsayle. *See* conne;
consail.
cunsence¹, consent 17/60 [OF
cunsence].
cupe¹, basket 9/137 [OE *cūpe*].
cu(p)pe, coppe¹, cup 8/14, 9/135,
etc. [OE *cuppe*].
cur-dogge¹, cur 17/78 [ME *curre* +
OE *docga*].
curre¹, coward 17/66 [obscure].
cursede³ *3pt.*, cursed 12/259; *3ptpl.*,
anathematized 2/53 [OE *cúrsian* B].
curteis², courteous 9/22 [OF *cur-
teis*].
curteisi(e), corteisy¹, courtesy
13/26, 77, 101 [OF *cur-, corteisie*].
curtiler¹, gardener 12/272 [OF
curtiller].
custe¹, qualities 10/9, 14/66; -es
pl. 6/50 [OE *cyst*].
custe; cupep, cupest; cupe. *See*
kisse; kype; conne.
cup², known 20/104 [OE *cūp*].
cwakieð³ *3prpl.*, tremble 18/30
[OE *cwacian* B].
cwalm-hus¹, torture-chamber 18/2
[OE *cwealm* + *hūs*].
cwap. *See* quod.
cwene¹, woman 17/51 [OE *cwene*].
cwike², living 18/29 [OE *cwic*].

dæde; dædes; dæl; dære; dæðe.
See ded; ded(e); del; deore; dep.
day(e)¹, day 3/23, 13/17, etc., dæi
6/73, daize 16/46, deai 19/23;
dæis, dayis, -es *g.* 2/41, 31/16,
33/3, deies 11/13; daies *pl.*
12/48, 153, dæis 2/60, dæzes
6/171, dawes 8/257; daghen,
dazen, dawe, dahzen, *dpl.* 6/223,
224, 19/60, 21/13 reign 6/165; *be
dæies*, by day 2/19; *a day*, during
the day 5/39; *god day*, farewell
9/169 [OE *dæg*].

daies-liht¹, daylight 24/2 [OE
dæges līht].
dale¹, valley 10/1, 13/4; -es *pl.*
6/131; -en *dpl.* 6/175 [OE *dæl*].
dam(e)¹, lady 5/77, 31/30, mother
38/3 [OF *dame*].
damishel, damoisele¹, maiden
38/1, lady-in-waiting 7/67 [OF
damisele, damoisele].
dare³ *1pr.*, cower, lie still 28/78;
-eð *3pr.* 11/14 [OE *darian* B].
darknep³ *3prpl.*, grow dark 13/4
[cf. OE *deorc, *dearc*].
dapeyt⁹, a curse on 8/172, 13/135
[OF *dahait*].
dawe³ *3prs.*, may dawn 13/125,
31/40 [OE *dagian* B].
dawe(s). *See* day(e).
deadliche, diadlich(e)², deadly
3/20, mortal 19/72, 88 [OE
dēadlīc].
deai; deað(e). *See* day(e); dep.
declyn¹, decline 32/25 [OF *declin*].
ded², dead 5/111, 7/65, etc., dæde
6/75, dede 23/3, dedh 38/43
[OE *dēad*].
ded(e). *See* dep.
dede¹, deed 12/223, 13/65, etc.,
work 38/70; *pl.* 10/185, -en
17/14, dædes 2/56; *wipp dede*, in
his deeds 15/63 [OE *dǣd*].
dede(n). *See* do(n).
dedestounde¹, hour of death 36/10
[OE *dēap* + *stúnd*].
def², deaf 31/34 [OE *dēaf*].
deze, deie³, to die 7/85, 9/40, etc.;
1pr. 29/15, 36/53; *1prs.* 36/26,
32; deide *3pt.* 5/83; *3pts.* 9/100
[ON *deyja*].
deies; del. *See* day(e); deuel.
del¹, part 8/268, 10/123, 20/196,
dæl 3/5, 14 [OE *dǣl*].
dele³, to grant 28/76 [OE *dǣlan*
A].
delit¹, pleasure 17/60 [OF *delit*].
deluol², calamitous 5/26 [OF *deol*
+ OE *full*].
deme¹, judge 10/205 [OE *dēma*].

deme³, to judge 10/169; **demþ,
-eþ** 3*pr.,* utters 10/177, adjudges
10/199; **dem** *imp.* 17/98; **idemed**
ptp., decided 6/73, 21/83 [OE
dēman A].

demembred³ *ptp.,* dismembered
5/71 [OF *desmembrer*].

demliche⁴, obscurely 5/87 [OE
dimlīce].

deofles; deoluen. *See* **deuel; duluen.**

deope, depe², deep 6/95, thick
12/109; **deopen** *dpl.* 6/175 [OE
dēop].

deor, der¹, animal 6/81, 11/1, 10,
25; **deoren** *pl.* 6/127, 136, **deor**
18/42, **dor** 10/108 [OE *dēor*].

deorc, derk², dark 1/16, 5/86 [OE
de(o)rc].

deore, dere², dear, beloved 6/217,
7/24, 106, 17/67, glorious 6/147,
150, 17/97, 18/54, precious 17/96,
dære, costly 2/42; **deorre** *comp.,*
more precious 17/98, 20/176
[OE *dēore*].

deore, dere, duere⁴, dearly 17/100,
32/18, 37/16 [OE *dēore*].

deorly⁴, affectionately 31/29 [OE
dēorlīce].

deorewurðe², precious 17/96, 99,
etc., **deorwurþe** 1/5, **derewurþe,
-worþe** 20/163, 28/37 [OE *dēor-
wurþe*].

de profundis¹, a penitential psalm
38/75n.

dereð³ 3*pr.,* harms 11/29 [OE
derian A].

dereworþliche⁴, lovingly 28/76
[OE *dēorwurþlīce*].

derflike⁴, skilfully 11/17 [ON
djarf-r + OE *-līce*].

derkhede¹, darkness 5/84 [OE
de(o)rc + mutated form of
hād].

derne², secret 1/5, 13/65 [nWS
dérne].

dernelike⁴, secretly 11/29 [nWS
dérnlīce].

deshonur¹, dishonour 9/17 [OF
deshonor].

dest, deð. *See* **do(n).**

deþ, deað(e), ded(e)¹, death 5/33,
9/38, etc., **dæðe** 6/95, **diaþe**
19/84, **diþe** 9/23; **deaðes** *g.*
17/67, 68 [OE *dēaþ*].

deuel¹, devil 11/28, 29, etc., **dieuel**
16/7, **del** 31/34; **-es** *g.* 11/109,
19/48, **deofles** 17/42, 100, 132;
deueles, deoules *pl.* 2/17, 32/20
[OE *dēofol*].

dewes¹ *pl.,* dew 13/4 [OE *dēaw*].

diadlich(e); diaþe. *See* **deadliche;
deþ.**

dich¹, ditch 21/18 [OE *dīc*].

dide(n); dieuel. *See* **do(n); deuel.**

diȝele², hidden 10/2 [OE *dīegol*].

diȝelnesse¹, mystery 1/5 [OE *dīe-
golnes*].

diht³ 3*pr.,* composes 10/178; **idihte**
ptp., arrayed 6/233 [OE *dihtan*
A].

dim², dark 11/112 [OE *dimm*].

dinede³ 3*pts.,* might dine 5/23;
3*ptspl.* 5/25 [OF *di(s)ner*].

diner¹, dinner 5/110; **-s** *pl.* 5/26
[OF *di(s)ner*].

dinge³, to strike, beat 8/242 [OE
*dingan 3].

dint¹, blow 8/180, 190; **duntes** *pl.*
12/295 [OE *dynt*].

dyssh¹, bowl 7/40 [OE *disc,* from
L *discus*].

diþe. *See* **deþ.**

diuers², different 19/67 [OF
diuers].

diueð³ 3*pr.,* dives 11/97 [OE
dȳfan A, *dūfan* 2].

do(n)³, to do 2/69, 3/7, etc., act
8/17, 27/2, perform 10/130, 19/2,
cast 13/128, place 15/32, 20/96;
done *ger.* 3/15, 16, 12/236, 19/48;
do 1*pr.* 10/163, 12/44, 19/26,
advise 12/51; **dest, dost** 2*pr.*
10/49, 12/33, etc., act 9/162;
deð, doð 3*pr.* 6/99, 11/10, etc.,
dos 38/20, causes 11/96, 101,

20/60, 30/4, sends 19/69, 78, acts 20/37, sets 20/38, pains 36/21; doþ *2prpl.* 19/90, 91, commit 10/156; *3prpl.* 8/213, 12/217, 19/32, don 8/211; do *2prs.* 12/50, may give 12/192; *2prspl.* 19/90; *3prspl.* 10/106; *imp.* 13/156, 20/204, cause 10/210 35/47; *imppl.* 10/203; dudest *2pt.*, acted 4/43; dede, dide, dude *3pt.* 2/5, 4/5, etc., placed 2/9, 24, 28, inflicted 2/11, caused 12/67, carried out 19/17, took 19/40, sent 19/68; deden, diden, duden *3ptpl.* 2/11, 46, etc., cast 2/19, put 2/25, 27, etc., inflicted on 2/36; ido(n), do(n) *ptp.* 3/7, 24, etc., ended 5/108, 12/106, deprived 6/202, set 20/181; *dude . . . teche*, caused to be taught 5/3; *dude . . . on*, put on 6/137; *als he coupe þerwith do*, to do as well as he could with it 8/153; *do ringe*, to cause to be rung 12/251; *dede . . . harm*, harmed 16/32 [OE dōn].

dogge[1], dog 17/68, 69, etc.; -es *pl.* 8/212 [OE docga].

dogge-deouel[1], devil in the form of a dog 17/105 [OE docga + dēofol].

dogge-fahenunge[1], fawning like a dog 17/94 [OE docga + fahn + -ung].

dole[1], sorrow, grief 38/42 [OF doel].

dom(e)[1], judgment 9/62, 10/159, etc., authority 15/38, sentence 21/83; dom, -es *pl.* 6/115, 10/177 [OE dōm].

dor. See deor.

dore[1], door 12/27, 38/10; -en *pl.*, gaps 31/14n [OE duru, dor(a)].

dore-tre[1], bar of the door 8/179 [OE duru, dor(a) + trēo(w)].

dou[1], dough 12/256 [OE dāg].

doun(e). See dun(e).

doute[1], fear 31/4 [OF doute].

dragen, drahen, drawe[3], to drag,

attract, draw 11/106, 17/130, devise 32/11; drageð, draheð *3pr.* 11/14, 17/62, draghus, approaches 22/28; dragen *3prpl.*, approach 11/67, 90; droȝ, droh, *3pt.* 9/45, 18/53, drou, went 5/15, drew up 12/277; *drauh þe forþ*, take up 20/202; *drowen ut*, unsheathed 8/210 [OE dragan 6].

dragse[3], *imp.*, trail 17/132n.

drahtes[1] *pl.*, way of life 32/11 [cf. OE dragan].

drake[1], dragon 18/55; -es *g.* 18/5 [OE draca, from L draco].

drapen. See drepeð.

dred(e)[1], fear 8/90, 11/17, 12/89 [cf. OE -drǣdan A].

drede[3], to fear 32/3; dret *3pr.* 20/59 [OE -drǣdan A].

dreȝy[3] *imp.*, endure 35/25 [OE drē(o)gan 2].

dreim, drem[1], sound 10/21, outcry 21/87 [OE drēam].

dreynt[3] *ptp.*, drowned 31/31 [OE drencan A].

drench[1], drink 7/58; -en *pl* 6/228 [OE drenc].

dreng[1], a free tenant 8/31 [ON dreng-r].

dreori, dreri[2], gloomy, sad 14/77 21/87, 29/5 [OE drēorig].

drepeð[3] *3pr.*, kills 11/98; draper *3ptpl.* 2/26, 34 [OE drepan 5, ON drepa].

drihte(n)[1], lord, God 1/20, 2/81 etc., drihtin 2/83, 85, 15/8 driste 6/0 2; drihtenes, drih tines *g.* 2/82, 6/150; drihtene 6/10 [OE dryhten].

drinke[1], drink 12/143, 21/14, etc. dryng 4/11 [OE drinc, or drync]

drinke(n)[3], to drink 7/40, 8/15 etc.; -es *3pr.* 30/4; -eþ, -en *3prp* 10/105, 11/95; drync, drinke *imp* 7/20, 41, 51; dronc, dronk(e *3pt.* 7/7, 50, 55, 12/93; drounke *3ptpl.* 35/7; dronke *ptp.*, drun 31/31 [OE drincan 3].

driue(n)³, to hasten 13/192, expel
6/118; -eð 3*prpl.*, hunt 6/131,
drive 10/66; **drof** 3*pt.* 8/166 [OE
drīfan 1].

driwerie¹, love 13/76 [OF *druerie*,
druirie].

drof; droȝ, droh; dronc, dronk(e).
See **driue(n); dragen; drinke(n).**

dropes, -en¹ *pl.*, drops 5/90, 17/128
[OE *dropa*].

drou. *See* **dragen.**

droui², turbid 11/81 [OE *drōf* +
-ig].

drounken. *See* **drinke(n).**

droupne³ 1*pr.*, pine away 28/78
[ON *drúpna*].

drowen. *See* **dragen.**

drunch(e)¹, drink, water 12/14,
18/2 [OE *drync*].

drupie², dismal 17/30 [obscure].

dubbede³ 3*pt.*, dubbed 9/146 [OF
-duber].

duc, duk¹, duke, lord 3/2, 9/59,
etc. [OF *duc*].

dude(st). *See* **do(n).**

duelle, dwellen³, to linger, remain
8/4, 54, 32/20, 36/49; **dwellen**
1*prpl.* 8/165 [OE *dwellan* A].

duere. *See* **deore⁴.**

duȝeðe¹, valour 6/127 [OE *duguþ*].

duȝeðe-cnihtes¹ *pl.*, best warriors
6/117 [OE *duguþ* + *cniht*].

dulle², blunt 17/113, 117 [OE
*dylle].

duluen³ 3*ptpl.*, dug into 17/114,
117; **idoluen** *ptp.* 17/113, **deo-**
luen, cultivated 17/112 [OE
delfan 3].

dun(e), doun(e)⁴, down 5/105,
8/197, etc. [OE *dūne*].

dunen, -es¹ *pl.*, hills 6/131, 175
[OE *dūn*].

duneward⁴, down 17/64 [OE
dūne + *w(e)ard*].

duntes. *See* **dint.**

durlyng¹, darling 14/11 [OE *dȳr-*
ling].

durste³ 3*pt.*, dared 8/65 [OE
durran; dorste].

dutten³, to stop up, close 31/14;
hidut *ptp.* 33/44 [OE *dyttan* A].

dwellen. *See* **duelle.**

eadi, eadiȝe², blessed 16/3, 17/92,
18/61 [OE *ēadig*].

eadines(s)e¹, happiness 16/6, 25
[OE *ēadignes*].

eadmodliche⁴, humbly 16/2 [OE
ēadmōdlīce].

earding-stowe¹, dwelling-place
10/28 [OE *ēardungstōw*].

eardið³ 3*prpl.*, dwell 18/33 [OE
ēardian B].

earen; ech. *See* **er; euch(e).**

eche², eternal 16/60, 35/52 [OE
ēce].

eche³, to increase 30/11 (nWS *ēcan*
A].

echon. *See* **euchan.**

eddre¹, vein 12/45, **heddre**, blood
from a vein 12/43 [OE *ǣdre*].

ede; efne. *See* **eode; heouene.**

eft⁴, afterwards 14/58, 15/48, etc.
[OE *eft*].

efter. *See* **after.**

efterward⁴, afterwards 19/27 [OE
æfterw(e)ard].

egging¹, inciting 35/32 [ON *egg-* +
OE *-ing*].

egleche², valiant 14/6 [cf. OE
ǣglēca, āglǣca].

egre², eager 12/289 [OF *aigre*].

eȝȝwhær⁴, everywhere 15/23, 27,
53 [OE *ǣghwǣr*].

eȝte¹, goods 3/17 [OE *ǣht*].

eȝtetenþe², eighteenth 3/23 [OE
eahtatēoþa].

ej⁹, alas 25/5 [obscure].

eidel¹, anything 9/175 [OE *ǣnig* +
dǣl].

eie¹, wrath 18/42 [OE *ege*].

eye¹, eye 8/185, 199, etc., **eȝe**
32/29; **ehnen** *pl.* 17/80, 133,
18/8, **eȝene** 10/75, **eye** 28/17
[OE *ē(a)ge*].

eili³ 3*prs.*, may injure 18/30 [OE *eglan* A].

eilþurl¹, window 18/3n [OF *ueil* + OE *þyrel*].

eise¹, opportunity 17/61, heyse, ease 31/28, hayse, peace 8/59; eyses *pl.*, comforts 35/27 [OF *eise*].

eisfule², fearful 18/30 [OE *egesful*].

eiþer²,⁵ either, each 5/58, 9/103, 10/9, 18/10, aiþer 10/7, both 5/17, also, likewise 17/99 [OE *ǣgþer*].

ek(e)⁴, also 3/35, 8/132, etc., æc 6/52 [OE *ē(a)c*].

ekenn³, to add 15/29; ekedd *ptp.* 15/23 [nWS *ēcan*].

elde¹, age, old age 19/69, 77, 79 [nWS *éldo*].

elles⁴, otherwise, else 9/25, 10/106, etc. [OE *elles*].

elleswer⁴, elsewhere 12/208 [OE *elles hwǣr*].

elne¹, courage 18/47 [OE *ellen*].

emes. *See* eom.

emparour¹, emperor 22/4 [OF *emparour*].

ende¹, end 5/112, 9/129 etc., hende, 35/60 ænde 3/10, place 6/133, part 6/178, death 20/21; *atten ende*, at last, 5/59; *on, an ende*, in the end 15/64, 72, 20/47, etc. [OE *énde*].

endelong⁴, downwards along 18/53 [OE *énde* + *láng*].

endy³, to finish 10/*Int.* 3 [OE *éndian* B].

endinge¹, death 8/276, 20/209 [OE *éndung*].

ene(s)⁴, once 13/168, 20/159 [OE *ǣne, ǣnes*].

engin¹, device, plan 9/117, 121 [OF *engin*].

engles¹ *pl.*, angels 18/42, 20/133 [OE *engel*].

eny², any 7/36, 37, etc. [OE *ǣnig*].

enne. *See* an⁵.

eode³ 3*pt.*, went 7/59, 74, ede 12/69, hede 12/275 [OE *ēode*].

eom¹, uncle 2/3; emes *g.* 4/44 [OE *ēam*].

eorl, erl¹, earl 3/27, 28, etc., þerl 8/107, count 3/2; eorles *g.* 6/216; eorles, erles *pl.* 9/6, 14/5 [OE *éorl*].

eornen. *See* erne.

eorðe, erþe¹, earth, ground 5/89, 6/88, etc., ierðe 16/47, land 2/55 [OE *éorþe*].

er. *See* or⁸.

er¹, ear 32/29, ære 15/67, yare 19/93; earen *pl.* 17/44, 50, 51, eren 32/23 [OE *ēare*].

er(e)⁴, before, formerly 17/13, 18, 46, 20/36, 54, ær 2/75, ear 17/66; erour, erur *comp.* 10/160, 12/4; erest, eroust *sup.*, first 12/16, 124, 21/96, ærest 6/9, arst 16/32, 33 [OE *ǣr, ǣrra, ǣrest*].

er(e)⁸, before 5/113, 17/30, 21/74, 31/40, ær 6/172, her 8/15; er þen, before 28/74 [OE *ǣr*].

ere. *See* her(e).

erbere¹, garden 13/98 [OF *herbier*].

erewe. *See* arewe.

erien³, to plough 10/135; eried *ptp.* 11/12 [OE *erian* A].

erl, erles. *See* eorl.

erliche⁴, early 21/8 [OE *ǣrlīce*].

ernde¹, errand 31/22 [OE *ǣrende*].

erne³, to run 12/16, 36/23; eornen 3*ptspl.*, might hasten 17/21 [OE *ǣrnan* 3, *éornan* 3].

ers, hers¹, rump 32/14, 38/10 [OE *ears*].

ert. *See* art.

erðchine¹, furrow 11/12 [OE *éorþe* + *cine*].

erþe. *See* eorðe.

eruename¹, inheritance 16/51 [nWS *erfe* + ON *nám*].

es³ 3*pr.*, is 38/3, 4, etc. [ON *es*].

est¹, east 20/100, 28/42 [OE *ēast*].

este², gracious 10/95, 127 [OE *ēste*].

estren¹, Easter 2/80 [OE *ēastron*].

eten³, to eat 11/34; -eþ 3*prpl.*
10/103, heten 11/95; hete 2*ptpl.*
12/156; eten 3*ptpl.* 35/7; ete
3*pts.* 5/23; i-ete *ptp.* 12/98, 169
[OE *etan* 5].

eðeliche⁴, cheaply 17/99 [nWS
ēðelīce].

eu. *See* ȝe.

euch(e), ælc²,⁵ each, every 2/73,
6/42, 163, etc., æhc 3/15, ælche
6/37, ech 10/123, any 18/36;
alcne *am* 6/29; ælchen *dm.* 6/146;
ælchere, echere *df.* 6/135, 14/55
[OE *ǣghwylc*].

euchan, echon²,⁵ every 13/19, 23,
each one 5/17, 98 [OE *ǣghwylc* +
ān].

euele. *See* uvel(e).

eue(n)¹, evening 10/41, 19/9, etc.
[OE *ǣfen*].

euene⁴, directly 5/34 [OE *efne*].

euenyng¹, equal 20/84 [ON *jafningi*].

euer(e)⁴, ever, always 4/6, 7/53,
etc., heuer(e) 8/17, 88, 13/127,
35/21, 38/59, eure 9/166, 11/76,
14/83, eauer 17/71, æfre 15/61,
æure 2/37, 53, 16/11, 45, aure
16/37, 44; *æure umwile*, at regular
intervals 2/38 [OE *ǣfre*].

euerich(e)²,⁵ each, every 19/16,
20, 69, 35/51, eueril 8/245, 268,
eueri 8/8, 13/149, euervche
32/8, eauereuch, any 18/62,
æuric 2/14, 50, æurihce 3/34,
everyone 19/18; æuerælches *gm.*
6/165; *euerich mest*, almost everyone 17/51 [OE *ǣfre* + *ylc/ǣlc*].

eueruchon⁵, everyone 21/91,
heuereuchon 12/270 [OE *ǣfre*
+ *ylc/ǣlc* + *ān*].

fa, fo¹, enemy 17/99, 102, etc.; fon,
foos *pl.* 5/16, 34, etc. [OE *fāh*].

face¹, face 28/14 [OF *face*].

fader¹, father 5/12, 109, etc.; *g.*
6/33, faderes 21/52 [OE *fæder*].

faderles², fatherless 8/75 [OE
fæderlēas].

fæie, uæie², doomed 6/56, 105,
185, 191 [OE *fǣge*].

fæier, fæire. *See* feyr(e); feire.

fæstned³ *ptp.*, fastened 2/32 [OE
fæstnian B].

fagen², glad 11/68, 89. As ⁴, faȝe,
gladly 9/65 [OE *fagen*].

faght, faht. *See* fiȝt(t)e.

fayle¹, fail 38/53 [OF *faille*].

fayllard², deceitful 38/8 [OF *faill-ir*
+ *-ard*].

fayr(e), fayrer, fairest; fale. *See*
feyr(e); fele.

falle³, to fall 8/39; falleð, ualleð,
falt 3*pr.*, flows 6/179, falters
10/37, lies down 11/11; falleþ,
valleþ 3*prpl.* 9/148, 21/44, fallen, alight 11/16; falle 2*prs.*
28/74; valle 3*prs.* 31/4; fal *imp.*
35/35; fel, vel 3*pt.* 7/95, 8/188,
etc., happened 5/83, 91, 8/116,
vanished 36/55; feollen 3*ptpl.*
6/56, 90, etc., ueollen 6/58,
velle 5/90, fell; fel, befell 22/11
[OE *f(e)allan* 7].

falewe³ 1*pr.*, fade, decay 29/3; -eþ
3*prpl.* 20/16 [OE *f(e)alwian* B].

fals(e)², false, deceitful 13/41,
20/44, etc., ualse 17/17, fauce,
imitation 32/32 [OF *fals, faus*;
OE *fals*].

false³ to weaken 20/124; falsi
3*prs.* 17/131 [OF *falser*].

fare¹, journey 2/41, fate 36/44 [OE
faru].

fare(n)³, to go, journey, fare 8/51,
10/201, etc., uaren 6/225; fare
1*pr.* 10/91, 12/202; -eþ 3*pr.*
20/33; 3*prpl.* 21/21; fare(n),
3*prs.* 6/126; fare *imp.* 13/180;
-eþ *imppl.* 10/158; for 3*pt.* 2/1,
66, 6/183 [OE *faran* 6].

fast³ 1*pr.*, fast 25/7 [OE *fæstan* A].

faste⁴, firmly, securely 6/108, 8/82,
etc., vaste, vigorously 5/49,
near 6/0 5 [OE *fæste*].

fastliche⁴, fiercely 6/55 [OE *fæst-
līce*].

fe¹, wealth 8/44, 37/2, feo 20/70 [OE *feoh*].

fearlac¹, fear 18/22, 41 [OE *fær* + -*lāc*].

feaue², few 19/29, vewe 5/90 [OE *fēawe*].

febliche⁴, feebly 5/115 [OF *feble* + OE -*līce*].

feblore² *comp.*, weaker 5/59 [OF *feble* + OE -*ra*].

feccheð. *See* fettes.

fede, ueden³, to feed 8/100, 17/51; fede 1*pr.* 38/69; fet 3*pr.* 11/40; fedde 3*pt.* 13/118; *ptp.* 8/261 [OE *fēdan* A].

feȝe³, to accord with 32/31; iueied *ptp.*, joined 17/57 [OE *fēgan* A].

feht(e), fihte¹, battle 6/199, 203, 211, 17/129, army 6/53n, feoht, uproar 6/168 [OE *fe(o)ht*, *fiht*].

feyr(e), fayr(e)², fair, beautiful 7/32, 9/113, etc., vaire 10/15, veyr 20/83, noble, good 6/18, handsome 9/67, 71, 20/91, pleasant 13/152, 21/5, generous 29/24, fæier, proper 1/23, vair, large 5/14; fayrer, feyrure *comp.* 20/117, 38/46; fairest *sup.* 6/239, uairest 6/225, uæireste 6/154 [OE *fæger*].

feire, faire⁴, courteously 21/46, 73, nobly, excellently 9/5, 21/61, quickly 21/21, fæire, brightly 1/16 [OE *fægre*].

fel. *See* falle.

fel(l)¹, hide, skin 11/18, 37, wel 34/3 [OE *fell*].

feld³ 3*pt.*, struck down 8/232; *ptp.* 8/197 [nWS *fellan* A].

feld(e)¹, field 11/11, 31/13, battlefield 5/36, 69, 35/44, estates 35/3; -es *pl.* 6/106 [OE *fēld*].

fele, feole², many 1/19, 6/207, 8/274, etc., uele 10/20, ueole 17/40, fale 10/144, uale 10/189; *so felefolde*, in so many ways 20/11; *of feole volde*, in many ways 20/117; as⁴, very 29/30 [OE *fe(o)la*, *feala*].

fele³ 1*pr.*, feel 36/10; -eð 3*pr.* 11/18, 96; -en 3*prpl.*, smell 11/68 [OE *fēlan* A].

felede³, 3*pt.*, scared 8/67 [ON *fæla*].

felefolde, in so many ways 20/11 [OE *fela* + OA *fáld*].

felle. *See* fille.

felons¹ *pl.*, evil-doers 9/30 [OF *feloun*].

felounye¹, felony 8/264 [OF *felonie*].

fen, fenne¹, mud 28/74, marsh 4/25, 6/158 [OE *fenn*].

fend(e), feond¹, fiend, devil 11/51, 17/63, etc., ueond 17/28; -es *g.* 13/18; feond, -es *pl.* 18/41, enemies 6/62 [OE *fēond*].

feng, feð; feo; feoȝelen; feollen. *See* foangen; fe; foȝel; falle.

feondliche², deadly 6/209; as⁴, furiously 6/93 [OE *fēondlic*, -*līce*].

feor, fer²,⁴ far 17/50, 74, 20/153, 29/31, high 6/167, a long way 7/29, 42, 75, from afar 8/254; fir *comp.*, farther 18/40 [OE *feorr*; *fierr*, *firr*].

feorren, ferrene⁴, afar 17/67, from afar 21/35 [OE *feorran*].

ferde¹, army 6/63, 166, 183, verde 6/154, levies 10/212; -en *pl.* 6/54 [nWS *férd*].

ferde³, 3*pt.*, went 6/112; -en 3*ptpl.* 10/211, 21/75, lived 21/13 [OE *fēran* A].

fere¹, outward appearance 20/79 [OF *afe(i)re*].

fere¹, fear 5/33 [OE *fær*].

fere¹, comrade, companion 12/120, 13/80, 104; ueren *pl.* 17/11; *to . . . fere*, as a companion 13/35 [OE *fēra*].

ferlik, ferlys², marvellous 8/222; as¹, marvels 22/11 [OE *fǽrlīc*, ON *ferlīki*].

ferlyng¹, farthing 4/10 [OE *fēorðling*].

ferrs¹, verse, metre 15/30, 32, 34 [OE *fers*, from L *versus*].

ferst(e). *See* first(e).

ferþe², fourth 8/183 [OE *fēorþa*].

feste¹, feast 8/257, 9/154 [OF *feste*].

festen³, to establish 1/23, bind 8/82; -eð *3pr.* 11/111; -en *3prpl.*, fasten 11/91 [OE *fæstan* A].

feteres¹ *pl.*, fetters 8/82 [OE *feter*].

fettes, feccheð³ *3pr.*, fetches, obtains 11/5, 22/36; fetes *3prpl.* 8/254; fette *3pt.* 9/152 [OE *fetian* B, *feccan* A].

feþ¹, faith 1/23 [OF *feid*].

feþeren¹ *pl.*, quill pens 6/26 [OE *feþer*].

fiede¹ *3pt.*, wrote 6/26 [OE *fēgan* A].

fiele¹, fiddle 28/43n [OF *viele*, infl. by OE *fiþele*].

fif, fiue², five 1/7, 12/29, 13/160, 186 [OE *fif*].

fifte², fifth 8/189 [OE *fifta*].

fiftene², fifteen 6/209 [OA *fiftēne*].

fifty², fifty 8/46, 29/23 [OE *fiftig*].

fiȝt(t)e³, to fight 5/107, 13/90; faht *3pt.* 6/197; faght *3ptpl.* 22/15 [OE *fe(o)htan* 3].

fihs; fihte. *See* fyssh¹; feht(e).

fikelare, uikelare¹, flatterer 17/13, 18; -es *pl.* 17/1, 45 [OE *ficol* + *-ere*].

fikele, vikel², fickle, treacherous 13/22, 20/12 [OE *ficol*].

fikeð³ *3pr.*, flatters 17/94 [OE *-fician* B].

filde¹, plain 13/180n [OE *filde*].

filet¹, head-band 32/32 [OF *filet*].

fille, felle¹, one's fill 7/51, 11/23 [OE *fyllo*].

fillen, fulle(n)³, to fill, fulfill 15/11, 17/62, 21/11, fill out 15/22, 31, 32; fil *imp.* 8/14; fulde *3pt.* 7/16, 49; fylden, fulden *3ptpl.* 2/15, 17, 21/14; ifuld *ptp.* 9/6 [OE *fyllan* A].

fyn¹, finish 8/22 [OF *fin*].

fyn², gracious 20/182, 28/24 [OF *fin*].

finde(n)³, to find, discover 2/41, 8/42, etc., fynd 22/35; findeð, uindeð *3pr.* 6/177, 11/104, vind 12/253; fond *1pt.* 7/79, 9/16, founde 12/214; fond *3pt.* 7/61, 12/21, etc., funde 9/77, founde 12/73, fonde 13/72, fand, provided for 2/60; fonden *1ptpl.* 19/11; funden *3ptpl.* 8/56, 21/28; founde, funde *3pts.* 6/11, 8/49, etc.; ifunde, ifounde *ptp.* 13/136, 20/55, 160, 21/90, fonde, found out about 13/42 [OE *findan* 3].

fingres¹ *pl.*, fingers 17/102, 104, 28/27, vingres 21/60; fingren *dpl.* 6/26 [OE *finger*].

finnes¹ *pl.*, fins 18/33 [OE *finn*].

fir. *See* feor.

fir(e), fur¹, fire 9/34, 76, etc., fuir 35/21, sparks 6/195 [OE *fȳr*].

first(e), ferst(e), furste²,⁴ *sup.*, first 7/91, 8/159, 13/71, etc., verst(e) 5/93, 19/28, werst 5/62, uirste, nearest 6/133; *wiþ þe vurste*, along with the first 7/13 [OE *fyrest*].

fyssh, fihs, fis¹, fish 7/36, 37, 10/103, etc.; fisches, fisses, fiscen *pl.* 6/159, 11/67, etc. [OE *fisc*].

fyssh³, to fish 7/39 [OE *fiscian* B]

fysshere¹, fisherman 7/28 [OE *fiscere*].

fysshyng¹, fishing 7/45 [OE *fisc* + *-ing*].

fle(n), fleo(n)³, to flee 5/103, 107, 8/193, etc., flæn 6/62; flænne *ger.* 6/93; ulih *3pr.* 6/132; fle *3prs.* 8/172n; flih *imp.* 17/107; flæh *3pt.* 6/106; flugen, -æn *3ptpl.* 2/45, 52, flowe 5/51, fluȝen, charged 6/87 [OE *flēon* 2].

flede³, to flow 18/39 [OE *-flēdan* A].

flehen¹ *pl.*, fleas 17/72 [OE *flēa*].

fleye³, to fly 8/186, 200; **flihinde**
prp., of the air 18/34; **fliʒt** 2*pr.*
10/89; **fleoð** 3*prpl.* 6/167, 18/34;
fle, flo *imp.* 10/33, 12/38; **flowen**
ptp. 12/31 [OE *flē(o)gan* 2].

flerd¹, deceit 11/53 [OE *fléard*].

fles, flesch, fleshe¹, flesh 10/83,
11/108, 17/112, 117, 19/43,
flehs, flesc, meat 2/42, 10/103;
flæshess *g.* 15/1 [OE *flǽsc*].

flet³ 3*pr.*, floats 11/60; **fleoteð**
3*prpl.* 18/33; **floten** 3*ptpl.* 21/18
[OE *flēotan* 2].

flih; flihinde. *See* **fle(n); fleye.**

flikereð³ 3*pr.*, hangs round 17/93
[OE *flicorian* B].

flo. *See* **fleye.**

floc, flok¹, flock 6/100n, 12/29,
company 8/24, 15/38 [OE *flocc*].

flod(e)¹, flood 6/10, 198, 21/2, 16,
20, water 6/103, sea 7/83, 26/2;
-es *g.* 21/3; *pl.*, seas 18/33 [OE
flōd].

flore¹, floor, house 38/9 [OE *flōr*].

floten. *See* **flet.**

flour, flur¹, flower 20/151, 33/28,
treasure 13/148 [OF *flour*].

flowe; flowen; flugen, fluʒen.
See **fle(n); fleye; fle(n).**

fluhte¹, flight 17/135 [OE *flyht*].

fnast¹, breath 10/44 [OE *fnǽst*].

fo. *See* **fa.**

foangen³, to take, receive 3/16;
feð, foð 3*pr.*, begins 17/29, 63;
feng 3*pt.* 21/94; **ifonge** *ptp.*
21/82 [OE *fōn* 7].

fode¹, food 11/16, 18/2 [OE *fōda*].

foʒel, fowel¹, bird 6/105, 13/50,
etc.; **fuʒele(s), foweles** *pl.*
6/123, 167, 13/6, etc., **feoʒelen**
6/159, **uoʒeles** 6/164, **fules** 11/9,
16, **fugeles** 11/12, **fuheles** 18/34,
fugheles 25/2 [OE *fugol*].

fol. *See* **ful⁴.**

fol¹, fool 29/9, 17, **foul** 22/28; **-en**
gpl. 37/3 [OF *fol*].

fol², foolish 20/80, 36/48 [OF
fol].

folc, folk(e)¹, people 1/17, 6/169,
etc., **uolc** 6/50, 120, army 5/21,
6/112, 185, 191, 8/89; **follkess**
g. 15/58; *loandes folk*, commonalty
3/6 [OE *folc*].

folde³, to clasp 28/27; **folden,
uolden** *ptp.*, thrown down 6/56,
90 [OA *fáldan* 7].

folgen, follʒhenn³, to follow
11/112, 15/4, etc.; **folegeð, foleweþ, follʒheþþ** 3*pr.* 11/104,
14/96, 103, 15/63; **follʒhe(nn)**
3*prspl.* 15/47, 60 [OE *folgian*
B].

foly¹, folly 22/28 [OF *folie*].

follost. *See* **fulluht.**

fomen¹ *pl.*, enemies 12/288 [OE
fáh + mann].

fon; fond(e), fonden. *See* **fa;
finde(n).**

fonde(n)³, to try, attempt 9/133;
fonde *imp.* 35/45; *to fonde*, when
tested 13/22, to see 28/8, 14
[OE *fándian* B].

foos; for. *See* **fa; fare(n).**

for, vor⁷, because of, by reason of
2/52, 4/27, 6/124, etc., for the
sake of 6/30, 7/48, 86, 37/14, for
the benefit of 2/5, 3/8, 8/44, as
4/14, 6/119, 12/123, in order to
obtain 8/73, 12/161, 14/68, 15/73,
17/94, 98, 19/6, 29/34, with a
view to 10/113, 188, 16/63,
36/14, in requital of 2/81,
11/43, 13/94, 178, 15/72, 16/17,
18, 49, 55, 19/81, in support of
9/110, as the price of 21/84, in
place of 6/39 [OE *for*].

for, vor⁸, since, because 2/3, 14,
5/6, etc.; *for þæt, þatt*, because
3/20, 15/66; *for ðan*, despite this
14/104, because 16/30 [OE *for*].

forbaren³ 3*ptpl.*, spared 2/47, 49
[OE *forberan* 4].

forbeddi³ 1*pr.*, forbid 13/179 [OE
forbēodan 2].

forbisne¹, example 11/25, parable
19/2, 27, 86 [OE *forbisen*].

forrblendedd³ *ptp.*, blinded 15/38 [OE *for* + *bléndan* A].

forcursæd³ *ptp.*, excommunicate 2/54 [OE *for* + *cúrsian* B].

forcuðest² *sup.*, most wretched, horrible 6/136, 18/12 [OE *forcúðest*].

forde, uord¹, ford 6/54, 97 [OE *fórd*].

fordemed³ *ptp.*, doomed 6/120 [OE *fordēman* A].

fordo(n)³, to destroy 11/56, 18/46; *ptp.*, ruined 2/56 [OE *fordōn*].

fordriuen³ *ptp.*, driven about 11/85 [OE *fordrīfan* 1].

foren, uore⁴, in front, before 6/78, 17/114 [OE *foran*].

foreward, -werde¹, agreement 4/41, 19/6, 7 [OE *forew(e)ard*].

forgilte², sinful 16/4 [OE *forgylt*].

forʒelde³ *3prs.*, may reward 12/226 [nWS *forgéldan* 3].

forʒet³ *3pt.*, forgot 18/22 [OE *forg(i)etan* 5].

forʒeue³, to forgive 12/175; *1pr.* 12/225; **forrʒife** *3prs.* 15/43; **forʒef** *imp.* 12/209; **forʒiue** *ptp.* 9/126, lost 9/141 [OE *forg(i)efan* 5].

forʒeuenesse¹, remission 12/295 [OE *forg(i)efnes*].

forholen³ *ptp.*, concealed 2/83 [OE *forhelan* 4].

forke¹, pitchfork 31/19 [OE *force*].

forlete³ *1pr.*, abandon 10/36; **forleten** *ptp.* 1/17 [OE *forlǣtan* 7].

forlore(n). *See* **furleosen**.

forsake³, to renounce 13/131, 37/2; **forsoke** *2pt.*, neglected 4/44; **forsake** *ptp.* 12/177 [OE *forsacan* 6].

forst¹, frost 31/5 [OE *forst*].

forstod³ *3pt.*, prevented the use of 6/97 [OE *forstándan* 6].

forsw(e)olhe(n)³, to swallow 18/20 51; **-swelh** *3pt.* 18/58. [Cf. OE *swolgettan* A and *forswelgan* 3.]

forsworen³ *ptp.*, perjured 2/13, 54 [OE *forswerian* 6].

fort⁸, until 10/41, 12/17 [OE *fórþ tō*].

forte, -to, uorte, -to⁸, to, in order to (with inf.) 3/15, 16, 4/4, 5/10, etc. [OE *for tō*].

forteoþ³ *3prpl.*, lead astray 14/99 [OE *fortēon* 2].

forþ⁴, forth, forward 6/33, 83, 8/91, 9/61, etc., **uorð** 6/85, away 6/235, 10/211, out 9/45, 17/32, over 9/49; *forþ mid*, as well 1/19 [OE *fórþ*].

forþedd³ *ptp.*, furthered 15/6, 13 [OE *fórþian* B].

forðfare¹, death 6/237 [OE *forð* + *faru*].

forþi⁸, because, therefore 2/2, 76, 8/269, etc., **vorþi** 10/65, **forþe** 10/69, **forrþi þatt** 15/58 [OE *for þȳ*].

forþingketh³ *3pr.*, displeases 19/26 [OE *forþencan* A].

foruaren³ *ptp.*, destroyed 6/120 [OE *forfaran* 6].

forrwerrpenn³, to reject 15/37; *3prspl.* 15/75, 78 [OE *forweorpan* 3].

forwunded³ *ptp.*, mortally wounded 6/208, 214 [OE *forwúndian* B].

fosterlinges¹ *pl.*, foster-children 6/207 [OE *fōstorling*].

fot(e), uot(e)¹, foot 4/36, 5/23, 25, etc.; **fet** *pl.* 2/22, 23, 5/73, etc., **vet** 17/115; *on fote*, afoot 8/101, 29/12 [OE *fōt*, pl *fēt*].

fotmen¹ *pl.*, infantry 5/102 [OE *fōt* + *mann*].

foul; foul; foule; founden; founden. *See* **fol**¹; **ful**⁴; **ful(e)**; **finde(n)**; **funde**.

four(e)², four 6/13, 7/60, 17/91 [OE *fēower*].

fourti, furti², forty 8/257, 19/75 [OE *fēowertig*].

fow, vouh², variegated fur 13/116, 20/28, 106 [OE *fāg*].

fowerti3þe², fortieth 3/24 [OE *féo-wertigoþa*].

fox, vox(e)¹, fox 6/121, 131, etc., **wox** 12/12, 33, etc.; **foxes** g. 11/18, 37, 47 [OE *fox*].

fox¹, trickery 11/53 [OE *fox*].

foxing¹, trick; *doð ... a foxing*, acts like a fox 11/36 [OE *foxung*].

frakel(e)², deceitful 14/71, 20/12 [cf. OE *frēcelnes*].

fram. *See* **from.**

frame¹, help, benefit 11/26, 15/9 [ON *frami*].

freboren², noble 21/35 [OE *frēo + boren*].

freme¹, benefit 3/8 [OE *fremu*].

fre, freo², noble 20/6, 25, 94, 28/8, free-born 9/21 [OE *frēo*].

frend, freond¹, friend 14/37, 16/39, 19/25, 20/129, kinsman 12/133n; **ureondes** g. 17/29; **freonden** pl. 6/74, **frend** 12/160 [OE *frēond*, ON *frændi*].

frer(e)¹, friar 12/266, 31/19, etc.; **-en** pl. 12/262 [OF *frere*].

freseþ³ 3pr., freezes 31/5 [OE *frēo-san* 2].

fret³ 3pr., eats 11/23 [OE *fretan* 5].

frith¹, wood 26/1 [OE *fyrhþe*].

fro⁷, from 8/16, 124, etc. [ON *frá*].

frogge¹, frog 10/85; **wroggen** pl. 12/256 [OE *frogga*].

from, fram⁷, from 4/21, 6/10, 9/90, etc., **urom** 17/44, 49, 54, by 2/66, away from 9/130 [OE *from, fram*].

fromward², liable to vanish 20/45 [OE *from + w(e)ard*].

frouer¹, solace 6/39 [OE *frófor*].

frouh², brittle 20/44 [OE **frōh*].

frount¹, forehead 28/14 [OF *front*].

frountel¹, band worn on forehead 32/31 [OF *frontel*].

frourede³ 3pt., comforted 18/1 [OE *frófrian* B].

fruit¹, fruit 22/33, 35, 38 [OF *fruit*].

frumþe¹, beginning 14/36 [OE *frymþ*].

fuel-kunne¹, race of birds 10/65 [OE *fugolcynn*].

fugeles, fugheles, fuheles; fuir; fules. *See* **fo3el; fir(e); fo3el.**

ful, fulle², full 2/15, 11/1, etc., unrestricted 6/123, satiated 21/17, **uulle**, avowed 6/70 [OE *full*].

ful⁴, full, quite, very 4/13, 8/6, 7, etc., **fulle** 6/98, foul 13/116, **fol** 7/64, 31/29, 32/18 [OE *full*].

ful(e), foule,² foul 7/104, 8/195 10/32, 40, 87, 17/45, 33/44, **wle** 10/35, evil-smelling 2/22, vile 17/50, 78, 32/14, 35/31; **as⁴**, disgracefully 5/77, **wl**, poorly 10/31 [OE *fúl*].

fulle(n), fulde(n). *See* **fillen.**

fully⁴, very 28/6 [OE *fullíce*].

fulluht¹, baptism, christianity 6/18, 15/2, **follost** 6/0 19 [OE *fulluht*].

fulste¹, help 6/245 [OE *fylst*].

fulste³ 3prs. may help 6/0 25 [OE *fylstan* A].

fulþe¹, filth 12/165, 17/19, 48 [OE *fylþ*].

fultume¹, help 3/1 [OE *fultum*].

funde, founden³, to go 20/51, 36/52; **fundeð** 3pr. 6/166, tries 18/46, 51 [OE *fúndian* B].

funde(n); fur. *See* **finde(n); fir(e).**

furg¹, furrow 11/11 [OE *furh*].

furleosen³, to lose, be deprived of 20/130; **forlore(n)** ptp. 20/159, damned 1/17, 2/54, 33/19, 35/12, 36/15, worthless 2/13, 19/52 [OE *forléosan* 2].

furmest(e)² sup., first 12/21, 32/15 [OE *fyrmest*].

furste. *See* **first(e).**

furþer⁴ comp., more forward 14/35 [OE *furðor*].

ga(n). *See* **go(n).**

gabbe³ imp., lie 12/121 [OF *gabber*].

gaddes¹ pl., goads 8/123 [ON *gadd-r*].

gadered. *See* **gederede.**

gadering[1], council 2/7 [OE *gader-ung*].

gæde. *See* **yede.**

gæildes[1] *pl.*, forced payments 2/38 (OE *g(i)éld*].

gær(e); gæt; gaf. *See* **zer(e); zet(e); ziue(n).**

gay[2], fair 28/38 [OF *gai*].

gayt[1], goat 38/20 [ON *geit*].

gal[1], song 20/126 [cf. OE *galan* 6].

galieð[3] *3prpl.*, bay 6/130 [OE *galan* 6].

galle[1], gall 8/40, 17/123 [OE *g(e)alla*].

galoun[1], gallon 7/17 [OF *galon*].

galwe-tre[1], gallows 8/43 [OA *galgtrēo*].

gamc(n), gome[1], pleasure, sport 12/24, 13/33, 21/5, 10, 23, 51, 35/8 [OE *gamen*].

gan, gon[3] *3pt.*, did (with inf. as equiv. of simple past) 5/53, 6/14, 79, etc.; **gunnen** *3ptpl.* 6/96, 99, 235, 13/102, **gonnen** 6/196, **gounnen** 12/283 [OE *ginnan* 3].

gandre[1], gander 11/6 [OE *gandra*].

gange[3], to go 8/164; **-en** *3prpl.*, up **gangen**, go ashore 11/92 [OE *gángan* 7].

gapeð[1] *3pr.*, gapes 11/64; **geapede** *3pt.* 18/18 [ON *gapa*].

gart(e)[3] *3pt.*, caused 8/108, 230 [ON *gøra*].

gast, gost[1], spirit 4/21, 11/108, 18/46 [OE *gāst*].

gaste[3], to spoil, ruin 29/8 [OF *gaster*].

gat[1], way, road 38/31 [ON *gata*].

ge. *See* **heo.**

gederede[3] *3pt.*, gathered 4/18; **gadered** *ptp.* 2/4 [OE *gad-, gæderian* B].

geineþ[3] *3pr.*, avails 13/155 [OF *gaignier*].

geld, gelt[3] *3pr.*, rewards 11/20, 41; **yeld, zelde** *imp.*, pay 19/15, requite 35/40; **zeld** *3pt.* 9/176;

izolde *ptp.*, given 9/171 [OE *g(i)éldan* 3].

gelte[1], guilt, sin 16/17, 49, 56, **gilt** 9/85, **guld, gult** 9/37, 36/9 [OE *gylt*].

gemme[1], gem 20/163 [L *gemma*].

genge[2], usual 10/98 [OE *genge*].

genow[1], open jaws 18/18 [obscure].

gentil[2], gentle, noble 5/63, 13/61, 28/39 [OF *gentil*].

geren[1] *pl.*, clothes 32/25 [ON *gørvi*].

gersume[1], treasure 9/135 [ON *gørsemi*].

gesse[3], to try 7/81 [obscure].

gest. *See* **go(n).**

gest[1], romance 8/259; **-es** *pl.* 8/241 [OF *geste*].

gestes[1] *pl.*, guests 2/60 [OE *g(i)est*].

get. *See* **zet(e).**

get[1] *pl.*, goats 12/167 [OE *gǣt*, pl. of *gāt*].

gif. *See* **zef.**

gigelot[1], foolish woman 32/17; **-es** *pl.* 32/25 [obscure].

gyle[1], deceit 14/93 [OF *guile*].

gilt. *See* **gelte.**

gyn, ginne[1], trap, contrivance 12/77, 82, 86, 103, 32/24, plan, device 4/31, 9/133, 12/125, ingenuity 12/72 [OF *(en)gin*].

girdil, gurdel[1], girdle 21/7, 37/5 [OE *gyrdel*].

gistni[3], to entertain 21/34 [OE *g(i)est* + *-nian*, cf. *g(i)estning*].

gistninge[1], feast 12/255 [OE *g(i)estning*].

gyuen. *See* **ziue(n).**

glad[2], happy, glad (at) 6/63, 12/249, 21/66, 35/7, **glade** 36/2, **gled(e)** 20/52, 92; **gladur** *comp.* 10/19 [OE *glæd*].

gladieþ[3] *3prpl.*, make happy 13/31 [OE *gladian* B].

gladnesse[1], happiness 9/71 [OE *glædnes*].

gle, gleo[1], pleasure 13/59, 20/126,

141, 37/3, sport, amusement
9/155, **gleu** 8/245 [OE *gléo(w)*].
gleam[1], sun-beam 18/15 [OE
glǽm].
gled(e). *See* glad.
glede[1], fire 8/91 [OE *gléd*].
gleyue[1], sword 8/217 [OF *glaive*].
glevmen[1] *pl.*, musicians 8/242 [OE
gléomann].
glides, glyt[3] *3pr.*, glides 8/224,
20/32; **glod** *3pt.*, shone 1/16;
iglyden *ptp.*, vanished 20/71
[OE *glídan* 1].
glistinde[3] *prp.*, glittering 18/6;
glistnede *3pt.* 18/15 [OE *glis-
nian* B].
glod. *See* glides.
glotoun[1], glutton 7/18 [OF *glotoun*].
glouen[1] *p.*, gloves 6/210 [OE
glófe].
gnede[2], miserly 8/97 [OE *gnéðe*].
go(n)[3], to go, happen 7/87, 8/152,
9/28, etc., **gan** 17/74, walk 9/94,
29/12, pass by 12/108, live
12/163, 13/83; **go** *1pr.* 30/18;
gest, gost *2pr.* 17/12, 36/32; **goþ**
3pr. 11/11, 24, 20/34, 21/57;
3prpl. 9/70, go about 10/109; **go**
3prs. 36/27; **go, ga** *imp.* 12/34,
53, 55, etc., enter 17/111; **goþ**
imppl. 19/12, 57; **igo(n), go(n)**
ptp., journeyed 13/91, 21/50,
passed 19/46, 31/21, pierced
30/3, **igan**, gone 17/60; *so ihc
mote go*, as I hope to thrive 9/91;
ne gest tu nout þe one, you are not
alone in this 17/12; *goþ forþ*,
advances 20/40 [OE *gán*].
God(e), Godd[1], God 2/76, 3/8,
4/23, etc.; **Godes** *g.* 1/22, 3/1,
etc.; *God wolde*, would to God
28/28 [OE *god*].
god(e)[1], good (thing) 11/49,
12/147, etc., **goed** 12/39, 46,
good 19/93, benefit 2/5, 10/136,
property 2/18, 47; **-es** *g.* 18/28
[OE *gód*].

god(e), goed[2], good 2/76, 77, 5/13,
27, etc., kindly 2/11, noteworthy
5/82, pleasant 6/103, 10/95, 127,
firm 19/36, bright 28/17, honest
38/29; *mid gode rihte*, very rightly
16/17 [OE *gód*].
goded[3] *3pt.*, adorned 2/63 [OE
gódian B].
godeman, -mon[1], householder
19/12, 25, 30, **goodman** 19/4, sir
17/11; **-men** *pl.*, nobles 5/85,
108, sirs 8/1 [OE *gód* + *mann*].
godewebbe[1], fine cloth 6/44 [OE
godwebb].
godnesse[1], goodness 16/14, 27,
61, 28/45 [OE *gódnes*].
godspel(le)[1], gospel 15/17, 25, 28,
19/4, 48, 86, **godespelle** 19/1;
-ess *g.* 15/7, 15, etc. [OE *gód-
spell*].
gold(e)[1], gold 2/5, 20, 4/26, etc.
[OE *góld*].
gold-ringe[1], gold ring 9/150 [OE
góld + *hring*].
gome. *See* game(n).
gome[1], man 8/7 [OE *guma*].
gon, gonnen. *See* gan.
gore[1], dress; *ounder gore*, among
women 13/150 [OE *gára*].
gos[1], goose 11/6 [OE *gós*].
gossip[1], friend, crony 12/116, 209,
220, 243 [OE *godsibb*].
gost; gounnen. *See* gast; gan.
gra[1], devil 18/21 [cf. ON *grá-r*].
grace[1], grace 5/38, 17/43, 20/170,
protection 5/48, mercy 5/107
[OF *grace*].
graciouse[2], gracious 28/38 [OF
gracious].
gradde; græte. *See* grede; gret(e).
gray[2], gray fur 20/28, 106 [OE
grǽg].
gram(e)[1], anger 9/74, 38/68, injury
10/49, danger 21/3 [OE *grama*].
granti[3] *3prs.*, grant 9/120, 19/95;
igranted *ptp.* 9/128 [OF *granter*].
grap[3] *3pt.*, seized 18/22 [OE
grípan 1].

gras, gres¹, grass 10/138, 14/33, 30/2 [OE *græs*].

gras³ 3*pt.*, terrified; *ham gras*, horror fell on them 18/6 [OE *(a)grīsan* 1].

grede³, to call out 5/53, 8/96; 3*prs-pl.*, may pray 36/47; gred *imp.* 17/81, 86; gredde, gradde 3*pt.* 7/96, 12/282 [OE *grǣdan* A].

grey², grey 31/19 [OE *grǣg*].

grene², green 10/18, 29/3, 30/1, fine clothes 13/116, ill 30/16 [OE *grēne*].

greowe; gres. *See* groweþ; gras.

gret(e), griat(e)², great, large 5/90, 8/168, 250, etc., grǣte 6/164, greth 8/132, swollen with anger 10/43; greater, grettere *comp.* 10/74, 19/76 [OE *grēat*].

grete³, to greet, welcome 13/33; -eþ 3*pr.* 10/*Int* 1; grette 3*pt.* 8/184 [OE *grētan* A].

gretynge¹, greeting 20/205 [OE *grēting*];

greu; griat(e). *See* groweþ; gret(e).

grylle², severe 29/34 [obscure].

grim¹, excitement 8/246 [OE *grimm*].

grin¹, halter 2/30n [OE *grīn*].

gris¹, young pig 21/12 [ON *gríss*].

grislich(e)², horrible, fearful 5/82, 10/99, 18/5, 21; -loker *comp.* 5/89 [OE *grislīc*].

griþ¹, peace 8/61, 10/101 [OE *griþ*].

griþbruche¹, breach of the peace 10/156 [OE *griþbryce*].

gromful², fierce 18/29 [OE *gram* + *full*].

grounde, grund(e)¹, ground, earth 5/50, 105, 6/56, etc., bottom 11/81, 12/74, 91, floor 7/9, bottom of the sea 11/97, lowest part 20/154; grunden *dpl.* 6/90; *to grounde ibroȝt*, defeated 5/55; *to grounde*, to the bottom of the

horn 7/56; *bringeþ . . . to grounde*, causes to fall 13/137 [OE *grúnd*].

grounde³ 3*pt.*, established, made firm 4/15, 36/11 [cf. OE *grúnd*].

groweþ³ 3*pr.*, grows 24/3; greu 3*pt.*, increased 8/246; greowe 3*pts.* 14/32 [OE *grōwan* 7].

gruchchede³ 3*ptpl.*, grumbled 19/21 [OF *gruchier*].

grund-stalwrþe², very stalwart 8/134 [OE *grúnd* + *stǽlwurþe*].

grundwal¹, foundations 20/124 [OE *grúndw(e)all*].

grure¹, horror 18/22 [OE *gryre*].

gulcheð³ 3*pr.*, vomits 17/26 [obscure].

guld. *See* gelte.

guldene², golden 21/70, 81 [OE *gýlden*].

gult. *See* gelte.

gultelese², innocent 21/97 [OE *gylt* + *-lēas*].

gurdel. *See* girdil.

ȝæn⁷, against 15/35 [OE *gegn, gēn*].

ȝaf. *See* ȝiue(n).

ȝare, ȝaru², ready 6/53, 10/202 [OE *gearu*).

ȝare, ȝore⁴, long ago 9/15, 13/42, 17/35, for a long time 12/169 30/8 [OE *geāra*].

ȝat¹, gate 12/20 [OE *geat*].

ȝe⁴, yea, yes 10/154, 12/176, 207 [OE *gēa*].

ȝe, ye⁵, 2*pl.*, ye, you 3/4, 6/69, etc.; ȝou *a/d.* 9/19,21/3, etc., ȝew 3/21, 22, you 8/3, eu 10/*Int.* 1, *Int.* 2, 215, 20/118, ou 12/214, 215, 216, 17/43, 44, yu 19/13, yw 19/59; ower, our *poss.adj.* 5/54, 10/158, 17/43, 50, yure 19/59, ȝoure 21/31 [OE *gē; ēow; ēower*].

ȝef, ȝif, if⁸, if 3/18, 7/36, 37, 9/39, etc., gif 2/51, 69, gef 11/60, yef 19/2, 51, 87, 88, 89, hif 38/16 [OE *gef, gi(e)f*].

ȝeȝe³ 1*pr.*, call 31/35; ȝeieð 3*pr.* 17/65 [nWS *gēgan*].

K

ʒeld(e). *See* geld.

ʒeme¹, heed 21/68 [nWS *gēme*].

ʒent⁴, at a distance 7/75 [OE *geond*].

ʒeoluh², yellow 17/32 [OE *geolu*].

ʒeond⁷, over 6/131, throughout 6/182 [OE *geond*].

ʒeoue, ʒeue(þ). *See* ʒiue(n).

ʒer(e), gær(e)¹, year 2/1, 59, 7/34, etc., ʒeare 3/24 [OE *gē(a)r*].

ʒerne⁴, eagerly 12/15, 93, 15/10, yorne 20/1 [OE *géorne*].

ʒerrndesst. *See* ʒiernen.

ʒet(e), yete, ʒit, ʒut(e)⁴, yet, up to now 5/7, 47, 6/238, 240, etc., get 2/3n, 11/59, gæt 2/95, in addition 6/173, 15/3, again 9/96, 15/19 [OE *gēt(a)*, *gī(e)t*, *gȳt*].

ʒettunge¹, acquiescence 17/60 [OE *gēat-an* + *-ung*].

ʒiernen³, to desire 16/51; yhernes 3*pr.* 22/1; ʒerrndesst 2*pt.* 15/12 [OE *géornan* A].

ʒif. *See* ʒef.

ʒimston¹, gem, precious stone 6/144; -stanes *pl.* 18/9 [OE *gimstān*].

ʒinge; ʒit. *See* ʒunge; ʒet(e).

ʒiue(n), yeue³, to give 10/189, 16/51, 19/13, 59, gyuen 2/40, ʒeue 9/164, ʒeoue 17/125, gef 38/58; yefþ 3*pr.* 19/82; ʒiueþ, ʒeueþ 3*prpl.* 10/195, 198; ʒeue, yeue 3*prs.* 7/90, 8/22, 12/34, 20/209; gef, yef *imp.* 19/16, grant 38/80, 81; ʒaf 3*pt.* 9/46, 10/55, etc., gaf 8/190, yaf 19/18; iafen, yeuen 3*ptpl.* 2/9, 8/218 [OE *g(i)efan* 5].

ʒiuernesse¹, greed 21/15 [OE *gīfernes*].

ʒiueðe¹, gift; *wes ʒiueðe*, was given 6/96 [OE *gifeðe*].

ʒond⁷, throughout 6/14 [OE *g(e)ond*].

ʒoʒelinge¹, guggling 10/40 [imitative].

ʒong¹, walk, gait 35/14 [OA *geong*, *-iong*].

ʒonge³, to go 12/61 [OA *geonga* 7].

ʒongling¹, youth 9/67 [OE *geongling*].

ʒore. *See* ʒare⁴.

ʒunge, yung(e)², young 8/30, 116, etc., ʒonge 5/24, ʒynge 7/88; ʒungen *dpl.* 6/39 [OE *geong*, *gung*, *ging*].

ʒungemen¹ *pl.*, young men 21/21, 61, etc. [OE *gung* + *menn*].

ʒut(e). *See* ʒet(e).

ha. *See* heo; hi.

habbe(n), haue(n)³, to have, possess, get, take 4/11, 6/119, etc., abbe 5/110, han 12/87, hafenn 15/72, 76, haf 38/30, 54, 62; habbe, haue 1*pr.* 7/33, 42, 8/268, etc., abbe 5/114, 115, hafe 15/6, 7, etc., haw 38/46; hauest 2*pr.* 12/47, 54, etc., hastu 38/12, hafs 38/66; haueþ, hafeð, haþ 3*pr.* 4/10, 25, 6/73, 117, etc., hafð 16/5, 7, has 22/31, ha 31/9, hauet 33/42, 44; habbeþ 1*prpl.* 19/23, 61, hafenn 15/4, habeþ 19/67; habbeþ 2*prpl.* 9/10, 181, etc., haue(n) 8/259, 270; habbeþ 3*prpl.* 3/7, 6/223, etc., habbeoð 6/165, 223, hauen 11/100n, han 28/57, 59, haueþ 36/38, haf 38/29, as 38/83; habbe 2*prs.* 17/123, 20/159, 3*prs.* 32/17, 32, abbe 5/45; haue *imp.* 9/47, 16/4, 10, 14, haw 27/6; habbeþ *imppl.* 5/54; hedde heuede 1*pt.* 12/134, 135; heuedest 2*pt.* 12/177; hedde, heuede hadde, hauede, 3*pt.* 2/3, 7/63 8/90, 202, etc., hafuede 6/109 hafden 6/152, hafde 6/209 hede 12/288, hefde 18/23; hed den, hadde(n) 3*ptpl.* 2/11, 19/20 etc., hefden 2/18, adde 5/33 afden 6/0 9, haueden 8/112 265; ihaued *ptp.* 13/63 [OE *habban* C].

ꞕad¹, order (of canons) 15/5 [OE *hād*].

ꞕæʒe, hæʒere, hæh, hæhʒere. *See* heh.

ꞕælden³, to bend, incline 6/85; **halde** 3*pt.*, followed 6/111, poured 21/60; **halden** 3*ptpl.*, advanced 6/193 [OA *hældan* A].

ꞕæne², mean, humble 6/119 [OE *hēan*].

ꞕærnes, hernes¹ *pl.*, brains 2/25, 8/181 [ON *hjarni*].

ꞕæþeliʒ⁴, contemptuously 15/40 [ON *hæðiliga*].

ꞕæued; haf, hafenn; hafde; hafde(n). *See* heaued; habbe(n); heaued; habbe(n).

ꞕaʒel¹, hail 10/98 [OE *hagol*].

ꞕay⁹, alas 38/18 [obscure].

ꞕayse. *See* eise.

ꞕaiward, -wart¹, hayward, man responsible for hedges, 12/26, 31/24, 27 [OE *hægw(e)ard*].

ꞕal², whole 6/228 [OE *hāl*].

ꞕald, halde(n), haldeþ. *See* holde(n).

ꞕale¹, corner, nook 10/2 [OE *h(e)alh*].

ꞕalechen¹ *pl.*, saints 2/57 [OE *hālga*].

ꞕaleð³ 3*pr.*, carries 11/8 [OF *haler*].

ꞕaleweiʒe², healing 6/228n.

ꞕalf¹, half 2/59, 12/4, 8, side 5/17, 42, 18/10; **heluen** *dpl.*, sides 6/135; *a Godes half*, for the sake of God 5/34; *o fowr half*, in every direction 17/91 [OE *h(e)alf*].

ꞕali, holi², holy 2/83, 8/36, etc. **hallʒhe** 15/7, etc., **aly**, god-fearing 38/84; *holi bok*, bible 13/136 [OE *hālig*; *hālga*].

ꞕalymotes¹ *pl.*, manorial courts 32/28 [OE *h(e)all* + *gemōt*].

ꞕalle¹, hall 21/40, 43, 59 [OE *h(e)all*].

ꞕalm; halp. *See* helm; helpe(n).

ꞕals¹, neck 2/33 [OE *h(e)als*].

ꞕalsinde³ *prp.*, heart-felt 17/89;

halse *imp.*, pray 17/106 [OE *h(e)alsian* B].

halt. *See* holde(n).

halter¹, halter 10/124 [OE *hælfter*].

ham, hamsuluen; ham; hame; han; hand; handes. *See* hi; am; hom; habbe(n); an⁸; hond.

hand-dede¹ *pl.*, deeds 8/92 [OE *hánd* + *dǣd*].

handiwerc, hond-,¹ handiwork 16/10, 18/44 [OE *hándgeweorc*].

hantit, hauntes³ 3*pr.*, practises 37/18, frequents 38/41 [OF *hanter*].

harde², rough 5/79, cruel 35/18, 36/6 [OE *h(e)ard*].

harde⁴, heavily 12/195 [OE *h(e)arde*].

hardi², firm, strong 17/103 [OF *hardi*].

hare. *See* hi.

harm¹, harm 10/155, 16/32 [OE *h(e)arm*].

harm-dedes¹ *pl.*, harmful deeds 11/3 [OE *h(e)arm* + *dǣd*].

harpe¹, harp 10/22, 24 [OE *h(e)arpe*].

harping¹, harping 8/238 [OE *h(e)arpung*].

hasard¹, game at dice 8/239 [OF *hasard*].

hasel¹, hazel tree 13/3 [OE *hæsel*].

hasel-bou¹, hazel bough 13/106 [OE *hæsel* + *bōg*].

hat², eager 17/86 [OE *hāt*].

hate¹, hate 20/131 [OE *hete* infl. by *hatian*].

hatien³, to hate 17/48; **hate** 1*pr.* 29/1; **hates** 2*pr.* 38/20; -eþ, -ieð 3*pr.* 11/8, 19/89; -ieþ 2*prpl.* 19/89; -en, -ien 3*prpl.* 11/3, 9; -ed 3*pt.* 8/40 [OE *hatian* B].

hat(te). *See* hote.

hattren¹ *pl.*, clothes 31/6 [OE *hæteru* pl.]

haue(n). *See* habbe(n).

hauekes¹ *pl.*, hawks 6/101, 104, 35/2, 15 [OE *hafoc*].

hauntes; he. *See* hantit; hi; heo.

he[5], he, it, 1/2, 4, 2/2, 6/11, etc., ha 19/7, 8, etc., a 19/57; hine *am.* 6/33, 34, 7/89, etc.; his, is *g.* 2/3, 5, 14, 4/9, etc., hise, ise 2/9, 3/3, 7/23, 8/34, 19/53, hijs 8/47; him *a/d.* 2/12, 14, etc., *ethic d.* 4/19, 5/14, 21, etc.; *refl.* hine 6/60, 61, etc., him 11/40, 18/17, himself 12/126, -selue(n) 7/46, 16/33, 34, -selwen 35/52, -seolf 17/118, -sulf 17/3, -sulue 5/83 [OE *hē, hine, his, him*].

healden. *See* holde(n).

healent[1], Saviour 18/63 [OE *hǣlend*].

heastes[1] *pl.*, commandments 18/35 [OE *bǣs*].

heaued, heued[1], head 5/76, 8/185, 10/74, etc., hefed 2/23, hæued 2/24, hafde 6/143, hed 32/32 [OE *hēafod*].

heddre; hede; heffne. *See* eddre; eode; heouene.

hegge[1], hedge 10/17, 59, 31/8 [OE *hecg*].

heglice[4], with great ceremony 2/84 [OE *hē(a)hlice*].

heh, hei(e)[2], high, lofty, noble 12/31, 15/33, 17/5, etc., hæȝe 6/85, hæh 6/143, 163, heȝe 6/205, 32/32, hehe 18/26, heiȝ 21/19; heȝes *g.* 6/23; hæȝere, hæhȝere, haȝere *df.* 6/47, valiant 6/94, loud 6/129; *on heh, an hei, vpon hep,* loudly 5/53, 18/63, 31/35; heier *comp.* 16/37; heste *sup.* 28/36 [OE *hē(a)h*].

hehte. *See* hote.

heye[4], aloft, on high 8/43, 20/208, haughtily 35/10 [OE *hē(a)h*].

heiemen[1] *pl.*, nobles 5/4 [OE *hē(a)h + mann*].

heieð[3] *3prpl.*, exalt 18/32 [OE *hēan* A].

heiȝte. *See* hote.

heil[2], safe 11/76 [ON *heill*].

heyse; heyte; held, helden. *See* eise; hote; holde(n).

hele[1], health, safety 28/72 [OE *hǣlu*].

hele(n)[3], to heal 8/209, 13/153; -eþ *3pr.* 20/156; -ede *3pt.* 13/119 [OE *hǣlan* A].

hele[3], to conceal 20/63; -ieð *3prpl.* 17/46; -ien *3prspl.* 17/47; hel *imp.* 38/40; helede *3pt.*, protected 6/140 [OE *helan* 4, *helian* B].

helen[1] *pl.*, heels 18/57 [OE *hēla*].

helle[1], hell 8/16, 11/44, etc. [OE *hell*].

helle-dogge[1], dog of hell 17/91 [OE *helle docga*].

helle-ware[1] *pl.*, inhabitants of hell 18/29 [OE *hell-wara*].

helm, halm[1], helmet 6/143, 21/77; helmen *dpl.* 6/194 [OE *helm*].

help(e)[1], help, assistance 15/13, 45, 17/86, etc.; *to help of*, to the help of 4/32 [OE *help*].

helpe(n)[3], to help, avail 4/17, 37, 10/141, 15/24, 46; -eþ *3pr.* 20/63, 29/4, 8, helpit 34/5; help(e) *3prs.* 3/15, 38/61; help *imp.* 18/31, 44, 46, 35/58, 36/46; help, halp *3pt.* 9/123, 12/84, 17/34; hollpenn *ptp.* 15/71 [OE *helpan* 3].

hem(m), hemself. *See* hi.

hemme[1], dress 20/167 [OE *hem(m)*].

hen[1], hen 12/7; hennen *pl.* 12/28, 32, 35, 40 [OE *henn*].

hende. *See* ende.

hende[2], gracious 7/11, 13/10, 78, 38/50, courteous 9/22, 20/197, 33/41, gentle 9/182, 13/26, near 7/31; hendeste *sup.*, bravest 6/92, most courteous 21/33. As[1], fair one 28/55, 66 [OE *(ge)hénde*].

hendinese[1], politeness 13/101 [OE *(ge)hénde + -ig + -nes*].

heng, hengen[3], to hang 8/43, 38/80; heng, henged *3pt.* 2/21, 22, 6/147; hengen *3ptpl.* 2/23,

81; heng *ptp.* 38/82 [OE *hōn,*
hēng, 7; ON *hengja*].

enne, h(e)onne⁴, hence, away
4/26, 8/172, 10/66, 20/26 [OE
heonan].

ente³, to take, seize 28/71; hent
ptp 28/55 [OE *hentan* A].

eo. See hi.

eo⁵, she, her 6/227, 9/53, 180, etc.,
he 9/86, 20/56, 29/7, 32/14, 17,
20, 32, hoe 6/22, 13/15, 80, hue
7/5, 28/28, etc., hi 10/10, 29,
30, 32, 14/106, etc., ho 10/19,
33, etc., ge 11/5, etc., ha 17/101,
18/3, 4, etc., yo 38/47, 49, 51;
hire *g/d.* 6/35. 7/15, 9/11, etc.,
hure 9/134, ire 13/176, here
22/18, hir 38/51; *refl.* hire 16/3,
13, 17/62, 98, 32/13, hireselue
7/98 [OE *hēo, hī(e); heore, hire*].

eold, heolde(n); heom; heonne;
heore. See holde(n); hi; henne;
hi.

eorte, herte¹, heart 6/219, 7/44,
92, 101, etc., horte 10/37, 43,
huerte 28/56, 72 [OE *heorte*].

eorte-scheld¹, a shield for the
heart 17/126 [OE *heorte* + nWS
scéld].

eouen³, to raise 17/102; heueð
3pr. 17/5; hef *imp.* 17/103, 132;
3pt. 18/25; heuen *3ptpl.* 6/193;
heueð to heie up, exaggerates 17/5
[OE *hebban* 6].

eouene, heuene¹, heaven 8/62,
9/186, 16/46, etc., heffne 15/73,
efne 38/25 [OE *heofon*].

eowe, hewe¹, hue, appearance
13/40, 20/91 [OE *hēow*].

er. See er(e)⁸.

er(e)⁴, here 1/1, 3/19, 4/29, etc.,
ere 6/0 11 [OE *hēr*].

erandbere¹, go-between 38/56
[OE *ǣrend-* + *-bāre*].

erbherg³, to harbour 38/9 [OE
herebe(o)rgian B].

erbifore⁴, previously 12/222 [OE
hērbeforan].

hercneð³ *3prpl.*, listen 17/18;
hærcne, herkne *imp.* 6/36,
13/112, 147; herkneþ, -et *imppl.*
4/1, 8/1 [OE *he(o)rcnian* B].

here. See hi; heo.

here¹, host 10/212, ravaging 8/66
[OE *here*].

here¹, hairshirt 5/79 [OE *hǣr*].

here(n)³, to hear, listen to 8/4, 241,
15/70, etc.; here 1*pr.* 12/128,
22/12; -eþ *3pr.* 31/33; -enn
3prspl. 15/46; her *imp.* 18/46,
38/26; herde, herdi 1*pt.* 13/7,
100; *3pt.* 12/170; *3ptpl.* 9/119;
(i)herd *ptp.* 8/259, 270, 9/10,
181, 19/86, ihert 10/185, iheerd
19/56 [nWS *hēran* A].

here³, to hire 19/5; herde *3pts.*
19/12 [OE *hȳran,* OK **hēran* A].

heredmen¹ *pl.*, retinue 6/205 [OE
hīredman].

here-marken¹ *pl.*, banners 6/193
[OE *here* + *m(e)arc*].

herhedest³ 2*pt.*, harrowed 18/45
[OE *hergian* A].

herien³, to praise 13/37, be praised
17/41; heriende *prp.* 18/63;
hereþ *3pr.* 13/10; -ieþ *3prpl.*
18/32; iherd, yheryed *ptp.*
13/149, 28/36 [OE *herian* B].

herinne⁴, herein 9/44, 12/104,
17/75 [OE *hērinne*].

heryng¹, herring 20/86 [OE *hǣr-
ing*].

hernes. See hærnes.

herof⁴, of this 17/35, 20/197 [OE
hērof].

herone⁴, herein 17/35 [OE *hēron*].

hers. See ers.

hersum², obedient 16/62 [nWS
hērsum].

herte; hertou. See heorte; art.

herunge¹, praise 17/6 [OE *herung*].

herut⁴, out of here 17/75 [OE *hēr*
+ *ūt*].

heste; het. See heh; hote.

het = he it 15/49, 54.

hete¹, heat 19/24, 76 [OE *hǣtu*].

heten. *See* eten.

heterliche⁴, fiercely 17/78 [cf. OE *hetelīce*].

heþ. *See* heh.

heþen², heathen 2/46, 19/45, 59 [OE *hǣþen*].

heued; heuen; heuene. *See* heaued; heouen; heouene.

heueneking¹, king of heaven 33/30 [OE *heofoncyning*].

heuer(e); heuereuchon. *See* euer(e); eueruchon.

heueriche¹ *g.*, of the kingdom of heaven 19/59, 64, 92 [OE *heofonrīce*].

heueð. *See* heouen.

heui², heavy 8/133, 157, 12/278 [OE *hefig*].

hewe³ *ptp.*, cut, hewn 31/23 [OE *hēawan* 7].

hewe. *See* heowe.

hi, hie, he, heo⁵, they 2/9, 13, 3/11, 16/8, etc., hii 5/3, 5, 25, etc., ho 10/66, 76, etc., hoe 12/264, 13/10, 22, 23, 77, ha 17/109, 114, 117, 18/39, i 19/57; hi *apl.*, them 2/40, 14/30, etc., hij 19/55, is 11/8, his 19/22; here, heore, hoere, *gpl.*, their 1/16, 2/9, 12/272, etc., her 2/23, hare 4/15, hor 5/2, 3, hore 5/45, 49, 17/19, 44; hem, hemm, heom, ham *dpl.*, them 2/19, 8/38, 15/77, 17/18, etc., hom 5/5, 17, 33, 10/62; *refl.* heom 6/54, hom 5/31, hem 8/69, 13/162, 19/21, hemself 13/56, hamsuluen 17/46 [OE *hīe, hēo; heora; hīom*].

hi; hic; hidden. *See* heo; ic; hude(n).

hider⁴, hither 6/18, 7/72, 21/47, 50, 38/53 [OE *hider*].

hydeward⁴, hither 7/12 [OE *hiderw(e)ard*].

hidut; hie. *See* dutten; hi.

hye³, to hasten 31/35; hyeþ 3*pr* 20/21 [OE *hīgian* B].

hierto⁴, for this 16/62 [OE *hērtō*].

hif. *See* ʒef.

hihendliche⁴, quickly 18/4 [O *hīgendlīce*].

hilke; hir(e), hireselue. *See* ilke heo.

hire¹, wages 38/12n [OE *hȳr*]

hired¹, retinue, court 6/47, 51 [O *hīred*].

his; his, hiis. *See* hi; is.

hit, it⁵, it 1/16, 2/4, 24, 3/14, etc as anticipated subject, there (are) 8/27, 126, 11/77, etc.; his, its 6/148, 22/36; him *d.* 9/54, 5 12/261, etc. [OE *hit, his, him*].

hiþte¹, effort 31/11 [OE *hīgþ*].

hlauerd; ho. *See* louerd; heo; wha; on⁷.

ho⁹, oh 35/22.

hoal⁹, hail to 16/61 [OE *hāl*].

hode¹, hood 28/18 [OE *hōd*].

hoe; hoe; hoeld; hoere; hof. hi; heo; holde(n); hi; of.

hofþurst³ *ptp.*, thirsty 12/273 [O *ofþyrst*].

hoked(e)², hooked 10/79, 18/ [OE *hōced*].

hoker¹, derision 17/93 [OE *hocor*

hold², loyal; *his soule hold*, caref of the good of his soul 8/74 [O *hōld*].

holde¹ *pl.*, vassals 3/3 [OE *hōld*]

hold(e). *See* old(e).

holde(n), halden³, to hold, ke 3/22, 8/29, 9/108, etc., healde 3/12, esteem, regard 6/11 13/144, embrace 28/25, imprise 29/20; holde 1*pr.*, mainta 13/53, 87; halt, holdeþ 3*f* 19/94, 20/102n, 32/32, esteen regards 10/32, 13/59, obe 18/35; holdeþ 3*prpl.* 5/5, 13/1(holde 1*prs.* 10/59; 3*prs.* 17/4 healden 3*prspl.* 3/12, accou 3/20; hald, hold *imp.* 6/22 17/133, 27/5; heold 3*pt.* 2/9 61, 71, 6/47, heolde, went 6/18 held, ruled 8/61, hoeld, kept 12/5; heolden, heldeη 3*pt*

2/13, 8/69, **holde** 10/12, garri-
soned 2/14, held (to him) 19/41;
holde 1*pts.* 10/51; **iholde** *ptp.*,
accounted 10/145; *halдеð after*,
pursue 6/101; *holdeþ to*, keep to
5/7,9; *holdeð feor*, restrain 17/50;
hald up, lift 17/80 [OE *h(e)áldan*
7].
hole[1], hole 11/8, 18/52, **hol** 6/132,
holle 6/133, eye-socket 8/186,
wound 17/121; **holзes** *pl.* 6/125
[OE *hol*, *holh*].
holi. *See* **hali.**
holme[1], hill 6/132 [ON *holm-r*].
hollpenn. *See* **helpe(n).**
holte[1], wood 6/80 [OE *holt*].
hom. *See* **hi.**
hom[1], home 9/163, 178, 10/173,
etc., hame 38/4, 30, atom = at
hom, in their own country 5/3
[OE *hám*].
hond, hand[1], hand 8/50, 175,
9/107, etc., power 5/1; **honde,
honden** *pl.* 5/73, 12/102, etc.;
beren an honden, possessed 6/43;
handes sprede, to surrender 8/95;
hauede in his hond, ruled 8/107;
sholden in honde haue, should have
work in hand 8/127; *þurh his
honde*, because of his deeds
10/179; *bald of hand*, bold in arms
22/7; *in honde*, into her possession
28/55 [OE *hánd*, *hónd*].
hond-habbing[2], red-handed 9/30
[OE *hándhabbend*].
hondiwerc; honger. *See* **handiwerc; hungær.**
honge, hongi[3], to hang 5/115,
12/88, 232; **hongeþ** 3*pr.* 32/23
[OE *hángian* B].
honne. *See* **henne.**
honur[1], honour 9/9, 179 [OF
honour].
honoure[3], to honour 32/16; 3*prs.*
28/20 [OF *honourer*].
hope[1], hope 11/111, 16/11, 18/45;
for hope, in hope 31/14 [OE
hopa].

hope[3], to hope 5/47; **hopieð** 1*prpl.*
19/64; 3*prpl.* 16/18; **hopede** 3*pt.*
5/39, 12/79 [OE *hopian* B].
hor, hore. *See* **hi.**
hord[1], treasure 13/142, 28/71, safe-
keeping, archives 3/22 [OE
hórd].
horderwycan[1] *d.*, office of chamberlain 2/69n [OE *hórdere* + *wīce*].
hordom[1], adultery 9/16 [ON *hór-
dóm-r*].
hore[1], harlot 17/100 [OE *hōre*,
from ON *hóra*].
horn(e)[1], horn (drinking) 7/5, 15,
etc.; -en, -es *pl.*, horns (musical
6/129, 23/1 [OE *hórn*].
hors[1], horse 6/94, 8/94, 29/12
[OE *hors*].
horse-knaue[1], groom 8/126 [OE
hors + *cnafa*].
horte. *See* **heorte.**
hosebonde[1], husband 27/3; **husebondes**, farmers 11/3 [OE
húsbónda].
hosede[3] *ptp.*, wearing hose 31/37
[cf. OE *hosa*].
hosen[1] *pl.*, hose, greaves 6/140
[OE *hosa*].
host, ost[1], army 4/18, 5/14, 24, etc.
[OF *(h)ost*].
hot[1], heat 20/78 [OE *hát*].
hote[3] 1*pr.*, command, be named
12/36; **hot, hoot** 3*pr.* 19/90, 91;
hoaten, hoteþ 1*prpl.* 1/6, 3/10,
19; **hoteþ** 3*prpl.* 1/4; **hat** *imp.*
17/78; **hat, hatte** *passive* 2/86,
6/187, 38/47; **het** 3*pt.* 9/75, 121;
hehte, heiзte, heyte *pt. passive*,
was called 6/217, 12/271, 21/53;
ihote(n), ihate(n), *ptp.* 5/19,
6/1, 8, etc., **hi-hote** 6/08, **hote**
6/0 1 [OE *hátan* 7].
hotest[2] *sup.*, hottest 19/74 [OE
hát].
hou. *See* **hu.**
houene-tinge[2], reaching to the
heavens 10/97 [OE *heofone (ge)-
tenge*].

houeð³ *3pr.*, hovers 11/83; hoven *3prpl.* 11/69 [obscure].

houle; hounderstod; houndes; houndret; hounger. *See* ule; understanden; hundes; hundred; hungær.

houpbringe³, to bring up 12/126 [OE *úp + bríngan* 3].

houre; hous(e). *See* we; hus(e).

houssong(e)¹, matins 12/265, 270, 274 [OE *úhtsáng*].

hout. *See* ut.

hu, hou⁸, how, in what way 5/55, 7/72, 13/117, etc., hw 8/93, 14/15, etc., hwou 8/262, 267, ou 12/230, wou 27/2 [OE *hú*].

huckel¹, guise, appearance 17/29 [obscure].

hude(n)³, to hide 17/108, 32/14; hud *imp.* 17/111, 120; hidden *3ptpl.* 8/69 [OE *hýdan* A].

hudles¹ *pl.*, refuges, hiding-places 17/122 [OE *hýdels*].

hue; huerte. *See* heo; heorte.

hul¹, hill 21/19 [OE *hyll*].

hule. *See* ule.

hundes, houndes¹ *pl.*, hounds 6/102, 104, 130, 8/244, etc.; hunden *dpl.* 6/129 [OE *húnd*].

hundred¹, hundred 6/168, 212, 16/5, oundred 12/8, houndret 13/160 [OE *húndred*].

hundredfolde¹,   hundredfold 20/179 [OE *húndred* + OA *fáld*].

hungær, hunger¹, hunger 2/35, 44, 8/66, 11/10, hounger 12/13, 68, etc., honger 12/112 [OE *húngor*].

hungren³, to hunger 11/101; -eð *3pr.* 11/64 [OE *hyngrian* B].

hunke. *See* unnc.

hunten¹ *pl.*, huntsmen 6/130 [OE *hunta*].

huntseuenti², seventy 14/29n [OE *hundseofontig*].

hup. *See* up.

hupe³ *imp.*, hop, come 31/37 [OE **hyppan*, cf. *hoppian* B].

hurde¹, shepherd 14/10 [WS *hierde*].

hure. *See* heo; we.

hure⁴, certainly 10/11 [OE *húru*].

hurne¹, corner 10/14, 18/4 [OE *hýrne*].

hus(e), hous(e)¹, house 12/11, 27, 15/3, 31/27, 38/9, monastery 2/61, 12/261 [OE *hús*].

husebondes; hut. *See* hosebonde; ut.

huten³, to revile 11/4 [cf. Sw *hutta*].

hw; hw-. *See* hu; wh-.

hwile-stucche¹, fraction of time 17/95 [OE *hwílsticce*].

hwilynde³ *prp.*, in a transitory way 20/33 [cf. OE. *hwílende*].

i, in, ine⁷, in 2/41, 61, 84, 3/10, 22, 4/4, 6/18, etc., on, upon 5/17, 42, 58, 6/162, 10/172, 176, 20/38, 21/24, 37/14, 38/9, into 2/9, 19, 25, 6/61, 7/58, etc., during, in the course of 3/23, 12/111, 17/129, 18/47, 19/39, etc., at 20/45, 29/23, with 17/77, for 3/7, throughout 5/8, 15/16, by 3/11, from 11/5, in front of 17/133; *in tresour*, as a treasure 13/144; *ine is seruise*, to do his work 19/35 [OE *in*].

i; iafen. *See* ic; hi; ʒiue(n).

iay¹, jay 28/39 [OF *jay*].

iaspe¹, jasper 20/115, 173 [OF *jaspre*].

iauhteþ³ *3pr.*, chooses 14/69 [OE *ge-(e)ahtian* B].

ibe; ibede(n); iben. *See* be(n); bidde(n); be(n).

iber³ *3pt.*, bore 6/34 [OE *geberan* 4].

ibiden³, to suffer 6/76; ibod *3pt.*, possessed 9/166 [OE *gebídan* 1].

ibye, ibien. *See* be(n).

ibite³, to drink 7/25 [OE *gebítan* 1].

iblesced; ibore(n). *See* blesce; beren.

ibred³ *ptp.*, bred 10/146 [OE *ge* + *brédan* A].

ibringe³ 3*prs.*, may persuade 10/119 [OE *gebringan* 3].

ibroȝt. *See* bringe.

ibroide³ *ptp.*, made of rings 6/137 [OE *bregdan* 3].

ibroke; ibrouȝt, ibrouht, ibrout. *See* breke; bringe.

ibuld³ *ptp.*, built 9/5 [OE *býldan* A].

ic, ich, I⁵, I 2/35, 5/8, 111, 7/27, etc., ihc 9/11, 83, 12/159, etc., hic 13/7, 19/13, 26, etc., hi 13/187, 38/15, 17, etc.; coalescing with following word in Icham, Ichot, q.v.; me *a/d.* 4/1, 5/111, 7/12, etc.; mi, min(e) *poss.* 4/2, 5/115, 6/116, etc.; mire *df.* 6/118, 10/163; *refl.* me 18/53, meseoluen 6/118, miself 9/93, mesellfenn 15/22 [OE *ic, mē, mīn*].

icast(e). *See* caste.

icham³ 1*pr.*, I am 7/28, 35, 13/184, etc. [OA *ic am*].

icheose³, to choose 14/106; -eþ 3*pr.* 14/71 [OE *gecēosan* 2].

ichosen. *See* cheose.

ichot³ 1*pr.*, I know 28/5, 31/22, 34, etc. [OE *ic wāt*].

icleoped, iclepede; icnowe; icome(n); icoren(e). *See* clepe; knawe; cumen; cheose.

icoren, excellent 6/241. *See* cheose.

icouere³, to gain, win 14/107 [cf. OE *acofrian* B].

icrope; icume(n). *See* crepen; cumen.

icundur² *comp.*, more suitable 10/85 [OE *gecýnde*].

icweme³, to please 10/206 [OE *gecwēman* A].

idel², idle, unemployed 17/49, 19/10, 45, etc., lying 11/38, useless 15/41 [OE *īdel*].

idelnesse¹, vanity, emptiness 19/52 [OE *īdelnes*].

idemed; idihte; ido(n); idoluen; ieden. *See* deme; diht; do(n); duluen; yede.

i-entred³ *ptp.*, entered 19/62 [OE *ge-* + OF *entrer*].

ierðe; i-ete; if. *See* eorðe; eten; ȝef.

ifaie⁴, gladly 12/199 [OE *gefægen*].

ifere¹, comrade, companion 7/23, 12/172, 185; *pl.* 13/18 [OE *gefēra*].

ifere⁴, in company 13/9, 35/20 [predicative use of OE *gefēra*].

ifo³, to receive 9/56 [OE *gefōn*].

ifoan, iuan¹ *pl.*, enemies 3/20, 6/70 [OE *gefāh*].

ifonge; ifounde; ifuld; ifunde. *See* foangen; finde(n); fillen; finde(n).

ifurn⁴, formerly 14/100 [OE *gefýrn*].

igan; iglyden; igo(n). *See* go(n); glides; go(n).

igretinge¹ *pl.*, greetings 3/3 [OE *ge-* + *grēting*].

igranted. *See* granti.

ygraued, igrauen³ *ptp.*, engraved 6/149, 7/62 [OE *grafan* 6].

iȝolde; ihate(n); ihaued; iheerd, iherd. *See* geld; hote; habbe(n); here(n).

iherde, iherede, ihierde³ 3*pt.*, hired 19/34, 38, 42; iherd *ptp.* 19/55 [OE *gehýran*, OK *gehēran* A].

ihere³, to hear 8/11, 9/24, 10/120, etc., ihure 14/14; 1*pr.* 12/119; -eð 3*pr.* 17/53; *imppl.* 19/30; iherde 1*pt.* 10/3; 3*pt.* 6/184, 12/113, 21/55 [WS *gehīeran*, nWS *gehēran* A].

ihert; iholde; ihote(n); ihure. *See* here(n); holde(n); hote; ihere.

ihurnde², horned 18/10 [OE *gehýrned*].

ikaut, ikeiht³ *ptp.*, caught 12/86, 103; *habbeð swuch word ikeiht*, has such a reputation 17/34 [OF *cachier*, infl. by ME *la(c)chen*].

ikennen³, to distinguish 6/199 [OE *gecennan* A, ON *kenna*].

iknede[3] *ptp.*, kneaded 12/256 [OE *cnedan* 5].

iknowe[3] 2*prs.*, may realize 20/89; **ikneu** 3*pt.*, recognized 12/123 [OE *gecnāwan* 7].

iknowe; ilad; ilærde. *See* **knawe; lede(n); lere(n).**

ilærde[1], clergy 3/3 [OE *gelǣred*].

ilast, ilest[3] 3*pr.*, lasts 10/134, 25/1, is remembered 6/187, remains 20/22; **ilestinde** *prp.* 3/9 [OE *gelǣstan* A].

ilc(e), ilche. *See* **ilke.**

ile[1], sole (of the foot) 18/57 [OE *ile*].

ileawede[1], laity 3/3 [OE *ge-* + *lǣwede*].

ileorne[3], to learn 20/3 [OE *geléornian* B].

ilerde; ilest, ilestinde; ilet; ileued. *See* **lere(n); ilast; læten; leuen.**

ileueð[3] 3*prpl.*, believe 6/238 [nWS *gelēfan* A].

ilik[2], like 11/45 [OE *gelīc*].

ilka. *See* **ilkon.**

ilke[2], same, very (after þe, þis, þat, etc.) 6/187, 12/47, 99, etc., **ilche** 3/16, 34, **ilce** 2/80, **hilke** 6/0 28, **þilke** 7/68, 99, 9/154, etc., **þulke** 5/5, 59, 101 [OE *ilca, ylca*].

ilke[5], each, everyone 8/271, **ilc** 8/163, 15/34 [OE *ilca*].

ilkon[5], everyone 8/215, 22/25, **ilka** 22/34 [OE *ilc* + *ān*].

ille[2], stormy 11/84, sinful 13/72 [ON *ill-r*].

illing[1], evil 11/21 [ON *ill-r* + *-ing*].

iloke[3] *ptp.*, closed 12/20 [OE *gelūcan* 2].

iloket. *See* **loke.**

ilome[2], often 10/49, 187, 190 [OE *gelōme*].

imad, imaked(e). *See* **make(n).**

imeind, imenged[3], *ptp.*, mixed, mingled with 6/200, 10/18 [OE *méngan* A].

imeteð[3] 3*prpl.*, meet 6/102; **imetten** 3*ptpl.* 6/54 [OE *gemētan* A].

imetliche[2], of moderate size 6/179 [OE *gemetlic*].

imunt; in, ine. *See* **mint; i.**

inne(n)[4], in, inside, within 6/149, 160, 12/23, 71, **ine** 12/162, 19/79, **in** 18/57, 21/38; *þar, þet, þer* . . . *inne*, wherein, in which 2/26 17/58, 18/52 [OE *innan*].

inch[1], inch 8/141 [OE *ynce*, from L *uncia*].

inoh, inou, inouh[2], enough, much 5/84, 8/125, 12/24, etc., very 5/14, 87, 90, in plenty 12/288; **inoʒe** *pl.*, many 3/33, 6/123; *hadden onoh*, had enough (to do) 2/31; *inouh reðe*, quickly enough 17/4 [OE *genōg, genōh*].

inome. *See* **nimen.**

intel, inntill[7], to, into 3/35, 15/7, 65, 74 [OE *in* + ON *til*].

into[7], in, into 2/63, 5/1, 49, 6/108, etc., to 3/34, 5/36, 10/92, as far as 10/180, (to go) into, (to work) in 19/6, 34, 38, etc. [OE *intō*].

inward[4], inside 17/76 [OE *in-w(e)ard*].

ioye[1], joy, pleasure 8/234, 247, 13/102, etc.; **ioies** *pl.* 12/166 [OF *joie*].

iolyf[2], lively 28/39 [OF *jolif*].

ioustynde[2], padded 32/24n [OF *jouster*].

ipaied. *See* **paide.**

ipeint[3] *ptp.*, painted 10/76 [OF *peindre*].

iradi[2], ready 16/56, 62 [OE *gerǣde* + *-ig*].

ire. *See* **heo.**

iren, irn[1], iron 18/8, iron collar 2/32, 34 [OE *īren*].

iryhte[1], rights 20/130 [OE *gerihte*].

is. *See* **he; hi.**

is[3] 3*pr.*, is 1/5, 17, 2/27, etc., his 10/183, 33/41, **hiis** 12/106 [OE *is*].

isæh, isah. *See* iseo(n).

iscapen³ *ptp.*, created 16/6, 9, 15 [WS *gescieppan* 6].

iscrud; ise. *See* shrude; he.

ise¹, iron 10/126n [OE *īsen*].

isechen³, to seek, approach 6/170; -eð 3*pr.* 6/124, 132 [OE *gesēcan* A].

ised. *See* segge(n).

iseene², evident 13/165 [nWS *gesēne*].

iseʒ, isei(e); iseid. *See* iseo(n); segge(n).

iseined³ *ptp.*, sealed 3/21 [OF *seignier*].

isemed. *See* seme.

isemeliche⁴, peacefully 6/180 [OE *gesēm-an* + *-līce*].

isend. *See* sende(n).

iseo(n)³, to see 6/75, 20/39, 137, ise 5/88, iseen 35/59; isiist 2*pr.* 12/232; isihð 3*pr.* 17/53, 20/140; iseo *imppl.* 6/69; isei 3*pt.* 5/36, 92, 12/280, isæh 6/59, 155, isah 6/66, 91, iseʒ 10/20; iseye 3*ptpl.* 21/25; iseie 1*pts.* 12/218 [OE *gesēon* 5].

iserued; iset. *See* serue; setten.

isetnesses¹ *pl.*, terms of agreement 3/12 [OE *gesetnes*].

ishend. *See* shende.

ishilde³ 3*prs.*, may protect 13/177 [OE *gescīldan* A].

ishote; isiist, isīhð; islaʒe, islawe; isold. *See* scheate; iseo(n); slein; sellen.

isome², peaceable 10/157 [OE *gesōm*].

isomned³ *ptp.*, joined 6/176, gathered together 6/188 [OE *samnian* B].

isouʒt; isowen; ispild; isriue; istonden. *See* seche; sowe; spille; sriue; stonde(n).

istounge³ *ptp.*, stabbed 12/292 [OE *ge* + *stingan* 3].

istriend³ *ptp.*, born 16/46, 47 [nWS *strēnan* A].

isunde², safe; *makien alle isunde*, heal 6/227 [OE *gesúnd*].

iswonge; isworene; it; itake. *See* swong; swere; hit; take(n).

iþenche³, to comprehend 19/93 [OE *geþencan* A].

iðoled; iþonked. *See* þole(n); þannkenn.

iþraste³, to insert 6/210 [OE *geþrǣstan* A].

iþrunge³ *ptp.*, close 10/38 [OE *geþríngan* 3].

itide³, to happen 10/155 [OE *getīdan* A].

itold(e); itoʒen. *See* telle(n); te.

itravailed³ *ptp.*, worked 19/22 [OE *ge-* + OF *travailler*].

iturnd. *See* turrnenn.

ituðet³ *ptp.*, granted 18/24 [OE *getīþian* B].

iuan; iueied; iuel(e). *See* ifoan; feʒe; uvel(e).

iugement¹, judgment, verdict 9/2, 20, 31, 66, trial 9/25 [OF *jugement*].

iui¹, ivy 10/27 [OE *īfig*].

i-upped³ *ptp.*, made known 17/36 [OE *yppan* A].

iustise¹, punishment 2/11n, chief justice 5/64 [OF *justice*].

iwar², careful 5/43 [OE *ge-* + *wær*].

iweden¹ *pl.*, equipment 6/152 [OE *ge-* + *wǣd*].

iwend. *See* wende(n); wene.

iwepnet³ *ptp.*, armed 18/60 [OE *wǣpnian* B].

iwersed³ *ptp.*, prejudiced 3/18 [OE *w(i)ersian* B].

iwil¹, pleasure 19/26 [OE *gewill*].

iwis⁴, certainly 5/12, 18, 42, etc. *mid iwisse*, with certainty 12/234; 293 [OE *gewiss, mid gewisse*].

iwonne; iworht, iwraht. *See* winne(n); wurche.

iwrche³ 3*prs.*, may make 14/37 [OE *ge-* + *wyrcan* A].

iwreþþed³ *ptp.*, angered 14/86 [OE *gewrǣþan* A].

iwriten; iwuste. *See* writen; wite(n).

iwurþe(n)³, to be, become 14/77, 17/11, have one's own way 17/64; iwurðe 3*prs.*, may be done 18/48 [OE *gewúrþan* 3].

iwurðen. *See* wurþen.

kayser¹, emperor 20/112 [ON *keisari*].

kam; kan. *See* cumen; conne.

kanunnkess¹ *g.*, of a canon 15/5 [OE *canonic*, from L *canonicus*].

kare. *See* care¹.

kaske², vigorous 8/214 [ON *kask-r*].

kastel. *See* castel.

kelde³, to grow cold 7/44 [OE *céaldian* B].

kempe¹, champion 6/199, 8/143, 18/45, keppe 6/45; kenpen *pl.* 6/55 [OE *cempa*].

kene², brave 8/205, 17/66, forward 7/22, sharp 30/3, 31/6 [OE *cēne*].

keneleden; kenne. *See* knele; cun(ne).

kep³ 1*pr.*, care to 38/9, 28; -est 2*pr.* 13/114; -eþ 3*pr.*, lies in wait for 13/16; kep *imp.*, oppose 35/46; *na kep I*, I don't care to 38/9; *ne kep I non*, I care nothing for 38/28 [OE *cēpan* A].

keppe; kepte; keste(n); kesten. *See* kempe; kipte; kisse; caste.

ket¹, carrion 11/39 [ON *kjǫt*].

kimeð; kind(e). *See* cumen; cunde.

kinedom(e)¹, kingdom 6/52, 9/164 [OE *cynedōm*].

kineriche, kune-¹, kingdom 3/7, 35, 6/221, 229; kineriches *pl.* 6/207 [OE *cynerīce*].

kinewurðe², royal 6/105 [OE *cynewyrðe*].

king¹, king 2/1, 3/1, etc., kync 38/78; -es *g.* 2/78, 6/23, 145, 9/131; *pl.* 6/48, 22/22; kingen *gpl.* 6/68 [OE *cyn(in)g*].

kinne. *See* cun(ne).

kipte, kepte³ 3*pt.*, seized, snatched 7/102, 8/157 [ON *kippa*].

kirke¹, church 8/36 [ON *kirkja*].

kisse³, to kiss 9/148, 21/58; keste 3*pt.* 7/89; custe 1*ptpl.* 29/23; kesten 3*ptpl.* 16/64 [OE *cyssan* A].

kyþe³, to show, make known 29/21; cuþest 2*pr.* 10/90; cuþeþ 3*pr.* 14/67; cudde 3*pt.* 17/121; kud *ptp.* 6/52, 32/34 [OE *cÿþan*].

klene. *See* clene.

knarres¹ *pl.*, crags 10/97 [obscure].

knawe³, to know, realize 8/92; kneu 3*pt.* 7/45, 12/114, 21/54; knewe 3*ptspl.* 21/93; iknowe, icnowe *ptp.* 13/114, confessed 12/182, 13/60, knewe, recognized 32/34 [OE *cnāwan* 7].

kne¹, knee 8/135, 21/44, 45 [OE *cnēo(w)*].

knele³, to kneel 21/36; keneleden 3*ptpl.* 35/9 [OE *cnēowlian* B].

knyf¹, knife 7/101, 32/2; knyues *pl.* 7/96 [OE *cnīf*].

kniȝtchild¹, noble youth 21/36 [OE *cnihtcild*].

knyht(e), knith¹, knight, warrior 7/8, 79, 8/87, etc., kniȝt 5/63, cnipte 6/0 3, cniht 6/38, 154, 155, knict 8/32, knicth 8/77, 80; cnihtes *g.* 6/46; knyhtes *pl.* 14/6, 28/57, kniȝtes 5/50, cnihtes 6/88, 203, knythes 22/11; cnihten *dpl.* 6/82, 111 [OE *cniht*].

kok; kom(e), komen, komeþ. *See* coc; cumen.

kors¹, curse 12/201 [OE *cúrs*].

kouþe. *See* conne.

krake³, to be cracked 8/230 [OE *cracian* B].

kud; kun, kunne(s); kuneriche. *See* kyþe; cun(ne); kineriche.

lac¹, want 32/30 [cf. Dutch *lak*].

lackeþ³ 3*pr.*, is wanting 32/22 [cf. Dutch *lak*].

ladde¹, youth, lad 8/115, 31/36; -es *pl.* 8/122, 131, 214, ladden 8/145 [obscure].

ladden; læiden. *See* lede(n); leggen.

læn¹, reward 15/72 [OE *lēan*].

lærden, læreþ; læt, lætenn. *See* lere(n); lete(n).

læten³, to prevent, hinder 16/28; letteð 3*pr.* 11/19; ilet *ptp.* 3/18 [OE *lettan* A].

læwedd², unlearned 15/28 [OE *lǣwede*].

lage, laȝe; laȝe(n), lahe. *See* lowe; lawe.

lahfulnesse¹, law-abidingness 10/163 [OE *lag-u* + *-full* + *-nes*].

lahte³ 3*pt.*, thrust 18/12 [OE *lǣcan*].

lay. *See* ligge.

layke³, to play games 8/118 [ON *leika*].

layt. *See* leggen.

lam(e)², crippled 10/154, 38/67 [OE *lama*].

land(e), landes; lang. *See* lond(e); long(e).

lang-Fridæi¹, Good Friday 2/81 [OE *langafrīgedæg*].

lappe¹, loose fold of garment 7/103 [OE *læppa*].

lare. *See* lore.

large², generous 8/97 [OF *large*].

largesse¹, generosity 28/49 [OF *largesse*].

larspell¹, sermon 15/28 [OE *lārspell*].

lasse. *See* lesse.

last(e)² *sup.*, last 17/11, 19/16, 20, etc.; *a last of*, towards the end of 19/43 [OE *latost*].

laste. *See* lesse.

lasteles², without blemish 28/33 [ON *lǫst-r* + OE *-lēas*].

lastest³ 2*pr.*, slander 13/107 [ON *lasta*].

lasteþ, lesteþ³ 3*pr.*, lasts 13/148, 20/46; lestinde *prp.* 3/21; laste 3*prs.* 29/6; lastede 3*pt.* 2/36 [OE *lǣstan* A].

lat(e). *See* lete(n).

late⁴, late 12/81; latere² *comp.*, latter 17/24, 27 [OE *late, lator*].

lateþ; laþ(e), laðest; lauerd. *See* lete(n); loþ; louerd.

laue¹, remainder; *to laue*, remaining 6/211 [OE *lāf*].

launterne¹, lantern 28/22 [OF *lanterne*].

law. *See* lowe.

lawe, laȝe¹, law 10/133, 14/8, 31/36, lahe 18/43, custom 6/165, 7/6, habits 13/113, fashion 32/10; lawes *pl.* 8/28, laȝen 6/223, 224 [OE *lagu*, from ON pl. *lagu*].

lawing¹, laughter 35/13 [cf. OA *hlæhhan* 6].

leaf, lef¹, page 6/24, leaf (of tree) 20/48, 29/3; *pl.* 30/2 [OE *lēaf*].

lealte, leaute¹, loyalty 4/2, 28/52 [cf. OF *leal*].

leapeð. *See* lepeð.

leattre¹, text 17/116 [OF *lettre*].

leche¹, doctor 8/209, 13/151, 30/12 [OE *lǣce*].

lecherie, licherie¹, lechery 37/8, 18 [OF *lecherie*].

lechurs¹ *pl.*, lechers 20/149 [OF *lecheor*].

lectorie¹, cock-stone 20/172n (L *alectoria*].

lede. *See* leode.

lede(n)³, to lead, conduct 6/154, 8/89, 14/16, 28/67, led 38/44; ledh, led 1*pr.*, 38/44, 68, lydy 38/42; ledeð 3*pr.* 11/44; ladden 3*ptpl.* 35/2; ledde, ilad *ptp.*, treated 8/262, devoted to 35/8 [OE *lǣdan* A].

ledene¹, language 17/89 [OE *lǣden*].

ledy; lef. *See* leuedi; leaf.

lef, leof¹, dear, pleasant 6/41, 11/86,
etc., luef 4/38, lieue 16/39, leif
22/17; leoue *pl.* 17/49, 59, 71,
121, leofe 6/82; as¹, lover 30/11,
luef 7/106, 29/16; leuer(e) *comp.*,
preferable 9/168, 12/7, etc. [OE
lēof, lēofra].
leflich(e)², lovely 28/13, 20, pleasant 28/53 [OE *lēoflic*].
lefmon. *See* lemman.
leggen³, to lay, place 13/158; leið
3*pr.* 17/64; lei *imp.*, beat 17/105;
leide 3*pt.* 7/15, 8/50, etc., lay
down 6/24; leiden 3*ptpl.* 6/235,
smote 6/194, læiden, imposed
2/38; layt, leid, leyit *ptp.* 32/10,
38/66, 83 [OE *lecgan* A].
legges¹ *pl.*, legs 28/31 [ON *legg-r*].
leȝe¹, lye 32/30n [OE *lē(a)g*].
leȝe¹, grove 7/54 [OE *lē(a)h*].
leȝe³, lie, to lie, deceive 12/132,
29/28; legeð, legheþ 3*pr.* 11/52,
19/85 [OE *lē(o)gan* 2].
ley¹, falsehood 38/83 [cf. OE
lē(o)gan 2].
leie¹, flame 18/15 [nWS *lēg*].
leye(n). *See* ligge.
leyk¹, sports 8/128, 239 [ON *leik-r*].
leitede³ 3*pt.*, gleamed 18/15 [nWS
*lēgettan A].
lemman, lemmon¹, lover 9/47,
182, 29/16, etc., lefmon 20/4,
leofmon 20/87, 186, leouemon
20/110, 120 [OE *lēof* + *mann*].
lene², slight 13/159 [OE *hlǣne*].
lenest³ 2*pr.*, grant 32/1; lenedd
ptp. 15/8 [OE *lǣnan* A].
leneþ³ 3*pr.*, leans 31/19 [OE *hleo-
nian* B].
leng. *See* long(e)⁴.
lengore, lengour⁴ *comp.*, longer
(of time) 12/42, 29/6 [OE *lengra*].
lengðe¹, length; *on* lengðe, at length
11/110 [OE *lengþu*].
leode, lede¹, people, nation,
country 6/14, 20/105, etc.;
leoden, -an *pl.* 1/3, 9, 15, etc.
[OE *lēode*].

leof. *See* lef.
leofliche⁴, lovingly 6/25 [OE *lēof-
līce*].
leofmon; leop; leore; leorne,
leornia. *See* lemman, lepeð;
lore; lernenn.
leosen, leosien³, to lose 6/74;
lesis 3*prpl.* 22/6; yloren *ptp.*
31/16 [OE *lēosan* 2, *losian* B].
leote; leoue, leouemon. *See*
lete(n); lef; lemman.
lepeð, leapeð³ 3*pr.*, leaps 11/19
17/66; lep *imp.* 12/234; lep, leop
3*pt.* 6/152, 12/22, etc. [OE
hlēapan 7].
lere(n)³, to teach 10/113, 12/231,
etc., learn 36/37; lærep 3*prpl.*
1/18; lærden 3*ptpl.* 1/15; ilærde,
ilerde *ptp.* 1/3, 9 [OE *lǣran* A].
leredmen¹ *pl.*, clergy 2/53 [OE
lǣred + *mann*].
lernenn³, to learn 15/10; -eþþ 3*pr.*
15/63; leorne *imp.* 14/66; leorny
2*prs* 20/196; leornia 3*prs.* 6/31
[OE *lēornian* B].
les², deceitful 13/67, 20/12 [OE
lēas].
lesinges¹ *pl.*, lies 13/130 [OE *lēa-
sung*].
lesis. *See* leosen.
lesit³ *ptp.*, freed 38/34 [nWS
lēsan A].
lesse, lasse² *comp.*, less, smaller
5/33, 8/203, 17/9; laste *sup.*,
smallest 6/210 [OE *lǣssa, lǣst*].
lest(e)⁸, lest 31/4, 32/4 [OE *þe lǣs
þe*].
lesteþ, lestinde. *See* lasteþ.
lete(n)³, to let, allow 12/51, 88,
leote 17/63, let 20/192, to
abandon 10/114, læten, to judge
15/40; lat 3*pr.*, pretends 11/30,
31; leteþ 3*prpl.*, neglect 10/193,
esteem 10/196; lete 2*prs.*, may
cease 13/27; late 3*prs.* 8/17;
3*prspl.*; refrain from 29/19; let
imp. 4/11, 9/88, etc. lete 29/16,
lat 36/18; lateþ *imppl.* 10/151,

159; **let, lette** 3*pt.* 4/24, 17/107, caused to happen (followed by inf.) 5/21, 89/2, 200, etc., **læt** 2/63; **lete** 3*ptpl.*, caused to be 5/31; **let** 3*pts.* 21/38; **let(t)en** *ptp.* 12/40, 45; *lateþ beo*, stop it 10/157; *let hem shewe*, showed them 8/226 [OE *lǣtan* 7, ON *láta*].

lete¹, appearance 10/35 [OE (*ge*)-*lǣte*].

leth¹, hatred 22/31 [OE *lǣþþ*].

letteð. *See* **læten**.

leue¹, faith 11/105, 108 [OE *lēafa*].

leue¹, permission 12/25, 13/97, 21/73 [OE *lēafe*].

leue³ 3*prs.*, may grant, allow 9/184, 17/44, 20/207 [nWS *lēfan* A].

leuedi, ledy¹, lady 13/25, 82, 28/33, etc.; **ledy** *g.* 32/10; **leuedi(e)s** *pl.* 13/52, 32/16, 35/4 [OE *blǣfdige*].

leuen³, to believe 11/55; **ileued** *ptp.* 17/31 [nWS *lēfan* A].

leuer(e); leuide; lhoauerd. *See* **lef; libben; louerd**.

lhoupᵇ³ 3*pr.*, lows 24/7 [OE *blōwan* 7].

lhude. *See* **lude**.

lyard¹, grey horse 4/39 [OF *lyart*].

libben, liue(n)³, to live 2/69, 11/86, 20/24, etc., **libe** 12/42, **liuie** 12/165; **lyue** 1*pr.* 30/10; **liueð** 3*pr.* 11/76; **libbeþ, liuieþ** 3*prpl.* 10/108, 13/105, **libbet** 18/43; **libbe** 3*prspl.* 10/102; **leuide** 3*pt.* 18/3 [OE *libban* C, *lifian, leofian* B].

licame, lichame¹, body 16/55, 21/9 [OE *lic(h)ama*].

lich¹, flesh, skin 5/79 [OE *līc*].

liche¹, likeness 18/5 [OE (*ge*)*līc*].

licherie. *See* **lecherie**.

lichur¹, lechery 22/31 [cf. OF *licherie*].

licunge¹, relish 17/95 [OE *līcung*].

lydy; lie; lieue. *See* **lede(n); leȝe³; lef**.

lif, liue¹, life 6/74, 9/36, 12/227, etc., **lijf** 22/6, **life** 38/5, body 5/48, lifetime 12/211, way of life 15/5, maiden 28/20, 38/50, **liif**, life story 12/187; **liues** *g.* 19/84, 28/67, alive 8/110; *to pines lifes*, with your life 6/222; *o(n) liue*, alive 6/238, into life 20/17; *of liue haue do*, have killed 8/178 [OE *līf*].

lifdaie, -daȝe¹, life 6/202, 12/200; **-dayes** *pl.* 12/49 [OE *līfdæg*].

liften³, to raise 8/135, 137; **lift** *imp.* 38/64; **lifte** 3*pt.* 8/179 [ON *lypta*].

ligge, lien³, to lie (down) 2/34, 9/116, 21/12; **lies, lyht, lyþ** 3*pr.* 7/31, 23/3, 32/29; **liggeþ, lien, lys** 3*prpl.* 20/15, 35/20, 38/76, appertain to 2/68; **ly** 3*prs.* 38/10; **li** *imp.* 17/73; **lai** 3*pt.* 6/218, 8/129; **leie(n)** 3*ptpl.* 5/105, 6/212, lay 8/182; **leye** *ptp.* 7/33 [OE *licgan* 5].

ligtlike. *See* **lihtliche**.

liht, liȝt², easy 12/236, small 17/94 [OE *lēoht, līht*].

liht(e), liȝt¹, light 1/16, 20/134, 33/3, 36/66; *in lyhte*, openly 28/68 [OE *lēoht, līht*].

liht⁴, brightly 28/21 [OE *lēohte*].

lihtlich², easy 10/181 [OE *lēohtlic*].

lihtliche, ligtlike⁴, lightly 10/196, quickly 11/19 [OE *lēohtlīce*].

like², like 22/10 [OE (*ge*)*līc*].

likeð, likes³ 3*pr.*, is pleasing 6/81, 22/26; **lyke** 3*prs.* 14/48 [OE *līcian* B].

lilie¹, lily 28/49 [OE *lilie*, from L *lilium*].

limes¹ *pl.*, limbs 2/29, 5/73, 8/86n, **limen** 17/120 [OE *lim*].

limpeð³ 3*pr.*, is fitting 17/47 [OE *limpan* 3].

lyn(e)¹, linen 32/10, 22 [OE *līn*].

linde¹, lime tree 10/172 [OE *lind*].

lisse¹, remission 36/59 [OE *liss*].

list¹, desire 11/102 [ON *lyst*].

lisstenn³, to listen to 15/67; lusteþ *imppl.* 10/151 [OE *hlystan* A].

listneð³ *3pr.*, listens to 11/109; *imppl*, 11/10; lustnede *3pt.* 28/69 [OA *lysna*].

lïte, lute², little 5/6, 61, 114; *long ne lite*, big or little 8/228 [OE *lȳt*].

litel, lit(t)le, luitel, lutel², little, small, unimportant 8/6, 9/112, 10/198, etc. [OE *lȳtel*].

liðe² gracious 6/2, 25 [OE *līþe*].

liðe(n)³, to go, journey 6/14, 232, 240, carry 6/235; *3prspl.* 6/172 [OE *līþan* 1].

liðere³, *imp.*, beat 17/78 [cf. OE *liðere*].

liue, liues; liue(n), liuie(þ). *See* lif; libben.

lo, low⁹, lo, behold 5/1, 18/50 [OE *lā*].

loac, loc¹, sacrifice 16/49, 54 [OE *lāc*].

lockes, lokkes¹ *pl.*, hair 18/7, 28/13 [OE *locc*].

lodlich², hateful 10/32, 71 [OE *lāþlic*].

lof¹, head-band 2/30n [OE *lof*].

lofenn³, to praise 15/39, 44, [OE *lofian* B].

lofte¹, air; *vp o lofte*, aloft 32/26 [ON *lopt*, *á lopti*].

loh, lou³ *3pt.*, laughed 6/114, 12/23, 148; lowe(n) *3ptpl.* 8/163, 9/138 [OE *hliehhan*, *hlōh*, 6].

loht. *See* lop.

loke, lokin³, to see, observe, protect 7/35, 17/74; loki *1pr.* 10/56; lokest *2pr.* 32/1; lokieð, lokið *3prpl.*, look forward to the time 6/240, look to 16/19; loke *3prs.* 15/52; *imp.* 13/120, 15/54, 16/56, etc.; lokeþ *imppl.* 19/87; lokede *3pt.* 6/218, 8/148, 9/64, 21/95; iloket *ptp.*, ordained 18/43 [OE *locian* B].

loket¹, love-lock 32/29 [cf. OE *locc*].

lomb¹, lamb 24/6 [OE *lámb*].

lond(e), land(e)¹, country, land 2/15, 16, 5/4, 88, etc., loande 3/8, 17, estates 2/49, 20/105, neighbourhood 17/52; loandes g. 3/6; londe, landes *pl.* 10/92, estates 2/62, 67, 68, 70; *o londe*, in the world 11/66; *for al þe worldes lond*, for anything in the world 12/161 [OE *lánd*].

long(e), lang², long 6/194, 8/218, 9/165, etc., extensive 6/162; *iss lang uppo*, is dependent upon 15/59 [OE *láng*].

long(e)⁴, a long while 5/113, 8/165, 9/157, etc.; leng *comp.* 2/69, 10/42 [OE *lánge*; *leng*].

longing(e)¹, desire 13/5, 105, 20/201 [OE *lángung*].

lord; lordinges. *See* louerd; louerdinges.

lore, lare¹, knowledge, teaching 4/44, 11/109, 13/147, etc., leore 1/17 [OE *lār*].

lorþeines¹ *pl.*, teachers 1/19 [OE *lārþegn*].

losiæþ³ *3prpl.*, are damned 1/19; losyt *ptp.*, wasted 38/12 [OE *losian* B].

lossom, lufsum, lussum², lovely 20/93, 28/17, 33; lussomore *comp.* 28/12 [OE *lufsum*].

lost. *See* lust.

lostlase², lazy 31/36 [ON *lost-i* + OE *-lēas*].

loþ¹, song (of Solomon) 14/98 [OE *lēoþ*].

loð, lath¹, injury 8/76, 11/31 [OE *lāþ*].

loþ, laþ(e)², hateful 6/41, 10/65, 72, etc., loht 4/38, loþe 7/97; laðest *sup.* 17/104 [OE *lāþ*].

lou; loude. *See* loh; lude.

loue, luue¹, love 2/82, 4/27, etc. (personified) 28/53, 61, 69, luf(e) 15/10, 73, 38/22, 25; *for mi luue*, for love of me 9/89 [OE *lufu*].

loue-bene¹, lover's petition 30/13
[OE *lufu* + *bēn*].

louelich(e)², lovely 13/150, 28/30
[OE *luflic*].

loueliche⁴, lovingly 6/0 25 [OE
luflīce].

louerd, lauerd, lord¹, lord, the
Lord 8/64, 96, 16/4, etc., lhoauerd 3/1, laferrd 15/76,
hlauerd 16/10, 38, 53; lauerdes,
lordes *g.* 17/112, 19/17 [OE
hláford].

louerdinges, lordinges¹ *pl.*, lords
5/94, 9/9 [OE *hláford* + *-ing*].

loue-tiþinge¹, news of love 10/131
[OE *lufu* + ON *tíðinde* infl. by
OE *tīdung*].

louie(n), loue³, to love 9/185,
19/50, etc., lufe 38/8; loue, luf
1*pr.* 29/1, 38/15, 19; louest 2*pr.*
30/14; luuieþ 3*pr.* 19/89, 20/50,
54; luuieþ 2*prpl.* 19/89; lufenn,
luuieþ, luueþ 3*prpl.* 15/47,
19/94, 20/136; louie 2*prs.* 30/19;
luuie 3*prs.* 19/51; louede 1*pt.*
29/26, 28; 3*pt.* 8/35, 37, etc.,
lufede 6/51, luuede 9/105,
14/20, 17/107; louede(n) 3*ptpl.*
8/30, 21/5, luueden 2/76; loued
ptp. 30/5, 8 [OE *lufian* B].

loupe³, to run, hasten 8/174 [ON
hlaupa 7].

loure³, to scowl 32/17 [OE **lurian*
B].

lowe², mean, humble 5/7, 13/32,
laʒe 6/205, lage, weak 11/105,
law, low 23/3 [ON *lág-r*].

lowe(n). *See* loh.

lud², loud 10/6; ludere *df.* 6/114;
luddre *comp.* 17/86 [OE *hlúd*].

lude, loude⁴, loudly 8/96, 14/90,
lhude 24/2 [OE *hlúde*].

luef. *See* lef.

luf¹, lover 38/24 [cf. OE *lufu*].

luf(e); lufenn; lufsum. *See* loue;
louie(n); lossom.

lufte¹, air, heavens 6/167, 18/34,
37 [OE *lyft*].

luitel. *See* litel.

luke³, to keep safe 20/147; -eð 3*pr.*,
closes 11/71; -en 3*ptpl.*, drew
6/194 [OE *lúcan* 2].

lumes³ 3*pr.*, shines 28/21 [OE
*léomian B].

lunde¹, grove; *a lunde*, elsewhere
20/53n [ON *lund-r*].

lure¹, beauty 28/21 [OE *hléor*].

lurken³, to hide 8/68 [cf. ON
lurka].

lussum, lussomore. *See* lossom.

lust¹, pleasure 12/96, 100, 17/95,
lost 20/93, desire 17/60 [OE
lust, ON *losti*].

luste³ 3*pr.*, pleases 10/39; 3*prs.*
17/103 [OE *lystan* A].

lusteþ; lustnede; lute; lutel. *See*
lisstenn; listneþ; lite; litel.

luþer², dangerous 21/10 [cf. OE
lýþerlic].

luðerliche⁴, severely 17/79 [OE
lýþerlíce].

luue; luuede(n). *See* loue;
louie(n).

luue-ron¹, song of love 20/2 [OE
lufu + *rún*].

luueþ. *See* louie(n).

luuewende², loving 18/43 [OE
lufwende].

luuie(þ). *See* louie(n).

ma; made(n); mære(n). *See* mo;
make(n); mere.

mæssedæi¹, festival 2/64 [OE
mæssedæg].

mahe, mahte. *See* mai.

magt, mahhte¹, power, strength
11/99, 15/60 [OA *mæht*].

mai, mei³ 1/3*pr.*, am able to, can,
may 2/35, 5/115, 9/52, etc.,
maig 11/74, maʒʒ 106, 15/24,
46, 54; mowen 2*prpl.* 8/11,
13/12, 20/39, etc., mawe 14/14;
muʒe, muwen, mowe 3*prpl.*
10/62, 17/19, 32/3, may 38/80;
mahe 1*prs.* 18/49; muge 3*prs.*
3/17; muʒe, mugen, mowe

1*prspl.* 6/75, 11/26, 14/68; **miʒte,
mihhte** 1*pt.* 12/58, 15/30; **miʒt,
myht** 2*pt.* 9/48, 118, 10/64, etc.,
myhtes 2/41, 30/11, **miʒtest**
9/44, **mist** 10/78, **mayht** 20/31,
myhtestu 20/96, **maht** 29/20,
michtis 38/30; **miʒte, mihte** 3*pt.*
5/88, 9/39, 20/144, etc., **mahte**
6/60, **micthe** 8/42, **mouthe**
8/135, 229, etc., **mithe** 8/137,
140, 38/6, etc., **miʒtte** 12/112,
micht 38/16; **miʒte, mihte** 1*ptpl.*
5/47, 10/171; **mouthe** 3*ptpl.*
8/204, **miʒtte** 12/42, **myhte**
20/183, **miʒten** 21/17 [OE *mæg;
mage, muge; meahte, mihte, muhte*].
mai[1], maiden 9/105, 170, 30/18,
38/6 [OE *mæg*, ON *mæ-r*].
maide, maiden(e)[1], maiden, virgin
9/84, 13/171, 19/43, etc., **maydne** 8/83, **meiden** 18/18, 61;
mayd(e)nes *pl.* 7/60, 8/2, etc.;
maidene *gpl.* 6/225 [OE *mæg-
den*].
maydenhod[1], virginity 20/162
[OE *mægdenhād*].
mayden-mon[1], virgin 36/45 [OE
mægdenmann].
mayht. *See* **mai.**
main(e)[1], might, strength 12/279,
13/89, **mæine** 6/86 [OE *mægen*].
maine, meyne[1], retinue, company
9/144, 20/69n [OF *mai(s)nee*]
mayster, maistre[1], master 8/152,
154, 12/206, as title 10/168, 200;
meistres *pl.*, teachers 17/116;
maister curtiler, chief gardener
12/272 [OE *mægester*, OF *maistre*,
from L *magister*].
maistry, maistrie[1], mastery 5/39,
31/28n, force 28/64 [OF *maistrie*].
make(n), makie(n)[3], to make,
cause 4/4, 6/228, etc., **mac** 38/57,
to be made 3/13, 17/108; **make**
1*pr.*, feel 28/83, 36/36; **makest**
2*pr.* 19/22; **makeþ** 3*pr.* 9/145,
20/58, 28/44, 29/24, make out
to be 17/4, 9, 10, **maket**, per-

forms 2/85; **makeþ, -ieþ** 3*prpl.*
6/168, 12/29; **make** *imp.* 5/111,
16/25, 17/124; **makede, made**
3*pt.* 4/19, 6/16, etc., followed by
inf.=caused to be done 8/38, 39,
etc., built 2/14, 75, admitted
2/74, wrote 5/93, created 13/143,
macod, summoned 2/6; **maden**
3*ptpl.* 8/146; **maked, imaked(e)**
ptp. 3/13, 8/58, 12/72, 13/80,
imad 5/46, 19/7, done 2/12,
built 2/17, told 8/5, 23, 273,
uttered 13/130, created 13/35,
maced, employed 2/31; *dede
maken*, caused to be made 8/29;
maden hem glad, made merry 35/7
[OE *macian* B].
male[1], bag 8/48 [OF *male*].
man, mann(e), mon(e)[1],[5] man
2/10, 29, 5/6, 11, etc., as impersonal subject, one 8/40, 11/8,
19/84, etc., anyone 2/41, 20/57;
mannes, monnes *g.* 2/32, 13/153
etc., **mones** 13/35; **men** *pl.* 2/17,
18, 3/16, etc., **monnen** 6/109,
212; **manne** *gpl.* 10/144; *men of þe
toune*, citizens 5/104 [OE *mann*].
maneres[2] *pl.*, kinds 17/24, 22/2
[OF *man(i)ere*].
mangonel[1] *pl.*, catapults 4/16 [OF
mangonel].
mani, moni[2], many 2/29, 4/21,
5/13, etc., **manig** 15/22, 29,
much 10/178; **manie, monie** *pl.*
2/74, 6/182, 10/177, etc., **maniʒe**
16/5 [OE *manig*].
manifældlice[4], in various ways
2/86 [OE *manigféaldlīce*].
manion[2], many a one 5/51, 73, 94,
102 [OE *manig* + *ān*].
mankenn(e)[1], mankind 10/147,
16/27, 33, etc., **monkune** 32/6
[OE *mancynn*].
manred[1], homage 2/12 [OE *man-
rǣden*].
mar(e). *See* **more.**
marcatte[1], market 19/9 [lOE *market*,
from L *mercatum*].

marescal¹, marshal 3/29 [OF *mare-scal*].

martyr¹, martyr 2/84; **-s** *pl.* 2/21 [OE *martir*].

masse¹, mass 12/252; **massen** *pl.* 5/21 [OE *mæsse*].

maðeleð³ *3pr.*, tells 17/52 [OE *maþelian* B].

maðelild¹, tale-bearer 17/52 [OE *maþel-ian* + *-ild*].

maugre¹, in spite of 4/12 [OF *maugre*].

mawe¹, stomach 21/14, 31/38 [OE *maga*].

mawe; me. *See* **mai; ic.**

me⁵, impersonal subject, one 2/5, 55, etc., men 38/53 [OE *mann*].

mearke¹, crucifix 17/77 [OE *mearc*].

med¹, meadow 24/3 [OE *mǣd*].

mede¹, reward 8/102, 13/64, etc. [OE *mēd*].

medewe-gres¹, meadow grass 20/16 [OE *mǣdwe* + *grǣs*].

mei; meiden; meyne; meistres. *See* **mai; maide; maine; may-ster.**

meke, meoke², meek 13/55, 171, 18/18, 36/34 [ON *mjúk-r*].

mel, meel¹, meal 12/173, 247 [OE *mǣl*].

membres¹ *pl.*, parts 5/75 [OF *membre*].

men. *See* **man; me.**

mend³ *imp.*, soften 38/26 [OF *(a)mender*].

mene³, to complain 29/4; *1pr.*, mean 11/107, 38/48; **-eþ** *3pr.* 13/43, 14/51, signifies 15/17 [OE *mǣnan* A].

menestral¹, minstrel 21/29 [OF *menestral*].

menskful², graceful 28/7, 29 [ON *mennsk-a* + OE *-full*].

menur², minor; *frer menur*, Franciscan 37/7 [L *minor*].

meoke. *See* **meke.**

merci¹, mercy 8/96, 36/13 [OF *merci*].

mere, mære¹, lake 6/157, 177, 179 **mæren** *d.* 6/174 [OE *mere*].

merede³ *ptp.*, refined 20/115 [OE *merian* A].

mereuh², weak 20/44 [OE *mearu*].

meri(e), mirie, mvrie², pleasant 6/0 4, 21/5, 25/1, 35/48; **mur-gest** *sup.*, most pleasing 28/41 [OE *myrge*].

merk¹, darkness 11/44 [OE *myrce*, ON *myrk-r*].

merkest³ *2pr.*, ordain 18/40 [OE *mearcian* B].

mern², splendid 6/6 [OE *mǣre*].

meseoluen. *See* **ic.**

meshe³, to crush 10/84 [OE **mæscan* A].

messeboc¹, missal 15/16 [OE *mæsse-bōc*].

mest² *sup.*, most 5/70, 74, 13/20, etc., **meste** 9/13 [OE *mǣst*].

mete¹, food 7/3, 77, etc.; **-es** *pl.* 8/253 [OE *mete*].

mete(n)³, to meet, encounter 5/22, 109, 12/6, 7; **mette** *3pt.* 8/183, 12/242 [OE *mētan* A].

mete-custi², generous in providing food 6/37 [OE *mete* + *cystig*].

meten³, to measure out 21/68 [OE *metan* 5].

meþ¹, moderation 12/97 [OE *mǣþ*].

mi; micel, michel; micht, mich-tis, micthe. *See* **ic; muche(l); mai.**

mid⁷, with, along with 1/1, 2/17, 64, 5/13, etc., **mide** 10/190, by means of 2/16, 22, 34, 6/26, 48, etc., in 6/149, because of 12/89, in the act of 21/82 [OE *mid*]. *See also* **mið.**

midday¹, midday 19/8, 38, 74 [OE *middæg*].

middel¹, waist 28/29 [OE *middel*].

middelerd, -ærde¹, world 5/84n, 6/157, 11/54, **middeneard** 16/52 [OE *middangéard*].

mye³ *3prspl.*, may gnash the teeth 31/39 [OF *mier*].

miȝt(e), myht(e)[1], power, strength 13/11, 89, 20/138, 35/50, 36/63, micth 8/35; *mid here migt*, with all their strength 11/90; *wiþ miȝtte*, immediately 13/96; *of myht*, with power over me 28/7 [OE *miht*].

miȝt(e), miȝten, miȝtest, myht(e), mihtes(tu). *See* mai.

mikel[2], big, great 8/130, 11/99, 15/9, etc., mike 8/249, mik 8/255; as[1], mikle *pl.* 11/106, 107 [OE *mycel*, ON *mikill*].

milc[1], milk 10/105 [OE *meolc*, *milc*].

milce, mildce[1], mercy, pity 16/3, 4, 10, etc. [OE *milts*].

milde[2], gentle, mild 2/10, 10/128, 13/21, etc.; mildre *comp.*, more generous 10/197 [OE *milde*].

myle[1], mile 7/74, 8/204; *pl.* 5/92 [OE *mīl*, from L *milia passuum*].

min(e). *See* ic.

mynde[2], thoughtful 36/34 [OE *mynde*].

mine[1], game played with dice 8/239 [OF *mine*].

mynstre[1], monastery 2/64, monastery church 2/85 [OE *mynster*].

mint[3] *3pt.*, intended 2/69; imunt *ptp.* 12/244 [OE *myntan* A].

mynur[1], miner 20/123 [OF *minour*].

miracles[1] *pl.*, miracles 2/86 [OF *miracle*].

mire; mireȝpe. *See* ic; murþe.

mis[1], wickedness 17/7 [cf. OE *missan* A].

misdede, misse-[1], sins 12/182, 38/72 [OE *misdǣd*].

misdoð[3] *3prpl.*, err 10/192 [OE *misdōn*].

miself. *See* ic.

misferdest[3] *2pt.*, committed adultery 12/212 [OE *misfēran* A].

mysgilt[1], misdeeds 38/21 [OE *mis- + gylt*].

misliche[4], indiscriminately 10/195 [OE *mislīce*].

misrempe[3] *1prs.*, may go astray 10/209 [OE *mis- + rempan* A].

misse[3], to lose 36/62 [OE *missan* A].

misseyde[3] *3pt.*, insulted 8/49 [OE *mis- + secgan* C].

mist. *See* mai.

mistie, miþtie[2], mighty 6/0 25, 0 30. [OE *mihtig*].

miðᵗ, with 6/142, 11/46, 18/35 [perhaps from OE *mið* rather than *mid*].

mithe. *See* mai.

mythe[3], to hide 29/24 [OE *mīþan* 1].

mo, ma[2] *comp.*, more 5/101, 6/189, 8/219, etc. [OE *mā*].

mod(e)[1], heart, mind 6/6, 59, 11/50, etc., temper 10/8, 14/88 [OE *mōd*].

moder[1], mother 6/150, 9/46, etc.; *g.* 6/34, 36/43, 44 [OE *mōdor*].

modiȝnesse[1], pride 15/39, 78 [OE *mōdignes*].

molde[1], earth 20/15 [OE *mólde*].

mome[1], mother 38/37n, 39 [obscure].

mon. *See* man.

mon[3] *1pr.*, must 26/3 [ON *munu*].

mone[1], moon 18/36, 31/1, 18 [OE *mōna*].

mone[3], to make known 30/20 [ON *muna*].

monendai[1], Monday 5/18 [OE *mōnandæg*].

monge[3], to mingle 28/15 [cf. OE *gemóng* and *mengan* A].

moni(e). *See* mani.

monkynde, -kunde[1], mankind 36/8, 27 [OE *mann + cýnd*].

monkune; monne, monnen. *See* mankenn(e); man.

monþe[1], month 3/23 [OE *mōnaþ*].

more, mare[2],[4] *comp.*, more, further 2/39, 45, 4/5, 5/11, etc., mor 37/17, 38/15, mar 38/19, 20, again 4/30, 17/36, longer (of time) 7/93, greater 16/38, 36/42; *þe moare dæl*, the majority 3/5,

14; *lesse and more*, small and great 8/120 [OE *māra*].

moreghen. *See* **morghen.**

moreȝeninge, morweninge¹, morning 5/20, 10/140 [OE *morgen* + *-ing*].

mores¹ *pl.*, moors 4/25 [OE *mōr*].

morewe¹, morning 36/56 [OE *morgen*].

morewentide¹, morning 21/75 [OE *morgentīd*].

morghen¹, morning 19/19, 34, 64, 70, **moreghen** 19/5 [OE *morgen*].

morþre, murþre¹, murder 5/61, 80, 101 [OE *morþor*].

moruenne¹, marshes 6/100 [OE *mōr* + *fenn*].

mose¹, titmouse 10/69 [OE *māse*].

moste² *sup.*, greatest 8/234, 11/58 [OA *māst*].

mote¹, mound, hill 20/121 [OF *motte*].

mote³ *1pr.*, may 18/50, 33/8; **most** *2pr.*, must 12/207, 208, 20/150; **mot(e)** *3pr.* 8/19, 9/184, 18/40, 28/15, must 15/28, 29, 31/15, 32/30; **mote(n)** *1prpl.*, 8/18, 9/185, 186, etc., must 9/24; **mote** *1prs.* 10/52; **moste** *3pt.*, must 12/85; *3pts.*, should 2/69, 18/23 [OE *mōt, mōste*].

mournyng¹, grief 28/83 [OE *múrnung*].

mous¹, mouse 31/31; **mus** *pl.* 10/87 [OE *mūs, mȳs*].

mouþ(e); mouthe. *See* **muþ(e); mai.**

mowe³, to mow 8/225, reap 10/136 [OE *māwan* 7].

mowe(n). *See* **mai.**

mowen¹ *pl.*, corn stacks 21/26 [OE *mūga*].

muche, muchel(e)², much, great 4/20, 23, 6/57, 168, etc., **micel** 2/4, 60, 61, 64, **michel** 16/23, 29, 32, 25/6, **mulch** 26/4, many 16/50; **muchelere** *df.* 6/230; **muclen** *dpl.* 6/181 [OE *mycel*].

muchel⁴, much, greatly 12/98, 13/140, 17/107, 21/20, **michel** 8/60, **muche** 10/192 [OE *mycel*].

muge(n), muȝe. *See* **mai.**

mulne¹, mill 4/14, 10/86, 17/54 [OE *mylen*, from L *molina*].

mulne-post¹, mill-post 4/19 [OE *mylen* + *post*].

munec¹, monk 2/76; **munekes** *pl.* 2/50, 60, 74, 84 [OE *munuc*].

munten¹ *pl.*, mountains 6/182 [OE *munt*, OF *munt*, from L *mont-*].

murgest, mvrie. *See* **meri(e).**

murie⁴, pleasantly, tunefully 13/6, 24/9 [OE *myrge*].

murne³ *1pr.*, mourn, lament 25/7 [OE *múrnan* 3].

murþe¹, joy, pleasure 13/79, 103, **mireȝþe** 9/44; **-es** *pl.* 28/15, 44 [OE *myrgð*].

murþre; mus. *See* **morþre; mous.**

muþ(e), mouþ(e)¹, mouth 9/70, 11/69, 12/56, etc., words 13/169; *þurh his muþe*, because of his words 10/179 [OE *mūþ*].

muwen. *See* **mai.**

na; naam. *See* **no; nimen.**

nabbe³ *1pr.*, have not 12/39, 18/47; **nast** *2pr.* 32/2; **naueþ** *3pr.* 6/126, 10/182, 20/107, 112, **naþ** 21/49, 31/22; **nabbeþ** *3prpl.* 10/101, 107; **nabbe** *3prs.* 5/72, 32/14; **nadde, nedde** *3pt.* 5/107, 12/100, 169, 286, **nefde** 6/45, **neuede** 12/98, 20/84, **neddi** 12/99; **nedden** *3ptpl.* 19/49 [OE *nabban, næfde*].

nadoun. *See* **adoun(e).**

nadres, neddren¹ *pl.*, adders 2/25, 17/42 [OE *nǣdre*].

nænne; næs; næstieð; naȝt, naht. *See* **no²; nas; nestes; nawt⁴.**

nay⁴, nay 12/188 [ON *nei*].

nayled³ *ptp.*, nailed 36/6 [OE *nægljan* B].

naked², naked 8/6 [OE *nacod*].

nale. *See* **ale.**

nam³ 1pr., am not 10/166, 29/36;
nert 2pr. 17/10 [OA nam].

nam; name; namen. See nimen;
nome; nimen.

namore⁴, no more, no longer
10/215, 216, 12/65, 30/5, 35/35,
nammore 13/156, nomore 37/1
[OE nā + māre].

nan; nanes. See no²; non(e)⁵.

nap¹, cup 21/70, 81, etc. [OE
hnæpp].

nareu², narrow 2/27 [OE nearu].

narewe⁴, closely 10/68 [OE near-
we].

nas, nes³ 3pt., was not 5/61, 6/45,
9/63, etc., næs 1/16, 6/46; nere
1pts. 9/43; 3pts. 9/25, 89, 90, etc.;
3ptspl. 13/24, 34 [OE næs,
nǣron, nǣre].

nap. See nabbe.

naðelæs⁸, nevertheless 16/26 [OE
nāðelǣs].

napt. See nawt⁴.

nature¹, nature 19/75 [OF nature].

nauep. See nabbe.

nawt, naht¹, nothing 2/53, 17/91
[OE nā-wiht].

nawt⁴, not, not at all 17/73, 75, etc.,
nazt 9/163, napt 10/162, naht
36/35 [OE nā-wiht].

ne⁴, not (preceding verb) 2/5, 11,
3/17, etc.; coalescing with verbs
in nabbe, nam, nas, nelle, nis,
noztest, nolde, not, nul(e),
nuste; as⁸, nor 2/42, 45, 3/17,
etc.; ne . . . ne, neither . . . nor
2/33, 4/31, 8/44, etc. [OE ne].

nease¹, nose 18/11 [OM *neasu].

nease-purles¹ pl., nostrils 18/11
[OE næspyrl].

necheð³ 3pr., approaches 25/3 [cf.
OE nē(a)h].

necke, nekke¹, neck 8/195, 196,
9/95, 11/7 [OE hnecca].

nedde(n), neddi; neddren. See
nabbe; nadres.

ned(e)¹, need, necessity 12/276,
15/18, 61, etc., neode 20/107,

191; at nede, in necessity 8/9, 25,
87; at pisse nede, in this hour of
need 12/225; nede g., needs, of
necessity, 15/31 [OA nēd, nēod].

nefde. See nabbe.

ney, neh⁴, nigh, at hand 5/37, 6/66,
12/32, etc.; neh alle, almost all
15/15 [OE nē(a)h].

neizebore¹, neighbour 12/115 [OE
nē(a)hgebūr].

neiles¹ pl., nails 17/113, 116 [OE
nægl].

neilond, island 11/61, 88 [nWS
ēgland].

neyper⁴,⁸ neither 8/136, 9/99;
neouðer . . . no, neither . . . nor
6/103 [OE ne ǣghwæper].

nelle³ 1pr., wish not 9/124, 12/132,
188 nellic 21/3; neltou 2pr.
12/189 [OE nellan].

nemne³ 1pr., name 20/161; nempne imp., invoke 17/105 [OE
nemnan A].

nempnunge¹, invocation (of God)
17/77 [OE nemning].

nenne; neouðer. See no; neyper.

ner(e)⁴ comp., nearer 12/38, 22/28,
30/7; nexte sup., nearest 5/79
[nWS nē(a)r(a), nēxt].

nere; nert; nes. See nas; nam; nas.

nestes³ 2pr., nest 12/48n; næstieð
3prpl. 6/164 [cf. OE nest, nistian
B].

net¹, net 7/31 [OE nett].

neth¹, ox 8/133 [OE nēat].

nepere⁴, down 35/33 [OE niper
neper].

neuede. See nabbe.

neuer(e)⁴, never 8/90, 150, 10/122
etc., næure 2/21, 45, 46, neure
2/41, 6/45, 9/51, neuær 6/46
nauer 6/241, 24/12, naure 16/35
neauer 17/99, neaure 18/39
ner 31/11; neuermo, no mor
12/145; neuermore, never agai
4/7, 30, 36 [OE nǣfre].

neues¹ pl., nephews 2/9 [OE nefa

neuly, neulic⁴, soon 38/33, 52 [OE *nīwlīce*].

newe, neuuæ², new 2/63, 13/111; *makest newe*, renew 29/25 [OE *nēowe*].

nexte. *See* ner(e).

niȝt(e), nyht(e)¹, night 21/21, 61, 28/82, etc., **niȝtte** 13/93, **nicht** 25/5, 38/17, **nyth** 33/24; *nihtes g.*, at, by night 2/18, 20/60; *pl.* 8/274 [OE *niht*].

niȝt(t)ingale¹, nightingale 10/4, 13, etc., **niȝt(t)egale** 10/141, 161, 13/5, **nyhtegale** 30/1 [OE *nihtegale*].

nikeres¹ *pl.*, water monsters 6/160n [OE *nicor*].

nimen³, to seize, take 9/160; **nime** 3*prs.* 3/17; **nim** *imp.* 17/76, 35/41, 43; **nome** 2*pt.*, obtained 7/71; **nom** 3*pt.* 6/15, 16, 26, etc., **nam** 2/7, 16/1, 21/68, **naam** 19/43; **nome(n), namen** 3*ptpl.* 2/17, 47, 84, 6/234, received 5/5, 35/19; **inome** *ptp.*, captured, taken 5/94, 99, 9/30, etc.; *wei . . . nome*, advanced 5/34; *nom in to*, set out to 7/83; *hire nam to quene*, married her 9/153 [OE *niman* 4].

nine², nine 8/117 [OE *nigon*].

nis³ 3*pr.*, is not 6/103, 9/15, etc. [OE *nis*].

niþ¹, malice 15/38, 42 [OE *nīþ*].

niþfull², malicious 15/34 [OE *nīþfull*].

no, non(e), na, nan², no, none 2/5, 11, 12, 6/155, 7/25, etc., **noon** 19/26; **nænne, nenne** *am.* 6/45, 126, 155; **nanes, nones** *gm.* 6/46, 12/294, 18/47; *non so crafti mon*, no man so powerful 13/44; *non so fayr a may*, no maiden so fair 30/18 [OE *nān*].

no, na⁴, not, no 6/177, 8/173, 10/93, 18/21, etc.; *as*⁸, nor 6/103, 200, 38/9 [OE *nā*].

noble², noble 5/64 [OF *noble*].

nocht, nogt, noȝt. *See* noht⁴.

noȝtest³ 2*pt.*, ought not 9/84 [OE *ne + āhte*].

noht, nout¹, nothing 7/45, 12/39, 77, 13/34, etc., **nouth** 8/58, **nohut** 13/155, **noth** 38/40; *as vor noȝt*, as if they were nothing 5/57 [OE *nāwiht, nō-wiht*].

noht, nout⁴, not, not at all 4/10, 12/121, 153, etc., **noȝt** 5/78, 9/15, 25, etc., **nouȝt** 5/74, 21/3, 45, **nouth** 8/251, **nogt** 11/13, 30, etc., **nohut** 12/220, 13/37, **nouht** 14/42, 104, **nocht** 19/47, 81, **nowiht** 20/7, **noutt** 38/21 [OE *nā-wiht, nō-wiht*].

nohwiðer⁴, nowhere 18/38 [OE *nāhwider*].

nolde³ 3*pt.*, would not, was unwilling to 5/23, 25, 9/56, etc. [OE *nōlde*].

nom, nome. *See* nimen.

nome, name¹, name 6/148, 10/184, 11/47, etc.; *hire to name*, its name 11/2 [OE *nama, noma*].

nomen; nomore; non(e). *See* nimen; namore; no².

non(e)⁵, none, no one, not one 5/8, 72, 8/49, 64, etc., **nan** 2/43, **noan** 3/17 [OE *nān*].

nonesweis⁴, in no way 17/7 [OE *nānes + weges*].

norþ¹, north 20/100, 28/42 [OE *norþ*].

norþerne², northern 28/1, 3 [OE *norþerne*].

norþhalf², northside 5/29 [OE *norðh(e)alf*].

norþward², northwards 5/22 [OE *norðw(e)ard*].

norþwest², northwest 5/86 [OE *norðwest*].

nos¹, beak 11/7 [OE *nosu*].

not³ 3*pr.*, know not 12/160, 13/110; **nute** 3*prpl.* 10/106 [OE *nāt, nyton*].

note¹, duty 10/130, enjoyment 34/4 [OE *notu*].

note¹, music 13/3n [OF *note*].

noþyng¹, nothing 7/46, 12/111, 183, etc.; *noþinge longe*, not long 9/157 [OE *nān* + *þing*].

noti³ 1*pr.*, employ 10/129 [OE *notian* B].

nou; nouȝt, nouht, nout, nouth; nouþe. *See* nu; noht; nuþe.

nouþer, noþer², neither 10/101, 107, 154, 12/5, etc.; *nouþer . . . ne*, neither . . . nor 2/47 [OE *nā(w)ðor, nōþer*].

nowcin¹, distress 18/47 [ON *nauðsyn*].

nowiderwardes⁴, in no way 2/33 [OE *nāhwider* + adv. *-w(e)ardes*].

nowiht. *See* noht.

nu, nou⁴, now, at present 1/17, 20, 2/78, 4/29, etc.; as⁸, since 17/36 [OE *nū*].

nuȝte. *See* nuste.

nul(e), nulle³ 1*pr.*, wish not 10/*Int.* 2, 20/7, 30/10, nullich 7/25, nully 7/40; 3*pr.*, 31/35, 40; nulleð 3*prpl.* 10/186 [OE *nyllan*].

nuste³ 1*pt.*, knew not 28/11; nuȝte 2*ptpl.* 10/173n. [OE *nyste, nyston*].

nute. *See* not.

nuþe, nouþe⁴, now 9/69, 12/55, 99, 18/53 [OE *nū-þā*].

o. *See* of; on²; on⁵; on⁷.

oc, ok⁸, but 2/34, 47, 53, etc., also 8/190, 239 [ON *ok*].

octobre¹, October 3/23 [OF *octobre*].

of, o⁷, from, out of 1/11, 19, 2/7, 8, 16, 4/10, etc., hof 12/295, about, concerning, of 2/67, 68, 69, 5/44, 6/7, etc., of 3/7, 8, 7/7, 16, etc. on 16/4, 10, 11, 27, 35/42, etc., belonging to 2/67, 17/68, 19/31, because of, on account of 6/127, 170, 10/40, 18/7, etc., by 8/92, 9/128, 11/93, 12/56, 16/41, with 2/15, 7/49, 9/6, 21/14, etc., in 13/38, 45, 55, 14/8, 17/112, etc., over, above 8/71, 20/164, 33/32, to 5/83, containing 7/17, into 12/233, at 19/74; *out, ut of*, out of 12/1, 109, etc., away from 5/14, 19/79, excluded from 19/46; *of al þat*, for all that 5/78; *on of*, all there is to 10/82; *off þatt*, because 15/44 [OE *of*].

ofdrad³ *ptp.*, afraid 10/166 [OE *ofdrædan* A].

ofdryue³, to kill 20/23 [OE *ofdrīfan* 1].

offruht³ *ptp.*, terrified 18/22 [OE *of* + *fyrhtan* A].

offrede³ 1*pts.*, might offer 16/55 [OE *offrian* B].

ofrende¹, offering 16/54 [cf. OE *offrung*].

ofsei³ 3*pt.*, saw 12/10 [OE *ofsēon* 5].

ofserueþ³ 2*prpl.*, deserve 19/92 [OE *of* + OF *servir*].

ofslaȝe³ *ptp.*, slain 6/202, 204 [OE *ofslēan* 6].

ofspreng(e)¹, descendants 16/7, 35 [OE *ofspring*].

oft(e)⁴, often 7/89, 8/144, 10/36, etc.; oftere *comp.* 14/89 [OE *oft*].

ofþinkeþ 3*pr.*, repents 12/205 [OE *ofþyncan* A].

oftok³ 3*pt.*, overtook 21/29 [OE *oftacan* 6, from ON *taka*].

oȝen, oȝte; *See* owest.

ohte², brave 6/83 [OE *āht*].

ok. *See* oc.

old(e), ald², old 5/18, 71, 10/25, etc., hold(e) 8/30, 142; alden *dpl.* 6/39 [OA *ald*].

omidhepes⁴, in the midst 18/61 [OE *on middan hēapes*].

on. *See* an³.

on, one², one, a single 10/182, 12/7, 213, etc., o 4/10, 9/41, 12/266, 31/10, onne 2/31; *on and on*, one and all 12/197, 269; *þat on*, the one 13/8, 10; *vych o*, every 20/128 [OE *ān*].

on, one⁵, indef., a(n), one 6/138, 9/149, etc., o 14/28, 20/10, 49, 145, 163; þones *g.* 21/71; ore *df.* 10/17, 172, 176 [OE *ān*].

on, o⁷, on, upon 2/38, 62, 64, 81, 5/83, etc., **an** 6/122, **onne** 38/83, in 1/1, 9, 15, 2/36, 45, 3/1, etc., **one** 11/62, 94, 13/122, **ho** 38/46, of, about 13/115, 18/10, 22/2, 3, 4, etc., near 10/51, at 11/39, **one** 11/37, during 2/58, 78, 79, 12/211, by means of 21/42, into 6/6, 11/11, 17/135, against 8/211, 17/67, 22/32, with regard to 17/98, 29/2, from 6/135, 8/240, with 18/15, 52, as 15/41; *ieden on*, lived on 2/44; *foð on*, begins 17/29; *þet . . . on*, on which 18/54 [OE *on*].

onde¹, breath 11/14, 103, envy 20/132; *it smit an onde*, a breath came forth 11/65 [OE *ánda*].

one², alone, only 5/9, 16/7, 17/12, 36/26 [OE *āna*].

onfest⁷, hard by 6/5 [OE *on + fæst*].

onȝenes⁴, against; *cumen her onȝenes*, oppose 3/19 [OE *ongē(a)n + adv. -es*].

oni(e). *See* **ani**.

onlepi², single 16/24 [nWS *ānlēpig*].

onlicnes¹, likeness 6/150 [OE *onlícnes*].

onlukest² *sup.*, most solitary 17/56 [OE *ānlic*].

onne; onoh. *See* **on²,⁷**; **inoh**.

onoþer², another 20/4, 116 [OE *ān + ōþer*].

opdrowe³ *3ptpl.*, drew up 12/287 [OE *ūp + dragan* 6].

open², open 8/169, **ope** 12/27 (letters) patent 3/21, 20/194, obvious 17/7; **opene** *pl.* 17/109 [OE *open*].

openlice, -liche⁴, openly 2/56, 17/24 [OE *openlíce*].

opon. *See* **upon**.

opward⁴, on the way up 12/242 [OE *ūppw(e)ard*].

opwinde³, to wind up 12/75 [OE *ūp + windan* 3].

or⁴, before 8/150, 151 [ON *ár*].

or⁸, or 8/46, 48, etc., **er** 11/12 [OE *ōþer*].

orchard¹, orchard 13/98 [OE *ort-g(e)ard*].

ord(e)¹, point (of spear, etc.) 6/97, 35/46; *ord and ende, ende of orde*, from beginning to end 9/129, 10/207 [OE *órd*].

ore¹, mercy 14/55, 16/10, 11, etc.; *þin ore*, be merciful 12/189 [OE *ār*].

ore; ost. *See* **on⁵**; **host**.

oþe¹, oath 3/16; **othes, athes** *pl.* 2/12, 8/250 [OE *áþ*].

oþer, opre², other, another 2/50, 3/15, 10/7, etc., **oþir** 38/31, 77, the second 12/74, 76, 13/8, 11, 15/48, etc.; **oþeres** *g.* 10/9, 12/224; **oþere, oþre** *pl.* 1/18, 3/32, 34, 5/37, etc., **oþer** 8/177, **þopere** 9/127; *oþer-hwile*, at other times 14/92 [OE *ōþer*].

oþer⁸, or 2/23, 30, 51, 3/5, 14, 18, 5/23, etc., **ouþer** 32/29; *oþer . . . or, oþer*, either . . . or 8/94, 12/14 [OE *ā(w)þer, ō(w)þer*].

ou. *See* **ȝe**.

ouer⁷, over, across 4/24, 6/65, 12/22, 28/70, **ofer** 2/1, contrary to 2/46, throughout 3/35, 17/88, beyond 8/160, from 14/107, upon 17/101, along 31/26 [OE *ofer*].

oueral⁴, everywhere 8/38, 54, 12/9, etc. [OE *ofer (e)all*].

ouercaste³ *ptp.*, clouded, overcast 5/88 [OE *ofer + ON kasta*].

ouercome, -cumen³, to overcome 5/57, 17/102; **-come** *2pt.* 18/45; **-com, -cam** *3pt.* 6/48, 16/31; **-kome** *3pts.* 10/165; **-come** *ptp.* 13/184 [OE *ofercuman* 4).

ouerforð⁴, too far 17/61 [OE *ofer + forð*].

ouergart¹, arrogance 18/50 [obscure].

ouerguld³ *ptp.*, gilded 18/7 [OE *ofergýldan* A].

oferhede³ 3*pt.*, disappeared 12/90 [OE *ofergān, -ēode*].

ouermyhte³ 3*pt.*, had the power 2/50n [OE *ofermagan*].

ouerpreisunge¹, excessive praise 17/5 [OE *ofer* + OF *preis(i)-er* + OE *-ung*].

ouerseȝ³ 3*pt.*, looked scornfully at 10/30 [OE *ofersēon* 5].

oversmale², very small 10/64 [OE *ofer* + *smæl*].

ouersteiȝ³ 3*pt.*, rose above 21/20 [OE *oferstīgan* 1].

ouertake³, to overtake 8/229; -tok 3*pt.* 8/189 [OE *ofer* + ON *taka* 6].

ouervuel², excessively wicked 17/9 [OE *ofer* + *yfel*].

ouȝ⁹, oho 5/43.

ounder. *See* under.

ounderfonge³, to receive 12/196; underfenge 1*pts.* 16/54; -fan-gen, -fonge *ptp.* 2/2, 66, 19/61 [OE *underfōn*].

ounderstonde; oundred. *See* understanden; hundred.

ounrede², severe 35/28 [OE *un-(ge)rȳde*].

ountrewe², disloyal 13/41 [OE *untrēowe*].

ounwiis; oup; oup(p)on; our(e). *See* unwis(e); up; upon; we.

ouris. *See* ure.

ous. *See* we.

ouste¹, haste 6/234 [OE *ofost*].

outdrawe. *See* utdrow.

ouþer. *See* oþer⁸.

owe², own 5/2, 7, 9, 7/108, awene 6/35, auȝene 16/59, ahne 17/89 [OE *āgen*].

owel¹, flesh-hook 10/80 [OE *āwel*].

ower. *See* ȝe.

owest³ 2*pr.*, have (to), be bound (to), possess 35/56; oȝen 3*prpl.*, owe 3/11; oȝte 1*pt.* 9/40, 86; ahte 3*pt.* 14/28; ahten 3*ptpl.* 6/9 [OE *āgan, āhte*].

owiht¹, anything 17/30 [OE *āwiht*].

pades¹ *pl.*, toads 2/26 [OE *pad(d)e*].

paens¹ *pl.*, pagans 19/52, 54 [OF *paien*].

paide³ 3*pt.*, paid 17/97, 19/18; ipaied *ptp.*, content 5/81 [OF *payer*].

pal, pel¹, costly cloth 20/146, 21/94 [OE *pæll*].

palais¹, palace 9/5 [OF *palais*].

palmere¹, pilgrim 7/68, 69 [OF *palm(i)er*].

pape¹, Pope 2/66 [OE *pāpa*].

paradis, parays¹, Paradise 33/33, 35/19 [OF *paradis, parais*].

par amours⁴, with all (my) heart 29/26n [OF *par amour*].

parlement¹, parliament 8/113 [OF *parlement*].

parting¹, departure 9/46 [OF *part-ir* + OE *-ing*].

paruenke¹, periwinkle 28/50 [OE *perwince*, OF *pervenke*].

passen³, to go 4/24 [OF *passer*].

passiun¹, passion, suffering 17/124, 131; -es *g.* 17/106 [OF *passiun*].

pater noster¹, the 'Our Father', Lord's Prayer 8/272, 38/71.

patriarke¹, patriarch 21/2, 4; patriarches *pl.* 16/16, 19/35, 65 [OF *patriarche*].

peyne¹, grief 36/17 [OF *peine*].

pel. *See* pal.

pelryne¹, pilgrim 7/50 [OF *pel(e)-rin*].

pende¹, enclosure 7/32n [cf. F *pendre*].

peny¹, penny 19/6, 17, 18, etc. [OE *peni(n)g*].

peolien³, to poll 17/16 [OE **peo-lian* B].

peres¹ *pl.*, pears 22/37 [OE *peru*].

pertre¹, pear-tree 22/37 [OE *peru* + *trēo(w)*].

pes, pees¹, peace 4/4, 10/152, 13/68, 35/53 personified, 28/60 [OF *pes*].

pycchynde³ *prp.*, driving in 31/13 [obscure].

pye¹, magpie 31/37 [OF *pie*].

pikes¹ *pl.*, pikes 12/62, 284 [OE *pīc*].

pilken³, to lop 17/16 [cf. OE *pilian* B].

pine¹, pain, torment 12/142, 16/17, 17/106, etc., anxiety 20/60; -es *pl.* 2/36 [OE *pīn*].

pinin³, to torture 17/118; -eþ *3pr.* 36/17; -ed, -eden *3ptpl.* 2/20, 80; -ed *ptp.* 2/21, 81, longed 7/94 [OE *pīnian* B].

pining¹, torments 2/20, 80 [OE *pīnung*].

pipe¹, pipe, whistle 10/22, 24 [OE *pīpe*].

piping¹, piping 8/238 [OE *pīpe*, + -*ing*].

pite¹, pity 5/74 [OF *pite*].

place¹, place 20/176, battlefield 5/39 [OF *place*].

plaid, plait,¹ argument, dispute 10/5, 159 [OF *plaid, plait*].

plaiding¹, dispute 10/12 [OF *plaid* + OE -*ing*].

plantede³ *3pt.*, planted 2/74 [OE *plantian* B].

plawe¹, sport 32/8 [OE *plagu*].

pleye³, to enjoy oneself 20/133 [OE *plegan* A].

pleyntes¹ *pl.*, complaints 28/61 [OF *plainte*].

plente¹, plenty 8/255 [OF *plente*].

ploȝe¹, sport, play 6/123, 161 [cf. OE *plagu*].

plow¹, plough 8/124 [OE *plōg*].

poer, power¹, strength, force 5/56, 28/60, army 5/28 [OF *pouer*].

pole¹, pool, lake 6/161 [OE *pōl*].

pond. *See* pund.

porpos¹, intention 5/16 [OF *po(u)rpos*].

porter¹, doorkeeper 9/136, 21/38 [OF *port(i)er*].

pot³, to kick 4/36 [lOE *potian* B].

pou(e)re², poor 8/58, 101, 17/15 [OF *pov(e)re*].

pound; power. *See* pund; poer.

prechede³ *3pt.*, preached 5/33 [OF *prech(i)er*].

prechur¹, preacher 19/56 [OF *prech(e)or*].

preȝe, preye³, to pray, ask, invite 7/86, 31/27; *1pr.* 30/9, 13, 19; *imp.* 33/6 [OF *preier*].

preyse³, to praise, be praised 8/60; -eð *3pr.* 17/3, 13 [OF *preis(i)er*].

prelates¹ *pl.*, prelates 22/22 [OF *prelat*].

prenne¹, pin, fastening 21/71 [OE *prēon*].

prest, preost¹, priest 6/1, 8/136, 202, etc.; -es *pl.* 2/49, 5/21, 8/33 [OE *prēost*].

prest², eager 22/25 [OF *prest*].

pride. *See* prude.

prikie³, to spur, hasten 5/53 [OE *prician* B].

prime¹, first division of the day 12/264n [OE *prīm*, from L *prima hora*].

princes¹ *pl.*, princes 22/22 [OF *prince*].

pris¹, prize 20/164, 32/8, 33/32, advantage 9/112, 21/11, value 13/142, 158, 17/98 [OF *pris*].

prisun, priso(u)n¹, prison 2/9, 19, 9/4, 13/128 [OF *prisoun*].

priue², secret; *priue membres*, genitals 5/75 [OF *prive*].

priuilegies¹ *pl.*, grants of immunity from taxation 2/67 [L *privilegi-um*].

profiete, prophete¹, prophet 16/64, 17/111, 19/56; -es *pl.* 16/16, 19/40, 65 [OF *prophete*].

proude, prute², proud 13/138, 14/5, 35/14; pruttest *sup.* 6/136 [OE *prūd, prūt*].

prouesse¹, excellence 28/50 [OF *proece*].

prude, prute¹, pride 4/20, 5/46, etc., pride 22/30 [OE *prȳdo, prȳto*].

pulle¹, pool 21/18 [OE *pull*].

pulten[3] *zptpl.*, put (the weight) 8/130 [OE *pyltan*].

pund[1] *pl.*, pounds 8/46, 9/174, **pound** 4/3, **pond** 9/172 [OE *púnd*].

put, putte[1], pit, well 12/71, 113, 117, 17/45, etc. [OE *pytt*].

put[1], putt 8/162 [OE *pút-ung*].

putten, puten[3], to putt 8/140, 151, 158; **putte** 1*pt.*, made 28/61; *zpt.* 8/159, placed 21/71; *zptpl.* 8/138, thrust 8/217 [cf. OE *pútung*].

putting[1], putting (the weight) 8/164, 237, **puttingge** 8/149 [OE *pútung*].

quakede[3] *zpt.*, trembled 9/74 [OE *cwacian* B].

quam. *See* **wha.**

quarterne[1], cell 2/25 [OE *cweartern*].

quaþ. *See* **quod.**

qued(e)[2], wicked 12/200; **as**[1], evil 12/210, 224 [OE *cwēad*].

quehte[3] *zpt.*, shook 6/88 [OE *cweccan* A].

quelle[3], to kill 9/84, 113 [OE *cwellan* A].

quene[1], queen 6/23, 226, 7/11, 24, etc. [OE *cwēn*].

quene. *See* **quyne.**

questiuns[1] *pl.*, questions, difficulties 1/4 [OF *questioun*].

queþ. *See* **quod.**

quic, quike[2], living, alive 6/11, 37, 75 [OE *cwic*].

quiðes[1] *pl.*, sayings 6/244 [OE *cwide*].

quyne[1], woman 38/67; **quene** *g.* 14/101 [OE *cwene*].

quite[2], free 9/86, 17/58 [OF *quite*].

quite[3], to pay for 4/35 [OF *quiter*].

quod, quaþ, queþ[3] *zpt.*, said 9/83, 87, 12/33, etc., **quoþ** 7/69, **quodh** 8/173, **cwaþ** 10/151, 161, etc. [OE *cweþan, cwæþ* 5].

qwa. *See* **wha.**

qweðsipe[1], wickedness 11/2 [OE *cwēad* + *-scipe*].

rachenteges[1] *pl.*, fetters 2/30 [OE *racen(t)-tēah*].

radde; rædesmen. *See* **rede(n); redesmen.**

ræhzere[2] *df.*, fierce 6/49 [OE *hrēoh*].

ræode; ræueden; ræueres; rahte; ran. *See* **reode; reuen; reueres; reche; renne.**

rath[1], help; *was he rath*, he helped 8/75 [ON *ráð*].

raðe, reðe[4], quickly 11/21, 36, readily 17/4; **raþer** *comp.*, earlier 12/68 [OE *hraþe*].

rauen[1], raven 11/15 [OE *hræfn*].

reasde[3] *zpt.*, rushed 18/55 [OE *rāsan* A].

recche[3], to go 12/268; **-eð** *zpr.*, 18/36 [OE *reccan* A].

rec(c)he[3] *1pr.*, care, desire 10/58, 60, 12/228, **rechi** 13/191; **rec-cheþ** *zprpl.* 10/102; **route** *zpt.* 12/260 [OE *reccan* (*rēcan*), *röhte*, A].

reche[3], to reach, stretch 9/53; **rahte** *zpt.* 18/56 [OE *rācan* A].

red(e)[1], advice 9/151, 160, 14/95, 96, etc., plan 8/206, **reed**, help 12/192; *nimen to rede*, adopt as a plan 10/186; *what shal me to rede*, what shall I do 36/16 [OE *rēd*].

red(e)[2], red 6/149, 8/47, 21/67, 84, **reade** 14/31, ride 9/172 [OE *rēad*].

rede(n)[3], (i) to advise, guide, help 8/104, report 10/204; *1pr.* 13/27, 96; *zprs.* 12/130, 149, 246; **radde** *zpt.* 9/123; (ii) to read 22/25, red 22/2; *zprs.* 6/31; **redenn** *zprspl.* 15/24 [OE *rēdan* 7 and A].

redesmen, rædes-[1] *pl.*, councillors 3/5, 9, 14, 25 [OE *rēdesmann*].

redi², prompt, ready 5/43, 11/15, glib 13/146 [OE *rǣde* + *-ig*].

redliche⁴, quickly 18/59 [OE *hrædlīce*].

refen³, to be roofed 2/63 [OE *hrēfan* A].

refte. *See* **reuen.**

reȝhellboc¹, rule of an order 15/4 [OE *regol* + *bōc*].

reine¹, rain 5/90 [OE *regn*].

reyne¹, world 20/71 [OF *regne*].

rencyan¹, fine cloth,? of Rennes 20/106n [OF *rentien*].

renne², to run 8/204; **ran** *3pt.* 8/223, 37/15; **runnen** *3ptpl.*, fell 17/128 [ON *renna*].

rente¹, income 10/189, 195, 198; **-es** *pl.* 2/62 [OF *rente*].

reode, rǣode¹, reeds 6/102, 158 [OE *hrēod*].

rerde¹, voice 12/114 [OE *réord*].

res¹, fit of madness 20/10 [OE *rǣs*].

rest(e)¹, rest 7/90, 16/20, 18/36, 20/20, 35/53, resting place 33/12 [OE *rest*].

reste³ *imp.*, remain; *3pt.*, hung 18/54, 28/19; *reste wel*, a greeting 38/1 [OE *restan* A].

reðe. *See* **raðe.**

reue¹, farm-bailiff 12/26 [OE *rēfa*].

reuen³, to rob, deprive of 8/266; **refte** *3pt.* 8/94; **rǣueden** *3ptpl.* 2/40, 50 [OE *rēafian* B].

reueres, rǣueres¹ *pl.*, robbers 2/52, 20/149 [OE *rēafere*].

reuliche⁴, piteously 12/107 [OE *hrēowlīce*].

reuþe, reowðe¹, pity, grief, compassion 5/106, 16/13, 26, 17/101, **rewhþe** 16/10, **rewðhe** 16/14, cruelty 6/102, sorrow 6/169, occasion for pity 20/75; as⁴, pitifully 5/70 [cf. OE *hrēow*, ON *hrygð*].

reuþfule², pitiful 21/87 [ME *reuþ-* + *-full*].

rewe¹, place, company 32/35 [OE *rǣw*].

rewe(n)³, to regret, be sorry for 11/110, 13/117, 20/95, 21/92; **-est** *2pr.* 13/154; **-eþ** *3pr.* 4/42, 30/7; **rew(e)** *imp.*, have pity 29/13, 32, 36/19, 43, **reu** 38/23; *hi me reweð*, I have pity on them 16/20 [OE *hrēowan* A].

rybaudes¹ *pl.*, rogues 32/35 [OF *ribauld*].

ribe¹, rib 12/41 [OE *ribb*].

riceman¹, magnate, lord 2/14; **-men** *pl.* 2/44, 70 [OE *rīce* + *mann*].

riche¹, kingdom 6/119, 16/7, 8, etc. [OE *rīce*].

riche², powerful, great 6/190, 10/192, 20/25, 81, **rike** 22/9, rich 13/45, 47, 20/57, 70, splendid 8/258, 21/26, 39, excellent 6/49, 21/63, precious 9/45, noble 35/4 [OE *rīce*, OF *rīche*].

riche⁴, richly 38/62 [OE *rīce*].

ride. *See* **red(e)².**

ride(n)³, to ride 4/39, 5/28, 6/107, etc.; **-end** *prp.* 2/51; **ryd** *imp.* 14/44 [OE *rīdan* 1].

riȝt, riht(e), ricth¹, right, justice 3/16, 8/78, 16/29, **rith** 8/266, righteousness 6/41, 8/36, 71, **right** 22/29, **riȝte**, due 10/88; *wiþ riȝte*, rightly 9/40, 13/29 [OE *riht*].

riȝt, riht, rith⁴, straight, right 6/112, 8/195, 199, 10/158, 12/274, just 8/255, correctly 15/49, 55, **riþt** 29/17, rightly 15/60, quite 21/15, straightway 21/22; *riȝt swo*, just as if 10/76; *riȝt so*, just like 10/80; *riȝt suich*, just as if 10/110; *al riht swa*, in the same way 17/130 [OE *rihte*].

riȝte, riht(e)², right, proper, true 4/40, 9/29, 10/177, etc., **rist** 9/25, **rigte** 11/108, **richt** 19/13, **riȝtte** 35/43, **rith**, right (hand) 8/185 [OE *riht*].

ryhtfulnesse[1], virtue 28/46 [OE *rihtful* + *-nes*].

rihtwise, ricth-[2], righteous 8/37, 16/40 [OE *rihtwīs*].

rih(t)wisnesse[1], righteousness 16/25, 29, 58, 64 [OE *rihtwīsnes*].

rike. *See* **riche**[2].

rikelot[1], chatterbox 17/53 [obscure].

rim(e)[1], story 8/21, 23, 270, 273, metre 15/22, 51, 22/23, poem 20/193; **-es** *pl.* 22/1 [OF *rime*].

ryng[1], ring 7/56, 62, etc. [OE *hring*].

ringe[3], to ring; *do ringe*, to have rung 12/251 [OE *hringan* 3].

rise[1], twig, branch 10/19, 53 [OE *hrīs*].

ryse[3], to rise 36/51; **ros** *3pt.* 7/1, 36/55 [OE *rīsan* 1].

ristnesse[1], greatness 6/0 7 [OE *rihtnes*].

riue[2], plentiful 6/57, 20/19 [OE *rȳfe*].

riued[4], in great numbers 21/18 [OE *rȳfe* + *-ed*].

ro[1], peace 20/20 [ON *ró*].

robbeð[3] *3pr.*, robs 17/15; **-ed** *ptp.* 4/25 [OF *robber*].

roc[1], distaff 38/69 [cf. ON *rokk-r*].

rod(e)[1], cross 2/81, 5/83, 8/103, etc. [OE *rōd*].

rode[1], face 35/6 [OE *rudu*].

rode-scheld[1], the crucifix as a shield 17/131 [OE *rōd* + nWS *scéld*].

rode-steaf[1], crucifix 17/76, 79, 90, 104 [OE *rōd* + *stæf*].

rode-taken[1], sign of the cross 17/92, 18/59 [OE *rōdetācen*].

romans[1] *pl.*, romances 22/2 [OF *romans*].

romanz-reding[1], reading of romances 8/240 [OF *romans* + OE *rǣding*].

ronde[2], round 22/14 [OF *ronde*].

ros. *See* **ryse**.

rote[1], root 22/36 [OE *rōt*, from ON *rót*].

rotieð[3] *3pr.*, decays 11/15 [OE *rotian* B].

roun(e)[1], song 13/2, advice 35/32; **runan** *pl.*, writings 6/31 [OE *rūn*].

route[1], company 5/41 [OF *route*].

route. *See* **rec(c)he**.

rowe[1], row 13/54 [OE *rāw*].

rubie[1], ruby 28/46 [OF *rubi*].

ruggen[1] *dpl.*, back; *to ruggen and to bedde*, for garments and bedclothes 6/44 [OE *hrycg*].

ruȝe[2], rough 10/109 [OE *rūh*].

rume[3], to distend 21/7 [OE *rȳman* A].

runan. *See* **roun(e)**.

runde[3] *3pt.*, spoke secretly 9/78 [OE *rūnian* B].

rune[1], course 18/36 [OE *ryne*].

runnen. *See* **renne**.

runie[2], fierce 6/79 [OE **hrēon* + *-ig*].

rung[3] *imp.*, rise 17/80 [obscure].

rusien[3], to rush 6/79 [OF *ruser*].

sad[2], sated, weary 6/116, 20/50 [OE *sæd*].

sad; sade. *See* **sheddest; segge(n)**.

sadelbowe[1], saddlebow 14/43 [OE *sadolboga*].

sæ; sæde(n), sægen, sæin, sæiþ. *See* **se**[1]; **segge(n)**.

saght, seihte[1], peace, reconciliation 16/25, 22/16 [OE *sæht, seht*].

say(s). *See* **segge(n)**.

sayct, sauhte[2], reconciled 20/134, 38/57 [OE *sæht*].

sayles[1] *pl.*, sails (of a windmill) 4/16 [OE *segl*].

saisede[3] *3pt.*, seized 4/14 [OF *saisir*].

saystu. *See* **segge(n)**.

sake[1], strife, sin 20/62, sake 12/44, 36/33 [OE *sacu*].

sakke[1], sack 21/71, 89 [OE *sacc*].

sal. *See* **shal**.

sale[1], hall 7/3 [OE *sæl*].

salm[1], psalm 17/88 [OE *s(e)alm*].

salt(u). *See* shal.

salue[1], ointment 8/208 [OE *s(e)alf*].

same. *See* shame.

sammnedd[3] *ptp.*, gathered together 15/15 [OE *samnian* B].

sanctus[1], saint 1/1 [L *sanctus*].

sannt[1], saint 15/5 [OE *sanct*].

sanges. *See* song(e).

saphir[1], sapphire 20/115, 173 [OF *safir*].

sardone[1], sardonyx 20/173 [OF *sardoine*].

sariliche[2], horrible 18/55 [OE *sārig* + *-lic*].

sarpe; sarre; sat; sauhte; saule(s); saw. *See* sharpe; sore[4]; sitte(n); sayct; soule; se(n).

sawe[1], saying 13/95, 112, 178, verdict 32/9; -es *pl.* 13/111 [OE *sagu*].

sawter[1], psalter 17/69, 113 [OF *saut(i)er*].

scæftes, scaftes[1] *pl.*, spears 6/58, 196 [OE *sceaft*].

scærp(e); scal, scalt. *See* sharpe; shal.

scanen[3], to break 6/196 [OE *scǣnan* A].

scarne[1], contempt 17/93 [OF (*e*)-*scarn*].

scatered[3] *3pt.*, dissipated 2/4 [obscure].

sceld(es); scelde; sceolen; sceone; sceort. *See* sheld; shilde(n); shal; shen(e); short.

sceouen[3] *ptp.*, pushed 6/232 [OE *scūfan* 2].

sceppend[1], Creator 16/30 [nWS *sceppend*].

schadewe[1], shadow 18/17, 20/32 [OE *sceadu*].

schan; schaw, schawde. *See* schyneþ; shewe.

scheate[3] *3pt.*, darted 18/14; shoten *3ptpl.*, rushed 8/211; ishote *ptp.*, produced 10/23 [OE *scēotan* 2].

schef[1], sheaf 20/72 [OE *scēaf*].

schille[2], tuneful 10/143 [OE *scielle*].

schimmede[3] *3pt.*, shimmered 18/17 [OE *scīmian* B].

schyneþ[3] *3pr.*, shines 20/184; schan *3pt.* 18/17 [OE *scīnan* 1].

schrifte, srift[1], absolution 8/202, 12/196, confession 12/186, 17/21 [OE *scrift*].

schunien[3], to avoid 17/22 [OE *scunian* B].

schucke[1], demon 18/16 [OE *scucca*].

scille[4], eloquently 29/33n [cf. ON *skil*-].

scilwis[2], wise 22/33 [ON *skilvíss*].

scinnes[1] *pl.*, evil spirits 14/99n [OE *scinn*].

scynnes; scolde. *See* sinne; shal.

scole[1], university 29/29, 38/41 [OE *scōl*].

sconken[1] *pl.*, legs 6/140 [OE *scanca*].

scort. *See* short.

scot[1], reckoning, costs 4/35 [OE *scot*].

screwe; sculde(st), sculle(n); se. *See* shrewe; shal; so.

se[5], *def.art.*, the 16/2, 19/12, 17, 25, etc. [OE *se*].

se, see[1], sea 4/24, 6/231, 8/256, etc., sæ 2/1, 6/180; sees *g.* 11/81 [OE *sǣ*].

se(n)[3], to see, behold 5/106, 8/128, 233, etc., seo 20/31, understand 15/24; se, so *1pr.* 10/34, 36/5, 23, 28; syþt *3pr.* 31/11; sen, seoþ *3prpl.* 9/70, 11/87; se. *imp.*, help 33/5; seh, sey *1pt.* 7/21, 12/216; sei, saw *3pt.* 5/40, 8/150, 166, 221, 12/281, seȝ 9/104, sauȝ 21/92; seyen *3ptpl.* 21/39, 76, sehen 18/6, seghen 19/19, sowen 8/162; seȝe, soge *2pts.* 7/53, 11/60; seȝe *3pts.* 29/27; syen *ptp.* 38/46 [OE *sēon* 5].

sea-strem[1], sea current 18/39 [OE *sǣstrēam*].

seaude, seauede, seaweth. *See* **shewe.**

seche³, to seek 7/30, 76, 10/181, 30/10; **sohvte** *3pt.* 12/69; **isouȝt, soht** *ptp.* 21/89, attacked 28/57, obtained 32/17 [OE *sēcan* A].

sed¹, seed 10/137, 24/3 [OE *sǣd*].

sede(n). *See* **segge(n).**

segge¹, sedge 10/18 [OE *secg*].

segge(n), sigge(n), sugge(n)³, to say, tell, inform 5/114, 6/173, 12/207, etc., **sæin** 2/57, **sægen** 2/78, **sugen** 6/242, **seien** 11/59, 35/47, **seye** 36/25, say 38/18, pray to 38/72; **segge, sug(g)e** *1pr.* 13/122, 184, 14/104, 32/9; **seist** *2pr.* 10/50, 13/61, 69, etc., **saystu** 38/63; **seiþ** *3pr.* 5/17, 111, 13/17, 14/98, etc., **sæiþ** 1/20, **seieð** 11/49, says 30/14; **seggeð** *3prpl.* 17/116; **segge** *2prs.* 10/60; **segge, seye, sigge** *3prs.* 6/32, 8/272, 17/30; **sigge** *2prspl.* 21/30; **sei, say** *imp.* 7/71, 12/121, 229, etc., **seye** 14/42, 43; **seide** *1pt.* 17/13, 18, 46; *3pt.* 6/68, 219, 7/11, etc., **sede** 5/43, 45, 9/9, etc., **sade** 16/13, 37, 44, etc., **sæde** 16/3, 22; **seiden** *3ptpl.* 19/21, 21/79, **sæden** 2/56, **seden,** 19/36; **iseid** *ptp.* 3/15, 10/133, 14/100, 19/67, **ised** 14/94, **seyd** 8/268, **sehid** 12/210, **ised** 14/94 [OE *secgan* C].

segges¹ *pl.*, men 6/128 [OE *secg*.].

seghen. *See* **se(n).**

se-grund¹, bottom of the sea 11/75 [OE *sǣgrúnd*].

seȝ(e), seh(en); sehid, sei(e), seyd, seide(n); seie(n); sey(en); seihte. *See* **se(n); segge(n); se(n); segge(n); saght.**

seint(e)¹, saint 6/16, 17 [OF *saint*].

seist, seiþ. *See* **segge(n).**

sek(e)², ill 12/41; *bygan be sek,* fell ill 7/85 [OE *sē(o)c*].

sel, seel¹, seal 3/22, 20/194 [OF *seel*].

sel², good, pleasant 6/4; **sel(e)re** *comp.* 6/155; *þat hire þe selre beo,* that it might be the better for it 6/35 [OE *sēl*].

selcuth, seolcuð², marvellous, wonderful 6/157, 22/23 [OE *séldcúþ*].

sellen, sullen³, to sell 8/53, 21/48; **sule** *imp.* 17/99; **solde** *3pt.* 13/141; **isold** *ptp.* 9/130 [OE *sellan, syllan* A].

sellic¹, marvel, wonder 6/173 [OE *séldlic*].

sellic⁴, excellently, well 6/107, 112 [OE *séldlíce*].

seluer. *See* **siluer.**

semblaunt¹, appearance 9/8 [OF *semblant*].

sembling¹, assembling 8/125 [OF *(as)sembl-er* + OE *-ing*].

seme³, to load 21/67; **isemed** *ptp.* 21/84 [nWS *sēman* A].

semest³ *2pr.*, seem 29/33; **-eþ** *3pr.* 15/33; **sem(e)de** *3pt.* 18/14, suited 13/116; **semden** *3ptpl.* 18/8 [ON *sóma, sǽmdi*].

semly², lovely 28/6 [ON *sǽm-r* + OE *-lic*].

sende(n)³, to send 13/84, 86; **sende** *1pr.* 20/193; **send, sent** *3pr.* 3/3, 17/27, 19/73, etc., **sendeþ** 9/33, 10/*Int.* 2; **senden** *1prpl.* 3/21; **send** *2prs.* 16/19; *3prs.* 38/33, 52; **sent** *imp.* 28/2; **sende, sente** *3pt.* 7/67, 19/7, 35, etc.; **sende** *3ptpl.* 5/76; **(i)send** *ptp.* 3/34, 9/1, 20/205, **sent** 8/112 [OE *séndan* A].

sending¹, disgrace 11/42 [OE *scéndung*].

sene², plain, evident 29/2, 30/15 [nWS *(ge)sēne*].

senne; seolcuð. *See* **sinne; selcuth.**

seollic², wonderful 6/36 [OE *séldlic*].

seoluer; seorewe(n); seoruhful; seoruwe; seo(þ); seoðe. *See* siluer; sorewe; soreweful; sorewe; se(n); sythen.

seoue², seven 6/98 [OE *seofon*].

sere², different, various 22/2, 12, 23 [ON *sér*].

serekin², of various kinds 22/21 [ON *sér* + OE *cynn(a)*].

serewe(s). *See* sorewe.

sergant¹, servant 19/14, 17 [OF *serjant*].

serue, serui³, to serve 19/50, 57, etc.; serui 3*prs.* 19/51; seruede(n) 3*ptpl.* 19/36, 66; iserued *ptp.* 21/61 [OF *servir*].

seruise¹, service, work 19/3, 31, etc.; *ine is seruise*, to do his work 19/36 [OE *serfise*, from OF *servise*].

set, sete(n); seþþe(n). *See* sitte(n); sythen.

setle¹, throne 16/42 [OE *setl*].

setten³, to place, set 16/42; sete *imp.* 31/26; sette 3*pt.* 9/140, 18/55, set 6/143, allotted 2/62, wrote down 6/27, established 15/5; 3*pts.* 7/101; iset, set(t) *ptp.* 6/157, written 15/21, 51, 31/10 [OE *settan* A].

seue(n)þe², seventh 7/34, 8/198 [OE *seofoþa*].

seuesiþe⁴, seven times 9/12 [OE *seofon* + *síþum*].

shake³, to shake, move 31/11; ssok 3*pt.* 21/95 [OE *sc(e)acan* 6].

shal, schal³ 1*pr.*, am to, must, shall, will 8/21, 170, 10/206, etc., sol 10/121, sal 19/13, 59, 38/24, 58, sule 27/2; shalt 2*pr.* 4/7, 39, 7/38, etc., shaltou 8/173, schalt 9/38, 17/125, schal 14/62, scalt 16/47, 48, etc., salt 38/56, saltu 38/60, 62; schal, shal 3*pr.* 9/28, 10/135, 13/95, etc., scal 6/74, 37/5, sal 11/110, 112, 23/1, 35/30, ssal 21/36; shulenn 1*prpl.* 15/37, sceolen 1/23, ssole 5/57,

sculle(ð) 6/75, 84, sollen 19/3, 62, schule 31/32; schulle 2*prpl.* 9/92, 94, ssulen 21/80; shule(n) 3*prpl.* 13/128, 134, 15/40, etc., shullen 3/7, scullen 6/76, sulle 19/28, solle 19/80, schule 20/133, shal 29/35, shulle 32/20, ssulen 34/4; scule 2*prs.* 16/11; schulle 3*prs.* 10/169; sholde, shulde 1*pt.* 10/93, 12/138, 15/12, etc., shuldich 12/163, 181; sholdest 2*pt.* 10/54, 12/136, 180, sculdest 2/41; sholde, shulde 3*pt.* 4/30, 35, 8/134, etc., scolde 6/154, scholde 10/150, schulde 17/36, 56, sculde 2/2, solde 19/82; ssolde 2*ptpl.* 21/85; shulden, scholde(n) 3*ptpl.* 9/143, 12/264, 268, 14/16, 20/183, schulden 17/48, solden 19/57 [OE *sceal*, *sculon*; *scólde*].

shame, shome¹, shame, insult 8/83, 12/35, 99, etc., schame 10/50, 153, 183, same 11/42, sham 29/15, injury 8/56, scam 38/29, 65; *me to schame*, as a shame to me 9/17; *to same*, to their shame 11/48 [OE *scamu*, *scomu*].

sharpe, scharp(e)², sharp 4/15, 8/235, 10/79, 18/14, scærp(e) 2/28, 32, sarpe 11/22, impetuous 20/69 [OE *scearp*].

shawe¹, wood, copse 13/124 [OE *sc(e)aga*].

shcire¹, shire, county 3/34 [OE *scír*].

sheddest³ 2*pt.*, shed 36/65; sad 3*pt* 33/15 [OE *scēadan* 7].

sheld, scheld¹, shield 4/31, 10/118, 17/124, etc., sceld 6/78, 147; sceldes *pl.* 6/87, 89, 196 [nWS *scéld*].

shene, schen², fair, beautiful 29/1, 38/45, sceone 6/226 [nWS *scéne*].

shenche³, to pour out 7/2; shenh *imp.* 7/13 [OE *scencan* A].

L

shende³, to shame 13/11, 75, **ssende,** to destroy 5/17; **ssende** 3*pt.* 5/77; **ishend** *ptp.* 13/169 [OE *scéndan* A].

shep¹ *pl.,* sheep 12/167, 203 [OE *scē(a)p*].

shereþ³ 3*pr.,* changes direction 31/4 [cf. MLG *scheren*].

shewe, schewe³, to show, see 8/226, 32/33, tell 9/79, **showe,** to bring forward as witness 13/51; **seaweth** 3*pr.* 19/2; **schaw** *imp.* 17/134; **schawde, seauede, ssewede** 3*pt.* 5/82, 17/127, showed (himself) 19/44; **seaude** 3*pts.* 19/56 [OE *scēawian* B].

shilde(n), schilde³, to shield, protect (oneself) 10/62, 13/14, 56, 32/7; **s(c)hilde** 1*pr.* 10/57; 3*prs.* 8/16; **scelde** 3*pt.* 6/95 [OE *sc(i)éldan* A].

ship¹, ship 7/83; **sipes** *pl.* 11/85, 91; *to shipeward,* near a ship 7/80 [OE *scip*].

shoddreþ³ 3*pr.,* trembles 31/4 [cf. MLG *schoderen*].

sholde(n), sholdest; sholdres. *See* shal; shuldre.

shome², shameful 13/82 [OE *scamu, scomu*].

shonde, schonde¹, shame, disgrace 10/155, 13/48, 164, **sonde** 11/104 [OE *scánd*].

short, scort², short 2/27, 10/73, **sceort,** small 6/232 [OE *sc(e)ort*].

shoten; showe. *See* scheate; shewe.

shrede¹, morsel of food 8/99 [OE *scrēad*].

shreward¹, rogue 4/43 [OE *scrēawa + -ard*].

shrewe, screwe¹, slut 32/13, 18 [OE *scrēawa*].

shrude³, to clothe 32/13; **iscrud** *ptp.* 6/44 [OE *scrŷdan* A].

shulde(n). *See* shal.

shuldre, sholdres¹ *pl.,* shoulders 8/191, 28/26 [OE *sculdru pl.*]

shuldreden³ 3*ptpl.,* nudged 8/163 [cf. OE *scúldor*].

shulle(n). *See* shal.

shurte¹, shirt 7/103 [OE *scyrte*].

sibbe¹, bonds of kinship 10/101 [OE *sibb*].

sibsumnesse¹, peace, concord 16/22, 23, 64 [OE *sibsumnes*].

side¹, side 5/58, 6/141, etc.; **-es** *pl.* 8/223; **siden** *dpl.* 6/174; as⁴, widely 20/47 [OE *sîde*].

syen; sigge(n). *See* se(n); segge(n).

signefiance¹, interpretation 19/30 [OF *signefiance*].

siȝeð 3*prpl.,* move 6/128 [OE *sîgan* 1].

syht. *See* se(n).

siht(e), sihðe¹, sight 17/134, 20/141; *on syht,* in appearance 28/6 [OE *sihð*].

syk(e)¹, grief, sigh 29/5, 30/6 [OE *sice*].

siken³, to sigh 12/195, 17/30; **siked** *ptp.* 30/6 [OE *sîcan* 1].

siker², certain 12/58 [OE *sicor*].

sykyng¹, sighing (personified) 28/58, 62 [OE *sîc-an + -ing*].

siluer, seluer¹, silver 2/5, 20, 4/26, 8/73, **seoluer** 20/28 [OE *silfor, seolfor*].

syn⁸, since 38/31 [OE *siþþan*].

sinndenn³ 3*prpl.,* are 15/16 [OE *sindon*].

sinful(e)², sinful 11/43, 102, **sunfoul** 13/65 [OE *synnful*].

singe³, to sing 5/21, 8/241, 10/39, etc., write verse 10/*Int.* 2; **-inde** *prp.* 14/44; **singe** 1*pr.* 10/92, 132; **-es** 2*pr.* 24/11; **-eþ, -es** 3*pr.* 14/78, 30/1; **-eþ** 3*prpl.* 13/6; **sing(e)** *imp.* 24/2, 5, 9, recite, read 20/203; **song** 3*pt.* 10/20, 26, 144; **sungen** 3*ptpl.* 21/65; **sunge** 1*pts.* 10/122 [OE *singan* 3].

sinke(n)³, to sink 6/96, 11/96, 12/80, 239 [OE *sincan* 3].

sinne, senne, sunne¹, sin 4/23, 11/32, 12/165, etc., sin 38/65, 76; sunnes g. 36/59; sinnes, sunnen *pl.* 2/58, 12/177, 197, scynnes 38/74 [OE *synn*].

sipes. *See* ship.

sir(e)¹, father 38/3, (as polite form of address) sir 9/23, 83, 17/15, 38/2, 11, (preface to names and titles) Sir 4/28, 33, 34, etc. [OF *sire*].

sipe¹, time 6/105, 8/159, 15/48, 29/23; sithon *d.* 2/46n [OE *sīþ*].

sythen, sepþe(n)⁴, afterwards 2/48, 82, 7/52, etc., seoðe 6/229, sipe 8/187, since 21/66 [OE *sippan, seoþþan*].

sypt. *See* se(n).

sitte(n)³, to sit, remain, dwell 2/33, 10/115, 12/281, 21/8, 40, 31/30; -ende *prp.* 2/42; -est 2*pr.* 20/201, perch 10/89, sitest 13/106; sit, sitteþ 3*pr.* 10/86, 20/208, 31/7, 32/23; -eþ 3*prpl.* 13/54; -en 1*prspl.*, may perch 13/166; site *imp.* 17/73; sitte(þ) *imppl.* 4/1, 21/45; sat, set 3*pt.* 7/9, 12/30, 117, lasted 8/257, perched 10/15, 172; sete(n) 3*ptpl.*, perched 12/32, were gathered 14/1; sete 3*pts.*, might rest 11/62; *sitte softe*, to rest in comfort 32/27 [OE *sittan* 5].

siwed³ *ptp.*, pursued 28/62 [ONF *suer, siwer*].

sixe², six 8/197 [OE *siex*].

sixte², sixth 8/193 [OE *siexta*].

sixti², sixty 6/162, 176, etc. [OE *siextig*].

skape¹, harm 13/15 [ON *skaði*].

skemting¹, amusement 11/35 [ON *skemt-a* + *-ing*].

skere³, to free 13/15 [cf. ON *skærr*].

skyere¹, squire 7/8 [OF (*e*)*squier*].

skill¹, reason 15/42; skiles *g.* 17/60 [ON *skil*].

skirming¹, fencing 8/236 [OF *skirm-er* + OE *-ing*].

slake³ 1*pr.*, become weak 28/81 [OE *slacian* B].

slat. *See* slete.

slawðe¹, sloth 17/103 [cf. OE *slæwþ*].

sley², shrewd 12/262, happy 20/143n [ON *slæg-r*].

slein, slo(n)³, to slay 7/97, 28/63, 29/20; sloð 3*pr.* 11/32; sloh, slou 3*pt.* 5/85, 91, 8/180, 16/33, struck 6/201; slozen, slowe 3*ptpl.*, smote 5/50, 105, 6/55; islaze, (i)slawe *ptp.* 5/27, 6/203, 8/176, 21/78 [OE *slēan* 6, ON *slá*].

slep¹, sleep 12/267, 28/81 [OE *slǣp*].

slepe(n)³, to sleep 2/34, 21/12; -inde *prp.*, sleepily 17/75; slep 3*pt.* 2/56 [OE *slǣpan* 7].

slete³, to hunt 12/289; slat *ptp.*, baited 32/23 [OE *slǣtan* A].

slyt³ 3*pr.*, falls 31/3 [OE *slīdan* 1].

sloweste² *sup.*, slowest 31/12 [OE *slāw*].

smal(e)², small 11/73, 12/155, 248, slender 10/73, 28/29, thin 10/142 [OE *smæl*].

smaragde¹, emerald 20/174 [OF *smaragde*].

smecche¹ *gpl.*, of tastes 18/12 [OE *smæc*].

smellen³, to smell 17/48 [eME *smellen, smullen*].

smeortliche⁴, quickly 17/89, 18/25 [OE *smeort* + *-līce*].

smere⁴, scornfully 12/23 [OE (*gāl*)-*smǣre*].

smerte³, to smart 20/58; smeorte 3*prs.* 14/58 [OE *smeortan* 3].

smite(n)³, to smite, strike down 8/227, 10/78; -eð 3*prpl.* 6/104; smot 3*pt.* 8/196, 201, etc.; smite(n) 3*ptpl.* 5/76, advanced 5/49; *smiten a*, fought against 6/88 [OE *smītan* 1].

smið¹, smith 6/138 [OE *smiþ*].

smiððe¹, smithy 17/55 [OE *smið-ðe*].

smok¹, smock 32/14 [OE *smoc*].

smoke¹, smoke 2/22, 18/12 [OE *smoca*].

smoked³ 3*pt.*, smoked 2/22 [OE *smocian* B].

smorðrinde³ *prp.*, suffocating 18/12 [cf. OE *smorian* B].

snailes¹ *pl.*, snails 10/87 [OE *snægl*].

snakerinde³ *prp.*, approaching stealthily 17/72 [cf. OE *snaca*].

snakes¹ *pl.*, snakes 2/26 [OE *snaca*].

snawe, snou¹, snow 6/80, 10/98 [OE *snāw*].

snel(le)², brave 6/55, 204, active 20/150 [OE *snell*].

so, se, swo, swa⁴, so, thus, in this way 2/21, 26, 31, 5/4, 71, 7/22, etc., also 4/5, such as 11/100, to such an extent 16/7, where 19/9, similarly 19/77. As⁸, as, like 6/79, 99, 8/40, 91, 133, 9/72, etc., yet 6/177, as if 8/256, 10/77, 11/44, so 12/149, however 20/47; *so þat*, consequently 5/18; *swo swo*, just as 16/48; *so muchel so*, as much as 17/25; *be swo þet*, provided that 19/72; *also . . . so*, as . . . as 29/22 [OE *swā, swē*].

so; soffrede. *See* se(n); suffre.

sofnesse¹, gentleness 16/24 [OE *sōftnes*].

softe², gentle, mild 10/6, 13/68, 35/30, easy-going 2/10 [OE *sōfte*].

softe⁴, gently 6/235, 17/65, in comfort 32/27 [OE *sōfte*].

soge; soht, sohvte; sol, solde(n); solde; solle(n). *See* se(n); seche; shal; sellen; shal.

solsecle¹, marigold 28/51 [OF *solsecle*].

some², united 20/134 [OE *sōm*].

somed⁴, together 6/84, 17/26 [OE *samod*].

som; somer, someres; somne. *See* sum(e); sumer(e); sum(e).

sond¹, sand; *se-sond*, bottom of the sea 11/62 [OE *sánd*].

sonde. *See* shonde.

sonde¹, messenger 9/158, 20/103 [OE *sánd*].

sone⁴, immediately 5/31, 51, 8/81, etc., soon 5/28, 20/26; *wel sone*, very quickly 14/67; *sone se*, as soon as 17/71 [OE *sōna*].

son(e), sones; song. *See* sune; singe.

song(e)¹, song 10/11, 36, 46, etc.; -es, sanges *pl.* 13/99, 22/23 [OE *sáng*].

sor(e)², grievous, painful 8/190, 29/30 [OE *sār*].

sore¹ *pl.*, wounds 13/153 [OE *sār*].

sore⁴, sorely, grievously 4/42, 5/93, etc.; sarre *comp.* 17/118 [OE *sāre*].

sore³. *See* swere.

soregh³ 1*pr.*, grieve 25/7 [OE *sorgian* B].

sorewe, serewe¹, grief, sorrow 12/89, 14/49, etc. (personified) 28/65, sorȝe 6/96, sorw(e) 8/57, 26/4, seorewe 14/41, 97, 20/46, seoruwe 17/40; sorȝen, sere-wes, seorewen *pl.* 6/76, 20/19, 29/24 [OE *sorg*, **seorg*].

soreweful, sorhfulle, seoruhful², sorrowful 6/219, 17/38, distressing 36/54 [OE *sorgful*, **seorgful*].

sorewyng¹, grief (personified) 28/58 [OE *sorgung*].

sory¹, sorrow 38/36n [cf. OE *sārig, sorg*].

sori², sorry, wretched 4/21, 13/83, 17/39, etc. [OE *sārig*].

sory³ 1*pr.*, grieve 38/17 n [cf. OE *sārig*].

sorinesse¹, grief 9/72 [OE *sārig-nes*].

sote¹, madman 22/18 [OF *sot*].

soþ¹, truth 8/36, 12/121, 13/168, etc., soðe 6/242; *for, to sop(e)*, in truth, truly 9/28, 83, 15/55, etc. [OE *sōþ*].

soþ², true 10/167, 191, 12/157, etc., soðe 6/244; **soþere** *comp*. 6/27 [OE *sōþ*].

soðfeste², true 6/32 [OE *sōþfæst*].

soþ-saȝe¹, true saying 10/134 [OE *sōþsagu*].

sotlice⁴, foolishly 2/4 [OF *sot* + OE *-līce*].

soule, saule¹, soul 2/5, 5/48, 6/33, etc.; **sawle** *g*. 15/69, 74, 77; **soules, saules** *pl*. 5/45, 16/17, 35/12 [OE *sāwol*].

soule-cnul¹, death-knell 12/251 [OE *sāwol* + *cnyll*].

soum, soumme. *See* sum(e).

soure⁴, bitterly 32/18 [cf. OE *sūr*].

souþ. *See* suþ.

sowe³, to sow 10/135; **-eþ** *3pr*. 10/137; **isowen** *ptp*. 14/30 [OE *sāwan* 7].

sowen; spac; spæche. *See* se(n); speke(n); speche.

sparke¹, spark 8/91 [OE *spearca*].

speatewile², horrible 18/11 [obscure].

speche¹, speech, language 5/2, 5, 9, 13/152, etc., **spæche** 15/65, dispute 10/13, arguments 10/204, word 12/223 [OE *sp(r)ǣc*].

spede³, to succeed 8/93, 38/61; **spedde** *3ptpl*. 10/214; **ysped** *ptp*. 31/22 [OE *spēdan* A].

speke(n)³, to speak 5/2, 9/24, 82, etc.; **spekest(u), spekstu** *2pr*. 20/113, 169, 29/33; **-eþ** *3pr*. 17/43, 19/1, 20/98; *3prpl*. 9/70; **spac, spak** *3pt*. 9/21, 12/65, 16/44, 21/38; **speke** *3ptpl*. 5/3 [OE *sp(r)ecan* 5].

spel(le)¹, tale, story 10/216, 11/38 [OE *spell*].

spellen³, to speak, preach 15/18, 68; **spelle** *1pr*. 8/15 [OE *spellian* B].

spende³ *3pt*., squandered 4/9 [OE *(a)spéndan* A].

speouwen³, to vomit 17/21; **-eð** *3pr*. 17/25; **speu** *3pt*. 8/192 [OE *spīwan* 1, *spēowan* A].

spere¹, spear 4/31, 6/151, 10/118, 30/3; **-es** *g*. 6/97; **speres, -en** *pl*. 6/89, 195, 8/235, 12/292 [OE *spere*].

sperclede³ *3pt*., came in sparks 18/11[cf. OE *spearcian* B].

speten³, to spit 10/39 [OE *spǣtan* A].

spille³, to destroy, waste 10/116, 13/66, 134; **ispild, spilt** *ptp*. 10/123, undone 38/22; *of limes spille*, to be castrated 8/86 [OE *spillan* A].

spire¹, reeds 10/18 [OE *spīr*].

spis¹, spice 20/168 [OF *(e)spice*].

spite³ *imp*., spit 17/92 [OE *spittan* A].

splen¹, spleen 12/47 [OF *(e)splen*, L *splēn*].

sporeles², without spurs 4/39 [OE *sporu* + *-lēas*].

sprede³, to spread 8/95 [OE *sprǣdan* A].

sprengen³ *3ptpl*., sprung 6/195 [cf. OE *spríngan* 3, *sprengan* A].

springe³, to spread, spring, grow 13/108; **-eþ, sprin(g)þ** *3pr*. 10/138, 13/3, 109, 24/4, **springet**, gushes 33/26; **springes** *3prpl*., sprout 30/2; **sprong** *3pt*. 8/91, was born 13/172, began 36/56 [OE *spríngan* 3].

sprutteð³ *3pr*., sprouts 17/17 [OE *spryttan* A].

spuse¹, spouse 17/67, 100 [OF *(e)spouse*].

spusen³, to marry 9/150 [OF *(e)spouser*].

sriue³, to absolve 12/184; **isriue** *ptp*. 12/176 [OE *scrīfan* 1, from L *scribere*].

sr-, ss-. *See* sch-, sh-.

stabell², steadfast (warriors) 22/13 [OF (e)*stable*].

stadden³ 3*ptpl.*, looked on 8/144 [ON *steðja, stadda*].

staf¹, staff 35/37, 41; **staues** *pl.* 12/62, 284, etc.; **-en** *dpl.*, characters 6/149 [OE *stæf*].

stake¹ *pl.*, stakes 31/13 [OE *staca*].

stalworþi², brave 8/24; **-worþeste** *sup.* 8/25 [OE *stǣlwurðe*].

stan. *See* **ston(e).**

stan-ded², stone-dead 8/188 [OE *stān + dēad*].

stanes; stannt. *See* **ston(e); stonde(n).**

starc, starke², violent, strong 8/122, 131, 10/5, **stearc,** vile 18/16 [OE *stearc*].

starest³ 2*pr.*, glare 10/77; **steareden** 3*ptpl.*, shone 18/9 [OE *starian* B].

staþe¹, shore 6/4 [OE *stæþ*].

steappre² *comp.*, more brilliant 18/9 [OE *stēap*].

steareden. *See* **starest.**

stede¹, horse 8/10, 26, 88; **-en** *d.* 6/152 [OE *stēda*].

stede¹, place 11/13, 16/43; **-es** *pl.* 8/219 [OE *stede*].

stedefæst, -fast², firm, steadfast 3/9, 21, 11/107 [OE *stedefæst*].

stedefæstliche⁴, steadfastly 3/11 [OE *stedefæst + -līce*].

stel¹, place, position 4/15, 20/200 [OE *stæl*].

stel(e)¹, steel 6/137, 140, 10/126, etc. [nWS *stēle*].

stele³ 3*prs.*, may rob 20/59 [OE *stelan* 4].

stench¹, stench 18/16 [OE *stenc*].

steorest³ 2*pr.*, rule 18/39 [OA *stēoran* A].

steor(r)en¹ *pl.*, stars 18/9, 37 [OE *steorra*].

stephne; stereð. *See* **steuene; stireð.**

sternes¹ *pl.*, stars 8/182 [ON *stjarna*].

sterteþ³ 3*pr.*, leaps 24/8; **stirte** 3*pt.*, hastened 8/156 [OE *styrtan* A].

steuene, stefene¹, voice 6/114, 10/142, 38/26, **stephne** 20/203; **stefenen** *dpl.* 6/129 [OE *stefn*].

sty¹, path, road 31/26 [OE *stīg*].

stif¹, fierce 10/5, hard 10/79 [OE *stīf*].

stille², quiet, still 4/1, 8/69, 12/36, etc. [OE *stille*].

stille⁴, quietly 8/272, 10/115, 11/83, etc., fast 29/35; *lude and stille,* under all circumstances 14/90 [OE *stille*].

stinken³, to smell, stink 17/19, 44; **-inde** *prp.* 17/73; **stonk** 3*pt.* 12/94; **stunken** 3*ptspl.* 17/20 [OE *stincan* 3].

stireð, stereð³ 3*pr.*, stirs, moves 11/13, 78, 83; **sturieð** 3*prpl.* 18/38; **sture** *imp.* 17/80; **sturede** 3*pt.* 18/17 [OE *styrian* A].

stirte. *See* **sterteþ.**

stiward¹, steward 21/80, 88 [OE *stīw(e)ard*].

stoc¹, tree-stump 10/25 [OE *stoc*].

ston(e)¹, stone 8/130, 132, 14/38, etc., **stan** 17/111, flint 11/93, precious stone 20/116, 161; **stones, stanes** *pl.* 2/28, 12/62, **ston** 12/284 [OE *stān*].

stonde(n)³, to stand 7/79, 9/145, 18/49, be 36/4; **stond, stont** 3*pr.* 20/121, 31/1, **stannt,** is written 15/17; **stond** *imp.* 10/210, 35/35; **stod** 3*pt.* 8/148, 191, 222, 9/7, etc.; 1*ptpl.* 29/23; **stode(n)** 3*ptpl.* 6/153, 8/144, existed 6/229; **i-stonden** *ptp.*, existed 6/223; *stond wel,* be comforted 36/1 [OE *stándan* 6].

stongen³ *ptp.*, pierced 36/29 [OE *stíngan* 3].

stonk. *See* **stinken.**

store³, to garrison 4/22 [OF (e)-*storer*].

storis¹ *pl.*, stories 22/21 [OF (e)*storie*].

storm¹, storm 11/78 [OE *stórm*].

storue³ 2*pt.*, died 12/151; sturuen 3*ptpl.* 2/43 [OE *steorfan* 3].

stounde, stund(e)¹, space of time 5/61, 7/55, 12/213, etc., state, condition 20/158; stoundes *pl.*, times of trial 35/18 [OE *stúnd*].

stout², stately 28/38 [OF (e)*stout*].

strahte³ 3*pt.*, moved 18/17 [OE *streccan*, *streahte* A].

stremes¹ *pl.*, streams (of blood) 36/23 [OE *stréam*].

strende³ 3*pt.*, begot 6/0 34 [OA *stréonan* A].

strenges¹ *pl.* cords 2/24 [OE *stréng*].

strengþe¹, strength, force 2/71, 6/49, 94, etc., strenkþe 35/50 [OE *strengðu*].

strenkþen³, to strengthen 35/45 [cf. OE *strengðu*].

strete¹, street, road 5/106, 12/5 [OE *strǽt*, from L *stráta via*].

stryd. *See* strit.

strif¹, strife 32/4, 35/53, strijf 22/5, dispute 13/7, 12 [OE (e)*strif*].

strit³ 3*pr.*, strides 31/1; stryd *imp.* 31/26 [OE *strídan* 1].

striue(n)³, to dispute 13/166, 183 [OF (e)*striver*].

strok³ 3*pt.*, went 12/9 [OE *strícan* 1].

strompet, strumpet¹, harlot 32/11, 35 [obscure].

stronde¹, seashore 7/80 [OE *stránd*].

strong(e)², strong 6/71, 116, 163, 8/80, fierce 5/58, 10/5, 12, strang 22/5, deadly 13/28, severe 17/79, 25/4, painful, grievous 17/131, evil 18/16; as ⁴, deeply, excessively 12/195, 273 [OE *stráng*].

strout¹, contention 8/146 [cf. OE *strútian* B].

stude¹, place 6/187, 17/57, 18/16; *pl.* 10/189, -en 17/57 [OE *styde*].

studegið³ 3*prpl.*, halt 18/37 [obscure].

studeuest², steadfast 20/18 [OE *styde* + *fæst*].

stund(e); stunken. *See* stounde; stinken.

stupede³ 3*pt.*, stooped 9/59 [OE *stúpian* B].

sture, sturede, sturieð. *See* stireð.

sturnne², harsh, severe 6/40, 9/63, 32/4 [OE *stýrne*].

sturuen. *See* storue.

stutteð³ 3*prpl.*, cease 18/37 [ON *stytta*].

such(e), suich, swuch, swilc², such 2/57, 5/80, 10/153, etc., svich 8/60, swyhc 14/53; suilce *pl.* 2/56, swulche 6/48, 50, sweche 13/51, swuc(c)he 17/58, 108, swiche 19/70; *swulc* . . . *swa*, whichever 6/81; as⁸, as if 10/104, 110, 21/12, 40, etc. [OE *swylc*, *swelc*, *swilc*].

sucur(s)¹, help 9/36, 17/81 [OF *sucurs*].

suencten³ 3*ptpl.*, oppressed 2/15 [OE *swencan* A].

suere; suert; suete; suetyng. *See* sweore; sweord; swete; sweting.

suetly², lovely 28/25 [OE *swéte* + *-lic*].

suetnesse¹, beauty 28/51 [OE *swétnes*].

suffre³, to suffer 9/31; soffrede 3*pt.* 13/186 [OF *suffrir*].

suge(n), sugge(n); suich; suikes; suinc; suyre; suyt, suythe; suythe. *See* segge(n); such(e); swikes; swinc; sweore; swete; swiþe.

sukeð³ 3*pr.*, swallows up 11/72 [OE *súcan* 2].

sule; sule; sulle; sullen. *See* shal; sellen; shal; sellen.

sulf⁵, himself 17/8, sulue, very 10/69 [OE *sylf*].

sumdel², somewhat 2/78, 8/161, much 12/237 [OE *sume dǽle*].

sum(e)², some, a certain 10/136, 16/20, etc., **som** 12/18, **soum** 12/104, **soumme** 12/125; **somne** *am.* 12/192; **summes** *g.* 6/170; **sume, summe** *pl.* 2/26, 44, 6/99, etc.; as⁵, one 8/216, 10/112, 20/54; **sumne** *am.* 6/32 [OE *sum*].

sumer(e), somer¹, summer 10/1 n, 11/79, 13/1, etc.; **someres** *g.* 13/126 [OE *sumor*].

summ⁸, as; *swa summ,* just as 15/5, 6, 49 [OEN *sum*].

sumwher⁴, somewhere 31/23 [OE *sum + hwǣr*].

sumwile⁴, formerly 2/44, sometimes 10/6 [OE *sum + hwīle*].

sund², sound 11/76 [OE *(ge)-súnd*].

sune, sone¹, son 3/31, 5/15, 22, etc., **son** 38/38, 63; **sones** *g.* 36/63; *pl.* 5/100 [OE *sunu*].

sunfoul; sunge(n); sunne. *See* **sinful(e); singe; sinne.**

sunne¹, sun 18/36 [OE *sunne*].

suore(n). *See* **swere.**

suster¹, sister 17/71; **sustren** *pl.* 17/49, 59 [OE *s(w)uster*, ON *systir*].

sup, soup¹, south 20/100, 28/42 [OE *sūp*].

supe. *See* **swipe.**

sval³ *3pt.,* swelled (with anger) 10/7 [OE *swellan* 3].

swa. *See* **so.**

swain, swein¹, peasant 6/201, 8/32 [ON *sveinn*].

swart, suart², black, dark 5/87, 18/8 [OE *sweart*].

swat¹, sweat 17/128 [OE *swāt*].

sweatte³ *3pt.,* bled 17/128 [OE *swǣtan* A].

sweche. *See* **such(e).**

sweng³ *imp.,* brandish 17/91; **swengde, sweinde** *3pt.,* hung 6/141, pulled 18/57 [OE *swengan* A].

sweord, swerd¹, sword 6/141, 8/175, 198, etc., **suert** 36/11; **swerdes** *pl.* 4/15, 8/210, 21/77, **sweord** 6/194 [OE *swéord*].

sweore, suere, swire¹, neck 6/147, 9/97, 18/13, 19, **swore** 10/73, **suyre** 28/25, face 7/105 [OE *swéora, swíora*].

swere³, to swear 8/252; **swerie** *1pr.* 13/187; **-ien** *3prspl.* 3/12; **swore** *1pt.* 8/250; **sore** *3pt.* 28/65; **suore(n), isworene** *ptp.* 2/12, 3/25, 4/28, 33 [OE *swerian* 6].

swete, suete², sweet, lovely 9/68, 13/36, 20/203, etc., **suythe** 38/23, **suyt** 38/50; **swetture** *comp.* 20/151, 168; **swetteste, swettoust** *sup.* 13/58, 76, most fragrant 11/66. As¹, fair one 20/89, 28/73 [OE *swēte*].

sweting, suetyng¹, fair one, lover 28/2, 34 [OE *swēte + -ing*].

swiche. *See* **such(e).**

swift(e)², swift 6/101, 20/29 [OE *swift*].

swik³ *imp.,* cease 24/12 [OE *swīcan* 1].

swik(e)¹, treachery 11/46, 70 [OE *swic*].

swikedom¹, treachery 21/96 [OE *swicdōm*].

swikele², treacherous 12/86, 103, 13/38 [OE *swicol*].

swikes, suikes¹ *pl.,* traitors 2/10, 8/265 [OE *swica*].

swilc, swilk. *See* **such(e).**

swyn¹, boar 32/23 [OE *swīn*].

swinc, swinke¹, toil, labour 12/144, 15/40, 72, 21/27, **suinc** 2/60 [OE *swinc*].

swincful(e)², heavy, grievous 17/126, 127 [OE *swincfull*].

swire. *See* **sweore.**

swipe⁴, very 6/45, 107, 112, 158, 11/89, etc., **suipe** 5/38, **supe** 9/65, 176, 10/2, 12, quickly 6/93, severely 6/214, much 12/4, greatly, very much 12/110, 16/20, 18/51, **suythe** 2/15, 63, **swuðe** 17/40 [OE *swīpe*].

swyuyng¹, fornication 4/9 [OE *swīf-an* + *-ing*].

swo. *See* **so.**

swohninde³ *prp.*, swooning 17/65 [cf. OE *swogen*].

swong³ *3pt.*, swung 18/13; i-**swonge** *ptp.*, beaten 12/291 [OE *swingan* 3].

swore. *See* **sweore; swere.**

swote¹, lovely one 28/73 [OE *swōt*].

swuch(e), swulc, swulche. *See* **such(e).**

tabell¹, table 22/14 [OF *table*].

tabour¹, small drum 8/242 [OF *tabour*].

tachte, tæchepp; tælepp; tær, tærfore, tæronne; taȝte; tayn. *See* **teche; telep; þer(e); teche; þein.**

take(n)³, to take 7/103, 20/4, 64, consider 15/41, choose 20/192, betake oneself 37/9; **take** *1pr.*, bring forward 13/46, 70, 88; **-en** *3prpl.* 8/206; **tac, tak** *imp.* 7/19, 35/37; **toc, tock** *3pt.* 6/0 28, handed to 7/23; **toke** *3pts.* 7/36; **itake, take(n)** *ptp.* 12/43, 29/11, 19, etc., turned 12/178, undertaken 15/4 [ON *taka* 6].

taken¹, sign, omen 6/171, 18/54 [OE *tāc(e)n*].

tale¹, story 8/3, 5, etc., charge 13/146, argument 10/3, 162; **-en, -es** *pl.* 13/51, scandal 17/52 [OE *talu*].

talieð³ *3prpl.*, shout 6/130 [OE *talian* B].

taleuaces¹ *pl.*, bucklers 8/236 [OF *talevas*].

targi³, to delay 19/82 [obscure].

tatt; te. *See* **þat; þe⁵; þu; to⁷.**

te³, to go, advance 13/190; **tey** *3pt.*, pulled 12/279; **tuȝen** *3ptpl.* 6/65; **itoȝen** *ptp.*, brought up 10/147 [OE *tēon* 2].

tebroken. *See* **tobreke.**

teche³, to teach, inform, advise

5/3, 10/117, 188, 20/8; **1pr.** 20/88; **tæchepp** *3pr.* 15/49, 62; **tech** *2prs.*, 20/198; **teche** *imp.* 27/2; **taȝte** *3pt.* 9/173; **tachte** *3pts.* 19/57 [OE *tæcan* A].

techinge¹, teaching 19/37 [OE *tæcing*].

tedai; teforen; teȝȝ; tey. *See* **todai; tofore(n); þei; te.**

teyte², active, eager 8/214, 244 [ON *teit-r*].

tekenn⁴, in addition 15/19 [OE *tō-ē(a)can*].

telep, tælepp³ *3pr.*, blames 14/52, 15/39 [OE *tǣlan* A].

telle(n)³, to tell, narrate 2/35, 6/7, 8/3, etc., tell 22/12; **telle** *1pr.* 9/83, 13/104, tel, account 37/17; **-eð** *3pr.* 11/38; *3prpl.* 13/103; **telle** *3prspl.* 9/114; tel, **telle** *imp.* 12/197, 13/110, etc.; **tellep** *imppl.* 21/46; **tolde** *1pt.* 20/177, 28/54; *3pt.* 5/112; **told, itold(e)** *ptp.* 9/19, 129, 19/27, etc., accounted 8/143, reckoned up 13/52; *me telp of him lute*, he is thought little of 5/6 [OE *tellan* A].

temep³ *3pr.*, tames 13/174 [OE *temian* B].

ten², ten 6/109, 8/117, etc. [nWS *tēne*].

tendep³ *3pr.*, tends 9/34 [OE *(on)-téndan* A].

tene, tone¹, hardship, grief 21/72, 30/4, reproach 10/50 [OE *tēona*].

teone³ *3prs.*, may be angry 31/39 [OE *tēonian* B].

tenserie¹, protection money 2/39n [OF *tenserie*].

teose; ter. *See* **þis; þer(e).**

teres, tern¹ *pl.*, tears 36/20, **22** [OE *tēar*].

tes; tet. *See* **þis; þat⁵.**

teþ¹ *pl.*, teeth 11/22, 17/68, etc.; **teh** 31/39 [OE *tōþ, tēþ*].

tetireð³ *3pr.*, tears in pieces 11/2: [OE *tōteran* 4].

tetoggeð³ *3pr.*, pulls in pieces 11/22 [obscure].

th-; ti, ty. *See* þ-; þu.

tide¹, time, season 13/126, 20/45; tide, -es *pl.*, hours (canonical) 10/26, 19/33 [OE *tīd*].

til(l)⁷, to, towards 8/174, 220, 15/9, etc., into 15/57; as⁸, until 2/9, 11/77, 33/21 [OE *til*, ON *til*].

tilede³ *3pt.*, cultivated 2/55; tiled *ptp.* 2/42 [OE *tilian* B].

time¹, time 2/58, 8/45, 12/263, etc., reign 2/79, 8/28, ages 19/33; *in hys tim*, during his lifetime 22/10 [OE *tīma*].

tire³, to pull back 9/98; -eð *3pr.*, tugs at 11/39 [OF *tirer*].

tis. *See* þis.

tyt³ *3pr.*, befalls one 20/20 [OE *tīdan* A].

tith. *See* tuhte(n).

tiðinge¹, news 17/55 [ON *tíðindi*, influenced by OE *tīdung*].

tiwesday¹, Tuesday 5/20 [OE *Tīwesdæg*].

to⁴, too 8/165, 12/81, 98, 13/74, 182, 14/85, 17/5, 101, forward 17/66, 67 [OE *tō*].

to⁷, to, towards 1/22, 2/1, 6, 51, 3/3, 4/1, etc., te 35/17, (as a mark of the inf.) 2/31, 39, 69, 3/12, 13, etc., for, as a 6/15, 34, 44, 9/14, etc., into 2/25, 17/26, 62, 107, 30/3, at 9/148, 17/79, 19/16, as far as 4/30, 16/63, concerning 9/13, 10/83, against 7/101, in 12/97, over 21/60, until 28/67; *to dryng*, as a drink 4/11; *to . . . ward*, towards 4/40; *foren to*, in front of 6/78; *nimen to rede*, adopt as a plan 10/186; *al to*, up to 19/16; *te*, up to that time 19/55 [OE *tō*].

to¹, toe 8/220 [OE *tā*].

toberste³ *imp.*, burst, break 7/92; -bearst *3pt.* 18/61 [OE *tōberstan* 3].

tobreke³, to break 10/152, 12/63,

conclude 10/159; -breken *3ptpl.* 6/196, 17/117; tobroke, te-broken *ptp.* 12/19, transgressed 16/61 [OE *tōbrecan* 4].

tobrode³ *ptp.*, torn in pieces 10/104 [OE *tōbregdan* 3].

toc, tock. *See* take(n).

todai, tedai¹, to-day 19/2, 4, 11 [OE *tō dæge*].

todeld³ *3pt.*, squandered 2/4; -dæled, -deled *ptp.*, shared out 6/117, scattered 6/181 [OE *tōdǣlan* A].

todelueð³ *3pr.*, digs out 6/135 [OE *tō + delfan* 3].

todrawe³, to tear in pieces 31/34 [OE *tō + dragan* 6].

todreosen³, to decay 20/48 [OE *tōdrēosan* 2].

tofore(n), touore⁷, before, in front of 10/150, 205, 20/155, 21/44, etc., teforen 16/3 [OE *tō-foran*].

toforeniseide³, aforesaid 3/9, 13 [OE *tō-foran + gesægd*].

togadere, -gedere⁴, together 6/27, 9/92, 12/156, etc.; *al togadere*, everything 9/79; *make wel togedere*, reconcile 16/26; *kesten hem togedere*, kissed each other 16/65 [OE *tōgædere*].

toglide³, to vanish 20/43 [OE *tō-glīdan* 1].

toȝein, toȝeines⁷, against 6/184, 12/95, 17/134, toyenes, towards 19/41 [OE *tōgēan, tōgēanes*].

tohauwen³ *ptp.*, cut down 6/212 [OE *tōhēawan* 7].

toke. *See* take(n).

tokninge¹, sign 5/82, 91 [OE *tācnung*].

tolde. *See* telle(n).

tolleð³ *3pr.*, attracts 11/103, 17/76 [OE **tollian* B].

tome², tame 21/24 [OE *tam*].

tone; tonge. *See* tene; tunge.

toniȝt¹, tonight 12/191, 21/34, 36 [OE *tō + niht*].

top¹, crown of head 4/33 [OE *top*].

tornde. *See* **turrnenn.**

tosomne[4], together 6/192, 197 [OE *tōsomne*].

totere[3], to tear in pieces 8/212; -eþ 3*prpl.* 31/6 [OE *tōteran* 4].

totose[3], to tear in pieces 10/70 [cf. OE *tǣsan* A].

toun(e), tun(e)[1], town 2/75, 5/19, 29, etc., village 2/41, 51, farmyard 11/5, dwellings of men 13/1; **tunᴇs** *pl.*, villages 2/38, 40; *tounes ende*, outskirts of the town, village 38/49 [OE *tūn*].

toward[7], to, towards 5/15, 17/81, 118, etc., -**wart** 18/5 [OE *tōw(e)ard*].

trayling[1], long trailing garments 35/14 [obscure].

traytre[1], traitor 35/47; **traitors** *pl.* 5/54 [OF *traitre, traitour*].

trauail[1], wages 19/15 [OF *travail*].

tre[1], tree 22/34, 38, 38/82, wooden bar 8/129, 194, cross 36/6 [OE *trēo(w)*].

tredenn[3], to tread 15/37 [OE *tredan* 5].

trecherie[1], treachery 8/263 [OF *trecherie*].

treowe, trewe[2], true, loyal 7/69, 13/92, 120, etc., loyal subjects 3/11, 19; **treowest** *sup.* 20/5 [OE *trēowe*].

treowþe, treuthe, trowwþe[1], faith, loyalty 2/12, 3/11, 15/2, 62; **treothes** *pl.* 2/13; *on vre treowþe*, in loyalty to us 3/8 [OE *trēowþ*].

tresor, tres(o)ur[1], treasure 2/3, 4/9, 20/145 [OF *tresor*].

tresoun[1], treason 8/264 [OF *treson*].

tressour[1], head-dress 35/5 [OF *tresseour*].

tricchen[3], to deceive 4/7 [OF *trichier*].

trichard[1], trickster 4/6 [OF *trichart*].

ttisteþ. *See* **truste**[3].

trome[1], company, troop 8/8 [OE *truma*].

troud[3] *ptp.*, believed 8/251 [OE *trūwian* B].

trous[1], hedge-cuttings, brush 31/15, 25 [OE *trūs*].

trowwenn[3], to believe, trust 15/20, 36, 67; **trowwe** 1*pr.* 15/26; **treowest** 2*pr.* 20/42; **trowe** 3*prs.* 31/9 [OE *trēowian* B].

trowwþe. *See* **treowþe.**

truan[1], vagabond 38/35 [OF *truant*]

truke[3], to fail 20/122; -**ede** 3*pt.* 21/62 [OE *trucian* B].

truste[1], loyalty 20/93 [cf. OE **trystan* A].

truste[3] 1*pr.*, trust 18/48; **tristeþ** 3*pr.* 20/56 [OE **trystan* A].

tu. *See* **þu.**

tubrugge[1], drawbridge 21/32 [OE *tyge-* + *brycg*].

tuelfmoneþ[1], year 4/35 [OE *twelf* + *mōnaþ*].

tuȝen. *See* **te.**

tuhte(n)[3] 3*ptpl.*, met 6/186, 192; **tith** *ptp.*, intended 8/265 [OE *tyhtan* A].

tuye[4], twice 9/40 [OE *twiga*].

tukest[3] 2*pr.*, ill-treat 10/63 [OE *tucian* B].

tunder[1], tinder 11/93 [OE *tynder*].

tun(e), tunes; tunnderrstanndenn. *See* **toun(e); understanden.**

tunge[1], tongue 15/68, 17/27, etc., **tonge** 10/37, **tunke** 27/5; -**en** *pl.* 17/44 [OE *túnge*].

tunscipe[1], villagers 2/52 [OE *tūnscipe*].

tupace[1], topaz 20/172 [OF *topace*].

tur[1], tower, castle 9/18, 43, 115, 152, **tuur** 34/1 [OF *tur*].

turrnenn[3], to turn 15/9; -**eþ** 3*pr.* 15/75, directs 19/73; 3*prpl.* 21/86; **turnde, tornde** 3*pt.* 5/113, 6/0 24, 9/106; **turrnedd, iturnd** *ptp.* 20/78, translated 15/65; *turneþ aȝen*, turn back 5/56 [OE *túrnian* B].

turuf[1], turf 34/1 [OE *turf*].

tus. *See* þus.

twa, two[2], two 2/30, 51, 3/24, etc., **tuo** 12/73, **to** 5/26; *on to*, in two 8/196 [OE *twā*].

tweien[2], two 6/171, 213 [OE *twēgen*].

twel, twolf[2], twelve 8/161, 21/76 [OE *twelf*].

twenti[2], twenty 8/219, 232, 9/172, 174 [OE *twēntig*].

twybyl[1], two-edged axe 31/15 [OE *twibill*].

twifold[2], double 11/25 [OA *twifáld*].

twiȝȝess[4], twice 15/52 [OE *twiga* + adv. *-es*].

twincling[1], twinkling 35/11 [OE *twincl-ian* + *-ing*].

þa. *See* þe[5]; þe[6].

þa[4], then, thereupon 2/40, 16/37, 44, etc.; *þa . . . þa*, when . . . then 2/6, 10, 16, 6/152, etc.; *þa þe, ða þa*, when 6/36, 16/31 [OE *þā*].

þabbotrice; þæ; þær; þære; þærinne; þæt. *See* abbotrice; þe[5]; þer(e); þe[5]; þer(e); þat.

þah, þauh[8], though, even if 4/6, 6/191, 10/142, etc., yet, nevertheless 10/201, 17/2, 8, 35 [OE *þēah, þǣh*].

þai, þaim, þam. *See* þei.

þan[8], than 2/46, 75, 5/44, 89, etc., **þane** 10/39, 20/151, **þanne** 2/57, 8/151, 16/38; *for ðan*, because 16/30 [OE *þanne*].

þan, þane. *See* þe[5].

þanne[4], then, thereupon 5/25, 92, 8/51, 59, 111, 9/161, 11/71, when 8/197, 11/64, 79, ðan, afterwards 11/24 [OE *þanne*].

þannkenn[3], to thank 15/14, 45; **þonkede** *3pt.* 9/170; **iþonked** *ptp.* 6/115 [OE *þancian* B].

þar(e)[4], there 2/7, 67, 6/4, 130, etc., where 10/26, 94, 128, 136, 138, 20/122, 21/33; combined with *prep.* or *adv.*, it, that, them, which; **þarafter**, afterwards 10/45; **þarbiside**, nearby 10/25; **þarfor, þarefore**, therefore 31/24, 38/55; **þarinne**, therein, within 2/48, 11/11, 16/52, 20/125, 38/33; **þarmid**, therewith 10/81; **þarof**, with it 2/5, for it 2/54, thereof 10/206; **þarto**, to it 2/62, 11/90, with it 9/123, 10/105 [OE *þār(a), þǣr*].

þare. *See* þe[5].

þart[3] *2pr.*, thou art 31/38 [OE *þū-(e)art*].

þas. *See* þis.

þat, þæt, þet[5] *def.art.*, the, that (orig. neuter) 1/17, 19, 3/6, 6/41, etc., þut 5/56, 88, these 2/30, this 2/36, 16/58, 62; (emphatic) that, it, the same 2/27, 31, 34, 3/15, etc., **tet** 17/19, 39, 18/55; *þet weren*, these were 1/10 [OE *þæt*].

þat, þæt, þet[6], that, which, who 2/30, 31, 3/6, 11, 12, 4/23, etc., what, that which 5/74, 6/232, 236, 7/61, 63, 9/80, etc., with which 2/80, of whom 5/102, he who, the one who 6/31, 12/259, 14/46, 20/56, 21/96, for him who 12/97, whom 12/128, 19/73, 20/188, 38/15, to whom 13/89, 22/12, those who 18/6, anyone who 19/11; *þæt þæt, þatt tatt*, that which 3/5, 15/17, 20; *þat in his*, in whose 8/28; *þet . . . to*, to whom 17/46; *þet . . . inne*, in which 17/57; *þet . . . to*, to whom 19/37 [OE *þæt*, for OE *þe*].

þat, þæt, þet[8], that 1/23, 2/2, 10, 3/4, 11, etc., **tatt** 15/9, so that 2/33, 40, 5/33, 51, etc., until 2/25, 6/107, 10/213, 21/17, 22, as 8/11, because 10/34, 13/10, 17/17, 122, 19/26, the fact that 17/127, so that 38/56; *þat . . . ne*, but that 8/57, 91, 9/15; *þo þet*, because 19/49, since 19/53 [OE *þæt, þætte*].

þauh; þe. *See* þah; þu.

þe, te⁵ *def.art.*, the, this 1/7, 2/3, 4/2, etc., þeo 1/17, 17/57, 20/41, þa 2/32, þæ 2/71, þo 10/26, 16/5, 41, 19/1, etc.; þene *am.* 6/71, 154, 12/113, 126, etc., þane 3/23, 9/181, 10/193, 19/84, 92, þen 5/34, 10/165; þes *gm.* 6/23, 17/42, þas 6/145; þan *dm/n.* 3/15, 6/10, 100, 102, 12/55, etc., þen 1/19; þa *af.* 6/15, 16, etc.; þare *g/df.* 6/22, 210, 10/28, 31, 140, etc., þære 3/35, þere 6/186, 226, þer 17/90, 128, 18/25; þe *inst.* 17/17, 31, 98, 20/29, etc., te 15/25; þa, þo, þeo *pl.* 1/3, 4, 5, 2/18, 36, 3/12, etc., to 2/84; þan *dpl.* 3/9, 13, 6/38, 39, etc. [OE *se* (later þe), etc.].

þe⁶, who, which, that 1/4, 5, 10, 2/50, 68, 6/10, etc., þa 6/9, 153, þeo 1/18, whom 1/6, 2/18, 17/122, on which 6/73, that which 16/61; ðe . . . *to,* for which 16/8; ðe ðe, he who 17/14, 18/19 [OE þe].

þeau¹, virtue 17/47; þewes *pl.*, customs 10/113, qualities 20/90 [OE þēaw].

þed(e)¹, country, people 8/105, 15/20 [OE þēod].

þef¹, thief 12/102, 35/42; þeues, þeoues *pl.* 8/41, 20/149, 21/79 [OE þēof].

þefþe¹, theft 21/82 [OA þēofþ].

þeʒes¹ *pl.*, thighs 28/31 [OE þē(o)h].

þeʒ, þey⁸, though, although 9/101, 10/48, 111, 13/21, etc., þeg 10/146, þeyh 20/81 [OE þē(a)h].

thehte³ *3pt.*, retreated 6/61 [OE þeccan A].

þei⁵, they 8/69, 127, 144, 21/15, etc., þeʒʒ 15/40, 41, 70, 75, teʒʒ 15/59, 78, þai 22/16, 38/29, 80; þeʒʒre *poss.* 15/18, 42, etc., þer 22/6; þeʒʒm, thaim, þam *dpl.* 15/25, 22/26, 23/4 [ON þei-r, þeira, þeim].

þein, tayn¹, thane, warrior 6/46, 8/31; þeines *pl.* 6/83, 14/2, 20/13 [OE þegn].

ðellice², such a 16/47 [OE þyllic].

pen. *See* þe⁵.

þen⁸, than 12/8, 68, 13/125, 17/4, etc., þene 6/156 [OE þænne].

þenche³, to think, seem 19/52; þenke 1*pr.* 30/16; þencheð, ðenkeð 3*pr.* 6/81, 11/50; þenke 2*prs.* 35/29; þench, þenk *imp.* 13/115, 139, 30/8, 35/38, guess 7/57; þenkeþ *imppl.*, realize 5/56; þohhtesst 2*pt.* 15/9; þoʒte, þohte 3*pt.* 5/88, 7/10, 18/24, intended 5/22, 6/118, ðoʒte 11/56, þohute, hoped 12/13 [OE þencan A].

þene. *See* þe⁵; þen; þenne.

þenne, þeonne⁴, then, thereupon 6/169, 14/45, 17/32, etc., þene 12/64, when 6/80, 86, thence 10/148 [OE þeonan].

þennes⁴, thence 35/24 [OE þeonan + adv. -es].

þeo; þeo; þeonne; þeos; þeoues; þer; þer(e). *See* þe⁵; þe⁶; þenne; þis; þef; þei; þe⁵.

þer(e)⁴, there 2/2, 5/8, 21, 25, 7/33, etc., þær 2/66, ter 11/32, where 6/5, 164, 218, 8/54, etc., þær 15/23; combined with *prep.* or *adv.*, it, that, them, etc.; þerafter, -efter, þrefter, afterwards 9/157, 17/22, 18/54, according to it 17/98; þer aʒean, with it 17/21; þeraʒeines, before it 18/30; þer(e)fore, þer(e)uore, on that account 6/91, 8/274, 9/138, etc., tærfore 15/65; þerfram, thence 8/55; þerinne, therein 2/28, 6/233, etc., þær-inne 2/29; þer . . . inne, wherein 18/52; þerof, of it, because of it 7/38, 9/60, 11/89, etc., þeroffe 8/251, þrof 17/134; þeron, þere-onne, on, in it 6/144, 35/38, tæronne 15/19, þron, about it

18/24; þer þoru, by reason of them 5/27; þertil, thereto, 8/148; þerto, in addition, to it 5/67, 6/189, 8/4, etc., of it 20/107; þerute, outside 8/182; þerwiþ, -wit, with it 5/81, 8/138, 153; tær tekenn, in addition 15/19 [OE þǣr].

þerl; þes; þes, þese. See eorl; þe⁵; þis.

ðesternesse¹, darkness 16/5 [OE þēosternes].

þet; þewes; þi. See þat; þeau; þu.

picke², thick 10/17; as⁴, thickly 5/106, in crowds 5/51 [OE þicce].

þider⁴, thither 8/119, 120, 166, 12/12, etc., þuder 9/132, þidere 12/268 [OE þider].

þiderward⁴, in that direction 6/190 [OE þider-w(e)ard].

ðies; þilke; þin(e). See þis; ilke²; þu.

þing(e)¹, thing 6/36, 10/181, 11/66, etc., þink 38/77, anything 9/125, maiden 9/68, 13/58, creature 17/63, 35/31; þing(e), þinges pl. 3/10, 8/71, 9/29, etc., þinghe 8/66, creatures 18/29, 32; þingen dpl. 6/159 [OE þing].

þinke(n)³, to seem, think 7/47, 35/30; þincþ, þinkeþ, þuncheþ 3pr. 10/209, 13/50, 67, 21/31; þuncheþ 2prpl. 21/35; þouȝte, þoute, þuȝte, þuhte 3pt. 5/113, 6/4, 10/21, 23, 31, 12/94, intended 12/125; hu þincþe nu, how does it seem to you now 10/46 [OE þyncan A].

thir; þire. See þis; þu.

þis, þes⁵, this 2/1, 36, 58, 3/17, etc., þeos 6/24, 31, 18/26, þos 10/41, tis 11/10, 15/77, 18/18, 21/20, ðies 16/44, ðese 16/45, tes 17/72, þise 19/7, 27, 81; þas af. 6/14; þisse d. 6/72, 12/225, 17/41, 20/90, þise 19/13; þis, þeos pl. 1/9, 10, 15, 5/91, 6/32, etc., þuse

5/101, þas 6/219, þes 9/61, 138, 147, 20/176, ðise 11/72, teose 17/119, þos 19/13, 21, þese 21/43, 78, 86, thir 23/1; þisse dpl. 10/211, 17/10 [OE þes, þēos, þis].

þo. See þe⁵; þou.

þo⁴, ⁸, then 5/2, 12, 40, 7/78 etc., when 8/154, 11/54, 12/23, etc.; þo þet, until 19/14, because 19/49, 53 [OE þā].

ðogte, þoȝte; þohh. See þenche; þou.

þoht¹, thought 15/11, 47, 60, 16/24, etc., þoȝt 5/54, þohut 12/223, 13/38, 154, þout(e) 13/41, 152, resolution 17/77, sorrow (personified) 28/58, 63; þohtes, þouhtes pl. 17/73, 20/61 [OE þōht].

þohte. See þenche.

þole(n), þolie(n)³, to suffer, endure 9/38, 39, 99, 15/26, etc., ðoliȝen 16/60; þole 1pr. 36/8, 9, 33; þolest 2pr. 9/42; ðoleð 3pr. 16/29, 30; þolieð 3prpl. 16/17; ðolede 3pt. 16/31; þoleden 1ptpl. 2/58; 3ptpl. 20/77; (i)þoled ptp. 16/5, 19/24, 29/30 [OE þolian B].

þones. See on⁵.

þonk(e)¹, thanks, grace 5/72, 12/158, thought 6/6; hire þonkes, willingly 10/70 [OE þanc].

þonkede. See þannkenn.

þor(e)⁴, there 8/121, 140, 151, etc.; þorwit, therewith 8/100 [OE þār(a)].

þornes¹ pl., thorns 31/6, 14 [OE þórn].

þorte; þos; thosand; þoþere. See þrote; þis; þusend; oþer².

þoþwethere⁸, nevertheless 2/61 [ON þó(h) + OE hwæþer].

þou. See þu.

þou⁸, though 8/250, 36/45, þo 8/127; þohh þatt, although 15/78 [ON þó(h)].

þouȝte. See þinke(n).

þourhout⁴,⁸, through 36/29þuruth, throughout 8/52 [OE þurh-ūt].

þousent; þout(e); þoute; þrat. See þusend; þoht; þinke(n); þre- test.

þre, þreo², three 2/31, 6/28, 171 etc. [OE þrēo].

þrefter. See þer(e).

þrengde³ 3pt., pressed 2/28 [OE *þrengan A, cf. þríngan 3].

þreouold², threefold 17/49 [OE þrēo + OA fáld].

þreste³ 3pt., issued 18/12 [OE þrǣstan A].

þrestelcok, -kok¹, thrush 13/16, 73, 121 [cf. OE þrostle + cocc].

þrete¹, threat 10/58 [OE þrēat].

þretest³ 2pr., threaten 10/83; þrat 3pr. 28/63 [OE þrēatian B].

þretti. See þritti.

þreu³ 1pt., threw 7/58; þrewe 2pt. 7/70; þreu 3pt. 7/56 [OE þrāwan 7].

þridde², third 6/19, 17/2, 12, 36/51, 56, pride 15/3 [OE þridda].

ðrist¹, thirst 11/101 [OE þyrst].

þritti, þretti², thirty 4/3, 5/92, 6/87, 111 [OE þrītig].

þrof, þron. See þer(e).

þrote¹, throat 2/33, 10/24, 129, etc., þorte 10/143 [OE þrote].

þrumde³ 3pt., compressed 6/28 [obscure].

þu, þou, tu⁵, thou, you 2/40, 41, 4/6, 43, 7/12, etc.; þe, te obj. 7/93, 15/6, 13, 16/19, etc.; þin(e), þi poss. 4/39, 44, 7/51, 9/48, etc., ti 18/35, 48, 38/3, 24, 54; þines g. 6/222; þire df. 10/162, 14/57, 16/19; þe refl. 9/118, 14/44, 17/80, 92, te 17/111 [OE þū, þē, þīn].

þuder; þuȝte, þuhte; þulke. See þider; þinke(n); ilke².

þumbes¹ pl., thumbs 2/23 [OE þūma].

þuncheþ. See þinke(n).

þurh, þurȝ⁷, through, by means of 1/3, 9, 3/1, 6, 8, 15/2, etc., þur 2/85, þoru 5/38, 104, 13/170, 185, þureȝ 9/135, 151, þurch 19/36, 40, þorou 35/32, þuruh 17/36, 37, 43, þourh 36/63, in 15/60, þureȝ 9/29; þoru, through- out 5/84; þet . . . þurh, through which 1/3; al þoru, throughout 8/259; þurrh þatt, because 15/4, 77 [OE þurh].

þurrhlokenn³, to look through 15/34 [OE þurh + lōcian B, cf. þurhlōcung].

þurrhsekenn³, to search 15/34 [OE þurhsēcan A].

þurhte. See þurte.

þurles¹ pl., holes 17/108, wounds 17/120 [OE þyrel].

þurleden³ 3ptpl., pierced 17/115, 118 [OE þyrlian B].

þurst¹, thirst 12/67, 90 [OE þurst].

þurte³ 3pt., need, might 8/10; þurhte 2pts. 20/95 [OE þurfan].

þuruth. See þourhout.

þus⁴, in this way, thus 1/20, 5/1, 12/158, etc., tus 11/45 [OE þus].

þuse. See þis.

þusend, þousent¹, thousand 4/3, 6/87, 98, etc., þusen 2/34, 6/168, thosand 22/6 [OE þūsend].

þuster², dark 33/24 [OE þēostor, þȳstor].   þut. See þat⁵.

þwertouer⁷, across 18/53 [ON þvert + OE ofer].

þwerrtut⁴, completely 15/37, 50 [ON þvert + OE ūt].

væie; væireste, vaire, vairest. See fæie; feyr(e).

vald¹, valley, fold of land 6/61 [cf. OA fáld].

vale; valle, valleþ; valse; varen. See fele²; falle; fals(e); fare(n).

vaste², secure 10/17 [OE fæst].

vaste⁴. See faste.

vat. See what⁵.

ucchen³, to loosen 21/7 [OE iecan A].

uch. *See* vich(e).

uchan, vychon², each, every 20/45, 32/1, vch a 32/11, 13, vych o 20/128 [OE *ilc ān, gehwylc ān*].

veden; veyr; vel. *See* fede; feyr(e); falle.

velaghes¹ *pl.*, fellows, equals 19/22 [ON *félagi*].

vele. *See* fele.

velle¹ *pl.*, skins 10/109 [OE *fell*].

velle; vend; veole; veollen; veond; verde. *See* falle; wende(n); fele²; falle; fend(e); ferde.

vereden³ *3ptpl.*, bore 6/234 [OE *ferian* B].

veren; vers; verst(e). *See* fere; wurse; first(e).

verteþ³ *3pr.*, breaks wind 24/8 [OE **feortan* 3].

vertu¹, goodness, virtue 22/34, medicinal power 20/170n [OF *vertu*].

vet; ves; vewe. *See* fot(e); was; feaue.

ufen⁴, above 6/122 [OE *ufan*].

vich(e), uch², each, every 20/125, 176, 196, 28/69, 32/17, 24 [OE *gehwylc*].

viit; vikel; vikelare(s); villeth. *See* wiht(e); fikele; fikelare; wilen.

villiche⁴, cruelly, vilely 5/55 [OF *vil* + OE *-līce*].

vind, vindeð; vingres; virste; vytuten. *See* finde(n); fingres; first(e); wiþute(n).

ule, hule¹, owl 10/4, 26, etc., houle 10/207 [OE *ūle*].

vlih. *See* fle(n).

umbiyeden³ *3ptpl.*, surrounded 8/215 [ON *um* + OE *be-ēode*].

umwile⁴, at times 2/38n [ON *um* + *hwīle*].

unnc, hunke⁵ *dual.*, to the two of us 15/14, 43, 44, to you two 10/155n; unker, *poss.* 10/202, 204, 205, 15/40 [OE *unc, uncer*].

uncuð, unkuðe², strange 6/172, ignorant 11/70 [OE *uncūþ*].

undep², shallow 2/28 [OE *undēop*].

under, ounder⁷, under 7/54, 12/41, 47, etc., at the foot of 6/128, 36/1, within 15/5, 29/31 [OE *únder*].

underfangen, underfenge, underfonge. *See* ounderfonge.

unnderrfot⁴, underfoot 15/37 [OE *únder* + *fōt*].

underȝetest³ *2pr.*, perceive 17/71; -gæton *3ptpl.* 2/10 [OE *únderg(i)etan* 5].

understanden³, to understand 15/25; -stonde *1pr.*, am informed 28/54; hounderstod *3pt.* 12/77; ounderstonde *ptp.*, informed 13/39 [OE *únderstándan* 6].

underwrote³, to undermine 20/123 [OE *únder* + *wrōtan* 7].

undren¹, early morning 19/8, 37, 72 [OE *úndern*].

ungeinliche⁴, threateningly 18/19 [OE *un-* + ON *gegn* + OE *-līce*].

unhersum², disobedient 16/30 [nWS *unhērsum*].

unhersumnesse¹, disobedience 16/18, 33 [nWS *unhērsumnes*].

unilic², different from 6/146 [OE *ungelīc*].

unimete², numerous 6/183, 185, etc.; as⁴, excessively 6/160 [OE *ungemǣte*].

unirude², great 21/20 [OE *ungerȳde*].

unisele², uncanny 10/100 [cf. OE *unsǣle*].

uniselen¹ *pl.*, calamities 6/181 [cf. OE *unsǣl*].

univele², very many 6/159 [OE *un-* + *ge* + *fela*].

unlahfulliche⁴, unlawfully 28/68 [OE *unlag-u* + *full* + *-līce*].

unlede², feeble 14/102 [OE *ɩnlǣde*].

unlust¹, sloth 17/62n [OE *unlust*].

unmeaðlich⁴, immoderately 18/56 [OE *unmǣplīce*].

unmerret³ *ptp.*, unharmed 18/61 [OE *un-* + nWS *merran* A].

unmeþ¹, fault 9/37 [OE *unmǣp*].

unmilde², rough 10/61 [OE *unmilde*].

unnen. *See* an.

unneðe², anxious 6/59; as⁴, with difficulty 5/88 [OE *unēape*].

unnitt², unprofitable 15/41 [OE *unnyt*].

unricht¹, wrong 19/26 [OE *unriht*].

unride², huge 8/168, 11/63 [cf. OE *ungerȳde*].

unrihtfulnesse¹ injustice 10/164 [OE *unrihtful* + *-nes*].

unseheliche², invisible 18/28 [OA *un* + *segenlic*].

unsehene², unseen 18/23 [OA *un* + *segen*].

unselhðe¹, danger 17/20, monster 18/6 [OE *unsǣlp*].

unskil¹, lack of reason; *wið unskil*, immoderately 11/34 [ON *úskil*].

unsode³ *ptp.*, uncooked 10/103 [OE *unsoden* 2].

untellendlice², indescribable 2/20 [OE *untellendlic*].

unþewes¹ *pl.*, bad habits 10/114 [OE *unþēaw*].

unto⁷, unto 8/171 [obscure].

untrende³ 2*prs.*, may unroll 20/195 [OE *un-* + *tréndan* A].

unvele², evil 10/99 [OE *unfǣle*].

unwiȝt, unwiht¹, monster 10/33, 90, 18/5, 24 [OE *un-* + *wiht*, cf. *unmann*].

unwis(e)², foolish 6/40, 32/9, ounwis 13/157, ounwiis, ignorant 12/139 [OE *unwīs*].

unwreast², ignoble 17/101 [OE *unwrǣst*].

unwreoð³ 3*prpl.*, uncover, reveal 17/45; -wreon 3*prspl.* 17/46; -wreih 3*pt.* 1/4 [OE *unwrēon* 1].

unwurp², worthless 14/27 [OE *unwúrðe*].

unwurðede³ 3*pt.*, dishonoured 16/30 [OE *unwúrpian* B].

voȝeles; volc. *See* foȝel; folc.

volde¹, way 10/72, 20/117 [OA *fáld*].

volden; volf; vor; vord. *See* folde; wolf(e); for; forde.

vordrye³, to achieve 19/41n [cf. OE *fyrþran* A].

vore. *See* fore(n).

vorme² *sup.*, first 17/1, 3, 10, 24 [OE *fórma*].

vorte, vorto; vorð; vorþi. *See* forte; forþ; forþi.

vostermoder¹, foster-mother 18/1 [OE *fōstormōdor*].

vot(e); vouh; vox(e); up. *See* fot(e); fow; fox; upon.

up, oup⁴, up 2/22, 5/115, 9/7, etc., uppe 7/20, hup 38/64 [OE *úp*, *upp(e)*].

upon, uppon⁷, on, upon 8/47, 20/121, 36/51, uppe(n) 6/4, 14/76, 16/42, opon 7/105, up 10/15, uppe(n), on the banks of 6/186, 192, concerning, about 17/50, 30/16, oupon 13/139, at 18/18, throughout 15/35, opon, in, on 4/9, ouppon 13/20, uppo 15/50; *vpon heh, heþ*, on high 31/17, loudly 31/35 [OE *uppon*].

upriȝt⁴, upright 9/145 [OE *úprihte*].

ure¹, hour 19/22; ouris *pl.*, canonical hours 37/11 [OF *(h)oure*].

ur(e); vrefore; vreondes; vrom; us, us-seluen. *See* we; werefore; frend; from; we.

ut⁴, out 2/45, 8/89, 17/17, etc., hout 13/190, uut 19/5, hut 19/90, 33/26, forth 6/145; *ut of*, from 6/71, 92, excluded from 19/46, away from 19/79 [OE *út*].

utdrow³ 3*pt.*, drew out 8/167; utdrawe, out- *ptp.*, drawn 8/175, 21/77 [OE *útdragan* 6].

ute³ *imppl.*, let us 10/201 [OE *witon, uton, ute*].

uðe. *See* an³.

uðen¹ *dpl.*, waves 6/232 [OE *ȳþ*].

utlawes¹ *pl.*, outlaws 8/41 [OE *ūtlaga*, from ON *útlagi*].

utlete¹, outlet, pass 10/176n [cf. OE *ūt* + *lǣte*].

uuæren; uuan; uuaren. *See* was; winne(n); was.

uulle. *See* ful².

uvel(e), evele, ivele¹, evil, wrong 13/155, 17/9, 18/48, malice 8/50, evil man 17/14 [OE *yfel*].

uvel(e), evele, ivel(e)², evil, wicked 2/17, 58, 10/8, etc.; uvelne *am.* 14/95 [OE *yfel*].

uvele⁴, badly, vilely 5/81, 10/63, 14/69, 75 [OE *yfele*].

uuenden; uuere; uueron; uuerse; uuolf; uureccemen. *See* wene; wher; was; wurse; wolf(e); wreccemen.

uurythen³ *3ptpl.*, twisted, tightened 2/24 [OE *wrīþan* 1].

vurste. *See* first(e).

wa; wa; wæl; wæs, wæron. *See* wha; wo; wel⁴; was.

wagge³, to wield 8/89 [cf. OE *wagian* B].

way. *See* weȝe; wei⁴.

wai, wei¹, way, road, path 4/40, 5/34, 112, etc., weye 20/135 [OE *weg*].

wayke², weak 8/119 [ON *veik-r*].

wayleuay. *See* weilawei.

wayted³ *ptp.*, spied upon 29/18 [AN *waitier*].

wake³, to watch, be wakeful 20/60, 37/11; *1pr.* 28/82; -eþ *3pr.* 28/40; -ed *ptp.* 8/274 [OE *wacian* B].

waker², watchful 20/150 [OE *wacor*].

wal(le)¹, wall 12/10, 11, etc. [OE *w(e)all*].

wald¹, forest 18/42; walde, woldes *pl.*, hills 6/87, 122 [OA *wáld*].

wald(e); waldeð. *See* wilen; wealden.

walke³, to live, move, become 29/6; *1pr.* 26/4; -eð *3prpl.* 18/37 [OE *w(e)alcan* 7].

walleð³ *3prpl.*, flow 6/174 [OE *w(e)allan* 7].

walspere¹, spear 6/208 [OE *wæl-spere*].

walte¹, power 16/8 [OA *wáld*].

wam; wan; wan, wanne. *See* wha; winne(n); whan.

wanene, wonene⁴, whence 6/8, O8 [OE *hwanon*].

war. *See* whar.

war², careful 14/22 [OE *wær*].

war, wher⁸, whether 13/120, 31/13, 18 [OE *hwæþer*].

waraunt¹, protection 20/27 [AN *warant*].

ward⁷; *to Douere ward*, to Dover 4/40 [OE *-w(e)ard*].

ware¹ *pl.*, wares 8/52 [OE *waru*].

waren. *See* was.

warmen³ *3prpl.*, warm 11/95 [OE *w(e)armian* B].

warp. *See* weorpeð.

war-sæ⁴, where-ever 2/55 [OE *hwǣr* + *swǣ*].

warsipe¹, prudence 11/27 [OE *wærscipe*].

warð. *See* wurþen.

war-to⁴, whither 12/137 [OE *hwǣr* + *tō*].

was, wes³ *1pt.*, was 10/1, 29/29, etc.; weore *2pt.* 6/220; was, wes *3pt.* 1/1, 7, 2/2, etc., wæs 2/43, 66, 75, 76, ves 12/258; were(n) *3ptpl.* 1/3, 9, etc., wæron 2/13, 21, etc., uuaren 2/16, uuæren 2/21, waren 2/44, 16/8, 19/19, uueron 2/54, weore(n) 6/8, 181, etc., wer 8/111, woren 8/262; were *1pts.* 12/57; *2pts.* 12/60, 176, 219, 36/57; *3pts.* 5/47, 7/18, 65, etc., weore 6/64, 201, 237, wor(e) 8/142, 38/5, 43; weren *1ptspl.* 12/64; *3ptspl.* 12/204,

17/59, **weoren** 6/65; *was him with*, helped, guided him 8/62 [OE *wæs, wæron, wære*; ON *váru(m) pl.*].

wastme¹, fruit 16/41 [OE *wæstm*].

wat⁸, why 12/163 [OE *hwæt*].

wat mid⁷, what with 12/89 [OE *hwæt* and *mid*].

wat. *See* **what**⁵.

water(e)¹, water 6/65, 95, 12/71, etc., lake 6/162, 173, 182, sea 11/58; **wateren** *g.*, of the river 6/67; **-es, weattres** *pl.*, rivers 6/176, seas 18/41 [OE *wæter*].

waxe³, to grow, become 26/3; 1*pr.* 28/80, 30/16; **-eþ, -en** 3*prpl.* 30/1, come into mind 20/61 [OE *w(e)axan* 7].

wde. *See* **wode.**

we⁵, we 1/6, 23, 2/57, etc.; **us** *a/d.* 1/1, 3/6, etc., **ous** 4/23, 33/15, 42, 35/58; **ure** *poss.* 1/9, 15, 2/58, etc., **vr** 5/45, 31/27, **our(e)** 5/56, 12/54, etc., **houre** 12/35, 59, **hure** 19/1, our 33/21; **vs-seluen** *refl.* 3/22 [OE *wē, ūs, ūre*].

wealden³, to rule, possess, direct 16/52; **-est** 2*pr.* 18/31; **waldeð** 3*pr.* 6/115 [OE *wéaldan* OA *wáldan* 7].

weattres. *See* **water(e).**

wed¹, pledge 31/24, 25, 32 [OE *wedd*].

wed³ *ptp.*, maddened 17/68 [OE *wēdan* A].

wede¹, garment 5/79, 20/111, armour 8/94; **-es, -is** *pl.* 31/8, 37/3 [OE *wǣd*].

weder¹, weather 5/89, 11/84, 25/4, cloud 5/86; **-es** *pl.*, storms 18/40 [OE *weder*].

weder⁴, whither 12/244, 245, 13/191 [OE *hwider, hwæder*].

wee. *See* **whi.**

weȝe³, to carry 10/118; **weieð** 3*pr.*, presses upon 6/86; **way** 3*pt.*, weighed 12/237 [OE *wegan* 5].

wei¹, whey 10/105 [OE *hwǣg*].

wei⁴, away 12/53; *do wey, way*, stop 29/9, 36/7, 38/7 [OE *onweg*].

wey(e). *See* **wai.**

weylaway¹, woe, distress 35/17 [OE *weilāwei*].

weilawei⁹, alas, woe is me 17/32, 29/13, 25, **wayleuay** 38/18 [OE *weilāwei*].

wel⁴, well 4/13, 5/10, 6/21, etc., **wæl** 2/66, very 5/43, 77, 81, 7/29, etc., fully 2/40, 3/4, 8/46, 11/18, certainly 12/87, 15/9, 29/33, much 21/6, carefully 5/38, many 5/101, entirely 15/31; *wel abouten*, round about 8/117; *wel mo*, many more 8/219 [OE *wel*].

wel⁹, alas 23/1 [cf. OE *wel lā*].

wel. *See* **fel**(1).

wel(e), weole¹, wealth 13/47, 14/27, 34, 20/57, prosperity 35/17, 54, good fortune 9/139, 13/8 [OE *we(o)la*].

welcum⁹, welcome 38/2, 38 [OE *wilcuma*, infl. by *wel*].

weli², wealthy 20/108 [OE *welig*].

welle¹, spring, fountain 8/224, 16/14, 33/26 [nWS *welle*].

welneȝ⁴, nearly 10/44 [OE *welnē(a)h*].

wem(me)¹, mark, blemish 18/62, 20/165 [OE *wemm*].

wen. *See* **when.**

wende(n)³, to come, go, proceed 5/22, 25, 6/231, 19/82, etc., embrace 13/81; **-eð** 3*pr.* 6/133, 180; 3*prpl.* 19/72; **-en** 3*prspl.* 6/178; **wend(e)** *imp.* 7/12, 9/163, change 29/21; **wende** 3*pt.* 5/14, 20, 18/62, **went** 33/23, translated 1/7, turned 2/75, 6/24, 97, 8/193; **-en** 3*ptpl.* 6/108; **went, (i)wend(e)** *ptp.* 12/74, 35/16, **vend** 12/159, changed 13/170, translated 15/7, 57, 74; *hu hit is went*, what has happened 9/19; *wendeþ ut of*, turn away from 19/79 [OE *wéndan* A].

wene[1], hope 9/13; *buten wene*, certain 6/169 [OE *wēn*].

wene[3], to think, expect 14/45, 19/85; 1*pr.* 5/8, 7/21, 10/170, etc.; -est, -st 2*pr.* 7/27, 10/47; -eþ 3*pr.* 11/15, 18/51, 20/24, **wenþ** 10/136, considers himself 6/127; -en 3*prpl.* 11/17, 88; **wende** 3*pt.* 4/13, 16, 20, etc.; -en 3*ptpl.* 2/18, 52, 82, 6/62, etc., **uuenden** 2/2, **wende** 5/35; **iwend** *ptp.* 12/134 [OE *wēnan* A].

wenne; **weole**; **weorde**; **weore(n)**; **weorkes**. *See* **when**; **wel(e)**; **word(e)**; **was**; **werk(e)**.

weorpeð[3] 3*pr.*, casts; **warp** 3*pt.* 10/45; *weorpeð adun*, hangs 17/29 [OE *weorpan* 3].

weorrede. *See* **werrais**.

wepe[1], weeping 21/87 [cf. OE *wōp, wēpan* 7].

wepe(n)[3], to weep 14/81, 21/92; -inge *prp.* 9/62, 106, -inde 9/104; -eþ 3*pr.* 14/88, 92, 21/57; 3*prpl.* 16/18; **wep** 3*pt.* 12/107 [OE *wēpan* 7].

wepinge[1], weeping 36/7 [OE *wēp-an* + -*ing*].

wepmon[1], man 32/3 [OE *wǣp-mann*].

wepne[1], weapon 8/89, 93, 12/286; **wepnen** *pl.* 17/132 [OE *wǣpn*].

wer; **wer(e)**; **werchen**, **wercheþ**; **werd**; **weren**. *See* **wher**[4]; **was**; **wurche**; **world(e)**; **was**.

werefore, **vrefore**[8], wherefore, why 19/53, because 19/45 [OE *hwǣr* + *fore*].

weren[3], to wear 32/24; -eþ 3*pr.* 31/8; **wereden** 3*prpl.* 35/5 [OE *werian* A, cf. Gothic *wasjan*].

werien, **were(n)**[3], to defend, protect 3/12, 17/42, 20/30, 22/14; **werie** 3*prs.* 20/47 [OE *werian* A].

wery[2], weary 33/12 [OE *wērig*].

werk(e), **werrc**[1], work, deed 11/43, 14/20, 22, 15/12, etc.; -es,

weorkes, **workes** *pl.* 8/34, 19/48, 37/13, domestic buildings 2/75 [OE *we(o)rc*].

werkmen[1] *pl.*, workmen, labourers 19/5, 9, etc. [OE *we(o)rcmann*].

wermide[4], with which 12/112 [OE *hwǣr* + *mid*].

werne[3], to refuse, restrain 20/7, 33/39, 36/22 [nWS *wérnan* A].

werrais[3] 3*pr.*, makes war on 22/32; **weorrede** 3*pt.* 6/113 [cf. OE *werre*, from AN *werre*].

wers(e); **werst**; **werþ**; **wes**. *See* **wurse**; **first(e)**; **wurþen**; **was**.

west[1], west 20/100, 28/42; *by weste*, westward 7/29, 75 [OE *west*].

weste[2], waste 10/96 [OE *wēste*].

weste. *See* **wite(n)**.

wet[2], wet 32/30 [OE *wǣt*].

wete[1], wheat 21/67 [OE *hwǣte*].

wha, wa, wo[5], who 6/200, 10/204, 12/122, 127, **ho** 9/123, **qwa** 23/1, whoever, anyone 5/17, 8/79, 13/135, **hwo** 8/172; **hwas** *g.* 18/28; **wham, wam, wom** *a/d.* 12/181, 13/170, 29/4, 30/21, **hwan** 20/3, **quam** 22/10, 38/48; **whase**, whoever 15/28, 48, 63 [OE *hwā, hwās, hwām; hwā swā*].

whan, hwan, wan[4],[8] when 5/111, 114, 8/67, 221, etc., **whane** 9/178, **wonne** 10/38, **hwon** 17/31, **wanne** 19/70, 71, etc., **hwanne** 20/140, for the time when 6/240; **whænne swa**, whenever 6/166 [OE *hwanne, hwonne*].

whar, hwar, war[4],[8] where, wherever 10/64, 149, 171, **wha-swa-auere** 6/126 [OE *hwǣr, hwār*].

what, hwat, wat[5], what 2/78, 6/8, etc., **whæt** 6/60, **hwet** 17/74, 75, **quat** 22/34, **whet** 29/28, 31/8, 36/38, 39, **vat** 38/63 [OE *hwæt*].

what, hwat[8], how 17/15, 25/5 [OE *hwæt*].

what, hwat, wat[9], lo, behold 10/152, 173, 12/89, 163, 17/15, 25/5 [OE *hwæt*].

when, hwen(ne), wen(ne)⁴,⁸ when
12/75, 151, 17/60, etc. [OE
hwænne].

whener⁴, whenever 31/17 [OE
hwænne + æfre].

whennes⁴, whence 21/30 [OE
hwænne + adv. *-es*].

wher, hwer, wer⁴,⁸ where, wherever 7/71, 20/65, etc., **uuere** 35/1
[OE *hwǣr*].

wher. *See* **war.**

wherþurȝ⁸, by means of which
3/17 [OE *hwǣr + þurh*].

whet. *See* **what.**

whi, hwi, wi⁸, why 7/48, 10/186,
etc., **wee** 19/10 [OE *hwī, hwȳ*].

whider⁴, whither 31/9 [OE *hwider*].

whil(e), hwile⁸, while 4/8, 9/48,
20/46, etc., **wil(e),** 2/37, 8/6,
wule 5/85 [OE *þā hwīle þe*].

while, hwile¹, time, space of time
8/203, 9/3, 176, 20/22, **wile**
10/116 [OE *hwīl*].

while(n)⁴, formerly 6/236, 243,
21/5, 24/22, **wile** 10/112, **hwilem** 19/66, **whil** 29/29 [OE *hwīle,
hwīlum*].

white, wite, with², fair, white 8/48,
21/60, 34/3, 38/45, silver 7/26
[OE *hwīt*].

wi. *See* **whi.**

wy⁹, woe! 35/23n.

wicke, wicked(e)², wicked 8/66,
13/53, 72, 29/12, **wikke** 35/32,
wiked 37/1 [obscure].

wicteste. *See* **with.**

wicth, wiȝt¹, whit; *no wicth, wiȝt,*
not at all 8/97, nothing 21/62
[OE *wiht*].

wide², wide 18/58, 30/10, gaping
8/218 [OE *wīd*].

wide⁴, widely 6/14, 52, 8/169, etc.;
so wide so, however widely 13/91
[OE *wīde*].

widuen, -es¹ *pl.,* widows 8/33, 79;
widewene *gpl.* 12/201 [OE
wīawe].

wif, wiue¹, wife 12/154, 212, etc.,
woman 32/3, 38/60; **wiues** *pl.,*
6/13, 8/2; *to wyfe,* as a wife 38/6
[OE *wīf*].

wiȝele-fulle², wonderful 6/142
[OE *wīgol + -full*].

wiȝt. *See* **wicth.**

wiȝt¹, weight 9/12 [OE *wihte*].

wiht(e)¹, being, creature 18/30,
20/132, **viit** 27/1, **wyþt** 31/7;
wiȝte *pl.* 10/87 [OE *wiht*].

wikenn¹ *pl.,* duties 15/33 [OE
wice].

wil¹, trick 11/1, 99 [IOE
wīl].

wil², ignorant 8/149 [ON *vill-r*].

wil(e). *See* **whil(e); while;
while(n).**

wilcume², welcome 6/220 [OE
wilcuma].

wilde², wild, fierce 6/99, 10/100,
etc.; **wildis** *gpl.,* wantons' 37/3
[OE *wilde*].

wilde³ *ptp. See* note to 20/94.

wilderne, wildernisse¹, wilder-
ness, 6/125, 10/96 [OE *wildděoren,
-děornes*].

wildscipe¹, wantonness 6/124 [OE
wilde + -scipe].

wilen³, to desire, wish, be willing,
fut.auxil. 15/48; **wille, wil(e)** 1*pr.*
8/15, 12/131, etc., **wulle** 9/93,
164, **wole** 12/175, 30/20, **willi**
13/190, 37/1, **wul(e)** 20/8, 37/4;
wilt, wolt, wult 2*pr.* 12/244,
16/27, etc., **wille** 10/77, **woltou**
12/186, 196; **wil(e), wol(e),
wul(e)** 3*pr.* 8/4, 10/170, etc.,
wille 11/24, **wolle** 28/75; **willen**
1*prpl.* 2/78, 3/4, 19, 20, **uilleth**
19/2; **wulle, wolle** 2*prpl.* 10/152,
21/1; **wilen, willeþ, wullen,
-eþ** 3*prpl.* 6/170, 8/54, 11/18,
13/64, 15/70; **wolde** 1*pt.* 12/179,
15/66; **woldest** 2*pt.* 10/84, 16/54,
20/109, **wuldes** 11/59; **wolde,
walde** 3*pt.* 6/7, 7/61, etc.,
wulde 11/55, 56; **wolden, wald**

3*ptpl.* 8/164, 22/16 [OE *willan, wyllan; wólde,* OA *wálde*].

wiles[8], while 11/84, 35/44 [OE *-hwíles*].

wille, wil[1], will, pleasure, desire 8/271, 9/110, 11/33, etc., *diden al his herte wille,* did as he wished 8/70; *bi hire wille,* of her own will 8/85 [OE *gewill, willa*].

wilnest[3] 2*pr.,* desire 20/87; -e*þ* 3*pr.* 20/104, 148 [OE *wilnian* B].

wymmon, -man[1], woman 14/88, 95, 20/6, etc.; -men *pl.* 2/19, 6/233, etc., wimen 13/34, 37 [OE *wífmann, wimman*].

win(e)[1], wine 7/4, 49, 8/254, etc. [OE *wín,* from L *vinum*].

wind[1], wind 6/86, 28/1, 3; -es *g.* 20/14, 25/3; *pl.* 18/40 [OE *wind*].

winde[3], to go 12/76; **wond** 3*pt.* 12/22 [OE *windan* 3].

wyndou[1], window 29/23 [ON *vind-auga*].

wine-maies[1] *pl.,* members of the retinue 6/77 [OE *winemǽg*].

winyard(e)[1], vineyard 19/6, 7, etc., **winiærd** 2/74 [OE *wíngéard*].

winkin[3], to blink 17/63 [OE *wincian* B].

winne, wunne[1], joy, pleasure 6/230, 9/167, 32/5, **wnne** 34/6 [OE *wynn*].

winne(n)[3], to win, gain, obtain 5/39, 7/38, 11/16, etc.; **winnen** 3*prpl.,* strive 11/79; **wan, uuan** 3*pt.* 2/72; **iwonne** *ptp.* 5/114 [OE *winnan* 3].

winter[1], winter 11/79; **wintre** *pl.,* years 2/37, 58, etc. [OE *winter, wintru*].

wypede[3] 3*pt.,* wiped 7/104 [OE *wípian* B].

wirken. *See* **wurche.**

wis(e)[2], wise, learned 5/65, 10/145, etc., **wiis** 12/105; **wysuste** *sup.* 14/23 [OE *wís*].

wisdom(e)[1], wisdom 10/148, 178, etc., **wisedom** 11/27 [OE *wísdōm*].

wise[1], way, manner 3/18, 12/3, etc., way of life 14/46, 47, tune, melody 10/20, 54 [OE *wíse*].

wisliche[4], wisely 1/2 [OE *wíslíce*].

wisman, -mon[1], wise man 14/39, 22/27 [OE *wís + mann*].

wisse[3], to direct 8/104 [OE *wissian* B].

wit, wiit[1], intelligence 10/199, 12/70, 15/8, idea 12/124 [OE *witt*].

witches[1], *pl.,* witches 11/100 [OE *wicca, wicce*].

wite. *See* **white.**

wite(n)[3], to know 14/59, 15/56; **wot** 1*pr.* 8/46, 10/61, etc.; **wost** 2*pr.* 36/44, 38/48; **wot** 3*pr.* 5/10, 14/50, etc.; **witeþ** 3*prpl.* 13/123; **wite** 2*prs.* 9/117; 3*prs.* 15/55; **witen** 2*prspl.* 3/4; **wist** 1*pt.* 38/14; **wiste, weste, wuste** 3*pt.* 6/50, 10/10, etc; **iwuste** *ptp.* 5/30 [OE *witan, wát; wiste*].

wite(n)[3], to guard, defend 9/118, 20/6, 62, 158, 183, blame 9/85; -est 2*pr.* 20/152, 167; **wyte** 2*prs.* 20/148; *imp.* 6/222, 18/48, **wyt,** blame 36/35 [OE *wítan* 1].

witeʒe[1], prophet 6/243 [OE *wítega*].

witerliche[4], clearly, plainly 17/127, 134 [ON *vitr* + OE *-líce*].

with. *See* **white.**

with[2], active, courageous 8/115; **wicteste** *sup.* 8/9 [ON *vígt*].

wiþ, wit[7], with, along with 7/13, 8/52, 139, 17/72, etc., **wid** 6/0 3, **wiðe** 6/200, by, by means of 3/21, 4/15, 20, 36, 8/184, etc., against 6/40, 95, 10/56, 57, etc., in 9/16, 38/42, on 11/75, because of 11/99, 18/6, **wid** 25/6, towards 12/247; *wit þat,* so that 8/19; *þat, þet . . . wiþ(e),* with which 8/158,

18/60; *wiþ-alle*, because of everything 9/8; *wyþal*, as well 20/128 [OE *wiþ*].

wiþdrau³ *imp.*, put away 35/27; -draʒe 3*pt.*, pulled back 9/96; *ptp.* 9/66 [OE *wiþ* + *dragan* 6].

wiðerwine¹, adversary 16/31 [OE *wiðerwinna*].

wiði¹, willow 17/16 [OE *wīðig*].

wiþinne⁴, inside 7/32, 12/11, 13/57, 19/87, 21/71, during 7/99 [OE *wiþinnan*].

wiðsaken³, to deny 17/37 [OE *wiðsacan* 6].

wiðsiggen³, to deny 17/8 [OE *wiþ* + *secgan* C].

wiðseggunge¹, denial 17/61 [OE *wiþ* + *secg-an* + *-ung*].

wiþute(n), **wiþoute(n)⁷**, without 11/17, 98, 12/25, etc., **wiþhouten** 35/49, **vytuten** 38/53; as⁴, **wituten**, outside 38/10 [OE *wiþūtan*].

witt⁵, *dual*, we two 15/4, 37 [OE *wit*]; for oblique forms see **unnc**.

witnesse¹, testimony 13/46, 70, 88 [OE *witnes*].

witnesse³ *imp.*, bear witness 3/22 [cf. OE *witnes*].

wl(e). *See* **ful(e).**

wlatien³, to be disgusted 17/20 [OE *wlātian* B].

wlyte¹, beauty 14/63 [OE *wlite*].

wn-; wo. *See* **wun-; wha.**

wo, wa¹, sorrow, grief 12/2, 53, 13/23, 14/72, etc., misfortune 13/8; *wa wes him*, he was sorrowful 6/91 [OE *wā*].

wo⁹, woe! 35/23.

wod(e)², mad, furious 6/65, 86, 8/221, etc., **woed** 13/181 [OE *wōd*].

wode¹, woad 10/76 [OE *wād*].

wode, wude¹, wood, forest 6/85, 7/54, etc., **wde** 24/4; -**es** *pl.* 18/40, 30/1 [OE *wudu*].

wode-gore¹, forest 29/31 [OE *wudu* + *gāra*].

wode-shawe¹, woodland grove 13/179 [OE *wudu* + *sc(e)aga*].

woh, wouh¹, evil, wrong 6/41, 20/40, 42; *hauest wou*, art wrong 13/107 [OE *wōh*].

wok², weak 20/12 [OE *wāc*].

wol(e). *See* **wilen.**

wolawo⁹, alas 17/33 [OE *wā lā wā*].

wolde; woldes; woldest. *See* **wilen; wald; wilen.**

wolf, wulf¹, wolf 6/79, 12/108, etc., **volf** 12/148, **vuolf** 12/221, **wulues** *pl.* 10/104 [OE *wulf*].

wolle, wolt(ou); wom. *See* **wilen; wha.**

wombe¹, belly 18/58, 62, 21/7, 11, womb 16/42 [OE *wámb*].

won¹, world 28/9; *ful god won*, in great numbers 8/131, 210, 238 [ON *ván*].

won², pale 28/80 [OE *wann*].

wond; wonder. *See* **winde; wunder¹.**

wondrien³, to wander 6/99 [OE *wandrian* B].

woned, wonede(n). *See* **wune(n).**

wonene. *See* **wanene.**

woneth. *See* **wune(n).**

woning¹, dwelling 10/182 [OE *wunung*].

wonys. *See* **wune(n).**

wonið³ 3*prpl.*, lament 16/18 [OE *wānian* B].

wonne; wor; wore(n). *See* **whan; was.**

word(e)¹, word 10/208, 12/132, etc., **weorde**, name 6/187; *pl.* 1/22, 6/27, etc., **wordes** 9/119, 15/21, etc., story 21/1; **worden** *dpl.* 6/231, writings 3/34; *warp a word*, spoke 10/45 [OE *wórd*].

wordes, wordl, wordle(s). *See* **world(e).**

worhliche; workes. *See* **wurhliche; werk(e).**

world(e)¹, world 1/22, 5/8, 12/150, etc., **wordl(e)** 19/35, 43, 50,

wul(e); wule; wulde(s); wulf,
wulues; wulle(n), wulleð,
wult. *See* wilen; whil(e); wilen;
wolf(e); wilen.

wunde(s), -en¹ *pl.*, wounds 6/209,
227, 11/98, etc., woundes, -en
29/30, 34, 36/53 [OE *wúnd*].

wunder, wonder¹, marvel 11/10,
16/59, etc., atrocities 2/11, 35,
terrible things 20/74, wonderful
creature 11/94; as², wonderful
7/47, 21/69 [OE *wúndor*].

wunder⁴, wonderfully; *wunder ane*,
wonderfully 6/38, 40, etc. [OE
wúndor].

wunderlice, -liche⁴, wonderfully
2/85, 6/233 [OE *wúndorlíce*].

wune(n), wunie(n)³, to dwell,
remain 6/230, 9/44, etc.; wuneþ
3*pr.* 10/174, 11/75, 18/52,
woneth 8/105, wonys 38/49;
wunieð 3*prpl.* 18/43; wunnien
3*prs.* 6/239; wonede 3*pt.* 6/3;
-eden 3*ptpl.* 12/262; woned,
wont *ptp.*, accustomed 12/105,
23/4 [OE *wunian* B].

wunne. *See* winne.

wurche, werchen, wirken³, to do,
work, make, cause 15/12, 16/56,
37/12, 13; wurcheð 3*pr.* 6/125;
wurcheð, wercheþ 3*prpl.* 13/23,
163, 18/35; wurche 1*prs.*, com-
pose 20/2; wrahtest 2*pt.*, created
18/31; wurhte, wrohte,
wrouhte 3*pt.* 2/62, 6/139, built
20/114; wroht, iworht *ptp.*
6/142, 15/77, 32/16, ywraht
28/32, iwraht, created 18/34, 38
[OE *wyrcan, worhte*, OA *warhte*
A].

wurhliche, worh-², splendid 28/9,
40; as⁴, worthily 6/77 [OE
wurðlic, -líce].

wurmes, wormes¹ *pl.*, reptiles
18/42, worms 34/4 [OE *wyrm*].

wurse, wers(e), wors(e)², *comp.*,
worse 2/46, 6/200, etc., uuerse

2/37, 38, wrs 10/34, vers 22/38;
wurst, worste *sup.* 13/142, 17/13
[OE *wyrsa, wyrst*].

wurð¹, price 17/94, 97 [OE *wúrþ*].

wurþe, wrþ², worthy, honoured
5/11, worth 20/86 [OE *wúrþ*].

wurþen³, to be, become 15/64;
worþe 1*pr.* 12/191; wurð, worþ
3*pr.* 12/248, 16/45, lives 7/93;
worþeþ 2*prpl.* 21/83; wurðe,
worþe 3*prs.* 6/115, 12/96, 21/96;
werþ, warð 3*pt.* 12/66, 18/15,
60; iwurðen *ptp.*, happened
6/121, 236 [OE *wúrþan* 3].

wurði², worthy 11/48, 15/64 [OE
wúrþ + *-ig*].

wurðmund¹, glory 18/58 [OE
wurþmýnd].

wurtscipe¹, ceremony 2/64 [OE
wurþscipe].

wuste. *See* wite(n).

y; y; yaf; yare; ych; ye. *See* ic; i;
ʒiue(n); er; ic; ʒe. For past
participles in y- not entered
below, see the verbs concerned.

yede³ 3*pt.*, went 8/6, 19/5, etc.,
gæde, entered 2/25; yede(n),
ieden 3*ptpl.* 2/44, 19/13, 60 [OE
ge-ēode, pt. of *ge-gán*].

yef. *See* ʒef; ʒiue(n).

yeft¹, gift 8/249 [cf. OE *gift*].

yefþ, yeue(n); yeld; yete; yf. *See*
ʒiue(n); geld; ʒet(e); ʒef.

yfed³ *ptp.*, reared, brought up
31/18 [OE *fēdan* A].

yfere; yhernes. *See* ifere; ʒiernen.

yknowe³, to recognize 7/107 [OE
gecnāwan 7].

ylde¹, protection 20/96 [OE *hýldo*].

ylere³, to learn 8/12 [OE *gelǽran*
A].

ylong², dependent 30/21 [OE
geláng].

ymston¹, gem 20/153, 178; -e *pl.*
20/175 [OE *gimstán*].

yn¹, dwelling 4/30 [OE *inn*].

ynow; yo; yorne. *See* inoh; heo;
 ȝerne.
yorne³ *ptp.*, travelled 7/42 [OE *ge-
 úrnen*, from -*iernan* 3].
you. *See* ȝe.
youþe¹, youth 8/263 [OE *geogoþ*].

ys; ys; yu; yuel(e); yung(e);
 yure, yw; ywis. *See* he; is; ȝe;
 uvel(e); ȝunge; ȝe; iwis.
ywyueþ³ 3*pr.*, marries 14/75 [OE
 gewīfian B].
ywraht. *See* wurche.

Addenda to Glossary

bihalfues, bihalues⁷, beside 6/69,
 67 [OE *beh(e)alfe* + adverbial
 -*es*].

bihalue³, to surround 8/207.
bihalues⁴, near by 6/153.

Costantines *g.*, of the emperor Constantine, *d.* 337, 13/115.
Cotingham, Cottingham, Northants. 2/72.
Crist, Christ 7/90, 8/16, etc., Criste 12/159, 18/58, Christ 2/56; -es *g.* 12/193, 15/13, etc.
Cuþbert, St. Cuthbert, bp. of Lindisfarne 685–7, 1/11.

Daris, 9/173.
Dauið(e), David 16/40, 17/68.
Dorsete, Dorset 10/175.
Douere, Dover, Kent 4/40.
Douse, 31/30n.
Dunholme, Durham 1/11.
Dunston, St. Dunstan, abp. of Canterbury 960–88, 1/14.

Ealured, Alfred the Great, 871–99, 14/9.
Ebrewisse, Hebrew 21/64.
Ector, Hector of Troy 20/69.
Edward, Edward I 1272–1307, 4/43, Sir(e) Edward 4/38, 5/28; -es *g.* 5/37.
Egipte, Egypt 21/22, 66.
Egwin, Ecgwine, bp. of the Hwicce 693–717, 1/12.
Engle, the English 6/7; Englene *gpl.* 14/10, 11.
Engelond, England 4/25, 5/1, Englalande 2/6, Engleneloande 3/1, 29, 35, Englenelond(e) 6/9, 14/12, 17, Englond 8/52, Englelonde 14/24, Engelonde 20/101.
Englisc, English 1/9, 15, Englise 1/3, Engliss 5/7, Englisca 6/16, Ennglissh(e) 15/7, 10, etc.
Eouerwic, York 6/107, 112.
Ernleȝe, Areley Kings, Worcs. 6/3.
Estun, Easton Mauduit, Northants. 2/72.
Euesham, Evesham, Worcs. 5/20, 80, 85.
Eugenie, Pope Eugenius III 1145–53, 2/67.
Exodus, 1/8.

Faraones *g.*, of Pharaoh 21/85.
Floriz, 9/35, etc.
Frankys, French 22/24.
French, Frenchis, Frenss, French 5/3, 6, 6/20.

Genesis, 1/8.
Gileberd of Eisnesfelde, Gilbert of Elsfield 5/68.
Gloucetre, Glowchestre, Gloucester 3/28, 5/41.
Godrich 8/107.
Goldeborw, 8/260.
Goswhit, Arthur's helmet 6/146.
Grece, Greece 22/5.
Guldeuorde, Guildford, Surrey 10/*Int.* 1.
Gwy de Mountfort, Guy de Montfort, *d.* 1291, 5/96.

Hauelok, 8/5, etc.
Heleyne, Helen of Troy 20/65.
Helwis, 38/37.
Hengelond, England 8/106.
Henri, Henry I 1100–35, 2/4.
Henri, Henry III 1216–72, 3/1, 20/82, 101.
Henri, Henry de Montfort 5/46, 63.
Henri de Hastinges, first Baron Hastings, *d.* 1268, 5/98.
Henries *g.*, of Henry II 1154–89, 6/23.
Heoueshame, Evesham, Worcs. 1/12.
Hereford(e), Hereford 5/12, 14.
Herodes *g.*, of Herod 11/53.
Hyrtlingberi, Irthlingborough, Northants. 2/73.
Horn, 7/9, etc.
Hubert, 31/37.
Hue de Bigot, Hugh Bigod, justiciar 1258–60, *d.* 1266, 4/34.
Hue þe Despencer, Hugh Dispencer, justiciar 1260–1 and 1263–5, *k.* 1265, 5/64.
Hugo of Walteruile, Hugh de Waterville 2/72n.

Noruuic, Norwich, Norfolk 2/79.
Nubie, Nubia 9/27.
Numerus, Numbers 1/8.

Oswald, St. Oswald, bp. of Worcester 961–92, abp. of York 972–992, 1/12.
Oxeneford, Oxford 2/7.

Paradiis, Paradis, Paradise 12/140, 20/166.
Paris, Paris of Troy 20/65.
Paulin, St. Paulinus, abp. of York 625–33, bp. of Rochester 633–44, 1/14.
Piers, son of Peter de Montfort 5/99.
Peris de Mountfort, Peter de Montfort 5/65, 100, **Perres of Muntfort** 3/31.
Perres of Sauueye, Peter of Savoy, earl of Richmond, d. 1268, 3/29.
Pharaones g., of Pharaoh 21/70.
Porteshom, -ham, Portisham, Dorset 10/174, 213.
Pridwen, Arthur's shield 6/148.

Rachel, 21/53.
Radestone, Redstone, Worcs. 6/5.
Rauf Basset, baron of Drayton, k. 1265, 5/66.
Rauland, Roland, one of Charlemagne's paladins, 22/15.
Reneuard, Reynard the Fox in the Beast Epic 12/133.
Richard, earl of Cornwall, King of the Romans, d. 1272, 4/6, 8, etc.
Richard of Clare, seventh earl of Gloucester, d. 1262, 3/27.
Richard of Grey, second baron Grey of Codnor 3/31.
Rymenild, 7/1, 43, 88, 91.
Ripum, Ripon, WRY. 1/11.
Roberd, Robert of Gloucester 5/92.
Roberd, Robert de Montfort 5/100.
Rofecæstre, Rochester, Kent 1/14.

Roger, bp. of Salisbury 1107–39 2/7n.
Roger, the Chancellor, son of prec., 2/8n.
Roger Bigod, fourth earl of Norfolk, d. 1270, 3/28.
Roger of Mortemer, sixth baron of Wigmore, d. 1282, 3/32.
Rogingham, Rockingham, Northants, 2/71.
Rome, 2/66, 8/64, 10/112.
Ron, Arthur's spear 6/151.
Ruben, Reuben 21/47.

Sæxisce, Saxon 6/76, 90, etc.
Sæxlonde, country of the Old Saxons 6/71.
Salomon, Solomon 14/94, 17/43, 20/114.
San Dinis, St. Denis 38/38n.
Sanct Willelm, St. William of Norwich 2/86.
Sanctus Beda, St. Bede, d. 735, 1/1, **Seint Beda** 6/16.
Sannt Awwstin, St. Augustine, bp. of Hippo 395–430, one of the Latin Fathers, 15/5.
Sant Jhon, Jone, St. John 38/13, 27.
Sarazins pl., Saracens 22/16.
Saunsum, Samson 13/139.
Saxes pl., Saxons 6/96.
Scotlonde, Scotland 10/180.
Scottes pl., Scots 6/181.
Seint Gyle, St. Giles 7/73.
Seinte Marie, the Virgin Mary 19/44.
Sem, Shem 6/12.
Sereberi, Salisbury, Wilts. 2/8.
Seuarne-staþe, banks of the Severn 6/4.
Seuorde, Seaford, Sussex 14/1n.
Sexes pl., Saxons 6/98.
Sexlonde, land of the Old Saxons 6/92.
Sigrim, Isengrim the Wolf in the Beast Epic 12/128.
Symeon, Simeon 36/12.

INDEX NOMINUM, LOCORUM, ETC. 335

Simon of Muntfort, Simond de Mo(u)ntfort, Simon de Montfort, earl of Leicester, *k.* 1265, 3/26, 4/28, 33, etc., **Sir Simond** 5/12, 36, **Sir Simon þe olde** 5/18; **Simondes** *g.* 5/96.

Sir Simon(d) þe ȝonge, Simon de Montfort, son of prec., *d.* 1271, 5/24, 35, 109.

Spaygne, Spain 9/131.

Stanewig, Stanwick, Northants. 2/73.

Stephne, Stephen 1135–54, 2/1, 6, 37; -es *g.* 2/78.

Swiþþun, St. Swithin, bp. of Winchester 852–62, 1/13.

Tambre, Tanbre, the River Tamar 6/186, 192, 198.

Teuskesburi, Tewkesbury, Glos. 5/104.

Tristram, Tristrem, Tristram 20/68, 22/17.

Troy, 22/5.

Vnfrai de Boun, Humphrey de Bohun, second earl of Hereford and first earl of Essex, *d.* 1274, 5/95.

Vðeres *g.,* of Uther 6/145, 224.

Vtronomius, Deuteronomy 1/8n.

Wace 6/21n.

Walingford, Berks. 4/10.

Walis, Wales 5/13.

Wallterr, Walter, brother of Orrm, 15/1.

Walter of Cantelow, Water of Wurcetre, Walter of Cantelupe,

bp. of Worcester 1237–66, 3/26, 5/32.

Walteruile, *see* **Hugo.**

Warewik, Warwick 3/31.

Waryn, Warynne, John de Warenne, earl of Surrey, *d.* 1304, 4/24, 29.

Warin of Bassingbourne, 5/52.

Water of Wurcetre. *See* **Walter of Cantelow.**

Wawain, Wawan, Gawain 13/88, 22/13.

Welsse, Welsh 5/102.

Westnesse, 7/82.

Wygar, Arthur's mail-coat 6/139.

Wigemor, Wigmore, Herefordshire, 5/76.

Wilfrid of Ripum, St. Wilfrid of Northumbria, held several sees between 664 and his death in 709, 1/11.

Willam de Verous, 5/66.

Willam Mautrauers, 5/72.

Willam Trossel, 5/68.

Willelm Malduit, 2/71.

Willelm of Fort, earl of Albemarle, *d.* 1260, 3/30.

Wincæstre, Winchester, Hants. 1/13.

Wyndesore, Windsor, Berks. 4/12, 17, etc.

Wircetre, Wireceastre, Wirechestre, Wurcetre, Worcester 1/12, 3/26, 5/19, 32.

Witeȝe, Widia 6/139n.

Ydoine, Idoine 22/20.

Yrloande, Ireland 3/2.

Ysambrase, Isumbras 22/19n.

Yseude, Ysote, Iseult 20/68, 22/17.

PRINTED IN GREAT BRITAIN BY
J. W. ARROWSMITH LTD., WINTERSTOKE ROAD BRISTOL 3